The Sexual Imagination

The Sexual Imagination
from **Acker** *to* **Zola**

A FEMINIST COMPANION

edited by
Harriett Gilbert

JONATHAN CAPE

LONDON

First published 1993

1 3 5 7 9 10 8 6 4 2

First published in the United Kingdom in 1993 by
Jonathan Cape
Random House, 20 Vauxhall Bridge Road, London SW1V 2SA

Random House Australia (Pty) Limited
20 Alfred Street, Milsons Point, Sydney,
New South Wales 2061, Australia

Random House New Zealand Limited
18 Poland Road, Glenfield,
Auckland 10, New Zealand

Random House South Africa (Pty) Limited
PO Box 337, Bergvlei, South Africa

Random House UK Limited Reg. No. 954009

A CIP catalogue record for this book
is available from the British Library

ISBN 0-224-03535-5

Typeset by Textype Typesetters, Cambridge
Printed in Great Britain by Clays Ltd, St. Ives PLC

In memory of
the cat Colette
(1974-1991)
and of her magnanimous tolerance
of the editor's irritability

And my gratitude to the following for their support and assistance: Robin Hazlewood; Philippa Brewster; Debbie Licorish; Janet Palmer Mullaney of *Belles Lettres*, USA; and every one of the bullied, harassed and underrewarded contributors.

Contents

List of Illustrations

Introduction

Most animals share a drive towards sexual activity and gratification – having achieved which, we variously scuttle away to build a nest for our offspring, eat our partner, turn over and sleep. The human imagination, however, is reluctant to leave matters there.

Using this communal urge as a foundation, humans have constructed fabulous, imaginative palaces of sex and sexuality: many of which have little or no relationship to reproduction. Indeed, as feminists, gay liberationists and philosophers from Foucault to Fanon have shown, all human love is 'unnatural love'. Our understanding of what sex means, the forms in which we express and discuss it, the fantasies that we weave around it are entirely artificial, manufactured.

Not only does sexuality differ from culture to culture, from era to era, modified or redesigned by religion, politics, science, art, pornography, technology and social pressure, at any one time and in any one place it crackles with internal contradictions. Widely accepted theories may bear no relation to widespread practice; the theories themselves (of medicine, the church, the cinema, for example) may clash; crucially, and not only because of their anatomical differences, women are not inclined to construct the same sexualities as men.

This Companion is intended as a tourist guide to the structures that contain, explain and express our sexualities. Via alphabetically ordered entries, it explores not only such major monuments as Hinduism, Judaism, Christianity, Islam, Freudianism and feminism, but many of the quirkier, less familiar or more parochial sites: novelists, poets, painters and thinkers, forms of popular culture and resistance, modifications to and heresies against the prevailing articles of faith. Historically, its sweep is from the ancient world to the end of the twentieth century; geographically, from China to Australia, from Japan to the USA, via India, Africa, South America, the Caribbean and Europe.

Needless to say, such a project could never be exhaustive. A book which merely *listed* every person, movement, idea and artwork to have shaped our sense of sexuality would probably fill the shelves of a decent public library. And this book is more than a desiccated list. Its 350 entries, by an international team of feminist authorities on literature, art, religion, sexology, psychology, philosophy, sexual politics and more, are actually miniature essays.

Rather than pretend to the usual reference-book neutrality, the entries engage with their subject (sometimes argue with it), bring it to life and expand upon it, combining researched information with informed opinion. Moreover, they do this without either jargon or the terseness of dictionary shorthand, being written, instead, in language both graceful and accessible. For this to be possible, space was required – not that many contributors feel that space was what they were given – and, thus, a highly selective approach to the subjects to be covered. In part dictated by common sense – Freud, for instance, could scarcely be ignored – the selection is also inevitably governed by a mixture of circumstance, chance and whim. The imbalances are clear for all to see, but (in many cases despite concerted attempts to rectify them) they include an over-emphasis on western history and culture and a far sharper focus on literature than on any of the other arts.

Nonetheless, as their editor, I continue to be astonished by the range of the entries. Re-reading them, I feel like a conjurer who, having tapped her top hat in the hope that a pigeon or two might flap out, finds that she has released a swirling, multicolored flock of doves. Some are enormous, with wings that span centuries and continents; others are particular and small; intermingled, they form a bright and ever-rearranging kaleidoscope. Perhaps it would be more succinct just to say that the entries under the letter 'J' begin with an analysis of Jacobean Revenge Tragedy, then move through studies of Derek Jarman, Sheila Jeffreys and the novel *Jin Ping Mei* to end with Judaism.

Nor is it just the subject matter that demonstrates such variety. The contributors may share expertise, lucidity and feminist politics; this doesn't prevent them from differing widely on such contentious issues as pornography, the role of religion or the virtues of psychoanalysis. Not only the entries on individual people – Angela Carter's on Sade, for instance, or Sarah Lefanu's on Andrea Dworkin – but those on movements, or on such phenomena as prostitution, agony aunts, transexuality, bisexuality and female genital mutilation, are bound to provoke dissent from one quarter or another. All of which seems right and proper: especially since the polemic has not been allowed to distort factual accuracy and thus make the book unreliable as a resource.

Besides, for those who would like to pursue an argument with a contributor, or to read at greater length what they, or others, have said on a subject, most of the entries are followed by a selective bibliography, giving the most readily available editions of titles that are currently in print.

For those who are not that energetic, the book can be read like a novel: either in the traditional manner, starting at 'A' and ending at 'Z', which produces some eyebrow-raising neighbours (the Browns, Rita Mae and Helen Gurley, for example; Safer Sex and St Augustine); or else, in more postmodern fashion, by following the trail of cross references, the latter indicated by words picked out in bold letters both within the main text and at the end of each entry. In that way, Kathy Acker might send you to William Burroughs, for instance; Burroughs to Obscenity, Obscenity to Radclyffe Hall and Hall

to Havelock Ellis. Or Picasso might send you to Prostitution and Prostitution to Isabel Allende, Flora Nwapa or Nawal el Saadawi, from which latter you could move (among other entries) to Islam, Incest or Masturbation.

Whatever way you read it, the story that unfolds will be Byzantine: a tale of elaborate confrontations of fantasy, faith, assumptions, conclusions and behavior. Sex is sacrament. Sex is sin. Sex is aerobics for the psyche. Sex is the major cause of oppression and the major site of resistance . . .

In the constant battle for supremacy between sexualities, there is no easy way to distinguish the goodies' flags from the baddies'; nor, for that matter, any sure sense that only two armies are fighting. To understand sexuality as a political force, for example, could be the sign either of a feminist or a serious pornographic artist (or, of course, of a serious feminist pornographic artist). Meanwhile, that the Kama Sutra describes the role of the clitoris in sexual arousal does not, of itself, ally it to the women who have done the same thing this century. Differences of intention, perspective and context create different meanings. Cross-dressing in Kabuki theater is not cross-dressing in an opera by Cavalli.

Nonetheless, there are patterns to be seen. Across the globe and across the centuries, liberalism and repressiveness are engaged in a tug-of-war; women avoid, resist or fight the dominant male sexualities; and nature, God or science are invoked to prove that this or that practice is 'natural', then laws brought in to compel us to comply with our 'nature'. The story is often an ugly one – too often, sexuality is tangled with violence, cruelty and vile combinations of fear, stupidity and power abuse – but it is also alive with wit, with ingenious subversions and subterfuges, with glimpses of terrible sadness but also of hope.

My hope is that the book entertains and provokes as much as it informs. If sexuality is only an invention, it is nonetheless one of the richest, most complex and intriguing that humans have devised.

HG

The Sexual Imagination
from **Acker** *to* **Zola**

Acker, Kathy (1947-   )

An American writer whose early works were published by small American presses, Kathy Acker rose to fame upon the publication in London of three novels in one volume, *Blood and Guts in High-school plus 2* (London: Picador, 1984). She was educated at Brandeis University, where she studied with the philosopher Herbert Marcuse, later following Marcuse to California. She has written ten novels, texts for avant-garde performance groups and the screenplay for Bette Gordon's feature film *Variety* (Variety Films: 1984).

The initial impact of Acker's work in London seemed partly due to a general amazement that a woman should write so explicitly about sex. In person, Acker tended to be seen as a symbol, a shocking Statuette of Libertinism associated with extremist New York, the photographs of Robert **Mapplethorpe** and punk. Thus the woman was detached from the writing, allowing many to sidestep the more profound challenges of her work.

In Acker's books, elaborate delineations of sexual **sado-masochism** are always juxtaposed to relationships of political oppression, slavery and deprivation. It is the political relations which are understood as truly obscene, for there the position of victim is not self-chosen. Deeply influenced by Gertrude **Stein** and the Marquis de **Sade**, Acker is regarded as the literary mother of the movement called 'New Narrative', which has been described as 'equal parts gossip, kinky sex, and high theory'. The theory is post-structuralist, the sex tends to be painfully violent and the gossip takes the form of inserting real people – whether Kathy Acker or Rimbaud, Henry Kissinger or Prince – and history into the text. Acker's work is situated at the margins. Orphans, pirates, perverts and other outsiders negotiate the unreal cities of her texts, colliding with intransigent structures of oppression, achieving moments of sadistic or masochistic bliss and continually inquiring into the construction of identity: the original fiction. In an implicit critique of **patriarchy**, Acker's practice of plagiarism challenges both property and authority, undoing relations of ownership at the level of the text. Sexuality is never essentialist in Acker's work: her story 'Lust' in *The Seven Deadly Sins*, ed. Alison Fell (London: Serpent's Tail, 1987), although written in the first person, describes in loving detail intense sex between two men. Crucially, for Acker, the pleasures of sex and writing are inextricably tied up: as she has said, in relation to the conservative backlash, 'Books *is* safe sex'. Acker is an obsessive reader and it is the polymorphously perverse capacity of texts to overlap, repress, expose and ultimately to generate new hybrid writings that fuels Acker's work and makes her literary **pornography** into a contemporary philosophy in the bedroom.

LD

Don Quixote, which was a dream (London: Paladin, 1986; New York: Grove, 1986); *Empire of the Senseless* (London: Picador, 1988; New York: Grove, 1988); *Literal Madness* (New York: Grove, 1988); *Young Lust* (London: Pandora, 1989); *In Memoriam to Identity* (London: Pandora, 1990; New York; Grove, 1990)

See also: **Burroughs; Genet; Ottinger; Perversion; Warhol**

Acton, William (1814-1875)

A controversial surgeon and sexual theorist – at a time when the British medical profession was starting to take a proprietary interest in sex – William Acton trained in London at St Bartholomew's Hospital, studied **venereal disease** in Paris and returned in 1840 to practice in London. In books such as *The Functions and Disorders of the Reproductive Organs* (1875) Acton evoked a world where sexual activity was always dangerous to men: 'excessive' ejaculation, especially if achieved through **masturbation**, was, he claimed, likely to lead to weakness or even to epilepsy or a heart attack. Men should therefore undertake sex in sensible moderation and ensure that no act of **sexual intercourse** lasted for longer than 'some few minutes'.

Abstinence, however, was not the solution.

Whatever contemporary feminists such as Josephine **Butler** might have been arguing, husbands had a right to, and medical need for, regular intercourse with their wives, regardless of whether these wanted it at that moment or even at all. In fact, according to Acton, it would be extraordinary if wives *did* want it: normal women resembling children in not being 'very much troubled with sexual feeling'. The point was that a virtuous wife would permit her husband to have sex with her because, first of all, she wished to make him happy and, second, she wanted children – not for any other reason. Women who sought sex for physical pleasure were mentally ill, 'nymphomaniacs', and ought to be in lunatic asylums.

On the subject of **prostitution**, Acton was in some respects radical. He did not suppose for a second that prostitutes had sexual intercourse for pleasure and understood how poverty, unemployment and atrocious housing were often the causes of women seeking such work. The remedy that he proposed, however – that working-class women should all be trained for domestic service in Britain or the colonies – was not very much more attractive. Besides, he was quick to blame prostitutes for luring weak-bodied men into sin and for giving them **venereal diseases** (failing to see that the luring and infecting was at least as much men's responsibility) and was a supporter of the nineteenth-century **Contagious Diseases Acts** according to which a woman merely suspected of being a prostitute could be forceably given a vaginal examination and, if thought to be infected, imprisoned until she was 'cured'. In short, according to Acton, men were naturally weak and sexual because of the need to procreate the human race; while women, whose natural *a*sexuality should have been used to limit men's lust, were all too often mentally ill, devious, dishonest or corrupt.   *HG*

Ed. Sheila Jeffreys *The Sexuality Debates* (New York and London: Routledge & Kegan Paul, 1987)

See also **Sexology; Stead, W.T.**

Adultery

If a married person has **sexual intercourse** with somebody other than their legal spouse, they are said to be committing adultery. In theory, at least, most societies find such conduct reprehensible. It is likely to result in conflict, to disrupt the peace of the community and to damage the structure of couples and families that is meant to contain sexual energy. And in societies where private ownership and inheritance are important – today, almost all societies – women's adultery puts men at risk of leaving their possessions and titles to other men's children. It is commonly understood, for instance, that, so long as she behaves discreetly, the wife of a British aristocrat may have what adulterous affairs she chooses as soon as she has produced two legitimate sons: one heir; one spare.

Nonetheless, a wife's adultery is almost always and everywhere seen as more blameworthy than that of a husband. This is partly a simple matter of power. As men are most likely to be the judges, priests or other community leaders, what more obvious than that women should receive the most blame for social disruptions? This naked unfairness tends, however, to be veiled in spurious justifications. It is commonly decreed, for example, that women have a special role as the guardians of morality, making their *im*morality a double betrayal. Moreover, in such societies as that of Victorian Britain, it was maintained that a 'normal' woman had little or no sexual drive, her desires being focused on pleasing her husband, childbearing and childrearing. Thus, for a woman to commit adultery was not merely wrong but abnormal, unnatural, *disgusting*; while, for a man, it was what must sadly be expected.

This double standard is far from trivial. It has led to the most appalling injustices and cruelties: the stoning to death of adulterous women (not men) by the ancient Hebrews; the crucifying of adulterous women (not men) in seventeenth-century Japan; the removal from their children and the ostracism of adulterous women (not men) in nineteenth-century Britain. And although it would be wrong to pretend that adulterous men are never punished at all, when they are it is almost always more lightly than women. There are even circumstances in which the adultery of men is encouraged. If a man has a mistress or goes to brothels – in other words, is adulterous without threatening other men's marriages – then he frequently receives society's tacit, if not formal, approval.

For both the sexes, adulterous liaisons are inherently more exciting, or frightening, or traumatic than those blessed by marriage, which undoubtedly accounts for the subject's popularity in fiction. In nineteenth-century America and Europe, for example, when marriage was sorely overtaxed (being asked to supply all manner of social, financial, religious and personal contentment), such classic novels of adultery were written as Nathaniel **Hawthorne**'s *The Scarlet Letter*, Gustave **Flaubert**'s *Madame Bovary*, Leo Tolstoy's *Anna Karenina*. In all these novels, it need hardly be said, the female transgressors are finally punished by their authors, but even present-day novels by women, such as Carol Clewlow's *A Woman's Guide to Adultery* (1989), tend to reserve their sharpest raps on the knuckle for female characters: with the difference that, now, those brought to task are the unmarried women who have sex with other women's husbands. The adulterous men are still perceived as behaving in a way which, sadly, must just be expected.   *HG*

See also **Chastity**

Agony Aunts

Agony aunts are journalists who respond in print, on air or by post to queries put to them by readers and listeners on emotional, sexual, health, family and social problems. They are an international phenomenon. There's scarcely a nation or culture in the world that doesn't have its media oracles dispensing advice to anything between 50 and 2,000 men and women of all ages per month.

The first recorded agony aunt in Britain – possibly the world – was John Dunton, a London printer and bookseller. In 1691 he brought out *The Athenian Gazette*, a publication devoted entirely to questions from readers and his answers. Although he dealt with philosophical issues as well as affairs of the heart, his successors bowed to market forces and advised mainly on topics of personal relationships, love and sex. Until the end of the Second World War the predominant ethos of agony aunts was middle-class morality and the belief that women's personal aspirations and sexual fulfilment came a long way behind their duties to their menfolk, family and home. Then, in the 1960s, came the dramatic growth of the self-awareness and counseling movements. This opened out the agony columns to more explicit questions from readers and more realistic, non-judgemental approaches from the agony aunts. The majority of advisers now come from backgrounds of counseling, nursing or social work, and many are professional psychologists, therapists or medical practitioners.

The sexual content of problem pages depends on their context. Some publications don't pretend to offer anything more than a titillating read and their agony aunts follow suit. Others, who feel that their role is partly educational, present both men's and women's sexuality as something to be developed with confidence, pleasure and self-knowledge and provide straight facts about **contraception**, sexually transmitted diseases and sex techniques. For this they are often condemned by traditionalists for going too far in promoting women's autonomy and by feminists for not going far enough. The truth is that they respond solely to what they are asked. Their prime function, still apparently needed as much as ever, is to listen, to show that they've heard, to offer common-sense guidance and to provide information on all available sources of help.
                                    AW

Terry Jordan *Agony Columns 1890–1980* (London: Optima, 1988)

See also **Brown, Helen Gurley**

Aidoo, Ama Ata (1942-   )

The Ghanaian Ama Ata Aidoo was probably the first African novelist to touch, albeit obliquely, on the subject of lesbians. She did this in her first novel, *Our Sister Killjoy*, which brilliantly interweaves poetry, prose narrative and reverie to chart a quixotic journey from Ghana through Europe and home again, where the heroine's identity and social role are reaffirmed.

During her travels, Sissie makes friends with a German woman, Marija, who becomes infatuated with her. Sissie has imagined what 'a delicious love affair she and Marija would have had if one of them had been a man'; she 'became so absorbed, she forgot who she was, and the fact that she was a woman'. But she is disgusted by Marija's desperate embrace, offended both by the woman's sexuality and the fact that she is European, with all that this represents. When Marija cooks her a special meal she is also annoyed: ' . . . it is not sound for a woman to enjoy cooking for another'. That Sissie allowed herself to contemplate sex with Marija 'if one of them had been a man' shows that, although she comes from a society which positively forbids **homosexuality**, Aidoo recognizes how friendship between women can become sexual. But, she suggests, for African women **lesbianism** is not realistic.

The range of choices that Aidoo offers her heroine is different. Sissie rejects her eminently suitable male lover on grounds of ideology, refusing to play a passive appendage to his articulate and forceful self. She admonishes him for resorting to convenient stereotypes. 'It seems as if so much of the softness and meekness you and all the brothers expect of me and all the sisters is that which is really western. Some kind of hashed-up Victorian notions . . . at home the woman knew her position . . . But wasn't her position among our people a little more complicated than that of the dolls the colonisers brought along with them who fainted at the sight of their own bleeding fingers?'

In Aidoo's play *The Dilemma of a Ghost* the protagonist Ato returns home to Ghana with an African-American wife, Eulalie, causing disruption and bewilderment in his family. Things come to a head when the family assumes Eulalie is barren and Ato doesn't have the courage to explain that they are using contraceptives. Though he loves his wife, Ato lacks the sagacity to make his marriage work despite the cultural differences. At the end it is his mother who rescues the situation as she takes Eulalie under her wing, suggesting to us that there is a glimmer of hope.

For Aidoo, who comes from a matricentred society, in which a man inherits both his identity and material wealth through his mother, to present women as docile, ever-acquiescent creatures is not indigenous invention but colonial inheritance. Which is why, although Sissie may feel pain upon losing her lover, she is certain that her decision is right, and why the mother of Ato will probably succeed in saving his marriage. And witness how in another play, *Anowa*, when the wife chastises the daughter, the father says, 'Leave me out of this. This is your family drum; beat it, my wife.' He knows his place. The women, however, have strong ideas about womanhood, wifehood and fertility. The mother says, 'I want my child to marry a man, tend a farm . . . A woman like her should bear many children so she can afford to have one or two die. Should she not take her place at meetings among the men and women of the clan? And sit on my chair when I am gone? And a captainship in the army, should not be beyond her when the time is ripe!' But her daughter may never bear children. After years of unsuccessfully trying to have sex with her husband Anowa learns that he is impotent, a condition she likens to death since he can leave no offspring. 'My husband is a woman now. He is a corpse. He is dead wood. But less than dead wood because at least that sometimes grows mushrooms.'

NOB

Our Sister Killjoy (Harlow: Longman, 1988); *The Dilemma of a Ghost* (Harlow: Longman, 1965); *Anowa* (Harlow: Longman, 1965)

See also **Ba; Fanon; Lessing**

AIDS

Acquired Immune Deficiency Syndrome, or AIDS, describes a broad set of illnesses caused by the breakdown of the body's immune system due to the presence of the Human Immunodeficiency Virus (HIV). It was first encountered as a new type of immune-deficiency disease following the deaths of several young gay men in the USA in 1981. The HIV virus, previously unknown, was not isolated until 1983, and the existence of the virus was not made public in the USA until 1984.

AIDS quickly became a worldwide epidemic, affecting not only gay men but heterosexual men and women, with 108,176 people known to have or to have died from the disease by 1988 and ten million people thought to carry the HIV virus. Though AIDS is falsely believed to have originated in Africa, a misconception fueled by the racist idea of that continent as being malevolent and threatening, epidemiologists are unable to agree on its first geographical location. Western racism continues to suggest that AIDS is overwhelmingly an African disease, but in fact, by December 1989, 19,141 cases had been reported to the World Health Organization from the continent of Africa and four times that number, 88,233, from the continent of the Americas.

It is now known that a person with the HIV virus – a person who is HIV-positive or seropositive – can remain perfectly healthy for many years: on average, in the west, for around eight years. Contrary to popular mythology, HIV is not *casually* infectious. Its transmission requires the exchange of bodily fluids: primarily blood, semen and, to a lesser extent, vaginal secretion. There is still, however, no sign of a cure. The antiviral drug AZT (Azidothymadine) was believed until recently to increase the body's immunological defences, but serious doubts about its efficacy have now been raised. It can only be hoped that research will soon produce new, and less toxic, drugs.

From the beginning, government agencies and the media in the USA failed to take any fast or effective action. Instead of confronting AIDS as a catastrophic health epidemic in urgent need of funding and research for immediate treatment and possible cure, and instead of mounting mass education campaigns to prevent the main transmission routes via unsafe sexual practices and shared intravenous needles, government and media alike met the public fear and panic by naming scapegoats and blaming victims. This proved all the easier when, in the west as distinct from in Africa, AIDS initially spread among stigmatized or powerless minorities: male homosexuals, Haitians and then other Black groups, as well as among intravenous drug takers and, for a time, haemophiliacs. Indeed, in the grip of **homophobia** and racism, some Americans, as others would elsewhere, rejoiced over this new and deadly disease.

For many years it was left to politicized gay communities (first of all in the USA) to study the spread of the disease, devise and promulgate **safer sex** practices and agitate around AIDS, while learning and sharing the best ways to care for AIDS sufferers and protect those with HIV infection from the multiple abuses and discriminations they faced in every area of their lives.

In Africa, meanwhile, following the failure of an education program aimed at men, it is women who have taken over the design of campaigns to contain the epidemic. Their example might usefully be followed in the west, where AIDS is increasingly affecting heterosexual populations – its homosexual transmission having dropped dramatically – yet many heterosexual men, even those most at risk like intravenous drug users, refuse to use condoms or safer sex practices. And women, after all, have an interest in taking the initiative, since men pass HIV to women more easily than women to men.

Most western governments have, belatedly, been forced to promote more open discussion about sexual practices and the idea of 'safe sex'. Government AIDS campaigns in Britain, however, have carried an ambivalent message, often straightforwardly anti-sex and hence encouraging guilt and anxiety, neither of which has ever proved effective in preventing the sexual transmission of disease. The moral right continues to use AIDS to whip up

A

homophobia and a fear of sex outside marriage. More progressive, and more effective, forces combating AIDS today are aware that we can only surmount this disease when men as well as women (who have always been more aware of the possible dangers surrounding sex) take on full responsibility for their sexual activities. This requires early, more creative sex education for all, in a climate which promotes the freest possible discussion of all sexual matters.   *LSg*

Steve Connor and Sharon Kingman *The Search for the Virus: The Scientific Discovery of AIDS and the Search for a Cure* (Harmondsworth: Penguin, 1988)

See also **Foreplay; Gay Liberation; Maupin; Sexual Intercourse; Venereal Disease**

Akerman, Chantal (1950-   )

Alienation and separation are constant themes in the work of the Belgian filmmaker Chantal Akerman. They are echoed in a film style that rejects easy identification and constantly challenges audience expectations. Akerman resents her films being labeled as feminist, or even as women's films, but nonetheless her early work has always held a central place in discussions of Women's Countercinema: that is, of those films in the 1970s that used formal innovation as a way to deconstruct traditional cinematic methods and expose the ideology behind them, while creating an alternative, oppositional cinema.

Such films put women at centre stage but, at the same time, reject the seduction of audience identification, locating meaning in the formal construction of each shot, and of the film as a whole, rather than in character and a resolved narrative. Akerman's first feature, *Je Tu Il Elle/I You Him Her* (1974) examines the workings of desire, and the threat to the self of emotional involvement, through three episodes in the life of a young woman played by Akerman herself. The final episode features one of the first explicit portrayals of lesbian sex by a woman filmmaker. It not only attacks assumptions about sexuality – the sex of the protagonist's lover had not been previously mentioned – but is filmed in a deliberately de-eroticizing way, emphasizing clumsy physical reality rather that soft-focus sensual fantasy.

Akerman's work questions in particular the *priorities* of conventional cinema, according to which certain elements (such as sexual acts) are deemed to carry much more weight and cinematic interest than others, usually in inverse proportion to the amount of time they occupy in real life. So in *Jeanne Dielman, 23 Quai de Commerce, 1080 Bruxelles* (1975) the heroine's daily rituals of cleaning, cooking and shopping dominate the screen time, acquiring as much significance as, if not more than, the daily visits of the clients who pay her for sex. **Prostitution** is thus put into a startlingly different perspective, and all the baggage associated with mainstream cinema's usually sensationalizing and prurient portrayal of women as prostitutes is discarded.

In the later *Toute une Nuit/All Night Long*, Akerman takes the reverse tack: giving us, instead of an intense concentration on one individual, a series of key moments, meetings, partings and so on in the lives of assorted couples, with no extraneous details. Amy Taubin, writing in the *Village Voice* (31 December 1985), suggests that all Akerman's films 'derive from a single psychic source – the terror of symbiosis lurking not only in the thrills of romance but in the most casual connection'.   *PA*

Je Tu Il Elle/I You Him Her (1974); *Jeanne Dielman, 23 Quai de Commerce, 1080 Bruxelles* (1975); *Toute une Nuit/All Night Long* (1982)

Compiled by Angela Martin: 'Chantal Akerman's Films: A Dossier' in *Feminist Review* no. 3 (1979)

See also **Borden; Export; Gorris; Lesbianism**

Algolagnia

See **Masochism**

Allende, Isabel (1942-)

Born in Peru, raised in Chile (where she also pursued a journalistic career), exiled to Venezuela as a niece of the assassinated democratic President Allende, now married and living in California: Isabel Allende has led a life as rich and inventive as her novels. Although she says that she is not a 'political animal', there is in her work a clear, implicit criticism of the ways in which men use both women and political control.

Allende's first novel, *The House of the Spirits*, which became a bestseller in over twenty languages, relates the story of Clara, born with supernatural powers, whose spirit continues working through her granddaughter long after her death. It is this capacity of women to transcend normal human experience that permits them, where they can't resist it, to subvert men's force. Pancha García, an illiterate peasant and **rape** victim, is made to personify the passivity and suffering of sexually abused womankind, while Tránsito Soto is the prostitute who succeeds in trading her body for the means of manipulating male dictators.

Allende's next novel, *Of Love and Shadows*, is, in her own words, 'the story of a woman and a man who loved one another so deeply that they saved themselves from a banal existence'. If *The House of the Spirits* is closely modeled on Allende's own extended family, then *Of Love and Shadows* is also based on personal experience: of the years immediately following Pinochet's coup against President Allende. In it, Irene Beltrán has a considerably more straightforward (and passionate) relationship with her lover than the unenamoured Clara, the abused Pancha or the scheming Tránsito in *The House of the Spirits*, but **rape** again becomes the vehicle by which weak or humiliated men seek to reassert their **machismo**. Unlike in the **snuff movies** of the America where Allende now lives, however, death is incidental rather than integral to their sexual pleasure.

Men's brutality to women, and women's tenacity according to their own moral laws, is a theme continued in Allende's short stories. It is only in her third novel, *Eva Luna*, that a range of physical tenderness is admitted: Eva's relationship with Riad Hálabi has a delicate closeness born of mutual nurturing, his on account of her youth, hers on account of his physical handicaps.   *AHo*

The House of the Spirits (New York: Bantam, 1986; London: Black Swan, 1986); *Of Love and Shadows* (New York: Bantam, 1988; London: Black Swan, 1988); *Eva Luna* (New York: Bantam, 1989; London: Penguin, 1990); *The Infinite Plan* (London: Harper Collins, 1993)

see also **Garcia Marquez**

All Men are Brothers

See Shuihu Zhuan

Alther, Lisa (1944-   )

An internationally successful US writer – born in Tennessee, at college in Massachusetts, and now settled in Vermont – Lisa Alther has consistently written from a woman's perspective about the forms that sex has taken in the latter half of the twentieth century.

After twelve years of writing, Alther's first published novel, *Kinflicks* (1977), met with enormous commercial and critical success. Sitting at her mother's sickbed, twenty-seven-year-old Ginny Babcock reflects on an action-packed sexual history that spans the massive changes in attitude from the repressive 1950s through the swinging 1960s and on to the feminist and gay liberationist 1970s. There are hilarious passages concerning the adult Ginny's attempts to reach the western sexual nirvana: **orgasm**. At a time when the quest for this sensation was a serious matter for many feminists, Alther milked it for as many laughs as she could get. Nineteen-seventies **lesbianism**, linked here with self-sufficiency and radical politics, is a passing phase in this novel – one which ends in macabre fashion with the decapitation of a lesbian lover.

In *Original Sins*, which followed in 1981, sex is

equally important. The narrative charts the fortunes of five childhood friends from the Southern USA who, in various ways, take part in the social and sexual revolutions of the 1960s and 1970s. With characteristic wit, Alther critically examines both contemporary lesbian politics and the lives awaiting heterosexual women in suburbia. In her third novel, *Other Women*, published three years later, Alther turned her humorous, feminist lens on **psychoanalysis**, **heterosexuality** and lesbianism. Caroline, the lesbian protagonist, attempts to make a go of a heterosexual relationship. Honestly finding that this is not only unpleasurable but fraught with sexism, she opts to see her lesbianism as a choice that gives her the ability to shape her own life.

Entering the 1990s with *Bedrock*, Alther returned to the themes of her first novel, with additions that take into account the changes wrought by AIDS and by post-1960s attitudes to the **sexual revolution**. There is the usual use of wit to poke fun at lesbian feminism and religious fundamentalism, as well as mellow insight into casual heterosexual sex. Against this backdrop, a significant and sustaining friendship between two married women takes eighteen years to become successfully sexual. Although not nearly as well received as her previous novels, this text does provide, yet again, a thought-provoking commentary on late-twentieth-century sexual mores.   *CAU*

Kinflicks (New York: Dutton, 1977; Harmondsworth: Penguin,1977); *Original Sins* (New York: Dutton, 1985; Harmondsworth: Penguin, 1982); *Other Women* (New York: Dutton, 1985; Harmondsworth: Penguin, 1986); *Bedrock* (New York: Knopf, 1990; Harmondsworth: Penguin, 1991)

See also Fell; Miller, Sue

Amis, Martin (1949-   )

In his first novel, *The Rachel Papers*, the British novelist Martin Amis described male sexuality warts, or rather pimples, and all. The book's adolescent hero alternates between spot-squeezing, sexual **fantasy** and **masturbation**. This can be seen as either a deliberate exposure of the socially unacceptable aspects of maleness, or boasting about them.

Amis's two novels of the 1980s, *Money* and *London Fields*, fit this pattern, showing their plots from the viewpoints of variously unpleasant men who end up being sufficiently complacent about the sexism the novels set out to satirize that it comes to seem the novels' accepted view. The books' respective protagonists, loutish film director John Self, and Keith, an aspiring darts champion and petty villain, have a crude, vigorous life – both in efficacious action and unpleasantly captured speech patterns – which is denied to the vapid, virtuous people who surround them. Amis seems to subscribe to the myth that the good and sensitive are somehow less virile, and thus less interesting, than obnoxious brutes.

London Fields has a heroine whose eventually fulfilled longing for violent death is intended to take apart male mythology about women 'asking for it', yet ends up arguably perpetuating what it purports to demolish. It is perhaps also relevant that the one Amis novel to have a female protagonist, *Other People*, is revealed by its title's reference to Sartre's *Huis Clos* to be set in hell. Here, and in other writings about the Bomb, Amis writes very consciously as a father who cares about protecting his and his wife's children from the world outside; but who is also conscious that this very protectiveness is morally ambiguous. His importance is probably that, like other writers of his generation such as Ian McEwan, he has tried to take on and make his own the perception of maleness offered by feminist writers – even if the attempt ends up being as unpleasant as (and strongly resembling) the unregenerate traditional maleness aggressively upheld in novels by his father Kingsley Amis.   *RK*

Other People (Harmondsworth: Penguin, 1982); *Money* (Harmondsworth: Penguin, 1986); *London Fields* (Harmondsworth: Penguin, 1990; New York: Random House, 1991); *Time's Arrow* (Harmondsworth: Penguin, 1992)

See also Barker; Lynch

Androgyny

Androgyny is the possession by a single person of attributes of which society considers some to be female and others to be male. It is quite distinct from **hermaphroditism**, which is the possession by a single person of both sets of *primary and secondary* sexual characteristics, such as breasts and a vagina with a penis. Today in the west, for example, a tall, broad-shouldered woman in a flowery dress might be called androgynous, or a smooth-skinned man wearing make-up and moving in large and assertive gestures: a style at one time adopted by many male pop groups.

Androgyny isn't entirely a matter of style. Feminists' interest in the subject has focused mainly on the qualities of character – compassion, tolerance, loyalty, decisiveness – which cultures tend to allocate uniquely to one or the other sex, and on the way in which androgyny makes a nonsense of such allocation, revealing it to be at best a restrictive over-simplification. To quote Carolyn G. Heilbrun: the concept of androgyny 'seeks to suggest that sex roles are societal constructs which ought to be abandoned'. There are many who find this proposal misguided. Traditionalists cling to the vague idea that men should be men, women women, fearing that its abandonment would lead to social chaos or unisex tedium. Others, like the poet Adrienne **Rich**, believe that the concept of androgyny is too shallow, too weak, to deal with our real sexual conflicts. But it does seem likely that most of us are, in fact, to some extent androgynous: not in the sense of being closer to Female or Male on an imaginary scale, but in the sense that, when working at our best, we deploy whichever attributes are appropriate to a given situation regardless of whether these are designated female or male.

Also, despite the persistent claim that 'real' men like only 'real' women and vice versa, it is often precisely androgyny that attracts us. Compassion in a man, directness in a woman (neither of which society promotes) are commonly described as aphrodisiac, while stars such as Elvis Presley, Greta Garbo, Michael Jackson (to name but a few) are adored at least in part for projecting mixed gender messages. Indeed, the more strongly societies insist upon gender distinctions, the more their sexual fantasies are likely to involve androgyny. In Japan, for instance, where real-life gender roles are kept as polar as possible, transvestites host popular TV shows, drag shows are largely frequented by women, and the favourite pin-ups of teenage girls include the boyish woman wrestler Chigusa and a gay young man called Gilbert Cocteau who, hair tousled and with limpid eyes, is the fictional star of a **comic** book, *Shojo*, specifically aimed at young women. Similarly, a popular Japanese film by Shusuke Kaneko, *1999 no Natsuyasumi/The Summer of 1999*, features young women actors playing schoolboy lovers.

The question is whether androgyny is a game that requires and thus sustains the existence of strong sexual stereotypes – a frisson that leaves those restrictive structures safely standing – or whether it is the signpost to a future where society will truthfully reflect the complexity of every individual.   *HG*

See also **Bisexuality; Bryher; Cross-Dressing; Kabuki; Mapplethorpe;** *Orlando*

Angelou, Maya (1928-   )

Born Marguerite Johnson in St Louis, Missouri, Maya Angelou is a writer, composer, performer and theater director. The widest acclaim has been for her poetry and five volumes of autobiography. The poems are concerned with many facets of African-American existence, and those written about women, such as 'And Still I Rise' and 'Phenomenal Woman', show Angelou's affirmative belief in, and praise of, the black woman's beauty and sexuality.

Angelou's indomitable spirit is apparent in her first volume of autobiography, *I Know Why The Caged Bird Sings*, first published in 1969. At the age of eight she was raped by her mother's boyfriend, who was then found murdered after serving a one-day sentence for his offense. Young Maya, overwhelmed by these events, and by the remorse she felt for her rapist's death, committed herself to silence and did not speak for five years. When she spoke again her worry was whether she had become a lesbian or not. She 'solved' this dilemma by becoming pregnant by a neighborhood boy at the age of sixteen. In the subsequent volumes of her autobiography, her travels take her halfway around the world and through two marriages, yet nowhere does she discuss any psychological problems she might have had as a young woman, or express any rage at having been raped at so young an age. Her feelings, however, can be gleaned from various interviews she has given. She told George Goodman: 'I'm going to write in *Caged Bird* about all those black men with their fists balled up who talk about nation-buildin' time and then go home to rape their nieces and step-daughters and all the little teen-age girls that don't know about life . . . I'm going to tell it . . . because rape and incest are rife in the black community.' (In *Conversations With Maya Angelou*, 1989.)

Incest or the **rape** of young black women can be found in the works of other African-American authors, such as Alice **Walker**, Toni Morrison, Gayl Jones, James Baldwin and Ralph Ellison. Hortense Spillers explains this historically by pointing to the slave laws that inhibited any traditional rights of consanguinity. These laws stated that the children of slaves must 'follow the status of the mother'; hence 'fatherhood' was all but impossible for the African-American male, the responsibility of parental engagement unattainable, the 'name' given to his child fictive.

It is with this possibly unconscious awareness of history that Maya Angelou is able to forgive her rapist. The process enabled her to 'understand how really sick and alone that man was'. In *Conversations with Maya Angelou* she told Tricia Crane, 'I don't mean that I condone at all. But to try to understand is always healing.' In this way Angelou has helped black women to understand that, despite sexual abuse and the general misrepresentation of

their sexuality, they can survive and flourish. The popularity of her works since the 1970s means that this message has reached women worldwide. *SRU*

I Know Why the Caged Bird Sings (New York: Bantam, 1983; London: Virago, 1984); *Gather Together in My Name* (New York: Bantam, 1985; Virago, 1985); *Singin' and Swingin' and Gettin' Merry Like Christmas* (New York: Bantam, 1985; London: Virago, 1985); *The Heart of a Woman* (New York: Bantam, 1984; London: Virago, 1986); *All God's Children Need Traveling Shoes* (New York: Bantam, 1991; London: Virago, 1987); *Just Give Me a Cool Drink of Water 'Fore I Diiie* (New York: Random House, 1971; London: Virago, 1988); *And Still I Rise* (New York: Random House, 1978; London: Virago, 1986)

Ed. Jeffrey M. Elliot *Conversations with Maya Angelou* (Jackson/London: University Press of Mississippi, 1989)
Ed. Cheryl Wall '"The Permanent Obliquity of an In(pha)llibly Straight": In the Time of the Daughters and the Fathers' in *Changing Our Own Words* (London: Routledge, 1990)

See also **Hurston**

Anger, Kenneth (1930-   )

Although there are no more than six films by Kenneth Anger in distribution, he is the acknowledged master of experimental, underground film and his influence on commercial film has been profound. Having grown up in Hollywood – playing the Changeling in Max Reinhardt's *Midsummer Night's Dream* when he was four – he has remained fascinated by Tinseltown and, in two books, *Hollywood Babylon* and *Hollywood Babylon II*, has exposed many of its sleazy scandals and secrets.

Anger's first film *Fireworks* (1947), made when he was seventeen, is a lyrical evocation of the homosexual initiation of an adolescent boy, featuring sailors, blood, milk, mutilation and fireworks, all fused in an imagistic dream sequence. Anger has said, 'My films are primarily concerned with sexuality in people,' and they are indeed erotic to a degree that has forced him to work outside mainstream commercial film. He has also remarked that his 'concept of sensuality and eroticism is through suggestion and inference' and has described his films as 'keys to get frequencies through to the

Great Collective Unconscious'. His films pay tribute to an intensely personal vision in which magic, astrology, mythical knowledge and fascination with popular culture are intermingled. Anger is a devotee of the teachings of English occultist Aleister **Crowley**, who believed in the occult force of what he called Sex Magick, and Crowley's ideas are enshrined in all of Anger's films. *Fireworks* was praised by Jean Cocteau, with whose films it has something in common, and Anger went to live in Europe where he made *Rabbit's Moon* (1950) and *Eau d'Artifice* (1953).

Returning to America he made *Inauguration of the Pleasure Dome* (1954), a film of one of Crowley's dramatic rituals, wherein on All Sabbath's Eve the members of a magical cult assume the identities of mythic goddesses and gods, in this case Shiva, Kali, Lilith and Pan. It was followed by his best known short film *Scorpio Rising* (1963) which pioneered the use of a pop music soundtrack. Its influence is inescapable, from the work of Martin Scorsese and David **Lynch** to pop videos and MTV. *Scorpio Rising* is a wholly fetishistic film, a hymn to leather, bikers, flaming youth, casual sex and violence. It is also extraordinarily beautiful and potent, exploring death, gay sexuality and power through the ironic use of pop lyrics and a ritualistic obsession with Hollywood and its cults, all this subtly contrasted with the power of the emergent 'real' youth culture. The theme is continued in *Invocation of My Demon Brother* (1969) which includes footage of rock concerts, the Rolling Stones and Vietnam. This film is related to the dawning of the Age of Aquarius, a serious matter in occult terms, but the enormously powerful forces Anger evoked seemed to betray him; his star and protégé Robert Beausoleil stole much of the footage and later became involved with the Manson Family. Anger was confronted with many painful problems, including a lack of funding. He struggled on, working for ten years on a revised version, *Lucifer Rising* (1980). He has himself gradually metamorphosed into an almost mythic figure; a magical adept and much respected source of inspiration to generations of younger filmmakers. *EY*

Hollywood Babylon (New York: Crown, 1987; London: Arrow Books, 1986); *Hollywood Babylon II* (New York: Dutton, 1985; London: Arrow Books, 1986)

Ed. Jayne Pilling and Mike O'Pray *Into the Pleasure Dome: The Films of Kenneth Anger* (London: British Film Institute, 1989)

See also **Fassbinder; Genet; Jarman**

Apollinaire, Guillaume (1880-1918)

In the first decade of this century realism in all the arts was being eroded by the first modernist impulses. **Picasso** and Braque were conducting their Cubist experiments and poets were questioning the Symbolist inheritance. The work of the French poet Guillaume Apollinaire spans this period and is oddly poised between a lyrical, tender innocence and a more fantastical strain, heir to the excesses of Alfred Jarry. It is this latter element that was to be most pronounced in Apollinaire's pornographic writing.

Although he had many friendships, Apollinaire's life was drab and he labored in uncongenial jobs. His time as curator at the Bibliothèque Nationale fueled his intense interest in eighteenth-century **erotica**. In 1907 he started writing **pornography** in order to make money and produced *Les Memoires d'un jeune don Juan*. Although this is mundane pornography in the Victorian mode, featuring aristocratic **incest** and many frothing petticoats and lacy knickers, the touches of perversity and ironic humor presage his next work, *Les Onze Mille Verges*. In this controversial classic the poet of genius can certainly be glimpsed behind the pornographic hack and in many ways Apollinaire succeeds in transcending the considerable limitations of the genre. As in his poetry, which became increasingly experimental, there is an attempt to extend boundaries. However in the pornography this radical inventiveness inevitably takes the form of increasingly bizarre and depraved imaginings.

Les Onze Mille Verges is initially conventional

13

A

in its description of relentless, improbable sexuality but when the hero, Prince Mony Vibescu, is joined by the beastly working-class burglar-turned-valet Cornaboeux, excesses of flagellation and **coprophilia** give way to extreme **sado-masochism**, sexual murder and **necrophilia**. The second half of the book is set in the Franco-Prussian war and it is there that Vibescu meets Kilyemu, the gentle, loving Japanese prostitute, and kills her. From this moment he is irredeemably damned and a symbolic figure appears, the personification of Evil. She is a Polish noblewoman who achieves sexual satisfaction by torturing wounded Russian soldiers. Even Vibescu is ultimately revolted. 'He became aware of his own cruelty and his fury turned against the infamous nurse.' He kills her and, in one of the strangest episodes in pornography, uses her belly as a drum to summon the Japanese army. He is too late to redeem himself and is sentenced to die by the application of eleven thousand lashes, or *verges*, which provides the title with its pun on *vierges* (virgins). An allegorical strain is evident in the book's weird combination of the political and scatalogical. *Les Onze Mille Verges* was prophetic in heralding the advent of a century marked by nihilism, intellectual despair and indifference to mass suffering. The many bizarre elements add a surreal touch and it was Apollinaire who coined the term 'surrealism'. For feminist analysis the primary interest of the book lies in the way Apollinaire manipulates the reader into repeatedly confronting the point at which she or he passes from lust to disgust, and the relevance of this issue to any consideration of pornography.   *EY*

Memoirs of a Young Rakehell/The Debauched Hospodar (New York: Grove Press, 1969; London: Star Books, 1986); Les Onze Mille Verges or the Amorous Adventures of Prince Mony Vibescu (London: Peter Owen, 1989)

See also **Bataille**; *Torture Garden*

Aquinas, Thomas (c. 1226-1274)

Aquinas was born in the kingdom of Naples and became a Dominican friar, probably at about the age of sixteen. As far as we know he was celibate for the whole of his life. He writes about sex with the calm and rationality of a man largely untroubled by sexual appetite. His teaching on sexual relations is based, in part, on assumptions which would have been virtually universal in his day.

These assumptions included Aristotelian biology. The science of Aquinas's day assumed that Aristotle was right in saying that the male role in conception is the active one, women being merely incubators; also that the fetus is initially male and a slip must occur to make a female baby, which is, in that sense, defective. Therefore women are biologically flawed and so more liable to irrationality, sin and so on. Based partly on this biology, partly on common (not specifically Christian) philosophical theory and partly on the usual interpretation of the Bible, particularly the Genesis creation story, the assumption of Aquinas and his contemporaries was that women are necessarily under male authority. Interestingly, Aquinas discusses the question of whether God could have become incarnate in a woman and concludes that he could not, because women are subject beings, but this conclusion is reached only after a list of reasons why it *would* be possible for Jesus to have been a woman.

Aquinas is clear that marriage is good and sexual pleasure within marriage a gift from God. However, like his contemporaries, he assumed that the main purpose of sex is to beget children and that this must always be the underlying motive for having sex. The 'matrimonial debt', the right to **sexual intercourse,** is judged to be part of the marital contract, but women have as much right to it as men and husbands must be sensitive to their wives' needs. Aquinas also assumes that a marriage is automatically invalid if a woman is forced into it.

Aquinas's teaching has been enormously influential. Much Christian doctrine, and Roman Catholicism in particular, is still saying essentially the same about the main purpose of sex. Yet

Aquinas reflected rationally on the accepted scientific data of his day and might well have reached different conclusions had those data been different.

JW

See also **Celibacy; Christianity**

Arabian Nights

Arabian Nights, or in French *Les mille et une nuits*, is the title given to a collection of stories which emerged from an oral, folkloric, Arabic tradition. They were first translated from Arabic by Antoine Galland, a French scholar and traveller, between 1704 and 1717, and later by other Europeans, such as Sir Richard **Burton** who added a number of salacious footnotes.

If the source of the stories themselves is vague, the framework is undoubtedly Persian, being that of a book called *Thousand Tales* attributed to a Princess Homai, supposedly the daughter of Artaxerxes I. The structure of the collection is this: King Shahriyar, having discovered that his wife has been unfaithful to him, beheads her and resolves to avoid future disappointment by spending each night with a different woman who, in turn, will be beheaded in the morning. After a long succession of women have been thus chosen and despatched, it is the turn of Scheherazade. She captures his interest by telling him stories which, tantalizingly, she never has time to finish so that the king postpones her execution in order to hear the rest the following evening. After one thousand and one nights, she has not only cured his mistrust of women but also borne him three children and is thus allowed to remain with the king without the threat of execution.

Though such tales as 'Sinbad the Sailor' are well known to European children, thanks to the many bowdlerized translations and adaptations available, stories such as that of the Ensorcelled Prince are less familiar. The Prince discovers that he is being cuckolded by his adored wife, who prefers to him a leprous, paralytic slave who ill-treats and humiliates her. He attempts to kill the slave, but succeeds only in wounding him. When his wife discovers that it was her husband who attacked her lover, she puts a spell on him, turning him to stone from the waist down, and beats and tortures him every day. Finally she in turn is tricked and killed and the spell is broken. There are shorter tales, too, such as that of Abu Hasan, who 'let fly a fart, great and terrible' upon his wedding night and fled the land in shame (to fart is an appalling social solecism in Arab society), returning years later to discover that the night when he farted has become 'a date which shall last for ever and ever'.

Galland's version is an Orientalist fantasy, in which the Arabic vernacular is often toned down to suit eighteenth-century European manners. Sir Richard Burton, on the other hand, reveled in the bawdiness of tales designed for an all-male audience. The women in his version are chiefly depicted as wanton lechers; the alternative stereotypes being those of the beautiful virgin who is corrupted and suffers a cruel fate, or the pious and kind wife. Only Scheherazade is presented as beautiful, intelligent, virtuous and learned (although none of this prevents her remaining subject to the king). Indeed, in Burton's translation, the *Arabian Nights* entirely reinforces the European myth of Oriental promiscuity, with both men and women of the East perceived as driven primarily by lust.

SR

See also **Perfumed Garden**

Aristophanes

See Lysistrata

Armstrong, Gillian (1950-)

A gifted Australian film director, Gillian Armstrong has made a series of movies featuring women who are, in their own ways, ahead of their time: women who claim independence in matters intellectual, emotional and sexual. Her first film, *My Brilliant Career* (1979), featured Judy Davis as Sybylla, a headstrong, self-confident young woman raised in Outback Australia at the turn of the century and, despite the insecurities, yearning to be a writer. The next, *Starstruck* (1982), was a surprising but exuberant departure: a pop musical. Starring New Wave singer Jo Kennedy, it tracked the wayward adventures of a young, working-class woman determined to make it big in Sydney music biz and, while being sexually liberated and freely enjoying sex with a boyfriend, refusing to be easily had.

The theme of healthy sexuality and social freedom was explored more specifically in *Mrs Soffel* (1984), based on the true story of Kate Soffel, the wife of a prison warden who fell in love with a prisoner convicted of murder. It is set in gray, industrialized Pittsburg in 1901; we are back at the turn of the century. Within the confines of her grim and proper middle-class household, Kate Soffel (Diane Keaton) recovers suddenly from a debilitating three-month illness (one of those mysterious ailments that beset repressed and oppressed Victorian women) but nonetheless insists on keeping to a separate bedroom. It is clear that she does not want to sleep with her stuffy and controlling husband again.

While passing out bibles to prisoners, Kate becomes drawn to the plight of Ed and Jack Biddle, and especially drawn to the charismatic Ed (Mel Gibson) who seduces her with his ardent attentions and his religious debates. Believing the men to be innocent of their murder charge, Kate writes a passionate plea to the governor to review their case. Her husband is outraged: 'Do you need to see the doctor?' In his mind, her wilfulness makes her unbalanced and threatening. So Kate sneaks saws into jail to help the Biddles escape and when after the break-out, Ed unexpectedly comes to her house to take her away with him, she goes. As Kate and Ed make a desperate escape north in the deep of winter, it is clear that she is escaping her own prison of a formal, unhappy marriage and suffocating Victorian convention. While staying overnight in a farmhouse, Kate and Ed make tender love in their briefly held freedom. Armstrong manages to turn this potentially maudlin story into a strangely poetic romance, in which healthy, vital female sexuality is inseparable from freedom of choice and from men's and women's mutual recognition of each other as whole.

High Tide (1988) took Armstrong back to her native Australia. In it Lilli, a free-spirited drifter – Judy Davis again, now looking ragged but more fascinating – is befriended by a teenage girl who turns out to be the daughter she abandoned long ago. Though she finds herself falling in love with this winsome child, she also fears commitment and is drawn by the freedom of the road. In *High Tide* Armstrong recognizes that a woman's choices become more complex with time, and that there is more than one kind of courage – but in all her films we are shown that women want to, and can, enjoy sexual freedom, and that healthy sexuality is inextricably tied to healthy emotional and social situations.   SC

See also **Brontë, Charlotte; Hui**

Atkinson, Ti-Grace (1938-   )

Ti-Grace Atkinson, one of the early radical feminists in New York City, wrote critiques of sexuality that prefigured the lesbian-feminist critique of heterosexuality and the writing of such feminist theorists as Catharine A. MacKinnon and Andrea **Dworkin**. Atkinson began her activism in the New York chapter of the National Organization for Women (NOW) and became the chapter's president, but her radicalism soon brought Atkinson and NOW to a parting of the ways. Atkinson then joined The Feminists, a radical feminist group that styled itself 'a political organization to annihilate sex roles'. The group's decision to limit women living with men to one-third of its membership drew much criticism from other feminists.

Atkinson's speeches were published in *Amazon Odyssey* (New York: Link Books, 1974). The speeches point to sexuality and reproduction as the means used by men to oppress women, to turn them from people into functions. Atkinson says that **sexual intercourse** is an institution: an institution that was created by and for men and is only in men's, not women's interest. The function of sex is to keep women subordinate; men enjoy it so much, writes Atkinson, because it reinforces their dominant position in society. However, Atkinson does not believe that free human beings would need either sex *or* love. Sex and love she sees as metaphysical cannibalism, a way that some human beings (men) have discovered to use others to ward off existential loneliness, instead of becoming autonomous. Love, like marriage and **vaginal orgasm**, is a scheme to convince women that subordination is in their interest. Love, says Atkinson, is the victim's response to the rapist; it is the gloss on women's situation that makes it seem bearable.

Although Atkinson's model for sex and love is **heterosexuality**, she also questions **lesbianism** because it is connected with sexuality. However, she strongly urges feminists to resist lesbian-baiting and at one point suggests that all truly radical feminists are political lesbians. But the frequent attribution to her of the quote 'Feminism is the theory; lesbianism is the practice' is neither correct nor does it reflect her thinking. What she does is to urge women to end their relations with men because even appearing in public with a man could reinforce the idea that women exist for men. However, willingness to take risks for the movement is, for her, the most important determinate of radicalism; she says that she cares more who women would die for than who they sleep with. Atkinson thought that a revolution would be necessary to end all forms of oppression and believed that radical feminism would be the leading force in that revolution, which would include coalitions with radical men.　　*CD*

Carol Anne Douglas *Love and Politics: Radical Feminist and Lesbian Theories* (San Francisco: ism press, 1990)

See also **Koedt; Political Lesbianism**

Atwood, Margaret (1939-　　)

Poet and novelist Margaret Atwood is one of Canada's most successful writers. Although Americans frequently claim her as theirs, she is a strong Canadian nationalist, acutely aware of cultural differences between Canada and the USA. Her early relationship with feminism was more ambivalent than her nationalism but, not surprisingly, given her acute sense of observation and her writerly ethos, her analysis of gender, sexual politics and writing as a woman is informed by feminism. In her 1976 article 'On Being a "Woman Writer": Paradoxes and Dilemmas' (*Second Words: Selected Critical Prose,* Toronto: Anansi, *1982),* she articulated the fairly common reservation that commitment to a political movement and good writing do not make good bedmates: 'the aim of a political movement is to improve the quality of people's lives . . . Writing, however, tends to concentrate more on life, not as it ought to be, but as it is, as the writer feels it, experiences it. Writers are eye-witnesses, I-witnesses.' But in fact this credo led to political commitment and activism, particularly in relation to issues concerning writers and human rights and national issues that affect Canadian cultural autonomy, and Atwood's focus on what the eye sees and on the 'I', especially in relation to women's lives and male-female relationships, brings her writing into dialogue with feminist issues.

In terms of sexual politics, Atwood tends to stay within the heterosexual paradigm of relationships, but graphically evokes the violences within these. Who can forget the sardonic, epigrammatic opening to her book of poems *Power Politics* (Toronto: Anansi, 1971)?

> you fit into me
> like a hook into an eye
>
> a fish hook
> an open eye

In *The Handmaid's Tale* (Toronto: McClelland and Stewart, 1985) Atwood hypothesizes a society of the near future in which reproduction and sexuality are rigidly controlled by a right-wing Christian fundamentalist state. The novel can be read as an illustration of the dynamics of public and private oppression, of public and private sexual politics, and of the ways these can be resisted. Told by Offred, reproductive handmaid to one of the commanders, the story focuses on Offred's experience of patriarchal repression and on her emergent resistance: expressed, ironically, through an illicit sexual liaison with the commander's chauffeur. At one level the novel explores this paradox, that sexuality can be both a site of oppression and a site of liberation. Pornographic sex is juxtaposed with memories of love and romance, but ultimately, for Offred, the confirmation of her existence lies in the body's desire: sexuality. In this novel as in other works, Atwood explores the popular fictions of romance – which makes it all the more curious that the film version of *The Handmaid's Tale* turned Offred into a straightforward, unquestioned, romantic heroine, in love with and rescued by her lover.

Atwood is fascinated by the tension that women experience between the *social* construction of gender and the individual desire for self-creation and freedom. She returns repeatedly to the socialization of the white, middle-class female in English Canada in the 1950s and 1960s, through the ironic vision of present-day adult protagonists. In this respect *Cat's Eye* (Toronto: McClelland and Stewart, 1988) is brilliant, particularly in its depiction of the way little girls police each other. Not a stereotypical feminist tract about the joys of sisterhood and female bonding, this novel demonstrates that fiction is sometimes ahead of theory in its investigation of human experience.   *DR*

The Edible Woman (Toronto: McClelland and Stewart, 1969; New York: Warner Books, 1989; London: Virago, 1980); *Surfacing* (Toronto: McClelland and Stewart, 1972, New York: Fawcett, 1987; London: Virago, 1979); *Lady Oracle* (Toronto: McClelland and Stewart, 1976; New York: Fawcett, 1987; London; Virago, 1982); *Selected Poems* (Toronto: Oxford University Press, 1976); *Dancing Girls and Other Stories* (Toronto: McClelland and Stewart, 1977; New York: Simon & Schuster, 1982; London: Virago, 1984); *Life Before Man* (Toronto: McClelland and Stewart, 1979; New York: Fawcett, 1987; London: Virago, 1982); *Bodily Harm* (Toronto: McClelland and Stewart, 1981; New York: Bantam, 1983; London: Virago, 1983); *Bluebeard's Egg* (Toronto: McClelland and Stewart, 1983; New York: Fawcett, 1987; London: Virago, 1988); *Murder in the Dark: Short Fictions and Prose Poems* (Toronto: Coach House Press, 1983; London: Cape, 1984); *Selected Poems II: Poems Selected & New 1976–1986* (Toronto: Oxford University Press, 1986); *Good Bones* (London: Bloomsbury, 1992)

Ed. Earl G. Ingersoll *Margaret Atwood: Conversations* (Willowdale, ON: Firefly Books, 1990)

See also **Heterosexuality; Romantic Fiction**

Ba, Mariama (1929-1981)

A Senegalese teacher and feminist, Mariama Ba became well known for her outspoken views in favor of women's education and against their oppression. Her novels *So Long A Letter* and *Scarlet Song* use these subjects as a background against which to explore the complexities of love and marriage in an African Muslim context.

Ba invests her heroines with certain liberal attitudes, to life, love, friendship and sex, which she encourages women universally to embrace. These heroines come from an Islamic society which sanctions polygamy, yet they warn both men and women against taking multiple marriage lightly, because of the jealousies it arouses and the sacrifices and constraints it demands from all sides. When men talk about the 'imperious laws' which govern them ('we aren't like women, it's in our nature'), the women to whom they are married see this as a ridiculous argument for the right to betray. Sex for the sake of 'variety' is degrading and Ba voices such sentiments vigorously through her female protagonists. Says Ramatoulaye in *So Long A Letter*: 'If you can procreate without loving . . . I find you despicable.'

Although the overriding themes in Ba's writing are abandonment and the inequality of the sexes, her novels challenge the stereotype of the docile African Muslim woman who caters only to the needs of her demanding African man. In Ba's fiction, first marriages have always been sacrificed to male lust and vanity and, as significantly, to the wiles of older women who, for social or monetary gain, sabotage the young wives' happiness. But except for Mireille, the French wife of Ousmane in *Scarlet Song*, the 'victims' in Ba's novels do not remain marital casualties. The African women appear culturally equipped to regard their experiences as educational, analyze their marital problems sociologically and question the aspirations of women in general. It is the white woman, unable to understand her husband's betrayal, who finally attacks him and murders their child. Ousmane, the husband, dreams up all kinds of sociological and historical justifications for his lust, but the truth is that he was 'thrown off balance by [Ouleymatou's] sexuality . . . What could Mireille's lack of sophistication do in the face of the provocative tinkle of beads around the hips, or the aphrodisiac potency of gongo powder? What could Mireille do against the suggestive wiggle of an African woman's rump?' His relationship with Mireille is complicated by the fact that he sees in her his own betrayal of his 'Africanness' and sees his other marriage as a way to save face in his community. Ba felt that education and women's liberation, rather than breaking up marriages, would strengthen the marital bond and ensure that women could not be so cavalierly discarded, their rights so easily violated. It would also mean that young women would be less willing sexually to stroke the vanity of (generally old and married) men for money.   *NOB*

So Long A Letter (London: Virago, 1982); *Scarlet Song* (New York and London: Longman, 1986)

See also **Fanon; Islam; Saadawi**

Baker Brown, Isaac (1812-1873)

Having trained at Guy's Hospital in London, Isaac Baker Brown practiced general medicine from 1834 to 1846 before becoming a surgeon *accoucheur*, or obstetrician. In this latter role he developed an interest in gynecological surgery and, in particular, in surgically removing women's clitorises.

This was more than just whimsical sadism. If, in Victorian England, the **clitoris** was a mystery to most of the public, the medical fraternity appears to have known about both it and its function. Well enough, in any case, for Baker Brown to connect its existence with women's **masturbation**, an activity then considered degenerate and dangerous in both the sexes. But Baker Brown specifically proposed that, in women, it led to hysteria, insanity, epilepsy, even to sterility, and thus advocated the removal of the clitoris to cure women suffering from any of these.

When, in the 1860s, he published several writings expounding this theory, he did encounter some criticism. But, to objections that masturbation could surely be cured less drastically, by 'moral treatment', Baker Brown retorted that there were cases where moral treatment just wasn't sufficient – and 'Are we, then, to forbid that surgery shall come to the rescue, and cure what morals should have prevented?' Others protested that clitoridectomy 'unsexes a woman'. Baker Brown laughed this out of court. 'The fact,' he wrote, 'that several of my patients have become pregnant after the operation is a complete reply to this objection.' Whether or not it was received as such, it is clear that the author took it for granted that, in a 'normal' woman, sexuality meant procreation. Indeed, his readiness to mutilate his patients ('either by scissors or knife – I always prefer the scissors') was at least as much to do with his concept of normality as it was with health. Among the symptoms that suggested to him that an operation was in order were 'distaste for marital intercourse', and a tendency to walk in the country alone and to 'come back exhausted'. (Other symptoms, read today, would seem to have been those of anorexia nervosa.)

Scissor-happy though a few of his colleagues might have judged him, Baker Brown was not so removed from the sexual mores of his time and place that anyone actually prevented him from practicing his craft. What finally got him expelled from the Obstetrical Society (in 1867) and brought his career to a sudden end was his failure always to *inform* his patients or their families what his 'cure' would involve.   *HG*

Balthus, *The Room*, 1952-54

Ed. Sheila Jeffreys *The Sexuality Debates* (New York and London: Routledge & Kegan Paul, 1987)

See also **Female Genital Mutilation**

Balthus (Balthasar Klossowski de Rola) (1908-   )

The painter Balthus, who was born in Paris, has never veered from a figurative style done in plastery paint in an earthy range of tones reminiscent of Renaissance frescoes. Many of his large, uncluttered canvases deal with the sexuality surrounding pubescent and pre-pubescent girls, the most powerful and outspoken dating from the 1930s and 1940s. It is very much a male view of female adolescent sexuality, with the few men seen as predators, or mere accessories, and cats symbolizing sexual knowledge. However, the urge to dismiss Balthus as the painter of parted legs is undercut by the surreal atmosphere of the works.

In 'The Dream' (1938) a young girl sits with closed eyes and one leg up on a stool, the crotch of her knickers revealed; below, a cat licks a saucer of milk. In 'La Chambre' (1952–1954) a **nude** young woman with socks, but no pubic hair, lies stretched backwards with parted legs over a chair; she faces a window whose curtain is being fiercely opened by a knowing, dwarfish woman who could be interpreted as throwing light on the subject of sexual abandonment. Several paintings allude to **lesbianism**. 'The Salon' (1942) pictures two adolescents, one on the sofa with her head thrown back, her legs parted and a cello on her lap, the other crouched over a book in a kneeling position on the floor; is it outrageous to see them as separate halves of one sexual situation? The far more explicit 'Guitar Lesson' (1934) depicts a young girl with her skirt lifted to her waist lying back across the knees of her older female teacher. The girl's hand almost touches the teacher's exposed breast while the teacher's hand rests close to her pupil's hairless genitals. A guitar lies on the floor, the banality of the metaphor redeemed by the cruel and dreamlike quality of the image.   *FB*

Musée d'Art Moderne, Paris

See also **Paedophilia; Rego; Surrealism**

Bannon, Ann (c.1935-   )

The author of a series of lesbian pulp novels published in the late 1950s and early 1960s in the USA, Ann Bannon has recently been rediscovered by lesbian readers on the republication of her novels by Naiad press. The novels are all set in the urban gay culture of 1950s Greenwich Village, New York. Although not the only pulp novels of their kind – during the same period many authors, male and female, were writing lesbian fiction, often for the pleasure of straight men – Bannon's were the most popular and described the most affirmative lesbian lifestyles.

Bannon's novels follow the lives and loves of three major characters, Laura, Beth and Beebo, tracing each woman's discovery of her **lesbianism** against a backdrop of the Butch-Femme roleplaying that characterized lesbian relationships of the period. At the time she was writing, Bannon (a pseudonym) was a young housewife whose experi-

ence of New York's lesbian culture was limited to the brief trips she made to the Village during her husband's absence. Despite this, her novels served as a reference point for many women who were struggling to come to terms with their lesbianism. She received scores of letters from women wanting support and information about a sexual and emotional possibility that was still largely invisible within mainstream culture. As Joan Nestle has stated: 'Buying an Ann Bannon book in the '50s was like coming out.'

If Bannon's importance in the 1950s and 1960s was as a reference point for an emerging lesbian identity, her relevance today, like that of Radclyffe **Hall**, is as a focus for debates about the relationship of lesbian history to contemporary lesbian politics. Like Hall's, Bannon's work has been vilified by lesbian historians looking for 'positive role models' because of its representations of Butch-Femme relationships and its occasional view of lesbianism as pathological. These negative aspects are certainly present in her fiction, but the novels can also be regarded as crucial interventions into 1950s debates about sexuality and women's role. By representing, through her narratives, a *variety* of lesbian characters whose journeys towards a lesbian identity are different from one another's, Bannon demonstrates that there is no singular definition or explanation of lesbianism and that, for many women, lesbianism can be a choice rather than an imposed identity. Moreover, in representing the lives of the few married women in her novels as a drudgery and a degradation, her work stands as an early feminist critique of marriage and **compulsory heterosexuality**.   *DH*

Odd Girls Out (Tallahassee: Naiad, 1986); *I Am A Woman* (Tallahassee: Naiad, 1986); *Women in the Shadows* (Tallahassee: Naiad, 1986); *Journey To A Woman* (Tallahassee: Naiad, 1989); *Beebo Brinker* (Tallahassee: Naiad, 1986)

Diane Hamer ' "I Am A Woman": Ann Bannon and the Writing of Lesbian Identity in the 1950s' in *Lesbian and Gay Writing* ed. Mark Lilly (Basingstoke: Macmillan, 1990)

See also **Microcosm; Romantic Fiction; Taylor; Wilhelm**

B

Barker, Howard (1946-)

Among those playwrights who have dominated the British theater for the last two decades, Howard Barker is both one of the most controversial and one of the most intriguing on the subject of sexuality. Like such contemporaries as Howard Brenton (with whom he is often confused) and David Hare, he began his career writing typical 1970s state-of-the-nation plays that explored the relationship between class and capital. Since the early 1980s, however, he has developed a bold, poetic language and written a series of anti-naturalistic history plays. *Victory* (1983), *The Castle* (1985), *Pity in History* (1986) and *The Bite of the Night* (1988) all mock the received idea of history and question the difference between truth and myth. And, increasingly, Barker's plays have dealt with issues of desire, emphasizing sexuality as the most important part of individual consciousness.

In an interview in *City Limits* magazine in October 1986, Barker declared that 'it is always easier to talk about a writer's problems than to try to come to terms with the sex. Politics is street talk whereas sex is unarticulated, even in bed. I have rejected discretion entirely and my characters articulate sex at their greatest level of reality. A reversal goes on in my plays. The unspoken becomes the revealed, and the normal pattern of communication, what passes for naturalism, is abolished.' Barker's 1986 act of 'creative vandalism' on *Women Beware Women*, a **Jacobean revenge tragedy** by the seventeenth-century Thomas Middleton, is one of several plays that have considered the liberating and redemptive possibilities of fucking. Carefully editing four acts of Middleton's and grafting on a final act of his own – where, instead of all being killed off, the characters find liberation through sex – Barker berates the British left's inability to deal with the politics of desire and argues that sexual revolution can lead to political revolution.

The new play takes issue with what Barker regards as Middleton's diseased sensibility – 'Middleton says lust leads to the grave. I say desire alters perception' – and yet it is no less confused and con-tradictory than its seventeenth-century counterpart. In Barker's version the final **rape** of Bianca is depicted as class revenge, which seems at odds with his ideas on sexual freedom, while his suggestion that rape can lead to raised consciousness is deeply offensive to most women. While Barker strives to explore sexuality and desire (most notably in *The Castle*), his efforts are continually thwarted by the manner in which he either marginalizes women, or uses them as convenient symbols (Helen of Troy in *The Bite of the Night* is systematically dismembered and mutilated, seemingly as a punishment for her sensuality and the desire she engenders) or creating women characters who are entirely like men, particularly in the way they express their sexuality. Even in *The Castle*, a play that specifically explores sexual desire within the context of male destructiveness and female compassion, the impression is of a playwright who, while despising the tyranny of men, denies the strength of women. In Barker's plays sex is a commodity, a weapon, a political statement, a means of raising self-consciousness. It is never an expression of love.   *LG*

See also **Amis; Hitchcock**

Barnes, Djuna (1892-1982)

During the 1920s a group of extraordinarily talented expatriate women, many of them lesbian, gathered in Paris. They included Natalie Barney, Romaine Brooks and Janet Flanner. Djuna Barnes, a woman of exceptional beauty and distinction, was a member of their circle and is considered to be one of the most important women writers of that period.

Barnes had been a journalist in New York and in 1915 published *The Book of Repulsive Women*, a collection of macabre, sexually explicit rhymes and *fin-de-siècle* drawings whose obscurantism alone allowed it to escape the censor. The book reveals a conflicting attraction and repulsion toward women's bodies, a disconcerting ambivalence more explicitly apparent in a later work, the privately distributed *Ladies Almanack*, an ornate, witty account of the lesbian characters in Paris. In it, high-flown comic rhetoric contrasts vividly with an unflinching insistence on the grosser aspects of female physicality, producing an effect strikingly at odds with the evasive, conventional romanticism of Radclyffe **Hall**, the other noted lesbian writer of the time. The *Ladies Almanack* takes the form of a Sapphic calendar listing 'the tides and moons' of the ladies, their 'distempers', 'spring fevers, love philters and winter feasts' and celebrates 'the little Difference which shall be alien always'. This combination of mock-heroic language and contemporary irony is typical of Barnes's distinctive style.

While in Paris, in 1928, Barnes published her most successful novel, *Ryder*, a bawdy, mock-Elizabethan account of her baleful and eccentric family. Her personal life was bisexual and distressed. She fell deeply in love with Thelma Wood, an expatriate sculptor, and when their anguished affair ended in 1932 wrote her masterpiece, *Nightwood*. This book was enthusiastically championed by T.S. Eliot who wrote the introduction and remained a life-long friend. It is a searing exorcism of Barnes's affair with Thelma Wood, who appears as 'Robin Vote', un untamed, primeval force. The episodes are linked by the soliloquies of one Dr Matthew O'Connor, a tragic philosopher, beribboned and perfumed, who was based on a notorious expatriate transvestite, abortionist and wit. His voice, by turns anguished, **camp** and motherly, allows Barnes to reflect in her disturbing, convoluted prose on the restrictions imposed by rigid societal sex roles. Barnes was a woman of exquisitely subtle sensibility and the structure of the book, which is almost sculptural in its distancing techniques, enables her to express extreme emotional pain with no hint of orthodox bohemian angst.

In 1940 Barnes returned to New York and lived for another 42 years as a near-recluse in Patchin Place, Greenwich Village. Her final work, a drama called *The Antiphon* (New York: Farrar, Straus and Cudahy, 1958) was impenetrable to the point where it seemed deliberately to repel and thus, possibly, reflected her growing misanthropy. The satirical sophistication of her lesbian books, her tortuous gothic investigations of her family history and the terrible pain and deep compassion of *Nightwood* combine to reveal a great stylist incapable of a conventional response who has proved to be a notable role-model to subsequent generations of lesbian feminists.   *EY*

Ryder (New York: St Martin's Press, 1980); *Nightwood* (New York: New Directions, 1946; London: Faber, 1950)

Andrew Field *Djuna: The Formidable Miss Barnes* (Austin: University of Texas Press, 1966)

See also **Bisexuality; Lesbianism; Stein**

Bataille, Georges (1897-1962)

As a philosopher, critic and novelist, French writer Georges Bataille has exerted an enormous influence on two generations of the French avant-garde: first on the Surrealists of his own generation and then on the influential theorists of the 1960s and 1970s, a group which included Roland Barthes, Jacques Derrida, Michel **Foucault** and Julia **Kristeva**. His erotic fiction is probably more disturbing to the reader than anything else ever written on the subject of sex. The classic elegance of his prose and sophistication of his thinking make **obscenity** a secondary issue, but there is no doubt that his novels pose a powerful and shocking challenge to the consciousness.

Bataille's childhood was disturbed. His father, apparently syphilitic, died blind and paralysed and Bataille documented his feelings about this in his first pseudonymously published pornographic work *The Story of the Eye* (1928). Although Bataille struggled with and finally rejected Catholicism, it remains a prominent issue in his work, in the same perverse and decadent sense as in the writing of, for example, Charles **Baudelaire** or Jean **Genet**. Bataille was involved in a number of left-wing projects from 1929–1939 and, after the Second World War, founded the journal *Critique*. He remained closely involved with new intellectual developments in the arts, was deeply influenced by Nietzsche, and worked for forty years as a librarian.

In 1970 Gallimard started publishing his complete works, the final volume, volume XII, appearing in 1988. There have, however, been relatively few English translations, many provided by the British firm of Marion Boyars.

Bataille was a high priest of the perverse. Briefly, his philosophical and religious writings investigate our loss of 'intimacy': that is, a sacred state, pure animal existence. Human self-consciousness dooms us to treat nature and ourselves as instruments and objects; we are imprisoned by rationalism and the process of production and cannot attain the unfettered boundary-less state of being 'like water in water'. We may glimpse it briefly – and this is the link to his erotic novels – through violent excess and debauchery. Such states also induce an agony of total existential self-awareness. Thus there is an emphasis in his novels on fleshly extremes: mutilation, sacrifice, ritual. This emphasis on perverse excess involves self-loathing, fascination and the transgression of all societal taboos of sex and death. His novels are replete with harsh and vivid images of corruption, terror, necrophilia and other sexual extremes. This is philosophy made flesh. Bataille flays the perceptions of the reader, forcing a primal confrontation with the self; metaphorically drenched in 'blood, sperm, urine and vomit' it is difficult not to be shaken by the power and depths of Bataille's vision and the strength and elegance of his writing. Language and sex; sex and death: Bataille achieves an unholy communion unique in literature.   *EY*

The Story of the Eye (San Francisco: City Lights; Harmondsworth: Penguin, 1982); *Blue of Noon* (London: Marion Boyars, 1986); *L'Abbé* (London: Marion Boyars, 1988); *My Mother, Madame Edwarda, The Dead Man* (London, Marion Boyars, 1989); *Literature and Evil* (criticism) (London, Marion Boyars, 1976); *Eroticism* (philosophy) (San Francisco: City Lights, 1986; London: Marion Boyars, 1987); *Theory of Religion* (New York: Zone Books, 1989); *Visions of Excess* (Minneapolis: University of Minnesota Press, 1985)

See also **Pornography**; *Story of O;* **Surrealism**; **Tantrism**

Baudelaire, Charles (1821-1867)

The French poet Charles Baudelaire remains the supreme artist of eroticism. His name has become synonymous with an image of decadent **sensuality**. Rich perfumes; smouldering candles; tapestries; heavy velvets; etiolated, feline women twisting sinuously in gloomy chambers: the intoxicating aura of a heady exoticism clings to his work. Indeed, so perfectly does Baudelaire's poetry correspond to what has become a debased notion of romantic decadence, and so perfectly does Baudelaire himself represent the popular idea of the poet as dandified, tormented, doomed, that it has become increasingly difficult to separate the man and his work from the myth. Perversity, **masochism**, drugs: the realities of Baudelaire's life have become the currency of every semi-intellectual rock band going through a heavy-lidded esthetic phase.

Baudelaire's influence has been profound, although many of the most obviously decadent poses associated with his work belong more properly to the generation of writers who succeeded him and who are known as Symbolists and Decadents. While certainly possessed of an exquisitely refined sensibility, Baudelaire's work is more remarkable for its strength and for the poet's ability to wrench single-handedly into being a language of alienation that foreshadows all the wastelands of the twentieth century.

Baudelaire's life and his work are inseparable. His early devotion to his mother was replaced by more ambiguous feelings when she married a General Aupick, whom Baudelaire disliked. His family caused him much wretchedness, allowing him very little money throughout his life; they in turn felt that he was a wastrel, a neurasthenic idler who ran up vast debts. They disapproved, too, of his twenty-year involvement with the mulatto woman Jeanne Duval to whom he addressed many of his poems. It was a tortured and masochistic relationship and the poems in the 'Jeanne Duval Cycle' combine sensual longing, despair and disgust. There were poems addressed to two other women, Marie Daubrun and Madame Sabatier, but there is a central mysteriousness to all Baudelaire's sexual relations, a quality echoed in the haunting, poignant aspect of his love poetry. Less mysterious was the syphilis that finally killed him. His poems are always a marriage of heaven and hell that defines all the central torments of love: sensual enslavement, worship, repulsion, self-loathing. Again and again a cycle is repeated in Baudelaire's work, as when, in his 'Voyage à Cythère', a voyage of hope ends in ashes, dust, bitterness and despair.

Rain in the city, the red glare of a street lamp: Baudelaire's langorous visions are set against his urbane modernity but, underlying this, is a spiritual struggle, a religious quest that has drawn comparisons with Dante. His pursuit of sin and redemption anticipates much of the tortuous twentieth-century battle with the nature of evil and of human vice. *EY*

Selected Poems (New York: Grove Press, 1974; Harmondsworth: Penguin, 1975)

See also **Bataille**

Beale, Philippa (1946-   )

An English artist born in Winchester and educated at Goldsmith's College, Philippa Beale breaks boundaries between advertising and fine art, using both photographs and text. She employs multiple repeating images and is known for her deconstruction of female desire, especially through such works as 'The Rough and the Smooth' (1979) and 'Baby Love' (1981). In the former, Beale wittily describes the desirable 'points' of two types of men, ironically reinforcing stereotypes through text and photographed fragments of the male body: ears, neck, jaw, hands. 'Baby Love' explores the confusions between nurturing and sexual desire, using a modern version of the woman-younger man relationship with texts extracted from magazine articles about motherhood. Beale is director of studies at St Martin's College of Art and Design, London. *JM*

See also **Colette; Neel; Women's Images of Men**

Philippa Beale, *Rough Being Gentle*, 1980

Beardsley, Aubrey (1872-1898)

The English illustrator Aubrey Beardsley has been described, by Brigid Brophy, as 'the most intensely and electrically erotic artist in the world'.

Beardsley worked almost exclusively in black and white and, in association with two short-lived 1890s periodicals, *The Yellow Book* and *The Savoy*, was one of the first major artists to work exclusively for print, his imagination stimulated and freed by the texts that he illustrated: Alexander Pope's 'The Rape of the Lock', for example, and works by Juvenal, Lucian, Edgar Allen Poe and Ben Jonson. He also did some fine drawings to accompany his only sustained piece of writing, the elaborate and sexually explicit fantasy *Under the Hill*, but his greatest work was inspired by Oscar **Wilde**'s play *Salome* and the Aristophanes 'sex war' drama *Lysistrata*.

Whatever his source, the world that Beardsley calls into being is wholly his own. His style – the elegant line, the brilliant counterpointing of black against white, of blank space against intricate pattern, the constant visual *double entendres* – is unmistakable. So, too, is the eroticism – elegantly perverse, sometimes sardonically oblique, some-

B

Aubrey Beardsley, *The Toilet of Lampito*, 1896

times dazzlingly explicit – that informs his work.

Beardsley mocked and occasionally despaired of late nineteenth-century respectability. The penis, anxiously minimized or concealed in the salon art of the time, was central to his fantasies. His work on *Salome* turned into a high comic battle with his anxious publisher, John Lane, and it is surprising how much – by puns and symbols, or by sexual references so unexpectedly explicit that at first glance they're invisible – Beardsley managed to smuggle past Lane's censoring gaze. The *Lysistrata* drawings, published in a strictly limited private edition, are outrageously frank, exquisitely beautiful and oddly moving; Beardsley's Athenians, with their enormous erect penises, are at once symbols of an impossible virility and of hopeless frustration.

Beardsley's vision is not, however, phallocentric. Every part of the body, and every last detail in a room or a garden, is sexualized. In Brophy's brilliant psychoanalytic account of his work, she argues that it is, in the phrase coined by Sigmund **Freud**, 'polymorphously perverse': Beardsley's sophisticated vision remains that of the child for whom sex isn't just genital, who hasn't established strict sexual categories, for whom 'everything is a jewel, and everything a sexual organ'. His imagination is fetishistic, masturbatory, androgynous; distinctions between the sexes are blurred, as is the line between desire and death. One of his most recurring self-images is the fetus, at once monstrous and comic, unformed yet already old. Beardsley worked for under five years, always in the shadow of the TB that killed him before he was twenty-six.

MW

Brigid Brophy *Black and White: A Portrait of Aubrey Beardsley* (London: Jonathan Cape, 1968); Brigid Brophy *Beardsley and His World* (London: Thames and Hudson, 1976); Ian Fletcher *Aubrey Beardsley* (Boston: Twayne Publishers, 1987)

See also **Obscenity; Sensuality; Androgyny**

Beauvoir, Simone de (1908-1984)

Simone de Beauvoir was born and educated in Paris. She was trained as a teacher of philosophy, and taught for some time before, at the end of the Second World War, becoming a full-time writer. She wrote several novels, among them *She Came to Stay* and *The Mandarins*, five autobiographical works and the book which was to make her world famous, *The Second Sex*, first published in 1949. In this book she developed a theory about women as 'the other' in Western culture, a theory which was largely derived from the existential philosophy expounded by her life-long friend Jean-Paul Sartre.

For de Beauvoir, adult sexual relations were inherently heterosexual. *The Second Sex* contains only a limited discussion of **homosexuality** (either for women or men) and what there is is brief and conventional in its acceptance of cultural stereotypes. Yet while de Beauvoir rejected homosexuality (which might have led her to validate the traditional form and understanding of heterosexuality) she was passionately, indeed almost pathologically, critical of motherhood and marriage. *The Second Sex* contains passages which portray motherhood in entirely negative terms. Despite the inherent essentialism of *The Second Sex* (which opens with a discussion of male/female biology in which male sexual function is described as active and female as passive) de Beauvoir has no wish to laud the capacity of women to bear children. In later life an active campaigner for abortion and **contraception**, de Beauvoir never modified her attitude to maternity, which she saw only in terms of its costs to women. For her, adult female sexuality was about freely chosen heterosexual relationships: at no point in her work did she raise the issues of the social construction of sexual desire or the emotional consequences of sexual difference. Consistently opposed to **psychoanalysis** de Beauvoir remained committed to a view of sexuality derived partly from existential theories of choice and freedom and partly from a belief in sexuality as fixed and static. Masculinity seldom poses a problem for de Beauvoir; indeed, her contention is that women should be

B

more like men in their attitudes and behavior. For feminists who validate the 'feminine' (whether in women or men) de Beauvoir's work remains problematic in its rigid distinction between male and female sexuality. *ME*

She Came to Stay (New York: Norton, 1990; London: Fontana, 1984); *The Mandarins* (New York: Norton, 1991; London: Fontana, 1984); *The Second Sex* (New York: Random House, 1989; London: Picador, 1988)

Deirdre Bair *Simone de Beauvoir: A Biography* (Seattle: S&S, 1991; London: Cape, 1990)

See also **Firestone**

Bedi, Rajinder Singh (1915-1987)

The Indian writer Rajinder Singh Bedi is best remembered for such post-Partition stories as 'Lajwanti' and the novel *Ek Chadar Maili Si/A Soiled Sheet* which won the Sahitya Akademi award in 1966. These works grasp the powerful social nettle of **rape** and use it as a symbol for the desecration of India, but Bedi's most reflective works are those in which the narrative grapples with ordinary social attitudes towards women.

Woman, Bedi notices, is considered a constant threat to family **honor**. To her in-laws she is also a beast of burden and a fecund child-bearer, while, to her husband, she is an unresisting source of sexual gratification. Three out of these four roles are directly related to her female organs and all dictate the quality of her life. Her suppressed sexuality acts as a furnace for male lust. After marriage, her husband's demands upon her body supersede her well-being. As a married woman with no maidenhead to protect, other men consider her fair game for sex, consenting or forced. The short story 'Grehan' ('Eclipse') of 1942 illustrates Bedi's observations by equating a woman's experiences with the cycles of the moon. Bedi juxtaposes the annual eclipse of the moon – caused by an assault on the moon by the demons Rahu and Ketu – with the cruelty of a husband and a mother-in-law to a pregnant woman, who, after she runs away, is raped. The moon as a symbol of female experience subsequently became a

recurrent motif in Bedi's work.

In *Ek Chadar Maili Si/A Soiled Sheet*, the cycle of the moon reflects woman's sexual desire. 'When a woman is audacious enough to unveil herself completely, I begin to see why the moon of the eighth day half-covers herself. Until one day, like the full moon, she uncontrollably throws off her veil, her blouse, her bra – and overwhelmed by her sexual hunger she bursts forth, depleting her most cherished treasure [modesty].' Darkness follows the moon's misconduct. Bedi also explores the erotic urges and inhibitions of women in the 1949 story 'Apne Dukh Mujhe De Do' ('Give Me All Your Grief'). Here he uses a wife's fear of losing her husband as the trigger for the emergence of her wanton Self. He further notes that men see a woman's uninhibited participation in sex as simultaneously 'life-giving' and 'life-draining' so that, through nourishing his need, she consumes him. This age-old fear is also reflected in images of the earth (woman) heaving up to devour the rain (sperm) in order to fulfil its female functions. *SH*

Dan-o-Dam/The Bait and the Trap (Lahore: Naya Idara, 1943); *Hath Hamare Qalam Hue/Our Hands Are Severed* (New Delhi: Maktaba Jamia, 1947); *Ek Chadar Maili Si/A Soiled Sheet* (New Delhi: Hindi Pocket Books, 1967); *Kokhjali/The Barren Woman* (New Delhi: Star Publications, 1970); *Rajinder Singh Bedi: Selected Short Stories* (New Delhi: Sahitya Akademi, 1989)

See also **Chugtai; Das; Indian Cinema; Manto**

Behn, Aphra (1640-1689)

Born in Kent, Aphra Behn visited Surinam (then a Dutch colony) in 1663 and, in 1666, was employed by King Charles II as a spy in Antwerp during the Dutch war. Her first play, *The Forc'd Marriage*, originally performed in London in 1670, was followed by some fourteen others in which she excelled at satiric comedy and caricatures of her contemporaries: a favorite theme being the consequences of arranged and ill-matched marriages. She also wrote poetry and was an early exponent of the novel, but, despite her success, she had to contend all her lifetime with accusations of lewdness, based on the current double standard whereby honesty and **honor** in a woman could refer only to her sexual conduct and could not exist in a woman who supported herself economically and who mixed with men in the public world.

Writing in a period long before **lesbianism** was defined as a pathological personality type, rather than as a variant of social behavior, Behn could cheerfully celebrate passion between women. She also wrote about women's desires for men, while simultaneously mocking male swaggering and impotence. Her poems on these themes employ comic reversals of the codes of traditional pastoral lyric: her nymphs, far from coyly fleeing proffered male embraces, are hot and lusty, only too eager to abandon their maidenhoods and chase their reluctant shepherd swains.   *MR*

Maureen Duffy *The Passionate Shepherdess* (London: Methuen, 1989)

See also **Daniels; Restoration Drama**

Belli, Gioconda (1948-   )

Perhaps the best known Nicaraguan woman poet, Gioconda Belli is now identified with the Sandinista revolution and the government of 1979–1990. Her writing combines her feminist and patriotic politics with eroticism and personal intensity – and the poems are often better performed than read in silence. Belli herself reads them powerfully in public and they have been set to music by several of her country's composers. Crowds of Nicaraguans, familiar with the words of her songs, have sung them aloud at rallies and festivals.

In seeking to embrace with her poetry the whole of human, specifically female, emotion, Belli has refused to discriminate between the personal and political. Aware that the revolution has to be fought for and defended on all fronts simultaneously, she has never ceased to work, both through the Sandinistas and her writing, to renew and refine her commitment to the revolution and to combat endemic

machismo. Her poetry renders even pregnancy and patriotism profoundly erotic. She writes of such previously taboo subjects as menstruation, **homosexuality** and female violence. From 1986–1988 she gave up her other professional work in order to complete a first novel, *La Mujer Habitada/A Woman Possessed*, which explores the linear relationship between women of the sixteenth and twentieth centuries in Central America and, thus, between indigenous and Hispanic cultures. It was published simultaneously in Nicaragua and Germany, where it won the prize for best literary work of the year.   *AmH*

Sobre la grama/On the Lawn (Managua: INDESA, 1974); *Linea de Fuego/Line of Fire* (Havana: Casa de las Americas, 1978); *Truenos y Arco Iris/Thunderbolts and Rainbows* (Managua: Nueva Nicaragua, 1982); *Amor Insurrecto/Love in Insurrection* (Managua: Nueva Nicaragua, 1985); *De la Costilla de Eva/Out of Eve's Rib* (Managua: Nueva Nicaragua, 1987; Connecticut: Curbstone Press, 1990); *La Mujer Habitada/A Woman Possessed* (Managua: Vanguardia, 1988); *Lovers and Comrades* (London: Women's Press, 1989)

See also **Allende; Kahlo**

Bellocq, Ernest James (1873-1949)

Bellocq was born in New Orleans, where he worked as a professional photographer for some forty years. His intimate and direct 'Storyville Portraits' form a unique document of prostitutes in the brothels of Storyville, an area famed as the birthplace of New Orleans jazz. Little is known about him and his photographs were never published or exhibited until after his death. This mystery, and the cracked, damaged surfaces of the glass negatives, add to their voyeuristic fascination. Louis Malle's film *Pretty Baby* romanticised Bellocq and the Storyville milieu and Bellocq also features as a fictional figure in Michael Ondaatje's jazz novel, *Coming Through Slaughter*.   *LH*

Museum of Modern Art, New York City; New Orleans Museum of Art

See also **Degas; Manet; Prostitution, Female; Voyeurism**

B

Ernest James Bellocq, one of a series of photographs of Storyville prostitutes

Benedict, Ruth (1887-1948)

In her popular book *Patterns of Culture*, published in 1934, the American anthropologist Ruth Benedict first suggested that **homosexuality** might be an alternative lifestyle, rather than a pathological state. She pointed out that, while it was considered an abnormality in 1930s society, other cultures in other times had honored their homosexual members. She used as examples Plato's *Republic* and the Native American custom of *berdache* in which certain men cross-dressed and lived as women. Where homosexuality was accepted, she wrote, homosexuals lived healthy lives. But where it was seen as perverse, then homosexuals found themselves at odds with the cultural standards of their society, a situa-

tion that led to internalized guilt, inadequacy, or a sense of failure. Thus homosexuality was not innately pathological, but certain people became so because they received no support from their society. She suggested a wider tolerance on the part of society and education for homosexuals in the cultural relativity of their situation so leading to a self-acceptance which would enable them to live full lives.

Patterns of Culture was written for the educated general public. Earlier in 1934 Benedict had published an article directed at psychiatrists and psychologists on the same theme. 'Anthropology and the Abnormal', in the *Journal of General Psychology* (no. 10, 1934), used various examples to show that what was considered normal was defined differently by each culture. Traits condemned by one culture might be honored in another. In a society stressing homosexuality, she wrote, most people would be homosexual.

Born Ruth Fulton, Benedict was married for over fifteen years to Stanley Benedict, a biochemist. After they separated she had two long relationships with women, but even before the separation she had been exploring her own sexual possibilities with friend and fellow anthropologist Margaret **Mead**. Coming from the tradition of nineteenth-century romantic friendship, which accepted intimate relationships between women, she did not see herself or her sexuality as pathological: an insight confirmed for her by her studies of cultural relativity in anthropology. Her observations on homosexuality were only a small part of her work, carefully placed within the context of questioning the concept of the normal in society, but she laid the groundwork for arguing that homosexuals should not be condemned as ill but accepted as competent individuals living a different, though not abnormal, lifestyle.   MC

Patterns of Culture (Boston: Houghton Mifflin, 1989); *Race: Science and Politics* (New York: Penguin, 1945; London: Greenwood Press, 1982); *The Chrysanthemum and the Sword* (New York: Dutton, 1974)

Margaret M. Caffrey *Ruth Benedict: Stranger in This Land* (Austin: University of Texas Press, 1989)

See also **Bisexuality; Gay Liberation; Le Guin; Lesbianism**

Besant, Annie (1847-1933)

If not before breakfast, then before her death, the British campaigner Annie Besant believed any number of improbable things: especially when, in later years, she became a convert to Theosophy. By the light of this quasi-Hindu philosophical system, founded by the Russian mystic Helena Blavatsky, she was sure that she met with astral guides, received magic letters from Tibetan Masters and was educating the future World Teacher, the suc-

cessor to Jesus Christ. She also believed her fellow Theosophist, Charles Webster Leadbeater, when he argued that, by making young boys in his care share his bed and learn to masturbate, he was doing no more than respond to a need that he had perceived in their auras.

In taking his side, Besant roundly declared: 'His only offence was that he gave a coterie of prematurely blasé young men some advice, which was exaggerated into a great fault and condemned as immoral teaching.' This was not, however, an indication that Besant was sexually ultra-liberal or even thought sex important enough to have serious views on at all. A woman of enormous energy and genuine moral and intellectual courage, she attacked the Victorian establishment on many fronts: first as the wife of a clergyman, from whom she eventually separated; then as a leading atheist; then as an active socialist, educational reformer and trades unionist. But Victorian sexual repression was an enemy she sidestepped. In her private life, it would seem that Besant abandoned sex with her marriage and, in public, she addressed the subject only as part of her firm belief that the 'oppressed and inarticulate poor' should have information about **contraception**.

Unlike most of the women who fought to make birth control more available, for Besant the issue was mainly the hunger of children, not women's sexual freedom. Tried in 1877 for helping to publish *The Fruits of Philosophy*, an implausibly titled birth-control book by a Boston doctor called Knowlton, she drew for the court a picture of 'little ones half starved because there is food enough for two but not enough for twelve'. But touching pictures were of no avail. Not only were she and her partner, Charles Bradlaugh, found guilty of having 'unlawfully and wickedly devised to corrupt the morals of the young', but the case gave Besant's estranged clergyman husband the grounds he'd been seeking to remove their eight-year-old daughter, Mabel, from her care. (He already had the custody of their son.) Although Besant went on to publish her own pamphlet on birth control, subsequently translated into several languages, on joining the

Theosophists she withdrew it from publication, believing that the 'evolved soul' should concern itself with higher things.   *HG*

Rosemary Dinnage *Annie Besant* (Harmondsworth: Penguin, 1986)

See also **Sanger; Stopes; Wright**

Bible, The

See **Christianity** and **Judaism**

Birth Control

See **Contraception**

Bisexuality

As used by **Freud**, the term 'bisexuality' referred primarily to a combination of masculine and feminine characteristics in the same person. This phenomenon was regarded by Freud (in sharp opposition to his contemporaries) as completely normal among young children. Among adults, however, the assumption of inappropriate gender roles in sexual fantasy or activity was classed as immature and potentially pathological. Evidence of sexual attraction toward both sexes was thus regarded (like unorthodox tastes in clothes or occupations) as a symptom of a problematic inner identity.

It is only very recently that doubt has been cast on the assumption that specific social roles – appearance, job interests, clothes – are in a one-to-one relationship to sexual desires. Although many psychiatrists believe that social behavior that breaks gender rules is symptomatic of specific sexual pathologies, feminism and **Gay Liberation** have raised questions about the link between the sexual and the social. For instance, it is beginning to be possible for people to assume 'butch' or 'femme' styles without their external appearance being regarded as an unequivocal sign of their preferences in bed. Today, the mixing of gender roles in a single person is generally called **androgyny**, while the term 'bisexuality' is reserved for the sexual identity of people who have, or want to have, sexual relationships with both women and men.

The 'psych' professions, and established straight society as a whole, regard bisexual behavior as immature and irresponsible, partly because it destabilizes the dichotomy of normal vs. pathological and partly because it implicitly attacks **monogamy** (both gay and straight). Among lesbians and gay men, people who call themselves bisexual are often patronized: it is assumed that they are 'really' gay but are unwilling to give up heterosexual privilege. The stereotype of bisexuals as unreliable fence-sitters is offensive to those people who are consciously fighting **heterosexism** while having both gay and straight relationships; nevertheless, the persistence of self-serving behaviors – such as established male politicians having a public marriage and a private gay sexual life – gives credence to the gay community's skepticism.

Bisexuals cannot be said to constitute a distinct social group, since there are no community institutions that would allow bisexuals to become a kind of 'third sex' or sexual orientation. One tends to define oneself negatively (not-this, not-that) and to live by crossing and re-crossing the boundary between gay and straight. This nomadic existence is often experienced as simultaneously liberating and oppressive. To challenge the oppressive aspect and provide support for its liberating potential, some bisexuals have called for the development of a bisexual community on a par with the gay community, a distinct social space in which to pitch a new tent. The desirability or otherwise of this project has given rise to heated controversy but, even if considered desirable, the project is unlikely to succeed since, no matter how versatile one is, each relationship is either homo- or heterosexual and, to that extent, there is no neutral territory.   *MV*

Mariana Valverde *Sex, Power and Pleasure* (Toronto: Women's Press, 1985; Philadelphia: New Society, 1987)

See also **Kinsey; MacInnes**

Borden, Lizzie

Coming from a privileged Ivy League background, Lizzie Borden studied painting and art history before becoming first an editor, then an independent filmmaker, setting up her own production company, Alternate Current. She has also edited *Heresies*, a feminist collective journal.

Borden's first feature film, *Born in Flames* (1983), is a radical futuristic feminist fable about sexual politics, race, class and the role of the media. The script was evolved in collaboration with the main characters and the style is formally inventive, both in its representation of women and in its use of contemporary women's music. It became something of a feminist classic, although there were many feminists who rejected its central utopian statement: 'Women can work together across class and race lines.'

Borden's next film, *Working Girls*, is more conventional in its style and deals in a non-moralistic way with **prostitution** as a viable economic alternative for middle-class women. Borden has said that the film is 'less about prostitution than about heterosexual codes of rituals in our culture'. The sex scenes, shot from the women's point of view, are non-voyeuristic, unerotic, demystifying and, in general, avoid explicit sexual detail. Borden exposes male bodies as vulnerable (bulging stomachs, for instance) and shows the women, rather than the men, in control. And the framing sometimes decapitates the male actors, making them as faceless as the punters in a real brothel.

The film's central conflict is not, in fact, between the women and the men, but between the prostitutes and their madam – and it's interesting to compare *Working Girls* with Marleen **Gorris**'s *Broken Mirrors*, which also deals with prostitution. While Gorris's film presents its women as victims of sadistic male sexuality, Borden's deliberately confronts the 'moralising stance of Women Against Pornography' – according to which prostitutes are both the victims of male lust and the guilty perpetuators of their own exploitation – and aligns herself with the position taken by the 1982 Barnard Conference on the Politics of Sexuality. Borden shares the conference's view that women's oppression is caused by the fundamental structures of society and that it is therefore not prostitution, but capitalism, that is the problem. Many feminists who had liked *Born in Flames* considered it contradictory that Borden could have made this subsequent movie. It is, however, precisely Borden's undogmatic feminism which allows her to tackle important but controversial issues for women. She is now planning a comedy film about a middle-aged couple who constantly argue but still have a vigorous sexual relationship. *US*

Regrouping (1976); *Born in Flames* (1983); *Working Girls* (1986)

Teresa de Lauretis *Technologies of Gender: Essays on Theory, Film, and Fiction* (Bloomington and Indianapolis: Indiana University Press, 1987)

See also **Akerman**

Bourgeois, Louise (1911-   )

Louise Bourgeois studied in Paris at the Ecole des Beaux-Arts before moving to New York in 1938 on her marriage to US art historian Robert Goldwater. She has three sons.

In New York, Bourgeois mixed with the emerging abstract expressionists and *emigré* French artists, studying with the Dadaist Marcel Duchamp. Drawing on the biomorphic side of **surrealism**, with its interest in abstract forms inspired by living organisms, she has invented a personal vocabulary of sculptural shapes. She works in a variety of media from bronze to latex, and in all sizes.

Although at first glance Bourgeois's work appears abstract, closer inspection reveals a host of allusions to the body, states of mind and sexuality. She has said that the motivation for her art comes from the meeting of her calm mother and anxiety-producing father and from her place in the middle of three children. She believes that making art can exorcise subconscious anxieties. A series of oils and prints from the 1940s, *Femme/Maison*, shows

B

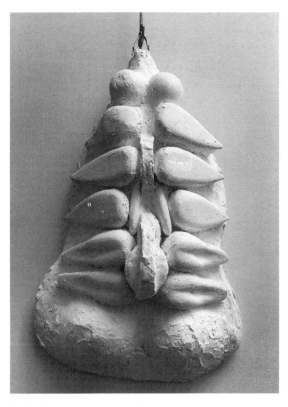

Louise Bourgeois, *Torso Self-Portrait, c.* 1963-4

women with houses for heads or bodies, a challenging visualization of women's place within the home. Her recognition by the US women's movement in the late 1960s was paralleled by her most explicitly sexual works. The *Cumul* series – worrying or not, depending on the viewer's response to clusters of drapery-covered mounds reminiscent of phalluses, eggs or breasts – is typical of the resonances set up by her forms. More outspoken is "Fillette" of 1968, a hanging (well-hung?) sculpture of male genitals which literally turns the male into a sex object. The blade-like "Femme-Couteau" (1969–1970), with a vertical slit exposed through wrapping, suggests a hostile response to penetration; "Femme Pieu" (1970), a heavy, limbless female torso reduced to powerlessness by its exaggerated shape, is an alternative expression of the vulnerability and fear roused by male sexual invasion. While it is unwise to overload a woman from the surrealist tradition with feminist consciousness, Bourgeois's ability to produce forms which cause her spectators to confront the unease and excitement aroused by sexuality makes her an artist of disturbing power.   *FB*

Works in the Museum of Modern Art, New York

D. Wye *Louise Bourgeois* (New York: Museum of Modern Art, 1982)

See also O'Keeffe

Brant, Beth (1941-   )

Beth Brant's Native American Indian name is Degonwadonti. Her tribe is the Bay of Quinte Mohawk, which is based in the Theyindenaga Reserve in Deseronto, Ontario. Although she has been writing only since the age of 40, Brant has twice received a Creative Artist Award from Michigan Council and her work has been published in a variety of US and Canadian Native Indian and feminist journals and anthologies. Her poetry was also included in *Naming The Waves: Contemporary Lesbian Poetry* edited by Christine McEwan (London: Virago, 1988).

Brant's commitment to her Native Indian and lesbian identity is a crucial element in much of her writing; she was first inspired to write on a trip through Mohawk valley. As the survivor of enforced treatment in a mental hospital, she has a rich understanding of what it means to have to fight for your life both personally and politically. In consequence her writing is a lyrical expression of the many injustices she has suffered, and sex, for her, is an act of deep and sustaining healing, one that brings women together in a safe, sensual and spiritual way. In one piece of prose entitled 'A Long Story', published in the collection she edited called *A Gathering of Spirit – A Collection of North American Indian Women*, Brant juxtaposes the 1890 American government policy of taking children from reservations to westernize them in faraway schools with a contemporary American government which has the power to take children from lesbian mothers. (Brant, who was married at 17, has three daughters.) Central to the narrative is the giving of comfort between women, a comfort that becomes a love-making where sexual contact is 'removing pain' and 'her mouth is medicine, her heart is the earth'. In another work, a poem in *Naming The Waves* called 'Her Name Is Helen', she gives an incisive portrait of a Native American lesbian who is unable to love herself because she walks in an America that has not loved Indians. Alienated from herself, she finds sex unimaginable.   *CU*

A Gathering of Spirit – A Collection of North American Indian Women (New York: Firebrand Books, 1984)

See also **Chrystos**

Brassai (Gyula Halasz) (1899-1984)

Born in Transylvania in the town of Brasov, from which he took his adoptive name, Brassai studied art in Budapest and Berlin before arriving in Paris in the early 1920s and working as a journalist. He was trained as a sculptor and took up photography only around 1929, encouraged by the photographer André Kertész, another Hungarian in Paris. Henry **Miller** was the friend who sometimes accompanied Brassai on the nocturnal jaunts that prompted him to use the camera as a journalistic tool. His first book, *Paris de nuit*, was published in 1933 and, although he did a variety of photographic work in the decades following World War Two, it is as the photographer of Paris by night and its secret vices that he is best known.

These pictures open up a world of dramatic light and shadow, of sex for sale and low-life rough and tumble. The camera seeks out intimacies: in cafés and homosexual bars; at the *bals musettes* and the Latin Quarter artists' dances; and inside brothels, from the cut-price production-line establishments to the high-class bordellos like the one frequented by Edward VII when Prince of Wales (and where he had a Hindu room specially created in homage to his mother, Queen Victoria, Empress of India). With their defiant criminal types, their archetypal prostitutes and assorted deviants, Brassai's scenarios invoke a world of heroism within

depravity. It corresponds to a mythic underside of Paris whose picturesque, romantic appeal for the wealthier classes was in part a nostalgic creation of cabaret life and popular song, intersecting with an old Paris where the bohemian tourists might encounter what Brassai called 'the beauty of evil and the magic of the lower depths'.

What makes these photographs so startling and gives them their coherence as secret glimpses of a Paris lost is their insistent obsession with looking. Sidelong looks, lewdly appraising looks, looks that exclude or betray, looks from above, from the wings of a stage, in mirrors and even, in one brothel interior, suggesting a view through a keyhole. Brassai's camera is a clever, knowing spy, a surrogate for **voyeurism**'s thousand eyes.   *LH*

Collection Bibliothèque Nationale, Paris

Brassai *The Secret Paris of the Thirties* (New York: Pantheon, 1977; London: Thames & Hudson, 1978)

See also **Bellocq; Degas; Zola**

Bray, Alan (1948-   )

See **Homosexuality in Renaissance England**

Brontë, Charlotte (1816-1855)

Charlotte Brontë was superbly suited to write about female independence, female passion and female loneliness. She was the sole adult survivor of her beloved sisters and brother, all of whom died either in childhood or early adulthood, the companion to a morosely grieving father, the would-be lover of a married man and, finally, the short-lived wife (she died as a result of pregnancy) of her father's curate, a man ill-equipped to understand her need for space and time in which to write.

Brontë's imagination, nurtured in childhood by shared fantastic games and writings, was also fed by the gothic and romantic traditions of English literature; her genius lay in her capacity to convey the

B

Brassaï, *The Wardrobe Mirror*, 1933

uncanny in terms of domestic imagery, to produce realism shot through with myth, to invent a prose peopled with the warring abstractions of a woman's psyche: Reason and Imagination fighting it out in stuffy drawing-rooms while Desire and Rage stalk the attics of the sub-text. *Jane Eyre*, first published in 1847, dramatized a penniless woman's search for autonomy and belonging; by insisting on the heroine's sexual and spiritual equality to the Byronic hero, Brontë aroused Victorian bourgeois wrath, even while the book proved a tremendous popular and critical success. Similarly with *Shirley* (1849) Brontë stirred up controversy by criticizing passionately the scorn heaped on unmarried, ageing women and by inventing a free spirit of a heroine who, being an heiress, could defy all the conventions before choosing her own mate. *Villette* (1853) is a superb study of sexual loss and unfulfilment, achieving its effects through a combination of heightened poetic prose, realistic character study and a gripping use of horror and **fantasy**.   *MR*

Jane Eyre (New York: Everyman's Classic Library, 1991; Oxford: Oxford University Press, 1980); *Shirley* (Oxford: Oxford University Press, 1981); *Villette* (Oxford: Oxford University Press, 1990)

See also **Brontë, Emily; Gaskell; Romantic Fiction**

Brontë, Emily (1818-1848)

Emily Brontë spent most of her short, outwardly uneventful life in Haworth Parsonage in Yorkshire; or roaming the moors, usually alone or with her mastiff, Keeper. When *Wuthering Heights*, her only novel, was published a few months before she died of consumption, her creation, Heathcliff, was branded 'diabolical'. How, the critics asked, could a vicar's isolated daughter have conjured up this convincingly evil anti-hero? There was speculation that Heathcliff must be based on Brontë's neurotic, opium-addicted brother Branwell, or (strangely) on her father's curate, the man who was later to marry her sister Charlotte. Another irritating but surpris-

ingly common interpretation of the book is to identify Brontë with its weak, worldly, cowardly heroine, Cathy.

A careful examination of the text, with the extra evidence of Brontë's mystical poetry, reveals that she was in love with God. The author cleverly disguises her devotion to immortality and spiritual power as a perverse *ménage à trois* for the masses: Cathy flees her twin soul to marry the insipid, secure Edgar; Heathcliff disappears then returns from an unnamed place to *murder Cathy with love*, so that they can be reunited in death. Heathcliff is not a man, but the earth: that is, heath-cliff. In dying, Cathy returns to the earth.

There is no sex in *Wuthering Heights*; Cathy and Heathcliff never kiss. Yet it is accepted as a passionate love story. Death, Brontë is saying, is sexy. While Cathy passively allows death to take her, to stop her from having to choose, Emily Brontë rose as usual at seven o'clock on the morning of her death, awaiting the event with thrilling, threatening composure, sitting upright on the sofa. She refused medical attention until she was certain that she would die. Death defiance had transcended to death control: Brontë willed it to happen. Her sexuality – her whole being – was expressed in the attraction to immortal power. In her last poem, 'No Coward Soul', she wrote: 'O God within my breast,/ Almighty ever-present Deity!/Life, that in me hast rest,/As I, undying Life, have power in thee!'   *CM*

Wuthering Heights (New York: Norton, 1990; London: Virago, 1990)

See also **Brontë, Charlotte; Ecstasy; Ghazal; Khusrau; Masochism; Mira Bai; Romantic Love**

Brossard, Nicole (1943-   )

A French Canadian radical lesbian feminist, Nicole Brossard has been commenting on the position of women – and on the specific way in which she sees **lesbianism** – since the early 1970s. She writes in French but seven of her twenty books have so far been translated into English.

Brossard's writing includes intellectual theory, poetry and novels, in all of which lesbianism plays a central role. The novels and poems are finely crafted explorations of the kind of radical feminist theory that questions the operation of language itself. Like Monique **Wittig** and Dale Spender, Brossard sees language as a formative agent, one that has invented woman as an inferior to man and which seeks to keep her in a subordinate place. This thesis has gained her the backing of Mary Daly, who in *Pure Lust* (Boston: Beacon Press, 1984) gives Brossard the accolade of being able to 'dream in female'.

The 'dream' is one that Brossard strives to make real by making language work *for* women, not against them, and this project is perceived in specifically lesbian terms. For the lesbian can 're-invent' herself in fiction and so subvert established man-made norms in both sexual, and textual, practice. Very much like Wittig, Brossard sees the existence of lesbian sexuality as revolutionary and disruptive, with the potential to wreak havoc in and out of patriarchal language. The final line of her experimental novel *French Kiss* reads, 'She rides above the delible ink': an assertive challenge to the power of man-made language to define woman. And in one of her essays she accuses men of taking the 'o out of open'.

Brossard's sexual politics place her firmly beside the radical feminists of her day, although her linguistic approach does limit her message in terms of accessibility. And, as with Mary Daly, her a-cultural emphasis on 'women' as an oppressed group leaves her open to charges of erasing issues of race and class and promoting the concept of the conditioned woman who cannot think for herself.   CU

Un Livre/A Book translated by Larry Shouldice (Toronto: Coach House Press, 1976); *Sold/out/Turn of Pang* translated by Patricia Claxton (Toronto: Coach House Press, 1980); *Mécanique jongleuse/Daydream Mechanics* translated by Larry Shouldice (Toronto: Coach House Press, 1980); *L'Amer/These Our Mothers or The Disintegrating Chapter* translated by Barbara Godard (Toronto: Coach House Press, 1980); *Amantes/Lovers* translated by Barbara Godard (Montreal: Guernica Press, 1986); *French Kiss/French Kiss* translated by Patricia Claxton (Toronto: Coach House Press, 1986); *The Ariel Letter* translated by Marlene Wildman (London: The Women's Press, 1988)

See also **Irigaray; Lorde; Stein**

Brown, Helen Gurley (1922-   )

A controversial figure with an unrepentantly frivolous style, as off-putting to right-thinking feminists as parts of her message are surprisingly appropriate, Helen Gurley Brown in 1965 took over a moribund Hearst Corporation magazine, *Cosmopolitan*, and turned it into a cultural force (as well as a rich source of parody) with foreign-language editions in seventeen countries. On newsstands, photographer Francesco Scavullo's flamboyantly glamorous covers rivaled any men's magazines in their celebration of plunging cleavage while, inside its pages, Brown's *Cosmo* told readers – over and over and over again – that it's smart to be sexy and sexy to be smart.

The lessons that Brown herself had learned, fleeing her small-town Arkansas background to an early career in seventeen successive secretarial jobs, are the backbone of her heavily *italicized* editorial gospel, with its strange combination of school-marmish severity and cosmetic obsession: work hard; look good; make the most of what you've got; and remember that 'fate has *something* to do with our success – but not much'.

While carrying the crucial *Cosmo* message of obtainable orgasms to deprived housewives and depressed working 'girls', among others, Brown has also repeatedly made the case for what can only be described as a sort of 'calculating courtesan' approach to female-male relationships. This can range from the exhortation 'Make your boss look good' to promoting tactically expressed admiration in marriage: '*Compliment* him – there is no such thing as too much flattery'. In matters of sex, a subject upon which Brown is particularly vociferous in her book *Having It All*, it leads her to such utterances as 'A delicately rosy, silky-satin, somehow innocent, always-vulnerable erect penis is *probably* the most fascinating object in the world' and 'If there is no man around, masturbate, of course, but sex with a man is what keeps you *womanly*.' At the same time, however, she can advise, 'Help with your own hands, if necessary; have him play with you *while* he is f-----g you. This is a fairly dumb analogy, but I think declaring to yourself that you *will* have an orgasm is not unlike a politician declaring that he will run for office. You have a better chance of getting nominated and elected if you 'declare' – very few politicians get *drafted*.'

The contradictions in Brown's philosophy are, in fact, in a weird way, what gives it its energy and persistent appeal; for many women, it seems, like to be reminded of their 'c-- power' (note, again, the letters coyly missing from Brown's phrase) at the same time as they are taking charge and managing their own lives. A onetime ad. agency copywriter, Brown's phrase-making talents can also be seen in the title of her early-1960s mega-bestseller *Sex and the Single Girl*, which was made into a film in 1964 and, shockingly for its time, offered frankly aggressive alternatives to the behavioral double standards assigned to unmarried women. And, while her word 'mouseburger' – used to describe those women like herself whose will must make up for deficiencies in such areas as looks and intelligence – may yet be in no dictionaries, nonetheless it cannot be forgotten by any reader who has ever come across it.   *MiS*

Sex and the Single Girl (New York: Avon, 1983); *Sex and the Office* (New York: Avon, 1983); *Having It All* (New York: Pocket Books, 1985); *The Late Show: A Semiwild But Practical Survival Plan for Women over 50* (Morrow, 1993)

See also **Agony Aunts; Foreplay; Masturbation; Orgasm; Sexual Revolution**

Brown, Rita Mae (1944-)

Best known now as a novelist, in the late 1960s Rita Mae Brown was an activist in the gay rights and feminist movements in New York City. In 1970, tired of the way in which gay men and heterosexual women misunderstood, or attempted to silence, the lesbian women working among them, Brown and other lesbian feminists wrote *The Woman-Identified Woman*, a paper arguing that **lesbianism**, describing nothing but a sexual practice, is a man-made concept devised to marginalize women who challenge men's prerogative. Women-identified women, it explained, define themselves in relation to women, make their greatest commitments to women and recognize women's supremacy; lust, with its complex ambiguities, is quite the wrong center of focus. Brown's 1976 collection of essays, articles and speeches, *A Plain Brown Rapper*, is a lucid and energetic amplification of these ideas: arguing that lesbianism, for women who call themselves feminists, is not so much a personal choice as a political necessity. 'Lesbianism, politically organized, is the greatest threat that exists to male supremacy. How can men remain supreme, how can they oppress women if women reject them and fight the entire world men have built to contain us?' Brown's first novel, *Rubyfruit Jungle*, published in 1973, is a funny, deliberately outrageous statement of pride in its heroine-narrator's lesbian identity. 'Molly Bolt,' ran the blurb, when the novel emerged from cult success to bestsellerdom, ' . . . an all American, true-blue gay – and proud of it.' The book is an escapist fantasy, with its heroine battling through poverty, illegitimacy and prejudice to become a beautiful, sexually irresistible super-achiever. Though impatient with sexual ambivalence and with what the narrator calls 'hang ups' – by which she mainly appears to mean sexual games-playing – and blithely asserting that lesbian sex, indeed sex in general, is unproblematic, it makes a refreshing antidote to the guilt-ridden gloom of most earlier lesbian fictions. In subsequent novels, however, Brown's energy seems to have slackened, to have tired of trying to force together the ethos of radical lesbianism with that of the righteous, puritanical, competitive American Dream. Indeed, in 1983, in an article in the Canadian magazine *Body Politic* (no. 95, July/August 1983), Brown renounced 'the whole ideology of the lesbian as the ultimate feminist and superior human being', describing it as 'pure horse shit'. Brown has also published poetry collections, including the memorably titled *The Hand that Cradles the Rock* (1971), and written both film and TV scripts. *HG*

Rubyfruit Jungle (New York: Bantam, 1983); *Six of One* (New York: Bantam, 1983); *Southern Discomfort* (New York: Bantam, 1983); *Sudden Death* (New York: Bantam, 1984); *The Poems of Rita Mae Brown* (California: Crossing Press, 1987)

See also **Clit Statements; Political Lesbianism**

Bryher (1894-1983)

Born Annie Winifred Ellerman, the British poet and novelist 'Bryher' changed her name when she began to be published. Her first prose works explored the dilemma of her own sexual identity. *Development* and *Two Selves* were both published as autobiographical fiction in the early 1920s. They record her rebellion against her plutocratic family's notions of femininity, her secret aspiration – shared with Havelock **Ellis**, whom she consulted at this time – to be a 'boy', and her attempt to integrate what she experienced as a 'feminine' social self with a 'masculine' inner self.

Her later historical novels have been classified as children's books because of an alleged absence of 'sex', but history – whether the period of the Norman Conquest in *The Fourteenth of October* or the Punic Wars in *The Coin of Carthage* – in fact allowed her to elude the conventions of the heterosexual plot and, by choosing young male protagonists, to write homosocial fiction. Her covert concern with gender roles also led her to write about acting and **cross-dressing** in an early essay, 'The Girl-Page in Elizabethan Literature' (*Fortnightly Review*, 1920), and in her most poetic novel, *The Player's Boy* (1953). The hero of this story is apprenticed to an older actor and takes the 'petticoat parts' in a company of traveling players; as their Elizabethan heyday gives way to a more sinister Jacobean era, he loses his illusions about life and recognizes death as 'but the giving over of a game that must be lost'. Thus Bryher's elegiac late fiction takes its place in the spectrum of lesbian writing that includes Mary Renault's historical novels and

Virginia Woolf's playful multiple life of Vita Sackville-West, **Orlando**.

Unable, as an (illegitimate) daughter, to inherit the financial empire of her powerful, shipping-magnate father, Bryher used her considerable legacy to promote her own interests in publishing, film, **psychoanalysis** and hellenic studies. She was a friend of Edith and Osbert Sitwell, Norman Douglas, Hanns Sachs and May Sarton, and also (directly or indirectly) the patron of many writers, among them James Joyce and Laurie Lee, but pre-eminently H.D. Bryher met H.D. in 1918 and remained the beloved 'sister' of this leading modern poet until her death in 1961. Bryher's love for H.D. is inscribed in her own writings: in the culmination of *Two Selves*, in her later memoirs, *The Days of Mars* and *The Heart to Artemis*, and in her Greek novel *Gate to the Sea*, as well as in the poems she published as 'Hellenics' (*Poetry*, 1920). H.D.'s love for Bryher is reciprocated in 'To W.B. (I said)', 'At Baia', 'We Two', 'Hyacinth', 'Halcyon' and 'To Bryher (Stars wheel in purple)'. Bryher made two marriages of convenience to protect her lesbian identity: the first in 1920 to Robert McAlmon, the American writer and editor of Contact editions; the second in 1927 to Kenneth Macpherson, who was H.D.'s lover and a gay man. With Macpherson she settled in a Bauhaus-style home in Switzerland and adopted H.D.'s daughter, Perdita, who later described herself as a 'child of two mothers'. *DC*

The Coin of Carthage: A Novel (New York: Harcourt Brace, 1974); *The Days of Mars: A Memoir, 1940-1946* (London: Marion Boyars, 1981)

Gillian Hanscombe and Virginia Smyers *Writing for Their Lives: The Modernist Women, 1910-1940* (London: Women's Press, 1987)

See also **Androgyny**

Burford, Barbara (1945-   )

A Black British writer who explores politics, passion and Black and lesbian identity in poetry, drama and prose, Barbara Burford has also maintained a commitment to medical research, seeing this as tightly connected to the enterprise of writing. For her, both areas of work involve an active search for meaning.

In 1984, The Women's Theatre Group successfully performed Burford's play *Patterns* and, in the following year, her poetry appeared in *A Dangerous Knowing: Four Black Women Poets*. Along with Gabriella Pearse, Grace Nichols and Jackie Kay, she uses poetry to affirm the cultural identity and the experiences of being Black in Britain, and the love and strength that can exist between women.

Her book of short stories *The Threshing Floor* followed and was acclaimed both inside and outside feminist and lesbian feminist circles. Throughout, its writing is alive with a poet's sense of language, image, magic, myth and creativity, suffusing the narrative with a Black sensibility. The title story is a novella and covers issues especially pertinent to the contemporary lesbian community. How is motherhood possible for lesbians? Is love between a black and a white lesbian viable? How does a lesbian deal with bereavement? Such social realism and emphasis on politics is more than matched by an appreciation of art as a healing process, with creativity here aligned to the attraction that develops between two Black women in contemporary Britain. The lesbian nature of this relationship is never moved into explicit sexual contact, but the relationship between the women is increasingly charged with awareness, with sex seen as the ultimate expression of love. The same perspective informs Burford's poetry and makes for a promotion of lesbian sex as an integral part of spiritual, political and sensual contact between women. In a poem entitled 'My Gift', for example, love is etched in images of sun, air and song. These are interwoven with daily acts of physical closeness such as 'taking your arm'. Sexual contact ends the poem, with 'leaning down/ to kiss, to be.' Characteristically, the sex is part of a process of becoming.   *CU*

A Dangerous Knowing: Four Black Women Poets (London: Sheba, 1985); *The Threshing Floor* (Ithaca, NY: Firebrand Books, 1987; London: Sheba, 1986)

See also **Brant; Chrystos; Parker; Sensuality**

Burroughs, William (1914-   )

During the 1960s, William Burroughs seemed an unlikely counterculture icon. Respectably dressed, with dry, patrician manners, he suggested an elderly banker rather than a man responsible for the most radical literary experiments of the post-war period.

Burroughs grew up in St Louis and was educated at Harvard. During the 1940s he encountered the other American writers who became known as the 'Beat Generation'. These included Jack Kerouac and Allen Ginsberg, who both tirelessly promoted Burrough's work. Alienated, intellectual and diffident, Burroughs was strongly attracted to the criminal underworld whose code of manners he preferred to that of conventional society. As a result he became a heroin addict and this experience was to provide a central metaphor in his work. As he analyzed the manner in which drug addiction controls the human organism, he became increasingly aware of the functions of power and control systems throughout society and the body politic, particularly in the sexual realm. 'In English-speaking countries,' he said, 'the weight of censorship falls on sexual words and images,' and all his work seeks to subvert and deconstruct such control mechanisms by a combination of savage satire, repeated emphasis on sexuality and societal taboos, and radical experiments with language and the form of the novel.

Although Burroughs was primarily homosexual, he contracted a common-law marriage with Joan Vollmer Adams and, in Mexico in 1951, accidentally shot and killed her. He retreated to Tangier, which became the 'Interzone' of his novels, and wrote *(The) Naked Lunch*, a violently fragmented postmodernist text notable for its bitterly satiric black comedy routines. The book establishes all his major themes: addiction as a model for control in a consumer society which forces us all into the role of addict or dealer; the world as a dystopia riddled with bureaucratic insanity, conspiracy, paranoia, and vulnerable to unspeakable forms of mutation, larval metamorphoses and alien psychic visitations. This world is old and dirty and evil, shot through with the running sores of corruption, rampant with scatological excess and peopled by quasi-human degenerates like the infamous Dr Benway who rips out tumors with his teeth. *Naked Lunch* was prosecuted for **obscenity** in Massachusetts in 1965 but the conviction was overturned, effectively ending literary censorship in the USA. Feminist critics have sometimes found the violence and misogyny of Burroughs's books to be offensive, but it is impossible to deny the force of his vision or the power of his influence.

Burroughs's early works *Junky* and *Queer* had displayed his cut-glass style in conventional narrative form, but *Naked Lunch* was a breakthrough. Afterwards he went on to perfect what he called the 'cut-up' method, insisting that totally random juxtapositions of text reveal new meanings and thus subvert control systems at their source: in language. He published several books in this mode before embarking on his great trilogy beginning with *Cities of the Red Night*. The trilogy combines a Boy's Own romanticized view of gun-fighters and pirates with Burroughs's habitual homosexual eroticism, at once lyrical and sadomasochistic. There is an increasing sense of nostalgia and loss in these books, although Burroughs continued with linguistic and textual experiments in his repeated attempts to shatter the deceitful uses of language in a depraved society and to try and find ways to evolve beyond the limitations of such a society and the prison of corporeal existence. *EY*

Junky (Harmondsworth: Penguin, 1977); *Queer* (Harmondsworth: Penguin, 1987); *Naked Lunch* (New York: Grove Press, 1984; London: Grafton, 1986); *The Soft Machine* (New York: Grove Press, 1966; London: Grafton, 1986); *The Ticket that Exploded* (New York: Grove Press, 1987); *Cities of the Red Night* (New York: Holt, 1982; London: Picador, 1982); *The Place of Dead Roads* (New York: Holt, 1985; London: Grafton, 1987); *The Western Lands* (Harmondsworth: Penguin, 1988)

Ted Morgan *Literary Outlaw: The Life and Times of William S. Burroughs* (London: Bodley Head, 1991)

See also **Acker; Genet**

Burton, Sir Richard (1821-1890)

A nineteenth-century scholar, orientalist and Arabist, Sir Richard Burton took a pioneering interest in **sexology**. Throughout his patchwork career as an officer, explorer and minor diplomat, he devoted his surplus energies to infiltrating, often in disguise, the more secret places of the countries in which he found himself – the brothels of Karachi, the holy cities of Medina and Harar (in Somalia), even the Mormon community in Salt Lake City – writing his observations up with particular emphasis on sexual mores.

In the Europe of his time, bourgeois morality was hostile to studies such as this, especially as Burton appeared to delight in deliberately shocking his readership with accounts of eunuchs in India, of pederasty and polygamy. But under the guise of orientalism it was possible for Burton to combine his interest in sexology with his passion for languages. His wide knowledge of Arabic and two dozen other languages enabled him to translate the **Kama Sutra** (1883), the **Perfumed Garden** (1886) and **Arabian Nights** (in 17 volumes) between 1884 and 1886. The latter Burton annotated with extensive footnotes on Muslim sexuality, presented as anthropological evidence but largely indulging a fantasy common in repressive Victorian Britain: of wild and debauched oriental sexual excesses. Indeed, his *Arabian Nights* was perhaps the most popular of all his works, fitting as it did into an image of the east similar to that conveyed by Eugène Delacroix's Moroccan paintings, for example, or all those slickly romantic pictures of oriental bathers and half-naked slaves that filled the annual exhibitions of the Royal Academy in London. *SR*

See also **Islam**

Butler, Josephine (1828-1906)

Josephine Butler was raised in a radical, devout Northumberland family and committed her life to helping and supporting prostitutes, while simultaneously working tirelessly to abolish their livelihood. This apparent paradox typifies much of her thinking and writing on sex.

Married to a University lecturer, the mother of a daughter who died when only five, Butler began her mission by opening a refuge for sick prostitutes. By 1869 she was President of the Ladies' National Association and, from this position, led the fight against the **Contagious Diseases Acts**, which punished prostitutes for the spread of **venereal disease**, yet winked at their clients. It was this double standard that roused Butler's wrath. She also argued that the Acts wouldn't work, and that the torture they inflicted on women was without political precedent, but it was to the double standard that she returned again and again, stripping it down to its naked illogicality. Unlike in the 1960s, however, when women were to ask for the same sexual freedoms as men, Butler and her supporters required that men adopt women's restraint: 'The essence of the great work which we propose to ourselves, is to Christianise public opinion until, both in theory and practice, it shall recognise the fundamental truth that the essence of right and wrong is in no way dependent upon sex, and shall demand of men precisely the same chastity as it demands of women.'

Deftly switching from rigorous and well-constructed argument to nauseous anecdotes about sobbing, repentant, golden-hearted prostitutes, Butler's writing most certainly helped to effect the repeal of the terrible Acts. It is nonetheless an uneasy mixture, and not just of literary styles. Compassionate, if patronizing, to women who hired out their bodies for food, Butler was totally intolerant of sex (outside marriage, in any case) for *pleasure*. Venereal disease was what such viciousness deserved and, indeed, what God gave it. Nor did Butler spare much thought as to what starving women would do for bread once **prostitution** was eradicated.

Similarly, despite her own courage in learning about and speaking and writing on subjects that ladies were meant to ignore, she advised young people that sexual matters were best not discussed, except in prayer, while the social purity movements with which she became for a while involved were notorious campaigners for the censorship of birth-control information. Although clear-sighted about power and class, about 'fallen' women and 'respectable' ones being made by men, not God, Butler was nonetheless blinkered by her dark and forbidding **Christianity**.   *HG*

See also **Acton; Stead, W.T.**

Califia, Pat (1954-   )

Pat Califia is a lesbian sado-masochist polemicist and writer. She has been active from an early stage in the San Francisco lesbian SM group Samois, and was responsible, along with Gayle Rubin, for much of the witty, energetic polemic in defense of that group and its sexuality during the feminist 'Sex Wars': the ideological confrontations between libertarian feminists and puritan, separatist feminists in the late 1970s and early 1980s.

Califia co-edited *Coming to Power*, the Samois collective volume of 1983, and – at times in provocatively extreme ways – accused anti-SM radical feminist lesbians not only of totalitarian instincts but of a cult of sexual boredom. Her lesbian sex manual *Sapphistry* (1980) took an aggressively libertine attitude not only to SM but to such other controversial matters as dildoes, sex with lesbian-identified transexuals and the sensuous cuddling of animals. Subsequent work in this vein, such as *The Lesbian SM Safety Manual* and *The Advocate Adviser*, has been equally useful, radical and rebarbative. Califia's erotic short-story collection of 1988, *Macho Sluts*, is of mixed quality, interesting partly for its early acknowledgement of the use by some lesbians of gay men for sexual fantasy (and vice versa) and its popularization of Dorothy Allison's 'wet test', the suggestion that the success of women's **erotica** and **pornography** should be judged by a simple physiological test. Califia's novel *Doc and Fluff* (1990) uses a mixture of **science fiction**, SM and co-dependency counseling tropes with limited success in a journey through a post-collapse America. *RK*

Coming to Power (Boston: Alyson, 1983); *Macho Sluts* (Boston: Alyson, 1988)

See also **Correct Sadist**; Lesbianism; Loulan; Transexuality; Sado-Masochism

Camp

Camp epitomizes the culture of the male homosexual underworld. Its essence is a mocking exaggeration, making a drama out of something trivial, an affectionate – or sometimes bitchy – puncturing of all pretension by taking it to an extreme. It often revolves around effeminacy. Camp gestures are a mincing walk, a limp wrist, a rolled eye and raised eyebrow; 'camping it up' means dramatizing these for effect. Camp talk often involves using feminine pronouns for men, ridiculing women and virility alike, harping on people's dress and appearance. In the male homosexual subculture, camp is often expressed in an elaborate slang, some of which is derived from parlaree (or parlyaree), the slang of the circus and the traveling theater, some from backslang and rhyming slang and some from an endless fund of camp inventiveness.

Camp style was used within the twentieth-century homosexual ghetto, but it was also used as a way of entertaining the 'straight' world. Many highly successful comedians have been camp; the British radio show *Round the Horne* was sparkling camp humor. But this public use of camp is ambiguous: on the one hand it is blatantly and perhaps proudly homosexual; on the other it is self-mocking and emphasizes the effeminacy which it implicitly deplores. Camp has been rejected for its obviousness by those who would like to blend in with straight society. Since **Gay Liberation**, it has been rejected by those who see it as an accommodation to oppression rather than a challenge to it. Nevertheless, the humor and camaraderie of camp, for all its double meanings, did foster a sense of community and resistance at a time when self-respect was being constantly corroded. With the opening-up of the ghetto, it is a moot point as to whether camp will survive: there are signs of it being transformed into a more challenging counter-culture. *MM*

See also **Homosexuality**; **Jarman**; **Vidal**; **Von Gloeden**; **West**

Carpenter, Edward (1844-1929)

'The subject of Sex is difficult to deal with.' So Edward Carpenter began his book *Love's Coming of Age*, first published in 1896. Certainly, he did not attempt the explicitness to which we have become accustomed one hundred years later but, along with Havelock **Ellis**, Carpenter was one of the major sexual radicals of his time and many of the issues about which he wrote are still alive today. Born into the English upper middle class and educated at Cambridge, Carpenter was much influenced by the American poet Walt **Whitman**'s ideas about manly love, comradeship and spiritual wholeness, and by H.M. Hyndman's socialism. He rejected the bourgeois respectability of his day and joined the university extension movement, lecturing in the industrial towns in the north of England. From 1885 onwards he was active in the Sheffield Socialist Society; he became a vegetarian and teetotaler, ran a market garden and later worked at sandal-making. Many of his friends were working-class men and some of them were his lovers, notably George Merrill, a Sheffield man, who he met in 1891 and who shared his house in a Derbyshire hamlet for the last three decades of his life.

Carpenter was a prolific writer of poetry and prose and immensely influential in British socialist and progressive circles from the mid-1880s onwards. Olive Schreiner, Edith Lees and her husband Havelock Ellis were among his friends. In *The Intermediate Sex* (1908) he set out the ideas of the **sexology** of the day and defended the idea of homosexual love, suggesting that homosexual men and women represent a new and more advanced type of human being. He linked homosexual liberation with the struggle of women and the transcendence of artificial gender difference; and he saw 'comradeship', especially between men, as bridging class divides, and love as an integral part of socialism in practice. *MM*

The Intermediate Sex (New York: AMS Press); *Selected Writings, Vol 1: Sex* (London: GMP, 1984)

Sheila Rowbotham and Jeffrey Weeks *Socialism and the New Life: The Personal and Sexual Politics of Edward Carpenter and Havelock Ellis* (London: Pluto, 1977)

Ed. Noel Greig *Edward Carpenter, Selected Writings, Volume 1: Sex*, with an introduction by Noel Greig (London: Gay Men's Press, 1984)

See also **Forster**

Carrington, Leonora (1917-)

The surrealist artist Leonora Carrington was born in Clayton Green, Lancashire, the only daughter of a highly successful textile manufacturer and an Irish Catholic mother. With her three brothers, she was cared for by a French governess, a religious tutor and an Irish nanny who filled her head with fairy-tales and myths, which set her on her quest into the magical realms explored in her painting, sculpture and writing.

Carrington's rebellious nature emerged early. In her young teens, she and a friend used to scandalize bourgeois ladies taking afternoon tea in a hotel by loudly discussing invented syphilitic symptoms. Similarly, a friend recalls the fourteen-year-old Carrington being introduced to the local priest and, wearing nothing at all underneath, pulling up her dress and demanding, 'Well, what do you think of that?' Scurrilous behavior excited and entertained this *enfant terrible* whose life, as well as her art, embraced surreality.

In 1937 the German-born painter and sculptor Max Ernst came to lecture on **surrealism** at the Amédée Oxenfant Art Academy, in London, where Carrington had just begun to study. Carrington was mesmerized and, aged nineteen, eloped to Paris with the forty-six-year-old artist. She made her debut in French society wearing a sheet, wrapped toga-style, which she soon threw off.

Carrington was Ernst's second *femme-enfant* (he had married Marie-Berthe Aureche in 1927) and the child-woman was the ideal image to fire the male surrealist imagination: the volatile mix of sexual awareness and childlike ingenuity; the element of instability, often bordering on madness; the easy access to the **unconscious**. But this left the child-woman vulnerable to failure in her *own* creative career. As an artist, Carrington was alienated from surrealist theory of woman as muse. However fantastic her imagery – strange animals, landscapes, birds, fruits – it remained firmly rooted in her own physical experience. As she has declared: 'I was never a surrealist . . . I was with Max.'

In her self-portrait of 1937, 'The Inn of the Dawn Horse', Carrington places herself on a chair in a room devoid of furniture, save for a rocking-horse hung on the wall and lavish gold curtains adorning the open window, through which a wild, white horse is visible galloping through the trees. In the foreground, Carrington is communicating with a lactating hyena, a nocturnal animal belonging to the fecund world of dreams. Behind the hyena is a patch of ectoplasm indicating that the hyena has materialized at Carrington's behest. Animals play a crucial role in Carrington's writing and painting – representing kindred spirits, guardians, extensions or reincarnations of humankind – and this is a scene of psychic communication: fearless, but with great intensity of emotion, captured in the direct stare of Carrington and the hyena at the viewer. The rocking-horse can be read as Carrington's childhood now behind her, while, ahead of her, lies the life of the nurturing female symbolized by the hyena. Meanwhile, her sexual imagination flies off as a white colt into an other-worldly realm. A Freudian would read the horse as a symbol of male power; it may also be seen as Carrington's sexual liberty. 'In l'amour-passion,' she has said, 'it is the loved one, the other who gives the key. Now the question: who can the loved one be? It can be a man or a horse or another woman.'

C

Leonora Carrington, *The Inn of the Dawn Horse*, 1937

In 'Portrait of Max Ernst' (1939), Carrington presents a white-haired Ernst clad in animal fur and bearing a lantern. The glass globe reveals a miniature rearing white horse which represents Carrington's wild spirit captivated by Ernst. But behind Ernst in the glacial landscape Carrington is also seen as the white spectral horse whose frozen stare has been likened to that of the horse in **Fuseli**'s 'The Nightmare'. A depth of field is set between Ernst and this white, soulful horse which is following its own path.

When, in 1959, André Breton invited Carrington to participate in an exhibition of eroticism, she visualized her own contribution thus: 'A Holy Ghost (albino pigeon) three metres high, real feath-ers (white chickens, for example), with nine penises erect (luminous), thirty-nine testicles to the sound of little Christmas bells, pink paws . . .' The exhibition was never realized, but the vision does give access to Carrington's evocative sexual imaginings. From the 1940s on, she adopted the classical technique of using egg tempera on small gessoed grained panels. The thinness of the paint application gives the work an added ghostly quality and lends it the appearance of ancient icons. Carrington continues to paint, sculpt and write, dividing her time between Mexico City and Chicago. She follows the teaching of Tibetan lamas. *PS*

Edward James Foundation, West Dean, Sussex; Young-Mallin Collection, New York.

The House of Fear, Notes from Down Below (London: Virago, 1989); *The Seventh Horse and Other Tales* (London: Virago, 1989)

Andrea Schlieker *Leonora Carrington: Paintings, Drawings and Sculptures 1940-1990* (London: Serpentine Gallery, 1991)

See also **Faery; Freud**

Carter, Angela (1940-1992)

Angela Carter was born in Sussex, England. Her first novel, *Shadow Dance*, was published in 1966; her last, *Wise Children*, in 1991. Around and between these came six other novels and three short-story collections, poetry, journalism and cultural history, scripts for radio, TV and the cinema.

In the worthy but mostly dull world of contemporary English letters, Carter's interest in and ease with sex, violence and exotica proved her dangerous and exciting. Yet novels like *The Magic Toyshop* – about sexual **voyeurism** between adults and children – or a tale like 'The Bloody Chamber', which plays long and hard with the conventions of nineteenth-century **pornography**, show Carter to have been less ludic, erotic or extreme than she at first appeared. Like Kathy **Acker**, with whom in scope and seriousness she had much in common, Carter has yet to be properly assessed. This is because, like Acker but unlike most other well known British or North American writers, Carter worked not within a parochial realist tradition but within one of highly literate fictiveness: which is to say that Carter was perhaps English literature's only genuine and unaffected postmodern novelist to date. The stories collected in *The Bloody Chamber*, for example, generally get read as feminist reworkings of old stories: 'Little Red Riding Hood', 'Bluebeard's Castle', 'Beauty and the Beast' and so on. On a banal level, they are, but the reworking process was being performed by a scholar who was critiquing more than simple, single-source stories; rather, she was exploring the tales' many actual and infinite possible versions. A novel like *The Passion*

of New Eve, playing with Hollywood representations of women, or *Nights at the Circus*, which reads at times like a direct fictionalization of Michel **Foucault**'s ideas, makes this scholarliness plain. And Carter's critique of sexuality and femininity was equally complex and equivocal: she loved manipulating the frissons inherent in writing about stereotypically grotesque heterosexual relationships, sexual violence and (particularly female) **masochism**.

The best way into Carter is via her long essay *The Sadeian Woman*. In part a defense and recuperation of **Sade**, this book also agitates in favor of 'the moral pornographer . . . who uses pornographic material as part of the acceptance of the logic of a world of absolute sexual licence for all the genders . . . [whose] business would be the total demystification of the flesh and the subsequent revelation . . . of the real relationships of man and his kind'. This is precisely what Carter's work was up to. And, as is clear from both the content and tone of *The Sadeian Woman*, the moral pornographer, Carter, was like Sade a deeply ironic operator. *JT*

The Magic Toyshop (London: Virago, 1981); *Heroes and Villains* (Harmondsworth: Penguin, 1990); *Love* (Harmondsworth: Penguin, 1988); *The Infernal Desire Machines of Doctor Hoffman* (Harmondsworth: Penguin, 1990); *The Passion of New Eve* (California: Harcourt Brace Jovanovich, 1977; London: Virago, 1982); *The Sadeian Woman* (New York: Pantheon, 1988; London: Virago, 1979); *Nights at the Circus* (Harmondsworth: Penguin, 1986); *Black Venus* (London: Picador, 1986); *Wise Children* (London: Vintage, 1992); *The Bloody Chamber* (Harmondsworth: Penguin, 1987); *Expletives Deleted: Selected Writings* (London: Chatto, 1992)

See also **Heterosexuality; Kaplan; Winterson**

Catullus, Gaius Valerius (c.87-54BC)

The poet Catullus came from a fairly wealthy, provincial family in Verona, North Italy, but, apart from a brief trip to Bithynia (now part of Turkey) as an assistant to the governor, he spent most of his adult life in Rome.

Catullus belonged to a group of poets who

C

immersed themselves in Greek poetry and were influenced by the early lyrical poets, notably **Sappho**, from Lesbos, and by the Alexandrian poets of the second and third centuries BC. Catullus's poems deal extensively with sex. There are four loose groups, the most famous of which is devoted to his mistress Lesbia (probably so named in honor of the Lesbian poets), a married woman. Another group is devoted to Juventius, a boy lover; while a few longer poems include marriage songs and mythological stories concerned with marriage. The final group is chiefly composed of poems to and about his friends – generally of a scatological nature – reflecting on current mores.

Catullus's Rome is a sexually voracious place where various forms of sexual activity seem to be going on all around. His attitude towards this is varied; he is no prude, but is censorious towards such forms of behavior as **incest**, which he regards as violating the important family bond. At the same time, he is almost voyeuristic and, in one of the Juventius poems, admits to using sexual language in order to excite others. The poems certainly provide an insight into the sexual practices and prejudices of the period: the idea, for example, that a man who fellates another, or is the passive partner in buggery, is thereby demeaned.

The Lesbia poems are romantic and expressive, the first truly personal, emotional poems in Roman literature. While Greek lyrical poetry tended to show women as the ones who suffered uncontrollable passion in love, Catullus takes on the role of tortured lover himself, in a then radical piece of 'role reversal'. He does this most famously in Poem 51, which is a direct translation of a Sappho poem. One could see Catullus as the prototype for the now familiar stereotype of the lovelorn romantic male poet. In the longer works, notably the two marriage songs, we see Catullus's ambiguous feelings towards marriage and its possible disappointments, although a number of writers are convinced that Catullus would have wanted to marry Lesbia had she been free, and he himself stresses his belief in the need for friendship with a woman, as distinct from having a purely erotic relationship. Catullus's

appeal lies perhaps most strongly in the fact that his voice as a lover, and as a salacious observer of his contemporaries, retains an uncertainty and ambiguity that we can still recognize today. *KH*

K. Quinn *Catullus – The Poems* (London: Macmillan, 1970)

See also **Bisexuality; Romantic Love**

Celibacy

A state of sexual abstinence pertaining to heterosexual, homosexual and auto-sexual activity, celibacy has two main forms: that which is chosen and that which is imposed. The first appears to be a positive state associated with productivity and political progress and not, as a rule, accompanied by 'regrets' – which may explain why, within the Christian context, the term has more often been applied to men than to women. Particularly among the clergy, celibacy has been seen as a 'higher' state; Catholic priests still take vows of celibacy while, within the Anglican community, permission for male clergy to marry is a relatively recent phenomenon. Women who become nuns, however, have taken vows of **chastity**.

All this contrasts sharply with enforced or imposed celibacy, which is frequently perceived as a negative state and associated with feelings of rejection, guilt and deprivation. In the west today this is partly because of an orthodoxy which maintains that sex is 'compulsory' and decrees that life without it is no life at all. And celibate members of the general public, as distinct from those in religious orders, are seen to be celibate by default: that is, because no one desires them as partners.

Married couples who have taken vows of celibacy have often been seen as leading a sanctified existence, but, since the introduction of Freudian concepts of sexuality, and the twentieth-century belief in sexual fulfillment, the premise that celibacy is a form of denial and is detrimental to one's mental and physical health has become increasingly accepted. In fact, this contrasts starkly with the little evidence available. The research of Sally Cline, for example, suggests that in Britain, in any case, there are many women who enjoy being celibate and see it as a more satisfactory perspective from which to view the other sex. For celibacy neither endorses the notions of female passivity and absence of desire, nor affirms the male 'drive'. Indeed, because it defies conventional male definitions of sexuality and of women's place in relation to men, it challenges the prevailing cultural standards. This is one reason that it is not always presented as a viable option for women. The most recent debates in the area suggest that, for many women who *choose* celibacy, it is not a matter of electing the polar opposite to sexual activity; rather it can be a new woman-centred form of sexuality.

This does, however, raise one fascinating issue: the difficulty of determining the period of abstinence required before a state of celibacy can be deemed to exist. Can one day, one week, one month without sexual activity be termed celibacy? Is a longer period required? What is the nature of *no* sexual activity? Does it mean no **sexual intercourse**, no activity with sexual overtones, no sexual *desire*? Does one sexual encounter of itself nullify the state of celibacy? Is it more a state of mind than a physical reality? Such questions have made it difficult for those who wish to assert that their celibacy is both a choice and a positive state of existence. Partly as a protest against the *compulsion* to be a sexual consumer, some women have tried to assert the active and political nature of their celibacy; they have insisted on removing 'sexuality' from their relationship with the opposite sex (and, in the case of their own sex, have neutralized it) and, in the attempt to delineate this consciously structured reality, have labeled themselves as radical celibates or sexually autonomous beings.   *DSp*

Sally Cline *Celibacy, Women and Passion* (London: Andre Deutsch, 1993)

See also **Aquinas; Christianity; St Augustine**

Chastity

Chastity is considered a virtue over a wide geographical area, but with somewhat varying connotations. It has also undergone a distinct evolutionary process in European thought. In general, it is no longer – and over most of Asia never was – strictly synonymous with either **virginity** or **celibacy**.

Although more often enjoined upon women chastity is perhaps somewhat less sexually evaluated than, say, aggressiveness. In the Renaissance, at about the same time that Juan Vives was advocating women's education as a means of inculcating them with chastity in its narrowest, most puritanical sense, Thomas Elyot, writing on the education of future statesmen, was recommending male chastity (which he termed 'continence'). Both reflected the view, found also in **Shakespeare**'s plays, that chastity constitutes a type of moral discipline: the practice of which, at least for the male, was a means of attaining and maintaining other admirable traits. (For the female, it was an end in itself.) Shakespeare's heroines were uniformly chaste; but chastity, in the senses both of sexual inexperience and sexual restraint, was also attributed to the hero in several of his plays. Even today, among certain Greek villagers for example, the virgin warrior youth is looked upon as the masculine ideal.

From medieval times and up to the Renaissance, marital chastity connoted marriage without sex, rather than sexual activity confined to marriage. Indeed, the early Christian church barely tolerated marriage, Jerome holding it acceptable only as it produced virgins. In the West, the Reformation slightly shifted the emphasis away from a strictly corporeal notion of purity. Nevertheless, this view still underlay many nineteenth- and twentieth-century writings, and is reflected also in the Hindu designation of menstruation as a temporary form of unchastity, as well as in the rapes perpetrated upon female Muslim political prisoners before execution to prevent their attaining paradise.

In both India and China, female chastity is enshrined in customs known if not admired in other parts of the world, but, while virginity is as usual considered the *sine qua non* of unmarried girls, it is wifely chastity (in the sense of extreme fidelity and devotion) that is celebrated. Among Hindus in India, the tradition of *sati*, or the immolation of a widow on her husband's funeral pyre, explicitly asserts that only the wife's chastity makes her eligible to participate in the ceremony. Similarly, in China, virtuous widows – many of whom demonstrated their virtue by committing suicide, for example by flinging themselves from the 'Pagoda of Chaste Women' in Fujian – are memoralized in the form of biographies of exemplary lives. What all these varieties of female chastity have in common is the magical power that they endow. This is best illustrated in the stories of virgin Christian saints, such as Joan of Arc, and in the divinity attributed to the Indian *sati*, a cult which has recently been revived. *DSt*

See also **Chinese Women's Resistance; Christianity; Hinduism; Islam; Lie Nu Tradition**

Chastity Belt

Also known as the Florentine Girdle, the chastity belt was at one time said to have been invented in Italy. More certainly, this metal contraption – designed to run between a woman's legs and, once locked into place round her hips, to prevent access to her genitals – first came into being in the course of the fourteenth century somewhere in Europe.

Principally used by husbands wanting to ensure their wives' sexual fidelity, chastity belts very soon became and still are a source of innumerable jokes about losing the key, possessing a spare key and so on: jokes that cannot have vastly amused the women subjected to the belts' humiliation. For although the belts were pierced with two tiny holes for the passage of menstrual blood, urine and feces, they would of course have been grossly unhygienic, leading to vaginal infections and ulcers if kept on for any length of time. And quite often they would

be kept on for months, even years, while women's husbands were on pilgrimage or fighting in the crusades – and, if the latter, in all probability raping the wives of defeated Egyptians, Palestinians and Syrians.

The ironies of the chastity belt are manifold, but perhaps the greatest is that its invention coincided with the cult of **romantic love** which positioned upper-class women, especially, on pedestals of awe-inspiring **chastity**. That this roseate image was sustained by an instrument of torture, about which everyone knew, reveals as clearly as anything can contemporary men's hypocrisy. Not for a second can they seriously have thought that 'ladies' were intrinsically purer, less sexual, more virtuous than themselves, but, by whatever means necessary, they were going to make them *behave* as though they were. And the crudeness of their method of last resort exposes the crudeness of their motive: obviously not to retain their wives' undivided love and affection, but to make quite sure that their lands and goods weren't inherited by someone else's bastard. According to Reay Tannahill in *Sex in History* (London: Cardinal, 1989) chastity belts were still being sold via surgical-instrument catalogues as late as the 1930s. These belts, however, as befitted an era of subtler sexual oppressions, were padded with rubber and intended to prevent **masturbation**. *HG*

See also **Female Genital Mutilation**

Child Sexual Abuse

The use of children by adults for sexual purposes, and adults' justification of the practice, is known as **paedophilia**. Child sexual abuse, by contrast, is usually, although not exclusively, identified with **incest** and the transgression of the incest taboo. It is also frequently marked by denial – of the fact and of its psychological implications – on the part of fathers, and this complicated dynamic presents one of the greatest obstacles for therapists working in situations where incest is suspected or is known to have taken place. Overwhelmingly, all the statistics show that father-daughter incest is by far the most widespread.

For feminists, key questions have turned on the long-term psychological consequences for survivors, on the power of men to control women and girls sexually and on the problematic assumptions of systems of family therapy which see the family as a collusive unit in which the mother 'knows' what is going on and fails to protect her daughter. Another issue that has been raised is the extent to which the theory of **infantile sexuality** is made problematic by the existence of *actual* scenarios involving the child and its parent. That said, it should be remembered that the sexual wishes of childhood, however willingly we acknowledge their existence, are not the sexual desires of adult life; indeed, as Jean Laplanche has argued most cogently, each child is presented with the 'enigmas' of the adult world and, before she or he can master them, is entitled to protection from them.

Clinically, the concept of 'informed consent' remains crucial. A small child, in a case of incest, has been coerced, however subtly, cannot freely assent and is usually left unable to integrate the loved and the hated father. The long-term psychological consequences for incest survivors are known to be very bad and the capacity to form stable and loving sexual relationships much impaired. Hence the need for early and appropriate therapeutic and statutory intervention and the provision of resources for political and educational action on incest as appropriate. Interestingly, there is some recent evidence to suggest that, where fathers are more involved in the day-to-day care of their children, they are less likely to abuse them sexually; social change in the direction of greater equality of roles in the raising of children may therefore have a significant preventive role to play.   *AS*

Jean Laplanche *New Foundations for Psychoanalysis* (Oxford: Basil Blackwell, 1989)

See also **Incest; Paedophilia**

Chinese Marriage Laws

The first marriage law of the People's Republic of China, passed in 1950, aimed to abolish the traditional system of arranged marriage and to replace it with a system of monogamous, free-choice marriage. 'The feudal marriage system based on . . . the supremacy of man over woman . . . is abolished. The New-Democratic marriage system, which is based on the free choice of partners, on monogamy, on equal rights for both sexes . . . is put into effect.'

Alongside the land-reform law of the same year, which extended rights of land ownership to women, the marriage law also granted women rights of divorce. Initial reaction was varied. Young people in the urban centers welcomed it as an attack on the power of the older generation, but the new law provoked widespread opposition in the countryside, where eighty per cent of China's population lived. Resistance to the new law effectively prevented young people from exercising their new rights and many young women committed suicide rather than acquiesce to parental authority. A second marriage law, passed in 1980, testified to the continuation of feudal marriage practices. It reiterated the illegality of venal contracts and 'acts of interference in the freedom of marriage'. However, it also extended the rights of divorce by introducing a new 'alienation of affection' clause.

Despite evidence that a large percentage of marriages in the People's Republic are still far from totally free of parental interference, young people's opportunities for meeting potential partners and their expectations of marriage are now very different from those of their parents' generation. Subservience to parental wishes has been replaced by negotiation and consultation. Although many contracts are still entered into for reasons of mutual convenience, love and affection increasingly feature as desirable conditions for marriage. However, in the process of the gradual elimination of feudal customs of marriage, the monogamous heterosexual union, legally registered, has become the only morally acceptable relationship within which sexual expression is sanctioned. The official discourse on sex-related issues suggests that extra-marital affairs are the harbingers of misery and chaos. Silence reigns over the issue of **homosexuality**, while women who choose not to marry are considered either psychologically unstable or promiscuous. **Monogamy** in its legally sanctioned form is thus identified as the single standard of normal sexual practice which, far from extending the principle of free choice, often seems to function as a new form of sexual and social tyranny. *HE*

Margery Wolf *Revolution Postponed: Women in Contemporary China* (London: Methuen, 1987)

See also **Romantic Love; Sexual Revolution; Yu Luojin**

Chinese Women's Resistance

With no rights of divorce or economic independence, and socially bound by a rigid code of moral conduct, women in traditional China had few means of escape from a destiny of absolute subordination to men. 'How sad it is to be a woman. Nothing on earth is held so cheap.' Nevertheless, women's resistance has been a constant feature of China's history. Besides participating in popular rebellions against state authority, often forming their own battalions independently of men, women wrote poetry exposing the injustices of being born female and condemning the brutal custom of footbinding.

The most common form of resistance, however, was escape. Female suicide was at times widespread. Chinese literature contains numerous stories of women who throw themselves down the household well, leaving their restless spirits to haunt their husband's household. Suicide statistics collected during the first two decades of this century indicated a high number of successful suicides among young wives in their early twenties. An alternative was to take vows of **celibacy** and enter Buddhist convents, or to join Daoist religious sects and secret societies, many of which upheld principles of sexual equality. In the nineteenth century, women in some parts of southern China were forming exclusive associations specifically designed to challenge their traditional destiny. Often called 'anti-marriage associations', they were composed of young women who swore to remain unmarried and undertook collectively to drown themselves if one of their number were threatened. By the early twentieth century women's resistance began to adopt a new form, acquiring the characteristics of an urban-centered women's movement.

The struggle for equal rights gathered momentum once the new republic was set up, to replace the overthrown Manchu dynasty, in 1911. Anti-footbinding associations emerged, alongside demands for women's education and suffrage. Women defied tradition by cutting their hair or adopting the dress of western men. The 'new thought' of the cultural and political awakening of the May Fourth period (1915-1921) injected further change into the women's movement. Journals appeared focusing on issues such as birth control and divorce. Influenced by western views on individual rights, women's emancipation became increasingly identified with the independence of the individual from traditional familial, marital and social constraints. The Confucian family came under attack as the principal unit of the traditional patriarchal system responsible for perpetuating women's subordination.

As heir to these tendencies, the Communist Party of China inscribed many of the principles of the May Fourth period into its own policies and women's resistance became increasingly identified with general goals of anti-feudal social transformation. The urban-centered feminism of the May Fourth period became, in the process, associated with a narrow, 'bourgeois' approach to revolution. *HE*

Elisabeth Croll *Feminism and Socialism in China* (London: Routledge, 1978)

See also **Chastity; Chinese Marriage Laws; Yu Luojin**

Christianity

Christianity was founded at the start of the first century on the life, work, death, resurrection and teaching of Jesus Christ. It had its roots in a world where, particularly among Jews like Jesus and his first followers, the subordination of women was taken for granted. There are signs that the earliest Christian communities allowed women unusual freedom and power but, in this respect, Christianity was quick to realign itself with current practice. In the fourth century the Emperor Constantine became a Christian and, from that time on, Christianity became entangled with the legislative powers of the Christianized West, so that it becomes hard to see what is 'Christian' and what is 'accepted custom' enforced by Christianized legislators.

A number of factors have a bearing on what Christianity teaches about sex, the first of which is asceticism. With the increasing wealth and power of the church, there also grew a movement intended to recall people to God. It laid stress on control of appetites and on willingness to die for Christianity: martyrdom. This was not primarily a hatred of the body or sexuality, although it was often expressed in such terms; it was intended as a means to channel energy into prayer and contemplation. Ascetic rules of life often bound communities of celibates together in single-sex, or monastic, groups. Although, ironically, the monasteries themselves often became immensely wealthy and powerful, from quite early on there is a widespread assumption that celibates are a better kind of Christian (despite the denials of, for example, **St Augustine**).

Dualism was the second factor to affect Christian teaching on sex. Christian theologians of the third to fifth centuries were greatly influenced by dualistic philosophies which made a distinction between body and soul, nature and reason and so on, and there developed an increasing tendency to undervalue the 'bodily' in favor of the 'intellectual'. Since women were, at least from the male viewpoint, bound up with the 'bodily' – sex, childbirth, breast feeding – metaphors that aligned women with the non-rational became prevalent.

That Christianity largely speaks of God as male tends to reinforce dualism, as does the fact of the maleness of Jesus. Although theoretically Christianity always insists that God is not sexual, pervasive male language and imagery, together with a belief that only men are 'rational', leads to a belief that God is, in some sense, more like men than women. It is also relevant that Christianity seldom made any attempt to challenge current social models. With the introduction of Christian marriage, religious sanction was given to existing male property rights and power over women – although it is true that practices varied from time to time and place to place.

Its asceticism and dualism, not to mention its Jewish roots, also mean that Christianity places strong emphasis on **heterosexuality** and the belief that the primary purpose of sex is to produce children. Sexual pleasure is good, but not an end in itself: hence traditional Roman Catholic teaching against **contraception** and the considerable muddle that all Christian churches are now in about **homosexuality**. *JW*

See also **Aquinas; Bataille; Celibacy; Donne; Ecstasy; Hinduism; Islam; Jarman; Judaism; Monogamy; Puritanism; St Paul**

Chrystos (1946-   )

A lesbian poet who emphasizes her experience as a Native American Indian, Chrystos has been writing since the age of nine. Her work first appeared in *This Bridge Called My Back*: *Writings By Radical Women Of Color* (New York: Kitchen Table: Women of Color Press, 1983) and she has subsequently contributed to *A Gathering of Spirit*: *A Collection of North American Women* (New York: Firebrand Books, 1984) and *Naming the Waves*: *Contemporary Lesbian Poetry* (London: Virago, 1988).

Chrystos has had first-hand experience of poverty and discrimination and this, along with her activist work with the lesbian and gay Native American community, provides her with an informed fury around many injustices. Disenchanted with what she perceived as a white, middle-class women's movement, she left that arena in the late 1970s, but still maintains a radical-feminist understanding of **lesbianism**. Recently interviewed in *off our backs* (volume xix, number 3, March 1989) she unequivocally stated: 'My sense of lesbianism is that by saying we want to love other women that's a deep rebellion against the patriarchy.' In the same interview she took a stand against **sado-masochism** in the lesbian community: 'Enjoying that kind of thing is a betrayal of history . . . particularly the use of the whip against Black people in slavery makes the idea of the whip nauseating to me . . . I have worn handcuffs put on by real cops. It's not sexy.' But, unlike those radical feminists who take a firm line against **pornography**, seeing it as an oppressive representation of subordinated woman, Chrystos has reservations about the use of censorship. She sees herself as a 'very sexual person' who has experienced censorship of 'how sexual a woman I was allowed to be'. Lesbianism, for her, is as sexual as it is revolutionary and she has equated lesbians with prostitutes as sexual rebels.

Many of Chrystos's concerns reappear in the first published collection of her poetry, *Not Vanishing*, where her use of language is as direct as it is eloquent. The love poems are tender, erotic and full of images conflating nature with lesbianism. In 'O Honeysuckle Woman', for example, she equates the opening of a flower in the honey-making process to women opening to each other in the act of lesbian love-making.   CU

Not Vanishing (Vancouver: Press Gang Publishers, 1988)

See also **Brant: Political Lesbianism; Prostitution**

Chughtai, Ismat (1915-   )

Screen-writer, novelist, short-story writer and multiple literary award winner, Ismat Chughtai was brought up in a progressive Indian family. The ninth of ten children, she was given an upbringing equal to that of her brothers and it is to this that she attributes the frankness of her writing. 'Even in those days sex was not a taboo subject in my house . . . We knew the facts of life very simply and very easily because they were openly discussed. That was a peculiar thing and we were all considered quite mad.'

Lesbianism, however, was not discussed, so that when Chughtai decided upon it as the theme for her story '*Lahaf*' ('The Quilt') in 1942, she thought it was something that women did 'because they can't go to prostitutes'. In the story, the lesbian sex is observed by a pre-pubescent girl who walks into her aunt's bedroom after hearing her talking to her maid and witnesses vigorous movements under the quilt. First published in *Adab-e-Latif/Belles Lettres*, it dropped an altogether unexpected bomb onto the literary scene, not least because of the realistic way in which Chughtai reproduced the language of women. Chughtai was bombarded with threatening and censorious letters before a few distinguished literary figures, mostly associated with the Progressive Writers' Association, wrote articles defending the story on the basis that it reflected reality. One of these was Sa'adat Hassan **Manto** who, in 1944, was prosecuted along with Chughtai by the Imperial Court of British India on a charge of **obscenity**.

This did not stop Chughtai exploring unusual sexual attitudes in her stories, particularly from the women's point of view. In '*Maujza*' ('The Miracle') of 1955, a wife who has had enough of sex and of housework learns to manipulate the sexuality of her husband and other women in order to change from victim to oppressor. She finds her husband a second wife and then, when her position is threatened by the co-wife's pregnancy, convinces him that pregnant women have an adverse effect on the health and sexual prowess of men. She regains her power by bringing in a third bride, then spends the rest of her life in luxury, controlling the women and her husband through their sexual impulses, having firmly appropriated prevalent male attitudes to redeem her own existence.   *SH*

Ek Baat/A Word (Lahore: Naya Idara, 1960); *Choten/ Wounds* (Lahore: Naya Idara, 1961); *Terhi Lakir/The Crooked Line* (Lahore: Naya Idara, 1962); *Do Hath/Two Hands* (New Delhi: Maktaba Jamia, 1962); *Quilt and Other Stories* (London: Women's Press, 1991)

See also **Bedi**; **Das**

Circumcision

In the male, circumcision means the removal of all or part of the foreskin covering the tip (*glans*) of the penis. Of possibly prehistoric antiquity, it is found in widely separated areas and among nomadic, agrarian and industrialized peoples. A bas-relief of the third millennium BC in Egypt shows an operation in progress.

After **St Paul** announced that there was no purpose in the observance of Jewish rituals, Christians replaced circumcision by baptism. Along with their dropping of the Jewish dietary laws, this was part of the process by which their religion became entirely separate from **Judaism**. The practice, however, was never forbidden and, among Coptic Christians, is mandatory. Among Muslims (except for Chinese Muslims) circumcision is universal but not a religious requirement; it is a social custom which has been retained and has spread.

It has been estimated that between one sixth and one quarter of males worldwide are circumcised at present. In some regions, such as north and west Africa, large regions of east Africa, Canada and the USA, the proportion rises to seventy-five per cent or more. In Europe it is rare, except for in the UK where the prevalence is about twenty per cent. But even there, the mid-century medical fashion in its favor has been reversed: in 1965, circumcision, except for medical indications such as phimosis (long and/or tight foreskin) ceased to be obtainable from the National Health Service. On the other hand, following a preference of Queen Victoria, male members of the royal family do tend to be circumcised.

With respect to esthetic considerations, only the ancient Greeks appear to have considered the uncircumcised penis an object of special beauty; Greek athletes, who competed in the nude, sometimes stitched up short or loose foreskins to produce a smoother, neater appearance. On the other hand, surveys of women generally indicate that they find the circumcised penis the more attractive.

Among some peoples, male and **female genital mutilation** are seen as complementary: the removal of the foreskin is viewed as the removal of a vestigial vagina, just as the removal of the **clitoris** is thought to be the removal of a miniature penis. In each case, the operation reduces the blurring of uncertainty of the sex, producing a more clear-cut man (or woman), fit for adult roles and responsibilities. In other societies, for example in the USA and Samoa, the reasons given are medical or hygienic. In particular, it is alleged that the low rate of cervical cancer among Jewish women is a result of the circumcision of the Jewish male, which inhibits the build-up of a possibly carcinogenic secretion (smegma) on the penis. Cancer of the penis is never found in males circumcised before the age of three – but it is, in any case, rare.

Among Copts, Jews and in modern hospitals, circumcision is performed shortly after birth. Among Muslims and many Africans, it is customary at later ages, often as a puberty rite but sometimes prior to marriage. The research of **Masters and Johnson** found no difference between circumcised and uncircumcised males in regard to the sexual pleasure they experience. A partial exception to this statement is the belief that circumcision results in a slight desensitization of the tip of the penis, thus permitting more protracted coitus before ejaculation occurs.   *DS*

See also **Emecheta**

C

Circumcision, Female

See **Female Genital Mutilation**

Clitoridectomy

See **Female Genital Mutilation**

Clitoris

To the naked eye, the clitoris is a tiny part of women's genitalia: a little, hooded, erectile bud at the front of the genital area. In fact, as with icebergs, most of the clitoris is hidden inside the body (the visible part is technically referred to as the *glans*). But more important is the fact that this organ plays a disproportionately major role in women's sexual pleasure, being the most sensitive, nerve-filled part of her genitals. Moreover, unlike the penis – which also acts as an organ of procreation and urination – sexual pleasure is the *only* role of the clitoris. As the English author Bernard de Mandeville put in 1724: 'All our late discoveries in anatomy can find no other use for the clitoris but to whet the female desire by its frequent erections.'

Indeed. And in many societies this fact seems to fill men with terror. Some have suggested that this is because they are frightened of being sexually exhausted by humans who appear even better designed than themselves for erotic enjoyment; others, that it is because men prefer to think of women as sexless in order to fend off worries about being cuckolded, or landed with another man's child. Whatever the reasons, the role of the clitoris is frequently ignored or misrepresented by male 'experts' – and, in societies where girls and women are discouraged from touching or exploring their bodies, frequently ignored or misunderstood by them too. In societies where a ritual is made of **female genital mutilation** (mutilation which always involves, at least, the excision of the clitoris), the organ inevitably has a higher public profile, but is commonly presented as being an ugly, unnecessary, misplaced penis, and thus far better removed. Another tack is to downgrade the clitoris to something infantile and vaguely shameful, as Sigmund **Freud** effectively did by proposing that a 'mature' woman, a woman who was neither perverted nor neurotic, was one who had shifted her sexual focus from her clitoris to her vagina.

Since Freud, it has frequently been maintained that women can have two kinds of **orgasm**, a clitoral or a vaginal kind. The latter is understood to be caused by penetration (in other words, by the kind of sex that can lead to procreation) and to be of a superior nature, while the former is understood to be caused by stroking or rubbing the clitoris and to be considerably less grown-up or satisfying or serious. The distinction is almost entirely fictitious. Certainly, a woman can feel great pleasure at having inside her vagina the penis of a man whom she loves or desires, but, unless her clitoris is also receiving some form of stimulation, the procedure is fairly unlikely to lead to her orgasm. The vagina, unlike the clitoris, is almost entirely nerveless.

The importance of the clitoris to women's sexual pleasure, whether in **masturbation, sexual intercourse** or other forms of sex, has in fact been pointed out on numerous occasions: by Helena **Wright** in the 1940s; by Alfred **Kinsey** in the 1950s; by **Masters and Johnson**; by Ann **Koedt**; by the countless women in the last twenty years who have helped one another to explore and understand their own bodies . . . It nevertheless remains the case that, within patriarchal culture at large, the *heart* of women's sexuality is seen to reside in their vagina and their womb. For men, sex may mean any number of things; for women, it must centrally mean motherhood.   *HG*

See also **Horney; Kama Sutra**

Clit Statements, The

Collective Lesbian International Terrorists (CLIT) were a small New York group who published several lesbian separatist 'statements' in 1974. These were energetically discussed in both North American and British women's liberation movements. Although the statements touch on several issues – the fashionability of **bisexuality** and the discovery of lesbians by the media; language; women and nature; consumerism; **monogamy** – the predominant topic is heterosexual or 'straight' women and why they are bad for lesbians.

The CLIT statements were not the first expression of lesbian separatism, defined as living separately from men. They were, however, the most public expression of a separatism from other women, a suspicion of contamination by male culture that extended itself even to lesbians who spent time with non-lesbian women. Straight women were variously described as agents for men, men in disguise, the real players of roles, or simply sexual partners to avoid. (Authors of the different pieces disagree about whether real dykes actually feel attracted to them.) Lesbians who had not sufficiently rid themselves of patriarchal attitudes were also attacked, as were gay men, but the language used against heterosexual women is extreme: 'The only difference between straight women and drag faggots is that faggots are real men.'

The tone is very much that of the earlier *S.C.U.M. Manifesto* by Valerie Solanas, quoted with approval. The statements are fascinating to re-read for their energy, their period-left rhetoric (lots of 'mind-fucks') and their jumbled airing of different feminist ideas. But although their anger against heterosexual women is all too clearly pained, the CLIT statements are chiefly remembered today for going too far: a comforting symbol of how 'reasonable' the rest of us were at the time. *R W*

off our backs (vol. IV, numbers 6 and 8, May and July 1974)

See also **Heterosexuality; Political Lesbianism**

Colette, Sidonie Gabrielle (1873-1954)

Sensuality in all its forms is the subject of the French writer Colette. She writes of food, of animals, of flowers, with as much passion as she writes of sex; often, indeed, with more. Her observation of sexuality is fascinated, frank and frequently cynical, while her response to the natural world is never jaded or cloying.

But Colette is not an ecstatic of the woodlands, either. Her natural worlds are the garden, designed and maintained; the kitchen, with its carefully created scents and flavors; and the boudoir, especially the boudoir. Women, in Colette's books, tend themselves like gardens which must be strictly weeded and kept up to scratch if they are to succeed in flowering. The femininity she describes so well is very much an artificial and constructed thing, one which is eventually allowed to relapse and relax into the sexless comfort of old age.

Of Colette's heroines, the eponymous Gigi and Léa in *Chéri* (the latter the book which, in 1920, secured Colette's literary reputation in France) are the best known. *Chéri* is a fascinating novel, provocatively and unexpectedly blending several of Colette's preoccupations. Léa is a wealthy courtesan whose household of servants and cellar of wines testify to a successful life as a professional woman. Her love affair with Chéri, half her age, comes to an end when he marries; but it is he, the young man with his whole life in front of him, who cannot come to terms with the loss of Léa (to old age, rather than to marriage) and kills himself. Their attachment mirrors the relationship of mother and child, a relationship which is central to Colette's work. She adored her own mother, Sido, and wrote about her at great length. She also sought the comfort of a quasi-maternal relationship – her own assessment – in lesbian affairs; most notably, after the break-up of the first of her three marriages, with 'Missy', the onetime Marquise de Belbeuf.

Eroticism between women is, for Colette, a twin theme with the narcissism which seems to play such an important part in the construction of the female that she celebrates so paradoxically and so superbly. Yet her attitudes to lesbian relationships, as well as to heterosexual ones, are never unambivalent. She cannot be claimed as a prototype feminist or lesbian. She traveled between worlds in a way that was shocking for, and to, her own time, and took copious notes as she went. She is ironic and perceptive about sexual relationships of various kinds and there is a lingering note of sadness in her work which helps to give it its originality. It is not the simple 'hymn to life' that some have supposed it to be. Colette writes, above all, of a profound and inviolable solitude at the heart of all human affairs – romantic, passionate or mundane – a solitude best comforted, she almost seems to say, by animals and by the pleasures of the table and the garden, rather than by the more complex and less secure pleasures and affections that human beings offer to one another.   *ALT*

Chéri and The Last of Chéri (New York: Ballantine, 1986; Harmondsworth: Penguin, 1990); *Ripening Seed* (Harmondsworth: Penguin, 1986); *The Vagabond* (Harmondsworth: Penguin, 1990); *Gigi* (New York: Dutton, 1973); *Earthly Paradise* (New York: Farrar, Straus, 1975); *Break of Day* (New York: Ballantine, 1983)

See also **Beale; Bisexuality; Compulsory Heterosexuality; Garcia Marquez; Menopause**

Comfort, Alex (1920-   )

Of all the 'how to do it' books on sex that have been published, Alex Comfort's *The Joy of Sex* is probably the best known. With millions of copies sold since it was published in 1972, it describes itself as the gourmet guide: an explicit sex manual that encourages people to experiment with and explore their sexuality. As with most sex-advice writers, Comfort's message is that 'anything goes' between consenting adults in private.

Some would argue that Comfort is a sex radical, who normalized many sexual activities previously seen as taboo and broadened people's definition of sex by celebrating variety: from flagellation to **fetishism**, from bondage to bananas, from group sex to gagging. But despite his wish to be non-judgemental Comfort isn't concerned to put lesbian or gay sex on his menu; the extent of his liberal tendencies is to promote heterosexual variation. And, even here, his challenge to the primacy of penetration is limited by his assertion that, although only one form of sexual pleasure, **sexual intercourse** is nevertheless, for most people, the *pièce de résistance*. Also, in pointing out how 'acceptable and normal' 'mild' sado-masochistic role-playing can be, Comfort helps to legitimate the association of eroticism with humiliation and pain, an association that feminists such as Andrea **Dworkin** perceive as encouraging **rape** and other forms of male violence.

The Joy of Sex and the equally successful *More Joy of Sex* (1975) were written for both women and men, whom Comfort assumes to be equal partners in the pursuit of pleasure. At the time of the books' publications, there were some who regarded this as part of the general encouragement of a new sexual freedom for women. But a closer look at the books reveals a bias towards meeting men's sexual needs and demands. From his liberal standpoint, Comfort regards women's dislike or fear of various kinds of sexual activity as being caused by inhibition and repression; women need to be helped (by men, of course) in overcoming their inhibitions and discovering new pleasures. What he fails to acknowledge is that many women who have negative feelings about sex do so not through guilt or prudery but in response to the sexual double standard and women's unequal relationships with men.

None of this has prevented a redesigned and revised edition from being published, as *The New Joy of Sex*, in 1991.   *DiR*

The Joy of Sex (New York: Pocket Books, 1987; London: Mitchell Beazley, 1986); *More Joy of Sex* (New York: Pocket Books, 1987; London: Quartet, 1988); *The New Joy of Sex* (New York: Crown, 1991)

See also **Foreplay; Heterosexism; Heterosexuality; Loulan; Sexual Revolution**

Comics, Japanese

The *manga*, or comic book, is the most accessible form of **pornography** in Japan today, being both readily available and cheap. It can be bought off the shelf at bookstores, convenience stores, railroad kiosks, and from vending machines in the street, not to mention at speciality neighborhood *manga* stores. It usually costs no more than a cup of coffee.

Not all *manga* are pornographic. There are some 1.6 billion comic books sold in Japan each year, most of them targetted at a very particular readership. There arc *manga* concerned with teenage romance, volleyball, ballet, cyborgs, computer games, sumo, fashion and so on. Of the total *manga* market, approximately 10 million sales each month are of pornography: the term, here, being used to describe those comic books which include explicit sexual scenes. But even within this working definition the diversity of target readerships is astounding. In the late 1980s, there emerged pornographic *manga* for teenage boys and girls (target age 12 and upward) while 'soft porn' *reediizu komikku* (comics for ladies) have been growing rapidly in popularity since the early 1980s. Among the pornographic comics for men are everything from the 'traditional' titles such as *Big Comics for Men*, which sell up to a million copies per issue, to those which deal with **sado-masochism** or the '**Lolita** complex'.

Two historical sources or precursors are frequently cited for the *manga*, the first being the woodblock print of the Edo period (1603–1868). The rapid development of this form of reproductive

Japanese *manga, c.* 1990

technology allowed the relatively cheap dissemination of multiple copies of an image or a text and two forms of woodblock are associated with present-day comic books: the *shunga*, or 'erotic prints', and the comic prints also known as *manga*. *Shunga* specialized in scenes of prostitutes and **Kabuki** actors, their images of heterosexual, lesbian, homosexual and autoerotic sex blurring the line between fantasy and reality. The Edo *manga* consisted of a sequence of images on a single woodblock, among which the pornographic ones might focus on human or animal sex, on bestiality or, occasionally, on unusual couplings across non-human species. They were invariably comic, in the sense of being humorous, which distinguishes them from their present-day namesakes which are frequently deadly serious in the level of violence and abuse that they represent.

The more recent precursor to today's *manga* is often claimed to be the *kamishibai* performance which gained great popularity in the immediate post-war years. A form of street storytelling, it was accompanied by images displayed on cards or scrolls, creating a separation of audible and visual narrative which is common within the dramatic tradition of Japan. In today's *manga*, a similar interplay between words and images continues to make the traditional point about representation's unreality.

A characteristic shared by the Edo *shunga* and present-day *manga* is the use of phallic substitutes, the intricately carved and textured dildoes of the Edo period having now been replaced by high-tec, battery-run implements of pleasure and torture. The two forms also make a point of transferring such everyday objects as paint brushes, candles, kitchen utensils and so on into the pornographic realm, a point of particular importance in present-day Japan where strict delimitations of space create a preponderance of de-erogenized areas in daily life. The displacement and, even more significantly, *r*eplacement of everyday objects operates simultaneously to familiarize the pornographic and to defamiliarize the everyday. The context in which the *manga* are read is also linked to this process, the most common time for reading them being when commuting, when the Japanese worker or student is

traveling between the private and the public domain; while being transported through geographic space, she or he is also transported through an imagistic textual space which blurs the boundaries of public and private and redefines both as potentially erogenous.

There have been attempts to explain the volume and popularity of pornographic *manga* as a safety valve, a fantasy outlet for suppressed male violence towards women. By contrast, they have also been seen as a catalyst for violence against women. Both interpretations oversimplify. For a start, neither offers any explanation for the popularity of pornographic titles among female readers, or the complex cross-over gay and lesbian readerships that have developed around the various sub-genres of pornographic *manga*. Despite strong anti-pornography campaigns mounted by Japanese feminists during the 1980s, the market for *manga* continues to grow (a hundred per cent annually from 1986 to 1989) and the range of titles also continues to proliferate. Ironically, the fastest growing segment of the market has been the women's *reediizu komikku*. There is much in the comics themselves that points, in overtly self-referential ways, to the fact that the sources of pleasure in these texts are to be found not in their relation to the extraordinary but in their relation to the everyday and, particularly, to the family.   *SB*

See also **Comics, US and European; Sado-Masochism; Ukiyo-E**

Comics, US and European

The comic strip as newspaper serial or comic book, or in its more fashionable incarnation as a graphic novel or *bande dessinée*, has a capacity to counterpoint image and word, to slow time and present incidents in a non-linear way at odds with standard perceptions, that might have made it more frequently a vehicle for subversive commentary, not least on sex and gender.

But the English-speaking world has been slow

to accept the form as a serious artistic genre, largely because of the panic kicked up by an odd alliance of the moral right, psychoanalysts and the Communist Party of Great Britain. In *Seduction of the Innocent*, published in New York in 1954, Frederick Wertham accused superhero comics of subverting gender roles: Wonder Woman was obviously lesbian propaganda; Batman and Robin unhealthy. The comics industry responded with a pre-censorship code analogous to Hollywood's **Hays Code**. For a decade, US comics avoided social problems and sexual matters, while in Britain the devoutly Christian Marcus Morris set up a group of comics which showed clean-limbed, square-jawed imperialists in space or western adventures, and their female counterparts in the intrigues of school and ballet companies.

In the 1960s, however, a struggle for readership between the two largest US comic companies, DC and Marvel, led to some innovation. An attempt to create a female readership – the comics market is traditionally ninety per cent masculine – reintroduced female characters in active roles, while super-heroines sometimes trashed villains by sensitivity and judo. Newspaper strips, aimed at adults, had more room for maneuver. Will Eisner's *Spirit* imitated Hollywood in placing good girls and bad girls in opposition but undercut stereotypes by having his sultry temptresses survive unrepentant.

There had always been pornographic comics, either in the shape of 'Tijuana Bibles' showing Disney characters having sex, or the glossily drawn SM (sado-masochistic) comics regularly quoted by artists like Allan Jones. Late 1960s alternative culture created its own tradition, often rebarbatively sexist but sometimes subverting the sexism of the male-dominated New Left by showing it satirically. The underground tradition has persisted, adopted by gay and feminist artists critical of its sexism but keen to use its freedom from censorship for their own agendas.

In the 1980s artists and writers influenced by the underground, and tired of the superhero conventions, accelerated the process of change. Sexually charged episodes of Alan Moore's *Swamp Thing*

Red Sonja, from *The Savage Sword of Conan the Barbarian*

led to the scrapping of the comics code, while the rise of specialist shops enabled independent publications to survive. Perhaps the most important of these were *Love and Rockets*, with its complex sexual intrigues in the Hispanic American community, and *Cerebus*, a free-flowing parodic novel with sexuality as a major theme and target. The impact of Moore on the mainstream, the pressure of the independents, obliged comics to deal with subjects other than superheroes, and to make those heroes who did remain vehicles for examining the neurotic compulsion to dress up in a costume to fight crime –

not least the implied sexual neurosis. In a sense, Wertham was right all along.

Meanwhile in France and elsewhere in Europe comics had always been taken seriously and so had a less interesting battle to fight. Much of the work of artists like Crepax and Manara plays prettily but uninterestingly around the fringes of softcore SM **pornography**; the more innovative work of Druillet and Bilal often sets up crude gender dichotomies between the mechanical and the organic, or between the direct and the messily confused. In Spain, post-Franco libertine anarchism has produced its own tradition of aggressively erotic noir thrillers with leftwing transexual hooker heroines.

RK

See also **Comics, Japanese; Sado-Masochism**

Compulsory Heterosexuality

Compulsory heterosexuality is the enforcement of **heterosexuality** as a political institution that is 'natural' for all women. Adrienne **Rich** introduced the term to a broad feminist readership in 1980.

Analyzing the phenomenon, Rich describes patriarchal power to enforce heterosexuality as 'a pervasive cluster of forces, ranging from physical brutality to control of consciousness'. Heterosexuality, 'a beachhead of male dominance', is most often pronounced to be the only normal mode of sexuality. Yet, given the primacy of the bond between mother and daughter as described by such researchers and theorists as Nancy Chodorow, Rich questions why women would swerve from woman-directed affection. Ultimately, the rupture of women from other women as emotional and erotic centers is accomplished through cultural ideology and then rigidified into social code. Mandated heterosexuality requires that lesbian experience be ignored, erased or labeled pathological or deviant. As such, the institutional status of heterosexuality not only disempowers lesbians but all women. And, by refusing fully to recognize lesbian experience, such **heterosexism** 'creates . . . a profound false-

ness, hypocrisy, and hysteria in the heterosexual dialogue, for every heterosexual relationship is lived in the queasy strobe light of that lie'. *LU*

Adrienne Rich *Blood, Bread, and Poetry: Selected Prose 1979–1985* (New York: Norton, 1986; London: Virago, 1987)

See also **Benedict; Colette; Dworkin; Hocquengham; Lesbianism; Patriarchy**

Contagious Diseases Acts, The

The Contagious Diseases Acts were a series of public-health measures in nineteenth-century Britain designed to contain the spread of **venereal disease** among soldiers and sailors. Under the first Act of 1864, a woman identified as a prostitute by specially recruited policemen and suspected of suffering from venereal disease was required to undergo a medical inspection. If she did not submit voluntarily, a local magistrate's court (with all the attendant publicity) could order her to do so. Where the internal examination confirmed infection, she could be detained for a maximum of three months in a hospital containing venereal wards.

The Act of 1864 covered eleven garrison towns and sea ports; in 1866 one more was added. The discretionary powers of the police were also increased: a woman needed only to be *suspected* of being a 'common prostitute' to be forced to submit to fortnightly inspections for the maximum period of a year. If an examination proved positive, she could be locked in a hospital ward for up to six months; if negative, a certificate was issued indicating her non-infection. The 1869 Act rescinded the practice of certification but extended the legislation to include six new towns and to increase the detention period to nine months.

Although the scope of the original Contagious Diseases Act was limited, part of a movement towards military reform, the Acts in fact reflected wider nineteenth-century British prejudices. And by 1869 extension of the Acts was actively being advocated, the argument being that such regulation

C

would improve public health, lessen vice and disorder and clean up **prostitution**. The National Association for the Repeal of the Contagious Diseases Acts, and the separatist Ladies' National Association for the Repeal of the Contagious Diseases Acts (LNA) led by Josephine **Butler**, were both formed in 1869. The repeal campaign argued that the legislation was repressive and legitimized discrimination on the grounds of sex and class. The LNA also pointed out that, by deliberately ignoring men, the Contagious Diseases Acts sanctioned a double standard of morality: male promiscuity was seen as the acceptable expression of male sexuality but female transgression of social norms was punished. Furthermore, the forced inspection of poor, working women was a violation of women's bodies tantamount to surgical **rape**.

The emphasis of the repeal campaign on the moral purity of women was very much a middle-class bias; it drew on an ideology which located woman firmly in the domestic and private sphere; after all, her moral and spiritual ascendancy were virtues of the home. The Contagious Diseases Acts were abolished in 1886, but the call for a strict code of sexual conduct for both men and women led to repressive social purity crusades and the formation of the reactionary National Vigilance Association which campaigned for widespread censorship of literature, music hall, the theater, even information about birth control. *GCL*

Judith Walkowitz *Prostitution and Victorian Society: Women, Class and the State* (Cambridge: Cambridge University Press, 1980)

See also **Acton**; **Contraception**

Contraception

For animals other than human beings, sex appears to have one simple function: reproduction. It is true that a female primate will sometimes initiate sex when she isn't 'in season' (in order to provoke a cuddle, it would seem, or some other gesture of affection) but, for the most part, non-human animals have sex only when the female's eggs are in a condition to be fertilized: in many cases, as infrequently as once a year.

For humans, of course, things are different. For a start, it is rarely the physical condition of a woman which determines when sex will occur; indeed, all too frequently even her mental and emotional conditions are overlooked. But even when a woman does instigate sex, a desire to get pregnant is only occasionally the motive. She may primarily or only want to demonstrate affection, elicit affection, stave off boredom, exercise power, do what society expects from her or, of course, experience physical pleasure and probably an **orgasm**. But because, when she instigates sex with a man, it is likely to become **sexual intercourse**, any woman who is not infertile risks getting pregnant unless she can prevent the man's semen from reaching her womb, or, in one or another way, ensure that none of her eggs can successfully be fertilized even if it does. The various methods by which this is attempted are collectively known as 'contraception' – and, if not always too efficiently, contraception has been practiced for thousands of years.

In Ancient Rome, the methods varied from plugging the womb with wool soaked in gum (which might have had some effect) to inserting pepper in the womb once intercourse was over (which certainly would not). The Ancient Egyptians also used plugs, one favorite material being crocodile dung, but also medicines concocted from herbs, roots, leaves and less fragrant ingredients. Today, those methods of contraception which women use without men's cooperation include the diaphragm, a dome-shaped barrier inserted high in the vagina; the coil (also known as the IUD or Intra-Uterine Device), which can only be placed in the womb by a doctor and works by preventing a fertilized egg from implanting and thus from developing; and the pill, which consists of one or more hormones whose effect is to stop eggs, right at the start, from preparing for fertilization. None of these methods is *one hundred per cent* effective – although, with the pill, when pregnancy occurs it is usually because the woman has forgotten to take it or taken it late – and

C

all can have side effects ranging from itching to a possible increase in the chances of cervical cancer.

Since 1992 there has also been a 'female condom' on the market, and this sheath designed for insertion in the vagina may yet become popular. For the moment, however, those methods of contraception with few or no side effects – the so-called 'natural' method, which requires careful timing of the menstrual cycle; last-minute withdrawal; the traditional condom – tend to be those that depend on a man's cooperation. And the problem with this is that men, throughout history, have shown themselves far less concerned than women about the risks and disadvantages of pregnancy and childbirth. Often, indeed, men have actively tried to prevent women learning that contraception was possible, to the point of bringing criminal charges against such would-be teachers as Annie **Besant** and Margaret **Sanger**. They have done so probably out of a well-grounded fear that, if women didn't automatically associate sex with maternity, they might enjoy their sexuality more and feel freer to experiment with it. This was, of course, precisely what happened when the pill became widely available in the West in the middle to late 1960s.

Where men *have* advocated contraception, like the English economist Thomas Malthus (1766–1834), this has usually been part of a strategy for limiting the numbers of the poor, not an attempt to improve the lives or the sexual pleasure of women. Alternatively, the condom has been promoted as a barrier to **venereal disease**, most recently now that **AIDS** has taken over from the earlier dangers of syphilis. And, because condoms do indeed have the dual ability to prevent conception and limit the chances of viruses being transmitted during sexual intercourse, it seems high time for a more equal share of responsibility between the sexes for ensuring that pleasure is paid for neither by imprisonment, unwanted parenthood, or death.

HG

See also **Sexual Revolution; Stopes; Wright**

Coprophilia

The fascination of very young children with their feces, although inconvenient, has generally been understood since **Freud** to be part of their normal development. But when adults are unduly fascinated by feces, to the point of obtaining sexual gratification from masturbating into them, or from smearing them over their body or simply from playing with them, they are considered by most psychologists to be indulging in regressive behavior: behavior technically known as coprophilia. (Coprophagia, in which satisfaction is obtained from eating feces, is a very rare variant on this.) Because the idea is disgusting to most nonpractitioners, even more so in some respects than sexual behavior that harms another person, pornographers intent on pushing readers' or viewers' responses to the limit frequently depict coprophilia: John Waters in his film *Pink Flamingoes*, for instance, or **Apollinaire** in his novel *Les onze mille verges*. *HG*

See also **Infantile Sexuality; Necrophilia; Obscenity**

Core, Philip (1951-1989)

An American-born artist and writer, Philip Core explored and celebrated issues of male **homosexuality**. After graduating as a Bachelor of Arts cum laude from Harvard in 1973, Core attended the Ruskin School of Art in Oxford and the Academia degli Belli Arti in Florence, before moving permanently to London in 1975. He died with AIDS in 1989.

Core's art is characterized by a combination of technical facility and sexual charge. He constantly experimented with different media and presented the human body in a variety of styles and scenarios which, whether obliquely or overtly, challenged the official British sexual orthodoxies of the 1970s and 1980s. He was concerned with placing homosexuality in a wide cultural and historical context and presenting homosexual acts as natural, joyous and

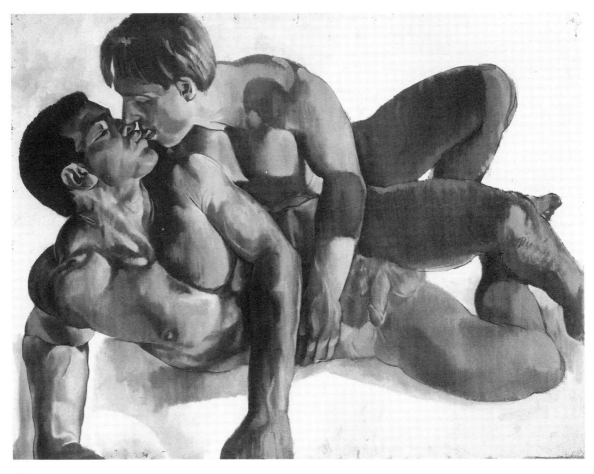

Philip Core, one from a series of paintings entitled *Sixteen Positions*, 1988

central, rather than as marginal to human existence. Core's best known works include the 'Pieces of Conversation' which show imaginary meetings between such cultural celebrities as Marcel Duchamp and Andy **Warhol**, Cocteau and **Colette**, Pinter and **Orton**; large-scale sculptures of neoclassical figures built up from layers of cut-out plywood; and a series of 'Black Pictures' which update and subvert the landscape tradition by depicting groups of men having sex in romantic rural nocturnes. But probably Core's finest (and certainly his most notorious) statement was the 'Sixteen Positions', which comprised an explicit gay paraphrase of erotic paintings by the Renaissance artist Giulio Romano. These were shown in London at the Old Bull Arts Centre in 1988.

Also in that year Core had a two-part retrospec-

tive entitled 'Claustrophobia' at Watermans Gallery in London. The title referred to the heterosexist Clause 29 of the 1988 Local Government Bill and was just one example of his active and articulate campaign against the suppression of any art inspired by homosexuality. Two days before he died Core appeared in court to fight against British Customs' confiscation of books and photographs which he was using as source material for his work.

Although he saw himself primarily as an artist, Philip Core also had a successful career as an erudite and unconventional writer on art and design. He published two books – *Camp: The Lie that Tells the Truth* (London: Plexus, 1984) and *The Original Eye* (London: Quartet, 1985) – as well as producing numerous illustrations and articles for publications ranging from *Vanity Fair* to *Zipper*. He was also

C

the photography critic for the *Independent* newspaper, but it was on their obituary pages that he produced some of his best work, appearing with greater and greater frequency as a champion and historian of the victims of AIDS, the disease that finally claimed his own life.   *LBu*

Philip Core *Paintings* 1975–85 (London: GMP, 1985)

See also **Camp; Gay Liberation; Jarman**

Corman, Roger

See **Exploitation Movies**

Correct Sadist, The

First published in 1983 by Vitriol Press, New York, *The Correct Sadist* was recognized at once as a classic in a field not noted for literary excellence, swiftly achieving a renown similar to that accorded Pauline Reage's earlier **Story of O**, another classic of sado-masochistic erotica.

The Correct Sadist is a combination of memoir, autobiography and philosophical speculation. Its author, Terence Sellers, was a renegade Catholic who early lost her faith and, in its stead, was converted to the writings of the Marquis de **Sade** and the fevered effusions of the French *fin-de-siècle* decadents, in particular **Baudelaire**, Lautreamont and Villiers d'Isle Adam. Her book with its ornate prose is to a large extent a purple pastiche of such writings.

The first section describes her temperament, 'in truth, worldly, sensuous and proud', and her belief in her 'innate aristocracy'. Such convictions, fueled by what seems to be a psychopathic loathing of ordinary heterosexual intercourse, propelled her into professional **sado-masochism**; she became Mistress Angel Stern, dominatrix. The middle section is a series of vignettes drawn from her professional experience. It is intended to act as a handbook for similar aspiring Superiors, and Sellers describes in detail all the equipment needed to set up in business as a successful dominatrix, from douche-bags and nipple-clamps to a variety of whips and riding crops. She covers a vast range of topics including basic etiquette for the slave, the cleansing of the slave, bondage, chastisement, torture, verbal humiliation, **fetishism, coprophilia** and transvestism. These instructions are interspersed with brief role-playing dramas which furnish the reader with a handy range of vituperative invective for use in such professional situations. The final part of the book describes a spiritual crisis wherein Sellers loses her sense of the parameters of power and control, leading to terrible doubts as to 'Who is the vampire and who the drained?' This debate is central to the sado-masochistic psychodrama wherein the slave can be seen to be exercising as much, if not more power than the Master.

Sellers has been criticized for her response; she favors a rigid 'classicism' in all areas of sado-masochistic role-play. She insists on style, perfection and dignity at all times and attempts to maintain the image of a 'flawless lady'. This means that the book is almost completely devoid of humor, apart from bitter jibes at the expense of the slaves whom she appears to detest above and beyond the call of duty.

Although Sellers intends to explain and illuminate sado-masochism, the anachronistic form and stylized language mean that the book really functions as a period piece of pure **pornography**. The master-slave debate has acquired intriguing ramifications in recent years as discussion of sexual politics has widened to include criticism of sexual modes that appear to perpetuate the power games of patriarchal sexuality, but Sellers's book remains, in essence, locked in the 1890s.   *EY*

The Correct Sadist (New York: Vitriol Press, 1983; Brighton: Temple Press, 1990)

Cross-Dressing, Men

Although there are examples of men dressing as women in order to disguise themselves – to enable seduction, for instance; to escape detection (Bonnie Prince Charlie); to engage in ritual performance (Japanese **kabuki** players); or to evade social constraints (English male actors playing women's roles until the mid-seventeenth century) – for obvious reasons this is much rarer than the reverse, female to male disguise.

Mainly because of the social oppression and supposed inferiority of women, much male cross-dressing is either 'illicit' or aggressive. In the first case, a secret and frequently fetishized wearing of women's clothes – especially women's underwear – for purposes of hetero – or homosexual arousal is common. Here it would seem to suggest either self-humiliation or a covert desire for a wider range of appropriate emotional responses. In the second case, cross-dressing can be used satirically, as an attack on women's identity. Such aggressive cross-dressing, always within the context of an 'act', inevitably caricatures the least attractive and most aggressive female stereotypes: the witch, the dame, the ugly sisters. Recent attempts to change this formula, as in the film *Tootsie* with Dustin Hoffman, raise interesting possibilities, but remain within the tradition of social satire: the audience is not confused even when the characters are.

The wearing of female clothes, or even adopting an effeminate style, has been labeled by a homophobic and defensive society as a homosexual activity, a 'pathological' denial of 'real masculinity'. This makes it difficult to assess the representational meaning of 'drag', a highly stylized and self-conscious transvestism popular in certain male homosexual groups. Like other elements of high **camp** it can feel like an uneasy mixture of mysogyny, cocking a snook at heterosexual norms, and self-derogation. But it can also be a strongly positive challenge to social convention and make a significant contribution to sexual politics. In addition, it is often hilarious: much funnier than the coyness and placatory nature of much public, approved, performance transvestism.

None of these uses of cross-dressing should be confused with the clothing choice of pre-operative transexuals, which seems to be a different activity altogether.   *SM*

Peter Ackroyd *Dressing Up* (London: Thames & Hudson, 1979)

See also **Homosexuality; Opera Seria; Shakespeare**

Cross-Dressing, Women

There appear to be four principal reasons why women choose to dress as men, the first being for disguise. Given the restrictions on women's lives in almost all historically recorded eras, there are numerous occasions for which mistaken gender-identity is crucial. Unfortunately women totally successful at such disguise are not found out, but James Barry (1799–1865) became a doctor, joined the army and then served as a colonial medical officer: all jobs unavailable to a woman. Her biological gender was not discovered until after her death. Thérèse Figueur (1774–1861) and Mary Anne Talbot (b. 1778) worked respectively as a sailor and a soldier until their retirement, when they reassumed female clothes and lived happily as women.

Religious ritual is another reason for women to assume men's clothes, many religions having specific times or occasions in which women cross-dress. These range from the defensive (women dressing as men before childbirth so that the gods will not envy them) to 'feasts of reversal'. **Christianity** has never looked very tolerantly on these ritualized occasions for embracing the anarchic – cross-dressing was declared one of the many symptoms of being a witch – but traces of this impulse remain in popular culture from the British pantomime to Mardi Gras.

Third, there is sexual politics. From Mrs Bloomer's Rational Dress Association onwards, women have used male dress or items of it to make political points about the oppression of women. In the first half of this century, in an attempt to give **lesbianism** a public presence, some gay women chose to wear full or partial male costume: the novelists Radcliffe **Hall** and **Colette,** for instance, and a number of the night-club acts of Paris and Berlin in the 1920s and 1930s. Although contemporary feminism has rightly come to be critical of the role-playing and male identification involved in male impersonation, it may still be seen as a courageous decision by individual women in a very different and difficult historical context. On other occasions wearing men's clothes seems to have been a way of explaining one's lesbianism to *oneself*: an expression of deep uncertainty and confusion. However, there seems to be very little evidence among either gay or straight women of the fetishization of men's clothes for direct genital gratification.

Fourth, there is performance, the deliberate and public assumption of men's clothing without any attempt to disguise biological gender. Joan of Arc is probably the most notable example of this process, but Queen Christina of Sweden, nineteenth-century music-hall artistes and, more recently, media stars like Greta Garbo and Annie Lennox have played with concepts of transvestism as part of their act. Such performances may be mounted for a number of reasons, often complex combinations of the three previously proposed motives. By and large, however, the models for women cross-dressing are aspirational rather than satirical; it is seldom critical in any way of masculinity or male supremacy.

SM

Sara Maitland *Vesta Tilley* (London: Virago, 1987)

See also **Androgyny**

Crowley, Aleister (1875–1947)

During his life Aleister Crowley had the dubious distinction of being known as 'The Wickedest Man in the World' or 'The Great Beast', appellations which he courted assiduously and considered flat-

tering. Born to parents who were members of the strict Plymouth Brethren religious sect, he was to die alone in a Hastings boarding-house, bankrupt and an incurable heroin addict. His life had been astonishingly varied; he was known as a poet, novelist, mountain climber, big-game hunter, chess expert and, most importantly, satanic occultist.

Crowley was sexually precocious and, during his education at Malvern and Cambridge, had sexual relations with both men and women. He joined the Golden Dawn, a respectable occult group whose members included W.B. Yeats and Arthur Machen, but was soon disenchanted with what he saw as their dull restrictive practices. He broke away in order to specialize in what he called 'sex magick' and magic of a generally darker hue. In 1912 he became involved with another occult group, Ordo Templi Orientis. Eventually, after worshipping, crucifying and eating a frog, he became a Magus, the group's highest order of magician.

Crowley had married Rose Kelly, sister of the painter Sir Gerald Kelly. He amused her by writing hard-core **pornography** and, by 1904 in Cairo, was using her to communicate with his 'Holy Guardian Angel', a spirit named Aiwass who helped Crowley dictate his creed into 'The Book of the Law'. The main tenets of Crowley's beliefs can be summarized in his slogans 'Every Man and Woman is a Star' and 'Do What Thou Wilt Shalt Be The Whole Of The Law'. The latter is not an invitation to total license; Crowley meant that one should discover one's true 'will' or nature through rigorous discipline and magical practices and then be true to it. His techniques of sex magic were an extraordinary *mélange* from occult and mystical history. They included the Oriental techniques of *karezza*, the retention of semen, and the use of the penis as a syphon to absorb vital male and female fluids. Crowley was also influenced by European occultists such as John Dee and Cagliostro and particularly by the nineteenth-century French magician Alphonse-Louis Constant who wrote under the pseudonym Eliphas Lévi. Crowley studied alchemy, astrology, the Quaballa, diabolism, the Rosicrucians, Egyptian rites and their Graeco-Roman descendants and incorporated aspects of all these belief systems into his philosophy.

Naturally Crowley had constant need of disciples and one of the earliest was Victor Neuberg, a young poet who joined Crowley at his Scottish home in 1909 and submitted to sleeping naked on gorse, vanquishing a demon called Choronzon and engaging in sado-masochistic sex acts with Crowley. Crowley also needed a Scarlet Woman for his rites and, from this time forth, despite his low opinion of women, always had one of his mistresses in attendance. He had divorced Rose.

Having acquired a considerable following among London writers, artists and bohemians, in 1920 Crowley established a magical community at his 'Abbey of Thelema' in Sicily. It seems to have been utter misery for the participants. His current Scarlet Woman, Leah Hirsig, had to tolerate being fucked by a goat; children died as a result of the insanitary conditions; and a young acolyte, Raoul Loveday, expired after being made to drink cat's blood. Crowley was expelled from Sicily by Mussolini in 1923. Bald, rouged, attired in full Highland dress and heavily addicted to heroin and cocaine, he returned to England where he spent the rest of his life writing, engaging in libel suits whenever he was defamed, which was frequently, and struggling with his drug dependency. Two novels, *Moon-Child* and *Diary of a Drug-Fiend*, despite being execrably written, are excellent guides to Crowley's life and beliefs. Although he died in obscurity, since the 1960s his work has again exercised a great influence. His books – Francis King's *The Magical World of Aleister Crowley* (London: Arros: 1977) provides a bibliography – and his magical paraphernalia command high prices. Film-maker Kenneth **Anger** introduced The Beatles, The Rolling Stones and Led Zeppelin to his work and, through them, a sort of half-baked black magic has been disseminated throughout heavy-metal music. He is held in high regard amongst contemporary occultists. For non-adepts it is impossible to assess whether his work contains anything of real power or value or whether he was merely a charismatic English eccentric with a prodigious sexual appetite.

EY

John Symonds *King of the Shadow Realm* (London: Duckworth, 1989)

See also **Wilson**; **Yin and Yang**

Daniels, Sarah (1957–   )

The first contemporary woman playwright to have a play produced on a main stage of Britain's Royal National Theatre (*Neaptide*, in 1986), the English writer Sarah Daniels is one of the few feminist dramatists to be accepted into the mainstream, despite a lack of male critical support, while swimming against the tide. A radical lesbian feminist, Daniel's plays are mind-expanding, funny, intoxicating and subversive. They highlight the inequitable power relations between men and women and question the presumption of **heterosexuality** and the sanctity of the nuclear family.

In her early comic plays, *Ripen Our Darkness* (1981) and *The Devil's Gateway* (1983), Daniels's heroines are middle-aged women pushed to the edge of madness by families who perceive them as walking food-dispensers, washing-machines and ironing-boards. Both Mary in *Ripen Our Darkness* and Betty in *The Devil's Gateway* make their escape, but only by coming to understand that the personal is political and to see the strength and solidarity of sisterhood.

The principal theme of *Masterpieces* (1984), a powerful and uncompromisingly angry work, is the link between **pornography** and violence against women. The central character is Rowena, a young social worker who giggles at her male relations' misogynist jokes and is, to begin with, naively oblivious to pornography. But, like Mary and Betty before her, Rowena evolves from unawareness to consciousness, from passivity to action and from acquiescence in a male-dominated society to rejection of man-made law – as she comes to understand that it is a short step from the dirty joke to the **rape** and violation of women. In her more recent plays

D

Daniels has tackled **lesbianism** and child custody (*Neaptide*), the threat to women from reproductive technology (*Byrthrite*, 1986), the exploitation of female workers (*The Gut Girls*, 1988) and the long-term effects of **child sexual abuse** (*Beside Herself*, 1990). In a theater which is dominated by middle-class heterosexual values, Daniels's voice is unique: a cry against the prevailing culture which presents the world from a fresh perspective.   *LG*

See also **Behn**

Das, Kamala (1935–   )

A well established poet both in English and in her native language, Malayali, Kamala Das has frequently written about sexual experience and its accompanying disillusionment. Her autobiography *My Story* became a cause célèbre with the Indian women's movement, catapulting her to phenomenal fame. Faced with a diagnosis of terminal cardiac illness, she had worked on it from hospital in order to 'empty myself of all my secrets' and 'depart when the time came, with a scrubbed-out conscience'. Originally serialized in a Malayali magazine, the book's confessions of dissatisfaction with sex and of extramarital romances profoundly offended Das's feudal family and friends, who ostracized her.

Das's outspoken views on sexual freedom for women endeared her to the young, but resulted in unwelcome advances from men assuming that such views must reflect personal promiscuity. The paradox, she wrote, was that 'My articles on free love had titillated many . . . It was obvious to me that I had painted of myself the wrong image . . . Sex did not interest me except as a gift I could grant to my husband to make him happy.' Married at fifteen with only a fleeting and guiltless lesbian encounter behind her, Das never quite recovered from the devastation of her first sexual experience with her husband. Of her wedding night she writes, 'Again and again through that unhappy night, he hurt me . . . By morning I could hardly move my limbs.' Never-

theless, in keeping with Hindu notions of wifely commitment, she felt she was 'deeply in love with him and would have undergone any torture to be able to please him, but my body was immature and not ready for love-making'. Subsequently she recalls sexual enjoyment with him only once, when, during her serious post-partum depression, he dressed her in his clothes and called her his 'darling little boy' and she 'shed my shyness for the first time and learned to surrender totally in bed with my pride intact and blazing'. It is not clear from Das's writing whether her extramarital liaisons included **sexual intercourse** but, if they did, her poems testify to her feeling of disappointment and emotional rejection. It was certainly little wonder that she looked for *Platonic* love outside her marriage, to counteract her husband's continued voracious demands on her body. Furthermore, it appears from her writings that her romances were no secret from him.

Das's story is the tale of many Indian women who 'thought love was flowers in the hair, it was the yellow moon lighting up a familiar face and soft words whispered in the ear' and, instead, experienced 'rejection, jealousy, and bitterness and grew old suddenly'.   *SH*

Summer in Calcutta (Bombay: Rajinder Pal, 1965); *The Descendants* (Calcutta: Writers Workshop, 1967); *The Old Playhouse and Other Poems* (Madras: Orient Longman, 1973); *My Story* (New Delhi: Sterling Publishers, 1976; East Glastonbury: Ind-US, 1988; London: Quartet, 1978); *Collected Poems, Vol 1* (Trivandrum: Navakerala Printers, 1984)

See also **Bedi; Chugtai; Manto; Yu Luojin**

Date Rape

'If she says No she means Yes'; male aggression and female passivity are normal; violence is sexy and men need to prove their virility by the number of women they have 'had': myths and stereotypes about **rape** are unfortunately often more abundant than facts. Particularly confusing to victims of date rape – women raped by someone with whom they have gone out dining, dancing or whatever – is the myth that, if you know the person, then rape is not rape. Yet innumerable studies, including US government statistics, have found that well over eighty per cent of all rapes are rape by an acquaintance.

In the USA, almost all date-rape statistics have come from college campus surveys, but date rape happens to widows, single women and divorced women who are supposed to be grateful for any man's attention and find themselves in a weird *déjà vu* of their adolescence, having to fend off people with whom they thought they were going to have a relaxed evening. The assumption is that those women can't be choosy, they are damaged goods and they are sex hungry.

The pressures of **compulsory heterosexuality**, gender roles, male-centered assumptions about the nature of sex, women's fear of male violence and verbal sexual coercion all contribute to the sexual pressure. Men also interpret women's behavior for their own convenience. For example, women often smile and giggle when they are afraid, especially when they are trying not to hurt a man's feelings. The problem of having to be nice when you're in danger is unique to women as an oppressed group, because we live and work with our oppressors intimately and are divided into one-on-one relationships. Thus, we are more easily conquered. And when you're not equal, honest and open, communication is impossible. The date rapist frequently creates the rules and then changes them, sometimes telling his victim, sometimes not. That is the most convenient use and abuse of power.

It is appalling that, in California, a bill needed to be passed in 1990 stating that, just because an alleged rapist had known the woman before, the jury could not *presume* that she had consented. But women saying 'No' to date rape is shocking US society in the way that women saying 'No' to their husband did a decade ago, because men's sense of entitlement from their physical power and purchasing power is being questioned. The date rapist often likes to think that he owns a woman, at least temporarily, by paying for a dinner or cinema tickets: a kind of mini-marriage.

What some recent US statutes have provided, with pressure from the anti-rape movement, is to require essentially a standard of affirmative consent for any **sexual intercourse** not to be considered rape. The woman has to say 'Yes' and the 'Yes' must be knowing and voluntarily and freely given – which means that she does not have to risk saying 'No' which the rapist could use as an excuse to use additional violence to subjugate her. This is especially dangerous where rapists are turned on by domination. The date rapist often likes to experiment with his 'friend' using pornographic scenarios whose most insidious power is the theme that women like to be conquered. *MS*

Ed. Maureen A. Pirog-Good and Jan E. Stets *Violence in Dating Relationships* (New York: Prager, 1989)

See also **Heterosexuality; Marital Rape; X, Laura**

Degas, Edgar (1834-1917)

Edgar Degas was a brilliant and original artist who exhibited with the Impressionists but differed from them in his concern with drawing and pictorial construction and his lack of interest in landscape. Born into a banking family in France, he studied at the Ecole des Beaux-Arts under a pupil of Ingres. It may be significant, given that over three quarters of his output was images of women, that he never married.

Although Degas is popularly known today for his paintings of ballet dancers, these are just one element in a body of work devoted to the depiction of women washing themselves, singing, doing the laundry, trimming hats or waiting for work in the brothel. These paintings and pastels, which show working-class women absorbed in their activities, are less conventional than his depictions of women of his own class and gave rise to accusations of **misogyny**. Charges that he was a voyeur and that he represented women as animals, cleaning themselves like cats, clung to him from the shocked reception of his pastels of women in the tub exhibited at the 1866 Impressionist exhibition. However,

D

Edgar Degas, *Waiting, (2nd Version)*, c. 1879–80

in an age when academic artists showed women as the object of voyeurs within the picture itself (women in slave markets, for example, or naked women asleep) and played on the link between their sexuality and their occupations (laundresses who worked in a steamy atmosphere with loosened clothes were an object of sexual curiosity, as were dancers and their protectors), Degas's unblinking depictions of what it feels like to stretch and yawn and have your hair brushed refuse to titillate his audience and are viewed with recognition by women.

Degas's most overtly sexual images appear in the brothel monotypes, possible done for private clients. In these velvety prints, the animal features, squat bodies and ungainly poses of the prostitutes epitomize late nineteenth-century views of the prostitute as obliging, stupid animal. Yet even here, the absence of coquettishness, the sense of female society in which the male is a necessary irrelevance (for example, 'The Madam's Birthday', c.1880) give a picture of a job as mundane as any other; while a scene of sexual congress, with the woman seen sitting from behind, is closer to documentation of a woman at work than to **erotica**.   *FB*

Ed. R. Kendall and G. Pollock *Dealing with Degas* (London: Pandora, 1992)

See also **Bellocq; Borden; Brassai; Manet; Prostitution; Voyeurism; Zola**

De Palma, Brian (1944-   )

Notorious for the **misogyny** and eroticization of extreme violence towards women in his films, American director Brian de Palma graduated from film school in the 1960s, part of the coterie of young male filmmakers (which included Martin Scorsese and Steven Spielberg) associated with the New Hollywood Cinema. A prolific filmmaker, he early gained a reputation for a flamboyant style and violence laced with cruel humor. His 1976 horror film *Carrie* intrigued many women by its complex

portrayal of the anguish of a repressed female adolescence – although in retrospect this probably owes more to the inspired casting of Sissy Spacek than to De Palma's intentions.

De Palma's speciality is the psychological thriller, verging on horror, with an emphasis on **voyeurism** both within the narrative and as a filmic strategy, using the subjective viewpoint to implicate – and to indulge – the (male) spectator. Obsessively influenced by Alfred **Hitchcock**, De Palma repeatedly plays on the idea of women as not just disposable but also, with calculated insult, as interchangeable. A dead wife is replaced by her identical daughter in *Obsession*: in *Body Double* one woman masquerades as another simply by wearing a wig and exposing her body (who's going to look at the face?); and in the infamous *Dressed to Kill*, De Palma's loving homage to Hitchcock's *Psycho*, one heroine is a good as another, which means that one can be slaughtered 'in a scene of unparalleled screen butchery' (*Sunday Times*, 28 September 1980) to leave room for the next.

This last film pushed back the boundaries of explicit violence within mainstream American cinema. De Palma's 'joshing Jack-The-Ripper approach to women, his flirting with pornography' (*New York Magazine*, 28 July 1980) made *Dressed to Kill* the focus for feminist protest in America and elsewhere as the apotheosis of the **Slasher Movie** and for its association of 'deviant' sexuality with psychological disturbance: the killer is a deranged transvestite. Challenged by critic Marcia Pally in *Film Comment* (vol. 20, no. 5, September–October 1984) De Palma refers to the use for entertainment of women in peril as 'a genre convention . . . like using violins when people look at each other . . . I don't particularly want to chop up women but it seems to work.'   *PA*

Carrie (1976); *Obsession* (1976); *Dressed To Kill* (1980); *Body Double* (1984)
'Pornography: Love or Death? The Sex and Censorship Debate' in *Film Comment* (vol. 20, no. 6, November–December 1984)

See also **Snuff Movies**

D

Detective Fiction, Golden Age

What was most noticeable during the 'golden age' of the detective novel – which is usually dated from the first novel by Agatha Christie (1920) to the last by Dorothy L. Sayers (1937) – is the almost complete absence of sex in any form. Reading any non-fiction text about famous crimes of the period, or looking at trial transcripts, reveals that love, lust and jealousy were equally popular motives for murder in the 1920s and 1930s as they have been at any time this century. Yet convention stated that, even when **adultery** or sexual blackmail were motives for crime, they could never be openly discussed, so, to avoid the problem, detective writers settled on money as their favorite murder motive. For this reason, those writers who chose to foreground sex in their fiction stand out.

The only writer of 'traditional' thrillers to use sex in a regular way was Dorothy L. Sayers. Since she has frequently been criticized for her 'reactionary' stance, it is perhaps surprising to find that she, almost alone of her peers, gave her characters sexual personae even when these were unnecessary to the plot. In particular, in choosing to give her two main characters, Peter Wimsey and Harriet Vane, explicit sex scenes, albeit written in French, and to give Harriet a sexual past unfashionable in a heroine, Sayers succeeded in breaking a few of the unwritten rules of 'golden age' detective fiction.

Sayers's near contemporary Josephine Tey (1896–1952) also pushed the boundaries by writing novels whose plots hinge on **lesbianism, crossdressing, incest** and **child abuse**; while Freudian psychology – and, hence, sexuality in all its forms – was used by the massively prolific Gladys Mitchell in many of her hundred-plus novels. But it was to take twenty years of shifting morality, coupled with the influence of the US 'hard-boiled' detective novel, for sex to be finally allowed to appear naturally and frequently in detective fiction. *LS*

See also **Detective Fiction, Hard-boiled**

Detective Fiction, Hard-boiled

The masters of hard-boiled detective fiction emerged in the USA in the 1930s. Raymond Chandler, Dashiell Hammett and, later, Mickey Spillane felt free to use the comparative freedoms of the US fiction scene to include sex as a major part of their writing. Their earthy private detectives, Phillip Marlowe, Sam Spade and Mike Hammer respectively, were faced with an array of *femmes fatales*, dodgy dames and easy women with whom they would frequently become sexually entangled, only to discover that the women were embroiled in whatever bad deeds were being investigated. Chivalry towards a woman was a concept virtually unknown to these men and they were not adverse to slapping one around, or plugging her with a bullet, if she cheated on them or did not play straight. The obverse of such bad treatment was that many of the women in the books by these 'hard men' were infinitely more enjoyable and rounded characters – particularly the women of Raymond Chandler – because, being bad, they were allowed to be sexual, independent and interesting.

One result of the increasing license to include sex in thrillers, which developed even further during the 1950s and 1960s, was that women writers in the 1980s who chose deliberately to emulate the hard-boiled style (but with female private investigators) were able to give their protagonists a sexual freedom uncommon in other kinds of fiction. The tradition of the lone sleuth drinking hard and picking up sexual partners along the mean streets could easily be translated into a feminist sexual self-determination: as it has been in the work of, Sara Paretsky, Sue Grafton and Liza Cody. In the novels of lesbian thriller writers such as Mary Wings and Barbara Wilson the tradition has allowed a fascinating freedom to write about lesbian sexuality in ways which would not have been possible within other conventional structures. The novels of a writer like Sara Schulman – which may not be thrillers by traditional reckoning but are certainly hard-boiled – even consider the urban underside of lesbian sexuality and issues such as those of **safer sex**. *LS*

See also Detective Fiction, Golden Age; Lesbianism; Machismo

See also Catullus; Ecstasy; Ghazal; Khusrau; Romantic Love

Donne, John (1572-1631)

Brought up a Roman Catholic, John Donne later renounced this faith, entering the Anglican Church in 1615 and subsequently becoming ordained. Not only was he one of the most celebrated preachers of his age, he was also an adventurer – who went on expeditions to sack Cadiz and to hunt treasure ships off the Azores – and the period's greatest non-dramatic poet.

Donne's poetry employs complex, ingenious arguments, complicated verse forms combined with seemingly spontaneous thought that loops and leaps about. Similarly, his use of metaphor is characterized by cunning sleight of hand, paradox, argumentative jokes. Just as might a lover's voice, the poems, through their form and language, woo, cajole, tease, flatter and insult. Donne openly despised the courtly ritual and euphemistic indirection of platonic love, choosing to celebrate the sexual quest: 'Love's not so pure and abstract as they use/To say, which have no mistress but their muse.' He has been criticized recently for confusing natural promptings with sexual imperialism – women as continents awaiting exploration – but we should perhaps be cautious of judging him solely in terms of modern feminist morality. His half-serious, half-ribald ingenuity, in any case, helps to defend him against simplistic readings. His erotically charged power relationships have a flexible grammar that allows the male speaker to be in the suppliant and masochistic position, especially in his religious poems where sexual images such as **rape** describe God forcibly penetrating the poet's soul. Donne's poems were first collected by his son John and published, after his death, in 1633.   *MR*

Ed. Helen Gardner *Elegies* and *Songs and Sonnets* (Oxford: Oxford University Press, 1965): Ed. Helen Gardner *Divine Poems* (Oxford: Oxford University Press, 1952)

'Dora'

Of Sigmund Freud's six celebrated case histories – 'Little Hans', 'The Rat Man', 'Schreber', 'The Wolf Man', 'A Case of Female Homosexuality' and 'Dora' – the last, more properly titled 'Fragments of an analysis of a case of hysteria ("Dora")' (1905), is probably unique in generating not only an extensive and enduring debate within the international psychoanalytic clinical community, but its own restaging as play, film and object of literary and feminist critique and commentary.

Freud treated the eighteen-year-old whom he named Dora in 1900, the year of the publication of his *The Interpretation of Dreams*. His treatment of the young woman is located within the evolution of his early theories of the transference, the **Oedipus Complex** (and thus of the vicissitudes of the seduction theory), dream interpretation and the sexual drive.

'Dora' was brought for treatment by her father, who urged Freud, in a famous phrase from the text, to 'try and bring her to reason'; by Freud's account, Dora's was a case of *petite hystérie*: nervous cough, hoarseness of voice, depression, *taedium vitae*. The family circumstances were Dora's concern, and the occasion for her many reproaches. Dora's unconscious motivations were Freud's concern. And on this hangs much of the fascination and ire that the case history has stimulated.

In essence, the situation was that Dora's parents had a friendship with Herr and Frau K and Dora's father was having an affair with Frau K, which the father at the outset denied. Herr K made a sexual advance to the fourteen-year-old Dora, which disgusted her. Herr K denied having done so. Freud's strategy was to interpret Dora's behavior and her dreams within the framework of a denied desire for Herr K and an unresolved oedipal desire for her father. Freud was convinced of the validity of his

D

interpretations, but Dora and many subsequent feminists were less so: in the case of the latter, centrally because Freud was unable to deal with 'the feminine and its relation to the mother'. Dora terminated the treatment abruptly. In time, Freud came to feel that he had failed to recognize Dora's homosexual attachment to Frau K as 'the strongest unconscious current in her mental life' and thus, in his words, had failed to master the transference. Yet, although he saw Dora's treatment as 'fragmentary', he was 'not inclined to put too low a value on [its] therapeutic results' and he responded to the news of Dora's marriage some years later with a retrospective observation about the 'second dream' within her treatment: it 'announced that she was about to tear herself free from her father and had been claimed once more by the realities of life'. On this note of certainty his 'Postscript' to the case ends.

In 1985 a selection of key papers by analysts, a historian and a number of literary critics appeared in the USA and in Great Britain. *In Dora's Case*: *Freud, Hysteria, Feminism* placed Dora's case 'at the center of the contemporary debate about the role of sexual difference'. It is an indispensable collection, a record of an ongoing cultural project. But, in a perceptive review of the book, Mandy Merck noted that 'our interest in this case is assumed to be political and aesthetic. Questions of illness . . . tend to be occluded . . . Or, pathology is discovered in Freud, who is variously described in this collection as authoritarian, pathologically phallocentric . . . perverse, boastful . . . neurotic . . . callous, aggressive and anxious . . . This displacement of pathology from the patient prompts me to register a question: is it characteristic of the feminist appropriation of psychoanalysis that the more we embrace it as an account of gendered subjectivity, the more we escape it as an account of individual illness?' This was, after all, the psychoanalytic trajectory: regardless of the justice of Dora's complaints about her family, and regardless of any shortcomings of clinical technique and insight, Freud did identify in her symptoms a series of clues to 'a disturbance in the sphere of sexuality', and in

her dream life a 'flight from life into disease', The point needs to be remembered.   AS

'Fragments of an analysis of a case of hysteria ("Dora")' in *Case Histories 1: 'Dora' and 'Little Hans'* (Harmondsworth: Penguin, 1977)

Ed. Charles Bernheimer and Claire Kahane *In Dora's Case: Freud, Hysteria, Feminism* (London: Virago, 1985)

See also **Child Sexual Abuse; Compulsory Heterosexuality; Psychoanalysis**

Drag

See **Cross-Dressing, Men**

Duffy, Maureen (1933-   )

See **Microcosm**

Dworkin, Andrea (1946-   )

The New York-based writer and activist Andrea Dworkin is probably best known for her writing and campaigning against **pornography**. In the painstakingly researched *Pornography: Men Possessing Women* she insists that the pornography debate is not about theories of representation but about *real* women and the real profits made out of those real women's bodies. Pornography, she maintains, is violence against women, not a cause of it; it is not only inextricably linked to the universal low status of women, but to **rape, prostitution**, battery and **incest**.

In the early 1980s Dworkin worked with Catharine A. MacKinnon on an amendment to US law that would allow women the right to bring civil complaints against pornographers. This was passed in the City of Minneapolis in December 1983. Her campaigning work on pornography as a civil-rights issue rests on the central tenet that male dominance

– and its manifestations in pornography and sexual violence – silences women, a case which she makes most forcibly in 'Against the Male Flood: Censorship, Pornography and Equality' (1985) and 'Pornography Is a Civil Rights Issue' (1986), both published in *Letters From a War Zone*.

Widely admired for her scholarship, her passionate belief in the importance of both literature and literacy, and the compassion with which she speaks on behalf of women, Dworkin is nonetheless distrusted by some feminists for her fiercely polemical style and has been criticized, wrongly, for holding a biological determinist position: for believing that a person's potential is primarily determined and therefore constrained by her sex (defined in chromosonal, hormonal and anatomical terms), giving rise to the phrase 'anatomy is destiny'. Dworkin early refuted this accusation in 'The Root Cause' (1975), printed in *Our Blood*. Since then, in *Right-Wing Women* (1983), she has explained the conformism and anti-feminism of conservative American women as a strategy of survival in a misogynist world; while in *Intercourse* (1987) Dworkin looked at the history of and meanings given to **sexual intercourse** in the works and lives of writers she admires, including Tolstoy, **Flaubert**, Baldwin and Singer. The book explores male fears of women's autonomy and charts the history of religious and secular control of women's sexuality. It is a difficult and challenging work, not least because it insists, unfashionably for the time, on the political nature of private sexual acts.

Dworkin has suffered astonishingly at the hands of both female and male critics. Castigated by men as a man-hater early in her career (see Alison Hennegan's analysis in *Gay News*, no. 228, November 1981, where she points out how often men – both gay and straight – confuse a woman's love for other women with hatred of men), with the publication of *Intercourse* she became a target for 'pro-pleasure' feminists (see Susanne Kappeler's illuminating article on feminist misreadings of Andrea Dworkin in the feminist journal *Trouble and Strife*, no. 12, Winter 1987).

In her fiction Dworkin makes audacious use of first-person narrative and centralizes a woman's experience of sex, offering a feminist perspective on the sexual confessional tradition of writers like Jean **Genet** and William **Burroughs**. Powerful but grim, her two novels, *Ice and Fire* and *Mercy*, articulate the subjective reality of rape.   SL

Woman Hating (New York: Dutton, 1976); *Pornography: Men Possessing Women* (New York: Dutton, 1989; London: Women's Press, 1981); *Right-Wing Women: The Politics of Domesticated Females* (New York: Putnam, 1983; London: Women's Press, 1983); *Ice and Fire* (New York: Grove Weidenfeld, 1987; London: Fontana, 1987); *Intercourse* (New York: Free Press, 1988; London: Secker and Warburg, 1987); *Letters From a War Zone: Writings 1976–1987* (New York: Dutton, 1989; London: Secker and Warburg, 1988); *Mercy* (New York: Four Walls Eight Windows, 1991; London: Arrow, 1992)

Pornography and Sexual Violence: Evidence of the Links: The Complete Transcript of Public Hearings on Ordinances to Add Pornography as Discrimination Against Women (London: Everywoman, 1988)

See also **Heterosexuality**; **Obscenity**; **Oral Sex**; **Russell**

Dyke

Formerly an insult addressed to lesbians, 'dyke' has now been reclaimed as a badge of pride and a mark of style. Whereas female chartered accountants and closeted politicians can be lesbians, only those with some kind of style – usually butch, but not only that – qualify to be dykes. Any given city or culture with a sizeable women's community has a large array of dyke styles and, although there are certain internationally recognized ones such as the track-and-field dyke and the leather dyke, some are local varieties. In London one can find 'Roots dykes', who combine elements of butch/lesbian clothing with clothes or accessories from their culture of origin (African, South Asian and so on). In Toronto one can find baseball dykes (who often do belong to the Not-So-Amazon softball league, a venerable community institution) and, in a grouping which overlaps slightly with the previous one, Birkenstock dykes, named after the footwear popular in feminist

E

intellectual circles. In California there are SM dykes, granola dykes and beach dykes. And practically everywhere one can find everyone's darling, baby dykes (who are, needless to say, just over the age of consent) and everyone's nemesis, bar dykes.

One may be a lesbian because of the inexorable force of the unconscious, but being a dyke is a willful act, an act of defiance, of creativity, of humor. Lesbians may exist for nasty reactionary politicians and for well-meaning sociologists, but dykes exist only for one another, dressing up, showing off and creating new meanings just for fun. And there's never just one kind of dyke.   *MV*

See also **Camp; Lesbianism**

Ecstasy

Although now popularized to mean almost anything intensely agreeable, ecstasy retains much of its original usage. It is a term to describe the ultimate state of mystical prayer: union with the godhead. The word derives from Greek: *ex*, out of; *stasis*, place (in the sense of stability, normality). Initially it was a medical term, but soon became used to describe a particular type of religious experience. In ecstasy, the initiate loses all sense of embodiment and becomes 'at one' with the divine.

In Shamanist and possession religions, this is a two-way experience: while the ecstatic becomes 'lost' in the divine, the god or ancestor or totem spirit can directly use the now 'available' body to express itself to the social community. In **Christianity** this social interaction is much less marked. Ecstasy is here a more private experience, always expressed as pleasurable; although, as in possession religions, there is usually a strong sense of non-volition or passivity. Ecstasy sometimes generates odd physical phenomena, which can be related to Freudian concepts of hysteria. These include levitation; stigmata (physical wounds often mirroring the wounds of Christ); extreme rigor; unnatural body temperatures.

More complex are the attempts by ecstatics to express their subjective experience. The only two women proclaimed 'Doctor' by the Roman Catholic Church, Catherine of Siena in the fourteenth century and Theresa of Avila in the sixteenth, received the title for their mystical theology: that is, their attempt to describe their ecstatic and other religious experiences. Both, along with others, wrote of ecstasy in intensely physical terms, using imagery that would now seem more in line with representations of sexuality, particularly **masochism**. Thus, among other things, Theresa wrote of being pierced through the stomach by a burning spear and Catherine of her 'mystical marriage' in which Jesus not only went through a marriage ritual with her but also removed her heart from her body and replaced it with his own. This form of expression subsequently became common, particularly among female ecstatics. These elements – almost certainly emphasized by Bernini's powerful and highly sensual sculpture 'St Theresa in Ecstasy', in which the saint is shown in what can easily be interpreted as a romantic version of post-orgasmic bliss – have led commentators to treat religious ecstasy as a sublimated expression of frustrated sexuality. This is a denial of the validity and context of ecstatics' experiences: it makes as good sense to see **orgasm** as a substitute for repressed religious experience.   *SM*

Theresa of Avila *The Life of the Holy Mother Theresa of Jesus* (London: Sheed and Ward, 1979)

See also **Brontë, Emily; Ghazal; Khusrau; Mira Bai; Romantic Love;** *Story of O*

Ellis, (Henry) Havelock (1859-1939)

'The greatest of British writers on sexuality, and during the inter-war years probably the most influential': so Jeffrey **Weeks** described Havelock Ellis in *Sex, Politics and Society* (London: Longman, 1981). Ellis qualified as a doctor but also wrote and edited works in literature, social policy and the popularization of science. A friend of Olive Schreiner, with whom he had a passionate correspondence until her death in 1920, he was married to Edith Lees, a writer, lecturer and lesbian. His account of their marriage can be found in the posthumously-published *My Life*.

The first six volumes of Ellis's major work, *Studies in the Psychology of Sex*, were published between 1897 and 1910 – in the USA, after the first volume, *Sexual Inversion*, was prosecuted in England. Ellis rejected the negative attitude of the Victorians and saw sex as the key to a fulfilling life, at its best when part of an intense psychological relationship. He adopted many of Richard von **Krafft-Ebing**'s categories of sexualities and presented many case histories, but he saw such variants as **coprophilia**, sadism and **masochism**, necrophilia, transvestism and inversion not as pathological but as part of a continuum, linked to procreative heterosexual sex through 'erotic symbolism'. In *Sexual Inversion* he argued that the homosexual orientation was inborn rather than an acquired vice or disease and (somewhat contradictorily) that everyone had something of the opposite sex in them and that children had homosexual as well as heterosexual impulses. He did much to counteract the prevailing stereotype of homosexual men as effeminate members of a perverted subculture but, as feminist critics have pointed out, his much shorter section on women gave wide currency to the stereotype of the mannish lesbian and may have played a part in the way that women like Radclyffe **Hall** lived their lives.

Ellis believed that women's sexuality was as strong as men's but more diffuse and more passive. So, although he was very important in establishing the twentieth-century idea of women's right to sexual pleasure and men's duty to ensure they got it, and although he was in principle committed to women's legal, political and professional rights, he also criticized the women's movement of the day for emphasizing equality with men and not recognizing that motherhood and menstruation gave women special needs for protection.   *MM*

Studies in the Psychology of Sex (California: Harcourt Brace Jovanovich, 1978); *My Life* (New York: AMS Press, 1939)

Sheila Rowbotham and Jeffrey Weeks *Socialism and the New Life: The Personal and Sexual Politics of Edward Carpenter and Havelock Ellis* (London: Pluto, 1977)

See also **Homosexuality**; **Infantile Sexuality**; **Lesbianism**; **Perversion**; **Sexology**

Emecheta, Buchi (1944-   )

Sex in the novels of the Nigerian author Buchi Emecheta is almost always demanded as the right of men; women seem to function perfectly well without it. Emecheta's two most popular fictions are both autobiographical. *Second Class Citizen* and *In the Ditch* chart the life of Adah, a young woman who marries neither for love nor money but because she is desperately in need of a quiet environment in which to study undisturbed for her university exams. When she forgoes the high bride-price she can command as a college-educated woman, her family is flabbergasted. But her husband Francis, she soon learns, is quite happy to have her work and support him both at home and, when they move there, in England. 'To him a woman was a second-class human, to be slept with at any time, even during the day, and, if she refused, to have sense beaten into her until she gave in . . . There was no need to have an intelligent conversation with his wife because, you see, she might start getting ideas.' Sex, then, without **contraception**, is the only way to keep a wife in her place. But Adah is also a survivor and a realist and soon realizes that her intelligence and sexual allure do not cancel each other out, but are assets to help her get a job and a home in which to bring up her five children.

In *Double Yoke*, Nko has to choose between being a 'good girl' or a feminist in a Nigeria where 'feminism means everything that is bad in women'. After Nko is seduced by her fiancé he wonders how, if she is a good girl, she could have given in. His loss of faith in Nko shatters her and leads to her moral corruption, when she is preyed upon by a lecherous old professor. She learns too late that one is better off 'using one's brain power than bottom power.

E

They may try to tell you that your bottom power is easier and surer, don't believe them.'

In Emecheta's novels men appear to assume that women's sex is up for grabs by the highest bidder. But although the heroines are constantly reminded of their inferior status, by men and by the society around them, many, if not without a struggle, rise above this. Debbie, the militant gun-toting middle-class heroine of *Destination Biafra*, is the antithesis of what we are constantly told an African woman should be: she 'wanted to do something more than child breeding and rearing and being a good passive wife to a man whose ego she must boost all her days'. Her affair with a white man may embarrass her family and scandalize her community – which is disgusted by, among other things, the uncircumcised penises of white men, which 'hang down like wet intestines' – but she takes her pleasure from him and makes no compromises, enjoying sex on an equal footing with him.

Emecheta paints pictures of societies in which men are unconvincing heads of families, either terminally insensitive or useless at providing their families with even the bare necessities. It is the women who hold families together. Where men are resistant to change, even when it results in their downfall, women are resiliant, enterprising and perfectly capable of living without them. *NOB*

In the Ditch (London: Allison & Busby, 1974); *Second Class Citizen* (London: Allison & Busby, 1979); *The Bride Price* (London: Allison & Busby, 1976); *The Slave Girl* (London: Allison & Busby, 1977); *The Joys of Motherhood* (London: Allison & Busby, 1979); *Destination Biafra* (London: Allison & Busby, 1982); *Double Yoke* (London: Ogwugwu Afor, 1983)

See also **Circumcision; Mizoguchi; Wa Thiong'o**

Erotica

Although, like **pornography**, erotica means the explicit depiction of sex in pictures or words, especially when designed to arouse desire, the terms are very rarely used as though they were interchange-

able. Pornography is generally a term of abuse, while erotica is a non-judgmental or even approving description.

Erotic art has existed in almost every culture, its function usually a complex mixture of sexual stimulation and sex education. The prints in Japanese pillow-books, for instance, were intended to be kept by the bed for instruction, but doubtless also aroused the viewers' need and desire to be instructed. Conversely, the seventeenth-century French erotic book *L'Ecole des filles*, although pretending to be sex lessons given by an older woman to a younger one, certainly had the primary function of stimulating men's lust. (The English diarist Samuel Pepys is known to have bought a copy, even though, once he had read it, he dismissed it as the 'most bawdy, lewd book that ever I saw', then burnt it.)

In many cultures, religion is involved as well. The *Kama Sutra*, most famously, is far from being the simple book of 'positions' perceived by ignorant non-Hindus. It expresses a religious philosophy according to which the sensual life is as worthy of respect as the spiritual. Indeed, erotic art almost always speaks to needs besides the physical: the need to celebrate (God or ourselves); the need to organize and understand; the need, as in **Kabuki** theater, to defy a political, social or moral establishment. And if this complexity makes it hard to categorize the erotic arts of eras remote from our own – are the pre-historic representations of round-bellied, large-breasted women, for instance, primarily about fertility, sexuality or both? – it makes it equally hard to be sure about the intentions and effects of erotica today. This matters because so many people position it in a moral opposition to pornography.

Pornography being the newer term (it was coined in the nineteenth century) and associated with mass-produced writing and images, many, especially in the art world, will reserve 'erotica' to distinguish well made, complex, intelligent sexual artefacts – probably old and certainly expensive – from those churned out for the hoi polloi for speedy financial gain. In this distinction, artistic judgment and snobbery are so tightly entwined that it is frequently hard to work out where one ends and the other begins. Nor does the snobbery stop at the works itself; as the trial of D.H. **Lawrence**'s novel *Lady Chatterley's Lover* revealed, an art work can, by implication, be harmless erotica when there are only a few select people who have access to it, dangerous pornography once their 'servants' can pick up a copy in the high street.

When feminists make a distinction between erotica and pornography, the criteria are somewhat different. Since most of them focus on pornography – either because they would like to ban it or because they would like to argue *against* its being banned – they tend to leave erotica to be defined by default. To generalize, because of course there is never an absolute feminist position, erotica for most feminists would be a representation of sex which did *not* imply that women like pain, humiliation, rape, did *not* conflate sexual excitement with violence or with women's degradation or torture.

Of those who have been more positive, Gloria Steinem has described erotica as sexual imagery or writing which 'contains the idea of love, positive choice, and the yearning for a particular person': an overall concept with which many would agree but which others find rather too saccharine. As Ellen Willis put it in *Beginning to See the Light* (New York: Knopf, 1981): 'This goody-goody concept of eroticism is not feminist but feminine' and derives from the belief that sexual excitement is 'an aggressive, unladylike activity'.

More recently, in her Introduction to *Erotica: An Anthology of Women's Writing*, Margaret Reynolds has offered the following, somewhat more open definition: 'Eros, the blind boy. Under one tradition he was the son of Aphrodite and Hermes. Love, realised in the body of a woman rising out of the sea, unites with speech and exchange in the winged messenger of the gods. These are the two strands in the erotic. The body's craving and the mind's release.' In common with Steinem's understanding of the word, this one not only refers to 'love' but to some kind of outward momentum, some traveling of the self towards another. The book's anthologized writings, however, range from

Elizabeth David's sensuous description of Calamata olives to an excerpt from Pat **Califia**'s sado-masochistic *The Calyx of Isis* – 'The knife travelled the inside of Roxanne's thighs. The girl had spread her feet as far apart as her manacles and chain permitted . . . ' – the first of which might not seem obviously sexual, the second of which a great many people (both feminist and apolitical) would certainly label pornographic. Is it really the case that, as Ellen Willis has also said, 'In practice, attempts to sort out good erotica from bad porn inevitably come down to What turns me on is erotica; what turns you on is pornographic'? It probably isn't the turn-on factor, but some kind of equally subjective assessment does seem to be involved in the sorting of sexual representations into two moral categories. It may be time to recognize that the ways in which sex is depicted, and the ways in which those depictions are received, are far too various and complex to be understood in such a dualistic fashion.   *HG*

Ed. Margaret Reynolds *Erotica: An Anthology of Women's Writing* (London: Pandora, 1990); ed. Michele Slung *Slow Hand: Women Writing Erotica* (New York: Harper Collins, 1992); Peter Webb *The Erotic Arts* (New York: Farrar Straus, 1983; London: Secker and Warburg, 1975)

See also **Greek Vase Painting; Obscenity; Ukiyo-E**

Exploitation Movies

Low-budget, fast-turnover movies, made under a strongly commercial imperative and aimed predominately at the (male) youth market that makes up the bulk of ticket sales, exploitation movies are characterized by a cinematic shorthand: minimal, straightforward storylines and easily recognizable character types, frequently cheap remakes of more upmarket productions, and leavened with a required quota of nudity, sex and violence. Associated with populist genres such as **science fiction**, biker flics and prison movies, their speed of production and frequently youthful exponents mean that they are likely to reflect fads and trends, social and

E

cinematic. Drug culture, punk nihilism and the impact of feminism have all been grist to the mill.

The genre is epitomized in the USA by the films produced since the 1950s by Roger Corman who, in 1970, co-founded New World Pictures and, later, New Horizons. Corman is quite explicit about the requirements of his films. Witness his briefing to Jonathan Kaplan before the latter made *Night Call Nurses* (New World, 1972): 'Exploitation of male sexual fantasy, a comedic sub-plot, action and violence, and a slightly-to-the-left-of-centre sub-plot . . . frontal nudity from the waist up, total nudity from behind, no pubic hair, get the title in the film somewhere and go to work . . . ' (quoted in 'The Art of Exploitation, or How to Get into the Movies' in *Monthly Film Bulletin*, vol. 52, no. 623, December 1985).

Paradoxically, however, the formulaic demands of the genre lay it open to subversion and, so long as those demands are met, can leave room for great freedom, a trend encouraged by Corman's left liberal leanings. Strong female roles in the 1970s were more likely to be found in exploitation than elsewhere. And the maverick quick-buck ethos, often employing inexperienced, non-union personnel, has made it a route into filmmaking for women – in the same way as the low-paid sector of any other industry. The American films of Stephanie Rothman in the 1970s are often cited for their subversive, proto-feminist content, slipping sexual politics into the titillation. And a film such as Abel Ferrara's *Ms .45/ Ms .45 – Angel of Vengeance* (Navaron Films, 1980) offers the female spectator the indulgence of a **Rape and Revenge** fantasy while satisfying the expectations of the male audience through the increasingly fetishistic outfits the heroine wears – evoking the dominatrix of SM fantasy.   *PA*

Pam Cook 'Exploitation Films and Feminism' in *Screen* (vol. 17, no. 2, 1976)

See also **Slasher Movies; Snuff Movies**

Export, Valie (1940-   )

Born Waltraud Lehner, in Austria, Valie Export has gained an international reputation as an avant-garde filmmaker, videomaker, photographer and performance artist. She also writes on contemporary art history and feminist theory and has organized and contributed to many international art exhibitions and film festivals.

An important theme in all Export's work is the making visible of women's repressed body language, perceived as the effect of patriarchal socialization; contorted poses come to be the signs of an enforced adjustment to a male-defined idea of beauty. Export argues that the oppression of women, the manner in which women are reduced to their physical nature, is inextricably linked with and perpetuated by their representations in art.

Since 1967 Export has made a series of short feminist and experimental films, including . . . *Remote . . . Remote* which painfully depicts female self-mutilation, showing a woman relentlessly snipping bits of skin from her fingertips until she has made bleeding wounds. *Unsichtbare Gegner/Invisible Adversaries*, Export's highly acclaimed and prize-winning first feature film, is about female identity, representation, culture and environment. The ambiguous **science-fiction** plot, about the earth being colonized by 'Hyksos' in the guise of aggressive men, gives Export the pretext to incorporate her experimental strategies imaginatively and effectively. Anna, a photographer, experiences her identity as divided between self-definition and male-definition. Throughout the film she encounters her double, in mirror reflections, cardboard cut-outs, video feedback and dream images; in one scene she is split between her mirror reflection, which applies cosmetics, and her other, observing self that no longer wants to fulfill this male-defined role. The science-fiction plot is thus a device to engage with feminist ideas about women's relationship with their bodies and to show the problem of self-representation, given the prescriptive female representations in art throughout the centuries.

Export's subsequent films continue to explore

esthetic and formal issues in a variety of formats, although some previous feminist admirers have been highly critical of her move towards greater accessibility. Others, however, agree with film theorist Alison Butler when she claims that Export's films represent 'one of the most exciting contemporary feminist challenges to both mainstream and avant-garde cinema'. *US*

Menstruationsfilm (1967); . . . *Remote . . . Remote* (1973); *Unsichtbare Gegner/Invisible Adversaries* (1976); *Menschenfrauen/Human Women* (1979); *Die Praxis der Liebe/The Praxis of Love* (1984); *Unica* (1988)

'The Real and its Double: The Body' in *Discourse* (vol. 11.1, Fall/Winter, 1988)

See also **Akerman; Graham; Nude; Voyeurism**

Faery

The Land of Faery is the world of the **unconscious**, of desires and fears mostly sexual. The early Christian church in the West tried to suppress it by the doctrine of original sin which made any manifestation of sexuality, outside the purpose of procreation, sinful and liable to terrible punishment in this life and the next. Forced into an underworld of the imagination, sexual **fantasy** invented alternative beings to embody its drives. Many are made over from the earlier religious systems replaced by **Christianity**: witches, elves, the fairy king and queen, spirits of place, water and earth, half-human hybrids. Illicit passions, **adultery**, pre-marital sex and **incest** find their outlet in tales of seduction by the fairies, shape-changing, wicked stepmothers and phallic hairy goblins who labor naked all night in the maid's milk turning it to butter while she sleeps.

Such stories were told by women to children until the nineteenth century but they also exist for every generation in an adult fictional form which allows the audience – either singly, as in reading, or collectively, as in the cinema – to suspend its disbelief and experience often repressed emotions through the metaphor of the supernatural.

Medieval romance provided just such a version, drawing on figures largely from Celtic mythology for its personae and, through them, dealing with such subjects as cannibalism, illegitimacy, incest, adultery and the quest of the unformed personality for identity in the pursuit of 'adventure'.

In each age the supernatural will reflect the sexual concerns of the time. The Victorians with their interest in children's sexuality, and its unacceptable manifestations in child **pornography** and **prostitution**, turn to the fairy forms which are diminutive and childish; pre and post the 1914–1918 war, the preoccupation with male **homosexuality** produces Peter Pan and the clubbable male friends of *The Wind in the Willows*, while we in our time have shifted shape into space where we can fly among the stars and fight demons. For another aspect of erotic supernaturalism is its need to clothe itself in exotic but convincing dress. As space itself is gradually mapped and explored, the stories change from encounters with 'bug-eyed monsters', the modern manifestation of bogles, giants and so on, to the fall of civilization, as in Malory's *Morte D'Arthur*, which is always allied to illicit sex and frequently replays some version of the oedipal myth.

The recent surge in reports in the USA and Britain of satanic cults connected with sexual acts, in particular involving children, is the latest manifestation of forbidden desires clothing themselves in the supernatural, with the devil as 'black' father imposing his sexual will on those in his power. Whether the stories of such practices are true or false is largely irrelevant except to those who might become their victims. They are reported and believed and so form part of the supernatural furnishings of the human imagination. *MD*

Maureen Duffy *The Erotic World of Faery* (London: Cardinal, 1989)

See also **Fantasy Fiction; Child Sexual Abuse**

F

Fanon, Frantz (1925-1961)

The Guadeloupe-born psychiatrist and philosopher Frantz Fanon caused a stir in the early 1950s with the publication of *Black Skins, White Masks*, a fiery treatise on race and the alienation of blacks which also tackled the sensitive issue of sex across color lines. Fanon believed that blacks and whites were crippled by ignorance and prejudice and that, until they freed themselves from their complexes, healthy social and sexual encounters could not occur between them.

Fanon argues that, in the French territories, colonialist propaganda so distorted the minds of those colonized that they came to believe in the existence of a naturally ordained hierarchy which placed the blackest person on the lowest rung and the whitest at the top. He illustrates how, in the Antilles, lighter-skinned people were regarded as more 'civilized' and how, as children of mixed unions married upwards on the color scale, rejecting the attentions of darker suitors whom they imagined inferior, the myth continued to feed upon itself. This process, which Fanon refers to as 'lactification', occurred from generation to generation until no trace of black ancestry was apparent. To move in the opposite direction on the color scale was strongly discouraged.

Fanon was aware as he wrote that black men in the American south were being lynched and castrated (a more brutally symbolic cancellation of black male sexuality by white males cannot be imagined) for merely observing white women too closely. He argued that relationships between black men and white women had nothing to do with love and everything to do with desire on the part of the man; since the white woman had for centuries been forbidden him she symbolized the apex of achievement. Yet the black man's feelings towards her were necessarily ambivalent. Black men, argued Fanon, were propelled by revenge to be the 'master' of a white woman and inflict upon her what her ancestors had inflicted for centuries upon his foremothers.

Although *Black Skins, White Masks* is an extremely complex and cathartic commentary on an oppressive system, it is also a heavily male-centered analysis which represents women mainly as the spoils of inter-racial conflict. The black man is characterized as the unwilling victim of this system, using sex to right historical wrongs. While he is complex, the black woman is fickle and calculating, a consistently willing victim fueled only by the desire to be white. The white female, on the other hand, as she transgresses all the laws of her society to love a black man, is self-sacrificing.

Importance was rarely attached to sexual relations between black women and white men, both because of the frequency with which they occurred in colonial situations and the obvious lack of choice on the woman's part.

Fanon's writing, although deliberately provocative about sexual politics, can be understood only within its historical and sociological context: as a plea from a man whose ideas and analysis are shaped by his own victimization. He rightly refers to the perverting influence of colonialism on sexual relations as 'poisonous' since, where revenge and lactification are intended, genuine affection, respect and self-respect are unable to flourish. Scratching the surface of French colonial rule, Fanon reveals a sore that doesn't disappear with the colonizers but eats into society's fabric, damaging its psyche and its sexual and social mores. *NOB*

Black Skins, White Masks (New York: Grove Weidenfeld, 1989; London: Pluto, 1986)

See also **Aidoo; Ba; Burford; Lessing; Macinnes; Mapplethorpe; Walker**

Fantasy Fiction

As a commercial publishing category, fantasy subdivides into horror fiction and heroic fantasy, overlapping extensively with **science fiction**. These genres have standard preoccupations that bring sexual metaphor into play even if sex and gender are absent from the foreground of the text.

Two standard themes of heroic fantasy are the quest for a cure for the world's pain and the reconciliation of the mundane world with **Faery** – the partly sexual nature of the quest evinced by the way it so often involves rings, swords and grail cups. Reconciliation myths such as Hope Mirlees's *Lud-in-the-Mist* (1928), alongside their quests for explicitly fantastic balances, oppose and reconcile bourgeois marriage with more sensual arrangements. Following quests and reconciliations to satisfactory conclusions is, for some adolescents, a vicarious rite of passage.

The predominately female audience of fantasy has been attributed by some male science-fiction writers to female distaste for the 'logic' of hard science fiction; more probably it has to do with the extent to which, from the 1930s, heroines like Catherine Moore's Jirel of Joiry or Joanna **Russ**'s Alyx offered positive identification in active roles. The downsides of this have been the tendency of much fantasy to engage in unthinking nostalgia for feudal and other hierarchical societies and the fact that the protagonists' agenthood is often acquired by buying into male society.

Horror fiction is almost always a metaphor for the sexual. Mary Shelley's *Frankenstein* (1818) deals with all sorts of repressed anger towards those who have formed and deformed the self, while Bram Stoker's *Dracula* (1897) links polymorphous sexual predation and venereal disease in mutually negative reinforcement. The power of these myths lies partly in the deep-seated anxieties of the writers, but each period has its horror themes. The 1920s work of H.P. Lovecraft, with its tales of shapeless Old Gods corrupting civilization with slime, combines obsessive fear of the organic with eugenicist racism; while, in the 1980s, male writers like Clive Barker became obsessed with solitary razor boys and flayings, their stories rich in anxieties about the raw messiness of sex. Rarely, aside from by writers like Lisa Tuttle, do female anxieties get addressed. A largely feminist vampire literature including writers in the vein of Anne Rice and Chelsea Quinn Yarbro has used the vampire myth to examine sexuality and the Good Man: if all men are predators, perhaps the safe lover is the man who is explicitly so.

Stephen King argues that horror writing pro-vides necessary and progressive catharsis. His novels show liberal American small-town values winning, and the socially marginalized brought into the center; he has shown abused women coming to terms with their past through a literally separate struggle with demons from space or haunted hotels. King's reactionary side, however, means that almost all his temptation scenes are seductions.   *RK*

See also **Comics, US and European**

Fantasy, Sexual

In the case history '**Dora**', Sigmund **Freud** wrote that a symptom signified the representation of a fantasy with a sexual content. It was a formulation pinpointing a key relationship within **psychoanalysis**: between a wish and its **repression** into the **unconscious**, with the symptom as a 'compromise formation' containing within it the repressed wish. Challenging this concept of fantasy was one of contemporary feminism's initial engagements with 'Dora': could not Dora's flight into illness be seen as her protest against the network of deceptions, collusions and flirtations in which she was a pawn? But Freud's position in 'Dora' is intransigent: despite the predisposition to hysteria in Dora's family background, especially given her father's syphilis, Dora is herself an agent and was libidinally invested in more than one of the significant adults of her circle.

In general, the psychoanalytic concept of fantasy is that it has a relatively stable nature and that the fantasy scenarios may bear little or no relation to what is commonly referred to as 'external reality'. Moreover, Freud also proposed 'primal' fantasies operating in the pre-history of the **Oedipus Complex**: nor did he restrict fantasy to the spheres of conscious or unconscious. An example of fantasy as a stable structure might be found in Freud's characterization of the 'conditions for loving': the subject *always* positions him- or herself in relation to an unavailable object, an injured third party in need of rescue and so on. Here, the fantasy nature of the

F

desire and its scenario may or may not be consciously accessible.

A rather different, pre-verbal fantasy mode (and one which must therefore be linguistically mediated) is perhaps best exemplified by the Kleinian notion of unconscious fantasy: here, an infant is represented as destroying, attacking, devouring its mother in fantasy. This mental configuration is inferred from clinical work, and its symbolic forms, at a later stage.

Fantasy has recently become a particularly important issue in relation to the question of **child sexual abuse**. Prompted largely by the work of Alice **Miller** and Jeffrey Masson, both non-practicing psychoanalysts who cite feminist writing on **incest** as an inspiration, there has been renewed controversy about whether Freud acted in bad faith in abandoning the seduction theory, the theory that children were in fact seduced, in favour of the theory of the Oedipus Complex. Actually, Freud never denied that incest occurred; he was trying to work at a different level; to theorize structures of fantasy. Analysts of all schools would probably argue that real seductions (actual incest) are pathogenic for the individual: that is, that they have pathological consequences. But the aim, for psychoanalysis, is to locate a place for fantasy and its effects without ruling out a place for actuality. The two terrains are different. *AS*

Sigmund Freud 'A special type of object choice made by men (Contributions to the psychology of love, 1)' (1910); 'Some psychical consequences of the anatomical distinction between the sexes' (1925) in *On Sexuality* (Harmondsworth: Penguin, 1977)

J. Laplanche and J.-B. Pontalis *The Language of Psycho-Analysis* (London: Hogarth Press and the Institute of Psycho-Analysis, 1973)

Farce

'Farces show the disguised fulfilment of repressed wishes', said the critic Eric Bentley. This is certainly true of French farce, typified by such plays as Georges Feydeau's *La puce a l'oreille/A Flea in Her Ear* (1907), in which a wife's erroneous belief in the impotence of her broker husband leads the entire extended family to a brothel, where all find themselves in a series of compromising situations. Chandebrise, the broker, is plunged into a dark night of the soul, coming face to face with his doppelganger, and for all the other characters life will never be the same again: their experience defies reality; everything becomes possible; 'repressed wishes' are consciously acknowledged and bourgeois values and sexual mores can no longer go unchallenged.

In English farce, with such notable exceptions as the work of Joe **Orton**, who exploited the genre to very different ends, the situation is entirely different. From the nineteenth-century court farces of Arthur Wing Pinero, through the Aldwych farces of Ben Travers, to the 1960s Whitehall farces produced by Brian Rix, the protagonists are portrayed as innocents abroad whose experience of a world turned upside down leads them not to liberation but to a wider embracement of traditional values. The very titles of many contemporary British farces – *No Sex Please, We're British*; *When Did You Last See My Trousers?* – hint at a naughty but not too nasty world where sexual titillation comes via the hero's inability to hang on to his outer garments. Sex is suggestive, rather than explicit. In this world husbands are essentially loyal, but easily tempted, and wives dull. The objects of desire are flighty women burdened with frilly silk underwear and foreign accents. For the purposes of plot, the men may find themselves having to dress in their wives' clothing, but there is no suggestion of transvestism and any form of sexuality which threatens the marriage-centered hierarchy is treated as a mildly titillating deviancy.

Whether British farce of this nature will continue to thrive is open to debate. Leslie Smith in *Modern British Farce* (London: Macmillan, 1989) argues that 'the conflict between the rational and the animal, between civilised restraint and primitive impulse, between id and ego, authority and license may take different forms in different ages, but it is a permanent feature of human nature, and one which most farces exploit for their own humorous or subversive purposes.' But although Orton and other playwrights – such as Edward Bond in *Early Morning* (1968) and Caryl Churchill in *Cloud Nine* (1978) – have used farce to lampoon sexual hypocrisy and establishment values, and although Alan Ayckbourn has used it to subvert suburban mores, the form seems increasingly an historical curiosity unable to reflect honestly today's social and sexual complexities.   *LG*

See also **Cross-Dressing; Repression**

Fassbinder, Rainer Werner (1945-1982)

A prolific writer and director, with over thirty feature films and many hours of TV to his credit by the time of his death from a drugs overdose at the age of thirty-seven, Rainer Werner Fassbinder was the most controversial of the filmmakers forging the New German Cinema of the 1970s.

Fassbinder's work was intimately connected to his personal life: literally, in the close-knit group of actors and actresses with whom he surrounded himself, making the emotional dynamics of off-screen relationships a potent undercurrent to the on-screen performances. Ronald Hayman, the author of *Fassbinder, Film Maker* (New York: Simon and Schuster, 1984), believes that all Fassbinder's films reveal his preoccupation 'with dramatising the battle between the male and female halves of his psyche'. His outsider status as a gay man – manipulatively bisexual when he chose – with no desire for social acceptability, gave him a striking freedom to explore his own vision, providing cinematic expression to those usually denied it: the lonely; the dispossessed; those deemed ugly and inadequate in a society dominated by the pursuit of success and the acquisition of beauty. For example *Angst essen Seele auf/Fear Eats the Soul* (1973) uses the doomed love affair between a middle-aged cleaner and a young Moroccan 'guest-worker' to expose the prejudice and hypocrisy of West German society.

Sex and sexual relationships are used in Fassbinder's films as a microcosm of wider social relationships. In those that deal specifically with the post-war German society of the economic miracle, including *Lola* and *Die Ehe der Maria Braun/The marriage of Maria Braun*, sex is opportunist and corrupting: a means to an end, but also a powerful force shaping society. The personal and the political are inseparable at every level; since, for Fassbinder, power is the key, the use and abuse of it are the bases for all sexual, social and political interchange. To be in love is to be ripe for exploitation and corruption, and to be the object of love is corrupting, as all power is corrupting. Fassbinder's last film *Querelle – ein Pakt mit dem Teufel/Querelle*, adapted from Jean **Genet**'s novel, makes a perfect epitaph: an intensely personal statement that is the most uncompromising portrayal of male homosexual sensibility to come from a major filmmaker. *PA*

Die Bitteren Tränen der Petra von Kant/The Bitter Tears of Petra von Kant (1972); *Angst essen Seele auf/Fear Eats the Soul* (1973); *Faustrecht der Freiheit/Fox and his Friends* (1974); *Die Ehe der Maria Braun/The Marriage of Maria Braun* (1978); *In einem Jahr mit 13 Monden/In a Year with 13 Moons* (1978); *Lola* (1981); *Querelle – ein Pakt mit dem Teufel/Querelle* (1982)

Ed. Tony Rayns *Fassbinder* (London: BFI, 1979)

See also **Anger; Bisexuality; Homosexuality; Jarman; Warhol**

Fell, Alison (1944-   )

Born in Dumfries, Scotland, and raised in villages in the Highlands and the Borders, Alison Fell moved to London in 1970 to work in the Women's Street Theatre Group and on the feminist magazine *Spare Rib*. Originally trained as a sculptor, she now writes poetry and novels.

Fell's poetry combines an attentiveness to the rhythms and vocabulary of her Scottish background with a free use of the modern vernacular of the city and is distinguished by lyrical, lilting lines that make the explicit sexual and political content all the more startling. For Fell engages passionately,

F

wittily, angrily and tenderly with female desire, particularly in its longing and frustrated aspects. Men are courted, cursed, deprecated, blessed; male fears and anxieties are ruthlessly dissected, even as female **orgasm** is wittily celebrated for its absence as much as for its presence. Fell also deals with the tentative reaching out towards each other by women and friends, and the power of mothers to bruise and reject their daughters. Her novels mostly stay within the confines of naturalism, although her latest works include poetic monologues and fantasy. Her poetry collection, *The Chrystal Owl* (1988), plays with different forms and includes the impressive 'Fantasia for Mary Wollstonecraft'; her most recent novel is *Mer de Glace*.   MR

The Chrystal Owl (London: Methuen, 1988); *Mer de Glace* (London: Methuen, 1991)

See also **Alther; Heterosexuality; Miller, Sue**

Female Genital Mutilation

It is estimated by the World Health Organization that over eighty million women and girls in the world have undergone some form of the genital surgery euphemistically termed 'female circumcision'. As functional parts of the female external genital organ are removed, the correct terminology for this surgical intervention is 'mutilation'. Clitoridectomy, or removal of the **clitoris**, is a focal point of the operation, which thus bears little comparison to male **circumcision**, the circumferential removal of the foreskin.

Female genital mutilation covers a wide spectrum. At the simplest end, the clitoris, with or without the labia minora, is excised. At the extreme end, however, this is accompanied by removal of the anterior two thirds of the labia majora. The remaining labia majora is sewn together leaving a small opening the size of a matchstick for urination and the passage of menstrual blood, the opening having to be widened to allow the consummation of marriage. Excision is currently widely practiced by dif-

ferent ethnic groups in more than twenty countries in western, eastern and parts of northern Africa; infibulation, or stitching up, is reported to affect nearly all the female population of Somalia, Djibouti and the Sudan, except for the non-Muslim south, as well as a small percentage of women in Mali, Senegal and the Gambia. Recently female genital mutilation has been reported to be practiced in Europe by minority communities originating from areas of the world where the practice is endemic.

Some theorists date the practice as far back as the fifth century BC, while others state that it was current among the aristocracy of ancient Egypt, as a sign of distinction, and affirm that traces of infibulation can be found on Egyptian mummies. Other countries involved are pre-Islamic Arabia, ancient Rome and Tsarist Russia. In England in the nineteenth century clitoridectomy was practiced by surgeons to treat psychological disorders. The reasons given for excision and infibulation of females vary from one community to the other, but generally fall into five categories: psychosexual, religious, sociological, hygienic and esthetic. Commonly the clitoris is believed to be an aggressive organ, threatening to the male and even endangering the birth of a child. The woman who has not had a clitoridectomy is believed to be incapable of controlling her sexuality. Infibulation is an added precaution, to maintain **virginity** and **chastity** in girls and fidelity in married women.

The few studies which have been done on sexuality and circumcised women, while pointing to delayed sexual response in circumcised women, do not completely rule out their ability to experience some sexual pleasure and even **orgasm**. But this is only one side of the story. The worst consequences of infibulation can occur during childbirth, as women who have been stitched up must be cut early on in their labor, risking an excessive loss of blood. There are also human-rights concerns about all forms of genital mutilation, for in ninety per cent of cases these are performed without anesthetics and with the use of crude knives, razor blades and stones. Children have to be held down by five to eight adults and, in some cases, are so bewildered that they bite through their tongues.

Interestingly, it is the very women who have suffered all this pain who tenaciously guard the custom, which makes campaigning to stop the practice difficult. That women condone practices detrimental to their health and that of their children is, however, an indication of their general powerlessness in a heavily traditional patriarchal society. Earlier attempts by colonial governments and missionaries to ban the mutilation failed because African nationalists capitalized on their intrusion and used it as a focal point for resistance to colonialism. And many elite Africans see female genital mutilation as a non-issue compared to the myriad other problems – famine, abject poverty – faced by the people of Africa and are angered by what they see as a disproportionate interest taken in it by westerners, even by such critics as the African American writer Alice **Walker**, whose novel *Possessing the Secret of Joy* (1992) courageously confronts the subject. In the last two decades, however, there has been a significant involvement of African women in campaigns against female mutilation and, as a result, the contentiousness surrounding action to stamp out the practice is decreasing. We are still a long way off from uprooting the practice in modern society, but at least awareness of this social evil is gaining ground.   *ED*

See also **Baker Brown**; **Masturbation**

Fetishism

Fetishism is the focusing of sexual interest on certain objects (underwear, shoes), materials (fur, leather, rubber), or parts of the body (hair, feet) to such an extent that arousal is possible only or mostly through the presence, actual or imaginary, of these things.

The term first became popular through Richard **Krafft-Ebing**'s *Psychopathia Sexualis* published at the end of the nineteenth century. He justified its use along the lines of an analogy: 'adoration of separate parts of the body (or even articles of clothing)

on the ground of sexual urges, frequently reminds us of the glorification of relics, sanctified objects, etc., in religious cults'. In the Roman Catholic as well as the Greek Orthodox church, the adoration of icons and holy relics for themselves has always been strictly prohibited and seen as leading away from the Word and into a heretic fixation on 'graven images'. Similarly, for the western missionary, fetish cults equaled blasphemy in that they represented a power (demon) independent of a central unifying god. The western conception of fetishism is of a leading astray from the word of truth and it is in this sense that fetishism comes to be classified as a sexual **perversion**: from *per-vertere*, turning aside from truth or right.

In the writings of Sigmund **Freud** fetishism finds a specific articulation as a *male* perversion: a denial by men of women's castration; acceptance of which is, for Freud, the basis of adult sexuality. The fetish is a substitute phallus, a phallus out of place, with which the woman is fitted in order to reassure the man against the threat of castration.

Fetishism has acquired a wealth of connotations ranging from the investment of the meaningless object with powers of attraction (commodity-fetishism) to the degrading media representation of women's bodies as an accumulation of titillating fragments ('tits and arse'). It has thus been seen as a symptom both of capitalism and patriarchy, in its double aspect of glorifying objects and objectifying women: a perspective which means, yet again, that the fetishist is always male, while the woman becomes the fetish itself, the perfect object, star, icon (see Laura Mulvey's 'Visual Pleasure and Narrative Cinema' in *Screen* 16, no. 3, 1975). Such theorizations of sexuality, though conceived within a feminist critique, can end up leaving women's desire out of the picture.

As an alternative it can be said that, while emerging within the framework of a phallic order, the fetish threatens that order by fixing sexuality away from its 'proper' manifestation and focus of attraction – that is, the genitals of the opposite sex – and ultimately away from the gendered body altogether. It moves sexuality towards a preoccupation with the fragment, the inanimate, the meaningless, and since the fetish is an object out of place, its power erupts outside a hierarchy of 'normality' and 'morality'. Fetishism is classified as a perversion in that it pushes to the limits and disrupts a phallocentric, or penis-focused, sexual order. *TP*

See also **Sensuality**; **Voyeurism**

Firestone, Shulamith (1945-   )

A Canadian feminist who moved to New York in 1967, Shulamith Firestone was extremely influential as an activist and a theorist. She helped Pam Allen to start the first New York women's group, Radical Women, she co-edited *Notes from the First Year* and, in 1969, she worked with Anne **Koedt** on a manifesto and a set of 'organizing principles' for a widespread radical feminist movement of consciousness raising, action and theory.

Firestone's most famous theoretical work is *The Dialectic of Sex: The Case for Feminist Revolution* (1970). Of all the attempts to separate women's sexuality from reproduction, this is perhaps the most extreme: in the sense that it did not merely point out that, however they may overlap, motherhood and women's sexuality are not the same, but looked forward to a time when advances in the technology of reproduction – the development of cloning, the invention of artificial wombs – and the end of the closed, traditional family would liberate women from carrying, bearing and being the principal rearers of children. Because Firestone located the oppression of women in their unfair vulnerability as mothers, rather as Simone de **Beauvoir** had done in *The Second Sex* (1949), she believed that they would achieve full human status only when freed from it.

The Dialectic of Sex was important for its explicit challenge to Marxist theory: its demonstration, using Marxist methods, that sexual relations underlie economic ones. It also shaped the agenda for many subsequent feminist writings by exposing

the family as a suspect structure and drawing the links between sexism, class injustice and racism. However, by ascribing women's oppression to a single, straightforward cause – what's more, to women's own biology – the book inevitably raised a fair bit of controversy. As Scarlet Friedman put it in her paper 'Heterosexuality, Couples and Parenthood: A "Natural" Cycle?' (1979): 'Apart from the questionability of the assumptions about women's defencelessness, which seem to presuppose a continual state of childbearing for each and every woman, and that women are dependent only upon men rather than upon each other or upon the rest of the men and women in the society, the major difficulty with this approach is its reductionism.' Equally strong objections have come from those who believe that looking to male-controlled technology for women's liberation is about as useful as looking to factory farming for chickens' liberation. *HG*

The Dialectic of Sex: The Case for Feminist Revolution (London: Women's Press, 1980)

See also **Atkinson**; **Frye**

Flaubert, Gustave (1821-1880)

Gustave Flaubert was born into a doctor's family in northern France. He studied law in Paris but, in 1843, suffered the first of a series of 'nervous attacks' (now thought to have been epilepsy) which, coupled with a healthy private income, enabled him to give up the law to write.

Flaubert was one of a number of French 'Post Romantic' writers who shared a disdain for and a revolt against the bourgeoisie, the provincial middle classes. In his best known novel, *Madame Bovary* (1856), he describes a provincial doctor's wife, bored with her insipid life, who satisfies her romantic longings with affairs and extravagances which ultimately lead to her downfall. Despite the 'moral' ending, in which Madame Bovary dies, the book was prosecuted for **obscenity** as 'an outrage to public morals and religion'. Flaubert made

Madame Bovary and her sensual longings sympathetic and appealing; he identified with her revolt against a restricted life. 'Madame Bovary,' he said, 'c'est moi.'

L'Education sentimentale/Sentimental Education, completed in 1869, charts the gradual disenchantment of its hero, Frederic, with his romantic dreams and illusions. This novel also shocked, partly by its apparent claim that the happiest moment in a man's life is when he first enters a brothel (by which Flaubert wanted to suggest the moment of supreme anticipation when Frederic's sexual and emotional future lies before him, and his dreams and illusions are still intact).

Flaubert seems to have had a somewhat alienated emotional life. In his early years he spent a good deal of time with prostitutes, as was normal for the time and his class, but he was especially fascinated by them and by the idea of 'biblical fornication' which they seemed to embody. He was also a fervent admirer of **Sade** and strong themes of cruelty and **sado-masochism** run through his more exotic, historical novels – *Salammbô* (1862) and *La Tentation de Saint Antoine/The Temptation of Saint Anthony* (1874) – whose eroticism shocked even his friends. He never married and his longest relationship with a woman, the poet Louise Colet, was conducted largely by post. He died of an apoplectic stroke in 1880.   KH

Madame Bovary (New York: Bantam, 1987; Harmondsworth: Penguin, 1970); *Salammbô* (Harmondsworth: Penguin, 1977); *L'Education Sentimentale/Sentimental Education* (New York: Dutton, 1984; Harmondsworth: Penguin, 1970); *La Tentation de Saint Antoine/The Temptation of Saint Anthony* (Harmondsworth: Penguin, 1983)

See also **Adultery; Dworkin; Prostitution; Romantic Love**

Footbinding

See **Lie Nü Tradition**

Foreplay

Foreplay, as the word so precisely conveys, is a ludic prelude to something more important and serious: **sexual intercourse**. That, at least, is the view expressed in most sexual writing by men, where kissing and stroking and licking and fondling, not just of the genitals but all the body, are generally presented as necessary games to arouse a female partner, to make her vagina wet enough for 'proper' penetrative sex to take place. This attitude is obviously preferable to that which ignores women's pleasure altogether – whether through ignorance, indifference or a positive desire to cause pain – but it is, nonetheless, misguided.

On the one hand, it is possible for a woman to want penetration without more ado, especially if that ado is labored, mechanistic and dutiful. Women do not invariably need to be coaxed to sexual arousal. On the other hand, more women than not would prefer it if manual and oral stimulation were *not* abandoned for intercourse the moment they'd begun to get wet. Approximately sixty per cent of them, according to surveys from the 1930s onwards, find it hard or impossible to come when having sexual intercourse. Although, for men, the grip of a vagina round the penis will usually lead to **orgasm**, for women, who generally require direct or indirect pressure on the **clitoris** to come, sexual intercourse, which may not provide this, can be a frustrating experience. As Anne **Koedt** wrote in 'The Myth of the Vaginal Orgasm', foreplay 'works to the disadvantage of many women, since as soon as the woman is aroused the man changes to vaginal stimulation, leaving her both aroused and unsatisfied'.

Many conclude that women and men are sexually incompatible. But, as gay men have started to learn through experimenting with various forms of non-penetrative **safer-sex** practice, and a few heterosexual men have discovered through trying to please their partners, when so-called 'foreplay' becomes the whole game it can satisfy men just as deeply as women. Besides being safer, in terms not only of health but of unwanted pregnancies, it can also be richer, more imaginative, more physically expansive and subtle. HG

See also **Comfort**; **Wright**

Forster, Edward Morgan (1879-1970)

After an unhappy boyhood at public school, E.M. Forster went up to Cambridge in 1897, where, at King's College, he found close and congenial friends. The atmosphere of free intellectual discussion and the stress on the *importance* of such discussions were to have a profound influence on his writing.

Forster's travels in Italy and Greece gave him material for his early novels: satiric comedies dealing with the bumblings and fumblings of the English middle classes abroad. A certain self-censorship can be read into these sparkling works' examination of heterosexual relationships, for, although traces of Forster's own **homosexuality** subvert the plots, it never dangerously intrudes. It was not until after his death that Forster's homosexual novel *Maurice* could be published, alongside his homo-erotic collection of stories, *The Life to Come*.

Maurice charts a young man's search for love and sexual fulfillment among his fellows, exploring the hypocrisy of Edwardian sexual mores and the tenderness and frankness possible between men of widely differing social classes. The stories employ a delightful mixture of comedy, romanticism and bawdiness to erotic effect. Both works suggest that sexual play and lust can break down the class barriers traditionally separating potential lovers, even as they also suggest that this carnivalesque subversion can reinforce the very power structures it attacks.

All through his life Forster took a firm stand against censorship, involving himself in the work of PEN and the National Campaign for Civil Liberties, working against the suppression of Radclyffe **Hall**'s novel *The Well of Loneliness* and appearing as a defense witness during the trial of the publishers of D.H. **Lawrence**'s novel *Lady Chatterley's Lover*. Perhaps he fought so courageously against the censorship of other writers' work precisely because he felt obliged to censor his own: a poignant contradiction. MR

Where Angels Fear to Tread (Harmondsworth: Penguin, 1989); *A Room With a View* (Harmondsworth: Penguin, 1990); *Howards End* (Harmondsworth: Penguin, 1989); *A Passage to India* (Harmondsworth: Penguin, 1989); *Maurice* (Harmondsworth: Penguin, 1975); *The Life to Come* (Harmondsworth: Penguin, 1989)

See also **Carpenter**; **Obscenity**

Foucault, Michel (1926-1984)

Michel Foucault was a French philosopher and leading contemporary thinker whose writings on sexuality have transformed contemporary debates on sexual politics. His main and best known work in the area is *The History of Sexuality*, of which Volumes IV to VI were never completed.

First published in 1976, *The History of Sexuality* issued a challenge to the current notions of how social control was exercised through the repression of sexuality: ideas popular among sex radicals such as Wilhelm **Reich** and which formed the theoretical basis of the **sexual revolution** in the 1960s. It was argued that sexuality within capitalism was controlled from above by those in power who, for centuries, had sought to repress its natural expression in the name of increased production. Against this 'repressive hypothesis' Foucault argued that the modern form of sexuality, far from having its natural expression censored by the application of power, was in fact talked about constantly in the hundred years immediately preceding the so-called 'sexual revolution'. Sexuality, he argued, was no natural phenomenon but was in fact brought into being by this urge to talk about it, this 'incitement to discourse'.

The imperative to 'discover', observe and study human sexuality operated primarily within the practices of medicine and the law. The medical establishment and the newly developed science of sexology concerned themselves with tracing sexuality's causes, describing its dominant forms of expression and cataloging its deviations; the judiciary sought to contain its unruly outbursts. The body of information and knowledge thus produced within medicine and the law Foucault called 'discourses'; the deployment of sexuality within these formal discourses was, he argued, as much a mechanism of power as the prohibitions placed upon sexuality as a result.

One of Foucault's main targets was **psychoanalysis**, a practice which he believed had replaced the church as the modern form of confessional, in which the secrets of one's sexuality could be told. The principles of psychoanalysis relied on the understanding that sexuality was the core of one's being and the motive force of human action. Foucault's writings on sexuality also challenge how 'power' has been conceptualized within left-wing thinking. Power, Foucault suggested, does not stem from a singular source imposed from above. Power is productive rather than repressive, and is brought into being through the creation of knowledge: hence, the medical establishment's imperative to 'know' the facts of sexuality was simultaneously an exercise of power over the individual subject of sexuality. This relationship Foucault designated 'the power-knowledge axis'. Power was always already present and its operation took place at multiple local sites: in the clinic, the psychiatric hospital, the courtroom and the gaol. The medical, legal and other institutional practices within which power resided were, moreover, often conflicting and contradictory rather than monolithic or coherent.

Foucault's importance to feminist theory has been to deconstruct any unified notion of individual identity. The human subject can no longer be regarded as a pre-formed individual standing outside culture, but must be seen as formed wholly within it, a product of these multiple and competing discourses. Thus his theories have problematized feminist political agendas by divesting feminism of the notion – popular from the 1970s via the work of Anne **Koedt**, Ti-Grace

Atkinson and others – that women's 'natural sexuality', repressed by centuries of patriarchal oppression, can be rediscovered by stripping away the layers of 'false consciousness' to get to the authentic core underneath. Rather, women's sexuality, and indeed any concept of 'woman' itself, is a socially constructed identity, a product of discourse.

An application of Foucault has also led to the deconstruction of notions of 'lesbian', 'gay' or 'homosexual' as pre-given or unified identities. These identities too are historically constructed, since the creation of a homosexual identity, an event which Foucault dated from the work of Westphaal in 1807, was predicated on the same discursive practices through which power was exercised. However, for Foucault power is never present without resistance. This bringing into being of the homosexual 'as a species' within science simultaneously enabled individual homosexuals collectively to resist the interventions of medicine and the law.

Foucault died of AIDS in 1984: an ironic fate for someone whose thinking has transformed contemporary ideas about the relationship between **homosexuality** and medical knowledge.   *DH*

Histoire de la Sexualité/The History of Sexuality: Volume 1, An Introduction (Paris: Gallimard, 1976; New York: Random House, 1990; Harmondsworth: Penguin, 1990)

See also **Freud; Ellis; Hirschfeld; Hocquenghem; Weeks**

Freud, Sigmund (1856-1939)

Born into a middle-class Jewish family in Moravia, then a part of Austria-Hungary, Sigmund Freud lived the greater part of his life in Vienna, leaving for London with his family in 1938 when Hitler invaded Austria. He founded **psychoanalysis** in the 1890s and saw it become an international movement by the time of his death.

Freud became a doctor in 1881 and, initially,

specialized in neuroanatomy and neuropathology. In 1885 he spent some months under Jean-Martin Charcot at the Salpêtrière, the hospital for nervous diseases in Paris, and, on returning to Vienna, set up in practice as a consultant in nervous diseases. An initial collaboration with Josef Breuer, in treating hysteria by allowing patients to range over their past in words ('abreacting' a forgotten psychical trauma), led, gradually, to the system of ideas known as psychoanalysis, with the technique of hypnosis giving way to the new technique of 'free association'.

Studies on Hysteria (1895), co-authored with Breuer, includes the first account of the psychoanalytic transference; from 1895 to 1905 Freud worked on the theory of the **Oedipus Complex**, on dream interpretation and on tracing the course of development of the sexual drive from infancy to adulthood. The theorization of the **unconscious** and the processes of **repression**, of mourning and narcissism, and of psychoanalysis in relation to anthropology, belong to the years up to and including the First World War. Between 1920 and 1923 Freud turned his attention to what is known as the structural theory of the mind, revising (but not jettisoning) his earlier model of a dynamic unconscious opposed to the conscious mind, to accommodate a tripartite division of the mind into agencies of the id, ego and super-ego. *Beyond the Pleasure Principle* (1920) posited the compulsion to repeat as a cardinal principle of mental life; and, in 1930, in *Civilization and Its Discontents*, Freud discussed the problem of human destructiveness, seeing it as a manifestation of the death drive.

As more women began to work in psychoanalysis after the First World War, Freud began to revise his views on the sexual development of women; at the end of his life he returned to a study of cultural life, especially religion: 'My interest, after making a lifelong detour through the natural sciences, medicine, and psychotherapy, returned to the cultural problems which had fascinated me long before.' It is Freud's fascination with the roots of cultural life in the vicissitudes of the sexual and the irrational that, among other things, marks his genius. So does

his refusal to make a demarcation between the origins of the normal and the pathological in mental life, stressing the circuitous pathways by which the 'normal' comes into being.   AS

On Sexuality (Harmondsworth: Penguin, 1977); 'Femininity' in *New Introductory Lectures on Psychoanalysis* (Harmondsworth: Penguin, 1973); *On Metapsychology: The Theory of Psychoanalysis* (Harmondsworth: Penguin, 1984)

Peter Gay *Freud: A Life For Our Time* (New York: Doubleday, 1989; London: Dent, 1988)

See also **Child Sexual Abuse; 'Dora'; H.D.; Horney; Infantile Sexuality; Kakar; Krafft-Ebing; Kristeva; Lacan; Miller, Alice; Penis Envy**

Frye, Marilyn

Marilyn Frye is a lesbian theorist who has written a number of essays that have had a significant influence on the feminist movement in the USA. Many of the essays are included in her book *The Politics of Reality: Essays in Feminist Theory*, published in 1983. She teaches philosophy at Michigan State University in Lansing, Michigan.

Frye has written about how lesbians are invisible in patriarchal society – even the dictionary definitions of sex do not include lesbian sex. She identifies herself as a lesbian separatist and, in her essay 'Some Reflections on Separatism and Power', notes that a form of separation is involved in many different kinds of feminist action not usually seen as separatist: abortion, for instance, or the creation of battered women's refuges. In more recent years she has coined the term 'lesbian connectionist' to emphasize that the point of separatism is the people with whom one is connecting. Among her other essays are 'On Being White: Toward a Feminist Understanding of Race and Race Supremacy' in which she suggests that the heterosexual imperative is, for white women, deeply involved with the perpetuation of the white race. White male objections to white women becoming lesbian involve the desire to perpetuate white as well as male

Henry Fuseli, *The Nightmare*, 1781

supremacy. Refusing to accept the privileges derived from being connected with white men can, she suggests, be anti-racist as well as anti-patriarchal.

In a recent essay, 'Lesbian "Sex"', Frye attacks that **sexology** which compares the frequency of sex in lesbian couples and in heterosexual couples. It is, she says, like comparing oranges with apples: lesbian sexual expressions take much longer and are more intimate than heterosexual intercourse.   *CD*

The Politics of Reality (Trumansburg, New York: The Crossing Press, 1983); 'Lesbian "Sex"' in *Lesbian Philosophies and Cultures* (Albany: University of New York Press, 1990)

See also **Fanon; Heterosexism; Lesbianism; Patriarchy; Rich**

Fuseli, Henry (1741-1825)

Henry Fuseli was Swiss by birth, English by adoption, and became a Royal Academician in 1790. Originally Johann Heinrich Füssli, he italianized his name during a stay in Rome (1770-1778), where he studied painting, teaching himself by copying Michelangelo. He began exhibiting in England on his return from Italy. He had had an earlier, aborted career as a Protestant clergyman, a calling forced on him by his father, himself a painter.

Fuseli's is an art of the late eighteenth-century gothic imagination, combining eroticism and grotesquerie in a full-blown Romantic expression of the fears and desires that lurk behind the conscious, rational mind. His extravagances earned him one critic's harsh judgement as 'the fittest artist on earth to be appointed hobgoblin painter to the devil'. His best known painting is 'The Nightmare', particularly the version exhibited at the Royal Academy in 1782 (there were many others); Sigmund **Freud** had a reproduction of it on the wall of his study. In this erotic phantasmagoria a woman lies on a couch, her back slightly arched, her head thrown back. On her lower belly squats a lascivious goblin that stares out of the picture, while a creature resembling a donkey watches avidly from behind a curtain. The female body, flimsy draperies clinging to its curves, undulates across the center of the picture, glowing palely out of the surrounding darkness and its terrors. 'The Nightmare' is a disturbing and powerful image of an orgasmic abandon whose most likely source is **masturbation**. The picture's bestial night intruders recall the incubi of witch-lore who feature prominently in the Inquisition's *Malleus Maleficarum* as instruments of diabolic copulation. Here, however, the monsters conjured by the persecutors of female sexuality are released for the sake of female pleasure.   *LH*

'The Nightmare' is in the Detroit Institute of Arts. Other works by Fuseli are held in the Tate Gallery, London, The Fitzwilliam Museum, Cambridge, and the Goethe Museum, Frankfurt.

See also **Munch**

García Márquez, Gabriel (1928-)

A man of many countries, both Latin American and European, Gabriel García Márquez has his roots planted firmly in his native Colombia. He first came to international attention with his novel *One Hundred Years of Solitude* (translated into English in 1970) whose hundreds of thousands of readers worldwide were apparently avid to learn about the sprawling family history of the Buendía clan. In 1982 he won the Nobel Prize for Literature.

Like Isabel **Allende**, García Márquez learnt many of the stories he incorporates into his novels at his grandmother's knee. He is also the originator of what the west so sloppily calls 'magical realism' – as well as being the genre's most coherent denouncer. He wishes his readers both to accept the magical in the everyday *and* the literal truth of his characters' lives. In terms of sexuality, this truth incorporates the gargantuan appetites of José Arcadio in *One Hundred Years of Solitude* through to the more tranquil, marital indulgences of Dr Juvenal Urbino in the later *Love in the Time of Cholera*. Indeed, as García Márquez has grown older, so have many of his principal characters, their desires changing accordingly: Dr Urbino remains devoted to his wife to the point of accepting her lie to him in order that he might regain the conjugal bed.

Throughout García Márquez's novels and stories, women tend to play the stronger part. Sometimes this is conveyed through their nicknames – 'The Elephant', 'Big Mama' – at others it is they who call the names and have the best lines. Nora Jacob in *In Evil Hour* feels 'a kind of frustration at the bad luck of having in secret a man who seemed to her to be made for a woman to talk about'. What sets the women apart and dazzles the men in García Márquez's stories is, frequently, the power of older women simply to endure. The books are rich in widows, elderly spinsters and worshipped wives who have an inner strength from either the security of established sexuality or the transcendence of earlier, conflictive passions.   *AmH*

One Hundred Years of Solitude (New York: Avon, 1976; London: Picador, 1978); *The Autumn of the Patriarch* (New York: Avon, 1977; London: Picador, 1978); *In Evil Hour* (New York: Avon, 1980; London: Picador, 1982); *Chronicle of a Death Foretold* (New York: Ballantine, 1984; London: Picador, 1983); *Love in a Time of Cholera* (New York: Knopf, 1988; Harmondsworth, Penguin, 1989); *No One Writes to the Colonel* (New York: Harper Collins, 1979; London: Picador, 1979)

See also **Colette**

Gaskell, Mrs E.C. (1810-1865)

Elizabeth Cleghorn Gaskell spent her formative years in Cheshire, Stratford-upon-Avon and the north of England. Marriage to a Unitarian minister working in a poor parish of Manchester brought her first-hand knowledge of the sufferings of the industrial poor under capitalism, experience that she put to acclaimed use in the novels she began to write after bringing up her large family.

A thoroughly professional writer, valued by peers such as Charles Dickens and Charlotte **Brontë**, Mrs Gaskell shocked contemporary critics by her willingness to explore subjects such as unmarried motherhood and the relationship between money and morality. Her radicalism extended itself to a use of literary motifs which anticipated the hypotheses later put forward by Sigmund **Freud** on the connections between suppressed desire and anger and their emergence through dreams, slips of the tongue and fainting fits. The novel best exemplifying Mrs Gaskell's impressive ability to link and explore industrial unrest and sexual conflict is *North and South*, first published in 1855, which makes sense of a passionate love affair between an idealistic, somewhat snobbish clergyman's daughter and a ruthless mill owner by grounding it in the Victorian realities of strikes, starvation, industrial illness and class warfare. The novel is structured by sexual metaphors which continually hint at the heroine's inexpressible desires and constantly subvert her attempts to conform to traditional ideas of correct feminine behavior. Similarly, the book's happy ending can be read as an ironic comment on women's status as sexual commodities owned by the men who marry them. *MR*

North and South (Harmondsworth: Penguin, 1970)

See also **Repression**

Gay Liberation

Gay Liberation began in New York in 1969, on the day that a group of homosexual people, enjoying themselves at the Stonewall Inn, were harassed yet one more time by the police and, instead of accepting it, rolled up their sleeves and fought back. The immediate result was a riot. The greater result was a worldwide transformation of homosexual politics and culture. Inspired in part by the Civil Rights movement, not only gay men but lesbian women were finished with creeping about in the shadows, protected by nothing but a wry sense of humor and a haphazard, underground support system.

That, at least, is the simplified version. In the more complicated 'real' world, even today there are homosexual people who resolutely cling to the shadows, their motives ranging from a genuine preference for darkness, ambiguity and danger to an equally genuine and well-founded fear of losing their friends, their job, their children, their freedom or even perhaps their life should they openly admit their sexuality. From this, it should be clear that Gay Liberation is still more a hope than a fact. That hope, however, is not without enormous importance.

First and foremost, Gay Liberation has saved many people from self-disgust: not only making them 'proud to be gay' but, conversely, by questioning in depth the values of **heterosexuality** and (in partnership with feminism) exposing so many of these as seriously flawed. Traditional beliefs about the meaning of 'family', the nature of friendship, the role of ex-lovers, the primacy of procreative sex, the sanctity of **monogamy**, the structure of power within relationships: all these and more have been thrown in the air as homosexuals have given new thought and value to their *own* experiences, no longer seeing themselves as outcasts but as part of a cultural vanguard.

Gay Liberation has also provided the spaces for this kind of thinking to proceed, with its public and therefore accessible clubs, centers, conferences, help-lines, bookshops, books and magazines. And besides being vehicles for debate, these highly visible structures have enabled the kind of co-operative, quick-moving action that is currently being taken in response to **AIDS**. Although there are many good arguments why those who have chosen not to 'come out' (in other words, not to let it be known that they are lesbian or gay) should have that decision respected, the importance of openness to Gay Liberation should equally be understood. In a perfect world, no sensible person would wander around with a label defining her or his sexuality – if only because, in practice, our sexualities are far too complex and shifting to fit on a label – but, while the world remains intent on misrepresenting, denying or trying to eradicate **homosexuality**, then voluble counter-assertions are obviously vital.

That Gay Liberation appears to be largely an affair of homosexual men is because, in the early years of the movement, a number of women who were actively involved decided that their interests, priorities, ways of proceeding and ultimate aims would fit rather better within feminism or some form of lesbian separatism. As outcasts, lesbians and gay men most certainly constructed overlapping cultures and saw one another as allies, but the sexual desires of women for women could not, in fact, be further removed from those of men for men – and even within those two polar extremes there are endless distinctions and differences. Although both sexes do, of course, still co-operate on certain ventures, what Gay Liberation has achieved for both is the freedom to explore what their sexualities actually mean to them, rather than struggling beneath a dark blanket, woven and thrown on them by heterosexuals, of fictitious homogenous 'perversion'.   *HG*

See also **Bisexuality; Brown, Rita Mae; Camp; Core; Dyke; Heterosexism; Hocquenghem; Homophobia; Jarman; Lesbianism; Maupin; Political Lesbianism; Radicalesbianism; Safer Sex; Vidal; Weeks**

Genet, Jean (1910-1986)

When Jean Genet died in 1986 he was, despite his previous literary notoriety, largely forgotten. He had abandoned the writing of novels and plays and vanished into obscurity. There were a few rumors: he was nomadic, a barbiturate addict, deeply involved with political groups. Then his last great work, *Prisoner of Love*, an account of his life with the Black Panthers and the PLO, was posthumously published and it became clear that an extraordinary clarity and unity of purpose had illuminated his entire life and writing.

Genet's life is easily mythologized. He was the archetypal literary outlaw. Illegitimate, abandoned at birth, by the age of fifteen he was shut away in a reform school in northern France. Branded a thief, he made what Jean-Paul Sartre considered an existential decision to be a thief and, in the 1930s, followed a criminal career as both a thief and homosexual prostitute throughout Europe. His first novel, *Our Lady of the Flowers*, was written while in Fresnes prison in 1942, to be followed by *The Miracle of The Rose, Funeral Rites, Querelle of Brest* and the autobiographical *The Thief's Journal*. In 1947 he was reprieved from another gaol sentence by the intervention of Sartre, Gide, Cocteau and other literary figures. Genet also wrote several important and controversial plays including *The Balcony* and *The Maids*. In 1952 Jean-Paul Sartre published a vast, hagiographical study, *St Genet, Actor and Martyr*, which enshrined the writer as an existential hero but may have contributed to his withdrawal and increasing lack of interest in literature.

In all Genet's work he identifies himself completely with the most pitiful and wretched outcasts from society: pimps, convicts, murderers. To him, sainthood, illumination, union with the Absolute lie in degradation, humiliation, deviance and **perversion**. He finds tenderness in hatred and exquisite liberation in betrayal and treachery. A complex symbolism informs his macabre, lyrical prose. Flowers, roses, angels, daggers, sailors, saints and sinners: his world is a hall of mirrors wherein the sacred and profane commingle, identity slips into metamorphosis and appearance and reality are endlessly fluid. Eroticism is central to all his writing. His sub-world of gangsters and criminals is ruthlessly divided into masculine and feminine, active and passive sexual partners. His homosexual passions are continually aroused and thwarted; the virile male who responds can no longer be revered as the embodiment of **machismo**. Genet was essentially a solitary, an onanist. Sartre called *Our Lady of the Flowers* 'an epic of masturbation'.

Eventually Genet came to question language, fiction and the very act of writing. In *Prisoner of Love* the Black Panthers and the PLO have come to replace his earlier fantasies of death, beauty and courage in male-dominated outlaw groups. 'It was completely natural for me to be attracted to people who are not only the most unfortunate but also crystallize to the highest degree the hatred of the West.' The book is dense with the contradictions that arise in his earlier work, with mystical atheism and anarchic submission. *EY*

Our Lady of the Flowers (New York: Grove Weidenfeld, 1987; London: Faber, 1990); *The Miracle of the Rose* (New York: Grove Weidenfeld, 1988; Harmondsworth: Penguin, 1989;) *Funeral Rites* (New York: Grove Weidenfeld, 1987; London: Faber, 1990); *Querelle of Brest* (New York: Grove Weidenfeld, 1989; London: Faber, 1990); *The Thief's Journal* (New York: Grove Weidenfeld, 1987; Harmondsworth: Penguin, 1990); *The Balcony* (New York: Grove Weidenfeld, 1985; London: Faber, 1991); *The Maids* (New York: Grove Weidenfeld, 1988; London: Faber, 1989); *Prisoner of Love* (London: Picador, 1990)

See also **Acker; Burroughs; Fassbinder; Masturbation; Prostitution, Male**

Ghazal, The

The ghazal has been the premier form of Persian lyric poetry since around 1000 AD. Its name derives from the Arabic *gha-za-la*, to dally or to flirt, to talk amorously. Ostensibly a love poem denouncing social and religious orthodoxy in Muslim society, it contains strong homosexual pederastic overtones.

The form's divine dimension was developed by the Sufis, early Muslim mystics, who used its array of sexually charged characters to reiterate the mystic quest. The Beloved symbolizes God, characterized as a ruthless and beautiful woman, who now grants and now withdraws her attention from the Lover in favor of his Rival. An Indo-Persian couplet by the thirteenth-century mystic poet Amir **Khusrau** illustrates this theme: 'My Beloved is Pari-like, cypress-statured and rosy-cheeked/From head to toe she wreaks havoc on hearts.' The poet-lover, contrary to international literary norms, strives to be enslaved and even unmanned by Her enchantment, since annihilation of his ego or Self facilitates complete union. The saki (wine-bearer), once the much-desired boy-lover, is the spiritual guide, potently enhancing the ecstasies of union for the lover.

In addition to the more conventional indicators of beauty – narcissus eyes, flowing ringlets, a rosebud or wine-dispensing goblet mouth – there exists a stock of weapon imagery to describe the Beloved. She has eyebrows like bows, lashes like daggers, glances like arrows or lightning. This last, in mystic terms a reference to the burning bush at Sinai, is also commonly applied in Urdu-speaking society to the destructive charms of courtesans. Thus the godhead is a heartless beauty and wanton whose charms destroy her lover by enticing him away from social obligation: signifying the God-love which causes the mystic to repudiate worldly connections. The goddess-harlot dualism is not unique; it can also be seen in the harlot-priestesses of ancient European huntress-goddess cults. Likewise, weaponry is associated with primordial huntress cults, the axe and the arrow both being sacred to Artemis.

The hedonistic exuberance of the ghazal contributes to its universal popularity, as it flouts social mores to celebrate sexuality and exult in a sexual longing heightened by drunken revels and spring madness in a manner reminiscent of the Bacchanalia. Its romantic images explain its particular popularity among courtesans, the earliest patrons of the genre, who set the verses to semi-classical dance music. Its musical performance adds to its continued vitality in the mass culture of the Indo-Pakistani sub-continent.   *SH*

D.J. Matthews, C. Shackle and S. Husain *Urdu Literature* (London: Urdu Markaz, 1985)

See also **Mira Bai; Romantic Love**

Golden Lotus, The

See **Jin Ping Mei**

Goldman, Emma (1869-1940)

Emma Goldman, who arrived in the USA as a Russian immigrant in 1886, was a working-class revolutionary, a feminist and a leading anarchist. Her charisma and heroic dedication made her a myth in her own time, the legendary 'Red Emma'. With Alexander Berkman she edited and published the anarchist paper *Mother Earth* and traveled all over the USA as a labor activist and public speaker. She saw suffrage law reform as an inadequate solution to female oppression and fought passionately for women's sexual freedoms. As a trained midwife, she worked in New York's Lower East Side and had intimate knowledge of the hardship and suffering caused by unwanted pregnancies among poor women.

Goldman's pioneering work on birth control always related it to women's rights and a sexuality free of conventional marriage and its legal bonds. In this she was more radical than any of the noted campaigners who came immediately after her. She also defended **homosexuality**, a stance that was rare at the time even among the advocates of 'free love'. Her own love affair with Benjamin Reitman, fellow-anarchist and birth controller, was a passionate but stormy one. Between 1893 and 1917 she was arrested and imprisoned a number of times on such charges as inciting to riot, publicly advocating birth control and obstructing the draft. As a result of her activism, in 1919 she was deported to the USSR, which she left two years later, critical of Soviet centralism. She died in Toronto.   *LH*

Living My Life (New York and London: Pluto, 1988)

See also **Besant; Contraception; Kollontai; Sanger; Stopes; Wright**

Gorris, Marleen (1948-)

Marleen Gorris's feature films deal eloquently with the human condition, but human in this case meaning women's, not men's. This is why the Dutch film-maker's first feature, *De Stilte Rond Christine M/A Question of Silence*, divided cinema audiences along gender lines to an extreme degree, and evoked howls of outrage and moral posturing from male critics who scrabbled apoplectically at phrases invoking Stalin, Hitler and Herod. Gorris commented at the time, 'I did think that feminists would be able to get the small jokes in it and that on the whole women would understand better. But I never thought it would be so little understood by men. At the time I'm absolutely sure that I didn't realise the gap was so great, so unbridgeable.'

The basic premise of *De Stilte Rond Christine M/A Question of Silence* is that three women, strangers to each other, spontaneously murder a man, simply for *being* a man, and in doing so gain the understanding and unspoken endorsement of other women who have perceived the workings of patriarchal society. This bald description belies the film's imaginative power and allegorical truth, qualities recognized by the audiences of women who applauded and cheered it in commercial cinemas – even normally undemonstrative British audiences – expressing not just appreciation of a feminist perspective on the battle of the sexes, but gratitude and even relief at the catharsis of being for once invited to share a gut, emotional reaction to the endless grinding down that is the reality of sexual inequality.

Technically and visually conventional, Gorris's work is powerful because of her ability to dramatize ideas and give genuinely cinematic form to abstract concepts. Working within established genres – the thriller, the murder mystery – in order to subvert them, she uses their familiarity to seduce audiences into entertaining radical, feminist ideas. The concept that *all* men benefit from the subjugation and dependence of women and have a vested interest in perpetuating their own power underlies both *De Stilte Rond Christine M/A Question of Silence* and Gorris's second feature *Gebroken Spiegels/Broken Mirrors*. The latter is an even more uncompromising and much darker critique of male-female relationships, in which sex, (male) power and money are inextricably linked and are all used by men to humiliate and degrade women, keeping them in a state of dependence. This is the evidence behind the events in the first film and, this time, there is none of the exhilarating laughter which was so empowering at the end of *De Stilte Rond Christine M/A Question of Silence*. Instead, there is the implication that women can refuse to concede to male manipulation, although not necessarily without cost.   *PA*

De Stilte Rond Christine M/A Question of Silence (1981); *Gebroken Spiegels/Broken Mirrors* (1984)

Jane Root 'Distributing "A Question of Silence": A Cautionary Tale' in *Films for Women*, ed. Charlotte Brunsdon (London: British Film Institute, 1986)

See also **Akerman; Borden; Export; Rape and Revenge Movies**

Graham, Roberta (1954-   )

An Irish artist living in Britain, Roberta Graham is one of many women artists who, over the past decade, have attempted to redefine visual representations of the female body. She has worked across a variety of media, including film and performance, but her light-box images of the early 1980s represent perhaps her best known and most striking work. Appearing as large-scale transparent photographs, the works are mounted within a deep frame to allow illumination of the image from behind, ideally being shown in a darkened space which underscores the quasi-religious implications of the imagery. In speaking of this series, Roberta Graham has said, 'I find the whole erotic experience is very much to do with the presence of mortality and fragility because it's the strongest sense of awareness of another person – you're touching someone else's physical structure, feeling the bones, hearing the heartbeat – the whole experience goes far deeper than images, which is what I'm trying to get across.'

Roberta Graham's imagery stands in fundamental opposition to the constant barrage of cosmetic images with which western culture surrounds us. It directly exposes and willingly embraces the sense of mortality which has been systematically suppressed in the genre of the **nude**, mostly through an overwhelming bias towards youthful subjects. Graham rejects the superficiality of most popular and traditional imagery of women's bodies by calling attention to the actual structures of the body beneath its surface, as in 'Whether the Storm'. In this image, the figure of a young woman (Graham herself) peels back her flesh to reveal the body's interior in an admission of vulnerability which may be read on an emotional level as well as a physical one. But the image is also an incitement to wonder at the remarkable complexity of the body's structure. The fullness of erotic consciousness in Graham's work is thus at once apprehensive and celebratory, an implicit acknowledgement of sexuality as a striving for life which owes its existence to the fact of death.

The effects of Graham's imagery are achieved by means of complex procedures through which she combines photographs, medical diagrams, X-ray imagery and the internal illumination of the light-box format. Titles are often of signal importance in the work, since Graham frequently uses them to extend the possible meanings of her images. 'Whether the Storm' – a title devised after the fact, when the artist noticed how the pattern of blood vessels resembled bolts of lightning – suggests the violent emotions evoked in sexuality. At the same time it questions the nature of that violence, or intensity, and the ability of the body and psyche to withstand it. Once such questions are raised, the

G

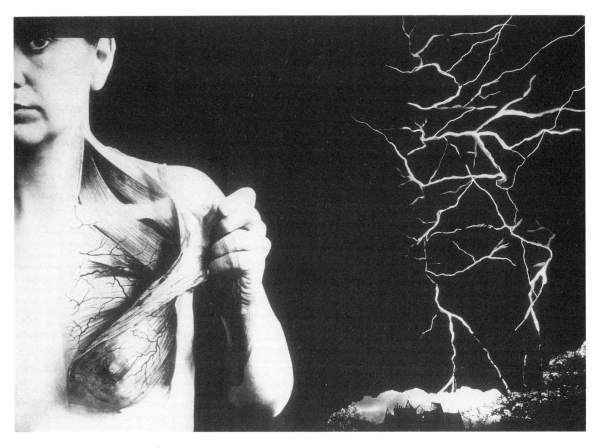

Roberta Graham, *Whether the Storm*, 1982

image itself seems to expand its meanings. One possible implication in this case is an acknowledgement of the insufficiency of ordinary sexual communication. In tearing away the body's surface, the image may suggest the irrational longing to go beyond the limits of sexuality itself, in an impulse to brave physical harm or even death for the sake of more complete union with another.   *SuB*

TEN. 8: Body Politics (no. 25, 1987)

See also **Export; Kahlo; Miller, Lee; Morreau; Voyeurism**

Grahn, Judy (1940-   )

One of the earliest US gay activists, Judy Grahn is a working-class woman who grew up in Chicago and New Mexico. Her first lesbian relationship, in 1959, happened at a time when secrecy was the norm for such a lifestyle. Forced to leave the armed forces with a dishonorable discharge, she had to undergo the indignity of family and friends being officially informed that her **lesbianism** was a 'crime'. Unprepared to accept the discrimination that she experienced in employment and housing and the physical abuse she suffered for refusing to look like the prescribed woman of the time, Grahn quickly became involved in trying to change things. Wary of personal attacks she published articles, prose and poetry under pseudonyms throughout the 1960s and contributed to one of the first lesbian periodicals, *The Ladder* (1957-1972). As early as 1964 she produced an article for *The Sexologist Magazine* in which she argued against the then predominant definition of lesbians as 'sick'.

Throughout the 1970s Grahn published and began to perform accessible poetry that included working-class women's experience. This, along with her lesbianism, enabled an early working relationship with the Afro-American lesbian poet Pat **Parker**. A powerful selection of the two women's work was recorded on *Where Would I Be Without You, the Poetry of Pat Parker and Judy Grahn* (Olivia Records, 1977). Grahn's drive to promote her sexuality as a viable one has led her to research gay culture, one result of which, *Another Mother Tongue: Gay Words, Gay Worlds*, made her the 1985 winner of the Gay Book Award of the American Library Association. Her deepening interest in women's spirituality forms the central theme of her first novel *Mundane's World* (1988) in which she creates a woman-centered world where issues of sexism, race and class are not in evidence. Lesbianism is more than a sexual choice for Grahn; it is one rooted both in a political position and a primary allegiance to women.   CU

The Work of a Common Woman: Collected Poetry (California: Diana Press, 1978); *The Queen of Wands* (California: The Crossing Press, 1982); *Another Mother Tongue: Gay Words, Gay Worlds* (Boston: Beacon Press, 1984); *The Highest Apple: Sappho and the Lesbian Poetic Tradition* (California: Spinster's Ink, 1985); *The Queen of Swords* (Boston: Beacon Press, 1988); *Mundane's World* (California: The Crossing Press, 1988)

See also **Political Lesbianism**

Greek Vase Painting

Greek vases, especially Attic vases of the late sixth to fourth centuries BC, show a variety of heterosexual and homosexual activity.

While there are many types of vase, ranging from huge storage jars to tiny perfume bottles, the ones on which the sexual scenes are generally depicted are those pots intended for use at drinking parties: cups, wine coolers and so on. These would have been used almost exclusively be men and the prostitutes who accompanied them to the parties, and would certainly not have been used by 'respectable' citizens' wives who, on their vases, had to make do with edifying mythological scenes. The sexual scenes show heterosexual sex in a variety of positions, but commonly with the woman sitting on top of the man. One could speculate whether this was truly the commonest position or whether it reflected male fantasies, since in many ways these cups fulfilled the function of present-day 'girlie magazines'. The women represented are invariably prostitutes or **hetaira**.

Another recurring theme is that of satyrs having sex with maenads. Both these mythological beings were attendants to Dionysos, the wine god, and thus appropriate as decoration. Satyrs were rather hairy men, usually with horses' tails and pointed ears (although they were depicted with less and less hair over the years. They appear to symbolize the unrestrained physical desires and are usually seen raping the maenads rather than being involved with them in mutually pleasurable activity.

Satyrs are frequently shown with erections in otherwise non-sexual contexts and often masturbating with glee. They also perform a number of other party tricks, such as spinning wine cups and even larger vases on their erect penises.

Women's masturbation was a subject of enormous male interest and is believed to have been the most common sexual outlet for citizens' wives, whose sex lives were otherwise rather inactive. While there is no known representation of human male masturbation on a vase, women are frequently shown using dildoes (they were in common use), or carrying them, or with baskets full of them.

Homosexuality tends to feature in a romantic, rather than erotic, style on the vases, with scenes of courtship and seduction. When intercourse occurs it is frequently shown face-to-face and intercrurally (between the thighs) rather than as buggery. This contrasts with the heterosexual sex, which is shown in positions where the partners do not face one another. Anal intercourse with women is frequently

Greek cup by Makron, *c.* 480 B.C.

shown and much attention is drawn to women's buttocks beneath their diaphanous clothing.   *KH*

There are collections of Greek vases in the British Museum, London, the Louvre, Paris, and Kerameikos, Athens

John Boardman *Athenian Red Figure Vases: The Archaic Period* (London: Thames & Hudson, 1975)

See also **Erotica;** *Lysistrata;* **Pornography; Prostitution**

Greer, Germaine (1939-   )

In many people's minds, feminism and the Australian-born writer Germaine Greer are inextricably linked. The publication of Greer's *The Female Eunuch* in 1970 coincided with the great expansion of feminism and, in Britain, the book was the first bestseller dealing with feminist ideas. In the eyes of the mass media Greer became 'the high priestess of women's liberation' and her exhibitionism guaranteed that the media would focus on her exploits as representative of the emergent women's movement. Greer's elevation to the status of high priestess was perhaps unfortunate. Her views were always somewhat idiosyncratic; indeed, more recently, she has

cultivated this idiosyncrasy to the point of becoming one of the media's tame eccentrics. But in the early 1970s Greer was part of the Underground Press, writing regularly for *Oz*, a magazine later prosecuted for attempting to 'corrupt the young'. She shared the sexual philosophy of that group, a philosophy which linked sexual self-expression with an opposition to the stuffy and repressive establishment. In *The Female Eunuch* Greer applied ideas about sexual liberation and sexual freedom to the position of women and argued that women's equality could be achieved only if women could free themselves from sexual repression.

Although views on sexual liberation were part and parcel of a radical consciousness of the time, many women had begun to feel reservations about the relevance of this doctrine to women's position. In a telling exchange in *Oz* in 1970, Michelene Wandor questioned the relevance of Greer's calls for 'clit power' and 'Lady Love your cunt', ending with a wistful question about where Germaine had been at the first Ruskin Conference, in February 1970, the moment that most define as the start of the British women's liberation movement. Indeed, even at this early point, many feminists were worried that the doctrine of sexual freedom was just another way in which women were to be put at the disposal of men. But it was Greer's version of sexual freedom which received the widest attention and came to be synonymous, in the public's mind, with women's lib.

Throughout the 1970s feminist theory diverged further from Greer's. Her main forum was a column in the *Sunday Times* where she wrote tough and radical pieces on abortion and **contraception** and drew attention to the **rape** of Bengali women. However, she appeared out of touch with the developing interests in feminism, including the growing critique of sexual liberation, **pornography** and psychoanalytical explorations of sexuality. In 1984 Greer published *Sex and Destiny*, which appeared on the surface to be a total reversal of her previous views on sexual freedom. Now she argued that sexual freedom was a con and that many women from 'primitive', non-westernized societies had far greater status than women ensnared by the constant pressure towards sexual performance and accomplishment. She railed against contraception and abortion as damaging to women's bodies and argued instead for the joys of inventive pregnancy-avoidance, such as coitus interruptus which she claimed was successfully and pleasurably practiced by Tuscan peasants. The book drew fire from all sides. Feminists accused her of ignoring their arguments and hence making a fool of feminism in the public eye. Anthropologists called her views of primitive societies crass, and Tuscans suggested that her view of their sexuality might be a little romanticized.

Greer's volte-face in *Sex and Destiny* was pretty universally derided but the book had more in common with *The Female Eunuch* than might at first appear. Underlying much of Greer's writing is a belief that the significance of sex should be reduced. In the 1970s she believed that the way to do this was by treating sex as no more important than 'drinking a glass of water' – hence her approval of Alexandra **Kollontai**, who thought the same – while in her more recent book, *The Change*, she welcomes the **menopause** as a release, among other things, from sexual activity. But her strategy has always been hopelessly idealistic. She has even posed nude for a 'radical' porn magazine, failing to take on board how sexist such an institution is. Most feminists criticized the spurious freedoms of the **sexual revolution** long before Greer wrote *Sex and Destiny*.

However, as she has aged and feminism has fragmented, Greer's irreverent utterances on male and female sexuality have come into their own. Freed from the burden of speaking for feminism, Greer appears more as a sniper from the sidelines. It is a role better suited to her wit and idiosyncrasies.

RC

The Female Eunuch (London: Paladin, 1971): *The Change* (London: Hamish Hamilton, 1991)

See also **Psychoanalysis**

Hacker, Marilyn (1942-   )

Marilyn Hacker is one of the more influential poets writing in English (and French – she lives in Paris and Manhattan) today. This is largely because of her fearlessness in combining 'traditional' poetic form with a bold content and a language that is on-the-edge contemporary. *Love, Death and the Changing of the Seasons*, her fifth book, published in 1986, indicates in its title a major theme of Hacker's work: love, and its lack, explored in every definition, every possibility.

The books which preceded *Love, Death . . .* follow the sensibility of a questioning, then disappointed, heterosexual woman: who begins the third book, *Taking Notice*, thinking 'I wish I were a Lesbian' and ends it trying to figure out what to do now that she is. The speaker in these poems doesn't *choose* her sexual identity, she discovers it; but, as the process is presented to us in virtuoso verse, we read and experience a melding of sexuality and intellect, passion and the music of language, with plenty of lusty erotic detail. Now the curious and the uninitiated can ask '*Is* it better with a woman? Will I write – or sing or build or live – better?' As Hacker examines the depths of sexuality, her writing on all planes feels more powerful. She lovingly explores sensory details so that the wine and cheese are as exciting and gratifying as a lover's caress – and the lovers' caresses are hot. If it's not better, it reads better.

Love, Death . . . is a novel in verse once described by Hacker as 'girl meets girl, girl loves girl, girl loses girl'. Intensified sexual awareness on the part of the reader and writer makes for a heightened interpretation of other experience, notably in Hacker's most recent book, *Going Back to the River*, where the complex relationships with mothers, mothers-in-law, daughters and friends are written with the empathy of one female sexual being to another. This is reminiscent of the poetic vision of Adrienne **Rich**; indeed, epigraphs from Rich's work appear frequently in Hacker's pivotal *Taking Notice*, where she wrote: 'We may be learning to tell the truth.' For a generation brought up hearing such iconic US avowals as 'We destroyed the village in order to save it', 'I am not a crook' and 'It's all in your head', honesty has gone underground. Poet Muriel Rukeyser wrote, 'What would happen if one woman told the truth about her life?/The world would split open.' Telling the truth about women's sexuality – to open up, bring to light, come out – is what Hacker shows us in her poetry.   *KW*

Presentation Piece (New York: The Viking Press, 1976); *Separations* (New York: Knopf, 1976); *Taking Notice* (New York: Knopf, 1985); *Assumptions* (New York: Knopf, 1985); *Love, Death and the Changing of the Seasons* (New York: Arbor House, 1986; London: Onlywomen Press, 1987); *Going Back to the River* (New York: Vintage, 1990)

See also **Alther; Heterosexuality; Lesbianism; Sensuality**

Haggard, Sir Henry Rider (1856-1925)

The son of an English squire with estates in West Norfolk, in the 1870s Rider Haggard worked for the colonial service in South Africa. After his return, he read for the Bar but turned to writing imperial romances. He is best known for his Zulu epics and for his African narratives involving the exploits of a hunter-adventurer named Allan Quartermain. Of the latter genre, *King Solomon's Mines* (1885) is the most famous. In 1887 Haggard produced his other best seller, *she*, whose eponymous heroine became a late nineteenth-century symbol of the contradictory male fantasies which circulate around the figure of woman.

Haggard's heroine, the awesomely named She-who-must-be-obeyed, belongs to the tradition of British Romantic and late-Victorian *femmes fatales* who appear in such literature as Keats's *La Belle Dame sans Merci*, Coleridge's *Christabel*, George MacDonald's *Lilith*, Oscar **Wilde**'s *Salome* and Bram Stoker's *Dracula*. Part Medusa and part Circe, She (also called Ayesha) is the powerful and independent evil Phoenician queen who rules over a tribe of cannibals in a world where women hold the

reins of power. However, in her quest to be reunited with her long-lost lover, her destiny and power are inextricably linked with men. Her secret of immortality is stolen from a male philosopher-sage and her attempts to use her powers to create a lover in her image only result in her final decay to a 'little hideous monkey-frame'. In the context of contemporary evolutionary theory, this simian form is by no means arbitrary, nor is it coincidental that Haggard's queen is located in the heart of Africa. Female sexual identity, as described by the medical science of the nineteenth century in Britain, revolved around an idea of woman as 'body': as other to man with his capacity for reason, stability, education and progress. Similarly, those who were racially 'different' were perceived, like women, as primitive, inimical to culture and civilization.

The dualities in Haggard's narrative, of angel and whore, good mother and evil temptress, express late-Victorian British sexual anxieties, as the New Woman of the century's close moved forward to sexual equality. The novel's ending reinscribes on the changing social and political scene a conservative vision of womanhood: like Lilith in George MacDonald's tale, Ayesha is allowed peace only when her will is broken and she relinquishes her overreaching feminine desires.   *GCL*

She (Oxford: Oxford University Press, 1991); *Ayesha* (California: Borgo Press, 1980; London: Dover, 1978); *She and Allan* (California: Borgo Press, 1980; London: Ballantine, 1978); *Wisdom's Daughter* (Salem: Ayer, 1978)

Sandra Gilbert and Susan Gubar *No Man's Land: The Place of the Woman Writer in the Twentieth Century* (Yale: Yale University Press, 1989)

See also **Fantasy Fiction; Munch; Rops**

Hall, Radclyffe (1880-1943)

Radclyffe Hall has gone down in history as the lesbian who wrote *The Well of Loneliness*: a novel that caused moral outrage when it was first published in 1928. Hall was born into a wealthy family and, despite her parents divorcing when she was three years old, she had a comfortable up-bringing: her education at home being followed by a year at King's College, London. At twenty-one she inherited the kind of wealth that meant that she did not have to work. Materially sheltered, with a home in London and a house in the Malvern Hills, she used the time on her hands to write – and not unsuccessfully. Her fourth novel, *Adam's Breed*, published in 1926, won two literary prizes.

Hall's first endeavors were in poetry, however, and between 1906 and 1915 she produced several volumes of mawkish verse, the bulk of which revolved around her feelings for women. Her attitude to her sexuality was very much shaped by **sexology**, a growing science at the turn of the nineteenth century. Sigmund **Freud** having broken the silence around the topic of sex in general, others in Europe, taking a lead from him, broke the even greater silence that surrounded **homosexuality**. In Britain, in 1897, Havelock **Ellis** had begun to publish his *Studies in the Psychology of Sex* in which he used the phrase 'sexual invert' to describe the homosexual. His theory was that anybody attracted to their own sex had, trapped within them, the body of the opposite sex. These much-to-be-pitied individuals deserved others' tolerance and understanding since they constituted a 'third sex' and were unable to control what were (for them) natural passions. At the time, this theory appeared a logical justification for women like Hall: it gave her the biological right to take on a masculine appearance and insist on being called John. She shared the last twenty-eight years of her life with Lady Una Troubridge, who had left a husband to be with her.

The Well of Loneliness is very much a manifesto for the 'invert' theory; indeed, Havelock Ellis provided the novel with a stamp of theoretical approval by writing the introduction to the first edition. The narrative plays out the consequences for the invert of social prejudice; it also has autobiographical strands. Included in it is a painful estrangement from a mother who has no time for her daughter's particular sexuality, which mirrors Hall's frosty relationship with her own mother. Like much of the book, it is an emotional scenario

with which lesbian readers have easily been able to identify. In direct line with the 'invert' theory, the lesbian protagonist, Stephen Gordon, grows up with disdain for the feminine and a 'natural' inclination to the masculine. She is prone to falling in love with women with an ease and a passion beyond her control. An illicit liaison with a married woman results in her expulsion from the family estate but she eventually finds true love with Mary: a fictional recreation of the 'normal' woman who can be attracted to the invert. However, the fact that Stephen cannot give her children, along with the stigma that life with an invert will place on her, persuades Stephen to manipulate Mary into the arms of a man. The narrative ends with an impassioned plea for tolerance, addressed to the reader by the now-lonely Stephen.

Taken to court under the Obscene Publications Act, the book fell foul of censorship law and future British publication was banned; an act that served only to increase the curiosity of both the general and the lesbian public worldwide. In Hall's lifetime the book was translated into eleven languages and sold over one million copies. Although an important milestone, it has always had a mixed reception. For years it was the only widely available fictional representation of attraction between women and, although lacking explicit sex scenes, acted as a validation for the feelings of its lesbian readers. But the rise of both the gay and women's movements from the late 1960s caused a significant change in the way that the book was seen; with late twentieth-century critiques of homosexuality that favor a theory of 'preference' above one of inborn 'biology', and interpret gay sex as both subverting and questioning **heterosexuality**, *The Well of Loneliness* has become an anachronism.   *CU*

The Well of Loneliness (New York: Doubleday, 1990; London: Virago, 1982)

See also **Bannon; Lesbianism; Obscenity**

H

Hanscombe, Gillian (1945-   )

Born in Australia, the writer Gillian Hanscombe has lived in Britain since 1969. In the 1970s she took a leading role in the fight to change public attitudes to lesbian motherhood. With Jackie Forster she researched and wrote *Rocking the Cradle: Lesbian Motherhood* (1981), the major tenet of which was that sex and procreation were not inseparable: women, at least, can gain satisfaction from sexual activities unrelated to the conceiving of children. The book also urged men to take up mothering and suggested an end to marriage. Hanscombe herself was in one of the first underground self-help groups successfully to introduce artificial insemination by donor into the lesbian community in Britain. She gave birth to her son in 1979.

Hanscombe's writing is marked by a willingness to voice the contemporary lesbian experience and engage in debates on sexuality. Her novel *Between Friends* (1982) is written in one of the oldest literary forms: an exchange of letters between characters. Through the feminist lens of each female protagonist a variety of lesbian and heterosexual politics and practice is examined. Two lesbians initially differ: one is the mother of a son; the other a confirmed lesbian separatist who has made the political decision to withdraw from anything and anybody male. One of the two heterosexual protagonists is engaged in sex without penetration with a husband who fully supports the exploration of sex beyond patriarchal limits. Another is unable to see the abusive infidelity of her husband. Her friendship with the lesbian mother founders when she refuses to believe that her husband has raped this close friend. Political positions around sex both shift and are re-evaluated in a text that fleshes out theory with human, recognizable characters. Hanscombe also writes poetry, while her short stories have appeared in lesbian anthologies since 1984.   CU

Hecate's Charms (Sydney: Khasmik Poets, 1975); *Rocking the Cradle: Lesbian Motherhood* (London: Peter Owen, 1981); *Between Friends* (London: Women's Press, 1990); *Flesh and Paper*, with Suniti Namjoshi (Seaton: Jezabel Tapes and Books, 1986)

See also **Burford; Firestone; Livia**

Harlequin

See **Mills & Boon**

Hawthorne, Nathaniel (1804-1864)

Born into a prominent Puritan family at Salem, Massachusetts, Nathaniel Hawthorne is best known for his novel *The Scarlet Letter*, a solemn romance set in seventeenth-century Boston. Like much of Hawthorne's other **romantic fiction**, this novel is a pessimistic portrayal of the consequences of concealed guilt, a theme that grows directly out of the writer's Puritan background.

Most readers of Hawthorne are struck by the overwhelming agony suffered by his characters as they struggle for absolution from secret, often sexual, sin: an absolution which, in most cases, they never achieve, because their creator is so thoroughly ambivalent about his own Calvinist heritage with its emphasis on total depravity and original sin. Hawthorne was never able either to embrace or disavow these doctrines completely. Having come from an American culture of the nineteenth century, in which man was supposed to be the head of the household, and from a background of strong Puritan forefathers who upheld the notion of the superior male as a symbol of industry and economic stability, Hawthorne found his role as a writer extremely difficult to justify. At the same time he was appalled that his female contemporaries were gaining more recognition in the literary marketplace than he was. He grew increasingly resentful toward all women who, independent from men, make their way in the world.

The narrative device that Hawthorne contrived in order to deal with his ambivalence about his artistic vocation and his envy of women writers' success was to create both chaste maidens whose acquiescence to male authority is rewarded, and powerful, dark, sexually alluring women (like Hester Prynne in *The Scarlet Letter*) who are forced to acknowledge the error of their ways and do penance. In his fiction, this damnation of a strong, autonomous female character always comes as something of a surprise to the reader because, in every case, Hawthorne's initial presentation of her is positive. She begins as a vital, passionate, creative being; then gradually Hawthorne changes his narrative stance toward her, portraying her more and more as a temptress, an Eve who must be domesticated. By the end of the narrative she has repressed both her independence and her sexuality in order to embrace a conventional definition of woman. In this paradigmatic plot structure, the woman, through an act of willful self-denial, chooses a spiritual salvation which is actually a kind of emotional damnation and, ultimately, a betrayal of the 'wisdom of the human heart' that Hawthorne initially seems to champion. *SMe*

Hawthorne: Novels (New York: Library of America, 1982); *Hawthorne: Tales and Sketches* (New York: Library of America, 1982)

Nina Baym *The Shape of Hawthorne's Career* (Ithaca, New York: Cornell University Press, 1976)

See also **Adultery; Flaubert; Puritanism**

Hays Code, The

A series of hotly publicized Hollywood sex scandals after the First World War led to a clamor for film censorship. In 1922, largely to fend off federal legislation, the movie moguls formed a self-regulating body – The Motion Picture Producers and Distributors of America – with former Postmaster General and strict Presbyterian Will H. Hays as its first head. By 1930, continued pressure from the puritans forced this body to draw up the Motion Picture Production Code, known as the Hays Code, an infamous charter stating what could not be shown in American movies. Drafted by a Roman Catholic publisher and a Jesuit priest, administered (until

1954) by another keen Roman Catholic, Joseph I. Breen, and pressurized by the powerful National Legion of Catholic Decency, founded in 1934, the Code kept a stranglehold on all Hollywood production. Until the by then unstoppable forces of change resulted in the introduction of film classification in 1968, any film which did not earn the Code's seal of approval risked almost certain death at the box office.

Although the Code's list of limitations embraced many different issues – the treatment of crime, profanity, liquor, religion, national feelings – its predominant concern was sex; and it is on this score that it has been most ridiculed, criticized and condemned. With the emphasis on wholesome family entertainment which would uphold 'the sanctity of the institution of marriage and the home', it followed that 'adultery . . . must not be explicitly treated, or justified, or presented attractively'; 'excessive and lustful kissing, lustful embraces, suggestive postures and gestures are not to be shown'; 'complete nudity is never permitted'; 'indecent or undue exposure is forbidden'; 'dances which emphasize indecent movements are to be regarded as obscene'; 'the treatment of bedrooms must be governed by good taste and delicacy'; and, of course, that 'sex perversion' (the nearest the Code came to mentioning **homosexuality** or **incest**) 'or any inference to it is forbidden'.

On the surface the Code could not be accused of being sexist. Neither men nor women must be seen to infringe its tenets. But two women were to prove its biggest banes. The come-hither looks, sashaying hips and salty double entendres of Mae **West** in her self-scripted films *She Done Him Wrong* (1933) and *I'm No Angel* (1933) caused uproar among the bluenoses and contributed directly to the formation of the Legion of Decency, which was to insist that the Code be more rigorously enforced. Conversely, Jane Russell – or, more precisely, her cleavage – was instrumental in bringing about the Code's demise. In 1943, via the 'undue' exposure of Russell's 'mammaries' in his indifferent Western *The Outlaw*, millionaire producer Howard Hughes offered the Code its most serious challenge yet. After a long battle with Breen, Hughes finally released the film in 1946 without a Seal and showed that the public, by now agog with curiosity, as well as made more mature by war, would flock to see it anyway.   *MH*

Leonard J. Leff and Jerold L. Simmons *The Dame in the Kimono: Hollywood Censorship and the Production Code* (London: Weidenfeld and Nicolson, 1990)

See also **Comics, US and European; Obscenity**

H.D. (1886-1961)

Hilda Doolittle's **bisexuality** leaves its historic trace in a separation between the writings published in her lifetime and those unpublished until after her death. Her reputation as an innovatory modern poet was made over the gender-free signature 'H.D.: Imagiste' at the time of the First World War. By 1925, when her first *Collected Poems* appeared, she had silently turned to fiction, encoding her sexualities and her marginalized position as a woman writer in a series of autobiographical novels. *Her* (1927) fictionalizes H.D.'s triangular relationship with fellow-poets Ezra Pound and Frances Gregg, while *Asphodel* (1922) recalls her arrival in London from the USA in 1911 and her desire to live without marriage as a 'modern woman'.

In fact, H.D. married the British writer Richard Aldington in 1913 and the politics of their open marriage and poetic rivalry informed her later novel, *Bid Me to Live* (1950), which also challenges D.H. **Lawrence**'s doctrine that 'man-is-man, woman-is-woman'. H.D. was grateful that she 'never slept with D.H.L.'; her only surviving child was conceived with his friend Cecil Gray. In the same year, 1918, she was associating with Havelock **Ellis** and advancing her own theory that 'the brain and the womb are both centres of consciousness' and there is 'no great art . . . without great lovers'. Her *Notes on Thought and Vision* (1919) thus endorses both female sexuality and **homosexuality** at a time when both were considered abnormal by medical science. H.D. had been influenced by Dora Marsden's vivid discussion of gender in the pre-war publication *Freewoman* and was a literary editor of its successor, *The Egoist*.

H.D.'s meeting in 1918 with the wealthy young British writer Winifred **Bryher** shaped the lives of both women. Their sexual relationship was short-lived and both had love affairs with other women but they remained companion-lovers until H.D.'s death. Bryher recalls H.D.'s beauty as 'truly Greek' and the Hellenism of much of H.D.'s writing encodes a fascination with 'gender-bending'. *Hedylus* and *Hyppolytus Temporizes* (both 1925) explore this theme, and *By Avon River* (1949) celebrates **Shakespeare** as a bisexual artist.

In the early 1930s H.D. undertook **psychoanalysis** with Sigmund **Freud**, having experienced a writing block that he identified with her sexual ambivalence. He also diagnosed a 'mother-fixation', but his theories of femininity and female homosexuality were incompatible with H.D.'s sense of her own creativity. *Tribute to Freud* (1948) recalls their collaboration and their conflicts, including *his* resistance to being the mother in transference and *her* resistance to his theory of castration. The most creative period of H.D.'s career ensued: in embattled London, during the Second World War, she produced among other works her great poetic *Trilogy* (1944) and her prose memoir *The Gift* (1943). Both are works of spiritual searching that, by lyrical and narrative means, critique **patriarchy** and recover the maternal principle embodied by H.D. in the phrase 'born of one mother'.

The heterodox inheritance of Moravian Christianity, with its love feasts, bodily symbolism and sex equality, was now enriched by H.D.'s study of ancient mystery religions and her increasing commitment to the esoteric traditions represented by writers such as Denis de Rougement. Her last poetic works, *Helen in Egypt* (1954) and *Hermetic Definition* (1960), also draw on Freud's theory of Eros and Thanatos to explore female consciousness of male violence in both love and war. Her memoir of Pound, *End to Torment*, bears out H.D.'s complicity in what has been called 'romantic thralldom' to dominant men, yet she saw clearly the **misogyny** of patriarchal culture and her poems give voice to the heroines and goddesses of a revisionary feminist mythology. Moreover, the female eroticism of such volumes as *Hymen* (1921) and *Heliodora* (1924), no less than their music and imagery, connect H.D. with the greatest woman poet of antiquity. **Sappho**'s vital presence in H.D.'s poetry and prose is mirrored by H.D.'s presence in the poetry and prose of Adrienne **Rich**. Hence H.D.'s recent recovery by feminist critics and her belated recognition as a woman modernist of the same generation as Virginia Woolf and Gertrude **Stein** have been of special inspiration to lesbian writers and readers. H.D.'s reaction to this posthumous homosexual identity would be equivocal; but, from the work of five decades, her poems for Bryher are a rare garland.   *DC*

Notes on Thought and Vision & The Wise Sappho (San Francisco: City Lights, 1982; London: Peter Owen, 1988); *Hedylus* (Connecticut: Black Swan Books, 1980; Manchester: Carcanet, 1980); *Her* (New York: New Directions, 1981; London: Virago, 1984); *The Gift* (New York: New Directions, 1982; London: Virago, 1984); *Trilogy* (Manchester: Carcanet, 1973); *By Avon River* (Connecticut: Black Swan, 1989); *Tribute to Freud* (New York: New Directions, 1985; Manchester: Carcanet, 1970); *Bid Me to Live* (Connecticut: Black Swan, 1983; London: Virago, 1984); *Helen in Egypt* (New York: New Directions, 1974; Manchester: Carcanet, 1985); *End to Torment* (New York: New Directions, 1979; Manchester: Carcanet, 1980); *Hermetic Definition* (New York: New Directions, 1972; Oxford: Carcanet, 1972); *Collected Poems 1912-1944* (New York: New Directions, 1983; Manchester: Carcanet, 1984)

Rachel Blau DuPlessis *H.D.: The Career of That Struggle* (Brighton: Harvester, 1986)

See also **Colette; Lesbianism**

Hemingway, Ernest (1899-1961)

Of all American male writers, Ernest Hemingway is probably the one most identified with masculinity. The image of Hemingway as macho conqueror grew from headlines about his big-game hunting as well as his three divorces. The essential Hemingway appeared to be a highly-sexed adventurer for whom physical hardihood included sexual prowess. His four wives and other lovers seemed to be as much trophies of his bravado lifestyle as his animal skins and mounted heads.

Hemingway's fiction did much to encourage that popular image. His tough, laconic protagonists could love passionately, but only if they found a submissive woman who was also as brave and defiant of cultural norms as they were. Nick Adams in *In Our Time* (1925) is content alone; Jake Barnes in *The Sun Also Rises* (1926) and Frederic Henry in *A Farewell to Arms* (1929) love only one woman – and the romance in each case is short-lived. Short-lived too are the most sexually satisfying relationships in Hemingway's fiction: those between Robert Jordan and Maria in *For Whom the Bell Tolls* (1940) and between Harry and Marie Morgan in *To Have and Have Not* (1937). In the former novel the earth-moving scenes became the classic image for the power of heterosexual intercourse and, more directly, the power of Robert Jordan.

Hemingway's comments about writing helped to create a sexual text for his readers. He often used the metaphor of writing as making love, with the physical satisfaction of writing well mimicking sexual satiety. He continually made public his woman chasing, his hunting and fishing escapades, his war reporting – even when, during the 1950s, most of his bragging about his physical prowess seemed pathetic rather than convincing. His suicide in 1961, head blown to bits in the vestibule of his home, was an angry disavowal of the macho power and control he had claimed for so many years.

In the past decade, particularly with the publication in 1986 of Hemingway's *The Garden of Eden*, written probably from the late 1940s into the 1950s, critics have begun to appreciate the complexity of both Hemingway's sexuality and his fictional representations of the sexual. The **lesbianism** between Catherine and Marita becomes a part of the author's sexual profile, and the macho figure becomes androgynous, if not actively bisexual. Perhaps Hemingway's fiction was dominated less by lovers than by men alone, beginning with Nick Adams, emphasized in the 1927 story collection

Men Without Women and brought to maturity with Colonel Cantwell in *Across the River and Into the Trees* (1950), Santiago in *The Old Man and the Sea* (1952), Thomas Hudson in *Islands in the Stream* (1970) and even the lonely memoirist of *A Moveable Feast* (1964). In his 1990 study *Hemingway's Quarrel with Androgyny* Mark Spilka poses the most complete portrait of a writer who created all segments – male and female – of the sexuality he both loved and feared.   *LWM*

In Our Time (New York: Macmillan, 1987); *The Sun Also Rises* (New York: Macmillan, 1987); *A Farewell To Arms* (New York: Macmillan, 1987; London: Panther, 1977); *To Have and Have Not* (New York: Macmillan, 1988; London: Panther, 1977); *For Whom the Bell Tolls* (New York: Macmillan, 1988; London: Panther, 1976); *Across The River and Into the Trees* (New York: Macmillan, 1988; London: Panther 1977); *The Old Man and the Sea* (New York: Macmillan, 1987; London: Panther, 1976); *A Moveable Feast* (New York: Macmillan, 1988; London: Panther, 1977); *Islands in the Stream* (New York: Scribner, 1970; London: Grafton, 1990); *The Garden of Eden* (New York: Macmillan, 1987; London: Grafton, 1988)

Mark Spilka *Hemingway's Quarrel with Androgyny* (Nebraska: University of Nebraska Press, 1990)

See also **Androgyny; Lawrence; Miller; Stein**

Hermaphroditism

Extremely rarely, babies are born with both female and male sexual organs. Their condition is known as hermaphroditism and, although there are various ways in which they may be treated or may naturally develop, the importance we attach to knowing early on whether we are 'a girl' or 'a boy' means that it is usual to raise such infants *as though* they were one or the other sex, even while, physically, they are not. The interesting point for all of us is that, whether raised as a girl or a boy, hermaphrodite children will usually conform to whatever behavior is expected from their sex of adoption.   *HG*

See also **Androgyny**

Hetaira

Of the several categories of prostitute found in the Greek city states of the fifth and fourth centuries BC, hetaira, also referred to as 'courtesans', were the most expensive. They led very different lives from, say, the streetwalkers of the period.

The Athenian system in particular had brought about a social polarization between 'good women' and whores. The citizens' wives did not go out of the house much, wore concealing clothing, did not expect sex more than three times a month and were inadequately educated. Hetaira were supposed to have combined physical beauty with intelligence and artistic talents, wore diaphanous clothing, accompanied men to drinking parties and probably had more frequent sex. The distinction was famously summed up by the fourth-century orator Demosthenes: 'We have mistresses for our enjoyment . . . wives for the bearing of legitimate offspring.'

Hetaira either offered themselves to the highest bidder each night, or sought a number of 'regulars', or established themselves as the partner of a well-known man. In the latter capacity, many gained political influence. Aspasia, the companion of the politician Pericles, was undoubtedly the most famous woman of her period; while the Egyptian rulers the Ptolemies, in the Hellenistic age, were also reputed to be much influenced by hetaira. No doubt the hetairas' sexual repertoire was more extensive than that of the wives and it was recognized, says David M. Halperin in *One Hundred Years of Homosexuality* (London and New York: Routledge, 1990), that prostitutes were used to provide sexual pleasures considered degrading to the provider, such as fellatio. Hetaira were more financially independent than other women, and there are extensive records of their donations to temples. If unsuccessful in finding a long-term male protector, they could survive in old age by training slave-girls and running brothels.

The emphasis by historians on **homosexuality** in ancient Athens has led to a general ignorance of the role of the hetaira, but their prominence seems to suggest that rich and aristocratic men sought the company of intelligent, educated women as partners. However, as Sarah B. Pomeroy has pointed out in *Goddesses, Whores, Wives and Slaves*, while there are numerous instances of hetaira attempting to live as wives, there are no recorded instances of wives becoming hetaira: from which she concludes that the marital status was still the more desirable. What it suggests to me is that the life of a woman in classical Greece was chiefly circumscribed by the need to find a male protector.   *KH*

Sarah B. Pomeroy *Goddesses, Whores, Wives and Slaves* (New York: Schocken Books, 1975)

See also **Greek Vase Painting; Prostitution**

Heterosexism

Heterosexism was a term first taken up by the women's liberation and gay movements in the late 1970s to denote the system that oppresses lesbians and gay men. Up to that point, many had used the world **homophobia** to label anti-gay attitudes or behavior, but homophobes were mentally disturbed individuals, analogous to claustrophobes or kleptomaniacs. Heterosexism conveyed the systematic nature of the phenomenon: so pervasive in our culture that even lesbians and gay men can and do exhibit anti-homosexual behavior and beliefs.

The deliberate relationship of the word to 'sexism' is also important. As sexism was the most popular term in the 1970s to describe the system in which women are put down, are even trained to put themselves down, heterosexism came to stand for a large and not always coherent set of bad attitudes, actions and applications. Not all feminists accepted it without question: the issue of whether the oppression that lesbians and gay men suffer is a side-effect of sexism (as men try to force women into marital roles) or has any independent existence was hotly debated. It remains an interesting question. Certainly, the term was taken up most vigorously by lesbian feminists who believed in at least some separate organizing by lesbians. However, it is now more or less ubiquitous as shorthand for (particularly) those attitudes that many people do not even recognize as undermining homosexuals. Many would move to stronger language to describe legislative or physical attacks on lesbians or gay men, but, in explaining why St Valentine's Day is bad news, we would probably say that it's heterosexist, a celebration of sexual love to which homosexuals are definitely not invited and for which we are allowed no public alternative.

The term heterosexism may be recent, but the phenomenon it tries to capture is not. In no known society have heterosexual and homosexual relationships had the same value. Attitudes to sexuality of any persuasion vary enormously from society to society but, in most, **homosexuality** has been illicit, illegal, taboo, or all three. The use of the term heterosexism – with its emphasis on how societies encourage heterosexuality and discourage homosexuality – is itself dramatic evidence of how much things have changed for lesbians and gay men in the west in the past two decades. In many societies there was and still is much more than a system of encouragement or discouragement: sexual acts between people of the same sex were or are punished severely, even by death. In most societies even today it is impossible for same-sex lovers to set up home together; openly lesbian women and gay men, in many places and periods, have faced ostracism in their cultures; while the very *possibility* of loving someone of your own sex in any way akin to **heterosexuality** has often been entirely denied.

Can we even talk of 'lesbians' or 'gay men' in cultures which so thoroughly denied or deny the possibility of our existence? Certainly there has been same-sex love in many different kinds of societies but it has often been explicitly forbidden. Heterosexism, in that sense, can exist where lesbians and gay men do not: it is frighteningly effective.

RW

See also **Compulsory Heterosexuality; Foucault; Gay Liberation;** *Homosexuality in Renaissance England;* **Weeks**

H

Heterosexuality

The condition of finding the other sex sexually attractive, or the act of having sexual relations with a member of the other sex, are known as heterosexuality: the 'hetero' part of the word meaning 'other' or 'different'.

There have been a few, of whom Sigmund **Freud** was probably the most important until very recently, who have tried to show us that heterosexuality – rather than being the 'natural' condition, from which some deviate only because they are seriously wicked or ill – is in fact the result of a complex and therefore entirely fallible process. But even Freud believed that it was the most *desirable* condition and, although almost every society tries to control heterosexual behavior – to limit the forms that it can take, the situations in which it can occur, the meanings that can be attributed to it – they too tend to consider it 'better' than other forms of sexuality. Moreover, even in the post-Freud era, it remains a common, popular belief that heterosexuality has to be 'natural'. Isn't it a fact that opposites attract? Isn't it God's, or nature's way of perpetuating the species? Don't people just *do* it, instinctively?

But instinct, in humans, is rarely straightforward and seldom if ever do we search for sex for the reason that non-human animals do, uniquely through some biological imperative. While it is true that far more people consider themselves to be 'naturally' heterosexual than lesbian or gay and, in practice, most who are sexually active are active with the other sex, even here there is a certain amount of ambiguity. Large numbers of self-defined heterosexual people admit to fancying, having fancied, having affairs with or having had affairs with people of their own sex. In a survey of sexual behavior and opinions conducted in 1983 by the British magazine *Woman*, almost all of whose respondents were primarily heterosexual, nearly one in ten of the unmarried women (the married ones weren't asked) admitted to having 'made love with another woman'. In a similar survey of men published four years later, seven per cent of those who were currently married or having an affair

with a woman admitted that, in the past, they had had a 'romantic friendship' with a man, and half described this friendship as having included physical sex. The truth would appear to be that, even as adults, many of us retain a considerable amount of sexual flexibility.

Nonetheless, the majority either does not or else cannot admit it, whether to themselves or others. Many, even when not homophobic, claim to have only ever been aroused by a person of the other sex, and often say that it is precisely their 'otherness' – of skin texture, smell, genitals, outlook, social role or whatever – that excites them. The erotic nature of difference, strangeness, is an observable phenomenon, but the differences between men and women, while undeniably real, are considerably fewer and less than societies pretend. Besides, humans differ in many other ways than in their sex. Is it the case that we really don't *know* why most of us live heterosexually, having devoted so much of our time to attempting to work out why some of us don't?

Of course, since the early 1970s, this imbalance has been modified, with **Gay Liberation** and feminism shifting the spotlight away from **perversion** to shine it on 'normal' sexuality. The predominant feminist view of heterosexuality is that it is merely one choice among many – albeit a choice with particular dangers, including physical, for women – but that, in practice, innumerable people who would *not* have chosen it freely are being coerced into doing so by a complex of legal, economic, religious and cultural forces and sanctions. The reason for this is that it is in the interests of the **patriarchy** that as many women as possible should focus their emotions on men and feel competitive with women, should depend upon men's assessment of their appearance, opinions and behavior, should easily be maneuverable into pregnancy, marriage, unpaid housework and detachment from the public sphere. From this, rather fewer feminists conclude that even in simply being attracted to or having sex with a man, regardless of the nature, style or structure of the relationship, a woman becomes a collaborator with the patriarchy.

This last view is not entirely logical. While it is

certainly true that heterosexuality is thrust upon us – indeed, with such force that one sometimes wonders how confident of its 'naturalness' the guardians of morality really can be – this does not of itself make the choice of it undesirable. What is not to be desired is that women, or men, should be unaware that choices exist or, if aware, should feel pressurized or frightened into making the wrong one.

What is also not to be desired, of course, is that heterosexuality be seen as a package no part of which can be changed. Both as individuals and collectively, we need to negotiate ways of being erotically involved with the other sex – should that be what we desire – which please and satisfy ourselves, as distinct from the patriarchal state.   *HG*

See also **Clit Statements; Compulsory Heterosexuality; Dworkin; Heterosexism; Jeffreys; Rich**

Heyer, Georgette (1902-1974)

There are perhaps three main reasons for the continuing popular success of the English novelist Georgette Heyer. One is her profound understanding of the classic components of the plot of the **romantic fiction** genre and her ability to deploy them with wit, a light touch and an elegantly concealed erudition. The second is her creation of a fantasy Regency world peopled by feisty, sharp-tongued heroines and dashing, sexy aristocrats: a world from which suffering, loss and poverty have been magically exiled and in which beauty, intelligence and courage in women are always rewarded with happy marriages. Heyer's novels are skilled and sensitive pastiches of Jane Austen's, spiced with a dash of Charlotte **Brontë**, and drawing, like them, on a long tradition of female gothic and romance.

The third ingredient of Heyer's success is the way that her plots touch on and resolve **unconscious** human dramas originating in unfulfilled childhood fantasies and desires. Her books' erotic

charge often derives from the acting-out of forbidden impulses. So, for example, her heroines often dress up as boys in order to escape tyrannical parents and taste the freedom of the streets and exclusive male clubs; men dress up as women as part of thrilling madcap Jacobin adventures; tyrannically charming male guardians can be fought and fallen in love with as safe substitutes for the forbidden oedipal father. Similarly, the novels draw on the guilty childhood pleasures of looking and being looked at, touching and being touched. All this delightful chaos and disorder speeds the narratives along, but doesn't disrupt their conventional resolution: a safe **heterosexuality** always reigns in the end.   *MR*

Devil's Cub (California: Buccaneer Books, 1984); *Regency Buck* (London: Heinemann, 1952); *Faro's Daughter* (London: Heinemann, 1952); *These Old Shades* (New York: New American Library, 1988; London: Heinemann, 1952)

See also **Cross-Dressing; Oedipus Complex**

Hinduism

The religious phenomenon which has come to be known as Hinduism includes many belief systems, texts and traditions. However, there are certain key concepts which have evolved and been maintained over a span of 5,000 years.

Hinduism is profoundly concerned with the human condition and means to transcend it. Moksha – self-realization and release from a cycle of rebirths – is achieved by acting in accordance with Dharmic laws to which all earthly and godly beings are subject. Dharma is the order inherent in the universe and must be maintained to avoid Adharma, disorder, taking its place. Central to Moksha and Dharma is Karma, the theory of action which holds that the self is eternal but bound to the material world by the cycle of rebirths. There are many ways of achieving Moksha, but the following paths have a bearing on sexuality.

First there is the path of the householder. This enjoins the individual to pursue wealth and merit

H

(artha) and love and esthetics (kama), albeit in an orderly manner. This is reflected in the Brahamic prescription for the four stages of life: celibate studentship; family duties; community service; and, finally, the renunciation of all worldly ties. Another path, the path of devotion, involves the worship of a personal god, exemplified in the treatment of Lord Krishna as a beloved with whom union is sought. In the path of renunciation, the renunciate seeks to conquer, through meditation and yoga, all physical and mental manifestations of desire. Finally, the path of Tantra is based on the Tantra scriptures and the cult of the Mother Goddess. The tantric believes in the supremacy of the feminine principle of the universe. Sex is seen as the central metaphor for creation and is as integral a part of ritual as the worship of the yoni, or divine vulva.

Human sexuality has a central position in Hindu thought, as a metaphor for the divine creation of the universe, and sex is regarded as sinful only where it is socially illegitimate. Hindu tradition has not, however, been lacking in proponents for the suppression of women and women's sexuality. The concepts of Dharma and Karma have been exploited to suppress not only women but also non-Brahmanic castes. The notion that the individual has determined his or her condition in the present by the quality of actions in a past life is a powerful argument to prevent people breaking out of designated roles.

The life of the Hindu woman has been typified by deification in theory and denigration in practice. Revered as a mother, her status is enhanced by her capacity to produce sons. Some sources hold that a woman's primary Dharma is Pativrata: the worship of her husband. Women are considered sexually more passionate than men: the sexuality of wives and daughters is a constant threat to be controlled. Further, a woman is considered unclean and a source of pollution while menstruating or giving birth. Child marriage, female infanticide, sati (self-immolation on the husband's funeral pyre), the prohibition of widows' remarriage and purdah are the many practices that have served to exclude women from full social participation.

Despite the increase in female literacy in India, the emergence of such frightening practices as the burning of brides for providing insufficient dowries reflects the continuing view of women as commodities; while the media in present-day India, particularly the popular Hindi cinema, continue to depict the ideal of Hindu womanhood as **chastity**, purity and singular faithfulness in the face of gross ill-treatment and cruelty from men. The inspiration for this is drawn mainly from Sita, a character in the *Ramayana* epic.

Islam and **Christianity** have both contributed to reinterpretations of Hindu thought and to redefinitions of the role of sex and of women: via purdah, for instance, or the association of sex with original sin. In the colonial period, thinkers such as Raja Ramohun Roy attempted to present Hinduism as a monotheistic religion in Judeo-Christian terms: for instance, by translating Moksha as 'salvation'. And organizations such as the Arya Samaj have come into being, to proselytize and to offer a means of conversion to Hinduism. Both developments point to a self-perception by Hindus as an endangered species. It is perhaps an irony that the Hindu phenomenon, which was remarkable for its capacity to absorb heterodox ideas, is now, due to political pressure, becoming more limited in its definition as a religion. *NR & KV*

See also **Das; Indian Cinema; Indian Sculpture; Judaism; Kakar; Kama Sutra; Manto; Tantrism**

Hirschfeld, Magnus (1868-1935)

Magnus Hirschfeld was among the most prolific of the pioneering sexologists of the late nineteenth and early twentieth centuries in Europe. Even before his famous study of **homosexuality**, *Die Homosexualiatat des Mannes und des Wibes/Homosexuality of Man and Woman* (1925), he had written a classic work on transvestism, a term that he introduced to describe **cross-dressing**. But Hirschfeld is perhaps best known for *Sexual Anomalies and Perversions* (1938), a summary of his works.

In 1919, Hirschfeld fulfilled his ambition to found the world's first institute for **sexology**. Situated in one of Berlin's finest buildings, his institute was a center for research and soon gained worldwide recognition. Among the many services that it provided were a marriage-counseling service, the first in Germany, medical and legal advice in criminal cases and public sex education. As a Jew, Hirschfeld was frequently attacked by the Nazi press and, in 1933, while he was abroad, the institute was ransacked by Nazis, books and papers being removed and later burnt in a public ceremony. Unable to return to Germany, Hirschfeld tried unsuccessfully to settle in the USA, before finally retiring to Nice, in France, where he died.

Hirschfeld had a major influence on the development of sexual categories and, in particular, on the notion that homosexuality is the characteristic of a certain kind of person, an intermediate or third sex. Although he believed that homosexuals were 'born like it', Hirschfeld rejected the view held by others, such as Havelock **Ellis** and Richard von **Krafft-Ebing**, that homosexuality was a disease or a defect. In addition to his efforts at classifying people and their problems, Hirschfeld was one of the first to apply the new knowledge of 'sex hormones' to an understanding of sexual behavior, asserting that sexual behavior depended on the action of hormones in developing the 'sexual personality'.

Hirschfeld also actively sought to bring about social and legal reform, especially where homosexual men and lesbians were concerned. In 1897 he formed the Scientific-Humanitarian Committee, whose major aim was the abolition of the German law against sodomy. Large numbers of German lesbians, as well as homosexual men, belonged to this organization. Hirschfeld also worked with a number of film directors to produce so-called 'sexual enlightenment films' in an effort to overcome prejudice and ignorance. He appeared, for example, with the German actor Conrad Veidt in the film *Anders als die Andern/Different from the Others* (1919), a plea for the reform of anti-homosexual laws.

Hirschfeld later became leader of the World League for Sexual Reform which, in addition to working for the removal of laws against homosexuality, was concerned with reforming marriage and divorce laws, laws against abortionists and the provision of birth control. *DiR*

Sexual Anomalies and Perversions (Miami: Brown Book, 1948)

See also **Lesbianism; Reich; Sexology; Weeks**

Hitchcock, Alfred (1899-1980)

Alfred Hitchcock began his movie career in the early 1920s, designing titles for silent films. He went on to make more than fifty films, first in England and then, from 1939, in Hollywood. Most of his best and most famous movies – *Notorious, Dial M for Murder, Psycho, Rear Window, Marnie, North by North-West, Vertigo* – are thrillers. Although there are exceptions such as *Rebecca*, a romance with murder at its core, and *The Birds*, an apocalyptic fantasy, by and large Hitchcock *uses* his elaborate thriller plots, with physical violence mirroring psychic violence and enacted crimes betraying inner anxieties and guilts.

Hitchcock has become something of a test case for women movie buffs: reviled as an arch-misogynist, or praised for his insight into **misogyny**. In her influential 1973 essay, Laura Mulvey used Hitchcock to support her argument that, in mainstream cinema, women are objects of the sadistic, voyeuristic male gaze – although she does admit that he explores, rather than endorses, the 'implications of the active/looking, passive/looked at split'. Subsequent studies have concentrated on Hitchcock's exposure of the male insecurities that can emerge in **voyeurism, fetishism** and sadism, on the tension between his fascinated identification with femininity and his sometimes brutal retreat from it, or on his thoughtful account of relationships between men and women.

Horror and disgust occasionally break out of control. There is little to be said for the infamous stabbing-in-the-shower scene in *Psycho*, or the prolonged strangling in *Frenzy*. But *Vertigo* is a dazzlingly intricate story about, among other things, sexual idealization and the disillusioned hatred that inevitably accompanies it. *Rear Window* deals memorably with voyeurism. Its hero (James Stewart), immobilized by a broken leg, nervous of committing himself, and projecting his sexual fears, fantasies and problems onto the neighbors he watches obsessively, is viewed ironically; while Grace Kelly as his sleek, slick fiancée develops into a complicated, sympathetic woman. The eponymous Marnie (Tippi Hedren as another of Hitchcock's neurotic blondes) is allowed even more complexity. The film is a portrait of a sick relationship; if Marnie is frigid, evasive and trapped in the past, her husband (Sean Connery), apparently protective, is in fact possessive and controlling. The key scene is a **rape** and Hitchcock insists on its brutality. But he also shows it from the point of view of both characters and, challenging our too-easy assumption that rape is always and absolutely about a victim and a villain, uses it, paradoxically, as a turning-point from which both characters can grow and change.   *MW*

Rebecca (1940); *Notorious* (1946); *Rear Window* (1954); *Vertigo* (1958); *North by North-West* (1959); *Psycho* (1960); *Marnie* (1964)

Laura Mulvey 'Visual Pleasure and Narrative Cinema' in *Screen* (Vol. 16, no. 3, 1975) William Rothman *The Murderous Gaze* (Cambridge, Mass.: Harvard University Press, 1982) Tania Modleski *The Woman Who Knew Too Much* (London and New York: Methuen, 1988)

See also **Barker; De Palma; Slasher Movies; Voyeurism**

Hocquenghem, Guy (1944-1988)

A political theorist, journalist, novelist and filmmaker, Guy Hocquenghem was one of the founders of the **Gay Liberation** movement in France and of the Revolutionary Homosexual Action Front (FHAR).His non-fiction book *Homosexual Desire*, written in the early days of the movement, is one of the best examples of what was revolutionary about

it. Hocquenghem's aim was not to justify **homosexuality** but to attack the whole system of family and reproductive sexuality which generated 'anti-homosexual paranoia'. He drew on the psychoanalytic theories of Jacques **Lacan** and the anti-psychiatry of Gilles Deleuze and Felix Guattari – *L'Anti-Oedipe: Capitalisme et Schizophrénie* (Paris: Editions de Minuit, 1972) – and showed homosexual desire, which he associated with the anus, as only part of an unbroken flux of desire. But, he argued, capitalist ideology has transformed the **Oedipus Complex** into a social characteristic and so located pre-Oedipal anal desire in certain 'perverse' individuals: homosexuals. Hocquenghem died with AIDS in 1988.   *MM*

Le Désir Homosexuel/Homosexual Desire (Paris: Editions Universitaires, 1972)

See also **Weeks**

Homophobia

'Homophobia' was once much used to describe the aversion to lesbians and gays – indeed, to the very idea of **homosexuality** – exhibited by a number of heterosexual people. Although it has now by and large been replaced by '**heterosexism**', the term did have its specific uses and meanings. The 'phobia' component, indicating an extreme and abnormal fear, stressed the *illogicality* of hating gayness, implying that the condition was neurotic. More specifically, many who used it did so in the belief that people who were frightened by homosexuality were frightened, most, by their own repressed attraction to members of the same sex. The US feminist Audre **Lorde** defined the term as follows: 'The fear of feelings of love for members of one's own sex and therefore the hatred of those feelings in others.'   *HG*

See also **Heterosexuality; Misogyny; Repression**

Homosexuality, Female

See Lesbianism

Homosexuality, Male

Homosexual simply means having a sexual propensity for one's own sex, but recently many women have wanted to disavow a category that lumped them in with men and have adopted the word 'lesbian'.

Homosexual activity and desire have probably existed in all human societies – and among many species of animal as well – but they take a variety of social forms and have different social meanings in different cultures. Homosexual relations are not always taboo. The pattern of relations between men and youths in classical Greece (pederasty) is probably the best known institutionalized form. But there are many cultures, especially in parts of New Guinea and island Melanesia, where homosexual activity with an older man is an essential part of male puberty rites. There are others, notably cultures of native North American peoples, where there is institutionalized **cross-dressing** through which a boy can become initiated as what anthropologists call a 'berdache' and live his life as a woman, including marrying a man.

In Judeo-Christian cultures homosexuality is disapproved of, and acts like sodomy (anal intercourse), especially between two men, have often been severely punished. An institutionalized but stigmatized form has arisen only over the last 300 years, with some men defined as 'homosexuals' (which incidentally makes the rest 'heterosexuals') and thought to be a different kind of person, often sick or perverted, and living a whole life organized around their sexuality. But in fact, in modern western societies – and, increasingly, worldwide – probably forty per cent of men have had some homosexual experience, most commonly manual or oral-genital contact. A much smaller group, probably five per cent of men, have mainly homosexual

contacts. Most of these men have a homosexual identity and lifestyle, in the sense that they organize their domestic and social lives around their homosexual relationships. Over the past three hundred years a lively subculture has developed. At first it was marked by effeminacy and cross-class relationships. At some time in the twentieth century it adopted the circus argot 'parlaree' and extended it in a specifically **camp** direction, defining the rest of the world as 'straight'. Since about 1970 the subculture has become much larger and more varied: there are gay newspapers and magazines, gay theater, gay arts, gay businesses and a specifically gay political voice, though this is not nearly as well organized elsewhere as in the USA. Many homosexuals now live in settled partnerships but, in the general subculture, compulsory **monogamy** is less respected and one-night stands and more casual encounters are common.

A reasoned defense of homosexuality began to be made in the second half of the nineteenth century by writers like Karl Heinrich Ulrichs in Germany and Edward **Carpenter** in England. In the early twentieth century, under the leadership of Magnus **Hirschfeld**, Berlin became the center of efforts to abolish anti-homosexual laws, but under the Nazis some hundreds of thousands of homosexuals were sent to the concentration camps, where they wore a pink triangle on their uniform. After the war, the defense of homosexuality by the homophile movement in the English-speaking world usually took the form of claiming that homosexuals were manly, monogamous, moral and respectable, differing only in their sexual orientation: which might be immature and unfortunate, but was beyond their control. In England and Wales the law was finally reformed in 1967 to permit homosexual acts between consenting men in private, providing they are both over twenty-one.

The **Gay Liberation** movement has taken a more critical stance towards the family and towards sexual repression. It has encouraged many men to 'come out' as openly gay and 'gay pride' has displaced both camp self-mockery and the apologetics of the homophile movement. This has enabled the gay male community to deal very positively with the impact of **AIDS** since its appearance in the 1980s.

MM

Jack Babuscio *We Speak For Ourselves* (London: SPCK, 1976)

See also **Anger; Core; Ellis; Fassbinder; Foucault; Genet; Isherwood; Jarman; Lesbianism; Maupin; Orton; Paedophilia; Prostitution, Male; Vidal; Weeks; Wilde**

Homosexuality in Renaissance England

In *Homosexuality in Renaissance England* (1982) the British writer Alan Bray argues that until the end of the seventeenth century male homosexual behavior occurred within the existing patterns of social life: in schools, the military, the church, the relations of master and servant. The prevailing image of the sodomite was one of wide-ranging debauchery, the man with his mistress on one arm and his catamite, or kept boy, on the other. A great shift took place, however, at the turn of the century, when **homosexuality** developed its own distinctive social forms and institutions. Gathering places in London were known as 'molly houses' and those who frequented them were characterized by their persecutors as effeminate and as 'woman-haters'. There was a series of pogroms, instigated by the Societies for the Reformation of Manners, involving raids, trials and hangings in 1699, 1707 and 1725-1726. Bray's work confirms the now established view among historians of male homosexuality that the homosexual as a distinct kind of personal identity, and a developed homosexual subculture, are not universal but have developed relatively recently. However Bray disagrees with Jeffrey **Weeks** and Michel **Foucault**, both of whom place the major change at the end of the nineteenth century. *MM*

Homosexuality in Renaissance England (London: Gay Men's Press, 1982)

Randolph Trumbach 'Sodomitical Subcultures, Sodomitical Roles, and the Gender Revolution of the Eighteenth Century: The Recent Historiography' in ed. Robert Perks Maccubbin *'Tis Nature's Fault: Unauthorized Sexuality During the Enlightenment* (Cambridge: Cambridge University Press, 1987)

See also **Heterosexism; Homophobia**

Honor

Honor is a matter both of personal virtue and public reputation. In both respects, the term has historically been – and over much of the world remains – sharply differentiated by gender. Moreover, evolution of the term has opened a gap between the regions of northern Europe and North America and those of southern Europe, Latin America, the Middle East and Asia. In the former, while it is still quite common and considered appropriate to speak of national honor, references to personal honor (as distinct from the broader concept of ethics) seem outdated. In the latter regions, in addition to national or community honor, it is still common to attempt to protect and fight for personal status according to a recognized code of procedure.

According to the moral division of labor that characterizes the classical code of honor, that of a man is the more broadly delineated. It includes the honor of his lineage and immediate family, as well as that due to his own achievements and attributes: especially, in the last resort, his courage, defined as the willingness to kill or be killed. By contrast, the honor of a woman consists almost entirely of a reputation for sexual propriety. Hence, somewhat confusingly, it is also known as 'shame', since prudent sexual behavior mimics bashful or shamefaced conduct. However, it does not simply comprise correct sexual behavior, but also having that behavior under appropriate male control. What makes life particularly restrictive for women in 'honor' societies is that their conduct and reputation reflect not just upon themselves but on all members of their family. Furthermore, every aspect of female behavior is considered to imply sexual propensities.

Thus drinking, or argumentativeness, or assertiveness in general are considered signs of sexual disrepute.

Taken to extremes – as they are, for example, in some Christian and Muslim societies in the Mediterranean region – considerations of honor require women to live in seclusion, have no contact with unrelated men, take no part in public life and remain under the perpetual guardianship of males. This not only makes them obvious targets for men seeking to discredit other men; it encourages and almost requires men to avenge any true or rumored infraction of sexual propriety in any related woman (wife, daughter, sister, mother) by killing the man involved; or, more frequently, the woman (and sometimes both). In northern Europe this same code of honor was pervasive during the Renaissance and traces of it can be found in quite recent northern-European literature. For example, in Jane Austen's *Pride and Prejudice* it is assumed that the reader will grasp that the impropriety of which Darcy accuses Elizabeth's father lies in his having exposed his wife and daughters to public ridicule. And, more recently still, the tragedy and pathos of John Le Carré's superspy Smiley derives from the *known* infidelity of his wife.   *DSt*

See also **Chastity; Christianity; Islam; Saadawi**

Horney, Karen (1885-1952)

Trained as a doctor in Freiburg, Karen Horney became a psychoanalyst, practicing in Berlin until 1932 and, for the last twenty years of her life, in the USA. She herself lived with a certain freedom from sexual conventionality, having affairs before, during and after her marriage and publishing a paper, in 1927, on 'The Problem of the Monogamous Ideal'.

During Horney's training analysis, she wrote in her diary about the shamefulness of getting the greatest pleasure from clitoral stimulation, according to Sigmund **Freud** an immature pleasure. But later, in the 'The Flight from Womanhood' (1926),

she said: 'I do not see why, in spite of its past evolution, it should not be conceded that the clitoris legitimately belongs to and forms an integral part of the female genital apparatus.' This paper was one of a series on female psychology which Horney wrote between 1922 and 1935, bringing her into more and more open disagreement with Freud. She pointed out the social conditions of inequality under which analytic theories of female sexuality were being developed, primarily by men.

Like Wilhelm **Reich** and Ernest Jones, Horney believed that girls experience themselves as fully female from the beginning: that is to say, vaginal sensation exists from infancy and, while a girl is well aware of the uses of her **clitoris** in **masturbation** (her own discovery, not an imitation masculine activity), she is also conscious of her vagina. The curiosity that small girls feel about penises is as much to do with desire as with envy and, where there is envy, it is conscious, natural and reasonable, since penises are very handy, satisfactorily visible and allow you to pee standing up. Boys and men, in Horney's view, experience an equivalent envy of the womb. Girls, in other words, do not have a fantasy of having been castrated. In so far as Horney made use of the idea of the castration complex, it was as a 'flight from womanhood', an attempt to identify with father as a result of father's 'rejection' of his daughter's seduction in the Oedipal period.

After Horney's move to America, where she became involved in the splitting into different factions of the psychoanalytic movement, she wrote more about the process of **psychoanalysis** in general than about sexuality in particular and increasingly emphasized cultural and social influences rather than biological ones. Feminist writers such as Adrienne **Rich** have stressed her achievement in redressing the bias towards masculinity with a due appreciation of what is essentially and enviably female. Others find her emphasis on a biologically determined difference in sexuality to be limiting, especially in her early writings, and ultimately untrue to the complexity of sexual experience, including our bisexual potential.   *GW*

H

Ten of Karen Horney's papers on sexuality are published in *Feminine Psychology*, ed. Harold Kelman (New York: Norton, 1966)

Susan Quinn *A Mind of her Own: A Life of Karen Horney* (New York: Summit Books, 1987; London: Macmillan, 1988)

See also **Koedt; Monogamy; Penis Envy**

Horror Fiction

See **Fantasy Fiction**

Hui, Ann (1947-)

Probably the most prolific Chinese woman filmmaker, and one of Hong Kong's top 'New Wave' directors, Ann Hui studied at the London Film School for two years before returning to Hong Kong in 1975. There she assisted in feature-film production and worked at the TVB television station before her directorial debut with the gripping thriller *The Secret* (1979). Her second feature *The Spooky Bunch* (1980) was a hilarious ghost-comedy, further distinguished by its female-led production team. *Boat People* (1982), a work sympathetic to the plight of Vietnamese refugees, gained her international fame.

Hui's films have ranged from comedy to thriller to kung-fu flick but, as a politically-attuned filmmaker, she has cast her female characters in a consistently interesting and individualistic light. Her most intellectual effort has been *Love in a Fallen City* (1984), which she adapted from a novel by the popular writer Eileen Chang. This nearly anti-romantic love story is set on the eve of the Second World War and the disintegration of traditional China and it opens with a scene from a Peking opera where a man and a woman mime a coy courtship. Meanwhile, living in the claustrophobic household of relatives who begrudge supporting her, a young Shanghai divorcée named Liu-su (Cora Miao) goes to Hong Kong with a family friend. There she becomes the unlikely object of desire of a wealthy playboy named Fan (Chow Yunfatt) whose attentions alternately attract and frighten her. For a month he courts her and their dialogues, about love, relationships and marriage, reveal much about the roles and expectations of the sexes. The sophisticated Fan appears to see clearly through the dishonesty of traditional sexual roles and believes that perhaps Liu-su can, too.

But are the lofty sentiments a disguise? Is Fan interested only in sexual conquest? Liu-su, a pragmatic Chinese woman with little to bargain with, wants a marriage proposal before any discussion about her feelings. Fan finally bursts out: 'I won't be so stupid as to spend money on marrying someone who doesn't love me. That wouldn't be fair. That wouldn't be fair to you either. But maybe you think marriage is just a form of long-term prostitution.' Liu-su, insulted, returns to Shanghai in a huff – where she finds herself in disgrace for allegedly having 'given in' to Fan. Three months later, a telegram from Fan brings Liu-su back to Hong Kong and here the couple begin an affair in earnest, living through the Japanese invasion of Hong Kong and working together to reconstruct their bombed home. Finally, they are ready to have a modern marriage of honesty and sharing and to dispense with the stifling play-acting of the past.

Hui's ninth and latest film, *Song of the Exile* (1990), is about the wrenching adjustments that a Japanese woman married to a Chinese man must make in post-war China. *SC*

See also **Kwan; Lie Nu Tradition; Yu Luojin**

Hurston, Zora Neale (1891-1960)

An anthropologist and writer, Zora Neale Hurston was born in the all-black, incorporated town of Eatonville, Florida. In a place without racism, her early years were filled with a positive sense of self and a nurturing sense of community. These transferred themselves to all her written work: fiction, folklore, theater and autobiography.

Black heroines before Hurston's time were

often 'tragic mulattas'. There were exceptions, such as Frances E.W. Harper's *Iola Leroy* and the heroine of Pauline Hopkins's *Contending Forces*, yet these novels treated their heroines as if they had no sexuality at all. Concerned with 'uplifting' the race, their authors tried to make their heroines 'pure', both fighting and following the traditions of nineteenth-century, white, southern literature, which declared that no woman of African blood, even the merest hint of it, *could* be pure. Slavery's children must expect a life of tragedy.

The heroine of Hurston's ground-breaking second novel, *Their Eyes Were Watching God* (1937), is far from tragic. In Janie Crawford, Hurston gave the black woman back to herself. Janie was the first African-American heroine to exercise sexual choice and gain selfhood. Disbelieving her grandmother's assessment of the black American woman – 'De nigger woman is de mule uh de world so fur as Ah can see' – Janie defies tradition, prescribed roles and male authority. Janie's grandmother is an ex-slave, which explains her vision of the world and the black woman's place in it, but Hurston's vision of African-American women was one of strength, defiance and power. Janie, unable to sustain her first, 'arranged' marriage to an older, propertied man, runs off with big-talking, ambitious Joe Starks, who becomes a mayor and requires silence and subservience of his wife. After Starks's death, Janie meets Teacake, the love of her life. The portrayal of their free and equal relationship was to alter the depiction of African-American women in literature. Hurston's strong female characters can also be witnessed in some of her short stories collected in *Spunk*.

Hurston's work in anthropology was also ground-breaking, in that she was the first African-American to investigate and record the traditions of her own people. In her second book of folklore, *Tell My Horse* (1938), she searches for truth in the voodoo practices of Haiti and Jamaica. In the middle of a voodoo ceremony, the question was asked: 'What is the truth?' And Hurston saw a Mambo priestess throw back her veil and reveal her vagina. She concluded: 'The ceremony means that this is

infinite, the ultimate truth. There is no mystery beyond the mysterious source of life.'

Hurston was a black voice among whites and a female voice among males. She was an extraordinary woman, ahead of her time. During the Harlem Renaissance of the 1920s and 1930s she was 'queen of the niggerati', yet she died poor and unknown. Twenty years later, the novelist Alice **Walker** had a headstone inscribed and placed near the site of her burial. It reads, 'Zora Neale Hurston: Genius of the South.'   *SRu*

Their Eyes Were Watching God (Illinois: University of Illinois Press, 1978; London: Virago, 1986); *Dust Tracks on a Road* (Illinois: University of Illinois Press, 1984; London: Virago, 1986; *I Love Myself When I Am Laughing, & Then Again When I Am Looking Mean: A Zora Neale Hurston Reader*, ed. Alice Walker (New York: Feminist Press, 1979); *Spunk* (Berkeley: Turtle Island, 1985: London: Camden Press, 1987)

Sandi Russell *Render Me My Song: African-American Women Writers from Slavery to the Present* (London: Pandora Press, 1989)

See also **Angelou; Lorde; Parker; Shockley**

Incest

Narrowly defined, incest is any sexual relation between family members. However, in the last twenty years, feminist theorists and activists have broadened our understanding of the term to include both physical and emotional incest and to place the act within the patriarchal context in which we live. For although some cases of incest involve either mothers or mother figures – and sometimes, too, both heterosexual and same-sex sibling incest can occur – the overwhelming majority of incest cases involve male adults and female children. Given the rights assumed by men within **patriarchy**, incest is essentially part of the submission expected of women within the system.

Where researchers once spoke about the taboo against incest itself, feminists have proven that the taboo is actually against speaking about the act. It is not possible to have something that happens to one in three girls (and probably one in eight boys) qualify as a cultural taboo. A central tenet within taboos is that almost no one ever practices them because of the extreme sanctions attached to them by a society. The sexual molestation and emotional appropriation of children by their parents or 'fathers' is part of the tacit power accruing to men within societies which say that men command the services of the various women within their households.

Incest is separate from, though related to, **child sexual abuse** because of the unique nature of the relationship between abuser and abused. Children love their parents very much and wish, if at all possible, to please them. This means that they will do many things at their parents' request that might well be resisted were they to be asked of them by a stranger. Children in a family are totally dependent upon their parents until they are mature enough to support themselves. To betray and violate that trust and special intimacy is to cause a trauma of a magnitude quite different from most others.

Incest robs children of their childhood, forcing upon them a sexual awareness before there is any context for having such feelings. It undermines any sense of safety or support within the family and home and fragments the child's developing sense of self to such a degree that most survivors require careful therapy in order to become functional adults. Common aftereffects include poor or light sleeping at night, because incest so often occurs at night; wariness about intimacy, since initial relationships were so devastating; body tension causing jumpiness at the slightest noise, because incest victims learn to hold their bodies so tight against the assault. While, of course, repeated occurrences cause increased terror and damage, a single incestuous incident is enough to produce lasting effects on the girl (or boy) to whom it happens. In all cases, physical or emotional, the child experiences a harmful reversal of roles in which she is asked to fill adult functions in order to 'take care of' some inappropriate need of the so-called adult. Incest experiences also teach children to triangulate relationships in later life, since they themselves are drawn into a destructive triangle whether the other parent or adult(s) in their household know of the incest or not.

When distinguishing between physical and emotional incest, most people tie actual penetration and genital contact to physical incest. Emotional incest is rather more difficult to pin down, but can be equally harmful to the victim. Often such incest occurs between a mother and her daughter or son and is characterized by an enmeshment or fusion of the parent with the child. The child is not allowed to have her own feelings or independent life, being told explicitly or by implication that her function is to listen to, care for and entertain the parent who is not able to get such needs met by an appropriate adult. The workings of this complex level of abuse may be seen in a classic novel on the subject: Radclyffe **Hall's** *The Unlit Lamp* (1924). Research into this kind of incest is much scarcer than work on father-daughter cases involving actual physical contact but, whatever the nature of the incest or the duration of its practice, the results are uniform: children stripped of their innocence and sense of safety and playfulness, growing up to be adults frightened of their own bodies and of intimacy with others.

While some cases these days are brought to court, in most instances the accused is not convicted because of certain attitudes towards children in the larger culture. Not really believing their children, cultures counter the pathetic stories of pain and abuse with such shibboleths as, 'Oh, you must be imagining that.' Until this fundamental discounting of children is corrected and until the underlying assumptions within patriarchy are replaced with a theory of families based on equality and mutual dignity, the high incidence of incest will continue.

TM

Toni McNaron and Yarrow Morgan *Voices in the Night: Women Speaking About Incest* (Pittsburgh, Pennsylvania: Cleis Press, 1985) Alice Miller *The Untouched Key: Tracing Childhood Trauma in Creativity and Destructiveness* (New York: Doubleday, 1990; London: Virago, 1990)

See also **Angelou; Kakar; Miller, Alice; Saadawi; Walker; Wharton**

Indian Cinema

Ever since the first Indian feature film was made in 1913, the country has been held in thrall by the big screen. The popular film industry in India is now the largest in the world and over a thousand films a year come out of the thriving studios of Bombay and Madras. Over the years, this ceaseless diet of addictive escapism has become an opiate for the vast numbers of hopeless poor in India; it has also replaced religion as the most potent moral force, both reflecting and dictating social behavior and duty.

Within the seething, tempestuous soap operas that make up the bulk of these films, powerful images of women have been created (mainly by men) which, in simple, dichotomous and coercive ways, determine the shape, size and behavior of Indian women. The options that they offer are straightforward. Good women are pliant, patient, sacrificial, asexual and dutiful mothers who dote upon all around them. Vamps gyrate on nightclub floors, wear tight clothes, have pointed breasts, voluminous hips, drink Black Label whisky, and smoke and come to a sticky end. Type three, the young, carefree college girl, is allowed to prance among the roses and mountains of Kashmir with her loved one – until she gets married and quickly converts to type one.

This is the Indian cinema at its worst and most predictable. The irony is that, in the beginning, and right through to the 1940s, women played more daring and unconventional roles and had more opportunities to display their sensuality and the power of that sensuality over men. Kissing on screen, bathing scenes and erotic dancing were common; the sexuality of women was not curtailed. And, as the industry gathered momentum, confident and passionate actresses like Meena Kumari, Nargis and Madhubala began to grip the nation with their amazing, liberated performances in films which dealt with difficult social issues. *Devdas* confronted the cruelty of forced marriages; in *Andaaz* Nargis played a young woman who was misunderstood and eventually destroyed because people could not accept her deep but platonic friendship with a young, attractive man. Meena Kumari played the sexually frustrated wife of a Nawab who spent his time with whores, and, in an unforgettable performance, enticed her husband to her bed by learning to drink and throwing herself at him. It is also interesting that, in the 1930s, two strong women – Durga Khote and Devika Rani, middle class and respectable – ended up controlling the biggest film studios in India. Nothing like that has happened since; these were stunningly creative times which, in the 1960s and 1970s, were replaced by mostly sterile and empty films: often bad imitations of western cinema, with utterly predictable roles for the heroines especially.

Since the 1980s a few talented young actresses have tried to reverse the trend. Among them, the most outstanding is Shabana Azmi, a beautiful, intelligent actress who has found huge success both in feminist films and in the popular cinema. Together with Smita Patil (who unfortunately died a few years ago during childbirth), Azmi has brought to the Indian screen an intelligent and sexual woman who initially took the country by storm. In films such as *Arth* and *Yeh Nazdikhia* she takes on the role of a wife whose husband is having an affair. In both films, Azmi is shown to have a passionately sexual nature and also the strength to live without her husband once he has abandoned her. Unfortunately, more disturbing trends are also beginning to appear in the Indian cinema. **Rape** scenes – often shown more to titillate than to get the audience to recoil in horror – are becoming more commonplace and younger Indian actresses are beginning to appear in scanty clothing and pulsating roles designed purely for the hungry eyes of Indian men. *YA*

See also **Hinduism; Rape and Revenge Movies**

Tenth century carvings from Lakshana Temple at Khajuraho, India

Indian Sculpture

Indian sculpture is remarkable for its sensual vitality and its interpretation of the erotic. This is perhaps surprising as the context of almost all Indian sculpture, whether in wood, metal or stone, is religious: as narrative friezes on temple walls or as statues for ritual use.

Of course, the sculptors were secular beings who delighted in the use of the female form as a decorative motif but, in the traditional Indian context, female nakedness is *not* a sign of the woman subject's submission to the male observer's gaze. Sexual attraction, a recurrent theme in Indian sculpture, is often depicted as active sexual love between two people, with the actions of each absorbing the other and the woman as active as the man.

The sculptors were also working within the confines of strict iconographical rules. Maithura figures, for example, representations of couples embracing or having **sexual intercourse**, are common decorative features on temples (those on the Konarak temple in Orissa being famous for their explicitness). The most usual explanation for them is that, being carved on the outside of temples, they symbolize a sensual life intended to contrast with the temples' austere and spiritual interiors. A Dampati pair, the representation of a husband and wife, is considered an auspicious motif especially for a temple doorway: openings being thought vulnerable to penetration by evil. Ardhnarisvara is the name given when a male deity, usually Lord Shiva, is represented as having a female half to his body. This symbolizes the essential unity and equilibrium of the male and female principles, both at the level of the human individual and that of the universe. Sculptures of the 'lingam' (divine phallus) and 'yoni' (divine vulva) rank alongside snakes and trees as auspicious symbols of fertility. They also represent the creative energies of deities. The lingam is usually represented as emerging out of the yoni, thus confirming the female as the matrix of all that exists.

The structure of Hindu temples deserves mention for being in itself a metaphor for the feminine as a matrix of creation. Basically, a temple consists of a raised, covered porch with a narrow passage leading to an inner sanctum – the *garbha-griha* or womb house – which shelters sculptural representations of a deity, or deities, or of the lingam and yoni. Essentially, Indian sculpture affirms the sexual mysticism of Hindu thought, particularly in its use of sexual symbolism as a metaphor for cosmic creativity and energy. *KV*

See also **Hinduism; Nude; Tantrism**

Infantile Sexuality

In psychoanalytic terms, infantile sexuality refers to the sexual drives and organization of infancy and childhood, conceived of as different from adult sexuality, while being the precursor of it. Adult sexuality, technically, is under the sway of the genitals; infantile sexuality involves pleasure (and the seeking out of remembered pleasure) at other sites of the body, the 'erotogenic zones', depending on the phase of development: oral; anal; phallic. It is in this sense that Sigmund **Freud**'s work is identified with an 'extension of the sexual': the sexual impulses of infancy are only gradually, and circuitously, brought under the dominance of the genital apparatus. The theoretical significance of Freud's writing on infantile sexuality is the link he made between the nature and manifestations of this early sexuality and the psychoneuroses of later life. Freud's *Three Essays on the Theory of Sexuality* (1905, with additions in 1910, 1915, 1920 and 1924) belongs with his *The Interpretation of Dreams* (1900) and *The Psychopathology of Everyday Life* (1901) as one of the founding documents of **psychoanalysis**. This is not only because it is Freud's key exposition of infantile sexuality, but because of the conceptual new ground it broke in seeing **perversion** as related to the vicissitudes of the sexual drive of all human beings, rather than as a problem of degeneracy or innate weakness in a discrete population. Because infantile sexuality is attached to one or other of the vital bodily functions (eating, excretion); has as yet no sexual object and is thus auto-erotic; is undirected in respect of a single aim (act); and because the infant and child's sense of shame, disgust and morality is as yet undeveloped, infantile sexuality is both 'polymorphous' and disposed to the 'perverse' in relation to 'what is known' (in Freud's words) 'as the normal sexual life of the adult'. Freud was making the assumption that this disposition to perversions was a general and fundamental human characteristic; other influences – environmental, parental, constitutional – interacted with the facts of infantile sexuality to determine the outcome in any one case. His radicalism thus lay in linking normal adult sexual practices with their perverse counterparts and giving them a common infantile origin; and in refuting turn-of-the-century popular opinion about the sexual innocence of childhood.

Freud's theorization of human sexuality is significant in another respect. He regards it as 'diphasic' in onset: that is, the sexuality of the two- to five-year-old gives way, after the **Oedipus Complex**, to the latency period, which is succeeded by the transformations of puberty. (It should also be noted that the matrix for Freud's presentation of the child's sexual development is its long period of dependence on its parents when compared with the sexual maturation of all other species.) Now the pursuit of pleasure comes under the sway of the reproductive function: to this end the component drives submit to the primacy of a single erotogenic zone and are directed to a sexual aim; both sexes now recognize the vagina's existence. Puberty is also a time of psychological transition and *Three Essays* discusses the emergence of new characteristics in girls and boys; while adding, in a famous footnote, that the terms 'masculinity' and 'femininity' remain little understood in science and should rather be thought of as modes of 'activity' and 'passivity' than as biological or social givens.

Freud consciously set himself against conventional morality in publishing *Three Essays*. Anyone who doubts the persuasive force of his argument could sample any passage from that work, which vividly evokes both the nostalgic and the inexorable

quality of desire and the subject's pursuit of pleasure, often at some cost to his or her psychic economy.   *AS*

'Three Essays on the Theory of Sexuality' in *On Sexuality* (Harmondsworth: Penguin, 1977)

See also **Child Sexual Abuse; Paedophilia**

Intercourse

See **Sexual Intercourse**

Irigaray, Luce (1932-   )

Luce Irigaray is a Belgian philosopher and psychoanalyst who first attracted the attention of feminists with her second book *Speculum de l'autre femme/Speculum of the Other Woman* (1974), which offered a critique of Freudian **psychoanalysis** and of western philosophy from **Plato** onwards.

Irigaray's main, and rather startling, point was that 'woman does not (yet) exist'. Western thought, she argued, was monosexual: there was only one sex and that sex was male. More controversially, she described it as hom(m)osexual. Woman was the scene on which representations were staged, the backcloth or the props, the mirror in which western man saw himself reflected. Like her contemporaries Julia **Kristeva** and Hélène Cixous, Irigaray is writing in a post-1968 context dominated by post-structuralist theory in philosophy and psychoanalysis. The erudition of *Speculum*, and the difficulty of its style, presents its readers with enormous problems of interpretation and, as a result, the importance of Irigaray's work is still a matter for lively debate.

In particular, readers have been intrigued by the concept of *parler-femme*/speaking (as) woman, which Irigaray introduced in her third book *Ce Sexe qui n'en est pas un/This Sex Which Is Not One* (1977). It seemed to imply the possibility of a different language stemming directly from woman's body. This impression was confirmed by the short poetic account 'Quand Nos Lèvres Se Parlent'/ 'When Our Lips Speak Together', which many readers took to be a celebration of lesbian sexuality. However, Irigaray's writing, with its preference for allusive and indirect language and a deliberate rejection of the distinction between theory and fiction, lends itself to multiple interpretations, and the meaning of 'speaking (as) woman' is still in dispute.

Since 1977, Irigaray has written another twelve books, of which most are currently being translated from the French. Her preoccupations now focus on the possibility of creating a social and cultural order in which women would be recognized as women: that is to say, as a different sex. She argues for a newly defined **heterosexuality**, which would no longer be a concealed monosexuality but a world in which women would have an identity in their own right, not simply as secondary or derivative beings. In its emphasis on the creation of a new order, her work has an undeniably utopian flavor; nonetheless, its radical critique of the presuppositions of western thought offers a challenge which is still being explored. *MWd*

Speculum de l'autre femme/Speculum of the Other Woman (Paris: Minuit, 1974; Ithaca: Cornell University Press, 1985); *Ce Sexe qui n'en est pas un/This Sex Which Is Not One* (Paris: Minuit, 1977; Ithaca: Cornell University Press, 1985); *Ethique de la différence sexuelle* (Paris: Minuit, 1984; Cornell University Press, 1993); *Parler n'est jamais neutre* (Paris: Minuit, 1985; New York: Athlone Press, 1993); *Sexes et parentés* (Paris: Minuit, 1987; Columbia University Press, 1993; *Le Temps de la différence* (Paris: Livre de poche, 1989; London: Routledge 1993)

Elizabeth Grosz *Sexual Subversions* (Sydney: Allen and Unwin, 1989; London: Unwin Hyman, 1990)

See also **Brossard; Lorde; Stein: Wittig**

Isherwood, Christopher (1904-1986)

A novelist and homosexual activist, Christopher Isherwood was part of the set of left-wing Oxford and Cambridge writers that also included W.H. Auden, Stephen Spender and Edward Upward. With Upward, Isherwood concocted Mortmere, an imaginary sinister landscape which Upward used for social commentary, Isherwood for whimsical imaginings, and both to express the explicit sexual angst of youths who had just heard of Freudianism. After finishing university, Isherwood went to Berlin in search of the sexual fulfillment that Britain's anti-gay laws denied him. In later years, he said of himself, 'For Christopher, Berlin meant boys', but it also meant the discovery of both his subject-matter as a writer and his approach to it. His sense of being outside society because of his sexuality enabled him to write with a certain detachment about sex, decadence and the rise of the Nazis in *Mr Norris Changes Trains* (1935) and *Goodbye to Berlin* (1939). 'I am a camera' was not only the title of the dramatization of the two Berlin novels, but also Isherwood's artistic creed at the time. The novels are *romans à clef*; Isherwood treats his subjects – Gerald Hamilton was Norris and Jean Ross Sally Bowles – as material for artistic treatment as if writing novels were a scientific experiment.

In later life, happy in his relationship with Don Bachardy and a convert to a variety of Californian religions, Isherwood looked back on his youth with a certain amount of disapproval, expressing an overstated concern that his past slumming with street boys involved an unacknowledged **sadomasochism** that made him inadvertently complicit in Nazism. This has been picked up by feminist writers like Sheila **Jeffreys** as a justification for puritan feminist positions. His late memoir of the Berlin days, *Christopher and His Kind* (1977), is nonetheless a particularly thoughtful account of Weimar **homosexuality**, in particular of the sexual historian Magnus **Hirschfeld**, and complements the early novels.

In old age, Isherwood found himself adopted by the liberated homosexual culture of California, a role he accepted more as a duty than a pleasure and which may have had as much to do with the film musical *Cabaret* (based on the early books) as with the books themselves. *RK*

Mr Norris Changes Trains (London: Methuen, 1987); *Goodbye to Berlin* (London: Mandarin, 1989); *Prater Violet* (New York: Farrar, Straus, 1987; London: Methuen, 1984);

A Single Man (New York: Farrar, Straus, 1986; London: Magnum, 1978); *Christopher and His Kind* (New York: Farrar, Straus, 1986; London: Methuen, 1985)

See also **Gay Liberation; Prostitution, Male**

Islam

Islam is the youngest of the Abrahamic faiths – the other two being **Christianity** and **Judaism** – and its adherents, Muslims, share many fundamental beliefs with Christians and Jews. The teachings of Islam derive from the revelations to the Prophet Muhammed in the early part of the seventh century. Like the other Abrahamic faiths, it is of Middle Eastern origin and to this day the Qur'an, the holy book which contains the guiding principles of Islam, is recited in Arabic.

The Islamic revelations broke new ground by granting rights to women that they would not possess in Britain, for example, until the late nineteenth century: the right to own property; the right of inheritance; the right to divorce. There are many references in the Qur'an and the sayings of the Prophet Muhammed to the status of women and the high esteem in which they should be held. An entire *surah* (chapter) of the Qur'an deals with the rights of women, family life and the mutual obligations of men and women towards each other. Marriage (which is a civil contract, not a sacrament as in Christianity) and family life are highly regarded and **celibacy** condemned; eroticism within marriage is condoned and consummation of marriage a requirement. The pleasure of sexual relations has no negative connotations; rather the opposite, as it prefigures the joys of paradise and is regarded as a divine gift, legitimate within social rules.

This balanced attitude, which forms one part of the Islamic celebration of life on this earth and anticipation of paradise, contrasts with the views of Islam and sexuality which, in conflict with one another, have prevailed in the west.

As Islam spread rapidly through the known world in the seventh century, it seemed threatening to the Christians. Thereafter Muslims were said to be lecherous and sex-crazed and the freedom of the men to marry four wives was caricatured. The requirement to treat all four equally, to seek permission of the first before marrying another and to marry widows for their protection were all overlooked. Overlooked, too, was the prohibition against fornication and **adultery**. In recent times, Muslims have often been accused of repressing women. While this is undoubtedly true of some Muslims in some societies – Islam is no more exempt from cultural accretions and individual interpretations than any other faith – what may seem to be repression is often, in fact, the desire to protect and to honor women. It is worth noting, in passing, that Islamic text and tradition stress the value of education equally for men and women, which is scarcely compatible with repression.

Men and women are equal before God; the Christian concept of woman as temptress, the source of evil, is absent from Islam. The Qur'an says that men and women were 'created of a single soul'. But the different biological functions of men and women mean that they have different functions in society: in western terms, they are not regarded as *socially* equal. To avoid injustice against women, Islam imposes upon men the requirement to deal with women at all times with sympathy and kindness.   SR

Ismai'l R. al Faruqi and Lois Lamya' al Faruqi *The Cultural Atlas of Islam* (New York and London: Macmillan, 1986)

See also **Ba; Burton; Ghazal; Hinduism; Honor;** *Perfumed Garden*; **Romantic Love; Saadawi**

Jacobean Revenge Tragedy

'Carnal, bloody and unnatural acts' is how Horatio, at the end of *Hamlet*, describes the events which have just taken place. Along with Thomas Kyd's *The Spanish Tragedy*, also first performed in 1600, *Hamlet* is one of the best and earliest examples of the Revenge Tragedy, a genre that was to reach its gory height during the Jacobean age.

The death of Queen Elizabeth I in 1603 and the accession to the throne of James I caused a crisis in the English identity and a sense of instability and disillusion that was to be reflected in the drama of the next twenty years. Elizabethan self-confidence gave way to a Jacobean world view which saw the worm in every apple. The Jacobeans were as much in love with death as the Elizabethans had been with life and nowhere was this more clearly reflected in their drama than in the attitudes to sex and sexuality. The easy bawdy of low-life characters in **Shakespeare**'s plays was replaced by a Puritan mentality which saw sensuality as diseased (over two hundred images of disease and corruption are crowded into John Webster's *The White Devil*) and sexual activity as a manifestation of political corruption. In plays such as Cyril Tourneur's *The Revenger's Tragedy* (1607), *The White Devil* (1612) and Thomas Middleton's *Women Beware Women* (1621), the lusts and excesses of courtly life are the heralders of disease and death. It is a world where putrefaction is disguised by perfume, dark deeds by glittering diamonds, and which had its real-life counterpart in the court of King James, where the system of patronage reached heights of corruption unexperienced during Elizabeth's reign and **venereal disease** was endemic among the favorites who surrounded the bisexual king.

Some critics have argued that the elements of sex and scandal, intrigue and violence that characterize Jacobean drama make it a decadent form. This is to mistake what the playwright depicts for the playwright's vision. There is a strong element of satire in the dramas, and they increasingly reflect the growing Puritan movement which despised the excesses of the monarchy. In Webster's *The Duchess of Malfi* (1613) the Duchess is a shining example of dignity and purity in a corrupt world dominated by her brothers, the lecherous and murderous Cardinal and the lycanthropy-struck Duke Ferdinand who harbors incestuous feelings for his sister. Most importantly, although the Duchess breaks the family code of **honor** by marrying

secretly and beneath her, this match for love rather than for dynastic alliance, money or property was an idea that was becoming increasingly important in Puritan thought. **Chastity** was highly valued, but **Puritanism** also offered more equality for women through the idea of a wife as a helpmate for her husband, bound not just by duty but by mutual affection. As the critic Margot Heineman has pointed out, tragedy occurs in *Women Beware Women* and Thomas Middleton and William Rowley's *The Changeling* because young women are treated as chattels, to be disposed of as fathers and guardians think fit. She writes: 'What is new in these plays is not so much the sexual situations as the ability of women to reflect on them in general terms, and the natural way in which exploitation by men is shown as contributing to aggressiveness and deceit by women.'

What is even more interesting is the ability of the playwrights of the period to present leading female characters such as Vittoria in *The White Devil* and Livia in *Women Beware Women* as multi-faceted and complex, capable of good and evil in contrast to the idealized heroines of Shakespeare's times. For the first time in the history of English theater these women are driven by lusts, desires and sexual jealousies which hitherto had been solely the provenance of male characters on stage.   *LG*

See also **Barker; Romantic Love**

Jarman, Derek (1942-   )

The British filmmaker and painter Derek Jarman began his career as a theater designer, working for the Royal Ballet and the London Coliseum before being invited by the controversial director Ken Russell to design *The Devils* (1970). A friend's Super-8 camera introduced him to filmmaking and he has continued to make personal, intimate films in this format, alongside and occasionally incorporated into his more public work.

Jarman achieved instant notoriety with his first feature, *Sebastiane* (1976) co-directed with Paul Humfress, which contained many of the elements that have kept him at constant odds with the British film establishment and the more conservative strands of British society. Based on the martyrdom of St Sebastian, the film is suffused with homoerotic desire, displayed in sensual, painterly visual images. The idiosyncratic use of Latin dialogue reveals Jarman's indifference to commercial considerations, his adventurous sense of humor and love of anarchronism (exploited in the subtitles) and his defiant disregard for the anti-intellectual stance of most cinema. The film was greeted with predictable moral outrage for its combination of gay desire, **sado-masochism** and religious iconography.

Describing *Sebastiane* in the press release as 'perhaps the first film that depicts homosexuality in a completely matter of fact way, such as another film might depict heterosexuality', Jarman added a comment that could equally apply to all his work: 'I did not want to make a moral comment on homosexuality within the film, the film in itself is a statement about our own sexuality.' Firmly independent – his sexuality, his politics and his artistic vision would not allow him to be otherwise – anticensorship and an outspoken critic of the British film industry and state, Jarman makes a strong argument for the existence of a discernible 'gay sensibility', located not just in the portrayal of men together but also in a sympathy for the outsider, a certain **camp** humor and delight in the incongruous, and in an empathy with the work of other gay artists: the paintings of the Italian Caravaggio, whom Jarman portrayed in the film of that name in 1986; the music of Benjamin Britten, visualized in *War Requiem* (1989); **Shakespeare**'s sonnets, used as the soundtrack for an elegiac celebration of male beauty, *The Angelic Conversation* (1985).

Jarman has been making pop videos since 1983 and, in 1989, collaborated on the Pet Shop Boys' concert tour. Of his many exhibitions of paintings and assemblages, the most recent, in 1992, was a show entitled 'Queer' at the Manchester City Art Gallery. Also in 1992 Jarman published the latest of his autobiographical writings, *At Your Own Risk*, continuing the collage of personal memories, reflections and discursions on life and art begun in *A Dancing Ledge* (1984) but now enthused with the additional perspective of Jarman's HIV-positive status.

In an interview in London's *What's On* magazine (27 April 1988) Jarman deliberately echoed the wording of the repressive anti-gay legislation known as 'Clause 28' just passed by the British Parliament: 'I made all my films, I say now, with the intention to "promote homosexuality", because why else?'   *PA*

Sebastiane (1976); *Jubilee* (1978); *The Angelic Conversation* (1985); *Caravaggio* (1986); *War Requiem* (1989); *The Garden* (1990); *Edward II* (1991); *Wittgenstein* (1993)

A Dancing Ledge (London: Quartet, 1984); *At Your Own Risk* (London: Hutchinson, 1992)

See also **AIDS; Core; Gay Liberation; Homosexuality**

Jeffreys, Sheila

Sheila Jeffreys is the best known exponent of revolutionary feminism, a political tendency which originated in the British women's liberation movement in the late 1970s. She is a writer and historian whose principal focus of attention has been on the history of women's resistance to sexual subordination. She was a founder member of **Women Against Violence Against Women** (WAVAW) and the Lesbian Archive.

Jeffreys's first book, *The Spinster and Her Enemies: Feminism and Sexuality 1880-1930*, published in 1985, examines feminist involvement in the Social Purity movement at the turn of the century. She argues that the women involved were in the process of developing a critique of male sexual abuse of women and children which included a call for feminists to abstain from sex with men. They were, she claims, politically defeated by the ascendency of **sexology** and the birth-control movement, both of which attacked spinsterhood and sought to recruit women back into **heterosexuality**. In this book Jeffreys warns feminists of the dangers, past and present, which she believes sexual libertarianism poses to feminist goals.

The idea that political ideologies which link women's freedom with sexual freedom are antithetical to women's liberation is further developed in Jeffreys's second major work, *Anticlimax: A Revolutionary Feminist Perspective on the Sexual Revolution* (1990). Here, her central concern is with the **sexual revolution** of the 1960s. She argues that its hidden agenda was to teach women to eroticize and enjoy their own subordination within heterosexual sex. Jeffreys contends that heterosexuality is the root of women's oppression and therefore incompatible with feminist struggle. The second book is also a critique of recent developments in the women's movement: the cross-fertilization between gay and lesbian culture which, Jeffreys believes, has lead to the proliferation of role-playing, **sadomasochism** and lesbian **pornography** in the lesbian community. Jeffreys's ultimate conclusion is that women's liberation will never be achieved if we cannot destroy the link between sex and power which underpins 'heteropatriarchy'.

Jeffreys's writings are highly controversial, as is her public persona. Critics feel that her demagogic style reproduces the worst aspects of leadership cults; it encourages followers rather than peers. Fellow historians have criticized her for continually steering her readers towards revolutionary feminist conclusions. The socialist feminist Margaret Hunt took issue with Jeffreys's work in *Feminist Review* (no. 34, Spring 1990), accusing her of avoiding any source material which would complicate her analysis and, therefore, glossing over the class-bound attitudes and biological determinism of some of her nineteenth-century heroines. Hunt, in common with many of Jeffreys's critics, does not accept an analysis which identifies heterosexuality as the fundamental site of women's oppression. Jeffreys's opponents feel that her work refuses to see women as sexual subjects as well as sexual victims, or to address aspects of women's oppression which do not relate to sexuality. She is also widely criticized for failing to acknowledge the ways in which race and class structure women's experience.

There is much that is vital, courageous and interesting in Jeffreys's work. She reminds us of the need for feminists to struggle against enforced heterosexuality and men's continued violence to women and children. Yet her assumption that a revolutionary feminist analysis and strategy springs naturally from this struggle will always be contested by the majority of feminists. *JE*

The Spinster and Her Enemies: Feminism and Sexuality 1880-1930 (London: Pandora Press, 1985); *Anticlimax: A Revolutionary Feminist Perspective on the Sexual Revolution* (New York: New York University Press 1990; London: Women's Press, 1993)

L. Coveney et al. *The Sexuality Papers: Male Sexuality and the Social Control of Women* (London: Hutchinson, 1984)

See also **Butler; Compulsory Heterosexuality; Contraception; Political Lesbianism**

Jin Ping Mei

Set in the household of a corrupt government official, *Jin Ping Mei* – translated as *The Golden Lotus* in 1939 by Clement Egerton – is an anonymous sixteenth century Chinese novel which explores the relationship between sex and power. It is remarkably naturalistic, with many examples of subtle characterization, particularly of women.

Sex in *Jin Ping Mei* often ends in death, rarely in life. Despite Ximen Qing's countless couplings with many different women (six wives, servants, prostitutes, various others), only two children are conceived. This is just one of the approaches the author uses to illustrate how Ximen Qing's immorality threatens harmonious family life and, ultimately, order in the Chinese empire. The sex scenes are sometimes pornographic, sometimes tender, sometimes ridiculous, but for the most part they are tedious: the desperation of the characters to secure or improve their status robs sex of any passion, emotional involvement or joy. Though the novel often shocks, this is mostly due to the reader's discomfort in witnessing human beings humiliate each other and degrade themselves.

Ximen Qing also has occasional liaisons with young male servants. This is disapproved of, but no more than his excesses with women: in China there was not then the prejudice against **homosexuality** that is traditional in western culture. It is regarded simply as further evidence of Ximen Qing's libidinous nature, which leads him to shirk his responsibility to his household and the government. Halfway through the novel, Ximen Qing obtains supplies of a powerful aphrodisiac which eventually brings about his downfall: its use encourages even greater sexual excess, further neglect of his duties and his early, horrific death during **sexual intercourse** with one of his wives.

With the exception of Ximen Qing's chief wife, the female characters in the novel are all, according to Confucian morality, flawed. And although it is made clear that, while women can lead men astray, it is men who must be held responsible, this is less enlightened than it might appear: women are thought to be incapable of exercising responsibility. In spite of this, and although the author follows convention in not trusting female desires, women's feelings are dealt with sensitively; the writer is apparently aware of the pain and frustration of the Chinese woman's lot. Certainly *Jin Ping Mei* displays none of the **misogyny** seen in some other Chinese novels – *Shui Hu Zhuan*, for example – from the same period.   *AR*

Jin Ping Mei/The Golden Lotus translated by Clement Egerton (London: Routledge, 1972)

See also **Jacobean Revenge Tragedy; Lie Nu Tradition;** *Rou Putuan*

Jordan, Neil

See Mona Lisa

Judaism

The Jewish interpretation of the story of Adam and Eve is different from the Christian one, in that it is interpreted neither as a 'Fall from Grace' nor as all Eve's fault. Nevertheless it does account for the fact that in human sexual relations, according to the authors of the Book of Genesis: 'your [Eve's and everywoman's] desire shall be for your husband and he shall rule over you.' So Judaism has continued to treat women as inferior to men, and to give them a lower legal status, but it has never demonstrated the sex- and body-denying tradition that **Christianity** developed.

There are those who hold that the traditional Jewish legislation about ritual purity was detrimental to women's interests. A woman was not allowed to have sex with her husband when menstruating, nor for a week afterwards, until she had gone to the ritual bath and become 'pure' again. Some think that this suggests a view of women as sexually dirty, but this is an incorrect reading of the concept of purity. Men were also ritually impure if they had nocturnal emissions, or a discharge from their genitals; touching a corpse rendered one ritually impure, as did various skin diseases. Ritual purity was about the leaking of bodily fluids which were seen as dangerous. The loss of blood was the loss of the life force and it is in this context that the menstrual laws must be seen. They must also be seen alongside a positive delight in sexual matters and an encouragement to have sex on the Sabbath, as well as a woman's having the right to sexual satisfaction from her husband (including, arguably, the right to get the rabbinic court to persuade her husband to divorce her if she was not satisfied sexually) and license being given for most sexual practices, if they gave pleasure, including almost certainly **oral sex.**

Indeed, one medieval Jewish teacher, Rabbi Moses ben Nachman (commonly referred to as Nachmanides), wrote that 'If we were to believe that intercourse is repulsive, then we blaspheme God who made the genitals; hands can write a Sefer Torah [a scroll of the five books of Moses, the Pentateuch] and are then honorable and exalted.

Hands can also perform evil deeds, and are then ugly. Just so the genitals. Whatever use a man makes of them determines whether they are holy or unholy.'

There is more along these lines. Women are supposed to enjoy the sexual act, although on the whole men initiate it. Sex is the greatest joy and, if not performed in an immodest way, is to be a source of endless delight. Nevertheless, Judaism produced its prudery too (though less prevalently than Christianity) and there are modesties in the sexual act and instructions undertaken by the very orthodox that include not looking at the spouse's naked body. But that is by no means the rule, and the delight in matters sexual in traditional Jewish texts, despite an emphasis on fidelity and modesty, is very appealing, as is the surprising but by no means infrequent injunction that the woman's wishes in **sexual intercourse** are to be taken into account and that she is to be wooed.

At the same time, it was considered a blessing to have a wife whose sexual tastes coincided with the man's. The author of the thirteenth-century Sefer Chassidim, the Book of the Pious, argues: 'All these sexual matters must take her wishes and his into consideration. If a man finds a wife whose wishes happen to coincide with his own in these matters, then he has obtained favor of the Lord and God has blessed the deed.'   *JN*

See also **Hinduism; Islam**

Kabuki

The colorful, stylized, traditional theater of Japan, which originated at the start of the Edo period (1603-1868) and developed into a theater of the masses under that repressive feudal regime, Kabuki is still enjoyed by a large audience. Today it is notable for its convention of male actors, *onna-gata*, impersonating all female parts.

Gender crossing, and the transsexual eroticism that goes with it, have been at the core of the Kabuki performance since its inception – although the originator of the tradition was a woman, a priestess called Kuni. In her historic performance of 1603, given in the precincts of Kyoto's Kitano shrine, the strikingly dressed Kuni portrayed a young dandy flirting salaciously with (female) prostitutes in a brothel. The impact was extraordinary. While the puritanical government authorities condemned it as a scandalous and corrupting 'evil', the public, for precisely the same reasons, raved about the performance. It was they who called it *kabuki*, an archaic word meaning 'tilt', which was slang at the time for 'outrageous', 'deviant', 'heretical'. Among Kuni's contemporaries were young militant samurai rebels who made themselves notorious as *kabuki* gangs; the term, with its subversive connotations, encapsulated not only the nature of public reaction to Kuni's performance but also the essence of Kabuki eroticism.

Early literature suggests that Japanese people were once unrestrained and liberal in their pursuit of sexual pleasure, not only in heterosexual but homosexual and bisexual contexts. For many, it seems, living was synonymous with making love. But, at the start of the Edo period, such liberalism came into conflict with the ascetic Confucian moral doctrines with which the new regime tried to take control of the volatile nation. For instance, marriage became mainly a political or economic arrangement (in which women were expected to be ideal wives and mothers, not lovers) and, while brothels were licensed for men's needs, **adultery** by women became an offense punishable by crucifixion. In the context Kuni's defiantly 'outrageous' performance evidently had a political as well as an erotic impact.

Ironically it was the authorities' repeated censure of early Kabuki performances that eventually brought about Kabuki's most eccentric convention, *onna-gata*. Women Kabuki players were banned in 1629 on account of their corrupting eroticism and **prostitution**; then, in 1652, came a ban on boy players on the same grounds. It was thus left to men to impersonate women if the Kabuki tradition was to survive. By the time these players developed the art of *onna-gata* toward the end of the century, the real-life conflict at the inception of Kabuki had been transferred to the stage, where unrestrained pursuit of passion by heroes and heroines invariably collided with their social and moral obligations, hurling them to inevitable destruction. The authorities won, but the art of *onna-gata* survived: a poignant reminder of Kabuki's revolutionary origins.   *AkH*

Ed. James Brandon *Studies in Kabuki* (Honolulu: University of Hawaii Press, 1978)

See also **Comics, Japanese; Cross-dressing; Opera Seria**

Kahlo, Frida (1907-1954)

Frida Kahlo is perhaps the most widely acknowledged Mexican woman painter of this century. Communists have called her work realist; André Breton, in common with many indigenous 'Mexicanists', claimed her as a natural surrealist. It was her husband, the painter and muralist Diego Rivera, who most respected her uniqueness. According to his assistant, 'He always seemed to be somewhat in awe of her work. He never said anything negative. He was constantly amazed at her imagination.'

Kahlo's paintings highlight the work of the Mexican artistic renaissance that began in the 1920s and 1930s. Full of references to indigenous culture in terms of image and color (including the decorated frames), they also divulge much of Kahlo's passionate **sensuality** and **bisexuality**. They show a three-way obsession: with Kahlo's body; with her 'shadow self' (or female lover); with Rivera. It has repeatedly been said that, of Kahlo's many love affairs, the most powerful was with herself; but, while it is true that she painted more self- than subject-portraits, art also worked for her as expiation. A horrific tram accident left her an intermittent invalid and robbed her of her prospects of maternity. Paintings such as 'The Broken Column' and 'Without Hope' (1945) reveal the unhealed wounds of the trauma even at twenty-five years' distance.

Rivera's polygamy and his numbers of illegitimate children served as a reproach and an agony to Kahlo. She painted him 'on her mind': her torturer as well as her lover. Even when their relationship had less of a sexual content, and she took younger male lovers, he remained her obsession and inspiration. While Rivera often appears as Kahlo's child (revealingly enough, in his paintings as well as hers), a more equal match is shown in her double portrait of women called 'Two Nudes in a Forest' (1939). While one adopts the typical 'Frida-with-Diego' pose, embracing her partner with one hand on her shoulder, the reclining woman caresses both the other's leg and her own sex. On one level, the picture represents Kahlo's two selves, id and alter ego, self and doppelganger; on another it connects to a post-Revolutionary obsession with *mestizaje*: the desire to create a mixed nation from pre-Colombian and hispanic roots, shown by having one nude black and the other white, both entwined among the delicately rooted vegetation of a 'virgin' jungle.

Perhaps the most celebratory sexuality in Kahlo's paintings lies in those not of people but of earth and fruits: for example, in the juicy lushness of 'Naturaleza Viva' (1952) or 'Fruits of the Earth' (1938). 'Viva la Vida' (1954), her last painting, shows a brilliantly colored arrangement of water melons cut into teeth, or lilies, one segment of which has the title and Kahlo's name hacked into it: a celebration of natural and creative lives then at their end.   *AmH*

Frida Kahlo Museum (The Blue House), Coyoacan, Mexico City

Oriana Baddeley and Valerie Fraser *Drawing the Line* (London: Verso, 1989)

See also **Belli; Colette; Graham; O'Keeffe; Surrealism**

Kakar, Sudhir (1938-   )

An Ericksonian analyst, Sudhir Kakar has been described as providing the best application of **psychoanalysis** to Indian culture. His clinical and cul-

Frida Kahlo, *My Nurse and I*, 1937

tural studies indicate that genital exploration and stimulation begin at a young age within the extended Hindu family. Myths acknowledging **infantile sexuality** include one about Brahma, the supreme spirit, falling in love with his new-born daughter Sandhya: as a corrective, Brahma curses the love-god Kama, while the daughter performs severe penances until Shiva promises that no creature will feel sexual desire before adolescence. In one ending of the myth the daughter is reborn as Arundhati, so pure that no man but her husband may desire her without being consumed by flames.

In another she returns as the goddess Rati: sexuality incarnate. As a counterpoint, young Indian women are surfeited with models of womanly purity to reinforce them against the sexual temptation on offer within the extended family. The favorite model of chaste womanhood is Sita in the epic poem *The Ramayana*.

Suppressed erotic impulses do not necessarily find release after marriage. Sexual ecstasy is frowned on by in-laws, fearful of being replaced in their son's emotions. Often, marriage is swiftly followed by childbirth and isolation from the husband due to post-partum taboos, leaving the woman sexually unfulfilled. According to Kakar, her erotic charge is transferred to her male infant in ways which, though not 'deliberately seductive or overtly sexual', arouse in him an intensity of feeling which he can only begin to comprehend later, alongside the knowledge that he cannot gratify his mother's desire. His ambivalence about his mother's sexuality and that of other mature women, who are simultaneously capable of great maternal love and 'contaminating sexuality', gives rise to a variety of hideous images: the *vagina dentata*, or 'toothed vagina'; poison-filled wombs; thunder-bolt weapons concealed within the vagina. 'Avoidance behavior' may result, causing women to 'extend a provocative sexual presence to their sons' and thus perpetuate the psycho-sexual pattern.

The Hindu male's sexual anxieties are compounded by religious texts which characterize woman as fire, her lap as fuel, her enticements as smoke. The flames are her vulva, the coals **sexual intercourse** and the sparks sexual pleasure. Gods must offer their 'seed' to this insatiable fire as oblation. Another text proclaims: 'The breast at which he suckled he now squeezes for pleasure. Ecstasy comes from the genitals that bore him. Once his mother, now his wife and now his wife, she will again become a mother.' *SH*

The Inner World (Delhi: Oxford University Press, 1989); *Shamans, Mystics and Doctors* with John M. Ross (Chicago: University of Chicago Press, 1990; Delhi: Oxford University Press, 1982); *Tales of Love, Sex and Danger* (Oxford: Basil Blackwell, 1987; Delhi: Oxford University Press, 1986)

See also **Bedi; Hinduism; Lawrence**

Kama Sutra, The

Long seen in the west as a spicy orgiastic manual, the Kama Sutra is nothing of the sort. Written in the third century AD by the religious and moral scholar Vatsyayana Maharishi (meaning 'The Great Seer'), the book was based on Hindu religious philosophy which recognized that a full human life demanded the development of three different elements: Dharma, the spiritual life; Artha, the social life; and Kama, the sensual life. All three, it was believed, existed in individuals in rudimentary form and had to be extended, developed and enhanced through discipline and education.

Vatsyayana's book concentrates mainly on Kama, but always within the context of Artha, so that the book is a sociological document. It traces in fine and detailed lines the kind of sexual behavior expected in different regions, among different classes and castes. For example, Vatsyayana proclaims: 'A man of low mind who has fallen from his social position and who is much given to travelling, does not deserve to be married; neither does one who has many wives and children, and one who is devoted to sport and gambling and who only comes to his wife when he likes.'

The book is also a celebration of sexual pleasure, male *and* female: something which is astonishing when one considers both the date it was written and the sexual mores of present-day India and Pakistan. As with the frescoes of Ajanta and the temple sculptures of Khajaraho – which contain extraordinary, voluptuous scenes of sensuous pleasure – although the focus of the book is the phallus, the sexual greed, need and power of men, women are seen as sexually active and demanding sexual gratification. 'If a male be long timed, the female loves him the more but if he be short timed, she is dissatisfied with him.' Thus, unlike **Ovid**'s *The Art of Love*, which is written entirely for men as a guide to the seduction and exploitation of women, the Kama Sutra devotes large sections to the sexual pleasure of women. For a book written thousands of years ago there is an extraordinary understanding of women's bodies: there is a graphic description of female emission during sex and an appreciation of the **foreplay** that turns a woman on. 'The man should rub the yoni of the woman with his hand and fingers (as the elephant rubs anything with his trunk) before he engages in congress until it is softened and after that is done he should proceed to put his lingham into her.'

This understanding and enjoyment of guilt-free

sexual pleasure was once unique to **Hinduism** among the world's great religions. Increasingly, however, intolerance – exacerbated by invasions and wars – led to the erosion of positive attitudes towards sexual fulfillment. The arrival of **Islam** with the Moghul invasion helped in this process and, together with British Victorian values, turned female sexuality into something hidden and shameful. Interestingly, the first English translation of parts of the Kama Sutra was made, in 1883, by the hedonistic Richard **Burton**, an orientalist who saw in the east all kinds of hidden, grotesque pleasures denied by tight Victorian Britain. His pornographic interest in the book stamped it with a reputation – maintained by orientalist anthropologists like Bronislaw Malinowski, who also saw the east as a bizarre, intoxicating but uncivilized curiosity – that has persisted to this day. And so it came to pass that a work of great sensitivity and innovation was reduced to a dirty joke. *YA*

Kama Sutra (New York: Berkley Publishing, 1984; London: Hamlyn, 1987)

See also **Indian Sculpture**; *Perfumed Garden*; **Yin and Yang**

Kaplan, Nelly (1934-)

A filmmaker and writer, Nelly Kaplan was among the first, in the late 1960s and 1970s, consciously to turn the tables on conventional cinema by presenting a woman's point of view and challenging received notions of acceptable female behavior: both cinematic and in real life.

Born in Buenos Aires, Kaplan arrived in Paris at the age of twenty. Here she met the celebrated filmmaker Abel Gance, working with him as his assistant over the next ten years, and founder surrealist André Breton, who became a friend and fueled her interest in the subconscious and the world of dreams. In 1961 she began a series of prize-winning short documentaries on art and artists, including one based on the secret diaries and erotic drawings of André Masson, which was heavily censored. She

was also publishing short stories, some erotic, under the pen name Belen.

Kaplan regarded herself as sympathetic to, but not part of, the emerging women's movement, and her films are distinctly different from most new women's cinema of the time in stressing the importance of fantasy as a liberating force and in working within the framework of entertainment films. Her first three features all subvert classic female stereotypes: the village whore who also has resonance as a witch figure; the dumb blonde; the sexually curious adolescent girl. In a world that allows women only to exist as sexual beings for men, her self-assured heroines are strongly in control of their own (**hetero**) **sexuality**, turning sex into a weapon and making it a source of power through the easy manipulation of male desire. Ironically, two of her films were marketed outside France to look like soft porn. Her first feature *La Fiancée du Pirate* (1969) was renamed *Dirty Mary* in Britain and *A Very Curious Girl* in the USA; while her third film *Nea* (1976), based loosely on a novel by Emmanuelle Arsan, became *A Young Emmanuelle*. The films' anarchic humor, hints of magic and female myth-making must have bemused the punters. Kaplan: 'Since the invention of cinema, women have been presented as either losers or housewives, but I like to turn things upside down so that in my films the woman always wins.' *PA*

La Fiancée du Pirate/Dirty Mary/A Very Curious Girl (1969); *Papa Les Petits Bateaux . . .* (1971); *Nea/A Young Emmanuelle* (1976)

Ed. Claire Johnston *Notes on Women's Cinema* (London: Society for Education in Film and Television, 1973)

See also **Akerman; Armstrong; Borden; Export; Gorris; Hui; Ottinger; Seidelman; Surrealism; Zetterling**

Khusrau, Amir (1253-1325)

A substantial body of verse in Khari Boli, an early version of Hindi/Urdu, is attributed to Amir Khusrau of Delhi: a Sufi mystic of Perso-Turkish ancestry and the author of some of India's finest Persian poetry.

poetry.

Khusrau adopted two Hindi verse forms, the doha and the pada. He also developed the practice of writing as a woman in the manner of the Krishna hymns which express love for the rustic god through the voice of the milk-maid Radha, who represents the yearning human soul. Khusrau assumes the identity of a bride to his spiritual guide, Nizamuddin Aulia of Delhi: the pre-marital phase symbolizing the unfulfilled human condition, marriage the achievement of union with the divine. Unlike the average mystic clamoring for union with an invisible God, Khusrau was constantly near Nizamuddin, the intermediary object of his spiritual desire. His female alter-ego therefore celebrates the joys of immanent union. Overwhelmed with passion after first encountering Nizamuddin, she rejoices in the loss of self in her all-consuming ardor.

One of Khusrau's best known verses describes the young woman shedding her identity after first meeting Nizamuddin's glance or 'look': 'I'll give up all for you, O Dyer/ for you've dyed me your own hue/From the presses of your passion you've fed me wine and made me passion-crazed.' The bulk of the poems cast Nizamuddin as the wayward bridegroom who is, nevertheless, 'evergreen' and much beloved, and the heroine talks in rustic terms of using innocent wiles and spells to bind him to her after marriage so that his eyes and thoughts will be for her alone. The erotic marriage-bed fantasy is also described: 'Khusrau all our wedding night I revelled with my love/The body mine, the heart my love's, thus body and heart entwined.'

A popular though unsubstantiated tradition alleges that, when in an ecstatic trance, Khusrau bedecked himself in full bridal regalia including the traditional marriage symbols of green, glass bangles and the streak of red powder in the parting of the hair that indicates total wifely devotion. He is said to have died after writing the following verse: 'The beauty sleeps on her bridal bed, her hair spread over her face/ Let's go Khusrau to our homeland, for night has come to this place.' *SH*

Wahid Mirza *Life and Works of Amir Khusrau* (Calcutta: Baptist Mission Press, 1935)
See also **Ecstasy; Ghazal; Hinduism; Romantic Love**

Kinsey, Alfred (1894-1956)

Alfred Kinsey, like Sigmund **Freud**, has been extremely influential in shaping beliefs about sexuality. *Sexual Behavior in the Human Male*, which he published in 1948 with co-authors Wardell Pomeroy and Clyde Martin, not only became an immediate bestseller but made him a household name. Then five years later came a sequel, *Sexual Behavior in the Human Female*, written with Paul Gebhard.

These 'Kinsey reports' were based on thousands of interviews with (mainly) white, middle-class American women and men. They aimed to describe people's sexual behavior and are particularly important for their documentation of *diversity*. Not only have they stimulated many subsequent studies, but the Institute for Sex Research, which Kinsey founded in 1947, continues to have an international reputation for research into sexual behavior.

Nonetheless, when first unleashed on the postwar USA, Kinsey's findings shocked a great many people: revealing, as they did, that a number of sexual practices generally thought to be rare, such as **masturbation**, **oral sex**, extramarital sex and premarital **sexual intercourse**, were, in fact, quite prevalent. Perhaps the most sensational 'discovery' was that homosexual behavior was far more common than had previously been realized. In the outrage that followed such revelations, Kinsey was accused of being anti-family and amoral, and his work was heavily criticized.

On the basis of his findings, Kinsey suggested that **homosexuality** and **heterosexuality** be considered as part of a seven-point continuum, ranging from exclusive heterosexuality to exclusive homosexuality. **Bisexuality**, in this model, was a statistical averaging of heterosexual and homosexual acts.

Kinsey's decision to define homosexuality in the terms of behavior was an attempt to challenge the popular belief in the 'homosexual personality type' and to create a more tolerant attitude towards homosexuality. But, in his attempt to change public opinion, he ignored the meanings that people give to behavior and the reality of sexual identity.

There is also an ambiguity in Kinsey's writings about the sexual drive. At times he emphasizes its debt to biology. For instance, he believes that the reason men tend to initiate and desire sex more than women is because they have a different brain chemistry, making them more likely to be aroused by erotic (or pornographic) stimuli. Related to this, he also accepts as a biological fact 'the greater submissiveness of the female and the greater aggressiveness of the male'. Feminist writers have criticized Kinsey (and the many other sexologists who share this view) for providing a model of heterosexual sex which legitimizes male violence towards women. At other points in his writing, however, Kinsey stresses the importance of social conditioning. For instance, he rejects the 'born like it' and hormonal explanations of homosexuality (as well as the notion of psychological 'causes') and, instead, suggests that it is primarily social attitudes which limit the possibilities of homosexuality.

Despite his plea for greater tolerance of sexual diversity, and his liberal attitude towards homosexuality, Kinsey reveals a bias towards marital heterosexuality and vaginal intercourse. Nevertheless, by documenting the remarkable variety of sexual behavior, Kinsey's work did undermine the narrow definition of sex as a drive to reproduce. His findings also challenged the validity of social policies, moral beliefs, laws, education and religious systems based on an assumption of (hetero)sexual similarity. *DiR*

Lal Coveney and others *The Sexuality Papers* (London: Hutchinson, 1984) Paul Robinson *The Modernization of Sex* (New York: Cornell University Press, 1989)

See also **Ellis; Hirschfeld; Krafft-Ebing; Masters and Johnson; Sexology**

Klimt, Gustav (1862-1918)

A painter and muralist born in Baumgarten, Austria, Gustav Klimt was one of the innovators of Art Nouveau. His success owes much to his early training as an artist-decorator at the School of Applied Art in Vienna. Mural painting was a flourishing art in his lifetime; his father had been a gold-engraver and his brothers were also artist-decorators. Klimt's work always demonstrates a respect for the wall surface, which frequently creates an interesting tension between the three-dimensionality of his figures and the flatness of their ornaments and surroundings.

Klimt received many public commissions and honors from the state yet, in 1897, he joined the Successionist Movement in Vienna and was its first president. One of the Successionists' aims was to encourage foreign, modernist work to be shown in Vienna and, further, for non-profit-making exhibitions to be sponsored by the state both at home and abroad. There was a strong desire for renewal in relation to the modern world, and to work from a first-hand experience of nature rather than to repeat themes and motifs from classical painting and decorative art. However, for himself, Klimt found the truth in pre-classical matriarchal mythology and symbolism. He seemed to see men (and himself, as a symbol of men) as agents of the female life force. He represented Fate, Justice and Strength all as female, and saw man as totally dependent upon the female will.

These ideas were not entirely foreign to a society which was much disturbed by the 'woman question'. In Klimt's formative years there was a close alliance between the Hapsburg aristocracy and the liberal upper-middle classes, in both of which women had considerable power, especially in esthetic areas of life. There was also an increased demand by women for more personal autonomy and for financial independence. Many men felt this as a threat to their power and masculinity. Many also felt that, should man succumb to the power of woman, he would lose his intellectual strength (depicted in art by many versions of decapitation by

K

Gustav Klimt, *Danaë, c.* 1907

Salome and Judith). Sex and death were closely connected in the minds of many in the nineteenth century, when sexually transmitted diseases were widespread and much feared: a connection foreign to us until the advent of AIDS. Many men believed that the beauty and desirability of women were snares to trap them, if the woman was 'good', into marriage, or into disease and death if she was 'bad'. Klimt, however, seemed to view women and his dependence on them and desire for them as positive. But when every theme for which he was commissioned became an example of his personal philosophy, he began to get into difficulties. In 1896 he was commissioned to paint the ceilings of the new university buildings in Vienna on three subjects: Philosophy, Jurisprudence and Medicine. He depicted Philosophy as a collection of bewildered, naked people arising like smoke from the head of an appraising woman. In Medicine we see the unending cycle of life and death, with only the female form of Hygeia, with her snake, to hint at healing. Jurisprudence is represented by an elderly, defeated-looking male nude, encircled by an octopus. He is being judged by three human women, one asleep, one indifferent and one coldly appraising. Higher up in the picture three supernatural Fates stand in judgement. They seem to have many

male heads at their feet. It is not surprising that these works caused a huge controversy; in no way did they represent how the modern faculties saw themselves.

Klimt's painting of Hope as a pregnant woman, the carrier of the future, was not very well received either, but his most famous painting, 'The Kiss', carries the same message in a more acceptable guise. A man dressed in a most glorious golden robe shelters a woman under its womb-like shape. She too is clothed in symbols of fecundity and plenty. They are isolated on a flower-strewn precipice.

Klimt's many paintings of society women show them as intelligent, powerful and in control of their lives, yet they too are clothed in garments that suggest fecundity. His Beethoven Frieze (1902) has recently been restored and can be seen at the Successionist Museum in Vienna. Although for Klimt the 'femme fatale' was a reality, he did not see sex as an act in itself but as a force of nature, leading to new life.
JM

See also **Munch; Schiele; Tantrism; Zola**

Koedt, Anne

Anne Koedt was a founder of the radical feminist movement in New York City and belonged to a number of the early radical feminist groups: New York Radical Women, The Feminists, New York Radical Feminists. She worked on the radical feminist *Notes From the First Year* and was an editor of *Notes From the Second Year, Notes From the Third Year* and the anthology *Radical Feminism*. In 1968 she wrote the article 'The Myth of the Vaginal Orgasm', one of the first radical feminist critiques of sexuality.

In 'The Myth of the Vaginal Orgasm' Koedt said that the female organ of arousal is the **clitoris**; there is no such thing as a vaginal orgasm, or orgasm by stimulation of the vagina without stimulation of the clitoris. Men have created the idea of the vaginal orgasm because they have orgasms inside the vagina and want to construct the idea of a parallel female response. They have defined women who do not have orgasms in classic, heterosexual intercourse as frigid: a definition which Koedt understood as political, at variance with women's anatomy. She suggested that men make this claim because it bolsters their domination of women, and because they fear that they would be sexually expendable if the vagina were not seen as the organ of women's sexual arousal.

Although critical of classical heterosexual relations, Koedt also criticized early lesbian feminists for suggesting that **lesbianism** was more feminist than **heterosexuality**. In her 1971 article 'Lesbianism and Feminism' she wrote that sex roles, whether acted out by heterosexuals or lesbians, are destructive. She expressed indignation at the idea that a woman had to have sex with other women to prove herself a radical feminist, saying that this suggests that women really *are* defined by those with whom they have sex, rather than their work. She also criticized lesbian feminists for sometimes discounting heterosexual radical feminists' views on subjects other than sex, simply because they are involved with men. *CD*

'The Myth of the Vaginal Orgasm' and 'Lesbianism and Feminism' in *Radical Feminism* ed. Anne Koedt, Ellen Levine and Anita Rapone (New York: Quadrangle Press, 1973)

Alice Echols *Daring to Be Bad: Radical Feminism 1967-1975* (Minnesota: University of Minnesota Press, 1989)

See also **Firestone; Orgasm; Political Lesbianism**

Kollontai, Alexandra (1872-1952)

A leading thinker and activist in the changes that swept through Russia in the early part of the twentieth century, Alexandra Kollontai was frequently attacked for her radical views on sexual love, erotic potential and sexual morality.

Kollontai aroused the wrath of her colleagues in the Bolshevik Party because she refused the dualistic approach to sex and politics, to inner and outer life, embraced by the majority of her male comrades. She advocated that women should be sexually self-determining and made enemies among conservative comrades – women as well as men – who despised her criticisms of the family, of the stultifying effects of conventional monogamous marriage and of women's forced economic dependence upon men. She believed that, in times of revolution, people have a heightened capacity to develop erotic sensitivity and a more developed form of sexual love. She advocated not indifferent promiscuity (as her critics alleged) but a series of monogamous relationships in which the person learns more and more about the complexities of sexual love, eventually being ready for a 'great love', a 'pure' relationship free from petty jealousies and possessiveness: a bond which feeds the erotic and political energy of both partners.

In her own life Kollontai searched for this kind of fulfillment with a man with whom she could be both 'erotic friend' and working comrade. Born into an aristocratic liberal family, at the age of twenty-six she left her husband and son for a life of political action (although she remained close to her son and found the separation hard). Ten years later she took her first lover, the Menshevik economist Petr Maslov. He was married and the affair was clandestine. Shortly after the revolution she married Pavel Dybenko. The difference in their age and class – he was younger than she, a sailor and soldier born of peasants – once again scandalized the Party. Afterwards she would write that her relationships left unmet 'the longing to be understood by a man down to the secret recesses of one's soul'.

During her travels around Europe as a Party worker she read and was influenced by the writings of Havelock **Ellis** and the emerging psychologists. Despite the scorn with which she was met, Kollontai continued to write and speak on love, sexuality and many facets of women's oppression. She was the only woman in Lenin's 1917 government but, by 1918, differences with Lenin forced her out. When Stalin came to power she was effectively sent into political exile: to a series of diplomatic posts in Scandinavia and Mexico. There, she turned to writing fiction. In 1922, in Oslo, she wrote a trilogy, *For the Love of Worker Bees*, as well as a short novel, *A Great Love*, which further explored women's frustrations at trying to find sexual, emotional and spiritual fulfillment in relationships with men while remaining independent and pursuing a political path. *JD*

For the Love of Worker Bees (Chicago: Academy Chicago Publishers, 1978; London: Virago, 1980); *A Great Love* (Salem: Ayer and Co., 1929; London: Virago, 1981); *Alexandra Kollontai: Selected Writings* (New York: Norton, 1980; London: Alison and Busby, 1977)

Cathy Porter *Alexandra Kollontai: A Biography* (London: Virago, 1980)

See also **Goldman; Greer**

Kono, Taeko (1926-   )

The world of the Japanese writer Taeko Kono is overshadowed by death, disease, sterility. Kono's uterus was affected by childhood tuberculosis and at the center of her novels there is often a woman incapable of bearing children. In the story 'Ants Swarm' (1964) a woman learns from a doctor that she is unable to give birth, and engages in an imaginary family life with a little girl – despite the fact that she has never previously desired a child. Indeed, she has taken precautions against conceiving all through her married life. In her imaginary child rearing, she abuses the girl, beating her and mentally torturing her.

The search for a meaning to sex when it is divorced from the possibility of childbirth becomes the preoccupation of many of Kono's protagonists. In such major works as *A Boy Friend* (1965) and *A Revolving Door* (1970) the women indulge in sado-masochistic sex in which they use their lovers' bodies purely for their own pleasure, as if to compensate for the pleasure their uterus has been denied. Kono's protagonists, however, are always positive, and assertive: if they are incapable of giving life and of forming a family in the 'ordinary' way, they still aggressively pursue the experiences of marriage, maternal love and sexual pleasure that 'ordinary' women desire.

In *A Pastoral Year* (1979), a woman, who has been told by her doctor that she must abstain from sex for a year, at first feels relieved to have been awarded this sabbatical. She accepts the occasion not as a forced prohibition, but as a self-chosen rest not only from sex but from sexual feelings. But desire for sex is so strengthened by its absence that she starts to engage in imaginary acts of **sado-masochism** which serve upon men the same injunction against sex that has been served on her.

For Kono, these women for whom sex is forbidden, or who find themselves to be sterile, represent women in general, their sexuality denied free fulfillment in order that it might better serve *men's*. Her fantasy sado-masochistic dramas are attempts by the suppressed to attain an existential sense of life. In her latest novel, *A Mummy Hunting* (1990) the protagonist kills her lover at his request at the height of their sexual pleasure: the ultimate fulfillment in an age when sex is no longer, of itself, the channel to an unknown realm. *NM*

A Boy Friend (1965); *A Revolving Door* (1970); *Blood and Shells* (1975); *A Pastoral Year* (1979); *A Mummy Hunting* (1990)

See also **Nwapa; Oshima**

Koran

See **Islam**

Krafft-Ebing, Richard Freiherr von (1840-1902)

The eldest child of an aristocratic family in Mannheim, Germany, and the grandson of the famous Heidelberg lawyer Mittermaier, Richard von Krafft-Ebing became a psychiatric consultant to the courts of Germany and Austria in his twenties and was frequently called upon as an expert on sex crimes by the courts of other countries. He was appointed Professor of Psychiatry at the University of Strassburg when only twenty-nine and published the catalog of 'psychopathological manifestations of sexual life' that was to secure his reputation in 1886. Although now largely discredited as a medical text, *Psychopathia Sexualis* remained enormously influential well into the 1950s and continued to feature on mail-order lists as a sensational 'tell-it-all' collection of weird-sex tales through the 1970s. For the last ten years of his life Krafft-Ebing held the prestigious Professorship of Psychiatry at the University of Vienna and was widely regarded as a leading authority in the field. Indeed, it was in his capacity as Chair of the Society of Psychiatry and Neurology in Vienna that he was publicly to dismiss Sigmund **Freud**'s 1896 presentation of the childhood seduction theory as 'a scientific fairytale'.

Krafft-Ebing stressed degeneracy as the determining factor in most 'abnormal' sex cases and appears to have found a left-handed aunt, at the very least, in each of the afflicted families he studied. **Masturbation**, as both sign and cause of degeneracy, is also emphasized, and Krafft-Ebing's oft repeated warning that children with a constitutional disposition (or 'hereditary taint' as he was to term it) would be likely to 'sink into dementia, or become subjects of severe degenerative neuroses or psychoses' if their masturbatory activities remained unchecked, has given license to several generations of parents, doctors and educators to police and punish young offenders 'for their own good'. Krafft-Ebing tells, for example, the 'disgusting story' of a little girl who not only taught her innocent sister to masturbate but continued to do so herself even after a white-hot iron had been applied to her **clitoris**. Another, it seems, carried on with the 'vice' even after she was married, with the result that five of her twelve children died early, four were hydrocephalic and two began to masturbate at an early age.

Although the vast majority of Krafft-Ebing's case histories were men (and, in the section on **fetishism**, exclusively so) he makes the point that women, though less likely to appear before the courts and less inclined to seek treatment (his two major sources of information), are equally disposed to sexual aberrations. It should be noted, however, that Krafft-Ebing makes no qualitative distinction between these aberrations: he presents the man who 'tore out the intestines and kidneys *per vaginum* of prostitutes' and the woman who 'soon recognized from the intensity of her love for her girlfriends and her deep longings for their constant society that it meant more than friendship' as simply instances on a continuum. What's more, he demonstrates how apparently innocent kissing can so easily lead to biting and how the playful tussling of young lovers might be the prelude to a foul murder of lust. 'The transition from these atavistic manifestations to the most monstrous acts . . . can be readily traced.'

In 1897 Krafft-Ebing gave his signature to the Scientific Humanitarian Committee's petition to decriminalize male **homosexuality** in Germany and, in 1901, published an article recanting his earlier insistence on homosexuality as a disease, giving credence instead to the theories of congenital anomaly then gaining currency. He also made it clear, however, that this new sympathy was not to be extended to homosexuals who had *acquired* their condition and certainly not to women who might be choosing **lesbianism** as a pleasurable alternative to pregnancy, disease or unwanted **sexual intercourse**.   *LBr*

Psychopathia Sexualis (Chelsea, MI: Scarborough House)

See also **Baker Brown; Ellis; Perversion; Sexology**

Kristeva, Julia (1941-   )

Julia Kristeva, a French psychoanalyst, literary theorist and linguist, brings her various interests together in her focus on the ways in which coherent, meaningful texts (of whatever kind) are constructed and disrupted. She is interested in the unacknowledged debt that texts owe to subjectivity – to the author's and reader's repressed or **unconscious** sexual impulses and drives – and in what it is that a

K

text must borrow and utilize, but leave unrepresented, regarding the author's body and corporeal (pre-)history.

Kristeva distinguishes between two kinds of energy or modes of organization, both of which find their 'corporeal origins' in the years of the child's earliest sexual development. Here Kristeva relies heavily on a Freudian and Lacanian model of sexuality, while making her own modifications to the theory. She calls these two forms of organization 'the semiotic' and 'the symbolic' and they are closely identified with, respectively, pre-oedipal sexuality and its oedipal reorganization. The semiotic is the energy or impetus provided by the pre-oedipal child's sexual drives, drives which are not yet distinct from each other, nor yet distinct from the functioning of the maternal body. This pre-oedipal, maternally dominated stage is considered by Kristeva to be feminine: the text must harness its energies, reorganizing them to form the basis of 'rhythm, intonation, punctuation', a material substratum necessary for any meaningful production but without any meaning itself. If either a meaningful text or a coherent subject is to ensue, the pre-oedipal semiotic requires order, structure, stability, and it is the oedipalized symbolic order which overlays and reorders the semiotic, creating the possibility of hierarchized, rule-abiding, grammatical, lexical and syntactical relations, as well as stable, more-or-less rational individuals capable of making heterosexual and homosexual object choices with suitable, non-incestual love objects.

In the 'normal' and even the neurotic subject, as well as in the coherent text, the semiotic remains subordinated to and in the service of the symbolic. However, in certain 'privileged' moments of social, psychical and discursive life, the semiotic overflows the boundaries of the symbolic, challenging and displacing the limits of coherence and cohesion. These privileged moments occur in the form of 'madness, holiness and poetry': a madness typified by the psychotic dissolution of the ego and stable sexual identities; a holiness exhibited not in pious devotion but in an excessive *jouissance*, a bliss that is clearly sexually gratifying while nevertheless remaining non-

genital; and in a poetry not represented in the canons of poetic greatness but rather in the transgressive literary practices of the avant garde, in whose texts the pleasure of pre-oedipal materiality outweigh the pleasures of oedipal rationality. Ironically, while Kristeva designates this overflowing of the semiotic as feminine, the best representatives – indeed, the only examples she speaks of in, for example, *Desire in Language* (1980) – are men, like Artaud or Beckett, who risk their stable phallic position within the symbolic order, risk their very sanity, in artistic production.   *EG*

La Révolution du langage poétique/Revolution in Poetic Language (Paris: Editions du Seuil, 1974; New York: Columbia University Press, 1984); *Desire in Language: A Semiotic Approach to Literature and Art* (New York: Columbia University Press, 1980; Oxford: Blackwell, 1982); *Pouvoirs de l'horreur/Powers of Horror: An Essay in Abjection* (Paris: Editions du Seuil, 1980; New York: Columbia University Press, 1982); *Histoires d'amour/Tales of Love* (Paris: Denoel, 1983; New York: Columbia University Press, 1987); *Soleil Noir: Dépression et mélancolie/Black Sun: Depression and Melancholia* (Paris: Editions Gallimard, 1987; New York: Columbia University Press, 1989)

Elizabeth Grosz *Sexual Subversions: Three French Feminists* (Sydney, London and Boston: Allen and Unwin/Unwin Hyman, 1989)

See also **Ecstasy; Freud; Horney; Irigaray; Lacan**

Kurosawa, Akira (1910-   )

In the work of the Japanese filmmaker Akira Kurosawa, men are placed in extreme predicaments in which their identity is shaken and, in the face of inner chaos, their dignity tested. In *Ikiru/Doomed* (1952), the protagonist, who learns that he has cancer, tries to find the meaning of life within the short time left to him. The Samurai in *Shichinin no Samurai/The Seven Samurai* (1954) fight a doomed battle for the oppressed peasants against the feudal lord. In *Kagemusha* (1980), a lower Samurai, ordered to mislead the enemy by becoming a dummy lord in place of the real lord, who is dead, is forced to question his identity as a shadow man. In *Ran* (1985), based on the story of **Shakespeare**'s *King Lear*, the identity of the lords and of their subordinate Samurai, of father and son, become confused and upset. Underlying Kurosawa's work is the world of the Samurai, or Bushi, and the philosophy of Bushido. The ultimate test of humanity is to maintain **honor** and dignity as a man.

Between men and women, the division is clear. Although Kurosawa rarely portrays women, in such works as *Rashomon* (1950) and *Ran*, in which women play an integral part, their sexuality is presented as being mysterious and dangerous to men. The sexuality of men, meanwhile, has no ambiguity: masculinity is that which stands against injustice and evil, even at the cost of men's lives. It is women's alluring and maneuvering sexuality which corrupts men or leads them astray from their pursuit of honor. While men's commitment to human dignity preserves hope for humanity, women are condemned for the dishonesty and cunning hidden in their ambiguous and often vicious sexuality. Even when women *are* honest and innocent, their sexuality is powerless, unable either to save men or to restore order to the chaotic world.

NM

Sugata Sanshiro/Sanshiro (1943); *Subarashiki Nichiyobi/One Wonderful Sunday* (1947); *Norainu/Stray Dog* (1949); *Rashomon* (1950); *Hakuchi/The Idiot* (1951); *Ikiru/Doomed* (1952); *Shichinin no Samurai/The Seven Samurai* (1954); *Kumonosu Jo/Throne of Blood* (1957); *Yojimmbo* (1961); *Tsubaki Sanjuro/Sanjuro* (1962); *Tengoku to Jigoku/High and Low* (1963); *Akahige/Red Beard* (1965); *Dodeskaden* (1970); *Dersu Uzala* (1975); *Kagemusha* (1980); *Ran* (1985); *Yume/Dreams* (1990)

Tado Sato *Kurosawa Akira no Sekai/The World of Akira Kurosawa* (Tokio: Asahi Bunko, 1986)

See also **Hemingway**

Kwan, Stanley (1957-   )

One of the most respected of Hong Kong's 'New Wave' film directors, Stanley Kwan treats sensitively both complex human relationships and female characters.

Kwan was apprenticed to director Ann **Hui** before moving on to make his own films, starting with *The Women* in 1985. His third film, *Rouge* (1987), featuring Hong Kong singer Anita Mui, is considered his masterpiece. It is also unusually frank in its depiction of the obsessive nature of erotic passion. In it, Fleur (Mui), a courtesan from the 1930s, returns as a ghost in search of the lover whom she met at a high-class restaurant-cum-brothel where she sang traditional Cantonese songs in male drag. The affair was doomed from the start, notably by the disapproval of the lover's respectable family; trapped in social roles beyond their choosing, the couple could discover freedom only with each other. As the world closed in, they found comfort in each other's arms and in smoking opium, until, in desperation, they agreed to a double suicide in order to join each other again in the hereafter. Fleur, alone, died.

Decades later, Fleur's returning ghost is lost in the bustle of modern Hong Kong. Her determined romanticism is compared to the pragmatic, humdrum relationship of the present-day couple who befriend her. The man's idea of a present to his girlfriend is a dowdy pair of new walking-shoes. The two make love perfunctorily. They take one another for granted. In the end Fleur finds her lover, now a derelict extra on a movie set where, ironically, they are shooting a grade-B ghost movie. By not taking the brave – and foolhardy – path of love, he has condemned himself to a living death. And there Fleur leaves him, returning a gold locket he gave her long ago, and takes her dream of love back to the other world.

Three Women in New York (1989) won Kwan the prize for best film at Taiwan's Golden Horse Awards. It is the story of three Chinese women – one from mainland China, one from Hong Kong, one from Taiwan – who become friends in the inhospitable climate of Manhattan. Taiwan's Sylvia Chang plays an ambitious actress battling racial stereotypes; China's Siqin Gaowa plays a newly-married woman who must learn to assert herself with her Chinese-American husband; Hong Kong's Maggie Cheung plays a successful businesswoman wrestling with conflicting sexual inclinations. In one of the rare Chinese films to deal directly with **homosexuality**, the businesswoman is shown trying desperately to bury a lesbian past. Kwan clearly recognizes the complex nature of sexual identity and is fascinated by female subjects. His next feature is to be based on the life of the legendary 1930s Shanghai actress, Ruan Lingyu, whose suicide at the age of twenty-five left only the cryptic note: 'Rumor kills me'.   *SC*

The Women (1985); *Rouge* (1987); *Three Women in New York* (1989)

See also **Lie Nu Tradition; Romantic Love**

Lacan, Jacques (1901-1981)

Probably the best known and most controversial psychoanalyst since Sigmund **Freud**, the French analyst and theorist Jacques Lacan has initiated what he calls 'a return to Freud', to the letter of Freud's own texts. These, Lacan claims, have been ignored or amended by neo-Freudians and Freudian revisionists, who have, as a consequence, ignored Freud's greatest insights.

As Lacan saw it, Freud's work rested on two cornerstones: the notion of the **unconscious** and the formative role of **infantile sexuality** in the constitution of the adult psyche and sexuality. In his re-reading, Lacan claims that **psychoanalysis** is concerned solely with language: it is only through language that it can gain any access to its objects of investigation and treatment. He claims that 'the unconscious is structured like a language' and that sexuality as such is a drive or a series of drives which are structured not by nature or instinct, but by signification and meaning. The unconscious can no longer be regarded as a seething chaos of sexual impulses seeking expression: rather, it is a very precisely structured and chartable system which, instead of being governed by the logic dictating consciousness, is governed by an entirely different logic. This defines not the movements of reason, but the movement of language: a movement which

induces, indeed requires, metaphors, metonymies, multiple meaning, ambiguities, undecidability. Sexuality too exhibits a logic of desire whose form is regulated by the subject's unconscious preservation of his or her life history, or at least its unconscious meaning for the subject.

Lacan's reconceptualization of the Freudian account of sexuality can be divided into two related components. First, he reinterprets Freud's problematic account of the **Oedipus Complex** and the stages of infantile sexuality in terms of signification rather than biology: the boy's and girl's sexual development is predicated not on the primacy of the biological organ, the penis, as in Freud's account, but on a signifier – indeed, the key signifier of patriarchal power relations, the key term initiating the child into language as a speaking subject – the phallus. The penis can never be identified with the phallus because the phallus is not a *thing* one has (as a boy) or lacks (as a girl); it is a signifier, a part of language that can exist only by circulation: that is, only through the desire of another. For Lacan, then, masculinity is that which (falsely) believes that it *has* the phallus while feminity is that which (falsely) believes that it *is* the phallus. The phallus remains the medium or dimension in which desire is expressed. Instead of seeing the Oedipus Complex in terms of the boy's recognition of the girl's castration, Lacan claims that the Name-of-the-Father (his reformulation of the Oedipus Complex) positions the child of either sex in a relation to the Father's Law, the law of **patriarchy**, in which it must choose to abandon the mother and take up a position of being, or having, the phallus. Incidentally, 'being' and 'having' are the two verbs by which other verbs are modified in both English and French.

Second, Lacan has controversially claimed that 'there is no sexual relation': by which he means that there can be no direct or unmediated relation between the sexes. He even claims that every love relation is always, in fact, a five-way relation, for it always involves a subject, a love-object, the image that the subject has of the object, the image that the object has of the subject, and the Other, the Oedipal Law which regulates sexual exchange. Courtly or chivalric love is in fact a form of male self-love, in which the subject loves his own projection of the beloved. *EG*

Ecrits (Paris: Editions du Seuil, 1966; New York: Norton, 1982; London: Tavistock, 1977); *Le Séminaire, Livre XI: Les quatre concepts fondamentaux de la psychanalyse/The Four Fundamental Concepts of Psychoanalysis* (Paris: Editions du Seuil, 1975; New York: Norton, 1981; London: Tavistock, 1977); *Le Séminaire, Livre XX: Encore* (Paris: Editions du Seuil, 1975)

Elizabeth Grosz *Jacques Lacan: A Feminist Introduction* (London: Routledge, 1990) Ed. J. Mitchell and J. Rose *Feminine Sexuality: Jacques Lacan and the Ecole Freudienne* (London: Macmillan, 1982)

See also **Kristeva; Romantic Love**

Lawrence, David Herbert (1885-1930)

Sexual liberator; phallic supremacist; late-Edwardian pornographer; last real author of the Great English Novel: these are the various popular ways of looking at D.H. Lawrence. Each has a certain validity. Because Lawrence is still widely read in British schools and universities, because his novels continue to reach wide audiences through their film and TV adaptations, because the 1960 trial of *Lady Chatterley's Lover* was such a landmark in the history of British censorship, the figure of Lawrence – ginger-bearded, tubercular, visionary – has passed beyond literary history and into popular myth.

Lawrence's innovations in writing about sexuality are many and bold. In the semi-autobiographical *Sons and Lovers* (1913) he writes with great candor (and much self-pity) about a sensitive young man dominated by his embittered, ambitious mother and so unable properly to connect with the women in his own life. In *The Rainbow* (1915) he chose to write about rootedness and ritual, family ties and sexual adventuring, from the point of view of a young woman. In the apocalyptic *Women in Love* (1920), originally to have been called Dies Irae, or Days of Wrath, the folly of modern men and women is shown to contribute to humanity's corruption. Finally, in *Lady Chatterley's Lover* (1928)

he managed, albeit posthumously, to break the taboo on explicit representations of sexual acts in British and North American literature, giving English literature a book of great libertarian energy and heteroerotic beauty into the bargain.

Lady Chatterley's Lover ends, however, not in multiple **orgasm** but in a celibate partnership which, for its author, 'passed beyond sex'. To call Lawrence a misogynist, as many do, is to understate and oversimplify his views on human sexuality, which are complex and bizarre. Like Sigmund **Freud**, Lawrence understood sexuality as a tangled bundle of primal energies and drives, sometimes healthy and life-affirming, often perverted and destructive. But, where Freud's attitude was basically scientific, Lawrence's was cultic and prophetic. In his mature works he rails against the modern world as corrupted beyond redemption, hopelessly out of touch with the sort of sex that could save it: 'The phallus is a great sacred image; it represents a deep, deep life which has been denied in us and still is denied. Women deny it horribly, with a grinning travesty of sex.' In his great novels, redemption and damnation both are expressed by specific sexual acts, which come to hold sacramental significance. Both *Women in Love* and *Lady Chatterley's Lover*, for example, culminate in acts of (heterosexual) buggery, seen as the point at which the life-force invades, commingles with and so defeats the forces of shame and death.

Lawrence's great achievement and interest lies with how, in successive works, he turned the matter of his own private obsessions into a massive pseudo-philosophical system, an overarching world-historical myth. People and places, whole races and civilizations, parts of the body and areas of the mind come to hold explosive emotional and moral meanings. These are impossible to map out definitively. Sometimes women are seen as the root of worldly evil; sometimes private property, machines, **masturbation**, the solar plexus are. He was not a systematic thinker but a sensualist and a solipsist. His ideas emerge from his writing, not vice versa. This makes it dangerous to come to any final view of Lawrence from any part of his work in

L

isolation. And this is why it is not possible ever to dismiss him as a homophobe or a repressed homosexual, as a simple misogynist or, indeed, as a fascist, although many bits of his writing certainly tend in some or all of these directions.   JT

Sons and Lovers (New York: Bantam, 1985; Harmondsworth: Penguin, 1987); The Rainbow (New York: Bantam, 1991; Harmondsworth: Penguin, 1989); Women in Love (New York and London: Penguin, 1990); Fantasia of the Unconscious and Psychoanalysis of the Unconscious (Harmondsworth: Penguin, 1990); Lady Chatterley's Lover (New York: Bantam, 1983; Harmondsworth: Penguin, 1990); A Propos of Lady Chatterley's Lover (New York: Haskell House, 1973)

Harry T. Moore The Priest of Love (London: Penguin, 1976) Kate Millett Sexual Politics (New York: Ballantine, 1980; London: Virago, 1977)

See also Celibacy; Hemingway; Lessing; Obscenity

Le Guin, Ursula K. (1929-   )

Ursula Le Guin started off as a fairly conventional North American **science fiction** writer, although her interest in anthropology – her parents were eminent figures in that discipline – did mark her out as rare, for the mid-1960s, in her imaginative grasp of other cultures and ways of seeing. It was the intersection of her development as a stylist with her growing concern with feminist and ecological themes which made her one of the dominant figures of the science fiction of the 1970s.

The Left Hand of Darkness (1969) is Le Guin's most important direct consideration of gender, dealing as it does with androgynous humanoid aliens whose physical gender alters according to attraction and circumstance, producing radically (some critics would argue, insufficiently radically) different social institutions. Le Guin responded to one criticism – that the narrator refers to all characters by male pronouns – by writing another story set on the same planet in which everyone is referred to by female pronouns, proving in the event that it is the reader's expectations as much as the author's intentions that matter.

The Dispossessed (1974) sets an anarchist utopia in opposition to a capitalist dystopia, and sets a scientist in anguished dilemma between a society that does not need his work and one which will abuse it. The complicated discourse of ethical checks and balances that Le Guin erects in this novel includes much consideration of sexuality and parenting: Shevek's responsibilities include co-parenting in an extended family, and his disillusion with capitalist Urras is triggered by a scene of sexual embarrassment. More recently Always Coming Home (1985) combines the portrayal of a radically different future society living in harmony with nature with a non-linear mode of narrative which refuses conventional 'story' in favor of songs, descriptions and fragments of legend. Le Guin sees this as an attempt to find a narrative mode that mirrors women's gathering rather than men's hunting. All of her work, particularly her children's books The Earthsea Trilogy, concerns itself with balance and respect, drawing on Native American and Taoist thought. Her feminism and the ecological concerns that interlock with it are aspects of this overall concern.   RK

The Left Hand of Darkness (New York: Ace Books, 1983; London: Futura, 1981); The Dispossessed (New York: Harper Collins, 1991; London: Panther, 1976); Always Coming Home (New York: Bantam, 1987; London: Grafton, 1988)

See also Benedict; Chrystos; Lessing: Mead; Russ

Lesbianism

Lesbianism is a twentieth-century, European term denoting sexual love between women.

Since the emergence of a lesbian feminist community after the **sexual revolution**, much energy and time has been spent trying to define the precise meaning of 'lesbian' and attempting to draw secure boundaries around this alleged species. These debates have not provided an agreed-upon definition for the lesbian community to offer as a replacement for the scientific, sexological definition of lesbianism as a socio-sexual pathology. However they have raised many interesting questions and perhaps the best that can be done is to list some of them.

Is non-sexual love among women a form of lesbianism? Were there lesbians in the Middle Ages, when the concept did not exist? Can non-European cultures which allow certain forms of love and sex between women to be said to contain 'lesbians'? Do women who sometimes sleep with men qualify as lesbians? Do women who don't sleep with anybody but constantly hang around with women qualify as lesbians? Is lesbianism inherently politically progressive? Will lesbianism always exist, or will it wither away once gender roles become insignificant?

Is lesbianism female **homosexuality**, or is it the sexual expression of feminism? Do lesbians therefore belong in the gay movement or in the women's movement? Is lesbian desire more nurturing and less aggressive than heterosexual desire? If so, why is there jealousy among lesbians? Are all women naturally lesbians because of the overwhelming infantile desire for the mother? Is any woman who calls herself a lesbian a lesbian, or is there some kind of test? What about formerly male transsexuals who desire women? What about the love between mothers and daughters, or between sisters? Is there even such a thing as 'lesbian sex' or is the very attempt to fix the content of sexual desire between women suspect?

After many years of sincere, engaged debate on these unanswerable questions, many lesbians now think that it is high time to put the is-she-or-isn't-she framework aside and ask: why do we ask these questions in the first place? Why do we think that it's so important first to decide who is part of our group and then to characterize this group with certain features that will distinguish it from other groups, eliminating all overlap in social life and all ambiguity in discourse? The one thing that comes through loud and clear in all experiential accounts is that sexual love between women has been made into a 'problem' by western patriarchal society and that this love-experience forces many women to become either victims or rebels or a bit of both. But, apart from this common experience of stigmatization and oppression, sex or love mean very different things in different circumstances, and the fact that the participants are all women does not suffice to fix the meaning of experiences.

The separation between lesbians and other women is, to a large extent, the product of medical discourse. Terms such as lesbian and **dyke** need to be claimed or reclaimed in order to fight **heterosexism**, but they sometimes feel like a ready-made dress that doesn't quite fit, especially for those women who have had important relationships with men in the past or who continue to be attracted to men. The clear need for a strong and publicly visible lesbian community does not mean that it is possible for anyone to be the Total Lesbian, any more than any woman, however feminine, can be the personification of Woman. Lesbianism is best defined as something one does, not something one is – and, as one does it, 'it' never stands still. The feelings change, their significance changes, the context changes. The definitional quagmires might be circumvented were lesbianism no longer seen as an inner identity with a single meaning, but rather as a social practice among people. And, like any other social practice, lesbianism is not a single 'thing' with one meaning but shorthand for a whole collection of experiences with multiple and shifting meanings. Complicated, yes, but also creative. *MV*

Lillian Faderman *Surpassing the Love of Men: Romantic Friendships and Love Between Women* (New York: Morrow, 1981; London: Women's Press, 1985)

See also **Aidoo; Atkinson; Bannon; Barnes; Bisexuality; Brown, Rita Mae; Chughtai; Ellis; Frye; Gay Liberation; Hall; H.D.; Jeffreys; Koedt; Lorde; Loulan;** *Microcosm;* **Ottinger; Political Lesbianism; Radicalesbianism; Rich; Rule; Sappho; Stein; Taylor; Transexuality**

L

Lessing, Doris (1919-   )

Doris Lessing was born in Persia of British parents who, when their daughter was five years old, moved to a farm in Southern Rhodesia. In 1949 she came to London with the manuscript of her first novel, *The Grass is Singing*, which imagines a complex emotional relationship, with sexual undertones and role reversals, between a white farmer's wife and her black servant. The book was published in 1950. The quintet of novels *Children of Violence*, published between 1952 and 1969, explores Martha Quest's inner and outer journeys between Rhodesia and post-war Britain and their apocalyptic culmination in AD 2000. The early novels in the sequence foreground Martha as a young woman struggling to come to terms with being daughter, wife, mother, lover, but, as both Africa and London, notions of home and of exile, move into the background, the sensual life is rejected and Martha too fades away, finally glimpsed as only one member of humanity facing apocalypse and rebirth.

Lessing's most important book, for at least two generations of women readers, is probably *The Golden Notebook* (1962), radical in form and content. Sections of conventional narrative ironically entitled 'Free Women' enclose and interrupt the four experimental notebooks of writer Anna Wulf, who is struggling with a writer's block as well as with domestic and political crises. Lessing made literary history by, for example, mentioning menstruation in the same breath as the British Communist Party, by probing the feminine mystique, by discussing how women's sexuality can be so often misunderstood by men. From today's perspective, her views on sexuality appear very much of their time – strongly marked by the same romanticism as that of D.H. **Lawrence** – while some readers have objected to her distinctions between vaginal and clitoral **orgasm** and to what seem stereotypical images of male homosexuals, even though she also parodies both these approaches. But Lessing did break new ground in daring to mix the personal so explicitly with the political: women writers following her are in her debt; what she achieved has passed into literary orthodoxy.

Lessing's later move into her own original form of **science fiction** allowed her to explore male-female sexuality in a more mythical fashion, notably in *The Marriages Between Zones Three, Four and Five* (1980) where her interest in Sufism becomes clear. Here she concentrates less on her characters' individual personalities and dramas than on their representing moments in the global flow of history: the ocean, not the drop of water.

MR

The Grass Is Singing (New York: Dutton, 1976; London: Grafton, 1989); *The Golden Notebook* (New York: Bantam, 1981; London: Grafton, 1989); *The Marriage Between Zones Three, Four and Five* (New York: Random House, 1981; London: Panther, 1981)

See also **Fanon; Kollontai; Le Guin; Russ**

Lie Nü Tradition

The famous Chinese *Biographies of Virtuous Women*, or *Lie nü zhuan*, was compiled in the first century AD to promulgate female **chastity**. Containing biographical sketches of filial daughters, ideal wives and mothers who would sooner meet death than disgrace, it survived for centuries as the principal authority on female conduct. Arches were erected before the houses of women who had distinguished themselves by their virtue and, although ritual self-immolation of widows was banned in the early Qing dynasty (1644-1911), the injunction on women to respect Confucian moral norms was rigidly maintained.

Indeed, as the new Manchu rulers attempted to consolidate their authority, by appealing to the conservative mores of their Han Chinese subjects, the *Lie nü* tradition acquired the characteristics of a cult. Chastity was required both of women whose betrothed died before marriage and of widows. Remarriage by a woman was widely considered a sign of promiscuity and, as such, subject to extreme social odium. Violation of the rule of chastity was a particularly serious offense for women prior to marriage, however, and one which could earn the offender and her family harsh punishment, including death.

The requirement that women be exclusively tied – in life and in death – to a husband whom their parents had chosen was physically represented by the practice of footbinding: a custom that became the symbol of status, grace and sexual desirability from the Tang dynasty (618-907) until the earlier part of the twentieth century. The authoritarian neo-Confucian philosopher Zhu Xi (1130-1200) was said to have been so shocked by the freedom of the women in the province of Fujian, where he held the office of prefect, that he ordered all females' feet to be bound so tightly that they would physically be prevented from indulging in lewd behavior. *HE*

T'ian Ju-k'ang *Male Anxiety and Female Chastity: A Comparative Study of Chinese Ethical Values in Ming-Ch'ing Times* (Leiden: Brill, 1988)

See also **Chinese Women's Resistance**

Lispector, Clarice (1925-1977)

Clarice Lispector's first novel, *Near to the Wild Heart*, was recently published as her last. As with many first novels, it is largely autobiographical; unlike many, it is autobiographical before the event, going beyond the nineteen years that Lispector had lived when she wrote it.

Ukrainian by birth and parentage, Lispector was brought up and lived in Recife and Rio de Janeiro, Brazil, and this is the background to a story whose pivotal figures are first a father and an aunt, then a Brazilian husband, Otavio. **Sensuality**, rather than sexuality, is the recurrent motif, and explored with that particular distaste deployed by the French Existentialists (a major influence). 'Her aunt's tongue and mouth were soft and warm like those of a dog. Joana closed her eyes for an instant, swallowed the nausea and the dark cake which were heaving inside her stomach, causing her to shudder from head to foot.'

The Hour of the Star (1977) was dedicated to 'the perfect couple', Robert and Clara Schumann, and 'to the deep crimson of my blood as someone in their prime'. Again, the main protagonist is a woman, Macabea, who is a failure both through her incompetence at work and her **virginity**. When a philanderer takes a passing interest in her, she is not transformed, as she had hoped, into a star with Hollywood appeal, but into a sterile anorexic. The tale's narrator is a man who cannot but 'think about Macabea's vagina, minute yet unexpectedly covered with a thick growth of black hairs – her vagina was the only vehement sign of her existence'. As for Macabea, 'She herself asked for nothing, but her sex made its demands like a sunflower germinating in a tomb.' In Lispector's longest novel, *The Apple in the Dark* (1961), her two most characteristic female protagonists find a place: Vitória, the elderly spinster whose courage has taught her to fear life, and Ermelinda, her young cousin, obsessively fearful of death. The arrival of a murderer, Martim, at their remote homestead sees an uneasy interplay between the three and death becomes the vehicle by which Ermelinda is brought to confront sex.

Lispector's short stories often focus on the stifling sexual repressions of upper-class society, which makes the gratuitously abusive attitudes towards homosexuals and spinsters assumed by some of her characters all the more shocking. Her central women characters, meanwhile, tend to be pushed to the point of absurd perversity: transferring their frustrated affections onto a zoo, for example, or onto a flock of chickens which, once cherished, must be devoured. *AmH*

Near to the Wild Heart (New York: New Directions, 1990; Manchester: Carcanet, 1990); *The Apple in the Dark* (Texas: University of Texas Press, 1986; London: Virago, 1983); *The Hour of the Star* (New York: New Directions, 1992; Manchester: Carcanet, 1986); *Family Ties* (Texas: University of Texas Press, 1984; Manchester: Carcanet, 1985)

See also **Repression**

L

Livia, Anna (1955-)

The Dublin-born author Anna Livia has been in the forefront of writing fiction, including **science fiction**, that debates the issues in and around radical lesbian feminism. She was on the collective that formed the first British publishing house with a commitment to radical feminist and lesbian feminist writing, Onlywomen Press, and contributed to the first collection of British lesbian feminist fiction, *The Reach* (London: Onlywomen Press, 1984).

Livia's first novel, *Relatively Norma* (1982) takes a witty look at the process of 'coming out' as a lesbian to friends and family. In *Accommodation Offered* (1985), the lives of three lesbians sharing a house are humorously observed through the eyes of their houseplants. At one point two women attempt to make love for the first time and one of them finds herself worrying about how to locate the **clitoris**. Did other lesbians, she wonders, 'use less medical terms for things'? Here, too, **pornography** is presented as an area of discord between men and lesbians, when one male character expects a lesbian to be sexually excited by the same material as he is.

Five years on and pornography features in the title story of Livia's second collection, *Saccharine Cyanide* (1990). Here, the radical proposition that all men oppress women is given credence by a narrative in which a lesbian faces the fact that her own brother may be involved in the distribution of hard pornography. In the same story, lesbian pornography is characterized as untenable because it is seen as undermining the radical feminist condemnation of all pornography for representing women as subordinate to men.

Livia's position on pornography is no bar to her fictional attempts at exploring all aspects of **lesbianism**. She often integrates the act of lesbian love-making into her narratives, in both evocative and humorous ways, but her perspective is always female-identified. In one of the stories in *Saccharine Cyanide*, for instance, she writes of the erotic charge between women as being 'cunt melting'. CU

Relatively Norma (London: Onlywomen Press, 1982); *Accommodation Offered* (London: The Women's Press,

1985); *Bulldozer Rising* (London: Onlywomen Press, 1988); *Saccharine Cyanide* (London: Onlywomen Press, 1990)

See also **Brown, Rita Mae; Hanscombe; Russ**

Llewelyn Davies, Margaret (1861-1944)

As general secretary of the **Women's Co-operative Guild** from 1889-1922, Margaret Llewelyn Davies played a central role in its development as a campaigning body for married working-class women in Britain. Forceful and persuasive – Virginia Woolf was of the opinion that she could 'compel a steam roller to waltz' – she focused the Guild on issues of relevance to its members, such as women's suffrage, men's marital right to sex, maternity care, combining inspirational leadership with a healthy respect for rank-and-file democracy. Her skills both in placing sexual politics on the agenda of public debate and empowering ordinary members is evident in her decision, in 1910, to use letters and opinions collected from the branches as the basis of the Guild's submission on divorce-law reform. The *Report & Evidence of the Royal Commission on Divorce and Matrimonial Causes* (1912) provided indisputable evidence, in the words of one commentator, 'that the very foundations of society are rotten'.

Llewelyn Davies came from a privileged but progressive background: her father was the Christian Socialist John Llewelyn Davies; her aunt was Emily Davies, the feminist who founded Girton College for women at Cambridge University. Her lifelong friend and companion, Lilian Harris, worked with her in the Guild. She never married. Yet, despite the social gulf dividing her from the married, working-class guildswomen, her personal charm and political convictions enabled her to win their trust and confidence. Traveling around the country and staying in guildswomen's homes, she learned of the hardship and suffering that characterized many of their lives. The wife is without 'economic independence' she wrote in 1915, 'and the law therefore gives the man, whether he be good or bad, a terrible power over her . . . the beginning and end of the working woman's life and duty is still regarded by many as the care of the household, the satisfaction of man's desires, and the bearing of children.' But, far from viewing these women as passive victims, she discovered that 'there is no class in the community who respond to organization and education more effectively, and whose enthusiasm for public work is greater'. During her years as general secretary, the Guild expanded from about two thousand to fifty thousand members and emerged as a significant element in local and national politics.

GS

Ed. Margaret Llewelyn Davies *Maternity: Letters from Working Women* (London: Virago, 1978)

See also **X, Laura**

Lolita

Vladimir Nabokov's *Lolita* is one of the rare books that has transcended literature and become a phenomenon. Humbert Humbert's paedophile obsession with his twelve-year-old stepdaughter is the perfect metaphor for forbidden, hopeless, compulsive passion destined to fail: because Lolita will grow up.

Nabokov's dark-haired fictional nymphet is virtually inseparable from Stanley Kubrick's blonde, teenage Sue Lyons in the film of the book – because the sophisticated but innocent Lolita is more of an icon than a girl. Obsession comes from within. Obsessive love is masturbatory self-love. Humbert, who makes Lolita his goddess, admits that she is sometimes 'a disgustingly conventional little girl'. His love for Dolores Hayes is the ultimate **masochism** metaphor. He is in love with his own failure and allows his obsession to destroy him, and her. Incapable of really loving Lolita, Humbert loves his vision of her. His sexual compulsion leaves her tarnished, sobbing herself to sleep, but the reader, the voyeur, accepts the crying child because she is a symbol as well as a little girl. And the detached involvement of the voyeur masks responsibility. Also, Lolita, who teases Humbert with childlike ruthlessness, is something of a sadist – until she indulges her own self-destructive crush on the corrupt playwright Clare Quilty.

It is testimony to the author's remarkable gift that he can convert the first-person account of a child molester into sensual, musical prose. Humbert is saved from being a monster partly through his own misery, and his willingness to sacrifice everything in pursuit of his perverse dream, and partly in comparison with Clare Quilty, who has no possessive, protective instinct towards Lo but uses her destructively and then discards her.

Stanley Kubrick's film doesn't have the unforgettable sensuality of Nabokov's *Lolita*. He invents James Mason's coat: the key to the film. Humbert (Mason) is both protecting and imprisoning Lolita. Lolita's rebellion against his inverted possessiveness and the pursuit of her passion for the playwright, Quilty (Peter Sellers) leads to her ruin. (The actress who played the part drifted into real-life obscurity.) Nabokov was born in St Petersburg but spent most of his life in Europe and the USA where, for eleven years, he was Professor of Russian Literature at Cornell University. He was a prolific writer – his other books include *Ada*, *Pale Fire* and *Laughter in the Dark* – and married with a son. He claimed that *Lolita* has no intentional message, or moral, but is an example of 'aesthetic bliss'. It is also a defense of the right of an artist imaginatively to examine the abhorrent.

CM

Lolita (New York: Random House, 1989; Harmondsworth: Penguin, 1989)

See also **Newman; Paedophilia; Romantic Love**

Look Back in Anger

First produced by the English Stage Company at the Royal Court Theatre in May 1956, John Osborne's *Look Back in Anger* is credited as the play which broke the mold of English drawing-room drama and introduced social realism or 'kitchen sink'

L

drama to the British stage.

The red-brick university educated Jimmy Porter is an angry young man, living in a dingy Midlands bedsit with his upper-class wife, Alison, and their friend Cliff, who helps Jimmy run a market sweet stall. Although the opening scene, with Alison ironing and the men reading the papers, suggests a cozy Sunday afternoon's domesticity, it quickly becomes apparent that the room is a battlefield, with Alison held hostage not only because of the class she represents but also because of her gender. 'When you see a woman in front of her bedroom mirror, you realise what a refined sort of butcher she is. Did you ever see some dirty old Arab, sticking his fingers into some mess of lamb fat and gristle? Well, she's just like that. Thank God they don't have many women surgeons. Those primitive hands would have your guts out in no time,' says Jimmy.

For Jimmy, sexual desire and violence are inseparable: 'There's hardly a moment when I'm not watching and wanting you. I've got to hit out, somehow,' he tells Alison. Even more disturbingly, it is Alison's sexuality and potential for motherhood that Jimmy finds most threatening: 'She has the passion of a python. She just devours me whole everytime as if I were some over-large rabbit. That's me. That bulge round her navel – if you're wondering what it is – it's me.' In fact, unbeknown to Jimmy, Alison *is* pregnant and, when her friend Helena comes to stay, unable to bear the emotional pain of living with Jimmy any longer she goes home to her parents.

The third act opens with Helena having replaced Alison both in Jimmy's bed and at the ironing board. But, when Alison suddenly returns, having lost the baby and possibly been rendered infertile, Helena departs leaving Jimmy and Alison to face the future alone. The play ends with the two of them playing a childish, sexually non-threatening game in which they pretend to be bears and squirrels: cuddly, furry little animals that will not hurt each other. Michelene Wandor, who provides an insightful analysis of the play in *Look Back in Gender* (London: Methuen, 1987) writes: 'The need for heroism (male) and sexual identity (male) are the subject matter of the play. Jimmy's anguish is expressed through the secondary castigation of a ruling-class which has left him nothing to fight for, and a woman whom he sees as a threat and has to destroy metaphorically. He is at least boss in how own home – a pyrrhic victory, since it is predicated on misogyny, a profound insecurity about male identity, and an uncertainty about the family model for the future.'   LG

Look Back in Anger (New York: Penguin, 1982; London: French, 1984)

See also **Oshima**

Lorde, Audre (1934-1992)

'What are the words you do not yet have? What do you need to say?' This question was asked by Audre Lorde, the African-American poet and polemicist, in 'The Transformation of Silence into Language and Action' in *Sister Outsider* (1984). Such questions occupied Lorde from childhood. Born in Harlem, in New York City, she felt herself to be 'different' early on; not only was she left-handed but she did not talk until she was five. Gloria Hull has noted that 'Lorde's first language was, literally, poetry'. Yet, in the 1970s, Lorde was outstandingly forthright in the debate on sexual politics. In speeches and essays like 'The Uses of Anger: Women Responding to Racism' and 'Sexism: An American Disease in Blackface', she addressed the feminist issues of her time from the doubly marginalized position of a black woman and a lesbian.

Lorde's intense concern with language was because of who she was. As a black mother and a lesbian in the white **patriarchy** of America, Lorde questioned a language that was not of her making; in *Sister Outsider* she said that she wanted to reclaim 'that language which has been made to work against us'. One of her most profound reclamations is her 'biomythology' *Zami: A New Spelling of My Name* (1982). This memoir not only offers intense insights into the lives of black

American lesbians, it simultaneously challenges the representative tradition of African-American autobiography.

In her life and in her poetry, Lorde struggled to present black women with role models that reflect female heroism rather than female victimization. She boldly came out as a 'Black lesbian poet' in 1970. After losing a breast through cancer, she took courage from the Amazons and refused to wear a prosthesis. According to Gloria Hull, Lorde achieved 'spiritual bonding with an ancestral and mythic past. The Amazons and warrior queens of Dahomey . . . have given her a family that cannot fail.' The Sotho warrior queen Mmánthatisi enters Lorde's poem 'Sisters in Arms', which reads: 'we were two Black women touching our flame/and we left our dead behind us'. Earlier poems, like 'Cables to Rage' and 'A Poem for Women in a Rage', express a necessary anger, while 'Love Poem' celebrates love between women with erotic explicitness: 'And I knew when I entered her I was/high wind in her forests hollow'.

Lorde validated anger as well as love, and saw a vital connection between them. In her essay 'Uses of the Erotic: The Erotic as Power' in *Sister Outsider*, she said: 'The erotic is a resource within each of us that lies in a deeply female and spiritual plane, firmly rooted in the power of unexpressed or unrecognized feelings.' Lorde recognized these feelings and expressed them in her life and in her art. *SRu*

New York Headshop and Museum (Detroit: Broadside, 1974); *The Cancer Journals* (San Francisco: Spinsters Ink, 1980; London: Sheba, 1985); *Chosen Poems: Old and New* (New York and London: W.W. Norton, 1982); *Zami: A New Spelling of My Name* (Trumansburg, New York: The Crossing Press, 1982; London: Sheba, 1984); *Sister Outsider* (Trumansburg, New York: The Crossing Press, 1984); *Our Dead Behind Us* (New York: W.W. Norton, 1986; London: Sheba, 1987)

Ed. Mari Evans *Black Women Writers: 1950-1980* (Garden City, New York: Doubleday, 1984)
Gail Lewis 'Audre Lorde: Vignettes and Mental Conversations' in *Feminist Review* (No. 34, Spring 1990)

See also **Brossard; H.D.; Irigaray; Parker; Shockley; Stein; Wittig**

Loulan, JoAnn (1948-   )

JoAnn Loulan is a lesbian who likes to talk about women doing passionate things together, including sex. She describes herself as a 'psychotherapist, sex educator and author specializing in the sexual and emotional concerns of lesbians'. In Britain she is best known as the author of two books on lesbian sex; in the USA she was known before being published, for her lesbian sexuality weekend workshops in California and her earthy, sometimes shocking, often hilarious lectures.

Loulan's work is two-faceted. She embraces pleasure, fun and the right to a self-chosen sex life. She also opens up discussion on a huge range of issues which can hinder enjoyment. She writes about the impact of **incest, rape**, alcoholism, **AIDS** and **homophobia** and discusses ways to have fun with sex if you are a woman with a disability, in a long-term relationship, celibate, aging, a parent and so on. She suggests 'homework' on all these topics: exercises to be done alone or with a partner.

Loulan's approach to sex is graphic and down-to-earth. Her books include diagrams and anatomical descriptions and a reminder that physical pleasure is about nerve endings. In her chapter on sex toys, she emphasizes that sex can be funny as well as fun. She steers clear of the debate surrounding lesbian **sado-masochism** but could never be described as prudish. If whips and chains are not included, premeditated sex, anonymous sex and fingers in vaginas in restaurants are. At the heart of the work is what Loulan calls the 'Willingness Model'. 'It starts with the premise that women can begin to have sex because we are willing. We do not have to be experiencing great desire or physical excitement: we can initiate sex because we want to.'

Loulan believes fiercely in women's right to enjoy themselves how they want to and in the way that is right for them. So, while she encourages an open-mindedness to the idea of trying lots of things to see if they are pleasurable, she is careful to emphasize every woman's right to be safe and really to listen to and take care of her feelings. If you have a hard time having sex because your body goes numb or you get flashbacks to scenes of abuse, then follow your needs: stop as often as you need to; cry when you feel like it, even in the middle of sex; take care of the hurt little girl inside. This acknowledgement of the child inside us is one way in which Loulan differs from most writers about sex. Her enormous popularity (her books have now sold hundreds of thousands of copies and her lectures are generally packed) lies in her successful mix of progressive, non-judgemental therapy, feminist politics, whacky humor, down-to-earth advice and a keen sense of the theatrical. *JD*

Lesbian Sex (San Francisco: Spinsters Ink, 1984); *Lesbian Passion* (San Francisco: Spinsters Ink, 1987)

See also **Comfort; Lesbianism**

Lynch, David (1946-   )

The American writer-director David Lynch can lay claim to two of the most honest and revealing films about male sexuality to have come from a male director. And the portrait they offer is distinctly unflattering. Working on a symbolic and allusive, as well as a narrative level, his films present a potent collision of Freudian imagery and American culture.

Made on a shoestring over a five-year period, Lynch's first feature *Eraserhead* (1976) instantly achieved cult success, becoming a staple of the late-night circuit. This surreal black-and-white fantasy, described by Lynch as 'a dream of dark and troubling things', ruthlessly follows the logic of dreams as it presents what is probably the clearest depiction of male sexual paranoia ever committed to film. Procreation results in an inhuman, ever-demanding, nightmare baby; the ineffectual hero is assaulted by strange worm things, sinks into a bed of putrescence during sex and is ultimately beheaded at a pencil factory, becoming the eraserhead of the title.

Lynch returned to sexuality ten years later with the mainstream but darkly subversive mystery *Blue Velvet*. This time, man as victim of his sexual fears is replaced by man as aggressor: male sexuality is

shown as brutalizing and degrading, infantile and violent, and rooted in the need for power and control. Which goes some way to explain why men were more likely to react with violent disgust to what *Time Out* (8-15 April, 1987) described as 'the most genuinely scary depiction of male-female relationships – and in fact all relationships – to hit the screen in years', while women could find the potential offensiveness of certain scenes surprisingly defused by the film as a whole, especially since the sexual threat that pervades *Blue Velvet* is for once genuinely polymorphously perverse and *not* directed only at women.

Having so graphically laid bare male sexuality for our examination, Lynch now seems to be simply indulging it. A more recent film, *Wild At Heart* (1990), is gross in its **misogyny**, reducing women to the decorative level of *Playboy* magazine, celebrating extremes of male violence while cavalierly laying moral guilt at the feet of the female characters and offering humiliation and sexual threat (only to women) as masturbatory fantasy. The enormously successful, late 1980s television series *Twin Peaks* (Lynch/Frost Productions), acclaimed for its achievement in showing that originality can have mass appeal, still, for all its enjoyable idiosyncrasy, recycles sex-oriented female stereotypes and bases its murder-mystery plot on the same old **rape** and murder of women. *PA*

Eraserhead (1976); *Blue Velvet* (1986); *Wild At Heart* (1990)

See also **Amis; Freud: Hemingway; *Look Back in Anger***

Lysistrata

Lysistrata is probably the best known play by the Athenian comic writer Aristophanes, many of whose extant works were written during the Peloponnesian War which dominated the politics of the late 5th century BC.

Lysistrata, named for its leading character, was first performed in 411 BC and deals with a sex strike, proposed by the heroine, in which all the women in Greece participate in order to force the warring city states, Athens, Sparta and their allies, to make peace. The Athenian women retire to the Acropolis but, after five days, are beginning to desert because of their own sex starvation. A man named Cinesias (which, colloquially translated, means 'fucker') comes to find his wife Myrrhine (or 'myrtle wreath', a euphemism for cunt) and, having thrown a purse to Lysistrata, parodying the gesture of a client paying a brothel-keeper, finally sees Myrrhine. Then, in the funniest scene of the play, Myrrhine entices Cinesias towards sex but always denies him at the last minute through a series of ruses. In the next scene, emissaries from Sparta arrive with huge erections and Lysistrata helps to negotiate a peace treaty.

The play contains many conventional features of Aristophanes's writing: a number of serious choruses, chiefly on the subject of peace; many double entendres and bawdy jokes; a portrayal of women as thoroughly libidinous and voracious. K.J. Dover in *Aristophanic Comedy* (California: University of California Press, 1972) stresses the Greek belief that women enjoyed sex more than men (nine times more, according to the myth of Tiresias) and had a lower resistance to sexual temptation. The women in the play are married: that is, the wives of citizens, who could not, according to Solon's recommendation, be expected to have **sexual intercourse** more than three times a month. Aristophanes portrays them as especially randy, since their men are permanently away on campaign, and complaining about the difficulties of obtaining dildoes with a war on. They are initially unwilling to accept the idea of a strike, but eventually swear an oath to resist both husbands and lovers and, although many desert the strike, it is ultimately male desperation that is the greater.

One or two points conflict with traditional thinking about the lives of citizen women. Here, they are referred to in several places as having lovers, despite the view that this was unlikely given their confined lives. It is also generally held that sex with wives was considered a duty rather than a pleasure, yet Lysistrata at one point says, 'No man

is ever happy if he can't please his woman,' and, in the central scene, Cinesias is shown to be very much in love with Myrrhine. But then Aristophanes's plays are noted for what we might now describe as their surreal elements, and perhaps the most surreal feature of *Lysistrata* is that, while brothel-keepers are mentioned by name, there is no suggestion that the men will relieve their sexual frustration with prostitutes – or, for that matter, with boys. On the other hand, this would have spoiled the happy ending.   *KH*

Lysistrata (Oxford: Oxford University Press, 1990)

See also **Beardsley; Hetaira; Plato; Zetterling**

Machismo

The Spanish noun *machismo* is translated as either 'virility' or 'masculinity cult'. In Latin America, the macho male is one who often proclaims his virility by having numerous children by numerous partners and, frequently, refusing to support them, in some cases even to acknowledge them except in boasting. If he lives with a woman, he'll treat her badly, abusing and humiliating her, often in front of other adults or her children. Whether this takes the form of verbal or physical violence, the woman is always made responsible for the aggression, being told that she 'asked for it' or that she likes being put in her place, knocked about, being shown who's boss.

In western countries, *machismo* is a term that has come into common usage with the advent of the women's movement in the late 1960s. It is used in an exclusively derogatory way, even by men: for instance, when speaking unfavorably of the selfish behavior of another, rather than when boasting of their own 'conquests'. While in the west *machismo* may not have quite the same connotations as in Latin America – with regard to a man's reproductive capacity or wife-battering – it applies, in an often more attenuated form, to men who fundamentally despise women, either bossing them around, continually criticizing and seeking to 'put them right', or affecting to love them while, in practice abusing and betraying them.

Sociologists look for the causes of this behavior in the power relations of a given society, often discovering that it is those men who feel inadequate or deprived of power in public life who mistreat women in their private life. More personalized interpretations often hinge on a man's relations with his mother, out of which he never seems to have grown, forever wanting to behave like a spoilt child, 'having his cake and eating it', and indulging in raging tantrums whenever the least thwarted. What is clear is that *machismo* points up the socially acceptable ways in which the genders express their aggression. Just as far more men than women go to prison for violent crimes, and women are nine times as likely as men to be 'driven crazy' and end up in a mental hospital, so some women punish themselves by tolerating the bad behavior of men whose aggression seeks a physically weaker victim. *AmH*

See also **Allende; Belli; Mastretta; Misogyny**

MacInnes, Colin (1914-1976)

The novelist and journalist Colin MacInnes was the great-grandson of Burne-Jones, the Pre-Raphaelite painter, and might usefully be seen as continuing both the Pre-Raphaelites' honorable attempt at a combination of hyper-realism and high-mindedness, and their regular collapse into a sentimental idealization that camouflaged bourgeois exploitation of the objects of their lust.

MacInnes's London novels, *City of Spades* (1957), *Absolute Beginners* (1959) and *Mr Love and Justice* (1960), capture very precisely a sense of a time and a place: the London of Nigerian students and first-generation immigrants, of a nascent youth culture and minor gangsterism, of sexual mores at the cultural cusp of the repressive 1950s and the libertine 1960s. Their combination of a slightly prissy narrative voice and an observing protagonist with racy, quasi-journalistic observations of social detail

marks them as literary descendants of Christopher **Isherwood**'s Berlin novels, while also looking forwards to the New Journalism.

MacInnes was bisexual, his *Loving Them Both* (1973) an early text on the subject of **bisexuality**. Some have caricatured it as *But Not Liking Either of Them Very Much* and MacInnes was not in huge sympathy with either feminism or **Gay Liberation**. Criticism of the reactionary aspects of his work – his **misogyny**, his colonialist appropriation of the black community in general and the sexual services of young black men in particular – has been tempered, reasonably, by the sense that he chronicled and perhaps helped to create a culture more progressive than his own work and behavior.

RK

City of Spades, Absolute Beginners and Mr Love and Justice (London: Allison and Busby, 1985)

See also **Fanon; Mapplethorpe; Sexual Revolution**

Manet, Edouard (1832-1883)

Edouard Manet studied in Paris with the artist Thomas Couture before developing an innovative style which minimized half tones and drew on contemporary subject matter. Though always mentioned in the same breath as the Impressionists, and friendly with and influenced by them all, he refused to show at their exhibitions, always hoping for the official recognition long denied him by his revolutionary art.

With 'Olympia' (1863) Manet produced one of the most controversial images of the nineteenth century. Posed by the model Victorine Meurent as a courtesan 'dressed' to receive a client in hair ornament, jewellery and slippers, it has lost none of its confrontational power today. **Prostitution** was a fact of Paris life at this period and Manet's decision to picture it was shared by **Degas** and Toulouse-Lautrec. *Nana*, Emile **Zola**'s novel about a prostitute, is also the subject of a painting by Manet. But 'Olympia' scandalized on two counts: socially

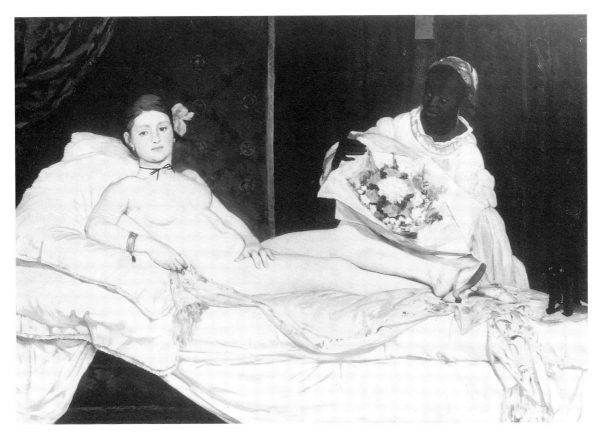

Edouard Manet, *Olympia*, 1863

because by confronting the middle-class audience with evidence of prostitution it broke the taboo separating the sale of sex from family life; artistically because far from looking pathetic, guilty or repentant, all artistically-approved representations which might have excused her intrusion into the gallery-going world, she stares straight out at the spectators, challenging them to deny her occupation. Her hand clamped over her thigh is a modern version of the classical *Venus pudica* pose – the modest Venus shielding her sex, famously adopted by Giorgione and Titian for their sixteenth-century nudes – but her insolent stare has nothing to do with the modest seductiveness of her predecessors. The fact that she will lift her hand for the gentleman whose bouquet the maid is holding is as much a parody of her classical antecedent as her name.

Manet also did several paintings of women in trousers, the most striking being 'Young Woman in

Spanish Costume' (1862). The exaggerated focus put on her legs and the top of her thighs by the tight breeches and pale stockings had an erotic charge in an age of crinolined respectability.   *FB*

'Olympia' is in the Musée d'Orsay, Paris; there are other works in most major museums.

See also **Androgyny; Degas; Nude**

Manto, Sa'adat Hassan (1912-1955)

Born in India during a time of political flux, Sa'adat Hassan Manto was attracted to the marxist oriented Progressive Writers' Association (PWA). On the publication of his third anthology of stories, *Kali Shalwar/Black Trousers* (1941), which contained writing of a largely socio-political bias in keeping with the PWA agenda, he was disillusioned by the swiftness with which some members dissociated themselves from him when the sexual content of a few stories received adverse criticism.

Other controversial stories followed, including 'Khol Do' ('Open It'), the harrowing tale of a pre-pubescent girl repeatedly raped during the 1947 partition of India whose father finds her half-dead in a refugee camp. When he points to a window saying, 'Open it,' the girl mechanically responds by untying the drawstring which holds up her trousers.

Manto's unfairly maligned stories deal not only with sexual horror but with sexual arousal and confusion in adolescent girls and boys. In 'Dhuan' ('Steam') of 1941, a pre-pubescent boy is impelled to touch freshly-slaughtered meat after smelling its faint odor; later, he gets an erotic thrill from imagining his older sister butchered and stroking her waist. In 'Blauz' ('Blouse') of the same year, a boy watches his sister sew a blouse which he later touches. The stories concentrate on the mysterious, compulsive essence of sexuality and the ways in which it is later used to exploit, particularly women. They also underline how similarly different kinds of women are used, be they respectably married wives or hired prostitutes.

The exposition of taboo topics in India's sexually repressed society resulted in a law suit for **obscenity** over 'Bu' ('Odor'), published in 1942. In this story, a man invites a low-caste woman in from the rain and here, as in many of the stories, the emphasis is on sexual enjoyment. The couple's subsequent love-making is a profound experience, mystical in nature, partly because the lovers can't speak the same language but mainly because the encounter is without commercial or social consideration. The natural bodily odor of the woman symbolizes, for the male protagonist, the essence of abandoned and meaningful love-making missing from both the taboo relations with prostitutes and the sanctioned one with his bride. The odor becomes a quest. Manto said that the story merely echoed classical Hindu literature – where woman symbolizes the earth, man a rain cloud, rainfall the sexual experience and the smell of earth released by the first monsoon rains, post-coital pleasure.   *SH*

Black Milk (Lahore: Al-Kitab, 1956)

Lesley A. Flemming *Another Lonely Voice: The Life and Works of Saadat Hassan Manto* (Lahore: Vanguard Books, 1985)

See also **Bedi; Chughtai; Hinduism; Lawrence; Rape; Rego**

Manusmriti

The Manava Dharma sastra, or the Law Book of Manu, is thought to have been written in the second or third century in India. Generally known as the Manusmriti, it is one of the earliest of the dharma sastras (manuals of human conduct) and has a lot to say about kingship, the origin of the four castes, and women. In dealing with castes and subcastes, it regulates and often forbids inter-caste social relations and marriage alliances, making caste mobility impossible and allowing a change of profession only in times of acute distress (although, even then, while a Brahmin may become a moneylender, a moneylender can never become a priest). It is for its injunctions to women that the Manusmriti has gained notoriety, however. While upholding women as mothers – 'A mother exceeds even a thousand fathers' – it forbids the remarriage of widows, prescibes the seclusion of women and recommends harsh punishments for **adultery**. When a woman committed adultery with a man of a lower caste, she was to be torn apart by dogs.   *KV*

See also **Chastity; Hinduism; Honor; Kama Sutra**

Mapplethorpe, Robert (1946-1989)

Robert Mapplethorpe was born in New York and studied painting and sculpture at the city's Pratt Institute from 1963-1970, when he began working as an independent photographer. After his first show in 1976 he had over seventy solo exhibitions

Robert Mapplethorpe, *Lisa Lyon*, 1983

and took part in numerous group shows throughout Europe and the USA. In the global art market of the 1980s he was a huge success. He is almost certainly the best known US photographer of nudes and his portraits of the monied and famous, of the SoHo beau monde and its hangers-on made him as much a vogueish New York phenomenon as Andy **Warhol**.

Mapplethorpe's death with **AIDS** sealed his status as a specifically gay artist. But, while some critics applauded his celebration of gay sexuality, others attacked what they saw as his estheticizing of **sado-masochism** and his voyeuristic subjection of black men to the white male gaze. And his female nudes, above all his studies of the bodybuilder Lisa Lyon, stirred doubts as well as enthusiasm.

Autonomous muscle-flexing woman? Or tamed phallic woman, taking the female body through its most threatening paces and returning it to normality?

Mapplethorpe's most disturbing moment of controversy was posthumous. An exhibition of his work provoked a right-wing onslaught on the arts when a Republican senator used it to introduce a legislative amendment restricting US government grants to the arts and entailing direct censorship in the public funding process. Yet **pornography** is remote from Mapplethorpe's esthetic. Bodies and faces, skin, hair and genitals present so many opportunities for the supreme formal control that was his hallmark. The highly polished sculptural qualities he brings to the human figure, the molding of analogies with classical natural forms, the abstracting of body parts, make the visual eroticism detached and stylized. For Mapplethorpe, gender, like the body's surfaces and musculature, is malleable. It's his knowingness, his ruthless awareness of instabilities in the body's signifiers of power, that has made him one of the most interesting photographers of his time.   *LH*

Robert Mapplethorpe: 1970-1983 (London: Institute of Contemporary Arts, 1983)

See also **MacInnes; Nude; Obscenity; Von Gloeden; Voyeurism**

Marital Rape

The **rape** of wives is the most ignored form of rape. In the USA, for instance, despite the fact that marital rape has at last been criminalized in most states, public concern about the offense is commensurate neither with the magnitude nor the severity of this traumatic and most common form of assault. Diana **Russell** found that fourteen per cent of the women who has ever been married – in her sample of 930 women residents of San Francisco – were willing to disclose that they had been raped by their husbands. But, because of extreme feelings of shame and a fear of being blamed, others may well have kept quiet about such experiences, so that the figure fourteen per cent could represent a gross understatement of the true prevalence of this problem.

Russell also reports, in *Rape and Marriage*, that rape by a husband and rape by a stranger are the two most traumatic forms of rape: that is, more traumatic than rape by acquaintances, dates, boyfriends, friends, lovers or unrelated authority figures. Thus her study demolishes the myth that rape in marriage is experienced as a relatively mild form of sexual assault. The frequent repetition of the experience, the painfulness of widespread victim-blaming (and self-blame), the complexities entailed in removing oneself from a marriage in order to try and end the rapes: all contribute to the extreme trauma reported by most of the women concerned. Russell further points out that the movements against both rape and battery have failed to confront the problem of wife rape. She cites a survey undertaken by Lynn Thompson-Haas of the Austin Rape Crisis Center, the goal of which was to find out how such organizations were meeting the needs of wife-rape victims. Thompson-Haas found that 'many sexual assault programs see marital rape as a "family violence problem," and many programs for battered women see it as a "sexual assault issue."'

Underlining the severity of wife rape is Jacqueline Campbell's finding, also quoted by Russell, that victims of wife rape are at greater risk of being murdered by their husbands, or of murdering them, than battered women who are not also sexually violated. In another study cited by Russell, Nancy Shields and Christine Hanneke report that women who are victims of battering *and* wife rape score significantly higher on scales of anxiety, paranoid ideation and psychotism – and are less likely to be able to enjoy sex – than battered women who have not been raped and women who have been raped by strangers. The glimmer of hope on the horizon is that marital rape has now been made illegal in Belgium, Denmark, Sweden, the USSR, Canada, most states in the USA, three states in Australia, Nicaragua, the Virgin Islands, Israel, Scotland and New Zealand. In England and Wales, an appeal court judgement in March 1991 appears to have set a precedent to make it illegal there too.   *LX*

Diana Russell *Rape in Marriage* (Indiana: University of Indiana Press, 1990)
David Finkelhor and Kersti Yllo *License to Rape* (New York: Holt, Rinehart and Winston, 1985)

See also **Date Rape; Sexual Harassment; Women's Co-operative Guild**

Masochism

Masochism is deriving sexual pleasure from one's own humiliation or pain, the latter also being called 'algolagnia'. The term was coined in the late nineteenth century by Richard von **Krafft-Ebing** from the practices described in the novels of Leopold von Sacher-Masoch, whose male heroes are usually at the mercy of cruel, dominating women for and through whom they suffer punishment, sometimes resulting in death. Masochism was pathologized by early western European psychiatry as the exaggeration of the 'normal' passive attitude during the sexual act, thus presenting 'a morbid degeneration of mental qualities specifically feminine'. Consequently, it has been seen as complementary to sadism in so far as the latter was held to represent a degeneration of active, masculine sexuality.

For Sigmund **Freud**, masochism is the seeking of punishment as a substitute for a transgressive sexual enjoyment, an eroticization of morality: the punishment ensuring the arousal that it originally attempted to suppress. This account of masochism sees it as a consequence of the child's incestuous wishes being repressed by paternal prohibition. It has been argued that the 'passion' of Christ on the cross, like that of the martyrs, constitutes a masochistic self-sacrifice and a feminization of the Son for the appeasement of the Father. A second Freudian account sees masochism as a primal manifestation of sexuality in which the suffering and arousal are central, the punishing agent secondary. This masochism has the self as its object and works through **fantasy**: a fantasy which can be seen as

introducing death as the ultimate sexual event, a death which is always about to occur but is always kept at a distance, anticipated. The essential feature of the scenario is suspense, waiting, deferred fulfillment of desire. In this account, passivity is not the essential attribute of the masochist, but a strategy adopted in order to ensure punishment, to lure the agent into fulfilling her or his place in the masochist's scenario. Thus, passivity and feminisation are simulated by the subject, male or female, in order for enjoyment to occur.

The traditional equation of women's desire with masochistic submission to a (male) authority, an equation which then annuls that desire, is corroborated by such lucrative pieces of erotic literature as Pauline Réage's *Story of O*, in which a woman incarcerated in a castle is educated by a group of men into total submission and the eradication of her will, until she perceives her femininity as existing solely for the master's pleasure. However, the exploration of masochistic scenarios in recent women's erotic literature, predominantly lesbian, suggests that most current definitions of both male and female masochism are too strictly bound within a clinical and phallocentric environment and that differences of masochistic desire and practice cannot be contained within the pathologizing frame.

TP

See also **Infantile Sexuality; Psychoanalysis; Sado-Masochism; Sexology**

Masters, William (1915-) & Johnson, Virginia (1925-)

William Masters and Virginia Johnson shot to fame with the publication of their first book, *Human Sexual Response* (1966), based on their research findings. Unlike their fellow American Alfred **Kinsey**, who had analyzed sexual behavior, Masters and Johnson were interested in studying sexual *response*: the physiological changes that occur during sexual arousal. They studied hundreds of volunteers, observing and recording bodily changes through various stages of arousal and **orgasm**. They measured penises, floppy and erect, photographed vaginas, timed rectal and vaginal contractions, determined the effects of sexual arousal on a person's breathing, heart rate, blood pressure . . .

Their methods, which included observing couples having sex and providing single men with surrogate partners, were as shocking to some as were their 'discoveries', especially those about female sexual response. According to Masters and Johnson, the Freudian distinction between the clitoral and vaginal orgasm is unjustified; the source of all female orgasms, whether through direct or indirect stimulation, is the **clitoris**. They also claimed that men and women are alike in sexual response: that they have similar physiological responses during arousal and orgasm. In fact, we need not have waited for the publication of *Human Sexual Response* to become aware of this – Kinsey had said much the same as early as 1953 – but, interestingly, such ideas had received little public attention. In addition to emphasizing the clitoral focus of female sexuality, Masters and Johnson demonstrated that women have a greater orgasmic capacity than men and are capable of multiple orgasms.

It is because of their work on female sexual response that Masters and Johnson have been seen as important contributors not only to sexual knowledge but also to the cause of feminism. And this is hardly surprising when one looks at the importance placed on sexual liberation in the first few years of the women's movement. Early feminists frequently cited the findings of Masters and Johnson as proof of the vaginal orgasm's mythical nature, and as a challenge to the idea that women could enjoy only **sexual intercourse** – or, for that matter, only enjoy sex with men. In hindsight, however, many feminists have criticized the assumptions behind 'sexual liberation', pointing out that the view of female sexuality portrayed by Masters and Johnson may have added new pressures on women to engage in sex when they didn't want to. It is also apparent from their books that Masters and Johnson are committed to promoting **heterosexuality** and marriage: all sexual relations are judged from a married, monoga-

mous, heterosexual standard; and their approach to the treatment of sexual problems reveals a concern with establishing sexual intercourse.

Masters and Johnson used their findings as the basis for developing a model of treatment for people with sexual problems. In 1970 they published *Human Sexual Inadequacy* which described their work as sex therapists. With a two-week treatment program and a reported high success rate, they offered a quick fix rather than psychotherapy or surgery. And their ideas – or perhaps, more accurately, the public attention they received – fueled interest in sex therapy and encouraged its growth from profession to lucrative industry.

During the 1970s Masters and Johnson turned their attention to **homosexuality**, leading to the publication, in 1979, of *Homosexuality in Perspective*. Where previously they had claimed that women and men are basically similar in terms of their sexual responses, now they claimed that homosexuals and heterosexuals are. But, although they stated that homosexuality was not a disease, they nonetheless claimed that they could usually cure it within two weeks. This work, and a subsequent alarmist book on **AIDS**, have been heavily criticized; it is for their early work that Masters and Johnson most deserve attention.   *DiR*

Paul Robinson *The Modernization of Sex* (New York: Cornell University Press, 1989)
Shelia Jeffreys *Anticlimax* (London: Women's Press, 1990)

See also **Koedt; Sexology; Sexual Revolution; Wright**

Mastretta, Angeles (1949-   )

Angeles Mastretta's first novel, *Arráncame la Vida/Mexican Bolero* (1986), propelled the Mexican literary world into a whirlwind. Set in the aftermath of the Mexican Revolution (1910-1920), it clearly satirizes the almost unbelievably named 'Party of the Institutionalised Revolution' that has now ruled Mexico for over sixty years. It also satirizes Latin sexual mores, particularly those of men:

men who expect their wives to be deflowered by them and so sweep girls (like the heroine Catalina) off their feet and from their houses at the age of fifteen; men who believe in maintaining various *casas chicas* (secret houses) where their mistresses and illegitimate families are installed; men who may regard courtly attentions to their wives by their political superiors as flattery of their good taste, but who kill rather than tolerate any reciprocal behavior hinting at their cuckoldry.

Catalina, whose husband's career embraces almost as much gangsterism as politics, succeeds by accepting the situation and by making it work for her. From the time when she learns from a fortune teller where the center of her sensuality is located, Catalina never ceases both to meet and to match her husband's schemes and desires. The cunning of women is portrayed alongside the idiocies of men, sometimes in ludicrous ways. When General Gómez gets drunk and looks likely to fall off a table, he accuses his wife – for lack of anyone more suitable to blame – of an incestuous relationship with her son. Somehow, 'Bibi struggled with the general's hands without losing her elegance.' Filial love, or rather the power that Latin women are suspected of having over sons, is also blamed (again, in masculine, usually military, outbursts) for turning the country's youth into homosexuals, as though male **bisexuality** weren't an accepted major part of Mexican relationships.

While notionally leaving politics to men, Catalina exercises power through the choice and manipulation of her lovers. Shortly before he dies, her husband concludes: 'I was right about you, you're bloody clever, like a man, that's why I forgive you your loose morals. I fucked with you better than anyone. You're the best woman *and* the best man I know, you bastard.' A feminist novel this is not. But one that portrays the stupidity and perversity of **machismo**, and the intelligence with which it is often resisted, it is.   *AmH*

Arráncame la Vida/Mexican Bolero (New York and London: Penguin 1991)

See also **Allende; Belli; Honor**

Masturbation

'Masturbation can be fun.' In the subversive 1960s 'tribal love-rock musical' *Hair*, this may have been the most subversive declaration of all. The word masturbation is generally used to mean stimulating one's own sexual organs for the purposes of sexual pleasure, and the act tends either to be ridiculed or venomously disapproved of.

The disapproval is usually part of a wider set of convictions. On the one hand, men shouldn't 'waste' their valuable, life-giving sperm; on the other, women should receive sexual pleasure, if they have to experience it at all, only from **sexual intercourse** with their husbands.

Both men and women have been punished for acts of masturbation – and various mechanical contraptions, from **chastity belts** to handcuffs, invented to prevent women doing it – but, by its nature, masturbation is difficult either to detect or prove where individuals are allowed any kind of privacy. This means that, in modern, western cultures, it has tended to be children (for whom privacy is scarce) who have been the most vulnerable to punishment.

Usually justified by the theory that masturbation drives people mad, such punishment has more often than not been grotesque. A nineteenth-century German child had a white-hot iron applied to her **clitoris** to cure her of wanting to touch it. At much the same time, a US doctor was recommending that masturbating boys be circumcised without an anesthetic. And, yet again in the USA, as recently as 1948, a five-year-old girl had her clitoris surgically removed to prevent her from stroking it.

Today in the west, where adults are concerned, masturbation is usually seen as a sign of social and sexual failure: pathetic, rather than dangerous. In English, to call a person a 'wanker' (a masturbator) is to accuse them of being not wicked but useless. Moreover, as part of this denigration, even to stimulate with one's hands the genitals of *another* person is likely to get one described as a masturbator: in other words, as someone who has inferior, marginally shameful sex.

There has, nonetheless, been retaliation. **Sade**, for one, could not see why 'spilling one's seed' should be seen as unnatural. In his 1791 novel *Justine* he argued that 'the ability we have in misplacing the vital fluid proves conclusively that it does not offend nature'. In *Annie Hall* (1977), the US filmmaker Woody Allen famously protested: 'Don't knock masturbation, it's sex with someone you love.' While the New Zealand poet Fleur Adcock has written, with wit and charm, 'Against Coupling': 'I write in praise of the solitary act:/ of not feeling a trespassing tongue/ forced into one's mouth . . . Five minutes of solitude are/ enough – in the bath, or to fill/ the gap between the Sunday papers and lunch.'

While masturbation inevitably lacks the surprise and compound eroticism of sex between two or more people – and usually needs some fantasizing to start it or to bring it to a climax – it also lacks the unpleasant shocks, frustrations and occasional dangers. And women, at least, tend to find it the surest way to achieve an orgasm. Indeed, of late, it has been quite common for popular women's magazines to run features on how to masturbate: with practical information on lubricants, shower heads, vibrators and so on. This is not so much because women are unable to imagine their own ways of masturbating – as *The Hite Report* (1976) revealed, most have – but more in order to remove the stigma, the sense of guilt or of shame. And it mightn't be such a bad idea if men's magazines were to copy this. Our needs for comfort, physical relief, sensual and sexual pleasure do not invariably have to be met by seducing, coercing or forcing someone else to provide them.   *HG*

See also **Baker Brown; Brown, Helen Gurley; Foreplay; Krafft-Ebing**

Maupin, Armistead (1944-   )

A novelist and gay activist, Armistead Maupin rose to ever-expanding cult acclaim through his *Tales of the City* sequence: six novels depicting the variant and sometimes conflicting life styles of the San Francisco of the late 1970s and the 1980s, particularly, but far from exclusively, the sexual life styles. The early volumes originally appeared as a newspaper serial and their slightly breathless tone derives partly from Maupin's need to get a climax – or at least a moment of humor or sentiment – into each episode. This sense of the immediacy of every moment was sufficiently in tune with how his readership felt about themselves for the serials to become popular.

The novels deal with the ongoing adventures of a group of men and women, straight, lesbian or gay, who have lived in, or been associated with the inhabitants of, the apartment block run by Anna Madrigal, a middle-aged woman with a mysterious past and a penchant for marijuana. What often seems an episodic arbitrariness usually turns out not to be so; the last volume of *Sure of You* (1989) ends with various denouements established as possibilities in earlier volumes. Maupin may not have planned this; it springs from his novelist's sense of human identity as a mixture of the essential and the contingent. His plots thus include a fair admixture of melodrama; at different times he has written about the aftermath of Jonestown, the discovery of a cult of Christian cannibals and all sorts of revelation of relationship and parenthood. The books capture their historical moment by reflecting its momentary concerns as well as by peopling it appropriately.

Part of the moment that Maupin found himself describing was the unfolding of the **AIDS** crisis, and part of his long-term importance is the way he has chronicled this convincingly in a series whose template he had long before created. His strong ethical sense and controlled sentimentality make his writing about AIDS sure-footed; it will, like the novels as a whole, stand as a record of the ways in which the San Francisco gay community chose to regard itself – in a skewed version of a standard American myth – as a saving fragment, a utopian exemplar of the good life, in adversity as well as in prosperity.

RK

Tales of the City (New York: Ballantine, 1987; London: Corgi, 1980)

See also **Core; Gay Liberation; Jarman; MacInnes**

Mead, Margaret (1902-1978)

An American anthropologist and the author of thirty-four books, Margaret Mead was primarily concerned with understanding the relationship between culture and personality. In 1925 she spent nine months on an island in Samoa carrying out field work with fifty adolescent girls. Her task was to look at a society radically different from the USA to see whether the turmoil of adolescence is biologically determined, and therefore universal, or determined by cultural factors.

In *Coming of Age in Samoa*, published in 1928, Mead describes an idyllic setting. Life for the Samoans is, she says, 'characterized by ease', with little conflict between people, no strong passions and a relaxed way of life. Adolescence, moreover, is a time of uninhibited lovemaking when girls choose and discard lovers at will before eventually settling down to marriage and childbearing. This relaxed attitude to sex might account for the lack of turbulence in adolescence, in contrast to the more puritanical sexual values of the USA in the 1920s.

Mead's work in Samoa has been criticized by Derek Freeman in his book *Margaret Mead and Samoa* (Cambridge, Massachusetts: Harvard University Press, 1983). Freeman questions Mead's field-work techniques and her assumption about sexual freedom, claiming that **virginity** is highly valued in Samoan culture and pre-marital promiscuity frowned upon. As one proof he cites a survey of young girls that he and his wife conducted, in which they found that seventy-three per cent of the girls were virgins. Unfortunately he does not describe his own field-work techniques for this survey. Freeman's book caused a sensation, not least because it is always good press when a prominent figure like Mead is attacked. But is it possible that Mead could have been so wrong about adolescent sexuality? Perhaps both Mead and Freeman are correct, but differ in their definition of lovemaking. In another Pacific island, Yap, a form of non-penetrative lovemaking, which allows for **orgasm** for both partners, is widely practiced before marriage. In a small, isolated, island community, birth control is crucial, as over-population would jeopardize survival in so precarious an environment. Mead is quite silent on the subject of birth control. Perhaps lovemaking for the girls in Mead's Samoa did not include penetration, while Freeman, taking a more masculine view, focused only on virginity.   *LC*

Coming of Age in Ssmoa (New York: Morrow, 1971, Harmondsworth: Penguin, 1971)

John Reader *Man on Earth* (New York: Harper Collins, 1990; Harmondsworth: Penguin, 1990)

See also **Benedict; Sexual Intercourse**

Menopause

The menopause is the natural process by which women cease to be fertile. It refers specifically to the last menstrual period, which occurs on average at the age of fifty and is precipitated by hormone changes, primarily a reduction in the amount of estrogen in the body.

The common myth that women lose sexual feelings and drive after the menopause dates back at least to Roman times. One theory that prevailed until the nineteenth century is that menopausal women decline sexually and emotionally because they retain toxic menstrual blood previously released during menstruation. More recently, gynecology, psychiatry and **psychoanalysis** have, in different and inconsistent ways, reinforced the idea that a woman's sexuality is inextricably linked to her fertility. For example, in the last century most menopausal women were viewed as suffering grief at the loss of their sexuality, while others were 'treated' for having 'erotic crises'.

Cultural traditions greatly influence perceptions of the menopause. Mexican Mayan women, who tend to marry early and experience repeated pregnancies until the menopause (when menstrual taboos and restrictions are also lifted), not surprisingly look forward to this life-stage. In western societies, however, this is less frequently the case. The Australian-born feminist Germaine **Greer** has written in praise of the menopause in *The Change* (1991) but, in general, Westerners dread it as a harbinger of old age, often requiring medical treatment, in particular hormone replacement therapy (HRT). Loss of sex drive, or libido, is still a frequently quoted symptom in medical textbooks. Testosterone, a hormone associated with male sexuality, is sometimes included with estrogen in HRT with the aim of increasing a woman's sexual desire. But female sexual desire is not primarily determined by hormones; adequate stimulation and a sensitive partner are much more important. And many women discover *increased* sexual pleasure after the menopause, especially if they have had heavy periods or problems finding a suitable contraceptive, and many enjoy sexual stimulation well into their old age, as illustrated in *The Hite Report* (New York: Macmillan, 1976). The only specific change associated with the reduction in estrogen is a tendency in some (though certainly not all) women for the vagina to be less well lubricated, which can lead to discomfort during **sexual intercourse**. Regular vaginal lubrication by **masturbation**, or an active sex life before the menopause, can help to prevent vaginal dryness, and lubricants and estrogen creams can also alleviate the problem. *MyH*

Myra Hunter *Your Menopause* (London: Pandora Press, 1990)

See also **Colette; Contraception; Kono**

Microcosm, The

An early novel by the English author Maureen Duffy, *The Microcosm* (1966) took **lesbianism** as its central theme at a time when neither feminism nor the **Gay Liberation** movement had publicly begun to challenge the assumption that all sexual practice should be heterosexual.

Originally conceived as a work of non-fiction, the novel is built on material gathered from British lesbians of the day. For Duffy, their great contradiction was having to live in secrecy in a London that was supposed to be at the heart of a **sexual revolution**. The text argues against this repression and proposes that to deny any one sexual preference is to diminish the whole of human possibility. The structure of the novel echoes this call for variety, employing a number of different narrative styles.

The lesbians in the book come from all walks of life, but most of them find themselves shoulder to shoulder in Duffy's fictional representation of the (now defunct) world-famous London lesbian bar, The Gateways. Here transformed into The House of Shades, the bar is where we are introduced to mid-1960s lesbian subculture. Women are strictly divided into roles that echo those of **heterosexuality**: some, the butch, wearing masculine attire and others, the femme, wearing feminine. (It is against the unwritten rules for butch women to relate to each other sexually; although, like heterosexual men, they may form relationships on a social level.) Outside the bar we are taken into the lives of several lesbians. Steve is a PE teacher, forced at work to brush off questions concerning her unmarried status. Cathy leaves her northern home and comes to London in search of herself; working as a bus conductor, she is able to wear trousers and attracts the support of a gay man who introduces her to other lesbians. Kay is a successful and rich hotelier who bemoans the fact that her job places strictures on the ways she can and cannot dress. Meanwhile, trapped in a stale and unsatisfying marriage, there is Marie. Her inclusion in the narrative is a telling reminder that marriage is not always proof of heterosexuality. The sex act between women has a low profile in the text and is alluded to with little explicit detail, beyond the fact that hands travel over bodies and climax is achieved.

Throughout the narrative, lesbian is considered to be something that you *are*: 'if it's in you it's got to come out'. One character looks forward to a time when 'we can all be what individually we are and nobody gives a damn'. The book proposes a liberal future in which lesbians would not have to live in their own microcosm but could take a full and open part in society. This 'what you are' perspective is at odds with later feminist and marxist sexual theory, which has argued for sexuality to be seen not as fixed but as a flexible component of behavior. The skillfully crafted text, however, which fully explores the various lives of lesbians from different classes, has deservedly received the accolade of being reprinted as a 'classic' by the feminist press Virago.   *CU*

The Microcosm (New York: Penguin, 1990; London: Virago, 1989)

See also **Bannon; Rule; Taylor; Wilhelm**

Miller, Alice

Alice Miller taught and practiced **psychoanalysis** in Switzerland for more than twenty years. Then, shocked by the amount of **child sexual abuse** she had encountered, she turned to writing books to explore the subject further. She was one of the first psychoanalysts to break with traditional Freudian theory and to advocate that children and adults who told of sexual abuse in childhood were to be believed.

Miller examines the whole range of abuse suffered by children at the hands of parents who are acting out their own lack of love and understanding in childhood. Her writings on the devastating effects of accepted child-rearing practice are beginning to have a profound impact, although she was at first scorned and ostracized in psychoanalytic circles.

To understand the phenomenal amount of abuse that she had come across, and wondering why other analysts hadn't reported similar findings, Miller went back to Sigmund **Freud**'s early writings. In 1896 Freud had published 'Studies on Hysteria' in which, with astonishment and reluctance, he recorded the frequency of sexual abuse among patients suffering from 'hysteria'. He concluded that the feelings arising from abuse suffered in childhood may be so successfully repressed that they remain **unconscious** and may only be reactivated and 'played out' again as an adult. But the scandal that this caused was so great that, within a few years, in order to preserve his reputation, Freud discarded these ideas and concluded that the sexual abuse in childhood reported by one female patient after another had never really taken place. To explain the symptoms they suffered in later life, and the stories they told about childhood abuse, he found, says Miller, 'the "solution" in infantile sexuality and the **Oedipus Complex** – in other words, his drive theory'. Under the weight of society's pressure – and in response to the command of obedience and deference to parents under which they themselves had lived – Freud and his followers, like so many others throughout history, had sided with the parent against the child.

Miller criticizes traditional practitioners of psychoanalysis for not believing their clients and, thereby, repeating their childhood trauma. For the clients would not have had to repress their feelings of acute distress, hurt, betrayal and confusion had there been someone at the time to believe them and to be prepared to take their side. Because her clients told her their stories in confidence, Miller uses already published biographies, often of famous people, to trace the history and consequences of childhood abuse. She believes that a wise counselor can help to break the circle of violence and abuse in which society is trapped. In a counselor or therapist, she says, we can find someone who is truly willing to understand us, making it possible to reclaim from the ocean of the unconscious the feelings of wounding that we suffered in childhood. By making those feelings conscious and extending compassion and love to the child who was hurt, and who is still inside the adult, we can be free of repeatedly 'acting from the place of the unconscious wound.' *JD*

For Your Own Good; Hidden Cruelty in Child-rearing and the Roots of Violence (New York: Farrar, Straus, 1983; London: Pluto, 1983); *Thou Shalt Not Be Aware: Society's Betrayal of the Child* (New York: Dutton, 1991; London: Pluto, 1985); *The Drama of Being a Child* (London: Virago, 1988); *The Untouched Key: Tracing Childhood Trauma in Creativity and Destructiveness* (New York: Doubleday, 1991; London: Virago, 1990); *Breaking Down the Wall of Silence* (New York: Dutton, 1991; London: Virago, 1991)

See also **Incest; Infantile Sexuality**

Miller, Henry (1891-1980)

Still one of the most controversial US novelists, Henry Miller never gave up his notions of sex as good male fun. Moving to Paris in 1930, the ageing satyr became the grand old erotician. Having abandoned the alimony and child-support payments to his first wife, living hand-to-mouth on remittances sent from New York by his second wife, he had one helluva fine time during his Paris years, which culminated in the publication of his first novel, *Tropic of Cancer*, in 1934. Its notoriously 'obscene' passages have not dated; the book contains the best comic sex scenes and the most passionate paens to language in English.

Lust is Miller's forte, not love. Plot is scant and one's feminism must be held in abeyance. *Black Spring* and *Tropic of Capricorn*, like the first *Tropic*, are uneven, but at their best exuberent and exhilarating. The later trilogy *The Rosy Crucifixion* (*Sexus, Plexus, Nexus*) fails.

Throughout his sojourn in the city of lovers, Miller read, wrote and rutted voraciously. 'Ye Gods! The first day of being a writer,' he says on 20 March 1922 in his first letter home. 'I feel I could turn out a book a month here. If I could get a stenographer to go to bed with me I could carry on twenty-four hours of the day.' In fact he did better than that. He got the writer Anais **Nin** into his bed. Not only was she brilliant and beautiful, she was married to a banker. Suddenly life was grand. Miller, most of whose female characters are merely walking cunts, nonetheless regarded Nin as 'my equal in every way'. They danced a sexual quadrille which embraced Nin's husband Hugh Guiler, who was handsome and far more sophisticated than Miller, and Miller's wife June, who was moodier than Nin but no less sexy.

Language was the ultimate aphrodisiac. The books he was reading – Ezra Pound's poetry, Walt **Whitman** – like the books he was writing, excited Miller. In his rambling letter of 24 August 1931, tucked into a sentence in brackets, comes the momentous announcement: '(I start tomorrow on the Paris book: first person, uncensored, formless – fuck everything!)' In a year, *Tropic of Cancer* was finished. Despairing of finding a publisher, he wrote to his friend and fellow Brooklynite Emil Schnellock: 'The worst coming to the worst, Anais will sell her fur coat and publish it privately.' The pornographic Obelisk Press, which had published Frank Harris's risqué *My Life and Loves* but rejected D.H. **Lawrence**'s *Lady Chatterley's Lover*, signed Miller. Fearing that prosecution for **obscenity** would eat into profits, Obelisk repeatedly postponed the book, publishing two years late and only when Nin guaranteed the finance. At the age of forty-three, the boy writer became a man.

It would be another quarter of a century before the courts allowed *Tropic of Cancer* to be legally imported into Britain or the USA and over half a century before Nin's unexpurgated journal appeared revealing the torrid details of her affair with Miller and his wife. The movie version *Henry and June* (1990) sparked yet another battle with the US censors. *AB*

Tropic of Cancer (New York: Random House, 1987); *Black Spring* (New York: Grove Weidenfeld, 1989; London: John Calder, 1968); *Tropic of Capricorn* (New York: Random House, 1987); *Sexus* (New York: Grove Weidenfeld, 1987; London: Panther, 1970); *Plexus* (New York: Random House, 1987); *Nexus* (New York: Grove Weidenfeld, 1987)

See also **Brassaï; Hemingway**

Miller, Lee (Elizabeth) (1907-1977)

Along with Tina **Modotti** and Suzanne **Valadon**, Lee Miller has a place in that company of women who were both the erotic object of the artist's gaze – the **nude** model – and themselves creators of images. Restless and much traveled, Miller's great physical beauty was the passport to a life whose nomadic glamor has acquired the posthumous radiance of myth.

Her career began in New York City when *Vogue*'s publisher, Condé Nast, spotted her potential as a model and she became a successful fashion-plate, elegant in the East Coast, thoroughbred style, photographed by Edward Steichen and other famous names. Pursuing her own aspirations as a photographer, she moved to Paris in 1929 and persuaded Man Ray to take her on as an apprentice. It is as his lover and the model for his most ravishing nude studies – images of blonde perfection – that she is still best known, and as a member of the Parisian surrealist circle (she later married the English painter Roland Penrose). She played the part of an armless statue in Jean Cocteau's film *Le Sang d'un poète* (1930).

Miller's photographic work was talented but sporadic: surreal Paris street scenes and fashion shots for the great couturiers; studio portraiture in New York; Egyptian desertscapes; *Vogue* assignment pictures of blitzed London and a brief moment of journalistic glory as a war correspondent. It was constantly disrupted and overshadowed by the image of Lee Miller, model. She posed nude not just for Man Ray, but for her father, with whom she had a closeness that one biographer says 'may have bordered on an unhealthy intimacy'. She also posed for herself, and her elegant portraits of other women often curiously echo her own style of

Theodore Miller, stereoscopic photograph of Lee Miller, 1928

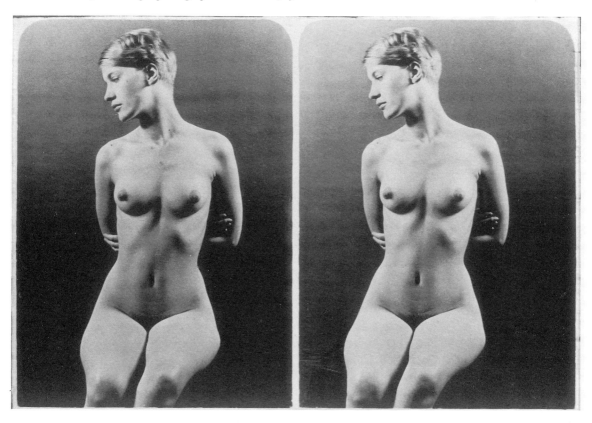

173

cool blonde beauty. There's a narcissistic mirror aspect to much of this that's almost perverse. She took horrifyingly eloquent photographs of the newly liberated concentration camps, then went on to be snapped in Hitler's bathtub, her combat boots on the mat and the Führer's picture beside her.

Independent and wayward, Miller was no victim, but a woman constantly on the move and remaking herself. Yet she also went on recreating herself as erotic object, apparently seduced by the images others had made of her and by their power to provoke desire.   *LH*

Anthony Penrose *The Lives of Lee Miller* (London: Thames & Hudson, 1985)

See also **Khalo; Surrealism; Voyeurism; Wharton**

Miller, Sue (1943-)

Sue Miller is one of the most popular writers of mainstream literary fiction in the USA. She began devoting herself to a writing career in the late 1970s when a series of grants enabled her to abandon the various jobs – teacher, psychological researcher, waitress, model – that had supported her. These experiences, plus her traditional family upbringing in Chicago, a Radcliffe education, marriage, motherhood and divorce, gave her the background to create the modern domestic situations she ably portrays.

Family crises, interpersonal relationships and sex – lots of it – are the stuff of Miller's stories. Her women, all heterosexual, often divorced, are usually equal partners with their men in deriving sexual pleasure. They make love willingly, frequently, guiltlessly. Even the children are sexually aware and playful. On the surface, sex in Miller's world is assumed to be healthy and pervasive.

But is it that simple? In *The Good Mother* (1986), the author's blockbuster first novel, later made into a movie, the sexuality of both Anna Dunlap and her young daughter conspires against them: they lose each other in a custody fight initiated, in effect, by the girl's sexual curiosity and exacerbated by Anna's love affair. 'Appropriate Affect', a story in the collection titled *Inventing the Abbots* (1987), features one of the few Miller women who 'in passion . . . was disappointed' by a 'rigid and unimaginative' husband. This grandmother's extended family is shocked – a daughter would almost rather see her dead – when a stroke damages her sense of inhibition and causes her to speak frankly about their sexual lives, past and present. Miller's second novel, *Family Pictures* (1990), describes the spiritual sexuality of Lainey Eberhardt, mother of six. When her third child is autistic, her psychiatrist husband blames her; when, to prove him wrong, she quickly produces three more 'perfect' babies, against his will, he is angry and ever more distant because of what he views as her abuse of sexual power.

Because all this is fiction, Miller's message – relayed symbolically rather than directly – is ambiguous. Her honest reporting of sexuality with its many forms, meanings and motives is refreshing, in that she neither recommends nor discourages, is neither graphic nor coy. Sex is presented as an inevitable influence, as how we are. Yet the consequences can be punishing. Perhaps she is reflecting the post-1960s tightrope that women must walk, where on the one hand they are variously allowed, encouraged or expected to be their natural sexual selves in their personal lives, but on the other their freedom is restricted by the law, the family, psychiatry, any of the social institutions overarching the individual.   *DJ*

The Good Mother (New York: Dell, 1987; London: Pan, 1987); *Inventing the Abbots* (New York: Dell, 1988; London: Gollancz, 1987); *Family Pictures* (New York: Harper Collins, 1991; London: Gollancz, 1990)

See also **Alther; Sexual Revolution**

Mills & Boon

See also **Romantic Fiction; Romantic Love**

With love and marriage as their territory, sex has always been implicit in Mills & Boon romances: from the company's first publications for the British market in 1909, through its purchase in 1971 by the North American romance house Harlequin, to its current worldwide mass market. But it is only in the 1920s, and then from the 1970s on, that sex scenes are actually described, obviously reflecting the moral codes of society at the time. In both periods the novels describe only heterosexual sex and there are no relationships between white characters and black, although, from the 1970s, Latin, Arab and Native American males are eroticized.

Sex and love are inextricably intertwined in Mills & Boon fiction. The implicit ideology is that sexual attraction is essential to love, that good sex is an essential expression of that love and that sex is better with love than without it. Indeed, in the 1970s and 1980s, the heroine often reaches **orgasm** only with the man she loves: the hero. In these books, it is only after she has acknowledged her love for the hero that the heroine has sex with him. More recently, however, the hero and heroine accept their sexual attraction for each other, act on it and only then realize that they love one another.

When descriptions of **sexual intercourse** were first permitted in both periods, **rape** was also described. In the 1920s it was rape by the hero of the heroine, but the present-day ethos takes the (for feminists unacceptable) view that, although the heroine might be raped by another man as a show of power over her, she is 'forcefully seduced' by the hero, as his feelings of frustrated desire and love and his anger at the heroine's continual denial of attraction to him overwhelm him. In both decades, however, in this type of book the hero eventually breaks down and begs the heroine for her love, so that the book ends on a note of female, not male, power: with sex seen as the male weapon, love as the female. *jD*

Carol Thurston *The Romance Revolution: Erotic Novels for Women and the Quest for a New Sexual Identity* (Urbana and Chicago: University of Illinois Press, 1987)

Mira Bai (1498-1547)

The life of Mira Bai, princess of Merta, Rajasthan, has largely been reconstructed through her poetry and an abundance of legends. A wandering ascetic is believed to have given her an idol of the sexually magnetic, dark god Krishna, who lifted a mountain to bring rain to drought-stricken Braj. Mira Bai fell so deeply in love with this mountain wielding cowherd that, during her marriage ceremony to the crown prince of Mewar, she addressed her vows to the idol. Her refusal to worship Mewar's patron-goddess Kali alienated both royal families. When Mira Bai's husband died in 1521 she broke royal tradition further by traveling with male peripatetics, dancing ecstatically in Krishna temples and chanting her love verses to him. Mira Bai writes that the murder attempts by subsequent rulers of Mewar, who thought her unchaste and a spy, were thwarted by Krishna, her protector.

Written in a mixture of her native Marvari and the language of Braj, Mira Bai's poetry is spontaneous and intense, containing an appeal which has preserved it to this day as part of the worship of millions in north India. Mira Bai truly believed that she was wedded to Krishna and chose for most of her lyrics the Madhurya Bhava (romantic style) of the Bhakta corpus, emphasizing that the love of man and woman, with all its agony and **ecstasy**, is the highest ideal of human interrelationship. Her poetry, usually set to specific musical modes (ragas), describes her as Krishna's wife, beloved and friend, and she often uses the erotic monsoon imagery of the Hindu tradition. 'The Dark-one lives in my heart/I cannot sleep/I will not drink of monsoon pools/The spring from Hari will quench my thirst/His body is strong and dark . . .' Sometimes the anticipation of consummation is explicit. 'The sound of his flute/Sets my body quivering/Mira says: Lord Giridhar/Quell this anguish now . . .'

It is only rarely that Mira Bai acknowledges her

M

lover as the transcendent, formless god of her fellow mystics. To her he is first her divine husband. It is widely believed that Krishna finally answered her appeals by taking her body from his temple, which she was last seen entering to take sanctuary from Mewar soldiers. When they followed her in they found only her clothes. *SH*

Usha Nilson *Mira Bai* (New Delhi: Sahitya Akademi, 1969)

See also **Ghazal; Khusrau**

Mirbeau, Octave

See Torture Garden, The

Misogyny

Misogyny, the hatred of women, is quite distinct from indifference to women, or from the eminently practical wish to exploit them. The latter, if only in the short term, can be seen as being in men's interest. Misogyny, an irrational terror of women as slimy, sexually devouring, frigidly castrating, emotionally unstable, brain-damaged and *different from men*, cannot. That said, misogyny is not a rare condition. Not only is it overtly present in violent acts against women as women – from **rape** to the burning of witches – it is also the quietly bubbling fuel for a plethora of anti-woman jokes, a maze of perplexing rules, laws and customs and a number of superficially calm but illogical antifeminist statements. And these, in turn, help to fill each new generation of men with their fathers' fear while simultaneously disguising it as rational, scientific and 'manly': so that, in practice, it is hard to disentangle the expedient reasons for men's oppression of women from the seriously disturbed. The hope in all this must be that, as we dismantle the practical patriarchal structures, so the misogynous, poisonous plant that clings to them and to which they cling will collapse and expire of malnutrition. *HG*

See also **Homophobia; Machismo; Patriarchy**

Mizoguchi, Kenji (1898-1956)

Born in downtown Tokyo, the son of a poor artisan, and receiving no formal education after elementary school, the filmmaker Kenji Mizoguchi consistently portrayed the lives of the oppressed: those who, both before and after World War II, formed the lowest social layer in the Japanese class system. In particular Mizoguchi showed their misery, their beauty and their strength through such female characters as prostitutes, or wives deserted by their husbands, drawn both from modern Japanese life and from classical literary texts.

Mizoguchi's Japan is a class-oriented, patriarchal society, one torn between rich and poor, between men and women. Through portrayals of the tragic struggles for survival of women of the oppressed class, those who are subject to dual oppression, he presents a biting criticism of Japanese society. Yet he is never pessimistic. While men in the upper class control money and power, making their women submissive to them, men in the oppressed class, who are deprived of both money and power, depend on their women for survival and the maintenance of pride. It is the women's instinct for survival and nurturing – their commitment to support, protect and care for those who depend on them – that preserves hope for human life and dignity.

The *Red Light District* (1955), Mizoguchi's last film, portrays the lives of the prostitutes in Yoshiwara on the eve of the passing of the antiprostitution bill. Yoshiwara is the traditional district of **prostitution**, secluded from the middle-class citizens, where the prostitutes work for brothel-owners who monopolize the licensed business. Democratic reforms, led by activists in the women's movement, abolished the system of licensed prostitution in 1955, leaving the prostitutes unemployed. Women in *The Red Light District* consider that selling their bodies is necessary to exist; also, to support their parents, husbands, children. Male customers visit the district desiring just one night of pleasure, but, captured by the women's soothing, enwrapping and manipulating sexuality, become frequent visitors. One prostitute becomes insane, deserted by a son who cannot accept what his mother does for a living, while another successfully saves money by cheating men and, at high interest, lending money to her fellow prostitutes. Mizoguchi's capitalist, sexist society continues to exploit women, but their sexuality is never stifled: rather, their nurturing, aggressive maternity forms the underlying force for will and hope in even the most devastating situations.   *NM*

Naniwa/Elegy (1936); *Gion no Shimai/The Sisters of Gion* (1937); *Yoruno Onnatachi/The Women of the Night* (1948); *Koshuku Ichidai Onna/ A Life of an Amorous Woman* (1952); *Ugetsu Monogatari/ The Story of the Rain and the Moon* (1953); *Sanshodayu* (1954); *Akasenn Chitai/The Red Light District* (1955)

Yoshitaka Yoda *Mizoguchi Kenji no Hito to Geijutsu/ Mizoguchi and His Art* (Tokyo: Tabata Shoten, 1983)

See also **Emecheta; Wa Thiong'o**

Modotti, Tina (Assunta Adelaide Luigia) (1896-1942)

In antithesis to Edward Weston, the photographer whose lover, model and pupil she was for some time, Tina Modotti always refused the name 'artist'. Weston's Whitmanesque vision put woman in the sensual and mystical realm of nature, leaving such images as 'Tina on the Azotea' to confirm the formal analogies between the female **nude** and the shells, rocks and peppers that he also photographed. Most histories of photography subsume Modotti into Weston's myth of the artist, forever enclosed in his images of her. But, more than any other woman, both with her camera and in her life, she crossed the boundary between being seen as esthetic, erotic object, and seeing.

Modotti was born in Italy, went to work in a textile factory at the age of twelve and, the next year, emigrated to the USA. After marrying the poet

and painter Robo in 1917, she began working as an actress in Hollywood silents. In 1923 she went with Weston to Mexico, where she became involved in anti-fascist and revolutionary politics, in close association with Mexican artists who included Diego Rivera and Frida **Kahlo**. In 1924 she exhibited jointly with Weston in Mexico City. Her work was much influenced by him formally, also by the German New Objectivity photographers, but her range is greater and her synthesis of political commitment and formal abstraction creates a dynamic poetic vision that validates the radical potential of a modernist esthetic. She photographed everyday peasant and city life, often using emblematic compositions to describe the elements in revolutionary struggle or to represent intellectual and manual labor; her photographs of women emphasize the physicality of their work, particularly in relation to the body's nurture of children. Modotti joined the Communist Party and worked as a journalist and editor in Mexico until she was deported for political activities in 1930. Continuing her activism, she then lived in Berlin and Moscow, in France and in Spain, where she was a reporter on a Republican newspaper during the Civil War. In 1939 she returned to Mexico, where she died. She is much commemorated and Pablo Neruda wrote a poem on her death.   *LH*

Museum of Modern Art, New York City; George Eastman House, Rochester; National Library, Mexico City; Comitato Tina Modotti, Trieste; Collection of Vittorio Vidali, Udine

See also **Miller, Lee; Mizoguchi; Wa Thiong'o**

Mona Lisa

An incisive cinematic exploration of the illusory nature of **romantic love**, *Mona Lisa* was directed by the Irish novelist turned filmmaker Neil Jordan. The movie boasts a fine script, co-written by Jordan and David Leland, and superb performances by the two leads: Bob Hoskins as the small-time hood, George, and Cathy Tyson as the high-class black prostitute, Simone, to whom George becomes chauffeur.

Feisty George returns from doing seven years in the pen, having taken the rap for a slimy gangland boss (Michael Caine). As his 'reward' George gets assigned as driver to the call girl Simone, whom we first see standing on the mezzanine level of a luxury hotel, literally looking down on George as he waits uncomfortably for his unknown passenger. Then the two meet and George very soon takes on the role of protector, fascinated by this beautiful woman whose stylishness, self-control and aloofness only add to her mystery. One evening, he asks about her customers: 'They fall in love with you?' Simone answers succinctly: 'Sometimes they fall for what they think I am.'

At the end of every evening, Simone has George drive her through the nocturnal hooker strips of London so that she can search for 'Cathy', another hooker, a friend, someone special to her. 'I promised I would look after her,' she explains. The shots of Simone seen in the rear-view mirror, her troubled eyes darting back and forth, her head pivoting about in search of the missing someone, are especially haunting. Eventually Simone sends George out to search for Cathy on his own. As a Cockney knight-in-shining-armor, he begins to prowl the strip joints, the peep shows, the porno shops, the tawdry nightspots of London where he sees more than he bargains for. In these places of degraded encounters, only deluded desire can hide the ugliness and cruelty. While George, of course, is also not free from the clutches of delusion. Having painted his picture of Simone, he has fallen in love with it and, when his illusions are smashed in a series of violent revelations, it becomes clear that Simone, too, is a relentless romantic. Except that her idealized love object isn't George.

Mona Lisa is a rare film in portraying a prostitute as flesh, blood and soul. Tyson, who was twenty when she made it, gives a stunning performance as a woman alternately unattainable, frosty, the object of romantic yearning, and painfully vulnerable as its desperate subject.   SC

Mona Lisa (1986)

See also **Prostitution**

Monogamy

Monogamy is the practice of taking one sexual partner for life – or, as indicated by the expression 'serial monogamy', one partner at a time. Monogamous marriage is essential to the nuclear family, the basic unit of western social order, and is a male-controlled institution forged for the domination of women, children and property.

Men's discovery of the connection between **sexual intercourse** and childbirth was probably the most crucial driving force behind the imposition of monogamy upon women. Biological fatherhood assumed increased importance with the accumulation of wealth, which men wished to pass on to their legitimate heirs, so that the notion of 'private property' became extended to children and to women, the sexual activity of the latter being strictly confined to and controlled by her husband to ensure that any children she might bear were his.

Two major factors have dictated the development of monogamy: religious belief and habitat. As **patriarchy** gained ascendance, female symbols of the divine waned along with the awe invested in motherhood. With male ascendancy came polygamy, the taking by a man of more than one partner at a time, and this prevailed throughout the early patriarchal period, particularly among the kind of nomadic communities, ruled over by clan chieftains, that we read of in the Old Testament. When and as this kind of community adapted itself to a more settled, agrarian life, blood ties became more sharply delineated. Wives and children could no longer be acquired, shed and shared at will since their labor was needed for the prosperity and survival of the individual family. Monogamy became the norm. Then the Hebrew God's relationship with the human community came, in biblical teaching, to be imaged in terms of a 'sacred marriage'. Monotheism, a belief in One God, became symbolically intertwined with the teaching on monogamy – except in monotheistic **Islam**, where polygamy remains enshrined in law – while **adultery**, prohibited by the seventh of the Ten Commandments, served as a metaphor for 'forsaking the Lord' (though a rigid double standard, involving heavier penalties for marital transgression by women, was what was actually practiced).

Under **Christianity**, marriage was completely transformed from a civil institution into a spiritual condition, a symbol of the eternal marriage of Christ and the church: a teaching which has been used to justify the ban on divorce (and all other forms of sexual repression practiced in western culture). But this symbolism was itself neglected as Christianity focused more and more intensely on **virginity** as the highest human estate. Monogamy became seen and taught in terms of damage limitation: the only thinkable but always inadequate compromise with the flesh.

With the demise of feudal theocracy and the rise of the concept of **romantic love**, the universal practice of arranged marriage was called into question and, around the sixteenth century, a new ideal of marriage, based on sexual attraction and mutual affection, came to prominence. For the first time the marital requirement to 'forsake all other' could be seen in positive terms: as a measure of the seriousness and intensity of a couple's desire for and commitment to one another. However, this new dispensation coincided with the rise of the bourgeois family and women's increased economic dependence therein. With this arose the belief that women were 'naturally' monogamous: nesting creatures who must 'tame' men into domesticity.

Romantic heterosexual monogamy is now being promoted as the coming state: as the way to combat **AIDS** and uphold 'family values'. Despite the fact that there are other ways of avoiding AIDS, and better ways of living than the nuclear family, the question of exclusivity and permanence – most commonly couched in terms of monogamous versus non-monogamous relationships – is one which now arises at some point in most long-term committed relationships. It is made even more pressing and perplexing for lesbians and gay men who have the additional pressure of prejudice against their liaisons, which are presumed to be automatically both transitory and promiscuous, and for whom there are no proper marriage rites, or rights, anyway. *SD*

Susan Dowell *They Two Shall Be One: Monogamy in Religion and History* (London: Collins, 1990)

See also **Celibacy; Chastity; Gay Liberation; Heterosexism; Judaism; Sexual Revolution**

Morreau, Jacqueline (1929-   )

A US-born figurative painter working on the representation of women from a feminist viewpoint, Jacqueline Morreau studied with Rico Lebrun in Los Angeles and completed a training in medical illustration before settling permanently in London in 1972. Technical skill and concern with depicting the human body have both remained central to her work, even when this commitment contravened feminism's 1970s rejection of oil painting as too traditional to be politically valid. Although Morreau's art is traditional in appearance, it is revolutionary in content.

Morreau was one of the four artists who organized **Women's Images Of Men** – a touring exhibition which opened at the Institute of Contemporary

Jacqueline Morreau, *She Who Spins*, 1988

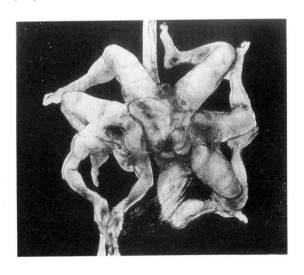

Arts and toured Britain in 1980–1981 – and, in her paintings and drawings, she has continued to express what she has described as 'the divided self'. Through metaphorical scenes, often derived from classical mythology, Morreau presents complex and often conflicting views of women which not only reclaim and represent familiar stories from a female perspective, but also act as allegories for the values of contemporary society. Subjects have included images of Siamese-twin women carrying out contradictory tasks, the Three Fates, Pandora, the embracing naked figures of Adam and Eve and of Psyche and Eros. Just as Greek mythology is underpinned by stratas of complex and ambiguous sexual messages, so are Morreau's paintings. A series of male and female figures in water, painted in 1990, combines confident handling of paint and line with an ambiguity of emotion. Morreau is one of the few artists to produce work that is both didactic and open to wide interpretation.   *LBu*

Jacqueline Morreau: Drawings & Graphics (Scarecrow, NJ 1986)

With Sarah Kent *Women's Images of Men* (London: Pandora Press, 1985)

See also **Graham**

Motion Picture Production Code, The

See **Hays Code**

Munch, Edvard (1863-1944)

Edvard Munch was born in Norway, studied at the Oslo School of Design and worked in Paris and Berlin where he was an influence on the development of German Expressionism. His mother died when he was five and he never married. His greatest work was done between 1892 and his breakdown in 1908, in particular the prints and oils associated with the 'Frieze of Life' cycle. Although artistically exciting, the works exhibit uncomfortable evidence of misogynistic ideas derived from Arthur Schopen-

hauer.

Munch is a painter of Woman with a capital W. Finding women both desirable and terrifying, he exhibits his unease in a woodcut of a vampire hovering over a skeletal male. A woodcut picturing a **nude** woman inside a man's head is a graphic depiction of his obsession. 'The Three Stages of Woman' (1894) epitomizes his attitude, with a manic red-haired nude, signifying sexual passion, centered between a virginal dreamer in white and an almost invisible older woman in black. 'Puberty' (1893), inspired by an etching by Felicien **Rops**, shows a young girl sitting naked and nervous on the edge of her bed, her eyes frightened, her body contained by the oval of her long arms, her hands crossed between her thighs. With its misplaced attitude of pity and horror, it is an example of the fascination with which a sensitive (and terrified) male of the time might view menstruation.

A powerless victim of her body when young, fit only to grieve or nurse when old, Woman in her prime has an irresistible destructive power. In 'Jealousy' (1895) Munch envisages the beloved with his rival. She is dressed in red, her breasts and sex revealed, a scarlet woman or whore of Babylon. The notorious 'Madonna' (1893) shows a red-haired woman, nude from the waist up, one arm pinned behind her, the other flung above her head which is thrown back in sexual abandon. Sperm shapes wriggle round the frame. It is an icon of a whole range of nineteenth-century male fears and fantasies about Woman as madonna, whore, vampire and life source, all-powerful in her control of men's desires. So powerful is she in her sexuality that, in 'Death and the Maiden' (1893), Munch paints her as the active partner in the embrace. In *La Revue Blanche* of June 1896, his compatriot August **Strindberg** described Munch's painting 'The Kiss' as 'The fusion of two beings, the smaller of which [the woman], shaped like a carp, seems on the point of devouring the larger as is the habit of vermin, microbes, vampires and women.'   *FB*

The Munch Museum, Oslo

See also **Klimt; Masochism; Misogyny**

Edvard Munch, *Death and the Maiden, c.* 1893

N

Nabokov, Vladimir (1899-1977)

See Lolita

Necrophilia

Necrophilia can be defined as a morbid attraction to corpses or, more particularly, as **sexual intercourse** with dead bodies. It is probably the ultimate social taboo, surpassing even cannibalism. So repulsive is the concept that it rarely appears as a crime on the statute books.

In 1979 a California mortuary worker, Karen Greenlee, was charged with interference with a burial. A self-proclaimed necrophile, she has provided an extraordinarily candid and detailed account of her sexual preference. 'The body is just laying there but it has what it takes to make me happy. The cold, the aura of death, the smell of death, the funereal surroundings, it all contributes.' She asserts that necrophilia is not at all uncommon among morticians. Sex murderers are by and large reluctant to confess to necrophilia. The Wisconsin ghoul Edward Gein (arrested in 1957) on whom Robert Bloch based his novel *Psycho* was a necrophile, as was London murderer John Christie (arrested 1953) of 10 Rillington Place. More recently, the homosexual serial killer Dennis Nilsen (arrested 1983) also had necrophiliac tendencies.

In literature, writers such as **Sade** and Georges **Bataille** have deliberately transgressed the taboo. Other authors, notably Edgar Allen Poe and some of the Gothic novelists, manifest strong unconscious necrophile urges in their work. Vampire novels from Bram Stoker's *Dracula* onwards express powerful erotic impulses towards morbidity. There are also a number of obscure minor novels which deal specifically with necrophilia: for example, Guy Endor's 1930s *Werewolf of Paris* which describes the famous case of the French necrophile Sergeant Bertrand. *EY*

Interview with Karen Greenlee in *Apocalypse Culture* ed. Adam Parfrey (New York: Feral House, 1990)

Harold Schechter *Deviant: The Story of Ed Gein* (New York: Pocket Books, 1989) Ludovic Kennedy *10 Rillington Place* (London: Panther, 1984) Brian Masters *Killing for Company: The Case of Dennis Nilsen* (London: Coronet, 1985)

See also **Obscenity**

Neel, Alice (1900-1984)

Although she had been working since the 1920s, it was not until the 1970s that US artist Alice Neel began to receive the attention she deserved. She was primarily a portrait painter and had steadily pursued her course through the decades when portraits – indeed, any kind of figurative painting – were out of fashion.

Neel painted the naked body only occasionally, but always to superb effect. Like other twentieth-century women, she challenged the conventional, idealized, anonymous **nude**, but she also subverted an even more insidious dream: that, in stripping off clothes, we can somehow strip off social convention to liberate an essential self, an essential sexuality. Neel's nudes are individuals. For her, the bare body is as psychologically expressive as the face and, sometimes, even more revealing of the social pressures which shape us.

Neel's naked bodies always bear the marks of their time, place and class. Her intense physical empathy with her subjects' vulnerability and mortality goes with a shrewd social understanding. A man dying of TB may be posed like a secularized Christ, but he is never more, or less, than a neighbor in Spanish Harlem. The pregnant figures (who include Neel's daughter-in-law Nancy) are modern urban women, tired, tense, thoughtful, rather than archetypes. A 1930s portrait of a woman in a blue hat and beads catches the careful chic that has become second nature. A portrait of the art critic John Perrault, sprawled across a bed in traditional female pose, enjoys his self-conscious pleasure as he collaborates with the artist in overturning an art-historical stereotype. While a sympathetically ironic double portrait of the feminist art historian Cindy Nemser and her husband acknowledges that even

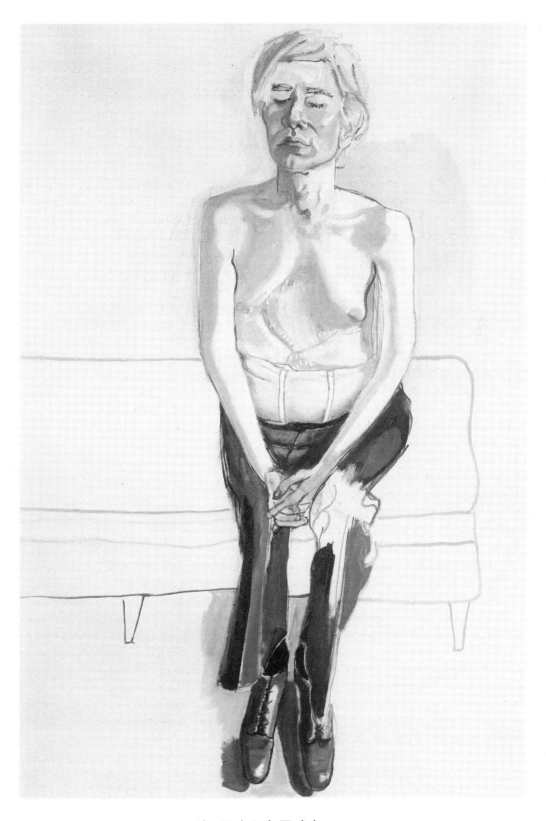

Alice Neel, *Andy Warhol*, 1970

liberated, liberal people can find it hard to discard their embarrassment at exposing themselves to Neel's cool gaze.

With some of her male nudes, that cool, analytic vision verges on cruelty. A remarkable, surreal 1930 portrait of a Greenwich Village eccentric called Joe Gould – his penis, sometimes stylized, sometimes described in disconcertingly meticulous detail, recurs five times – is a devastating comment on exhibitionism and impotence. And, in her best known portrait, a study of Andy **Warhol** not long after a near-fatal shooting, Neel's sympathy for the dreadfully wounded body is inseparable from her insight into the curious pleasures to be found in martyrdom, in **masochism**.   *MW*

Patricia Hills *Alice Neel* (New York: Abrams, 1983)

See also **Beale; Graham; Morreau; Voyeurism**

New Portuguese Letters

New Portuguese Letters, published in 1972, became famous as 'The Case of the Three Marias': its authors, María Isabel Barreno, María Fatima Velho da Costa and María Teresa Horta, being first subjected to scandalous attacks and then to prolonged legal action. The book consists of poetry and prose written in the form of intimate letters between three present-day women and contains a frankness in discussing sexuality not previously published under Portugal's lengthy Salazar dictatorship. It was all the more shocking that the taboo should have been broken by women, in particular women overtly writing from a feminist perspective.

Long before foreign-language translations were available, women's liberation groups in many countries had joined in protest at the censorship. International writers' organizations followed; *samizdat* copies of the text were circulated. The book was generally regarded as being not only of substantial artistic value, but also of pioneering value in treating openly such subjects as abortion, female **masturbation** and **sado-masochism**. In April 1974, the judge abruptly ended its trial, ordered all

the charges to be dropped and, proclaiming *New Portuguese Letters* to be a work of outstanding merit, urged its authors to continue writing.

María Isabel Barreno and María Fatima Velho da Costa were, in fact, already established writers, friends since adolescence who worked together in the Economics Ministry. María Teresa Horta was likewise a published poet and the literary editor of a Lisbon daily newspaper. The three had decided to share the experience of being 'progressive' or 'erotic' writers under Salazar's declining military dictatorship by holding weekly meetings to discuss their work. Out of these grew the unusual format of *New Portuguese Letters*, whose inspiration was the famous *Letters of a Portuguese Nun* written by the young Mariana Alcoforado to her wayward French lover in the 1650s. Although only five of those letters have survived, the intensity of their passion, pain and, finally, resolution has inspired many subsequent writers. The 'Three Marias' found in her a sister and a mentor, and together compiled a rare volume of poetry, letters and prose stories that is both lyrical and candid, erotic and cruelly honest.

AmH

See also **Obscenity**

Newman, Andrea (1938-   )

Andrea Newman is a British novelist and TV playwright who, since the mid-1970s, has had enormous popular success with her sagas of **adultery, incest, sado-masochism** and seduction among the middle classes. 'What you end up with is a genteel version of those Marquis de Sade fantasies in which the butcher, the baker and the candlestick maker find themselves all roped into the action,' has commented TV critic Clive James.

It was Newman's own TV adaptation of her 1969 novel *A Bouquet of Barbed Wire* that, in 1976, brought her to prominence in Britain. Twenty-four million viewers tuned in to the weekly seven-part series, in which a middle-aged publisher's marriage is destroyed by his lust for his daughter, Prue, and the revelation that both his wife and Prue are actually masochists. In the character of Prue the series introduced a favorite Newman stereotype: the innocent, manipulative, child-woman, teenage nymphet. The success of *A Bouquet of Barbed Wire* spawned a TV sequel the following year, *Another Bouquet of Barbed Wire*, in which the characters – minus Prue, who died at the end of the first play, a moral retribution – tried out the sexual permutations that they hadn't previously exhausted.

A Sense of Guilt, which was published as a novel in 1988 and transmitted as a TV play in Britain in 1990, was deliberately set half a decade before, in 1985-1986. 'I wanted it to take place at a time before there was any real awareness of **AIDS**; I didn't feel I could cope with any more complications,' said Newman. In it, the apparent harmony of family life is disrupted by the rakish Felix, who betrays the trust of friendship by having an affair with his best friend's stepdaughter, Sally, another nymphet. As in all of Newman's work, the shattering of a contrived moral order is an excuse to reassert an even more conservative world view, in which heterosexual couplings are held up for voyeuristic titillation while 'deviant' sex – Richard's unresolved homosexual feelings for Felix; Inge's multiple and violent sexual encounters – is punished with terminal unhappiness. The success of Newman's tangled tales owes much to the medium of TV, which has not only brought them a mass audience but lent them a tasteful, soft-focus glow that suggest that they may be naughty, but they're always nice.   *LG*

A Bouquet of Barbed Wire (Harmondsworth: Penguin, 1976); A Sense of Guilt (Harmondsworth: Penguin, 1989)

See also **Lolita**

Nin, Anaïs (1903-1977)

Despite a significant literary output, including such novels as *House of Incest* (1936), the French-born American Anaïs Nin achieved fame only with the publication, from the 1960s onward, of her *Diaries*.

This fame was increased with the posthumous publication of two **erotica** collections: *Delta of Venus* (1977) and *Little Birds* (1979).

Nin's novels are intensely written works, surrealist in their use of dreamlike images and other **unconscious** material, which expound what were considered at the time to be avant-garde social views. But Nin was convinced from an early age that her *Diaries* would be her major work – although 'diaries' is a somewhat disingenuous term to describe the heavily revised and edited books that were eventually published, very much written with the reader in mind and in what appears to be a self-conscious style. Indeed, Nin admitted that she found it hard to be truthful, and her editor, Gunther Stuhlmann, pronounced, 'Miss Nin's truth . . . is psychological.'

In 1940, when Nin had emigrated to the USA, her friend Henry Miller was asked to write pornography for a dollar a page for a private collector. He farmed the work out to friends, including Nin, who wrote him stories with her usual emphasis on sensuousness, circumstance and character – rather than on multiply-positioned repetitions of the sexual act – which provoked the collector to issue her an instruction to 'cut the poetry'. The chief interest of Nin's erotica lies in its reflection of a woman's viewpoint: its promotion of the idea that women can be interested in physical beauty and desire to have sex for its own sake, rather than as a means to an end; its assertion that women have a right to pursue their sexuality without condemnation. It is, however, instructive to compare the erotica with 'Henry and June', the section of Nin's *Diaries* which deals with her love affairs with Henry Miller and with June Miller, Henry's wife. Although, even here, one is left with a strong flavor of Nin the fabulist, the more realistic depictions of sex expose the total artifice of the erotica.   *KH*

House of Incest (Ohio: Ohio University Press, 1958); Diaries New York: Harcourt Brace Jovanovich, 1977; London: Peter Owen 1978); Delta of Venus (New York: Bantam, 1978; Harmondsworth: Penguin, 1990); Little Birds (New York: Bantam, 1980; Harmondsworth: Penguin, 1990)

See also **Sensuality**

Nude, The

The nude human form is the most heavily loaded subject in the western artist's repertory. It inevitably represents the viewer's private self, with which she or he identifies regardless of the gender of the representation. Yet it can also represent the viewer's 'other', who is not the self but is meaningful to the self. These two alternating and intermingling factors allow the viewer to project the whole range of emotions onto a nude, and artists, mindful of this or not, have used it to represent human emotions and attributes which reflect not only their own views but the attitudes of the time in which they worked. Most artists working in the public domain have been men; the representations have therefore been made from a masculine point of view for a male audience.

Because of the highly charged nature of the subject, women have long been deeply distressed by the ways in which male artists – and photographers in

Jean Auguste Dominique Ingres, *Angelica in Chains*, 1859

advertising and **pornography** – appropriate and misrepresent the female body. These artists have codified and employed all the known male sexual triggers in the construction of the desirable woman: the nude subject is anonymous, does not intercept the viewer's gaze (except as further enticement), displays her body as available and compliant. She shines, she looks delectable, inviting. And, above all, she is only an image; she will make no demands of her own. Although some women do find these constructions sexually stimulating, most feel degraded and insulted by the fact that women are portrayed only as sex objects. Similar stereotyped constructions of women are to be found throughout the annals of western fine and decorative art.

Homoerotic images were constructed on much the same lines, using such appropriate triggers as those seen in representations of St Sebastian, who, although bound and wounded, is still intact and inviting: lusciously vulnerable, just like the women.

Two men whose ideas on representation were frequently quoted in early feminist discussions on understanding the meaning of the female nude were Sigmund **Freud** and John Berger. They both elucidated in their work the prevailing masculine blindness to women as autonomous people. Freud claimed that the female nude is, in itself, a symbol of passivity, in that it demonstrates so clearly the absence of the symbol of power, the penis, and is therefore the inevitable site of voyeuristic fantasies of manipulation and possession. Berger claimed that woman is unable to look at the world for herself because she is always concerned with how she is being seen by others. In other words: man sees; woman is seen. Because these views seemed so entrenched, many women suggested that the nude should be banned entirely. She could never be free from negative interpretations. This led to a latter-day prudery and a tendency to a literal reading of metaphorical work. While not denying the unpalatable nature of many representations of the female nude, other women artists rejected the idea that the female nude must inevitably be read as passive: that would not only show an ignorance of art history, but would inhibit the feminist project of investing

Nancy Grossman, *Male Figure*, 1971

the nude with new and hitherto unexpressed understandings of women's real experiences.

The male nude was taken on by feminists only after years in which women actively reclaimed the power of seeing and telling. Margaret Walters's *The Nude Male* (1979) and the exhibition **Women's Images Of Men** (1980) presented men and **patriarchy** from women's point of view and gained acceptance for women as makers of meanings in the visual arts. Where clues to the gender of the maker were provided, the nude could now be read from a woman's perspective. Women artists felt increasingly able to use the nude, both male and female, employing this highly charged signifier to expand the meanings inherent in representations of the human body. In recent work it has been used, for example, to represent woman as god, woman as maker of culture, woman as mother (from a per-

sonal perspective), woman in celebration of her body, woman as victim of male cultural readings.

JM

Gill Saunders *The Nude: A New Perspective* (London: Herbert Press, 1989) Margaret Walters *The Male Nude* (Harmondsworth: Penguin, 1979)

See also **Graham; Manet; Mapplethorpe; Neel; Picasso; Schiele; Ukiyo-e; Voyeurism**

Nwapa, Flora (1931-)

Marriage, barrenness and the traditional restrictions placed on women in Igbo society form the backbone of Flora Nwapa's writings. In *Efuru* (1966), *Idu* (1970) and *One Is Enough* (1981) we meet three women all of whom, by their society's reckoning, are 'deformed'.

The eponymous heroine of *Efuru*, the book which earned Nwapa the distinction of becoming Nigeria's first woman novelist, is goodness incarnate. Unfortunately, this is not enough. In a society which demands that its women procreate, Efuru's misfortune is that she is not very fertile. She may be rich but, someone asks, 'Can a bag of money look after you in your old age? Can a bag of money mourn you when you are dead?' Her busybody neighbors decide that her husband should take another wife, since 'two men do not live together. To them Efuru was a man since she could not reproduce.' Efuru has no qualms about polygamy; however, when she finally gives birth to a girl, she still has not met society's requirements. A girl child is merely brought up to be a wife; a boy child confers status at birth, with education will bring in riches and, when he marries, will bring in daughters to help his mother through her old age.

In *Idu* and *One Is Enough*, the heroines (Idu and Amaka) also have difficulty conceiving. Amaka begins life as a decent woman but six years of a barren marriage have taken their toll. Dejected and despised by the community, she is effectively driven away from her husband. Idu succeeds in giving birth to one child, a boy, and, although her husband loves her and is satisfied, the villagers are not. In all three novels we see the havoc which meddling neighbors, invariably 'wise' older women, can wreak on a marriage. For them, love and happiness are secondary. 'Of what use is it if your husband licks your body, worships you and buys everything in the market for you and you are not productive?' No one perceives a contradiction in the fact that many other marriages exist which, although fruitful, are pairings of supremely ill-matched couples. Nor does anyone find it peculiar that men are never blamed for barrenness until their wives openly have affairs with other men and become pregnant.

In Amaka's case, she ends up in Lagos where she quickly embraces the city's basest values, acquiring great wealth in no time by sleeping with powerful men. Yet Amaka has no regrets; instead she regards her situation as the only freedom she has known: 'I don't want to be a wife any more, a mistress yes, with a lover, yes, of course, but not a wife . . . As a wife I am never free . . . I am in prison, unable to advance in body and soul . . .' But Nwapa shows that freedom doesn't necessarily elude village women. In Igbo tradition women have always turned to the virtuous goddess Uhamiri as their liberating angel. In a male-centered ethos, she comes to represent the freedom and peace which women can find within themselves. It is significant that, at one of the saddest moments of her life, Efuru is calmed and re-strengthened by a dream of Uhamiri: 'She had lived for ages at the bottom of the lake. She was as old as the lake itself. She was happy, she was wealthy. She was beautiful. She gave women beauty and wealth but she had no child . . . . Why then did the women worship her?'

NOB

Efuru (London: Heinemann, 1966); *Idu* (London: Heinemann, 1970)

See also **Kono; Lorde; Prostitution**

Obscenity

Obscenity is the state of causing outrage to, or offending against, accepted standards of decency. However, when applied to a representation, as distinct from actual behavior, it is often the case that the thing being shown – a married couple having sex, for example – is not considered indecent in itself, merely unsuited to public exposure.

Standards of decency vary, of course. The poems of **Sappho**, judged beautiful by contemporaries in Ancient Greece, were considered obscene and perverted by the scholars of Victorian Britain. Similarly, as Angela **Carter** noted in 1971, while modern Japanese **comics** show women being raped and killed with a graphic insouciance outrageous to most foreign readers, in the copies of *Playboy* imported to Japan from the USA each image of pubic hair will have been blacked out for the sake of modesty. Or take *The Well of Loneliness*, a British novel compared to the plague and banned for obscenity in 1928 (for daring to mention **lesbianism**) yet sold without any fuss in France, acquitted of being obscene in the USA and, half a century later, cheerfully broadcast in Britain by BBC radio.

Variety may be the spice of life, but problems occur where obscenity is considered a legal offense. Especially today, when communities tend to consist of a complex, shifting mixture of national, ethnic, class, religious and generational cultures, how is a court to decide which particular feelings it ought to protect? Or are feelings not really the issue? Is it the case that obscenity laws have always, in fact, protected not feelings but the interests of the male ruling class?

Consider the case of the invisible penis. In Europe, Japan and the USA, representations of the penis, especially the penis erect, are felt to be highly offensive: more so, even, then representations of women's genital organs. Yet few adult viewers can be ignorant of the functions and appearance of the penis, while at least forty-eight per cent of them, one would think, feel nothing but tenderness for it. Could it be that the men who manage the law have perceived a connection between exposure and vulnerability, concealment and power? This would certainly help to explain why such things as advice about **contraception**, sex education for children, and serious reports from sexologists have been regularly banned as obscene. Our capacity for outrage may be admirable, but it does no harm to bear in mind that it can also be manipulated, and to recognize that, on some occasions, we are being shocked into opening our eyes, while on others we are being *threatened* with shock in order to make us close them.   *HG*

See also **Beardsley; Besant; Burroughs; Chughtai; Comics, US And European; Flaubert; Forster; Hall; Hays Code; Kabuki; Lawrence; Manto; Mapplethorpe; Miller, Henry;** *New Portuguese Letters*; **Pornography; Sanger; Schiele; West**

Oedipus Complex

Sigmund **Freud**'s initial understanding of the structure of wishes represented by the Oedipus Complex came to him through his self-analysis in the 1890s, and marked a decisive shift in the evolution of psychoanalytic thought about the sexual impulses of childhood.

Freud had initially believed his female patients' accounts of their seduction by an adult male family member, although he doubted that the occurrence of **incest** could be as widespread in reality as his clinical evidence suggested. It was when he had a dream which showed him his own sexual desire for his mother that he felt that a critical understanding had been reached. This revelation, together with his other findings, led him to uncover what he claimed to be one of the most important psychic configurations of mankind, for which the myth of Oedipus provided the dramatic framework. He posited a sexual wish, on the part of every young child, for the parent of the opposite sex, alongside jealousy of the parent of the same sex and the wish to usurp that parent's place. Traditionally, one would say

that it is the resolution of this Oedipus Complex, with all its vicissitudes, which determines a person's characteristic forms of desire. 'Every new arrival on this planet,' Freud wrote in 1920, 'is faced by the task of mastering the Oedipus Complex; anyone who fails to do so falls a victim to neurosis.'

Freud's case history '**Dora**' was written in 1897 in the light of the collapse of his seduction theory and the emergence of his theory of dream interpretation and of the Oedipus Complex. In his later writings he explored both the motives for the disappearance of the Oedipus Complex and its different relationship to the castration complex in boys (that is, the boy's fear of castration) and girls (the girl's conviction that she has *been* castrated). In a short paper, 'The Dissolution of the Oedipus Complex', Freud proposes that the experiential and the 'preordained' both play their part in bringing about the Complex's end. Thus it is the girl's disappointment in her father, who fails to give her a longed-for child, which leads her to give up her wishes for him. The Oedipus Complex itself should be seen as determined by heredity, and as giving way to the next phase of development: latency and the formation of the super-ego.

The important distinction between boys and girls is marked in Freud's 'Some Psychical Consequences of the Anatomical Distinction Between the Sexes'. This paper argues that in boys the Oedipus Complex is destroyed by the castration complex, while in girls the Oedipus Complex is made possible by the castration complex. As with all Freud's later writings on women, his focus moves increasingly not only to the pre-Oedipal phase, but to the nature of the Oedipal girl's renunciation of her mother as love-object. But the Oedipus Complex never loses its significance, and the phallocentric dimension remains; thus, the idea of a weaker super-ego in women is related to their lack of motive for demolition of the Oedipus Complex, because their castration has already taken place.   *AS*

'The Dissolution of the Oedipus Complex' and 'Some Psychical Consequences of the Anatomical Distinction Between the Sexes' in *On Sexuality* (Harmondsworth: Penguin, 1977)

Rosalind Coward 'On the Universality of the Oedipus

Complex: Debates on Sexual Divisions in Psychoanalysis and Anthropology' in *Critique of Anthropology* (no. 15, 1980)

See also **Horney; Infantile Sexuality; Lacan**

Oh! Calcutta!

'Some time ago, it occurred to me that there was no place for a civilised man to take a civilised woman to spend an evening of civilised erotic stimulation,' declared the British theater critic and dramaturge Kenneth Tynan, outlining his plans for 'an international erotic revue'. *Oh! Calcutta!* (the title was a French pun; *O quel cul t'as*) opened in New York in June 1968 and transferred to London the following year, becoming a *succès de scandale* in both places despite poor critical response. The *New York Times* critic Clive Barnes summed it up: 'This is the kind of show to give pornography a dirty name.'

With unattributed contributions by some of the leading writers of the day, including Joe **Orton**, Samuel Beckett and Sam Sheperd, *Oh! Calcutta!* promised more than it delivered. As John Elsom points out in *Erotic Theatre* (London: Secker and Warburg, 1973): 'Despite the fact that *Oh! Calcutta!* was intended for enlightened couples, nearly all the fantasies, except perhaps the pas de deux, were male ones – chauvinist males at that . . . Women were there to be fucked, men were around to fuck them if they could.' And, for all its claims to be in the forefront of sexual liberation, the revue remained determinedly heterosexual (Tynan insisted that it must be choreographed by 'a non-queer') and a throwback to an era of Edwardian naughtiness and **voyeurism** that took delight in flashes of naked flesh. On this score, it was no more liberating than the dozens of striptease performances to be found in the Soho of the time and, in the long term, proved only the difficulty of acting sex on stage with honesty and (something that everyone knew) 'that group nakedness is considerably less arousing than the nudity of one desirable person': John Simon in *Uneasy Stages* (New York: Random House, 1975). *LG*

See also **Heterosexism; Sexual Revolution**

O'Keeffe, Georgia (1887-1986)

Georgia O'Keeffe was one of this century's most original and influential North American painters. Bleached bones against a red sky; a river bed snaked into parched earth: her paintings are stark, striking and sensual. One of her favorite themes was flowers: often a single blossom filling a huge canvas, the petals spread wide, opening out, with the viewer invited to look deep into the stamen and beyond. It was a theme that was, from the start, to arouse controversy over what many saw as its erotic, voluptuous imagery.

This was New York in the 1930s. The liberal intelligentsia was reading Sigmund **Freud** and D.H. **Lawrence**. When critics – including O'Keeffe's admirers – made the comparison between the flowers and a woman's vulva and **clitoris**, O'Keeffe was at first ambivalent. But soon she began to deny that she was using a sexual visual vocabulary. It is unlikely that her denial was out of prudery or coyness: she allowed her lover, then husband, the photographer and art dealer Alfred Stieglitz to take and show hundreds of photographs of her naked, or semi-naked, staring directly into the camera. Perhaps it was a sense of survival, a fear of being netted and pigeonholed, and, as such, part of a bigger issue. O'Keeffe was particularly angered by her treatment at the hands of male reviewers, who repeatedly wrote that she 'embodied the feminine', was 'gloriously female', was 'the poet of womanhood'. Early in her career, she privately acknowledged that she was expressing a female sensibility, but in the words of the critics she may have sensed a trap. And theirs *was* a curious assertion. For, although O'Keeffe's flowers may resonate powerfully with images of a woman's cunt, their erotic energy is quite at odds with the traditional concept of a passive feminine sexuality. They are painted in bold shapes and colors, their self-poise is unflinching and they appear to exist of and for themselves.

Perhaps even more galling to O'Keeffe was that critics would acknowledge her only as 'the greatest American female artist', refusing to allow any man to be outshone. These attitudes strengthened her

Georgia O'Keeffe, *Red Canna*, c. 1923

feminist views. She became friends with writers like Meridel Le Sueur, had a large female following and joined the National Woman's Party. Of her flowers, her comment became this: 'Well – I made you take time to look at what I saw and when you took time to really notice my flower you hung all your own associations with flowers onto my flower and you write about my flower as if I think and see what you think and see of the flower – and I don't.'   JD

Georgia O'Keeffe (Harmondsworth: Penguin, 1976)

Laurie Lisle *Portrait of an Artist: A Biography of Georgia O'Keeffe* (New York: Pocket Books, 1985: London: Heinemann, 1987)

See also **Bourgeois; Colette; Miller, Lee; Sensuality**

Opera

Opera sets language in tension with melody, plot against musical form. These conflicting forces, and the struggle to balance the rational and the sensa-

tional within them, have made opera among the most eloquent, intense and effective artistic modes for discussing the structures of sex and gender.

In the late eighteenth century, freer forms replaced the strict system of **opera seria**. The operas in which Mozart collaborated with Da Ponte – *The Marriage of Figaro, Don Giovanni* and *Così Fan Tutte* – are notable for a partnership of theatrical and musical structures at once naturalistic and formal; Mozart's powerful music subverts his collaborator's sometimes cynical formulations, particularly in respect of the sexual double standard. The sensibility of the music, its use of modulation to express characters' emotions, enhances the opera's liberal hostility to aristocratic and male privilege – which is less true of earlier work, like *The Abduction from the Seraglio*, where the emancipated English maid Blonde is a joke, and of the later vaudeville, *The Magic Flute*, where the Queen of the Night is a demonic threat to the assimilation of her daughter Pamina into utopian brotherhood.

Beethoven's *Fidelio* is the most memorable case of the way in which the Rescue opera, of which *The Abduction from the Seraglio* is an earlier example, became, in the era of Romanticism and Revolution, a metaphor for liberation: in which it was more often the heroine who saved the hero. This was as much a matter of theatrical sensation as of ideology, but it shifted audiences' attention to the heroine, as did the development of a style of singing that drew as specifically on the resources of the female soprano as earlier music had on the more brutal force of the castrato.

In *Opera: Or The Undoing of Women* (London: Virago, 1989) Catherine Clement suggests that nineteenth-century opera was obsessed with the death of the heroine, particularly the racially exotic heroine. Though examination of the body-count of operatic plots does not indicate such a bias, the obsession of nineteenth-century opera with sensation – and the comparative difficulty of using opera for comedy – did combine with the temper of the age to portray liberation from circumstance as possible only in madness or death. (And death produces such poignant closing tableaux.)

O

Death as liberation finds its most powerful expression in the operas of Wagner, particularly in *The Flying Dutchman* where the woman's death redeems the man, or *Tristan* where erotic passion is seen as necessarily the solvent of personal identity. The death of the lovers is here intrinsic to their love, where in Verdi – in *Otello*, say – it is imposed from without by character flaws and malevolence. Wagner's stretching of tonality mirrored his solipsistic world view, whereas Verdi's constant reference to formal technique, even at his most free-flowing, contextualizes sexual emotion and identity in a world of **honor**, duty and other demands.

In later Romantic opera, this opposition becomes an unhelpful model. Richard Strauss, the most gifted of Wagner's followers, used literary texts which put back into his operas the social complexity that Wagner by and large left out. Strauss is at his best at moments like the closing trio of *Der Rosenkavalier*, where sexual renunciation is mediated by the knowledge that social context renders it precisely *not* tragic. Clement's arguments come closest to validation in the works of Puccini, where heroines are sacrificed to sensation and spectacle, but the infantile Butterfly or the venal Mimi are given as much respect as the brilliant, heroic Tosca, and that respect is where Puccini's writing, constantly moving between the lyrical and the passionate, leads us.

The history of twentieth-century opera has been one of a quest for expressiveness. The use by Janàček and Britten of enhanced speech rhythms makes vivid their portrayal of tough survivors like Janàček's *Jenufa* and tortured (implicitly gay) outcasts like Britten's *Peter Grimes* and Aschenbach in *Death in Venice*; while Berg's exploration of formal limits mirrors the doomed Lulu's quest for sensation. Shostakovich's *Lady Macbeth of the Mtensk District*, with its powerful portrait of female agenthood pursued at all costs, takes to extremes the graphic depiction in music of **sexual intercourse**. *RK*

See also **Romantic Love**

Opera Seria

During the heyday of opera seria, in the late seventeenth and eighteenth centuries, sexual boundaries were being moved around in a remarkable way. The convention in **opera**, which survived much longer than its equivalent tradition in theater, was that female roles were played by men or boys, while the main interpreters of such roles as Orpheus, Solomon or Julius Caesar were castrati, men whose testicles had been removed before their voices had broken in order to preserve their pure sopranos. This custom was most prevalent in Italy, so that the most famous castrati – men such as Senesino and Farinelli – were usually Italian.

And something strange was clearly happening between the opera-going public and the castrati, who, at a time when communication was still far from speedy, were famous throughout Europe. Women fell madly in love with them, as did some men. Operas were composed for them by Handel and by Rameau. They were the equivalent of present-day pop stars. Then the age of the castrati passed (although the last Italian castrato survived into the twentieth century and his voice still exists on record) and women moved in to sing the great heroic roles: which, in opera seria, continued to be written for high voices. These 'trouser roles' for female sopranos and altos were written to great effect by such composers as Mozart (in his final opera seria, *La Clemenza di Tito*) and Handel, whose later operas, oratorios and rewrites of earlier operas were written for specific female singers who became known for their cross-dressed performances.

It has been argued that cross-dressed roles were, at this time, simply functional and had no sexual sub-text, that it is the sophisticated, post-Freudian twentieth century which has laid meaning on an innocent tradition. One look, however, at the libretto of Francesco Cavalli's *La Calisto* – in which, with knowing glances from writer to audience throughout, a woman plays a man disguised as a woman who seduces a woman, and a man plays a woman who is seduced by a woman playing a boy

O

– shows without doubt that spectators were expected to understand the titillating aspects of gender confusion from the very beginning of the genre. *LS*

See also **Androgyny; Cross-Dressing; Kabuki; Shakespeare**

Oral Sex

Oral sex is sex in which a person uses her or his mouth to stimulate another person's genitals: licking them, sucking them, nibbling them, or some combination of all of these. When the person being aroused like this is a woman, it is known as 'cunnilingus' (from the Latin for 'vulva' and 'licking'). 'Fellatio' (from the Latin for 'sucking') describes the oral arousal of a man. And, to switch from Latin to French, when two lovers simultaneously use their mouth to caress the other's genitals, the maneuver is called *soixante-neuf* (69) to describe the most convenient position.

Needless to say, most people prefer to have oral sex when their partner has washed. When, in the course of the seventeenth century, the French invented the bidet, the practice of oral sex in that country is said to have grown by leaps and bounds. Similarly, in the hygiene-conscious USA of the early 1970s, cunnilingus was practiced by fifty per cent more people than had done so twenty years before.

When mutually agreed to, oral sex can be the most subtle and heart-stopping pleasure imaginable. Men, however, have not infrequently ordered a woman to suck their cock – and to do so from a kneeling position – in order to establish male dominance, frequently hurting the woman's throat or choking her as a result. Of course, there's a certain irony in this, when so many men are frightened of putting their penis inside a vagina for fear that it will be bitten off by a set of entirely fictitious teeth, but forced fellatio clearly does have a resonance for both sexes. In Andrea **Dworkin**'s novel *Mercy* (1990), for instance, it constitutes the ultimate out-

rage committed against the heroine, a woman who has previously been repeatedly beaten, tortured and vaginally raped. *HG*

See also **Foreplay; Rape**

Orgasm

An orgasm is the most intense sensation of sexual pleasure, following which a man will almost always need to rest from sex, while a woman may find that she can immediately have yet another, and yet another, until her body, as distinct from her desire, is exhausted. For either sex, the aftereffect is usually one of profound satisfaction.

But in most cultures – Taoist China being one of the few exceptions – women's orgasms are not believed to be as important as men's. This strange idea may in part be explained as the product of wishful thinking, but it may also be explained by the fact that, while men unmistakably ejaculate semen at the moment of orgasm, women show few if any external signs. That the muscles of their vagina have gone into womb-melting rhythmic contractions is not very easy to spot with the naked eye.

It is also commonly held that women find orgasms harder to achieve than men and, in this, there is some truth. The most obvious reason is that **sexual intercourse** (the form of sex most available to a woman in a heterosexual partnership) frequently fails to provide any kind of stimulation to the **clitoris**, thus making it as difficult for women to come as men would find if it were their penis to be left unstimulated. There may also be a problem with timing. When men initiate sex it is usually because they are already physically aroused, whereas women, to quote the US psychotherapist JoAnn **Loulan**, 'do not have to be experiencing great desire or physical excitement, we can initiate sex because we want to.' The result of this is that a woman may well take longer to reach her climax because she was farther away from it when she started.

O

According to one strand of feminist thinking, women who care about orgasms are merely emulating the worst, most achievement-based aspect of male sexuality: dismissing the delights of the journey in their hurry to arrive. Again, there is something to be said for this. Whatever excited men may insist (some of them no doubt believing it), sexual arousal that *doesn't* result in an orgasm causes no physical harm and can, indeed, be pleasurably prolonged for nothing but its own sweet sake. Nor is there any good reason to believe, along with such theorists as Wilhelm **Reich**, that 'orgastic potency' is essential to everyone's psychic health, especially since Reich was convinced that the vagina was more important to women's sexual pleasure than the clitoris. Nonetheless, it has to be said that orgasms are a delight. And, with a bit of gentle and even indirect attention to the clitoris – preferably by a lover who knows and enjoys what she or he is doing – they are a delight that women can easily experience.   *HG*

See also **Alther; Brown, Helen Gurley; Koedt; Masters and Johnson; Snuff Movies; Stopes; Wilson; Wright**

Orientalism

See **Burton**

Orlando

Virginia Woolf's novel *Orlando*, first published in 1928, is one of the richest and least expected of her works. In it, fantasy, biography, literary and social history, feminist criticism and an open avowal of love combine. The book grew from and is a magnificent expression of Woolf's passionate friendship – briefly sexual, always erotic – with Vita Sackville-West, aristocrat and writer. Unimpressed by Vita's writing, Woolf was fascinated by her lineage and awed by Knole, the outstandingly beautiful Great House in which Vita spent her childhood. Her gen-

der debarred Vita from inheriting Knole, a perpetual source of intense pain which Woolf was quick to recognize. In *Orlando* Woolf did her best to restore the estate to Vita by making it and her the central characters in a narrative which moves through four centuries and which encompasses the transformation of a sixteenth-century Orlando, teenage and male, into a woman who, like Vita, is thirty-six when the book ends on Thursday 11 October 1928 (also, in reality, the date of *Orlando*'s publication).

Elements of Vita's own life – her early determination to be a writer and her daunting fluency, family law suits, Eastern travel, her passionate affair and elopement with Violet Trefusis and her marriage of very much more than mere convenience to the homosexual Harold Nicolson – are conferred upon Orlando and woven into a remarkably vigorous work shot through with wit and fantasy. But *Orlando* also addresses more public and pressing concerns. Two things are constant in Orlando's life: Knole, and her passionate determination to be a writer. For the woman she becomes at some point in the late seventeenth century, however, writing is fraught with peril and intractable difficulties. Things effortlessly easy for the male Orlando become almost impossible for his female self, not through incapacity or lack of courage but because of the part played by gender in shaping literature, markets, readers, criticism and esthetic judgements. Different historical periods offer women writers different apparent freedoms and constraints, all of which Orlando must confront. The book thus becomes a sustained enquiry into the nature of gender and its relation to the workings of the creative imagination. It explores in 'poetic', fictional form many of the ideas which Woolf later developed in her polemical essays, *A Room of One's Own* (1929) and *Three Guineas* (1938).

Remarkably in Woolf's writing, *Orlando* is stylistically and formally as sexual as its subject matter: its syntax is often tantalizingly ambiguous; proffered information is at the last moment withheld from the reader, gratification is constantly deferred or denied; and even the book's final and much debated image – of the wild goose flying overhead – evokes the mocking farewell of the beloved who refuses to be caught. In *Orlando* Woolf allows herself to be revealed as a consummate tease.   *AH*

Sexuality is no longer the focal point of Sally Potter's film *Orlando* (1992). At this end of the twentieth century perhaps it would not appear so daring to use the flirtatious lack of definition which in the novel offers the reader a frisson of excitement with Woolf's question marks surrounding Orlando's ambiguous sexuality. Tilda Swinton's androgynous appearance as she plays Orlando is not fetishized. Her casual delivery suggests instead the sense of a rather endearing, unexceptional *person* moving through time, who simply happens to be male and then female. If the irony of the novel is the teasing use of ambiguous or withheld information, it is the opposite in Potter's version, where the audience is empowered with knowledge through Swinton's constant ironizing asides. The camp element of **cross-dressing** which in the novel is part of the flirtation with the reader is always used in the film as a witty comment on the psychology of the age, where Orlando is seen as a man struggling through the heat in full wig and frock coat in a seventeenth-century desert expedition, or female Orlando is laced into a dress so wide in the eighteenth century that she cannot even walk down her long gallery, visually draped like the draped furniture round her, a mere belonging in her own house.

The final sequence sees Orlando, a late twentieth-century woman, no longer hampered by history, role or possessions but in charge of her own destiny, an angel above her promising a future where 'every man and woman are at one with the human race' and sexual roles no longer matter. Potter's *Orlando* is made very much in the spirit of Woolf's own thoughts on **androgyny**; she writes in *A Room of One's Own* that 'a great mind is androgynous. It is when this fusion takes place that the mind is fully fertilized and uses all its faculties.'   *SW*

Orlando (New York: Harcourt Brace Jovanovich, 1973; London: Panther, 1977)
Orlando (Dir. Sally Potter, 1992)

See also **Bryher**; **Ottinger**

Orton, Joe (1933-1967)

Joe Orton worked for three years as a playwright before being battered to death by his longtime lover, Kenneth Halliwell, in August 1967. During those years he set about cocking a snook at the British establishment with a clutch of exuberant, aggressive and morally anarchic farces that have been described as a 'celebration of sexuality in all its manifestations' and yet, ironically, enjoyed great commercial success.

Orton's **homosexuality** and how that was viewed by society were crucial to his art. 'Complete sexual license is the only way to smash the wretched civilization . . . . sex is the only way to infuriate them,' he said. In *Joe Orton* (London: Methuen, 1982) C.W.E. Bigsby argues: 'Orton replaced dialectics with excess. He sought the extreme as though to burn off the prosaic power of the real, the banalities of a bourgeois world for which he had complete contempt. He tried to make transgression itself a value, and in that process unregulated sexuality was an enabling strategy and a central fact rather than simply an image.'

In all Orton's plays sexual stereotypes are challenged and taboo sexualities – **incest**, homosexuality, nymphomania, transvestism, **necrophilia** and **sado-masochism** – become the unassailable norm in a world where authority is consistently shown to be absurd and where the sexual fantasies of the **unconscious** mind are the only true reality. As Michelene Wandor has written of *Entertaining Mr Sloane* (1964) and *Loot* (1966): 'The sexual anarchy in Orton serves as a revelation of what might be submerged behind suburban values, as a desperate explosion of unresolved desires, and profound anxiety about the nature of the family and the dominant role of the mother': *Look Back in Gender* (London: Methuen, 1987).

If both *Sloane* and *Loot* use a domestic setting to explode the myth of net-curtained suburban

O

decency, Orton's last play, *What the Butler Saw* (1966), takes the **farce** form to its logical conclusion by using the setting of a psychiatrist's clinic for a comedy of lost and mistaken identities. In *Prick Up Your Ears*, his biography of Orton, John Lahr wrote: 'Where *Entertaining Mr Sloane* aspired, in Orton's words, "to break down all sexual compartments", the wit in *What the Butler Saw* bombards conventional sexual attitudes while its situations dramatise society's compulsion to categorise.' In the end, Orton the playwright remains uncategorizable: a true original who understood the value of sex as a weapon and who learned, in Lahr's words, 'how to corrupt an audience with pleasure'. Or, as Orton wrote in his diaries: 'Much more fucking and they'll be screaming hysterics in no time.' LG

The Complete Plays (New York: Grove Weidenfeld, 1990; London: Methuen, 1976); *The Orton Diaries* (New York: Harper Collins, 1988; London: Minerva, 1989)

John Lahr *Prick Up Your Ears: The Biography of Joe Orton* (New York: Random House, 1987; Harmondsworth: Penguin, 1980)

See also **Burroughs; Genet**

Osborne, John (1929-   )

See Look Back in Anger

Oshima, Nagisa (1932-   )

In the world of the Japanese filmmaker Nagisa Oshima, violence is immanent in sexuality. From his first film, *Ai to Kibo no Machi/The City of Love and Hope* (1955), Oshima has consistently portrayed the existence of underprivileged youths who find no other way of expressing their frustrated sense of self than through sex and crime. From the Korean high-school student in *Koshikei/Capital Punishment* (1968), who rapes and murders a female classmate, to the phantom killer in *Hakuchu no Torima/Phantom Killer in the Daytime* (1966),

who rapes women after rendering them unconscious, sexual violence against helpless women is the only revolt against an establishment that denies these young men's existence. It is also the only way for them to show their pride and dignity in the face of oppression.

Underlying their assaults against women is a protest against the revolutionaries and leftist intellectuals of the 1940s and 1950s, whose failed revolution was responsible for depriving them of a meaningful youth. For them, sexual crimes are the ultimate denial of existing society, of both the oppressive establishment and the powerless intellectuals; it is their only way of proving their subjectivity.

In *Ai no Corrida/The Realm of the Senses* (1976), it is not so much criminal acts as deviancy and excess that channel frustration. The film's protagonists, Sada and Kichizo, engage in continuous lovemaking, doing anything in order to increase their pleasure. Their desire for sexual pleasure is a desire for life, making their commitment to lovemaking a pure act of *living*: an act which reaches its height (climax) when Kichizo willingly lets Sada strangle him to death.

Sex and violence as a frustrated expression of life and self return, with greater sophistication and references to the **unconscious**, in *Senjo no Merry Christmas/Merry Christmas, Mr Lawrence* (1983). Both the sadistic tortures that the Japanese sergeant inflicts on the American prisoners, and the Japanese captain's masochistic suppression of his tender feelings, are driven by sexual suppression. A new dimension of cultural conflict is also introduced, making the protagonists' frustrations yet more complex and psychopathological. NM

Ai to Kibo no Machi/The City of Love (1955); *Hakuchu no Torima/Phantom Killer in the Daytime* (1966); *Koshikei/Capital Punishment* (1968); *Ai no Corrida/The Realm of the Senses* (1976); *Ai no Borei/A Ghost of Love* (1978); *Senjo no Merry Christmas/Merry Christmas, Mr Lawrence* (1983); *Max Mon Amour* (1986)

Tadao Sato *Oshima Nagisa no Sekai/The World of Nagisa Oshima* (Tokyo: Asahi Bunko, 1987)

See also **Kono;** *Look Back in Anger;* **Machismo; Sado-Masochism**

Ottinger, Ulrike (1942-)

Ulrike Ottinger trained as a painter before becoming a filmmaker. Her work represents human sexuality as a fluid process and thus subverts the rigid distinction between femininity and masculinity. The main objective of her cinema is to renegotiate visual pleasure for the female, especially lesbian, spectator. From the outset, unlike many contemporary feminist filmmakers, Ottinger rejected a realist treatment of women's issues. Instead, she deploys exaggeration, artifice and parody.

Madame X – Eine absolute Herrscherin/Madame X – An Absolute Ruler (1977-1978) is a parodic feminist reworking of the pirate film genre. A group of women sail off on the Chinese junk Orlando to find adventure but, having broken with a male-dominated society, they reproduce only the same destructive rituals of domination and submission. Monika Treut, another filmmaker, notes that the movie represents neither female power nor its absence; rather, it is an ironic enactment of social reality and a complex role-reversal game in which signs and symbols of power – sado-masochistic leather gear worn as armor, the female figurehead as a phallic symbol – are heavily marked. Ottinger's esthetic strategies, if almost incomprehensible to the general (even feminist) public in the 1970s, have in the meantime become more accessible through similar developments in film and video art.

Freak Orlando (1981), based on Virginia Woolf's **Orlando**, relates the mythology of the social outcast through the ages. Orlando, a symbolic figure who undergoes several transformations in sexual and historical identity, encounters only compassion from other freaks but persecution, misunderstanding and cruelty from everyone else. Ottinger wants to show that men not only control the structures of power but also set the standard of normality. The film is, in her view, a 'satirical vision of a woman who sees history as that of the patriarchy'.

Although Ottinger's films still do not attract a wide audience, they have nevertheless become a focus of debate among many feminists, who acclaim her cinema for its contribution to new ideas on non-patriarchal forms of representation. Ottinger's insistence on mythologizing and estheticizing women's experience has retrospectively been validated by many critics as a more fruitful approach than the orthodox feminism of the 1970s which focused exclusively on subject matter.　　*US*

Berlinfieber/Berlin-fever (1973); *Die Betörung der blauen Matrosen/The Bewitchment of Drunken Sailors* (1975); *Madame X – eine absolute Herrscherin/Madame X – An Absolute Ruler* (1977–1978); *Bildnis einer Trinkerin/Ticket of No Return* (1979); *Freak Orlando* (1981); *Dorian Gray im Spiegel der Boulevard presse/Dorian Gray in the Mirror of the Popular Press* (1983–1984); *Superbia – Stolz/ Superbia – Vanity* (1986); *Usinimage/Industrial Image* (1987); *Johanna d'Arc of Mongolia* (1988)

See also **Acker; Akerman; Kaplan**

Ovid (43BC-17AD)

Publius Ovidius Naso came from a wealthy family in Sulmona in the Abruzzi region of Italy. He was educated in Rome and had planned a civil and judicial career, but gave this up to write poetry. In 8 AD he was exiled to Tomi on the Black Sea, for reasons which have never been satisfactorily clarified: it is generally held that he was connected with a scandal involving the Emperor Augustus's granddaughter, Julia, and this, in addition to his authorship of *Ars Amatoria/The Art of Love*, gave him a reputation as undesirable. Ovid's third wife, the only one to whom he was happily married, followed him into exile, where he died at the age of sixty.

Ovid was a prolific writer, and most of his works have survived. The best known of these is probably the *Metamorphoses*, a collection of myths concerning shape-changing: Daphne's transformation into a laurel tree, for instance. Of his other works, three deal particularly with love. *Amores/Loves* is a collection of elegiac poems, more notable for their use of literary forms and conventions than for any great emotional insight. Ovid's work is generally witty and, here, his deliberately exaggerated use of typical elegiac devices has been said to have dealt the death blow to Roman love elegy. The *Heroides* also deals with male-female relationships but, despite the occasional poignant passage and what male critics have seen as insight into female psychology, the work chiefly allows Ovid to have fun making comments on and critiques of myths through the device of letters sent by heroines to heroes, such as those from Dido to Aeneas.

The work on which Ovid's 'scandalous' reputation rests is the *Ars Amatoria*. This is written in a didactic style, parodying the Hellenistic authors of such educational epics as the *Phaenomena*, an astrological and astronomical work by Aratus. *Ars Amatoria* chiefly seeks to amuse. It poses as a handbook divided into three sections, two addressed to men (how to get her, how to keep her) and one to women (how to get him and keep him), the latter assumed to be either courtesans or married women who have affairs. Despite the book's reputation, it is no **Kama Sutra**. As the author himself says: 'Two lovers to their private couch repair; to pass the bolted door, my Muse, forbear.' Generally the advice, allowing for cultural and historical differences, is not dissimilar to that offered in magazines such as *Cosmopolitan*.

The chief advice to women is on how to look nice. This covers dress, cosmetics, hair, how to laugh nicely and the sexual positions that show off your figure to its best advantage. It does not deal with any sort of equal relationship; women are very much seen as male 'playthings' and love depicted as a game whose prize is sexual pleasure. It is a very frivolous book and Ovid claimed to have conquered love – '*Et mihi cedet Amor*' ('Even Love will yield to me') – although he did sufficiently acknowledge love's power to write a sequel, *Remedia Amoris*/*Cures for Love*. In his exile Ovid wrote *Tristia*/*Sorrows*, in which autobiographical work he insists that he was never the voluptuary that his knowing poetry suggests.   *KH*

Ars Amatoria (New York: Riverrun, 1988; Harmondsworth: Penguin, 1982)

See also **Brown, Helen Gurley**

Paedophilia

The difference between paedophilia and **child sexual abuse** is slight but significant. Essentially, as the words are used today, paedophilia means being attracted to and having sex with other people's children and being willing to *admit* the fact, to oneself if not always to others. In other words, it describes the non-incestuous use of children for sex by adults who, more often than not, are prepared to justify their behavior – instead of pretending that it hasn't occurred, or that, if it did, it was all the child's doing.

The most hideous examples of paedophilia – for example, those involving the abduction and sexual torture of infants – can, of course, be justified only by those who are seriously deranged. Where children close to adulthood, however, have been seduced, as distinct from forced, and obtain something positive like pleasure or love or security from the relationship, then the blacks and whites begin to create shades of gray.

Perhaps the most widely acceptable instance of what must, legally, be called paedophilia is when a man has sex with another who, were either of the couple a woman, would legally be considered 'of age' but, where homosexual acts are concerned, is still described as a child. More generally, there is a logical problem with the clear-cut ages at which societies deem that a child becomes an adult: obviously it cannot be the case that just before midnight a person is vulnerable, open to all kinds of pressures and deceits, ignorant or confused about their sexuality; then a second later is in control, informed, immune to coercion. The law necessarily restrains some people within childhood longer than it needs to, while propelling others into adulthood before they are ready. Nonetheless, a line must be drawn, and after puberty (accepting that this is a variable and variably drawn-out process) would seem to be the most sensible place to draw it. This isn't simply a matter of checking the gross imbalance of power which exists between adults and frequently smaller, relatively ignorant, financially dependent children. Power imbalances remain throughout life and, in sexual relations especially, can only be crudely policed. The crucial point is that pre-pubescent children – sexual though they most certainly are – are sexual in a quite different way from adults. And the inappropriate use of their sexuality causes them damage, no matter how loving, gentle or well intentioned the surrounding relationship.   *HG*

See also **Balthus**; **Infantile Sexuality**; *Lolita*; **Plato**

Parker, Pat (1944-1989)

One of the earliest Black feminists openly to acknowledge her **lesbianism** in her poetry, Pat Parker bravely risked the censure of the Black community. Raised in Houston, Texas, she spent her adult life in Oakland, California, where she worked as the director of the Oakland Feminist Health Center. Her poetry is clear, precise, often witty and always accessible, expressing her keen awareness of the power imbalances between the sexes.

'Womanslaughter' is the angry retelling of how a violent husband served a year in jail for the 'manslaughter' of his wife. Parker's anger, however, does not focus solely on the man, but is careful to encompass the sexist bias within the law itself. Always ready to address contemporary issues of sexuality, her approach could be humorous and pithy. She pronounced non-**monogamy** fine, for example, except where the non-monogamous woman happened to be one with whom she was in love. Disturbed by the rise, in the 1980s, of **sado-masochism** in the lesbian community, she wrote 'Bar Conversation', which was openly critical of a practice that re-enacted a powerlessness already far too available in everyday life. What lesbian sex meant for Parker is best exemplified in an erotic poem called 'Metamorphosis', in which lovemaking is tenderly described: 'you take these fingers/bid them soft – / a velvet touch/ to your loins.' Such softness is typical of how she experienced and expressed sex between women. Typical, too, is the

political note on which she chose to end that poem: describing such lovemaking as a 'revolution'.   *CU*

Child of Myself (California: Shameless Hussy Press, 1971); *Pit Stop* (California: Women's Press, 1974); *Womanslaughter* (California: Diana Press, 1978); *Movement in Black* (California: Diana Press, 1983); *Jonestown and Other Madness* (New York: Firebrand Books, 1985)

See also **Lorde**; **Shockley**

Patriarchy

Patriarchy means 'rule by the fathers' and, traditionally, the word has been used to describe societies where men head the families and kinship, titles, descent and so on are traced through the male line: in other words, the societies with which we are most familiar today.

According to most anthropologists, this is a relatively late form of organization; presumably because it depends upon men understanding their role in procreation. While it was believed that women bore children without any contribution from men, only a matriarchal system of descent and kinship could logically exist. But although there are many who believe that the early matriarchies were *ruled* by women – that it was women who made their laws and established their cultural values – there is no proof that the power of women has ever extended so far beyond the family. The rules of descent, though important, are not the whole of the power machine.

Similarly, men's power today would not be so universal, so great, if it consisted of nothing more than their being perceived as 'the head of the family' and having the right to pass their possessions and position to their sons before their daughters. If, as Kate Millett has written, 'patriarchy's chief institution is the family', it is nonetheless supported, magnified and extended by public structures: including the male-designed, male-run churches, schools, court rooms, professions and media. And 'patriarchy' is most used today to describe this *wider* complex of power: a complex which, crucially, reduces women to the status of exchangeable objects, their sexuality (among much else) defined and controlled by men.

Most feminists agree that a patriarchy is, to quote Zillah Eisenstein, a 'hierarchical ordering of society'. But if, within it, men order themselves according to various racial, class and economic criteria, they also arrange things so that *every* man can consider himself superior to, with power over, one or more women. In the sexual arena, this power allocation contributes to the ease with which men are forgiven such activities as **rape** (especially of their wife, or a prostitute, or a woman on a 'lower' social rung) and the blind, if embarrassed eye that so often gets turned to **child sexual abuse** by a father.   *HG*

See also **Incest; Misogyny; Monogamy**

Penis Envy

A key concept in Sigmund **Freud**'s theorization of female sexuality, penis envy refers to the 'momentous discovery which little girls are destined to make' (Freud, 1925) that they do not have a penis like their brother or male playmate. Penis envy begins with this first recognition of anatomical difference. The two most striking features of Freud's account are these: first, that the envy is instantaneous and that its psychical consequences for adult women are far-reaching and negative; second, that the equivalent experience for boys is a much more psychically evolved process.

Freud's account of the psychology of adult women relies heavily on the concept of penis envy, which it sees as implicated in, among other things, women's sense of inferiority, their proneness to jealousy and – because of the vicissitudes of the castration complex and **Oedipus Complex** in girls – their weaker super-ego. The question of penis envy is also inseparable from the wider issue of Freud's theory of sexual phallic monism – that is, the belief that neither little girls nor little boys acknowledge the existence of the vagina, even in the **uncon-**scious, before puberty – and his model of a little girl's relationship with her parents. According to this model, the little girl 'knows that she is without the penis and wants to have it' and holds her mother responsible for her lack of one. However, this wish for a penis is given up through the female Oedipus Complex and replaced by the wish for a child, to which end the girl 'takes her father as a love-object', focuses her jealousy on her mother and turns into 'a little woman'. The Oedipus Complex is itself gradually given up because the wish is never fulfilled. The two wishes – for the penis and for a child – remain 'cathected' (bound) in the unconscious and help prepare the female for her later sexual role.

Even though Freud attempted in his later writings on women to redress the explanatory balance by exploring the pre-Oedipal period of life, especially the early mother-daughter relationship, his work on women retained an undeniably 'phallocentric' quality. The notion that female sexuality and psychology could be so pivotally based on a 'deficiency' was initially criticized within **psychoanalysis** by Ernest Jones and Karen **Horney** in the 1920s and 1930s; and the criticism returned with the first wave of 1960s and 1970s feminism, especially in the USA and is perhaps best known through the work of Betty Friedan and Shulamith **Firestone**.

Subsuming penis envy in a wider critique of the uses to which popularized Freudianism had been put, Friedan argued that Freud was a genius, but that the psychology of women that he described – with its proneness to hysteria and other neuroses – fitted *fin de siècle* Vienna, not the mid twentieth-century world of the USA which had 'seized' on the concept of penis envy to account for women's frustrations. Consequently, his views on women should be modified in the light of broad social changes and new research data. Firestone approached the question of penis envy differently: the biological became a metaphor for the social, with penis envy as a woman's 'realistic' envy of men's social power. Although Firestone does not share Karen Horney's identification with Freudian theory, her position is in some respects similar to Horney's.

The sea change in feminist responses to psychoanalysis was effected by Juliet Mitchell's *Psycho-analysis and Feminism* (London: Allen Lane, 1974) which rightly argued that 'notorious concepts' like penis envy were meaningful only within their context in the larger theories of psychoanalysis. ' . . . in "penis envy" we are talking not about an anatomical organ, but about the ideas of it that people hold and live by within the general culture, the order of human society . . . The way we live as "ideas"? the necessary laws of human society is not so much conscious as *unconscious*.' However, despite the Lacanian emphasis on the unconscious and representation, and despite the general importance of Jacques **Lacan**'s attention to linguistic processes in both the theorization of psychoanalysis and the clinical experience of psychoanalysis, it is widely felt that the relationship between the 'penis' as an anatomical organ and the 'phallus' as privileged signifier of difference for both sexes remains unresolved within this tradition.

Within the International Psycho-Analytical Association there has been a fresh reconsideration of female sexuality since the 1970s. Janine Chasseguet-Smirgel's 'Freud and Female Sexuality' (1976) is a key contribution to this debate. Acknowledging the early work of Melanie Klein, Chasseguet-Smirgel argues that little girls and little boys are both knowledgeable about sexuality but that the knowledge is subject to a series of repressions. Such reconsiderations are a reminder of the relative lack of fixity of psychoanalytic thinking, within the basic conceptual framework of the unconscious and the sexual drives. It is probably also true to say that, within the various schools of psyhoanalysis, and especially since the work of Klein and of the object-relations theorists, the concept of penis envy has lost its hegemonic role in the discussion of psychical structure and psychical life, and is usually seen as itself defensive against a more primitive form of envy of the breast.   *AS*

Sigmund Freud 'Some Psychical Consequences of the Anatomical Distinction Between the Sexes' and 'Female Sexuality' in *On Sexuality* (Harmondsworth: Penguin, 1977); 'Femininity' in *New Introductory Lectures on Psychoanalysis* (Harmondsworth: Penguin, 1973).
Janine Chasseguet-Smirgel 'Freud and Female Sexuality: The Consideration of Some Blind Spots in the Exploration of the "Dark Continent"' in *International Journal of Psycho-Analysis* (1976, vol. 57)

See also **Infantile Sexuality**

Perfumed Garden, The

The Perfumed Garden is a study of sexuality dating from the sixteenth century. In the Arabic original, by Shaykh Nefzawi, both the sexual act and sexual relations between women and men are treated reverentially, as one of the bounties of God on this earth. First translated into French in the mid-nineteenth century, the work was rendered into English and privately published in 1886 by Sir Richard **Burton**. Like his translations of the **Arabian Nights** and the **Kama Sutra**, his *The Perfumed Garden* served to reinforce the western myth of oriental, lust-driven sexuality. Extra material was added – including more erotic stories and additional sexual positions – yet, even so, Burton lamented the absence of information on tribadism, sodomy and cunnilingus. In his hands, the work was transformed from a study of the joys of sex – comparable, perhaps, to some of the manuals more recently created by western authors, except that *The Perfumed Garden* is informed by Nefzawi's religious faith – into a salacious report on eastern mores. It is, regrettably, this version which has all too often been accepted by orientalists and other western readers.   *SR*

The Perfumed Garden of the Shaykh Nefzawi (Rochester, Vermont: Inner Traditions International, 1989; London: Panther, 1967)

See also **Comfort; Islam; Loulan**

Perversion

Perversion is a term used to describe forms of human sexuality which deviate from an assumed 'norm' of socially acceptable behavior, the latter defined according to heterosexual, reproductive sexuality. **Homosexuality** is the best known and most widely practiced of all the so-called 'perversions'.

Since the nineteenth century there has been a great deal of scientific interest in the perversions; sexologists from Havelock **Ellis** onward have attempted to trace the causes and to catalog the varieties of 'perverse' human sexual behavior, regarding it as a product of corrupted psychology (as opposed to 'inversion', which was seen as innate). One of the first challenges to this account of perversion was from Sigmund **Freud**. The distinction between inversion and perversion was irrelevant to Freud; rather, he regarded both as an extension of 'normal' sexuality. The concept of perversion appears in his work in two different senses: in the first sense it serves as a description of **infantile sexuality**, which he came to regard as 'polymorphously perverse'; in the second sense 'perversion' came to designate certain categories of adult sexual expression, including homosexuality, **masturbation**, **fetishism**, **masochism**, sadism, **voyeurism**, the roots of which can be found in infantile sexuality.

According to Freud, the sexual drives of young children, as yet ungoverned by the taboos and prohibitions placed on sexual expression within human culture, are pleasure-seeking rather than being reproductive in intent. For them, satisfaction is experienced across the body, rather than located exclusively in the genital region. Freud regarded infantile sexuality as perverse because it did not line up with a heterosexual reproductive imperative. For him, 'mature' adult sexuality was necessarily narrower and more exclusive than the infant's. Normal adult sexuality was both heterosexual and genitally organized around the penis's penetration of the vagina in **sexual intercourse**. In response to this 'norm', Freud used the notion of perversion in its second sense, to indicate those forms of sexual expression in adult life not governed by heterosexual penetration.

The list of the perversions was long. It included any form of sexual expression which was neither genital nor heterosexual. Clearly, with such a wide definition, it is likely that most human beings indulge at some time in their lives in some form of perverse behavior. Freud himself remarked that 'the less repellent of the so-called sexual perversions are very widely diffused among the whole population, as everyone knows except medical writers upon the subject'. Indeed, within this definition, even excessive kissing might be regarded as perverse, since it is not reproductive. Freud's use of the word gestures towards a critique of the cultural imperative that pushes everyone towards a heterosexual and reproductive norm: he regarded such a task as impossible and 'normality', therefore, as an ideal fiction. However, since Freud's time, his theories have been used as a means of pathologizing 'deviant' sexual behavior. Indeed, many feminists have argued that Freud's own usage of the term was intended in this way. Within psychoanalytic and psychiatric institutions, and in social-policy debates in Britain and the USA from the early twentieth century on, the perversions have been treated as forms of sickness, or as products of arrested development. The main target of medical intervention has been homosexuality, for which a variety of 'cures' – from surgical operations to aversion therapy – have been developed.

Since the beginning of **Gay Liberation** in the 1960s, sexual radicals such as Gayle Rubin in the USA have attempted to reclaim the word 'perversion' as a term of positive affirmation. The British writer and gay activist Jeffrey **Weeks** has recently translated the concept of 'perversity' into a politics of choice – *diversity* – which recognizes the existence of benign sexual variation.   *DH*

Gayle Rubin 'Thinking Sex' in *Pleasure and Danger*, ed. Carole Vance (London: Pandora, 1984)
Jeffrey Weeks *Sexuality and Its Discontents* (London: Routledge, 1985)

See also **Heterosexuality; Krafft-Ebing; Sexology**

Picasso, Pablo (1881-1973)

A painter, sculptor and printmaker, born in Malaga, Spain, Pablo Picasso worked chiefly in France from 1901 onward. Although he was an innovator in style, his whole output a search for the means to represent his visual experience in a new way, for content he accepted the conventions of European art. In Europe the female body had long been a traditional and widely accepted subject for artistic experimentation and, like most male artists, Picasso would not have questioned his right to use the female **nude** as he wanted.

The work of the impressionist artists, a number of whom were working in Paris when Picasso arrived there, implied a direct correspondence between what is seen and what is painted; but, by 1905, Picasso had rejected this assumption and, instead, worked toward the use of logical sculptural forms within the pictorial space, representing not the seen experience in the sense of photographic relationships, but the visual realities as he experienced them. (We too, for instance, have seen two eyes at different levels when we have been head-to-head with a lover.) The real breakthrough in Picasso's work came with his interest in African sculpture. His 1905–1906 portrait of Gertrude **Stein**, which incorporated ideas both from that and from classical sculpture, was a milestone in his break from nineteenth-century influences. During the eighty sittings for this work, he and Stein had crucial conversations on the subject of representation in art which influenced them both.

Picasso's controversial 1906 painting, 'The

Pablo Picasso, *Satyr and Sleeping Woman*, (from the *Vollard Suite*), 1936

Demoiselles of Avignon', incorporated forms which would lead to Cubism; its subject matter, however, the prostitutes in a famous brothel, looked back to the nineteenth century and the prurient artist as a voyeur. Cubism (1908–1916), a joint project with others, most notably Georges Braque, was an experiment in reducing the illusion of depth in the picture by fragmenting, flattening and rearranging forms on the canvas.

After the First World War, Picasso worked with the Diaghilev ballet. He married the dancer Olga Kokhlova in 1917. These events coincided with his return to whole and rounded classical forms. He painted monumental women as well as many mother-and-child subjects, especially around the time of the birth of his son, Paolo, in 1921. At about that time he also began to copy and to re-invent the work of the neo-classical painter Ingres, whose portraits and harem scenes contain many bizarre examples of distortions. It may be that it was these, or Picasso's attempts to reconcile Cubism with his neo-classicism, which led him to his own experiments with distortions of the female body. Or it may be that they were an expression of his lust-hate relationship with that body, as the work coincided with difficulties in his marriage with Kokhlova. For the rest of his life he alternated between varieties of Cubism and neo-classicism and, for most of these later periods, his principal subject was the female, mostly nude.

Picasso was a great enthusiast of bull-fighting and, from 1928, images of bulls began to appear in his work. In 1933 he produced the cover for the magazine *Minotaure* and a vast number of erotic bull drawings. In Greek mythology, the god Zeus disguises himself as a bull to rape Europa, a mortal woman, who proceeds to give birth to the minotaur – demi-God, monstrous animal – but, in most of Picasso's work, it seems that the rapist was the minotaur himself. The bull also represented the artist, as sacrificial victim, irrepressibly lustful, a demi-god in a world of uncomprehending mortals, and gradually its meanings increased to include male violence in general and war in particular: especially the Spanish Civil War of 1936 to 1939 and

the cruelties of General Franco (the victim is now often shown as a defenseless horse rather than a defenseless woman.) In an etching of 1936, a bull is killed by a woman representing peace – a case of wishful thinking.

Picasso had tremendous vitality and was, by many accounts, insatiable in his appetite both for work and for women. (These appetites seem often to be closely allied in creative people of either gender.) Picasso combined the two in his many representations of the artist and his model. Much of this work has a humorous intent – commenting on the absurdity and delight of both art and sex – but it is also about the transformation of life into art.

Among Picasso's best known works is 'Guernica' (1937), the culmination of his 'Minotauromacy' ideas. This large painting was made as a tribute to the Basque city whose civilian population was indiscriminately bombed during the Spanish Civil War. This work, many of his minotaur works and the series of weeping women that he made at about the same time display a darker side of Picasso's character, one which he showed infrequently, until his late self-portraits. One can view his depiction of women with unease, even anger, but they might also be viewed as self-portrait, or as portraits of his own needs objectified in the women he loved – for all his paintings of women are based on his lovers.

JM

Gertrude Stein *Picasso* (New York: Dover, 1984)

See also **Degas; Voyeurism**

Plath, Sylvia (1932-1963)

The daughter of a German mother and an Austrian father, Sylvia Plath was born and grew up in Massachusetts, USA. She was driven to succeed in terms of the American Dream, but, to her cost, fell foul of the contradictions buried in that dream: discovering, in those days before the current wave of women's liberation, how painfully impossible it was to try to be simultaneously a serious, committed writer and a man's ideal of the perfect woman. Marriage to the British poet Ted Hughes, after initially happy years, turned bitter. Plath nevertheless plunged into creating much of her major poetic work before finally committing suicide.

Currently acclaimed as one of the great poets of the twentieth century, Plath has nonetheless suffered from having her work read exclusively in terms of her life: some critics concentrating on her alleged neuroses and personality defects, others on her supposed death wish, still others claiming her as a pure feminist heroine. These ideological readings prevent any appreciation of how her art was not a simplistic mirroring of her life, how the 'I' of the poems is often a series of masks. Her work brilliantly employs sophisticated poetic techniques to map, in a complex way, inner worlds upon outer ones, often through the creation of myths and archetypes. The often fraught relationships between women – as mothers and daughters, as sexual rivals for men – are superbly explored in her work, as are women's attitudes to the sexuality of fathers, lovers and husbands. Plath's poems foreground feminine anger and desire in a way that has inspired women poets ever since.   *MR*

Collected Poems (New York: Harper Collins, 1981; London: Faber, 1981)

See also **Fell**

Plato (427–348 BC)

The Athenian philosopher Plato was one of the circle that surrounded Socrates. Plato wrote in the form of dialogues: conversations between Socrates and his followers which expounded various aspects of the former's philosophy.

The name Plato is most commonly associated with the 'Platonic relationship', commonly understood to mean a non-sexual relationship between two people who might reasonably be expected to be sexually attracted to each other. The original meaning, however, was far more specific; it referred to an ideal and chaste relationship between an older man and a boy, which Plato considered to be the highest form of love.

A number of Plato's dialogues deal with sexuality, chiefly of the homoerotic kind, but it is in his *Symposium* that Eros (sexual love) is discussed at greatest length. In this, a number of prominent Athenians are at a drinking party and each in turn expounds his view of love, with particular reference to homosexual love and the desire for beauty. The playwright Aristophanes tells a story to account for the origins of sexual love. He recounts that originally there were three kinds of double-bodied humans: female, male and androgyne. These humans attacked the Olympian gods and, as punishment, were split in two. The punishment left them distraught and very lonely and the two parts held each other closely in an attempt to reunite. Then the god Zeus took pity on them and moved their genitalia to a more 'convenient' position so that they could have the consolation of sex and procreation. From these three sexes there descended four types of humans: from the androgynes came men who are especially keen on women ('such as adulterers') and women who are especially keen on men; from the double-bodied men came homosexual men (who 'have the most manly nature'); and, from the double-bodied women, came women who form 'female attachments'. The division, however, has given us *all* a longing for fusion, for unity with our other half, with the result that 'the desire and pursuit of the whole is called love'.

Plato's political philosophy shows a liberal view of women. In the *Republic* he outlines his ideal City, one which would be ruled by the more enlightened members of society, the Guardians. Women, in his vision, would be Guardians as well as men – for, since both male and female sheepdogs are capable of guarding a flock, why should not the citizen flock also be guarded by both the sexes? The chief distinction between them, says Plato, is the bearing and begetting of children; if women are given the same education and allowed to exercise their strengths like men, they might be just as good Guardians. This doesn't seem wildly radical today, but it was fairly shocking at a time when women were often not allowed to go to the market on their own.

Recent radical criticism of Plato has praised him for the way he has taken the two Athenian stereotypes of woman – the dangerously over-sexed, over-stimulated being and the completely passive creature with no desire except for procreation – and created a more acceptable idea of an erotically responsive woman who also has the desire to procreate. Furthermore, he tried to erase the distinction between the lover and the beloved, the active and the passive, and show true love as being an expression of equal desire by both partners.   *KH*

Symposium (New York and London: Penguin, 1952)

David M. Halperin *One Hundred Years of Homosexuality and Other Essays on Greek Love* (New York and London: Routledge, 1990)

See also **Firestone; Hetaira; Heterosexuality; Homosexuality; Lesbianism;** *Lysistrata;* **Romantic Fiction**

Political Lesbianism

Political lesbianism, as an idea and a force within contemporary feminism, has developed primarily within white, western women's movements. It has been developed by women who identify variously as Radicalesbians, Radical Feminists, Separatists and Revolutionary Feminists. In essence, political lesbianism is grounded in the belief that **heterosexuality** is the basis of male domination. Its advocates therefore see **lesbianism** as a political, as well as a personal, choice.

In England, the most explicit political lesbian statement was made by a group of Revolutionary Feminists in Leeds in 1979. They argued that the radicalism and energy of feminism was sapped by heterosexual feminists who put men first. The paper defined lesbianism in terms both of giving up men and of 'woman identification'. It stressed that this did not entail compulsory sexual relationships with women.

Opposition to political lesbianism has emerged across the feminist political and sexual spectrum. It has been widely condemned for asserting that lesbianism is the only honorable option for feminists. Many feminists, irrespective of their sexuality, feel this to be a 'vanguardist' position which duplicates the prescriptive nature of ultra-left politics. It has also been condemned for reducing the multiple causes and manifestations of women's oppression to the heterosexual act. In some quarters it has been interpreted as being tantamount to an expulsion order directed at straight feminists in the movement. Bea Campbell, a lesbian Socialist Feminist, has particularly objected to the conflation between feminism and lesbianism which political lesbianism can imply. In an article in *Feminist Review* (No. 5, 1980) she argued that the history and meaning of lesbianism, as an erotic and emotional choice, needed to be protected, and heterosexual feminists' right to sexual self-determination defended. Some feminist lesbians would argue that the political lesbian imperative grew in response to anti-lesbianism within the women's movement. Lesbian anger and chauvinism, in this analysis, is the direct outcome of many straight feminists' reluctance either to express solidarity with lesbians or to see the relationship between **compulsory heterosexuality** and the oppression of women.

The political lesbianism debate has provoked fierce battles among feminists wherever it has arisen. If it is to be credited with anything, it is perhaps the demolition of the fallacy of fixed and immutable sexual identities: many women with no history of sexual attraction towards women did discover the possibilities of love between women in a feminist context. But, for many feminists, the simple injunction that women should become lesbians could never take account of the complex processes by which women can and do change their sexuality.
                    JE

See also **Atkinson; Brown, Rita Mae; Clit Statements; Jeffreys; Radicalesbianism**

Pornography

Pornography is one of the most fiercely contested moral issues of our time. Traditionally defined as sexually explicit, and therefore obscene, words or images intended to provoke sexual excitement, the term was first used in the 1860s to describe the photography of prostitutes: a modern, mass-produced form of erotic imagery. Today, however, there is immense disagreement over both its definition and significance.

It is customary to separate out three distinct positions on pornography: the liberal, the moral right and the feminist. The liberal position, manifest in the US *Presidential Commission* of 1970 or, in a more qualified way, in the British *Williams Report* of 1979, offers a non-evaluative definition of pornography as sexually explicit material designed for sexual arousal. It argues that there is no scientific evidence of pornography causing harm in society and, therefore, no sound reasons for banning it. While pornography may offend many women and men, it brings harmless pleasure to others; the *Williams Report* aimed to limit the public display of pornography to protect those who might find it offensive.

The position of the moral right, manifest in the British *Longford Report* of 1972, defines pornography as representations of sex or violence removed from their proper social context, or 'a symptom of preoccupation with sex which is unrelated to its purpose'. This purpose, according to the moral right, is procreation. Thus sex should be confined to marriage and pornography is a threat to family values. The moral right has always sought to suppress information on birth control, abortion and sex education in schools, while demanding rigid censorship of any explicit depictions of sex, particularly of 'perverse' and homosexual imagery.

Finally, there is the feminist critique of the sexism and exploitation of women represented in most pornographic material – which is also frequently racist. Recently, it is from *within* this position that the most passionate battles have been waged. Certainly, all feminists have seen the standard images of pornography as promoting and strengthening sexist and demeaning images of women. In its heterosexual versions, reducing women to flesh (or bits of flesh), it celebrates the idea of men's insatiable sexual appetite and women's ubiquitous sexual availability. In the 1970s, however, few feminists sought legal restrictions on pornography. The state and judiciary were seen as essentially patriarchal; **obscenity** laws were known to have always served to suppress the work of those fighting for women's control of their fertility and sexuality. Objecting to all forms of sexist representations, feminists set out to subvert a whole cultural landscape which, whether selling carpet sweepers, collecting census information or uncovering women's crotches, placed women as the subordinate sex.

In Britain, however, a more single-minded focus on pornography as being at the root of male violence and therefore male domination was becoming evident in feminist writings by the close of the 1970s. Many feminists re-defined pornography as material which depicts violence against women, and is in itself violence against women. It had been the popular writing of US feminists like Robin Morgan and Susan Brownmiller in the mid-1970s which first made a definitive connection between pornography and male violence: 'Pornography is the Theory, Rape is the Practice.' More recently, following through this logic to draft model legislation, which would allow any individual to use the courts to ban pornographic material, US feminists Andrea **Dworkin** and Catharine MacKinnon define pornography as 'a systematic practice of exploitation and subordination based on sex that differentially harms women'. Dworkin's *Pornography: Men Possessing Women* (London: Women's Press, 1981), undoubtedly the single most influential feminist text on pornography, argues that pornography is the ideology behind all forms of female oppression, indeed all forms of exploitation, murder and brutality throughout human history.

And yet, despite the growth and strength of the western feminist anti-pornography movement during the 1980s, particularly in the USA and Britain, a minority of feminists passionately reject Dworkin's analysis and its related feminist practice. They see it as a complete mistake to reduce the dominance of sexism and **misogyny** in our culture to sexuality and its representations. They know that men's cultural contempt for and sexualization of women long pre-dates the growth of commercial pornography and they fear, in today's political climate, that we risk terminating women's evolving exploration of our own sexuality and pleasure by forming alliances with, instead of combatting, the moral-right anti-pornography crusade. Blanket condemnation of pornography, they stress, discourages women from owning up to our own sexual fears and infantile fantasies, which are by no means free from the guilt, anxiety and eroticization of power on display in men's pornographic productions. What we need, according to feminists opposed to anti-pornography crusades, is not more censorship but more sexually explicit material produced by and for women, more open and honest discussion of all sexual issues, alongside the struggle against women's general subordinate economic and social state.   *LyS*

Ed. Gail Chester and Julienne Dickey *Feminism and Censorship: The Current Debate* (Dorset: Prism Press, 1988)

See also **Apollinaire; Bataille; Carter; Comics, Japanese; Erotica; Livia; Perversion; Prostitution;** *Rou Putuan*; **Sade; Snuff Movies;** *Story of O*; *Torture Garden*; **Walker**

Prayer-Mat of Flesh, The

See ***Rou Putuan***

Prostitution, Female

There is an opinion, expressed not only by misogynists but some feminists, that *all* women are prostitutes: in the feminist view, because all women are treated as sexual commodities and are, in general and ultimately, economically dependent on men.

Specifically, however, a prostitute is a woman who hires out her body, her conversation and her sympathy for a pre-arranged period of time at a pre-paid price, and is only rarely required to make an exclusive, one-man contract. By and large, she is free to negotiate with any number of customers.

But the customers, of course, are equally free to haggle over conditions and cost. Unlike a wife, whose terms of employment are largely upheld by cultural, social, legal and religious diktat, a prostitute is almost entirely at the shifting mercy of the marketplace.

The prostitute, then, is a saleswoman. She is also, however, a symbol. Most forcefully (but not only) in cultures influenced by **Christianity** she is made to embody what men perceive as women's 'dirtiness' and 'viciousness' – in other words, their sexuality – allowing 'ordinary' wives, mothers and daughters to be seen as sexless, pure, unthreatening to men's libido and to their control of family affairs. Although this absurd division is to the advantage of neither set of women, for prostitutes the effect is to turn them into outlaws: women who, if not always in theory then very often in practice, can be financially cheated, beaten, raped, maliciously harassed by the police and even murdered with impunity. It should be added that none of this is because men want them not to *exist*. Suitably controlled, prostitution is seen as a safety valve for such lusts as men would prefer not to take to their wives and – through various forms of taxation, control of brothels and so on – as an excellent source of income for churches and state.

That prostitutes should be seen as victims is not entirely surprising. As Susan Brownmiller put it in 'Speaking Out on Prostitution' (1971): 'Prostitution is a crime, gentlemen, but it is not victimless. There is a victim, and that is the woman.' Nonetheless, it is equally easy to understand prostitutes as heroines, winners. The temple prostitutes of ancient Greece and India, for instance, were probably far more valued and influential than their married contemporaries. More certainly, the **hetaira** of Greece, the geishas of Japan and the mistresses of European noblemen obtained and obtain more power, respect and economic and social freedom than most of their 'virtuous' sisters. The market might be run for men, and very largely by men, but prostitutes with exceptional talent, intelligence, shrewdness or luck can still extract a profit. For most, of course, the reality is much more uncertain, unhealthy, dangerous and squalid. Even so, it is not just men such as **Baudelaire**, Lautrec or **Degas** (to name but a few among many) who have seen in these women's life a forbidden, dark glamor; a number of women artists have used the image of the 'common' prostitute as a flawed ideal of sexual honesty, integrity and freedom. The novelists Nawal ed **Saadawi**, Isabel **Allende** and Flora **Nwapa** have written of prostitution as an *escape* as opposed to a rejection.

Many real prostitutes agree with this. In her autobiography *Working* (1988), the American prostitute Dolores French describes prostitution as a sexual liberation and says, 'Best of all, I was in control . . . By living off the money men gave me for sex, I was able to achieve the independence from men my mother had always wanted me to have.' But even she acknowledges the dangers and injustices inherent in her trade – from exploitation by pimps through taking the blame for spreading **venereal disease** to systematic or whimsical legal harassment – and, in common with prostitutes in the USA and elsewhere, is campaigning to get these eradicated. Sex, control and money might not, in an ideal world, be related; while they so obviously are, however, attempts to eliminate prostitution are not only doomed to failure but are rather less helpful to the women involved than their own, increasingly vocal attempts to improve the conditions under which it occurs.   *HG*

Dolores French with Linda Lee *Working: My Life as a Prostitute* (New York: Dutton, 1988)
Jess Wells *A Herstory of Prostitution in Western Europe* (Berkeley, California: Shameless Hussy Press, 1982)

See also **Acton; Adultery; Bellocq; Borden; Brassai; Butler; Contagious Diseases Acts; Flaubert; Gorris; Greek Vases; Manet;** *Mona Lisa***; Picasso; Pornography; Prostitution, Male; Rhys; Wa Thiong'O; Whitman; Zola**

Prostitution, Male

Male Prostitution is much less systematically institutionalized than female. It is similar, however, in that the clients are nearly always men – although there are scattered historical accounts of male brothels for upper-class women and the gigolo is often more than just a professional dancing partner. In Britain, some male prostitutes dress as women and solicit in the places where women do, but most of their clients probably know that they are men. In cities there are usually fairly well known pick-up places, often railway or bus stations and amusement arcades where boys and young men hang around waiting for male customers. These boys sometimes claim to have no homosexual feelings themselves and to be doing it for the money; they are often homeless and will accept meals and a bed for the night or for longer. Their clients are sometimes married men who are not part of the gay scene.

Within the gay scene itself there are some men who are known to be 'trade' – willing to take money for sex – but it is usually not a major part of their life. Some men work from home, advertising as escorts. These may specialize in **sadomasochism** or some activity that involves equipment; they are able to charge because they have something other gay men want to share. Otherwise, prostitution merges into the casual sex of many male clubs or pubs. Male prostitution in the third world forms a significant part of sex tourism, with men from rich, capitalist countries traveling to North Africa, Thailand, the Philippines and elsewhere to pick up (often under-age) boys. Amsterdam also has a world reputation as a center for male prostitution and brothels.   *MM*

See also **Cross-Dressing; Genet; Homosexuality; Isherwood; Prostitution, Female**

Psychoanalysis

Psychoanalysis is a clinical practice, a theory of the unconscious mind and the laws that govern it, and an interpretative tool in the study of social organization and cultural production. It is centrally organized around the concept of the **unconscious** and takes as its object of study the vicissitudes of the sexual drive, the processes of symptom formation and the repetitions and compulsions of adult life. In presupposing a radical separation between the conscious and unconscious mind, psychoanalysis raised the concept of unconscious motivation to a high level of explanatory power. The fascination with psychoanalysis stems from the fascination with the idea that we do not know ourselves as we think we do.

There has always been debate about the nature of Sigmund **Freud**'s conceptual framework. Freud himself varied in his formulations of the relationship of psychoanalysis to the science of biology, believing both that the foundations of the sexual drive would one day be found in biochemistry and that the psychoanalytic method should establish its own conditions of validation, independently of the evidence of science. Clinically, psychoanalysis is based on an analysis of the transference, a relationship whereby the patient is able to project all his or her infantile (and unconscious) conflicts on to the analyst because the analyst remains an object of **fantasy** for the patient, revealing nothing (or as little as possible) of his or her own views, personal situation, likes and dislikes and so on. The idea of 'working through' these early conflicts is what distinguishes a rigorous psychoanalysis (and analytic psychotherapy) from supportive therapy, or more goal-oriented and usually brief therapeutic interventions.

Psychoanalysis has developed via a number of schools. In the USA, ego-psychology became dominant, as did the medicalization of psychoanalysis. After the Second World War, US psychoanalysis, with its all too frequent notion that the healthy outcome of treatment for women was conventional feminine domesticity, was seen by feminists as con-tributing to a normative ideological climate for women. Lacanian psychoanalysis in France targeted ego-psychology for its fiercest criticism, seeing it as an adaptationist debasement of Freud's original subversive vision, with its critique of rationality and its attention to the unconscious as 'another place' of language. Because his career was long and included a series of key modifications to his thought, it is not surprising that different schools of thought draw from Freud a particular emphasis. Lacanians have tended to concentrate on the early Freud of *The Interpretation of Dreams* and the theorization of the unconscious; the American ego-psychologists on Freud's later writings on the structural division of the mind into id, ego and super-ego, the latter being, in part, heir to parental authority and injunction.

The third main development of psychoanalysis, object relations, is closely linked with child psychoanalysis. Beginning in the 1920s, child analysis rapidly became associated with the work of Melanie Klein and, arising from her contributions to British psychoanalysis, gave rise to a major refocusing of psychoanalytic thought: onto the relationship between infant and mother, an extension back in time of Freud's later concern with the pre-oedipal. (The work of Anna Freud, Freud's daughter and Klein's main rival in the field of child analysis, has traditionally been associated more with ego analysis and the analysis of the ego's defenses, than with object relations.) Currently, object relations, in different forms, is probably the dominant clinical perspective in US and British psychoanalysis; the different perspectives of Kleinian and Lacanian psychoanalysis are now some of the most significant areas for debate, and have important implications for feminism.

Psychopathology, in the psychoanalytic sense, is the study and theory of the 'flight into illness' through disturbance in the sexual drives. Illness is used here not in the physical or medical sense, though it should be remembered that much of the key work in understanding the psychosomatic disorders – pathological narcissism, autism and the other psychotic disorders – has been inspired by psychoanalysis, especially from the object relations perspective. Illness, in the traditional Freudian sense, refers to the subject's (unconscious) renunciation of, or inability to attain, conventional sexual (genital) maturity; Freud always maintained that the achievement of genital maturity was precarious and never fully complete. That said, the pathologizing of **homosexuality** has been a contentious issue within psychoanalysis for decades and remains unresolved. Although Freud was a liberal in his advocacy of the acceptance of homosexuals within the social order, he both does and does not, in his writings, problematize the notion of the normal sexual aim, the normal sexual object.   *AS*

Sigmund Freud *New Introductory Lectures on Psychoanalysis* (Pelican Freud Library, vol. 2)

J. Laplanche and J. –B. Pontalis *The Language of Psychoanalysis* (London: Hogarth Press and the Institute of Psychoanalysis, 1973)

See also 'Dora'; Foucault; Horney; Kakar; Kristeva; Lacan; Oedipus Complex; Penis Envy; Perversion; Repression; Sexology

Puritanism

In relation to sex, the word 'puritanism' is casually used to describe a fuddy-duddy prudishness. Real Puritanism, however, which sprang into being in the sixteenth century, was a movement to purify the Church of England of the ceremony, ritual and esthetic decoration that many felt were too 'Roman Catholic'. The movement also involved a belief, not only religious but political, in individual conscience and the values of the middle (as distinct from the upper) classes. Its emphasis on frugality, restraint, hard work and the family unit – in particular, where this last was concerned, on the father's right to replace the parish priest as the family's moral arbiter – was both to women's advantage and disadvantage.

On the one hand, the Puritan ethic placed a high value on housework and the education of children and, in consequence, on the women in charge

of these. Moreover, the virtuous Puritan husband ought not to get drunk, assault his wife, visit prostitutes or have mistresses and thus risk infecting his family or women outside it with **venereal disease**. On the other hand, if Puritans held that **sexual intercourse** was honorable and holy (the German Puritan, Martin Luther, even married a former nun), they most certainly did not believe in sensual extravagance, connecting excessive physical delight with death, disease and corruption at court. The more radical among them, the Quakers and Ranters, did in fact question the Christian insistence on **monogamy**, but the mainstream Puritan opinion of sex was that it should be, as Bishop Taylor put it, 'moderate, so as to consist with health'. Meanwhile, women outside the family unit, especially those suspected of witchcraft, continued to be harried, persecuted, hanged: from Hertfordshire in England to Salem in the USA.   *HG*

See also Hawthorne; Jacobean Revenge Tragedy

Qur'an

See Islam

Radicalesbianism

Radicalesbianism is a variant of **political lesbianism**. The first radicalesbian group was based in the USA in the early 1970s; since then, other groups have developed and re-worked the earliest theories, notably in France.

The US radicalesbians wrote a notorious 'position paper' called 'The Woman-Identified Woman' (1972) which asserted the political significance of **lesbianism** in unforgettably flamboyant terms: 'Lesbianism is the rage of all women condensed to the point of explosion.' Lesbianism was defined as an expression of political solidarity between women and a fundamental assault on male power.

Later radicalesbian theories have argued that lesbians defy the private appropriation of women and men and therefore pose the greatest threat to **patriarchy**. The French radicalesbian Monique **Wittig** repudiated lesbians' status as women altogether in her article 'The Straight Mind' in *Feminist Issue* (Vol. 1, No. 1, 1980), claiming that the category 'woman' is defined in relation to men and that lesbians exist outside this relation. Radicalesbians believe that the category 'woman' has to be smashed; they therefore do not call themselves feminists, since feminism recognizes and organizes around the existing category of 'woman'. The political consequence of this analysis is that most feminist struggles come to be defined as pointlessly reformist: battered women's refuges and reproductive-rights politics are seen as little more than 'band-aid' measures for the casualties of the sex war. Heterosexual women themselves come to be seen as either the willful or unconscious betrayers of their 'class'.

Radicalesbianism has attracted widespread criticism: French feminists have noted the uncanny resemblance of its most chilly and stentorian writings to left-wing dogma; the notion of 'reform' versus 'revolution' has been borrowed wholesale from 'hard-line' revolutionary socialist analysis. An article by Claire Duchen in the British radical feminist magazine *Trouble and Strife* (No. 2, Spring, 1984) describes radicalesbianism as a 'closed analysis' in that it sees 'one basic factor as explaining all others' and rejects the place of openness and contradiction in feminist politics. The idea that lesbians are somehow outside the category 'woman' has also been questioned: lesbians may escape men in the private sphere but are just as susceptible as other women to patriarchal control in the world at large. Arguably, the most damning criticism of this tendency is that it has constructed a theory, in the name of women's liberation, which is based on contempt for the majority of women.

Radicalesbian and political lesbian theories have, at their most incisive, clarified the limitations of a political analysis which sees lesbianism as no more than a civil rights issue or cultural phenome-non. They have highlighted the extent to which the oppression of lesbians is bound up with the social control of women as a whole. Their failures are identical to those of any radical politics which endorses a single strategy for change. *JE*

Ed. Sarah Lucia Hoagland and Julia Penelope *For Lesbians Only* (London: Onlywomen, 1989)

See also **Clit Statements**

Rape

Prior to the emergence of feminist theory in the late 1960s, thinking about rape (here defined as any sexual act committed against a woman without her consent) was dominated by a variety of male 'experts', principally in law and medicine.

The US attorney Catharine MacKinnon has asserted that legal definitions of rape are based on what men, not women, think violates women. From women's point of view, MacKinnon argues, rape is not prohibited but regulated. Thus, for example, in many jurisdictions, rape is perceived as a crime against men's property and, as owners of this property, husbands cannot legally rape their wives: which has led the feminist Pauline Bart to describe rape as a paradigm for sexism. Similar ideology has led to belief in a number of myths: that women precipitate rape; that women mean 'yes' when they say 'no'; that nice girls don't get raped; and that, once a rape begins, women relax and enjoy it. My research on convicted rapists indicates that men use these rape myths to justify their sexually violent behavior and that these justifications are also used legally to defend men accused of rape.

Psychiatry contributes another view of rape, based on a disease model. From this perspective, rape is a psychopathologically isolated, idiosyncratic act limited to a few 'sick' men. However, despite widespread belief in this explanation, there is little empirical support for the disease model of rape. Twenty years of psychological research has failed to find a consistent pattern of personality type or character disorder that reliably discriminates rapists from other groups of men, while other research has found that fewer than five per cent of convicted rapists were psychotic at the time of the crime. Current feminist research confirms that sexual aggression should be thought of as a continuum of behaviors, ranging from verbal street harassment and harassment in the work place to wife battering, rape and murder as endpoints. Likewise, men can be thought of as varying along a continuum of sexual aggression, with some more likely than others to commit sexually aggressive acts against women. Indeed, research conducted on male college students in the USA indicates that thirty to forty per cent admit to having engaged in sexually aggressive behavior – some of it rape – in dating situations.

In contrast to the medical model, in the feminist theory of writers such as Susan Brownmiller, Susan Griffin, Diana **Russell** and others rape is perceived as a singularly male form of sexual coercion: an act of violence and of sexual and social control that functions to keep women in their place. Feminists have also pointed out that, because it preserves male dominance, sexual violence benefits all men, not just those who actually rape. In support of the feminist perspective, research on pre-industrial societies reveals substantial variation in the frequency of abusive treatment of women. Rape and other forms of sexual violence towards women are found as regular features of violent patriarchal societies organized around the social, political, economic and sexual subordination and devaluation of women. Among western industrialized societies, rape rates vary but are increasing. For example, over the past twenty years reported rape rates have more than doubled in the USA and in England and Wales, although the reported frequency is still lower in the UK than in the USA. Thus, whereas the disease model assumes psychopathology and disassociates rape from normal men, feminist theory assumes that rape is an extension of normative male behavior, the result of conformity to the values and prerogatives that define the male role in patriarchal societies. Men do not rape because they are crazy but because they have learned that, in violent

patriarchal societies, rape is permitted and it is rewarding.   *DS*

Diana Russell *The Politics of Rape* (New York: Stein & Day, 1975) Catharine MacKinnon *Feminism Unmodified: Discourses on Life and Law* (Cambridge, MA: Harvard University Press, 1987) Diana Scully *Understanding Sexual Violence: A Study of Convicted Rapists* (New York/London: Unwin Hyman/ Harper Collins Academic, 1990)

See also **Allende; Angelou; Barker; Bedi; Date Rape; Dworkin; Hitchcock; Marital Rape; Mills & Boon; Misogyny; Patriarchy; Rape and Revenge Movies; Women Against Violence Against Women; X, Laura**

Rape and Revenge Movies

The popularity of the 'video nasty' *I Spit on Your Grave* (1980) fanned the emergence of the 'rape and revenge' genre in cinema. The basic narrative centers on a woman in a deserted house who is terrorized, raped and sodomized by a gang of men, one of whom is dominant, another of whom is mentally retarded: a personality combination that recurs throughout the genre, even when the assault is carried out by just two men. The woman in question recovers from her trauma to exact revenge by murdering her rapists, usually in a sexual situation.

There are minor variations on the theme. In *Death Weekend*, which moves into the 'woman in jeopardy' genre, Brenda Vaccares in the lead role kills all the men in self-defense before escaping in her car. Before this, however, she undergoes the degrading experience of being forced by the cretin of the group to paint her face in preparation for sex with him. Compliant at first, as he reaches **orgasm** she gores him with a shard of glass. Such sexual dishonesty is a regular feature of the genre, allowing the audience the vicarious thrill of participating in the **rape** and humiliation of a woman while, at the same time, attempting to provide contextual justification by allowing the woman to triumph in the end. There is little doubt that much of the material produced in this genre is exploitative. Camera angles are chosen to sexualize the women to the maximum, and the women are dressed in skin-tight tee-shirts, brief bikinis or baby-doll nighties. Cleavages, buttocks and crotches are thrown into focus during the rough-handling, there is binding and gagging of the female victims, who are seen as entirely helpless until the second half of the film, when the lust for revenge takes over. But, even then, they tend to use their femaleness and their sexuality to lure their victims to their death.

The Sisterhood (1986), another variant of the genre, considers castration to be just punishment for rape. This was remade in India as Zakhmi Aurat/Woman Wounded in 1988. Although a common feature of Indian films, rape is traditionally portrayed in the Indian cinema through a series of standard symbols: stylized close-ups of birds and beasts of prey and distorted male faces leaning inward indicate the process of rape, while a guttering lamp-wick, a shattered vessel or a torn garment inform the audience that the rape is over. Realistic brutality is thus avoided in the portrayal of rape and cameras are precluded from panning up the legs and into the crotches of scantily clad women – unlike in the west where extended thrusting, beating and verbal abuse are exposed in detail.

Indian filmic convention also demands that virtuous women kill themselves rather than survive a desecration of their **honor**. In a deeply patriarchal society, with a predominantly male audience, the will to live of heroines in rape and revenge movies requires explanation. The rapists are therefore demonized as powerful men who use their respectability in the pursuit of illegal activities; while the female avenger, now cast as a protector of society, gains the patronage of the goddess Kali, protector of women's mysteries and destroyer of demons. This patronage becomes manifest in the woman's superhuman strength. Other well known mythological references, such as the vastra harana (removal of clothes) from the Sanskrit epic Mahabharata, are also common. The mythological twist divests the genre of its exploitative value for men anticipating the thrill of rape, who are left instead

with the eternally perplexing threat of a wronged woman's power and their own haplessness. Such films are therefore only moderately successful at the box office. SH

See also **Exploitation Movies; Gorris; Indian Cinema; Slasher Movies; Snuff Movies**

Réage, Pauline

See Story of O

Rego, Paula (1935-)

The painter Paula Rego was born and brought up in the country outside Lisbon, an only child in a household where different generations of women influenced her, telling her stories drawn from Portuguese folklore and French culture. She later attended an English school in Portugal. Though her father was a liberal and anticlerical, the imagery of Catholicism and the church's association with the fascist regime of Salazar made their mark on her. With remarkable imagination and originality, her painting has consistently explored the nature of power as well as the reponses and retaliation of the disempowered: children and animals have been favorite protagonists of her work. She is able to confront issues of sexuality, especially young women's, with clear eyes and a degree of black humor. Her art carries an unmistakable frisson of carnal knowledge and its risks and pleasures, for it deals with the cruelty that can be found even in tender love, the violent longings that possess the most demure-looking young girls and the eroticism that charges the adulation of the male in traditional southern European families.

While studying at the Slade School (1952-1956) she met and married Victor Willing (d. 1988), the English artist, and they subsequently went to live in Portugal for six years, where Rego had three children and, for a time, found it hard to continue

Paula Rego, *The Family*, 1988

painting. She was freed, however, by the discovery of art brut, the spontaneous, free-associating processes of Jean Dubuffet, as well as by the novels of Henry **Miller**.

Rego has said, 'I paint to give fear a face,' and she is able to examine tabooed areas of behavior and experience. 'The Dogs of Barcelona' (1965), a major collage, commemorates the poisoning of strays by public order and offers a tragic metaphor

for other forms of wanton cruelty. The *Red Monkey* series of smaller canvases of 1981–1982 explores the relations of man and wife through comic-strip techniques and savage wit; the *Vivian Girls* sequence of large, graffiti-like oils which followed, in the mid-1980s, imagines the adventures of an unruly gang of adolescents. These heroines first appeared in *The Realms of the Unreal*, a long, illustrated fantasy novel by a Chicago hospital cleaner, Henry Darger (1892–1972), the kind of 'outsider artist' with whom Rego feels great sympathy.

In recent large works, 'The Policeman's Daughter' (1987) and 'The Family' (1988), Rego creates a world of memory and fantasy focused on the lives of little girls, showing them performing household tasks (cleaning boots, helping a man to dress) in a stilled, eerie atmosphere. The birth of a granddaughter inspired *Nursery Rhymes*, a series of etchings (1989) that seize the disturbing, enigmatic side of children's nonsense verse. Her compositions and subject matter recall the work of **Balthus** but the resemblance is superficial, for Rego's images do not contemplate languidly the appeal of young girls but convey the fierce potency of their daily routines and the inventiveness of their play. She always works indoors (for a time her London studio had no window at all) and her palette, once riotously exuberant, has become more subdued and nocturnal, appropriate to the expression of the realms of the unreal, where the humdrum duties of women and children's lives are transformed and the ordinary takes on a disquieting air of mystery and promise.

MWr

See also **Infantile Sexuality**

Reich, Wilhelm (1897-1957)

One of Wilhelm Reich's first publications, while working as a psychoanalyst in Vienna, was *The Function of the Orgasm* (1927). Reich believed that 'orgastic potency' was crucial for psychic health and also fairly rare, since it was not a question simply of having orgasms but of having orgasms that were truly releasing. He disapproved of any kind of double standard for men and women. In his view sexual experience was essentially similar for both, women's 'widely prevalent passivity' being an unhealthy result of factors such as economic dependence.

While Reich accepted that each person had the right to live sexually as they chose, he made no bones about thinking that heterosexual intercourse was to be preferred (clashing on this point with Magnus **Hirschfeld**). The acme of sexual experience resulted from a desire to 'penetrate completely' matched by a complementary desire to 'receive completely'. Unsurprisingly, he emphasized the role of the vagina rather than the **clitoris** in **orgasm**. Unlike Sigmund **Freud** but like Karen **Horney** he considered that vaginal sensation existed from earliest childhood. However, the participation of the whole organism in the sensations of orgasm was the important thing.

In the late 1920s and early 1930s Reich attempted to bring **psychoanalysis** and communism together, while also maintaining the centrality of sexuality. He set up 'sexual hygiene' clinics in Vienna and later in Berlin (where he helped to found the German Association for Proletarian Sex-Politics), published sexual information for children, offered advice to teenagers on **contraception** and analyzed fascism partly in terms of the general passivity induced by sexual **repression**. His clinics were popular, but he also provoked a great deal of hostility, including from the Communist Party and the Psychoanalytical Association of Vienna, both of which severed their connections with him. Moving to Scandinavia, he began to work more and more directly with his patients' bodies, encouraging the dissolution of 'character-muscular armor' with the reported result of 'streamings' of energy and emotion. He also started experiments on 'orgone energy'. From 1940 he worked in the USA, continuing individual therapy but also developing an 'orgone energy accumulator' and experimenting in weather control. In 1957 he died in the Federal Penitentiary in Lewisburg, PA, where he was serving a sentence for violating a Food and Drugs Administration injunction against all activity related to orgone accumulators.

In the late 1960s and early 1970s Reich's work, or the idea of it, experienced something of a vogue. While Reich had thought **monogamy** productive of sexual unhappiness, he never advocated promiscuity, seeing it as a flight from sexual reality. For himself, he practiced, more or less, serial monogamy.

GW

The Function of the Orgasm (New York: Farrar Straus, 1986, London: Souvenir, 1983)

Myron Sharaf *Fury on Earth: A Biography of Wilhelm Reich* (London: Deutsch, 1983) Juliet Mitchell *Psychoanalysis and Feminism* (New York: Random House, 1975; Harmondsworth: Penguin, 1975)

See also **Foucault; Sexual Intercourse; Sexual Revolution; Wilson**

Repression

Sigmund **Freud** believed that the concept of repression was the cornerstone of **psychoanalysis**. Wishes and desires that are unacceptable to the subject are repressed; the **unconscious** is the location of the repressed material. Most significantly, repression is a process of which the subject is unaware (and in this sense differs from suppression, a conscious process). Repressed wishes then find their expression in symptoms, as Freud argued in '**Dora**'. In *Three Essays on the Theory of Sexuality*, which dates from the same period of his work, Freud's view is that, in hysteria, repression affects the genitals most: there is displacement to other parts of the body, which then behave 'exactly like genitals'. It is a reminder of the pre-eminent role that Freud gave to sexuality and the subject's conflicts over sexuality in the formation of symptoms.

Repression is not, however, co-terminous with symptom formation alone. Repression of oedipal desire, for example (balanced in a complex way with the gradual giving-up of which Freud also speaks), should also be seen as prerequisite for *normal* development. Juliet Mitchell's *Psychoanalysis and Feminism* (1974) attempted to show that repression is also linked to the establishment of sexual difference. She argues that each sex psychologically represses the qualities of the other, thus psychically acquiring the social meaning of the biological sex of each.

When repression is thought of as repression of 'real' experience alone, we are in the domain of revisionist psychoanalysis, and Alice **Miller**'s work is probably representative of this. In it, oppressive,

sadistic parents inflict such pain on their child that the child must repress the experience in order not to hate the parents on whom it is dependent for care. This forms part of a theory which rehabilitates a pre-Freudian notion of the sexual innocence of childhood. However, repression as a structure connotes, in the first instance, the way in which unacceptable wishes and desires are held in the mind. *AS*

Sigmund Freud 'Three Essays on the Theory of Sexuality' in *On Sexuality* (Harmondsworth: Penguin, 1977) Sigmund Freud 'Repression' in *On Metapsychology: The Theory of Psychoanalysis* (Harmondsworth: Penguin, 1984) Juliet Mitchell *Psychoanalysis and Feminism* (Harmondsworth: Penguin, 1975)

See also **Infantile Sexuality; Oedipus Complex**

Restoration Drama

The restoration of Charles II to the English throne in May 1660 brought a flowering of drama which had been denied since play-acting was banned by the Puritans in 1642. As anti-Puritan feelings grew, a sexual revolution took place, led by the new king who, with his courtly wit, weary cynicism and sexual appetites, could well have served as a model for characters such as Willmore in Aphra **Behn**'s 1677 play *The Rover* or Dorimant in George Etherege's 1676 *Man of Mode*.

The theater of the time reflected the new age: an age of sexual and economic opportunism. As Robert Phelps wrote in his introduction to *Selected Writings of the Ingenious Mrs Aphra Behn* (New York: Grove Press, 1950): 'the best ingredient for guaranteeing the attention of a Restoration audience was sex. Politics was next best, but for a really sure-fire job it had better be sex.' But, while the king and his courtly circle, which included writers such as George Etherege and the notorious libertine the Earl of Rochester, enjoyed their sexual freedom, women remained victims of a double standard. Dorimant's mistress Mrs Loveit in *Man of Mode* is discarded when her charms fade and is presented as a pathetic figure of fun, damned for her sexual assertiveness. Likewise Olivia in William Wycherley's 1676 play *The Plain Dealer* is humiliated for behaving, both sexually and morally, in a manner that would have been perfectly acceptable in a man. The prolific Aphra Behn, who was proving her independence by earning a living as a writer, was chastised for writing bawdily (an accusation that brought a typically robust response from Behn, who demanded to be given the right to express herself as freely as men), while actresses on the Restoration stage, frequently treated as if they must be prostitutes, were forced to take refuge in the title 'Mrs', even if they were not married, in order to retain a modicum of respectability.

Restoration drama – and its successor, the comedy of manners exemplified by the work of writers such as Congreve, Vanbrugh and Farquhar – appears to deal freely and explicitly with sexual matters. But, with the exception of Behn and the other, less known female wits, Catherine Trotter, May Pix and Susannah Centilivre, the playwrights all filter sexuality through a perspective which exposes women who take the sexual initiative as whores and understands that the hero's intended must be sexually pure, sexually passive and, preferably, an heiress.   *LG*

See also **Prostitution; Puritanism**

Revolutionary Feminism

See **Jeffreys, Sheila**

Rhys, Jean (1890-1979)

Born and raised on the island of Dominica, West Indies, Jean Rhys went to England at sixteen where she studied for the stage and was briefly an actress. She married for the first of three times in 1919 and moved from London to Paris, thereafter dividing her time between the Continent and London. Ford Madox Ford introduced her first book of short stories in 1927. Prolific and moderately successful until the war, her work was then neglected until she published *Wide Sargasso Sea* in 1966. Her life resembled those of her pre-war heroines in that she was usually dependent on men for support and spent periods of time alone and poor.

In Rhys's fiction, sex is ideally a source and expression of nature and of natural joy. However, it is generally exploited and undervalued: women commonly become victims because they are seen and used as purchasable commodities by men. Respectable women become absorbed into the capitalist 'machine' as wives, while freer, more 'natural' women find only a precarious place in bohemian life. Waitresses, sales girls, chorus girls and models appear in Rhys's work as little if any better off than prostitutes or mistresses, either serving men, acting as attractive objects for men, or patronized and harassed by male bosses.

The price that these freer women pay is expressed variously as madness, depression, isolation, self-hate, craven yearnings for love, poverty, and **prostitution**. In the pre-war novels and stories, café society and street life, more or less squalid, complement bleak, empty rooms. The women are outcasts, often homeless. In *Wide Sargasso Sea* Rhys sets most her story in the beautiful and beautifully depicted nature of Dominica. This novel expresses her recurrent themes most completely, in a longing for home revealed on many levels. Her victim-heroines, allied to nature, music and painting, and to excruciatingly intense honesty of feeling, are not simply defeated. They express, if intermittantly, a vitality of mind and body that is scorned and used, but not shared, by their oppressors.

Rhys's treatment of sex shows the strength of her feminist assessment of capitalist exploitation in sexual relations. However, what no summary of Rhys's themes can do justice to is the beauty, clarity, wit, humor and esthetic innovation of her writing. Like Virginia Woolf, rejecting the rational cause-and-effect basis of nineteenth-century fiction, Rhys structures her work through what can be termed feminine groupings of memories, associations, impressions and images. Instead of the Victorian novel's concern with the complexities of individuals, Rhys portrays archetypal situations and achieves a remarkable expression of the common experience of women through characters who at first seem peculiar and outré. *GH*

Quartet (New York: Carroll & Graf, 1990; Harmondsworth: Penguin, 1987); *After Leaving Mr MacKenzie* (New York: Carroll & Graf, 1990; Harmondsworth: Penguin, 1991); Voyage in the Dark (New York: Norton, 1982; Harmondsworth: Penguin, 1990); *Good Morning, Midnight* (New York: Norton, 1986; Harmondsworth: Penguin, 1990); *Wide Sargasso Sea* (New York: Norton, 1982; Harmondsworth: Penguin, 1990); *Smile Please: An Unfinished Autobiography* (Harmondsworth: Penguin, 1990)

See also **Brassai; Colette**

Rich, Adrienne (1929-)

A US poet, theorist and activist, Adrienne Rich is widely recognized for her lucid explorations of gender representations. Focusing on an urgent 're-vision' of women's history in *Blood, Bread, and Poetry* (1986), she examines women's oppression and the enforced invisibility of lesbian consciousness, declaring lesbian eroticism 'the most violently erased fact of female experience' and excoriating **compulsory heterosexuality** as an institution that disempowers women. With relentless self-scrutiny she has worked toward a renewed sense of 'woman-identified' consciousness as 'a source of energy, a potential springhead of female power, curtailed and contained under the institution of heterosexuality'. Her prose study *Of Woman Born* (1976) is a feminist classic, an indictment of women's oppression as wives and mothers.

Rich is most highly regarded for her poetry which, since 1970, has graphed her evolving struggle as a feminist and lesbian. Although her technically accomplished first book of poetry *A Change of World* (1951) reflects her early lack of engagement with sexual politics, her poetry continued to evolve toward a more direct account of her life and its sexual, political and social contexts. She has written vividly of her own conflicts as a wife and mother

and of her anger at patriarchal violence and the domestic seclusion that she and other women have suffered. After 1970, she increasingly clarified personal and political issues. Her explorations of power – particularly the power to transform patriarchal structures – assumed greater urgency as she sought to validate women's experiences and urged their active assumption of self-belief and dignity. In 1974 she received the National Book Award for *Diving Into the Wreck* but rejected it as an individual, accepting the award with nominees Audre **Lorde** and Alice **Walker** on behalf of all women. Her search for a 'common language' – a quest for community among women, a 'drive to connect' – is explored most powerfully in *The Dream of a Common Language* (1978). As she writes in *Your Native Land, Your Life* (1986), she is 'the woman with a mission, not to win prizes/ but to change the laws of history.' *LU*

Diving into the Wreck (New York: Norton, 1973); *The Dream of a Common Language* (New York: Norton, 1978); *On Lies, Secrets, and Silence: Selected Prose 1966–1978* (New York: Norton, 1980; London: Virago, 1980); *The Fact of a Doorframe: Poems Selected and New 1950–1984* (New York: Norton, 1984); *Blood, Bread, and Poetry: Selected Prose 1979–1985* (New York: Norton, 1986; London: Virago, 1987); *Your Native Land, Your Life* (New York: Norton, 1986); *Time's Power: Poems 1985–1988* (New York: Norton, 1989)

See also **H.D.; Heterosexuality; Lesbianism; Patriarchy**

Rola, Balthasar Klossowski de (1908-)

See **Balthus**

Romantic Fiction

Romantic fiction is a term used to cover a wide range of popular writing that focuses on love relationships between women and men. It dates from the epistolary, sentimental and gothic novels of the eighteenth and nineteenth centuries, through Charlotte **Brontë**'s *Jane Eyre* (usually acknowledged as the major influence on subsequent romances) to a range of twentieth-century works such as Daphne du Maurier's *Rebecca* (1938) and Colleen McCullough's *The Thorn Birds* (1977). In general use, the term is now understood to denote the popular, critically derided publications of mass-market publishers such as Harlequin and **Mills & Boon**, based in Canada and Britain, which distribute worldwide, mainly through mail order, supermarkets and general stores rather than bookshops. It also embraces the work of a host of other (mainly women) writers, notably that of Barbara Cartland, the prolific and internationally successful 'Queen of Romance', best known for her celebration of virgin heroines, and the sex-and-shopping 'cliterature' of Shirley Conran, Judith Krantz, Danielle Steele and others.

Since the late 1960s, ironically in tandem with the rise of the women's movement, romantic fiction has become one of the most commercially viable literary genres. Apart from Harlequin's worldwide network and the success of romantic blockbusters, feminist novelists such as Marilyn French and Meredith Tax have used the romantic novel form, while Anglo-American publishing houses have begun to target teenage girls and pre-teens with adolescent romances. The US-based Naiad Press has tapped into a large market with its reprints of 1950s and 1960s lesbian romances by writers such as Ann **Bannon** and Valerie **Taylor**, as well as commissioning new lesbian **erotica**.

And as the genre has become a complex one, with many different characteristics and target audiences, so the novels have moved with the times to become more erotically explicit and suggestive. In the early 1970s the 'sweet romance' of courtship, **foreplay** and loving sex when the wedding date was set – still hugely popular, be it set in Restoration times, a hospital ward or on a remote Greek island – was challenged by a new sub-genre, initiated by Kathleen Woodiwiss's *The Flame and the Flower* (1972): the 'bodice-ripper', featuring **rape** and sado-masochistic sexual encounters. Indeed, many feminist critics have pointed to the violent

sexuality in most formula romances, comparing it with **pornography** aimed at men. The romantic hero, as Ann Barr Snitow argues, is 'a sexual icon whose magic is maleness'; the books emphasize 'phallic worship', with the heroine – a passive, cowed figure of the pornographer's imagination – awaiting breathlessly her sexual initiation. This is all too often a brutal and cold violation, but it's later explained to have erupted from the hero's overwhelming desire and love, thwarted by some earlier misfortune or emotional rebuff.

Romantic fiction shares with the romances of the Greek love poets, the medieval troubadours and the Romantic Poets associations with and qualities of dream, idealized setting and character, themes of love and adventure, and a happy ending. The stories are concerned primarily with the nature of desire and its fulfillment. Marriage becomes a resonant symbol of love reciprocated, the fusion of two separate selves in emotional and sexual union and, thus, the absolute satisfaction of the individual self's yearning to be made whole and complete. Feminist theorists like Janice Radway have turned attention to the appeal of such a narrative for women readers. They argue that it helps to allay the inevitable dissatisfactions inherent in women's daily domestic and sexual lives and offers a nostalgic re-enactment of those urgent, bewildering sexual encounters in adolescence and courtship, as well as material for erotic **fantasy** and masturbatory titillation. Romance reading offers recognizably stereotyped characters whose qualities, infinitely loving and nurturing but also omnipotent and punitive, speak to sexual fantasies which operate at an **unconscious** level and thus often at odds with our socio-political beliefs and practices. Sexual engagements exist in an apparently timeless, dream-like vacuum in which the eternal verities confirmed by sexual union are expressed by natural metaphors of flood, storm and earthquake. A far cry from social and sexual realism, such scenes offer readers space to explore and enjoy their deepest infantile fears, loves, hatreds and desires.

Thus the dominant hero, who is always the object of desire – even in lesbian romance, which also presents couples within a definably masculine-feminine power relationship – is simultaneously powerful, desirable father and caring, sensitive mother. In bed, these combined qualities enable him both to stimulate the heroine's 'deepest core' to achieve simultaneous **orgasm**, and to calm her deepest fears. The apparently subordinated and undistinguished heroine nonetheless embodies a magnetic sexual presence which overwhelms and humbles her partner, who must express true love and thus acknowledge his complete dependence.

The growing commercial success of romantic fiction suggests that women readers enjoy works which address our sexual needs and pleasures. Formula romance provides a playful arena for a woman to engage in an intensely eroticized power struggle of a kind she knows, in everyday life, produces other effects than mutual orgasm. It thus makes sense to consider contemporary romance fiction (as distinct from the historical family saga, which aspires to social realism) as a rapidly evolving form of female erotica.   *HT*

Janice A. Radway *Reading the Romance: Women, Patriarchy, and Popular Culture* (Chapel Hill, North Carolina: University of North Carolina Press, 1991; London, Verso, 1987);

Carol Thurston *The Romance Revolution: Erotic Novels for Women and the Quest for a New Sexual Identity* (Urbana and Chicago: University of Illinois Press, 1987)

See also **Heterosexuality; Heyer; Romantic Love; Susann; Virginity**

Romantic Love

Obsessive yearning for someone with whom one has scarcely exchanged a word; indulgence in sexual frustration; the equation of true love with suffering: although such things have probably occurred since human beings existed, for most of our history they have been seen as signs of tragic insanity. They did, however, form part of a poetic convention – first of **Islam**, later of Christendom – that gradually, through various vicissitudes and counter to all common sense, became adopted as the ideal model for real-life lovers to aspire to: the lifelong, monogamous, idealizing, anguished amalgam of **ecstasy** and sacrifice known as romantic love.

The early Arab songs of 'pure love' were invented out of necessity, Islamic imperialism having led to 'respectable' women being so secluded that even their prospective husbands might not see them, let alone talk with them, until they were safely married. Thus songs such as those by the poet Djamil were addressed to entirely imaginary women – projections of the poets' own fantasies – and glorified **chastity**, purity, fidelity and poignant, heart-broken suffering. Through Islamic conquest and influence, the form reached Spain, then France, becoming enormously popular (ironically) during the Crusades: the eleventh, twelfth and thirteenth-century wars between Christians and Muslims for the Holy Land. But the European idea of 'pure', chivalric or romantic love evolved into something more complex, in part because those women to whom the troubadours addressed their songs, comparatively liberated chatelaines now that their husbands were away at war, influenced the genre through their response. While retaining the essentials of distance (troubadour and lady were of different classes), chastity, fidelity and suffering, romantic love acquired a new, flirtatious and teasing quality; where it had previously been a substitute for sexual passion, it now became dangerously confused with it.

Through plays and novels, the concept spread geographically and over the classes and, as literary conventions will, continued to change as it traveled. In the seventeenth century, importantly, the understanding of romantic love as quintessentially *tragic* was overturned by the introduction, to novels, of happy endings. Then, in direct contravention of the rules, romantic love became associated with marriage: and not only, now, in literature but in life. The young of the bourgeois and servant classes, the novel readers, in other words, astonished their elders by swearing that 'love', as distinct from financial or other advantage, was reason enough to ally themselves to another person for life. The eighteenth century English surgeon, John Knyreton, was one of the many perplexed, writing of 'this strange, intoxicating distemper of love, which I have heard described as a disease'.

Today, pop lyrics, movies, television and the worldwide sale of novels from Harlequin and **Mills & Boon** all declare romantic love as addictive a fantasy as ever. But unfortunately, especially for women, it also remains a hazy ideal for *real-life* sexual and (in the west) matrimonial conduct, all the more potent for being, by now, so profoundly taken for granted. As distinct from lust, affection, respect or negotiated mutual support, romantic love, when removed from the page, is both dangerous and dangerously confused. First, as the French psychoanalyst Jacques **Lacan** has pointed out, romantic love is the love of oneself projected onto another; it is therefore fundamentally dishonest and in blatant conflict with reality. It also involves, or encourages, the perception of women as objects, a dismissal of their own sexuality, and the kind of game of 'seduction and resistance' that all too often overlaps with **rape**.

The troubadours' songs were not without religious connotations. At the minimum, they praised romantic love for being, unlike marriage, a divine gift; but, like the Persian **Ghazal** poets, they may also have conflated the beloved with the Beloved: in other words, with God. It needs to be borne in mind that romantic love is indeed a religion – man-made, consolatory, ecstatic, irrational – not an unchanging, integral part of the human emotional make-up.

HG

See also **Atkinson; Brontë, Charlotte; Brontë, Emily; Christianity; Flaubert; Khusrau; Kwan; Mira Bai;** *Mona Lisa;* **Opera; Romantic Fiction; Shakespeare**

Rops, Felicien (1833-1898)

Felicien Rops was a Belgian printmaker and painter who, after a conventional start as a satirist for Brussels journals, arrived in Paris, got involved with the symbolists and found his subject: women.

Felicien Rops, *Pornocrates*, 1896

Ideas about women and satanism meshed with Rops's Catholic upbringing to release an art that, at times, becomes blasphemous and pornographic. Among the works of the literary symbolists he illustrated were *Le Vice suprême* by Péladan, *Les Diaboliques* by d'Aurevilly and frontispieces to poems by Mallarmé. When his work is taken as a whole, the depictions of pretty women in cosmetics, Gainsborough hats and black stockings – the acceptable face of decadence – are canceled out by works showing a woman using an octopus to satisfy her sexual appetite, a crucified woman tempting St Anthony, women with the cloven hoofs of the devil. In 'Agony' a death's head eats the genitals of a **nude** woman.

Although Rops's reputation has fallen, in part because of the crude banality of his sexual vision, his skilled etchings influenced his contemporaries and his lurid view of female sexuality was shared by many.   *FB*

See also **Munch**

Rossetti, Christina (1830-1894)

Ill health disqualified Christina Rossetti from an active public life such as her famous brothers Dante Gabriel and William enjoyed. What it allowed her were the peace and solitude necessary for writing poetry. During her lifetime she published much prose and poetry in periodicals and anthologies, as well as many prose devotional works. Her output ranges from poems of fantasy and verses for the young to ballads, love lyrics, sonnets and religious poetry.

Rossetti was a devout High Anglican in an ascetic tradition who nevertheless, in her poetry, powerfully connected the spiritual and the erotic: exploring, among other themes, female desire, **masochism** and frustration, often through the use of imagery drawn from the natural world. To some extent her sexual references are coded – as with the image of a sunflower twisting to follow the scorching heat of the masterful sun – which is perhaps why she has only recently been read as poet to whom sexual themes are inescapably part of the subject matter. Her intense imagination and technical virtuosity are shown to powerful effect in the long narrative poem 'Goblin Market', whose complex symbolism plays off the tensions between divine and human love, self-sacrifice and desire, and memorably celebrates the sensuousness of sisterly love. The poem's **sensuality**, and its use of short, irregularly rhymed lines, make it utterly distinctive.
MR

A Choice of Christina Rossetti's Verse (New York and London: Faber, 1970)

See also **Brontë, Emily**

Rou Putuan

The pornographic content of this seventeenth-century Chinese novel probably accounts for the fact that, although regarded by some as a minor classic, it has largely been neglected by critics. Its attention to its women characters has led some scholars to suggest that the author was a woman, but, given the scope of the book and the restricted lives of women in imperial China, this is most unlikely. In all probability *Rou Putuan* was written by Li Yu (1611-1680), a dramatist and story writer famous for his hedonism and appreciation of women.

In plot terms, *Rou Putuan* is almost entirely about sex. The story is that of a young scholar who, as soon as he has initiated his bride in the uninhibited enjoyment of sex, leaves her at home while he journeys forth to have as many sexual adventures as possible. To facilitate this he has a dog's penis grafted onto his own. The many scenes of lovemaking are detailed and explicit even though they are described in conventional and poetic language. There is considerable use of wit and humor, and both men and women are viewed cynically, yet sympathetically. In many places the novel satirizes Chinese scholars; elsewhere, many of its elements parody *Jin Ping Mei*.

It is in the characterization of and attitude towards its female characters that *Rou Putuan* is most unusual for a traditional Chinese novel. The young hero is very considerate about the pleasure of his partners and, besides the physical attraction, there is often genuine affection between them. The author, too, pays great attention to women's sexual and emotional feelings. What the women experience is considered to be as important as the pleasure of the man, and assertive, experienced women are looked on more favorably than passive, conventionally virtuous ones. Sex is often described in the language of battle, or of diplomatic missions, but there is no dominant partner: the 'battle' or the 'negotiations' are always on an equal footing.

On the other hand it must be said that this mode of description, together with the parade of lustful, available women (whom the hero inevitably satisfies), makes the novel resemble modern western **pornography**. Although *Rou Putuan*'s undoubted literary value separates it from most of the latter, it does seem at times that the author's purpose was to titillate and vicariously gratify the egos of male readers (the novel's readership would have consisted almost entirely of men), rather than to produce a sincere exploration of male or female sexuality.   *AR*

Rou Putuan/The Prayer Mat of Flesh (New York: Ballantine, 1990; London: Arrow, 1991)

See also **Lie Nu Tradition**

Rule, Jane (1931-)

Jane Rule is a lesbian writer whose fine first novel, *Desert of the Heart* (1964), was rediscovered by many readers twenty years after its publication when it was adapted for Donna Deitch's successful feature film *Desert Hearts*. Rule has published novels, short stories, essays and a major study of writers ranging from Radclyffe **Hall** to Jill Johnston, *Lesbian Images* (1975). Born in the USA, she has lived in Canada since her early twenties, writing and teaching.

Rule is the George Eliot of twentieth-century lesbian writing: the subtle realism of her novels and stories marks them 'for grown-ups' in that they explore women's loving relationships without either the grief and guilt of much earlier lesbian writing or the eroticism and romance of more recent fiction. Her characters learn to love and survive across differences of age, health and social circumstances. For them, sex is 'one of the languages for loving rather than an identity'; being a lover is a status bringing with it responsibilities and pleasures no more important than those of a daughter, sister or friend; and these various relationships co-exist in every life. Such beliefs, stated in her autobiographical introduction to *Lesbian Images*, are manifest in all Rule's fiction. In novels like *Memory Board* (1987), small communities of women and men form around the

lesbian protagonists, communities which are exemplary in the way space is provided for individuals to be both separate and connected. But even in her early books like *Desert of the Heart* and *This is Not for You* (1970), where lesbian relationships are represented in a social environment which makes them much more vulnerable and often betrayed, the lovers are never isolated in high romantic style.

In contrast to the sympathetic and restrained intensities of the novels, Rule's essays on writing, art and sexual politics in contemporary Canada are feisty: the work of a 'hot-eyed moderate', as her 1985 collection is aptly titled. More of these essays appear in *Outlander* (1981), together with stories addressing the variety of lesbian lives with sharp humor as well as the intelligent compassion that is the hallmark of her writing.   *SS*

Desert of the Heart (Tallahassee: Naiad, 1985; London: Pandora, 1986); *This Is Not for You* (Tallahassee: Naiad, 1982; London: Pandora, 1987); *Against the Season* (Tallahassee: Naiad, 1984; London: Pandora, 1988); *Lesbian Images* (California: Crossing Press, 1982; London: Pluto 1989); *Theme for Diverse Instruments* (Tallahassee: Naiad, 1990); *The Young in One Another's Arms* (Tallahassee: Naiad, 1984); *Contract with the World* (Tallahassee: Naiad, 1982); *Outlander* (Tallahassee: Naiad, 1981); *A Hot-Eyed Moderate* (Tallahassee: Naiad, 1985); *Inland Passage* (Tallahassee: Naiad, 1985); *Memory Board* (Tallahassee: Naiad, 1987; London: Pandora, 1987); *After the Fire* (Tallahassee: Naiad, 1989; London: Pandora, 1989)

See also **Hanscombe; Lesbianism;** *Microcosm*

Russ, Joanna (1937-)

A US novelist and critic, Joanna Russ started to make her name as a **science fiction** writer in the early 1960s. Her progressive involvement in feminism coincided with the development of sf's New Wave. As a result Russ's semi-experimental variations on standard sf narrative modes, which declared war on their unthinking sexism – women portrayed as bimbo liabilities, scheming adventuresses or ravening matriarchs – had a wider readership than might have been the case in other times and genres.

The most important of Russ's novels is *The Female Man* (1975) which sets various universes, each containing a different state of play in the conflict between the sexes, in direct apposition and opposition to each other, making this a metaphor for the forces that determine and alter the identity of any individual woman. The novel is closely linked to her award-winning short story 'When It Changed', depicting a women-only utopia under threat from male visitors, and her earlier Alyx stories, which subjected many of the clichés of heroic **fantasy** to friendly subversion. Her non-sf novel *On Strike Against God* (1979) sets an autobiographical account of coming out as lesbian against some witty diatribes about the sexism, and condescending liberalism, of her coevals in the sf community. Russ's playful postmodernism is worn lightly: it is at all times a polemical tool and what is said always more urgent than the mode of expression. Her work exists fruitfully at the interfaces between artifice, witness-bearing and feminist propaganda.

Russ's *How To Suppress Women's Writing* (1983) is an elegant dissection of the pressures militating against the growth of a full tradition of women's literature, and her essays on the feminist controversies over **sado-masochism** and **pornography** have been sane pleas for sisterly moderation.

RK

The Female Man (Boston: Beacon Press, 1987; London: Women's Press, 1985); *On Strike Against God* (California: Crossing Press, 1985; London: Women's Press, 1987)

See also **Le Guin; Livia; *Orlando***

Russell, Diana (1938-   )

Born in South Africa, now living in the USA, Diana Russell is one of the handful of feminists who, in the early 1970s, subjected **rape** to a feminist analysis and revolutionized the way in which we understand it. In her first book on the subject, *The Politics of Rape: The Victim's Perspective* (1975), she argues that rape is the logical consequence of the sexist sex roles imposed on us in male-dominated societies.

A researcher and professor of sociology, as well as an activist and writer, Russell became one of the major organizers of the 1976 Brussels-based International Tribunal on Crimes Against Women. This speak-out included considerable testimony on rape, forced motherhood, **female genital mutilation, pornography, prostitution** and femicide (the killing of women *because* they are women, as in rape-murder). Together with the Belgian feminist Nicole Van de Ven, Russell documented this herstoric event in *Crimes Against Women: The Proceedings of the International Tribunal*.

Russell next embarked on the ambitious undertaking of trying to ascertain the prevalence of rape in San Francisco. Funded by the National Institute of Mental Health, her pioneering study resulted in the first book ever to be published on **marital rape**, *Rape in Marriage* (1982), as well as *Sexual Exploitation: Rape, Child Sexual Abuse, and Workplace Harassment* (1984) and *The Secret Trauma: Incest in the Lives of Girls and Women* (1986). This last book won the most prestigious award in sociology in the USA, the C. Wright Mills Award for outstanding social science research. Russell's brilliant study was also groundbreaking in its methodology, combining rigorous scientific methods with a sophisticated understanding of the *experience* of sexual victimization. Particularly startling were the unprecedentedly high rates of sexual assault reported by the 930 women residents of San Francisco: forty-four per cent for rape and attempted rape; thirty-eight per cent for **child sexual abuse**; sixteen per cent for incestuous abuse; four and a half per cent for father-daughter **incest** (including stepfathers); ten per cent for pornography-related sexual abuse.

Returning to the land of her birth in 1987, Russell interviewed sixty women in the anti-apartheid movement. Although these interviews did not focus on sexual assault, some of the women spoke of such experiences, particularly those who had spent time in prison.

Finding that the concept of 'femicide', about

S

which she had spoken publicly for years, continued to be ignored by feminists as well as by the public at large, Russell and the British feminist criminologist Jill Radford embarked on an anthology on this subject – *Femicide: The Politics of Woman-Killing* (1991) – in the hope that its publication would break the massive denial about the lethal consequences of **misogyny** in some societies.

Pornography has been another form of sexual exploitation to concern Russell. In 1976 she became one of the founders of the first feminist anti-pornography group in the USA, Women Against Violence in Pornography and Media. She was also among the first writers to undertake a feminist analysis of pornography; 'Pornography and Rape: A Causal Model' in *Political Psychology* (Vol. 9, No. 1, 1988) is her most influential article on the subject. In it she makes a seemingly irrefutable argument for the causative role of pornography in violence against women.

Russell is a firm believer in the efficacy of civil disobedience as a strategy for women. Indeed, she has been arrested three times for engaging in civil disobedience, twice in connection with the sexual assault of women. She is convinced that, if thousands of women were to follow the example of the women in the anti-apartheid movement in South Africa, or Nikki Craft in the USA (Craft has been arrested thirty times to date), that the women's movement would be significantly more effective in combatting the sexual terrorism that threatens our well-being and our lives. LX

The Politics of Rape: The Victim's Perspective (Chelsea, MI: Scarborough House, 1975); *Rape in Marriage* (Indiana: Indiana University Press, 1990); *Sexual Exploitation: Rape, Child Sexual Abuse, and Workplace Harassment* (California: Sage, 1984); *The Secret Trauma: Incest in the Lives of Girls and Women* (New York: Basic Books, 1986); *Lives of Courage: Women for a New South Africa* (New York: Basic Books, 1991); *Femicide: The Politics of Woman-Killing*, with Jill Radford (Boston, MA: Twayne Publishers, 1991; London: Open University Press, 1991)

See also **Dworkin; Patriarchy**

Saadawi, Nawal El (1930-   )

An Egyptian doctor, advocate of women's rights and author of more than fifteen books of fiction and non-fiction, Nawal el Saadawi, with her lucid portrayals of women in the Arab world, has caused aggravation to successive Egyptian governments, leading to her onetime imprisonment and the banning of her works both at home and in other parts of the Middle East.

Although her books explore sexuality, **female genital mutilation, incest**, love, marriage, divorce and so on within the boundaries of **Islam**, and her prognosis is decidedly grim, Saadawi reminds us that Islam doesn't have the monopoly on sexual repression. In Judeo-Christian ideology the sexual and economic oppression of women is glaring and, as with Islam, it begins within the confines of the patriarchal family unit. Saadawi argues that economic liberation is inextricably linked with sexual liberation and that the denial of one is the denial of the other.

In her non-fiction book *The Hidden Face of Eve* Saadawi criticizes puritanical Islamic notions which keep women ignorant of all things relating to the body and sex, and condemns the tradition which values a woman's unbroken hymen more than her limbs and often her life. A woman is not expected to enjoy sex and her worth plummets with the loss of her **virginity**. Men often marry inexperienced girls much younger than themselves (Egyptians refer to them as 'blind pussy cats') who haven't yet worked out their own physical, sexual or intellectual needs and are less likely to question their function as sex provider and childbearer. A woman or girl who is experienced is regarded as deformed. On the other hand licentiousness is encouraged for men. Since **masturbation** is forbidden and prostitutes are generally expensive, **rape** and incest are not uncommon and women are usually blamed for allowing themselves to be so molested. Saadawi notes one case in which a father, upon learning that his brother had raped his young daughter, conspired with him to kill the girl so that their good family name could not be sullied.

Because they are never told what to expect, girls are often seized with terror when they experience their first period. Meanwhile, under a cloak of secrecy, varying degrees of female genital mutilation are practiced, from clitoridectomy to infibulation, and the experience is sometimes so traumatic that frigidity among Arab women is common. Fear and ignorance propel sex into women's lives in such a way that it occupies many of their thoughts.

It is interesting that the fictional heroines Saadawi creates are very different: rebels, as a rule, whose desire for freedom expresses itself in many ways. *Woman at Point Zero* (1975) documents the life of Firdaus, a prostitute and an honorable woman who, terrorized by a pimp who forces himself into her life, kills him and, when her execution is demanded, embraces death as the ultimate freedom. Unrepentant in prison, Firdaus reflects, 'Now I realized that the least deluded of all women was the prostitute . . . She experiences the rare pleasure of . . . being completely independent and living her independence completely . . . That marriage was the system built on the most cruel suffering for women.' Bahiah Shaheen, the protagonist of *Two Women in One*, is a young medical student who falls in love and gives up the one thing society decrees an unmarried woman should not: her virginity. Whereas before she had imagined that sexual desire and her genitalia were abnormal, she finds sex uplifting and this discovery sets off a chain of events which liberates her from her former self and changes her perception of life entirely.   *NOB*

The Hidden Face of Eve (Boston: Beacon, 1982; London: Zed Press, 1980); *Woman at Point Zero* (London: Zed Press, 1983); *God Dies By The Nile* (London: Zed Press, 1985); *Two Women in One* (Seattle: Seal Press, 1986; London: Al Saqui Books, 1985)

See also **Ba; Honor; Patriarchy; Prostitution**

Sacher-Masoch, Leopold von (1836-1895)

See **Masochism**

Sade, Comte Donatien Alphonse François de (1740-1814)

Also known as 'The Marquis de Sade', 'The Divine Marquis' and so on, the man who should, correctly, be referred to as plain 'Sade' signed away his titles, including the aristocratic 'de', in 1790. (And to impute divinity, even ironically, to this proselytizing atheist is offensive.)

Republican; anti-clericist; sodomite; philosopher; pamphleteer; satirist; old lag; dramatist; flagellant; briefly, under the Terror, judge; glutton; libertarian: this unusual renegade French nobleman's other claims to fame are overshadowed because he has become synonymous with sexual violence. When the time came, in the mid-nineteenth century, for the classification and definition of sexual preference, his name was bestowed upon the practice of cruelty for the sake of sexual gratification on the basis of some of the ideas propounded in his pornographic novels: *Justine ou les infortunes de la virtue* (1791); another version of that novel, accompanied by an extravagantly malign sequel, *La nouvelle Justine, suivi de l'histoire de Juliette, sa soeur, ou les prosperités du vice* (1797); and *Philosophie dans le boudoir* (1795). (The manuscript of *Les 120 journées de Sodome, ou l'école du libertinage*, written during Sade's period in prison from 1778 to 1790, was lost and not rediscovered and published until the twentieth century.)

These novels are visions of a social and erotic dystopia, written as a conscious act of verbal terrorism against the state and its institutions, which Sade believed were immutably repressive. Sade defined art as 'the perpetual immoral subversion of the existing order' and saw sex in the same way. It is fair to say that, when the works of Sade are on sale to the general public, as opposed to the obsessed pervert, the whole question of the nature of human nature is under discussion. They were freely on sale during the period of the French Revolution, banned under Napoleon – when Sade himself was tidied away into a madhouse – and once again available in the 1960s. Sade's libertarianism, however, although extreme, is that of a lover of bondage. He is full of contradictions. Women are not the victims of aggressive male sexuality in his **pornography**; it is a question of the weak and the strong, a question of power.

Sade's world is one without transcendance, in which the human body is the only unit of measure, and that body – in its fleshy materiality, the ambiguity and transferability of its genders, the ease with which it breaks, the way it can penetrate and be penetrated and split and spill its various juices and convulse in the spasms of death or pleasure – is the entire theater of human consciousness, in which all relations of power are played out.

Janus-faced, Sade as philosopher looks back to the Enlightenment, which, having reasoned itself out of the idea of God, found it could not do without something in charge and substituted Nature. But Sade reasoned that Nature was indifferent to humanity, source only of a demonic energy. Sade's Mother Nature is Kali, the 'mad mother', and to behave in tune with her is, for him, to surrender oneself completely to the promptings of desire.

In the ferociously sexualized republic of his imagination, Sade promised women equal rights to sexual pleasure: 'Charming sex, you will be free; just as men do, you shall enjoy all the pleasures that Nature makes your duty.' This does not make him a proto-feminist, any more than does the presence of women among the monstrous libertines who populate his pages. But he remains immensely important as a writer for whom the sexual is always the political, not in terms of gender politics but in terms of a universal transgression. In *Philosophie dans le boudoir* the heroine, Eugénie, exclaims gleefully as she rapes her own mother while being herself anally entered: 'Here I am, at one stroke incestuous, adulteress, sodomite, and all that in a girl who only lost her maidenhead today!' Sade is no ordinary pornographer and it is foolish to treat him as such. He is much more dangerous than that. He did not write for money, but for love.

History gave Sade the opportunity to act out his most virulent fantasies in Paris during the Terror; he signally failed to take advantage and was imprisoned for opposing the death penalty. The remainder of Sade's literary output, novels, stories, plays, journalism of all kinds, runs to sixteen volumes in the 1966-1967 complete edition in French and betrays little trace of the polymorphously perverse passions that pervade his most famous work, which deals comprehensively with every sexual variation from anal intercourse to zoophily. Nobody seems to read any of that other stuff.   *AC*

Oeuvres Complètes (Paris: Cercle du Livre Précieux, 1966–1967)

Simone de Beauvoir *Must We Burn Sade?* (London: John Calder, 1962) Angela Carter *The Sadeian Woman: An Exercise in Cultural History* (New York: Pantheon, 1988; London: Virago, 1979)

See also **Acker; Burroughs; Flaubert; Obscenity; Orton; Perversion;** *Torture Garden*; **Valenzuela**

Sado-Masochism

A sexual and cultural set of ideas, rather than a medical term, sado-masochism (SM) is the complex of mutual, consensual sexual activities which involves, often in combination, the use of pain to produce pleasure, the use of costumes and role play and the use of performed fantasies of domination and humiliation. Participants place emphasis on prior consultation between partners as to the rules of the sexual game and on agreed, unequivocal code-words whereby activity can be terminated if, when and as soon as the partner taking the 'bottom' role ceases to find a particular activity, or the whole 'scene', pleasurable. There are extensive subcultures in Europe and North America built around SM and it is a major theme of Japanese **comics**. Lesbian and gay SM subcultures marginally intersect with the heterosexual one.

The subcultures' need for internal recognition has made their members adopt and adapt a variety of stock images – the biker's jacket, the whore's fish-net stockings – which have fed back into mainstream fashion through movements like punk. Gay SMers have adopted a color-coded system of back-pocket handkerchieves to indicate precise sexual tastes, not widely adopted in the other SM cultures. Lesbian SM style signals a particular interaction of sexual practice, political attitudes and post-punk bar **dyke** culture.

Feminist critics stigmatize SM as perpetuating stereotypes of heterosexual behavior, blurring the distinction between SM and non-consensual sadism or the entirely different complex of ideas that has been referred to by male psychologists as 'female **masochism**'. This critique ignores the fairly even distribution of roles in heterosexual SM; the slight preponderance of males demanding pushily to be whipped by dominant females might be taken as evidence of male selfishness, but has not been by such critics. A more complicated hostile analysis has come from radical separatists like Sheila **Jeffreys**, who claims that lesbians and gay men use SM to avoid recognition of powerlessness by imitating the power of the oppressing classes, instead of rebelling. This analysis further charges that SM is intrinsically racist, because it trades in images allegedly linked to Nazism and ignores the distaste for it felt by some black and Jewish women.

Most retorts to this analysis have come from lesbian SMers, because they are actively obliged to share space with the radical separatists. They have concentrated on clearing up slanders. Few sadomasochists wear Nazi uniforms or swastikas, even in the bedroom, and most of the 'Nazi regalia' referred to is, in fact, motor-cycle gear. Gayle Rubin has suggested that the stigmatizing of sexual minorities by lesbian separatists is an attempt by the latter to buy into the mainstream, or convince the mainstream that they are less threatening than sexual outlaws. She links this with the alliance of radical feminists with the political right on issues of censorship and **pornography**. Certainly, the regular presence of SM material on the 'shopping list' of the **Dworkin**-McKinnon ordnance and its rightwing imitators would imply such a link. The claim that lesbian and gay, or black and Jewish, SM practitioners identify with their oppressors is seen as hypocritical in the light of this alliance.

Defenders of SM have questioned the hidden agenda of Jeffreys and her ally Mary Daly. Creating

a massive outcry against SM has been the cover for an attack on *all* genital sexual behavior, lesbian, gay or heterosexual. Many lesbians see experimentation with SM as an attempt to put sex back into their sexuality and sexual politics. To create a single unitary model of correct sexual practice, they argue, is to ignore human diversity and to impose the biases of white, middle-class, academic women on others. It is also, implicitly, to reject the pleasure and productive ambiguities and tensions of fantasy and sensuality for an austere model of 'women's freedom' whose proponents advocate constant mutual policing. Lesbian SM writing like the anthology *Coming to Power* (1983) is optimistically utopian in its view of SM as play through which conflict can be acted out. The debate on SM is seen by both sides as dealing with broader issues than whips, chains and leather jackets.   *RK*

'Samois' *Coming to Power* (Boston: Alyson, 1983)

See also **Chrystos**; *Correct Sadist*; **Jarman; Kono; Oshima; Parker; Sade;**

Safer Sex

In 1983 Michael Callen and Richard Berkovitz wrote a pamphlet entitled 'How to Have Sex in an Epidemic'. It was the first attempt by gay people to initiate changes in sexual practice to protect people from the sexual transmission of **AIDS**. Safe or safer sex practices – most AIDS workers prefer to speak of safer sex, recognizing that some low-risk practices may not be a hundred per cent safe – were thus introduced and enacted before the isolation of the HIV infection responsible for AIDS was made public in 1984. Since that time extraordinary effort has been put into public-information campaigns by gay activists, following the pioneering work of the North American gay community, to promote individual and collective responsibility for safer sex practices.

The virus responsible for AIDS is now known to be carried in body fluids containing T4 cells (which are part of the immune system). These are concentrated in blood and semen, with a lower concentration in vaginal and cervical secretions and breast milk, and an even lower presence in saliva. Transmission can occur only when HIV infected body fluid enters the body of another, via breaks in the skin of the anus, mouth, vagina. This means that, for sexual transmission to occur – as distinct from infection through the sharing of needles, or through transfusion with unscreened blood – certain practices are far riskier than others. Heterosexual or homosexual anal or vaginal intercourse, without a condom, are the most risky sexual practices. The use of condoms for all sex which involves penetration is a safer sex practice, while mutual **masturbation** and manual sex (with the use of finger cots if there are cuts on the hand) are virtually free from risk. The use of latex barriers (squares of thin rubber) or dental dams makes **oral sex** safer.

In the absence of any vaccine against HIV it is clear that the only means we have today of preventing its spread is through changes in behavior, but in countries such as Britain and the USA government health agencies were slow to response to the AIDS epidemic. Even when they did, their warnings about AIDS were primarily aimed at heterosexual men and, particularly at first, were criticized by many AIDS activists for promoting a negative fear of all sexual encounter – straightforwardly linking sex and death – rather than positive thinking around safer sexual practices. But the unprecedented success of the safer sex campaigns in the gay community – in the USA it is estimated that around seventy-five per cent of gay men now always use safer sex practices, considerably reducing the incidence of new infection – has confirmed that a different approach can work. Some gay men have written of coming to feel comfortable with safer sex and beginning to enjoy the positive, imaginative side of it.

The male-oriented and sexually repressive message of much of government propaganda was also criticized by feminists for its failure to address women as sexually active people who, within the heterosexual population, have expressed a greater concern about AIDS than men. It is women, of course, who have always had to take greater res-

ponsibility for the undesirable consequences of sexual encounters with men: accidental pregnancy, infection, physical violence. But it is women who, because they only rarely exist as equal partners in sexual encounters with men, may find it harder to feel the self-confidence necessary to make demands for safer sex, even though many women are known to experience more sexual pleasure from the less risky forms of non-penetrative sex. Feminist AIDS activists have reported that women most at risk from AIDS infection – those closest to the HIV drug scene and usually poor – have complained of violence from their partners for demanding safer sex.

It is clear that a more generally successful campaign against AIDS will be one which re-educates everyone, women and men alike, to combine more open discussion and inventiveness around sexuality with responsibility and concern for others. As the US feminist AIDS activist Cindy Patton argues, we must all come to see safer sex as sexy, and give everyone the confidence and opportunity to become safer sex educators.   *LyS*

See also **Contraception; Foreplay; Gay Liberation; Venereal Disease**

St Augustine (354-430)

Augustine, Bishop of Hippo, North Africa, is one of the great writers of the Christian tradition. In the *Confessions* he tells of his lifelong search for God, through several of the religions of his day, and of his conversion to and continued wrestling with **Christianity**.

Augustine is often portrayed as one of the starting points for Christianity's distrust of the body and of sexuality. Much is made of the fact that he sent his mistress away when he was a young man hoping for an ambitious marriage. In the end, he did not marry and seems to have been celibate from the time of his conversion. His interest in sex is not that of a man tortured by lust but of one disgusted by lack of control. What he writes about sex falls largely into two categories.

First, there is sex as loss of rationality. Augustine speaks of involuntary erections, of night emissions and of the impossibility of rational thought during **sexual intercourse** as signs that sex is not 'rational'. Like most of the thinkers of his day, he took for granted a distinction between the soul and the body, the rational and the non-rational. The body and sex are, in themselves, good and God-given, but only if controlled by the soul. Augustine is clear that the body will be raised from the dead, but it will be a body completely responsive to the will. He himself seems to have found in **celibacy** a way of controlling his sexuality in an emotionally liberating way, but he recognizes married sex as good and a proper way of putting sex in perspective. He assumed that the better the relationship between a married couple, the sooner they would give up sex (the notion of sexual activity as a sign of human fulfillment being a modern one). Augustine insisted on the celibacy of his clergy, in part because of the current idea, not peculiar to Christianity, that the less sex you need the better you are, but also because celibacy freed you from family ties, from being drawn into the customs of society. It freed you, Augustine argued, from your culture.

Second, there is sex as a symptom of a disordered world. In Augustine's work, rational, controlled behavior is not an end in itself; its aim is to free the person from over-attachment to things other than God. Sexuality, pain, human suffering are all indications of the first human rebellion against God: the belief that life can be lived without God. Lust, the disordered seeking after pleasure, is not itself the primordial sin but it is a symptom of it. Augustine certainly believed that the human will was deeply disordered, sinful, but he does not speak of this primarily in sexual terms, nor does he believe the body and its needs to be evil. On the contrary, they are gifts of God. But, like all gifts, they serve the relationship between the giver and the receiver; we are not meant to be satisfied with the gift, but to long for God, the giver.   *JW*

Margaret R. Miles *Augustine on the Body* (Montana: Scholars Press, 1979)

See also **Aquinas; St Paul**

St Paul

St Paul was a missionary in the early years of the Christian church, having converted from **Judaism**. He traveled, preached and wrote during the middle years of the first century. Many of his letters to churches survived, at least in part, and were incorporated into the New Testament. Although they were written to address particular situations and so do not constitute a work of systematic theology, they have been mined by all succeeding Christian generations for their attitudes.

Paul does not treat fully the relationship between the sexes, but he has a number of theological themes that have a bearing on the issue. Like almost all his contemporaries, he takes for granted a certain order in the way the world works. He assumes that this order was given by God when he made the world and that it dictates a subordination of women to men, of animals to humans and so on, as set out in the Jewish scriptures in *Genesis*. Given this assumption, which Paul nowhere seriously questions, he does nevertheless expect that, within **Christianity**, subordinates will be treated with respect, as human beings equally called by God. No license is given for the treatment of women as property.

On the subject of flesh and the spirit, Paul was deeply aware of that part of human nature which often prevents us from living up to our ideals, and he calls this part 'flesh'. 'Flesh', however, does not have specifically sexual connotations. Although Paul does mention 'unnatural' sexual acts as a sign of God's judgment, it is not clear precisely what he means; sexual sin is just one more symptom of the way in which we fail ourselves (although Paul does think that sex has a particularly direct effect on those sinfully involved in it). The 'body', as distinct from 'flesh', is a good thing in Pauline theology. God made us and loves us as bodily beings; God the Son came to us fully embodied in a human being; God raises our bodies after death. The 'body' becomes one of Paul's metaphors for how the church ought to be.   *JW*

Mary Hayter *The New Eve in Christ* (London: SPCK, 1987)

See also **St Augustine**

Sanger, Margaret (1880–1966)

When the American Margaret Sanger first agitated for sex education and birth control, in the second decade of the twentieth century, she was carrying on a tradition begun nearly one hundred years previously. As early as 1824, Frances Wright, the first woman to speak publicly in the USA, advocated the use of **contraception** and argued for women's equality, the abolition of slavery and the political rights of workers. Her arguments were taken up by other women activists and, in the 1880s, Elizabeth Cady Stanton was urging women to question marriage, divorce and birth-control restrictions: 'As long as they filled their homes with infants, their own conditions grew worse and worse with every generation.'

This message had particular resonance for Sanger. The daughter of an Irish-born stonecutter father and a devout Roman Catholic mother who gave birth to eleven children, Sanger became a nurse after her mother died of tuberculosis, complicated by cervical cancer, when Sanger was sixteen. Nursing poor, immigrant families on New York's Lower East Side, she became increasingly aware that women's suffering was exacerbated by frequent childbearing. She was also aware that the Comstock Law, passed in 1873, made it illegal to mail, transport or import 'obscene, lewd or lascivious articles', including contraceptive devices and information on birth control. Incensed, she found herself drawn to socialists and anarchists who denounced these restrictions and put forward a program for women's emancipation. Emma **Goldman** became a mentor and, like Goldman, Sanger believed that women should be able to control not only their fertility but their sexual lives. **Monogamy** was not for her and she openly advised women to delight in **sensuality** and sexuality, lambasting the hypocrisy that gave men free rein in and out of the bedroom while proscribing women's roles in both spheres.

But, while Sanger joined Goldman on a number of campaigns, her focus remained health and sex education. In 1914 she began publishing *The Woman Rebel*, a magazine calling for revolution and sexual radicalism. Feminism was a popular topic and, of the women who were entering the paid workforce in record numbers, many were beginning to see birth control as part of a larger movement for gender equality. This atmosphere bolstered Sanger. Despite the post-office's suppression of the June issue of *The Woman Rebel*, merely for employing the term 'birth control', she decided to write 'Family Limitation', a pamphlet detailing how to *use* contraceptive devices, douches and suppositories. Not long after, in August 1914, she was arrested and fled to Britain to prepare her defense and rally support.

Although the federal government dropped its case against Sanger in 1916, she was still not satisfied. Just months before, Goldman had been arrested for her support of birth control and had served two weeks in jail; while Sanger did not champion Goldman during this period, the injustice meted out was not lost on the firebrand. Whatever the reason for the split between the two women, Sanger had not given up activism on behalf of birth control: in 1916 she opened a clinic in Brooklyn which was an explicit challenge to the law and, as soon as she had opened shop, was swamped with requests – 464 in nine days – from working-class women desperate for advice and assistance.

Not surprisingly, the clinic was quickly closed by the police. Staff were found guilty of violating the law and sentenced to thirty days in jail. By the time Sanger recovered from incarceration, the USA was gearing up for involvement in the First World War and the left was responding with a retreat from controversial positions on sexuality. Within several years the feminist movement also receded, as women's suffrage was won. Sanger adopted a new strategy, eschewing rallies and civil disobedience in favor of lobbying. Her American Birth Control League, founded in 1921, focused exclusively on monitoring legislation, arm-twisting legislators and doing research.

This time, the medical establishment was receptive: due, no doubt, to the growing acceptance of eugenics, a movement that argued that society could be perfected by keeping the physically defective, poor and 'mentally unfit' from reproducing. The movement got a particular boost from the Depression and Sanger worked tirelessly to add pro-birth-control riders to relief legislation. She often resorted to arguments that sound racist and classist a half century later; despite this, her eighty-six-year life never deviated from its course. She remained a feminist and her many love affairs are evidence that she also remained true to her independent nature. Furthermore, the growing acceptance of birth control as a fact of US life – it was officially legalized in 1965 – was in large part the result of her efforts. *EB*

Happiness in Marriage (New York: Pergamon, 1969); *What Every Boy and Girl Should Know* (New York: Pergamon, 1969); *Margaret Sanger: An Autobiography* (New York: Pergamon, 1971)

Lawrence Lader *Abortion 11* (Boston, Massachusetts: Beacon Press, 1973)

See also **Besant; Obscenity; Stopes; Wright**

Sappho (c. 600 BC)

Throughout the centuries, Sappho's poetry has become submerged in the continuing obsession with 'the perverse practices of women', as one commentator has expressed it, to which both she and the Greek island of Lesbos, on which she lived, have given their name. As in the case of so many other women writers, biography and work have become blurred. To prurient Victorians, Sappho was guilty of gross sexual **perversion** and therefore unfit to be read; modern scholars, finding her poetry more than suitable for serious study, have therefore decided to champion her innocence. Despite the fact that little or nothing is known of her life, except that she flourished around the beginning of the sixth century BC, controversy remains.

Often, discussion has centered not on the poetry itself but on the question of the existence of **lesbianism** – of its possible meaning – in ancient Greek society. On the one hand, Anacreon, a younger contemporary of Sappho, bemoans his unrequited love for a young girl 'because she is from Lesbos and gapes after another woman'; on the other hand, the verb 'to play the lesbian' seems to have referred to voracious heterosexual rather than homosexual activity.

When returning to the poems themselves, even feminist scholars have had to admit to difficulties. For one thing, all of them are fragmentary, some as brief as a few words or even letters; any statements about their context and meaning can therefore only be inconclusive. In addition, the lyric form used by Sappho and her contemporaries was then in its infancy: a revolutionary new form of literary expression which centered on the experience of the individual, rather than on the collective experience expressed in earlier epics. As such, it is extremely difficult, if not impossible, to ascertain how far the poetic voice, the 'I' of the genre, represented personal experience or a mere poetic convention.

However, what the recent feminist studies have emphasized is the indisputable **sensuality** of Sappho's poetry: her preoccupation with the physical world of female experience. 'For whenever I catch sight of you,' she writes of a lover confronted by the beloved, 'then my voice deserts me/and my tongue is struck silent, a delicate fire/suddenly races underneath my skin . . . ' Here, it is the immediacy of her description which beguiles, the freshness and vigor which seem as striking today as when the poem was first written, over two and a half thousand years ago. The same directness pervades Sappho's many celebrations of female beauty: a woman's 'radiant, sparkling face' (which the poet much prefers to the glint of chariots or armor, the panoply of male warfare). Whether she is mourning the loss of virginity crushed like a 'hyacinth on the mountains' or advising a bridegroom of his good fortune in his marriage to a honey-eyed bride, it is this emphasis, in a strictly segregated society, on female concerns and female values, rather than a more erotic explicitness, which characterizes Sappho's work. *JB*

S

Josephine Balmar *Sappho: Poems and Fragments* (Secaucus, NJ: Lyle Stuart, 1988; London: Brilliance Books, 1984)

See also **Catullus; H.D.**

Schiele, Egon (1890-1918)

An Austrian painter, Egon Schiele is best known as an idiosyncratic expressionist who produced explicit female nudes and obsessive self-portraits. The disturbing atmosphere and appearance of these works have meant that, although Schiele occupies a prestigious position in art history, there have been few comprehensive exhibitions of his work.

Schiele was a child prodigy and, at sixteen, his precocious drawing skills made him the youngest student at the Vienna Academy of Fine Arts. As the protegé of the artist Gustav **Klimt** he soon became a respected figure of Vienna's progressive art circles, which focused on Klimt's breakaway Secession group. Yet, at the same time as he was building a promising career, Schiele was using his art to explore his psyche. Not only did he produce studies of naked women and young girls, drawn with a jagged, expressive line that accentuates their emaciated bodies and splayed limbs, he also subjected his own body to a range of roles and fantasies. These raw, highly personal works are characterized by a potent mixture of crude, adolescent emotion and sophisticated technique.

Schiele often sold his drawings specifically as erotic images and, in 1912, his notoriety was assured when he was arrested and imprisoned for **obscenity** and one of his drawings publicly burned. Although there is no evidence that he ever had **sexual intercourse** with any of his pre-pubescent models, this has not prevented a myth growing up that he did. Pencil and watercolor drawings such as 'Self Portrait Masturbating' (1911) or 'Reclining Woman with Legs Apart' (1914) have been popularly viewed as evidence of his fevered appetites and tormented nature, while his premature death at twenty-eight in the great Spanish flu

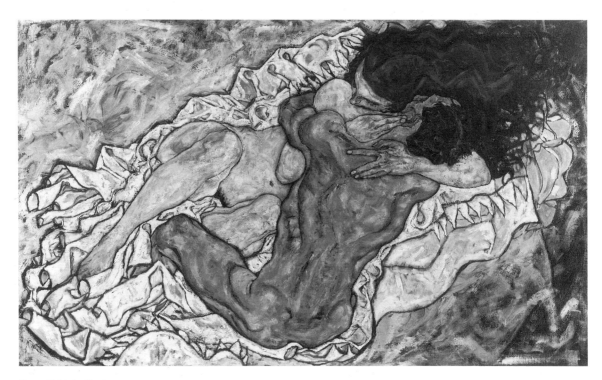

Egon Schiele, *Embrace*, 1917

epidemic of 1918, and the publication by one of his patrons, the writer Arthur Rossler, of a fictitious 'Jail Diary' four years later, also assisted in fueling his reputation as one of this century's troubled figures.

Yet, by 1918, the mood of Schiele's work had changed. He had married, experienced a world war and his wife was expecting a child. The last paintings still display a formidable graphic skill and a preoccupation with conveying psychological states, but Schiele's relationship with the model has become as much an exercise in form and texture as in emotional extremes. Instead of a stark line and an occasional vivid highlight, the mature female body of his 'Reclining Model' (1917) is richly painted and intricately integrated with the crumpled fabric which surrounds and partially covers it; while the interlocked, painterly figures of 'Family' (1918) also project a more gentle mood of melancholy. There is no way of knowing how Schiele's work would have developed but, myths aside, he is one of the first artists this century to have bared his innermost feelings in an uninhibited way.   *LBu*

Frank Whitford *Egon Schiele* (London: Thames & Hudson, 1981)

See also **Nude; Paedophilia**

Science Fiction

A mode of fantasy fiction that uses scientific and sociological extrapolation as a starting-point, science fiction (SF) has traditionally taken much of its subject matter from itself: writers constantly echo earlier treatments of the same themes to score polemical points. This has meant that the material – rockets, monsters, great cities, much of it already reflecting cultural anxieties and often highly charged with unacknowledged sexual metaphor – is always liable to be used for deliberate psychodrama. What is said here of the US and British genres is broadly true for the western and eastern European and the Japanese genres, which have followed their lead.

From H.G. Wells onwards, anxieties and arguments about sexuality and gender relations have served as part of the subject of SF. The gentle, esthetic Eloi of Wells's *The Time Machine* (1895), preyed upon by virile, cannibalistic, subterranean proles, are as much a metaphor for sexual roles as for class or for degeneracy. Wells's lectures on the constitution of Utopia regularly pause for a disquisition on the advantages of free love and eugenics. Much ink has been spilled on the exploitative side of Wells's belief in the sexual freedom of women; that the belief existed, however, needs to be recorded.

As SF developed as a publishing category and, in the English-speaking world especially, a type of magazine for adolescent boys, sexuality as an overt intellectual concern never entirely disappeared. The strain of SF that owed more to Edgar Rice Burroughs's hectic narratives of death-duels with six-limbed giants and hair-breadth escapes through Venusian jungles became dominant; sexuality was often steamily present in such narratives, both overtly and – particularly in the adventure fiction of Catherine Moore and Leigh Brackett – through metaphors of mental control and physical transformation and degeneration.

The US SF of the late 1940s and early 1950s concerned itself increasingly with political matters, largely because the McCarthy years made it attractive to discuss politics metaphorically. Ironically, Freudian orthodoxy made many otherwise progressive writers reactionary in sexual matters. The dystopian satires of Frederik Pohl and Cyril Kornbluth, for example, portray aggressive women as dangerous. The cult of the frontier in more right-wing authors, such as Robert Heinlein, paradoxically involves greater sympathy for women as agents, though only as secondary figures working on agendas set by male protagonists. Women, and others of the sexually oppressed, were portrayed sympathetically by Theodore Sturgeon, whose taste for anarchy made him suspicious of sexual and gender hierarchies.

Sturgeon's attitudes were an important influence on the SF New Wave of the late 1960s. But, where he preached equality from a position of privilege, gay SF writers like Samuel Delany and women SF writers like Joanna **Russ** did so from a position of angry intensity. The New Wave's insistence on higher literary standards made possible Russ's ludic postmodernism and Delany's lyrical verbal hyperrealism, both strategies adding a new sensibility to the genre whose manners they were engaged upon reforming. The portrayal of equality in New Wave SF owed much to the Utopian tradition in the novel and, specifically, to the tradition of feminist Utopias from Charlotte Perkins Gilman to Marge Piercy. For many New Wave writers, though, political programs were entirely secondary to more literary and eschatological concerns, or to drugs 'n' rock 'n' roll.

There persisted, and persists, a reactionary, technophile SF in which hierarchies of gender and class, and four-square linear narration, are far less mutable than the stuff of the universe itself. Nonetheless, SF has included in its subject matter every variation on sex and gender imaginable: alien races with seven sexes or none; post-Collapse matriarchies; survivalist fantasies of female subordination; incest with clones; time-traveling autoeroticism; languages that can only be spoken by one sex and languages in which pronouns define both a person who is sexually attracted and the person to *whom* they are attracted, regardless of gender. It is a matter for regret that SF so often ends up safe in the bosom of heterosexual **monogamy.**   *RK*

See also **Faery; Fantasy Fiction; Le Guin; Lessing**

Seidelman, Susan (1953–   )

Probably today's most successful US woman film director, Susan Seidelman has explored sex roles, sexual stereotypes and sexuality in her adept, exuberant comedies.

Seidelman caught the public's eye with her second feature *Desperately Seeking Susan* (1985), a stylishly produced and off-beat film about mistaken identity and identity-switching. Roberta (Rosanna Arquette) is a frustrated suburban housewife whose pleasures in life are getting her hair done, trying to make Julia Child meals for her uninterested husband and fantasizing about a more exciting romantic life. Her curiosity about 'Susan', who is sought by 'Jim' in personal ads, leads her into Manhattan to try to meet the mystery woman.

The pop singer Madonna plays the wild and irrepressible Susan; decked out in stiletto boots and provocative clothing, she is the 'whore' to Arquette's innocent housewife. Her on-again-off-again affair with Jim is as torrid and passionate as Roberta's relationship with her husband is tepid. However, after getting knocked on the head and suffering from amnesia, the mousy housewife undergoes a transformation; she is mistaken for Susan, lands a job as a magician's assistant and unwittingly finds herself in possession of stolen jewelry. If Susan is the 'bad girl', she is also the liberated woman in this film; she is her own woman, dealing with life on her own terms. Though the repressed Roberta does not become the libertine Susan, she has a sexual reawakening with a newfound boyfriend and learns to assert herself.

Seidelman has called her third film *Making Mr Right* (1987), a 'reverse Pygmalion'. In it, the lead is again a spunky young woman, this time an image consultant named Frankie (Ann Magnuson) who works in Miami, Florida. Frankie has just dumped her boyfriend – a handsome, glad-handing politician – after discovering his infidelity. She is working with a nerdy scientist (John Malkovich) to promote his android Ulysses (also played by Malkovich). In training Ulysses to become more personable and human, she creates the sweet, forthright, ever-considerate man of her dreams. To complicate matters, he falls in love with her.

The two 'real' men in the film are unable to win Frankie's affections: the scientist is an anti-social curmudgeon; the politician is suave but an unrepentant opportunist. Though *Making Mr Right* is farcical in tone, it has a darker subtext: modern men just don't seem right for modern women.

Two feature films by Seidelman appeared in

1989. In *Cookie*, a bratty teen (Emily Lloyd) tries to win the trust and approval of her father, a gangster just released from jail. In *She-Devil*, based on Fay Weldon's dark satire of female revenge against men, Ruth Patchett (Roseanne Barr) is a lumpy housewife who tries to do everything to please her feckless husband Bob. But glamorous romance novelist Mary Fisher (Meryl Streep) steals him away with money, material comfort and romance-novel sex. Ruth vows retribution and sets about methodically destroying everything Bob loves: house, family, career, freedom. The recurrent theme in Seidelman's films is that of women trying to break out of the crippling definition of being a 'good girl', whether to husband, mother or lover. Women must risk disapproval; being a 'bad girl' is taking control of one's life and trying to become a whole person.

SC

Desperately Seeking Susan (1985); *Making Mr Right* (1987); *She-Devil* (1989)

See also Heterosexuality; Lynch; Prostitution

Sellers, Terence

See Correct Sadist, The

Sensuality

Although 'sensuality' is often used to convey that a quality or state is not '*sexuality*', the two are more interrelated than that would imply. Sensuality concerns the senses – touch, sight, taste, smell and hearing – and, although a simplified reading of **Freud** might suggest that mature, non-perverted adults experience sex through touch to their genitals alone, in practice everyone knows very well that adult sexuality involves the whole gamut of the senses. Certainly, touch is the only one to be *indispensible* to sexual pleasure, but sight, smell, taste, even hearing (most people recognize 'a sexy voice'

or are turned on by certain words and phrases) are intimately involved in arousal and pleasure.

There is a theory that female sexuality is more widely sensual than male: that women experience erotic pleasure through more of their body, including their hearing, than penis-fixated men. At the moment of **orgasm**, certainly, there is evidence that women (if not all of them, always) are conscious of pleasure from head to toe while men feel it only in their genitals, but arousal and pleasure in both the sexes is very much connected with scent, sight, sound and taste. If it weren't, what would happen to the sale of oysters, perfume, telephone sex-lines and **pornography** in general?

For all that, it does seem true that women are more prepared to acknowledge and celebrate erotic sensuality, to accept, in a way that men find hard, that sex is not a discrete, containable, open-and-shut experience in which the genitals are always obviously involved. In Margaret Reynolds's *Erotica: An Anthology of Women's Writing*, for example, eating, giving birth and breast-feeding are presented as specifically sexual acts, while the French writer **Colette** understood sex as much the same kind of experience as eating, drinking, stroking a cat or smelling fresh flowers. Anais **Nin**, in the meantime, commissioned to write pornography for men, became so involved in the sensuality of fur, perfume and silk that she was sharply instructed to 'cut the poetry'; while, on the other side of the coin, novelists like Clarice **Lispector** have reveled in sensual *disgust*. Male writers, **Baudelaire** for instance, have also mixed sex with sensuality, but in art, in theory and – unfortunately – all too often in practice, the majority of men seem determined to keep their sensuality and sexuality locked in quite separate compartments. *HG*

Ed. Margaret Reynolds *Erotica: An Anthology of Women's Writing* (London: Pandora, 1990)

See also **Beardsley; Burford; Foreplay; Frye; Hacker; Kahlo; O'Keeffe; Oral Sex; Parker; Sappho**

S

Sexology

Towards the end of the nineteenth century, there developed in Europe a growing concern that sexuality should be seriously studied. This concern gave rise to a new discipline: sexology. In the first part of the twentieth century, writers such as Havelock **Ellis**, Magnus **Hirschfeld** and Richard von **Krafft-Ebing** played a leading role in establishing the study of human sexual behavior as a 'science' and, after the Second World War, sexology extended its influence through the work in the USA of Alfred **Kinsey** and, a decade or so later, of William H. **Masters** and Virginia **Johnson**.

Sexologists have sought to discover scientific truths about sexuality: to find out the natural laws that govern sexual behavior. They have busied themselves with labeling and cataloguing, defining and categorizing: the girls from the boys; the abnormal from the normal; the inverts from the perverts. They have also put forward as scientific truth an essentialist model of sexuality, one which assumes that sex is a natural instinct or drive. The natural direction of this instinct or drive is towards the opposite sex and, related to this, the most natural expression of **heterosexuality** is penetration of a vagina by a penis. It has also commonly been assumed, within sexological writings, that men have a stronger sex drive than women and that it is both a normal and important ingredient of sexual arousal for men to be dominant and women submissive.

The 'science' of sexology has had a profound influence on our beliefs about sex and sexual identity. It has shaped ideas about what is regarded *as* sex, what is considered sexually satisfying, what is thought to be normal. It has categorized people by their sexual desires and activities, most obviously as 'heterosexual' and 'homosexual'. It has constructed a view of female and male sexuality as polarized yet complementary, with submission meeting dominance and living happily ever after.

But this is not to say that the theories put forward by sexologists have gone uncriticized. Feminists, among others, have challenged their model of sexuality, arguing that sexuality is not naturally given but socially constructed. From this perspective, sexology has not so much discovered the truth about our sexual selves as invented it. For example, sexology, in association with the law, medicine and psychiatry, is said to have played an important role in constructing the notion of the lesbian, the homosexual and (by implication) the heterosexual person. Lesbian and gay identities are, in turn, a product of this categorization. From this perspective, it is also implied that concepts such as 'sexuality', 'sex drive', 'sexual behavior' – the object of study for sexologists – are not in fact concrete, finite, clear-cut entities, to be weighed and measured, but *ideas*. From a radical feminist perspective, sexology, despite its liberal involvement with issues such as birth control and abortion rights, can be seen as playing a crucial role in the oppression of women: in particular, by insisting that heterosexuality is natural and by eroticizing power differences. Some have even argued that the emergence of sexology in the nineteenth and early twentieth centuries was a response to women's growing opportunities and the emergence of a feminist movement. *DiR*

Sheila Jeffreys *Anticlimax* (New York: New York University Press, 1991; London: Women's Press, 1990)

See also **Foucault; Jeffreys; Perversion**

Sexual Harassment

Sexual Harassment is the use of sex to threaten, intimidate, denigrate, harm or dominate another person. From wolf whistles through the 'accidental' touching of buttocks to outright demands for sex, it reduces one human being to an object for use by another human being. **Rape** is the actualization of the threat behind sexual harassment, but sexual harassment on its own has uniquely grotesque aspects: ironically, because it does not have the status of physical rape.

First and foremost there is the phenomenon of suffering psychic harm without a corresponding physical harm (although many victims are unable to associate their emotional distress with the harassment until a number of years later). Second, this initial trauma is usually compounded by society's demand that the victim prove her or his innocence in initiating and perpetuating the harassment. Further, in countries like the USA, many people are acclimatized to the view of women as sex objects and skeptical of a claim of psychic harm without physical injury. Victim credibility is a particularly difficult problem in sexual harassment complaints where the victim is, for example, an African-American female and the perpetrator an Anglo-American male, or where there are other socio-economic differences between the perpetrator and the victim. Third, regardless of the victim's class, race or socio-economic status, the consequences of the victimization are made more severe by people's failure to understand how traumatic it can be. Indeed, depending on the interplay between its medium (auditory, visual, tactile, all three), its content (vulgar comments, outright demands for sex), its context (work, home, recreation, an isolated public place) and the relationship between the individuals (strangers, casual acquaintances, close associates, relatives), it can range from mild to severe.

In the USA, under certain conditions, sexual harassment in the workplace is a federal offense. And, in July 1991, it became a criminal offense in France. Outside the workplace, however, it is not illegal; it can even be a profitable and flourishing enterprise. The **pornography** industry is an obvious example, but other examples abound in movies, television programs, commercials, and in the course of other non-work-related events. Moreover, there is tremendous social and economic pressure, in today's society, to accept and become a part of this scheme of existence. This is true whether the victim seeks redress through the legal system or chooses to suffer in silence.   *OY*

Jane Caputi *The Age of Sex Crime* (Bowling Green, Ohio: Bowling Green State University Popular Press, 1987; London: Women's Press, 1988)

See also **Patriarchy**

Sexual Intercourse

A form of heterosexual activity in which the woman's vagina encloses the man's entering penis, then grips it while it is rhythmically thrust back and forth, intercourse is often presented as the only legitimate sexual practice: what most people mean when they talk about 'having sex'. This is notably true in Judeo-Christian cultures where sex is generally judged to be evil unless, as in unprotected intercourse, pregnancy can result. Even during the **sexual revolution** of the 1960s, when sexual pleasure began to be disentangled from procreation and other forms of delight were cautiously admitted, intercourse retained its status as the ultimate sexual act, everything else being relegated to **foreplay**.

Yet the irony is that a number of women find intercourse unsatisfactory. Whether because they worry more than men about getting pregnant by mistake (even when they have access to **contraception**), or whether because the thrusting doesn't invariably stimulate their **clitoris** (the vagina itself is nearly nerveless), or whether because of the pain it can cause if the woman isn't aroused and wet, every major survey this century, from Dickinson and Bream's in the 1930s to *The Hite Report* (New York: Macmillan, 1976), has shown that two-thirds of women would either prefer something else or no sex at all: except, of course, when and if they choose to conceive.

Such feminist theorists as Andrea **Dworkin** have argued that the reason a male-governed world prefers sexual intercourse is that it is a symbol of men's domination, forcing women who want to enjoy sex to learn to enjoy being dominated. Also according to this view, intercourse may not be *possible* unless the man has previously reduced the woman to an object in his mind; making it, therefore, not very different from **rape**. This analysis seems to ignore the fact that vaginas can sometimes be open, demanding, precisely desiring an object inside them – and that intercourse doesn't always involve the man being on top – but certainly male-governed churches and states have attempted to limit the options: perhaps to retain sex principally as a man's game, to discourage women from pursuing it and thus undermining the laws of inheritance and property; or perhaps to ensure that men and women stay divided, at odds, easier to rule. It's symptomatic that the advent of **AIDS**, one partial answer to which is avoidance of intercourse, has not prompted governments to advocate manual stimulation as a route of sexual pleasure but to advocate either the use of condoms or intercourse only within marriage.   *HG*

See also **Heterosexuality; Koedt; Masters and Johnson; Orgasm; Wright**

Sexual Revolution, The

Beginning in the mid-1950s, reaching its zenith a decade later, the sexual revolution was a global revolt, particularly by young people, against 'repressive' sexual beliefs, behavior and social structures. Its basic tenets were that sex was *good* (in part because pleasure was good and sex was pleasurable) and that it need be in no way linked to marriage, **monogamy** or child-producing; that parents should not have the power to restrict or to order their children's sex lives; that women no less than men were entitled to take sexual pleasure where they wanted; that sexual experimentation and variety, especially if heterosexual, were 'cool'; and that every aspect of sexuality ought to be freely discussed and represented.

That such ideas not only arose but were widely, if not universally, put into practice – substantially shifting the general attitude to marriage, divorce, illegitimacy, 'living in sin', **obscenity** – has been attributed to many causes. Benjamin Spock, the paediatrician whose best-selling *Common Sense Book of Baby and Child Care* (1946) had advocated a less restrictive approach to bringing up children, has been accused of instigating the revolution single-handed. More commonly, the principal cause is held to be the contraceptive pill, which became more and more available from the mid-1960s

onwards thus making it easier to disconnect sex from reproduction. In fact, of course, the causes were not only numerous and interlinking but varied from country to country. In post-austerity Britain, the sexual revolution began in a heady mixture of 'money to burn', teenage culture and pop music. In the USA, it was more closely linked to activism over Civil Rights and protest at the Vietnam war. In China, the context was the wider revolt against feudalism and the absolute power of parents to decide when and whom their children would marry.

Feminism, which was both re-ignited and radically changed by the sexual revolution, is nonetheless sharply aware of its failings and inadequacies: its emphasis on **heterosexuality**, for instance, its scorning of those who choose celibacy, its careless assumption that female desire corresponds precisely to male desire and consequent failure to question the ways in which power is at work between the sexes. Gloria Steinem has described it as 'a non-feminist phase of the 1960s that simply meant women's increased availability on men's terms', while Sally Roesch Wagner, in 'Pornography and the Sexual Revolution: The Backlash of Sado-masochism' (1982), wrote: 'The so-called "sexual revolution" should not be confused with actual sexual liberation. True sexual freedom will be possible only when we break the connection between sex and power.'

Other critics have included the French philoso-her Michel **Foucault**, who argued against the idea that some kind of 'natural' sexuality was being controlled and repressed by people at the top, proposing instead that sexuality, rather than having an existence of its own, was being continuously reinvented by all who talk or who write about it.

More ominous is the chorus of reactionary voices, all over the world, which has taken to blaming the sexual revolution for **AIDS**, the drug trade, violent crime, illiteracy, blasphemy and much besides, and would like to return us to some kind of pre-1950s moral utopia. Imperfect though it most certainly was – unfinished, it might be more accurate to say – the revolution did question, even topple, a number of sexual beliefs and habits that were

S

unquestionably damaging. A feminist who claims to have gained no benefit from it at all either wasn't alive in, or else has forgotten, the back-street-abortion, lesbian-silent, ignorant, dishonest 1940s.   *HG*

See also **Alther; Armstrong; Brown, Helen Gurley; Comfort; Contraception; Gay Liberation; Greer; Hui; Jeffreys; Miller, Sue;** *Oh! Calcutta!*; **Pornography; Reich; Sexology; Yu Luojin**

Sexually Transmitted Disease

See **Venereal Disease**

Shakespeare, William (1564-1616)

As Eric Partridge established in his scholarly study *Shakespeare's Bawdy* (1947), sex is spoken of freely in the plays of the English dramatist William Shakespeare. But, while sexual bawdy and banter are evident in almost all Shakespeare's work, it is difficult to agree with A.L. Rowse's assertion that 'Shakespeare is the sexiest great writer in the language . . . his mind, quite naturally and effortlessly, dripped sex at every pore.' Talking about sex is not necessarily sexy.

Despite some recent, largely unsuccessful efforts by modern directors to prove otherwise, **homosexuality** plays almost no part in the dramas, particularly when they are compared to the work of Shakespeare's contemporary Christopher Marlowe. Today, the thought of boys playing women whom the plot has required to dress up as men can carry a homoerotic charge; in Shakespeare's time, it was simply a device to make the task of the boy actors (there were no actresses) easier.

Similarly, it has been argued that Shakespeare's 154 sonnets, the majority of which appear to concern the writer's relationship with a young man, are evidence of his homosexuality. But, since the sonnets were almost certainly addressed to one of

Shakespeare's patrons, either the Earl of Pembroke or the Earl of Southampton, it is more likely that their intention, rather than being erotic, was to perform a literary exercise in courtly good manners. In so far as Shakespeare was concerned with sex as sex, it was primarily of the heterosexual variety.

With the exception of *Measure for Measure*, which puts its debate about **chastity** and **rape** center-stage, in Shakespeare's dramas sexual relations are presented almost entirely within a social and moral context; the sexual banter may be a kind of **foreplay**, but consummation can take place only in the marriage bed. As Germaine **Greer** declares in *Shakespeare* (Oxford: OUP, 1986): 'At the core of a coherent social structure as he viewed it lay marriage, which for Shakespeare is no mere comic convention but a crucial and complex ideal. He rejected the stereotype of the passive, sexless, unresponsive female and its inevitable concomitant, the misogynist conviction that all women were whores at heart. Instead he created a series of female characters who were both passionate and pure, who gave their hearts spontaneously into the keeping of the men they loved and remained true to the bargain in the face of tremendous odds.'   *LG*

See also **Heterosexuality; Jacobean Revenge Tragedy; Jarman; Kabuki; Opera Seria**

Shamanism

See **Ecstasy**

Shame

See **Honor**

Shockley, Ann Allen (1927-)

An African-American author, Ann Allen Shockley has done much to increase the profile of Black women and Black lesbians. Writing in *Conditions* (No. 5, 2 February 1979), she both criticized the racism that denied a comprehensive reception to writing by Black women and deplored the **homophobia** within the Black community. Her own fiction has never failed to weave these issues into its narratives. *Loving Her* (1974) was the first novel by a Black lesbian to look at the issues surrounding an inter-racial lesbian relationship: the white lover, for instance, is forced to confront racism when her Black lover moves in with her to a whites-only apartment; the Black lover to face the **heterosexism** of her own community. Love, however, conquers all, even the violence of a deserted husband.

In a collection of short stories aptly entitled *The Black and White of It*, Shockley takes a critical look at racism in the white lesbian feminist movement. In the novel *Say Jesus and Come to Me*, feminist sexual politics, **lesbianism** and racism are integrated into a narrative set in the contemporary Southern States of the USA. A Black woman preacher, Myrtle, feels that she cannot be open about the lesbian sexuality that she secretly explores with a string of willing lovers. Appalled by the vice and sexual violence that she encounters in one city, she begins a campaign aimed at bringing Black and white women together against a common enemy. She begins a meaningful relationship with another Black woman and publicly declares her lesbianism. When dealing with the sexual act between women, Shockley is unashamedly explicit, producing erotic writing that is characteristically clear and accessible. Describing Myrtle's desire to make love with a woman, for example, she writes of a 'pain in her groin', while lovemaking is also graphically described: 'Her fingers tangled below in the moist crevice of Travis, sliding into the pit of her . . .' *CU*

Loving Her (Indianapolis: Bobbs–Merril, 1974); *The Black and White of It* (Tallahassee: Naiad, 1980); *Say Jesus and Come to Me* (Tallahassee: Naiad, 1987)

See also **Fanon; Lorde; Parker**

Shuihu Zhuan

A sixteenth-century Chinese novel notorious for its anarchical violence and **misogyny**, *Shuihu Zhuan* is, in effect, a compilation of legends surrounding a gang of bandits who actually lived during the Song dynasty (960–1279) and it is full of heroic deeds and larger-than-life characters. It was written down in the late Ming dynasty and, in this form, is traditionally attributed (but almost certainly incorrectly) to Luo Guanzhong or Shi Nai'an. It has remained enormously popular ever since.

Though literally translated as *The Water Margin*, the work is also known in English as *All Men Are Brothers*. This alternative title is taken from a common saying in the novel and neatly expresses its central theme: only a handful of female characters appear; two of these are female heroes whose femininity extends no further than their names; the others are almost all singing girls, prostitutes or adulteresses whose sexuality is seen as being at best troublesome, more often destructive. In *Shuihu Zhuan* women are used to represent sex, and sex is seen as something that emasculates the individual hero and threatens the brotherhood of the hero gang. Most of the women meet a violent death, usually disembowelment or decapitation as an enraged hero reasserts his masculinity and reorders his priorities.

The only woman portrayed as 'good' (apart from the female heroes) is stereotypically virtuous, but in her case, too, her sexuality is destructive. Her attractiveness leads to her hero husband being persecuted and she eventually commits suicide in defense of her **honor**. This virtuous woman barely says a word and appears to be illiterate, in marked contrast to the other women, who can read and are assertive and relatively independent.

Sexuality in *Shuihu Zhuan* is repressed. The depiction of sex is brushed over quickly (there are none of the pornographic descriptions that can be found in other Chinese novels, although there are graphic descriptions of violence in the fighting scenes) but the novel is nevertheless disturbing in the attitudes it reveals: fear of women; the equation of sex with death. *AR*

Shuihu Zhuan/ *The Water Margin* (Hong Kong: The Commercial Press, 1963)

C. T. Hsia *The Classic Chinese Novel* (New York: Columbia University Press, 1966)

See also **Lie Nu Tradition; Theweleit**

Shunga

See **Ukiyo-E**

Slasher Movies

'Slasher movies' is a term coined to describe those films which take the genre of woman-in-peril a step further, to feature prominently women's terrorization, mutilation and murder, usually with sexual overtones.

The words are graphically descriptive. These murders involve hands-on contact, using knives and other blades, electric drills, chainsaws and so on: phallic weapons grotesquely parodying sexual intimacy in their desire to reach the flesh and in their invasion of the body. Death comes to women who are 'asking for it', both as a replacement for the sexual act and, frequently, as a punishment for sexual activity or sexual availability. In John Carpenter's *Hallowe'en* (Falcon International Productions, 1978), it's the virgin who survives. This film brought the slasher movie, usually cheap drive-in and late-night fodder, to a much wider mainstream audience. It was also highly influential in its use of the subjective camera, a cliché of the genre, allowing audiences the vicarious thrill of identifying with a powerful killer, unhampered by any moral or logistical constraints in a world of comic-book simplicity, and playing on the inherently voyeuristic nature of the genre.

Alfred **Hitchcock**'s *Psycho* (Shamley Productions, 1960) is an obvious forerunner, inspiring innumerable imitators, not least in the constant re-using of bathroom scenes as a simple way of removing a woman's clothing.

The 1970s saw a proliferation of these films, no doubt in part as a crudely vengeful response to the increasing militancy of women during the heyday of the new women's movement: independent, sexually liberated heroines made prime targets. Even where there are victims of both sexes, as in the many teens-in-peril movies or the infamous *The Texas Chainsaw Massacre* (Vortex/Henkel/Hooper Productions, 1974), men tend to be summarily despatched, whereas the fear, mental torture and deaths of the women are lingered over sadistically and graphically displayed. The US director Amy Jones attempted a feminist intervention with *The Slumber Party Massacre* (Santa Fe Productions, 1982), scripted by Rita Mae **Brown**, which climaxes with the killer's comically outsize phallic drill being symbolically castrated by the resourceful heroine. *PA*

See also **De Palma; Snuff Movies**

Snuff Movies

Snuff movies may be an urban legend: a nightmare fantasy started both by women's experience of actual male violence and by their disgust at representations of sexual violence towards women on video and in the cinema. But whether or not they exist in fact, what snuff movies *are* are movies in which – as the climax to acts of feigned or real sex – an actress is actually killed, for real, while the cameras continue to roll.

It should be said that no such film has ever been proved to exist. Nonetheless, in the mid-1970s, New Yorkers commonly believed that several, all made in South America, were in the possession of the police. Then, in 1976, a couple of 'ordinary' **slasher** filmmakers, Michael and Roberta Findlay, released a movie cobbled together from various scraps of their earlier footage with, as its climax, a newly-shot sequence in which, the story ostensibly over, a 'script girl' is shown informing the 'director' that she found the film sexually arousing and, apparently unaware that the cameras continue to turn, agreeing to sex with him then and there in the

S

studio. On 'noticing' that they are being filmed, the woman then tries to escape the man, at which he grabs for a nearby knife and, having said to the camera: 'You want to get a good scene?', slices the woman to pieces, cuts open her stomach and pulls out her palpitating organs. Although the sequence used no effects that hadn't already been used in a thousand drear horror films, the Findlays' ingenious (some might say cynical) choice of a title – *Snuff* – and the strength of the existing rumors combined to convince many people that what they were seeing was real.

That it wasn't may not be the important point (except, of course, to the actress concerned). The fact remains that people paid to watch what they either believed to be, or thought *might* be, a woman being tortured and killed for their entertainment. Were they all insane? Or were they merely, as many women are quite convinced, enjoying the usual, sadistic, heterosexual male pleasure, but magnified? Neither seems a likely or useful explanation. To bundle together all the forms of male **heterosexuality** and violence, including the ways that they are exploited, expressed and explored on screen, can only increase women's fear, not their understanding.

The specific function of 'reality', or apparent reality, in pornographic film has been more coolly examined by Linda Williams, a US film theorist, in *Hard Core: Power, Pleasure, and the 'Frenzy of the Visible'* (1990). Defining hard-core movies as those where the audience believes, often rightly, that what they are watching is actual sex, Williams convincingly argues that what they want is to see the elusive, frustratingly invisible spasms of an actual female **orgasm**. And, although she is clear that *Snuff* is an *exploitation*, not a pornographic, movie, she still relates it to hard-core porn in this respect: that, in its efforts to appear 'real' as distinct from merely realistic, it offers men the tantalizing prospect of finally seeing, if not a woman's orgasm, then a terrible, murderous substitute. 'Read in the context of pornography as opposed to horror, a flinch, a convulsion, a welt, even the flow of blood itself, would seem to offer incontrovertible proof

that a woman's body, so resistent to the involuntary show of pleasure, has been touched, "moved" by some force.' None of this makes less horrifying the lengths to which some men will go to know, to conquer, whatever they see as alien in women's sexuality. It does, however, illuminate them better than do generalized outrage and alarm.   *HG*

Linda Williams *Hard Core: Power, Pleasure, and the 'Frenzy of the Visible'* (California: University of California Press, 1989; London: Pandora Press, 1990)

See also **Pornography**

Stead, Christina (1902-1983)

Christina Stead's treatment of sexual themes in her novel *Letty Fox: Her Luck* (1946) earned her notoriety in the USA and censorship in her native Australia. The book was attacked as a slur on American womanhood for its portrayal of Letty, a 'typical New York Girl', finding her way through the middle-class milieu of political radicalism and predatory sexuality during the 1930s and the Second World War. The heroine tells her own story in a confidential manner reminiscent of Defoe's *Moll Flanders*, making pronouncements such as 'the ability to sell ourselves in any way we please is a step towards freedom' (out of women's former sexual slavery). A self-described 'sexual tourist', Letty declares that 'men don't like to think that we are just as they are' and memorably recounts the antics of male sexual teases (the 'hounds of love') and her bouts of unfulfilled lust.

Letty Fox is in fact a satire on US sexual mores of the period, saturated with current advertising slogans, Hollywood fantales and traditional sexual lore as well as the more material, financial considerations of the marriage market. Stead continued in this vein with her next two novels, *A Little Tea, A Little Chat* (1948), the portrait of a seedy capitalist Casanova, and *The People with the Dogs* (1952), where the hero's seductive charm lies in his passivity. Yet throughout the satires there also runs a deeply romantic notion of sexual passion as an anarchic creative force which constantly breaks through the social barriers built to contain it. In her autobiographical novel *For Love Alone* (1944) the association between sexual and social freedom is most forcibly articulated, the young woman's quest for love bringing her 'out of the womb of time' and into the 'cited plain' of human history.

Stead's romantic conception of the power of heterosexual love to liberate women from traditional femininity is accompanied by a sharp recoil against women's bonds with one another, particularly **lesbianism**. This is evident in several novels, especially in *Cotters' England* (1966). In interviews Stead dismissed the women's liberation movement as a lesbian plot to lead 'poor little struggling houswives' astray, insisting that men were women's 'natural allies'. Paradoxically, she is as well known for her critical portraits of men as for those of women. Many readers have found in her masterpiece, *The Man Who Loved Children* (1940), a profoundly disturbing account of patriarchal relations in the modern middle-class family overshadowed by the threat of father-daughter **incest** and the destruction of the wife-mother figure.   SS

The Man Who Loved Children (Harmondsworth: Penguin, 1987); *For Love Alone* (London: Virago, 1978; Australia: Sirius Paperbacks, 1987); *Letty Fox: Her Luck* (London: Virago, 1978); *Cotters' England* (London: Virago, 1980)

Susan Sheridan *Christina Stead* (Hemel Hempstead: Harvester/Wheatsheaf, 1988)
Chris Williams *Christina Stead: A Life of Letters* (Melbourne: McPhee Gribble, 1989)

See also **Patriarchy**

Stead, W.T. (1849-1912)

The son of a congregational minister, W.T. Stead was an influential journalist and editor in late-Victorian England who combined a non-conformist morality and crusading zeal with a sensational press style. Together with figures such as Josephine **Butler** and Bramwell Booth of the Salvation Army, Stead participated in the campaign against child **prostitution** and for the raising of the age of consent. His contribution to this campaign was the July

1885 issue of *The Pall Mall Gazette* which contained the notorious article 'Maiden Tribute to Modern Babylon'. The publicity this story generated pressured a reluctant government into hurriedly passing the Criminal Law Amendment Bill, raising the age of consent.

'Maiden Tribute' was a graphic exposé of child prostitution, 'white slavery' and the buying and selling of 'maidenheads' calculated to produce 'a shuddering horror that will thrill throughout the world'. Written with the help of a small team, Stead's account milks the horrors of the 'London Slave Market' for all it's worth. The 'forcing of unwilling maids' in 'secret chambers of accommodation houses' and 'padded rooms for the purpose of stifling the cries of tortured victims', the drugging of young, innocent girls and the buying of virgins for £5 are all written against the drama of parental irresponsibility, state complicity and corruption. The case of 'Lily' (Eliza Armstrong in real life), a virgin bought for £5, provides the heart-wrenching human-interest story at the center of this narrative: 'an industrious, warmhearted . . . hardy English' child, Lily is first inspected, then certified as the 'genuine article' and later drugged and raped. Her 'wild and piteous cry' must not 'fail to touch the heart and rouse the conscience of English people'.

Stead's 'secret commission' on child prostitution betrays a voyeuristic fascination with its subject. Its melodramatic language and images – the insatiable lust of wealthy male patrons (and their 'evil procuress') contrasting with the innocence of the 'yet uncorrupted daughters of the poor' – stem from the nineteenth-century social-purity rhetoric of protection and moral stewardship of the less privileged. Ostensibly written for both men and women, 'Maiden Tribute', by drawing on the sexual stereotypes of female passivity and male activity, in reality addressed only men – it was precisely men, after all, who initiated the cycle of corruption through their abdication of responsibility and lack of self-control. In fact, there was no real evidence of the widespread 'white slave' traffic of innocent girls or their false entrapment on the scale described by Stead, but his depiction enabled massive publicity for the campaign; also, by focusing

S

exclusively on false entrapment, the wider socio-economic causes of prostitution and poverty were avoided.

The Criminal Law Amendment Act entrusted the political, social and moral custody of subordinate groups to the state, adopting a distinctly interventionist approach. In this respect, by giving the state much greater power over the lives of working women, the bill went against everything for which Josephine Butler fought.   GCL

Alison Plowden *The Case of Eliza Armstrong: A Child of 13 Bought for £5* (London: British Broadcasting Corporation, 1974)

See also **Acton; Virginity**

Stein, Gertrude (1874-1946)

Tender Buttons (1914), published a few months after Gertrude Stein's fortieth birthday, is perhaps the only abstract book of **erotica** ever written.

The 'tender button' of the title is the **clitoris**. The book's subjects are touched on in the same way – now hard, now soft, now flirtatious, now steady – that works on the clitoris itself. At the time Stein was writing, acknowledgement of the clitoral **orgasm** by sexologists such as **Masters and Johnson** was half a century in the future. Even an advanced American woman such as Stein, who dropped out of medical school in her last term, would have garnered most of her knowledge of sexual anatomy from life.

The book is a maze of linguistic experiment and is in some ways meant to be comparable to cubist painting. As the critic Edmund Wilson noticed, *Tender Buttons* is hard to understand on purpose – because it speaks of the then unmentionable sex between women. 'The sister was not a mister. Was this a surprise. It was.'

A far more earnest account of Stein's first lesbian affair, *Q.E.D: Things As They Are*, was not published until four years after her death. Stein left the USA for Europe in 1901 partly to get over that affair. In Paris, she and her brother Leo established an artistic and literary salon which was frequented by **Picasso** and other up-and-coming modernists and a stream of US writers including Ernest **Hemingway**. In 1906, Stein sat for the famous Picasso portrait which now hangs in the Metropolitan Museum and wrote *Three Lives*.

Then, in 1907, along came Alice. Ousting Leo, Alice B. Toklas soon became Stein's significant other, acting as secretary-companion and co-hostess of the flourishing salon. Later Toklas set up the Plain Editions to publish Stein's more uncompromising experimental works. When Stein's *The Autobiography of Alice B. Toklas*, an astute, *faux naive* memoir of their life in Paris, became a huge bestseller, Stein returned to the USA for the first time in a quarter of a century. Toklas was with her. They were welcomed by headlines and embarked on a triumphant transcontinental lecture tour which transformed them into the most famous lesbian couple of their era or any era; although, at the time, few mentioned the hated l-word.   AB

Tender Buttons (California: Sun and Moon, 1990); *The Autobiography of Alice B. Toklas* (New York: Random House, 1990; Harmondsworth: Penguin, 1989); *Bee Time Vine and Other Pieces* (Salem: Ayer, 1953)

See also **Acker; Barnes; Brossard; Irigaray; Lesbianism; Lorde; Wittig**

Stopes, Marie (1880-1958)

Born in Scotland and educated as a botanist in London and Munich, in 1904 Marie Stopes became the first woman member of the scientific staff at Manchester University, her then speciality being the cellular structure of ovules and ova in tropical plants. This is not, however, the subject for which Stopes is famous, almost synonymous. The most celebrated British campaigner for women to have access to **contraception**, she came to that work via a tortuous and tortured route.

What happened, in essence, was that Stopes emerged from a three-year unconsummated marriage determined to learn what she could about what had gone wrong between her and her husband. This was no easy matter in 1914, when factual information on sex was jealously protected by the 'specialists'. Undeterred, she read every book on the subject in the British Museum and, much enlightened, in 1918 she published her own book, *Married Love*, designed to explain not only how marital sex could be pleasurable for women but how it need not inevitably result in pregnancy. In many ways it was a radical work – it even proposed that, during pregnancy, a woman might acquire sexual satisfaction from other forms of sex than **sexual intercourse** – and provoked as much interest as outrage. To those women who wrote for further advice, Stopes answered with passionate, florid exhortations that they ask much *more* from their sex lives (she described the female **orgasm** as 'wonderful tides') and, more practically, in 1920, she opened the first British birth-control clinic, making it all the more accessible by employing trained female nurses in preference to male doctors.

In constant battle with the Roman Catholic church, insulted by the establishment – in 1924 *The Times* refused to announce the birth of the daughter that she had had by a second marriage – Stopes nonetheless continued campaigning, writing (including poetry and plays) and running her clinic until her death. The clinic, still bearing her name, is open to this day.   *HG*

June Rose *Marie Stopes and the Sexual Revolution* (London: Faber, 1992)

See also **Besant; Sanger; Wright**

Story of O

First published in 1954, *L'Histoire d'O/ Story of O* is one of the classics of **pornography**, considered and criticized on a par with the works of **Sade** and Georges **Bataille**. Among these, however, it is unique in being found sexually arousing by a substantial number of women, including feminists: a fact which many find shocking and disturbing because, to put at its most straightforward, the novel concerns the systematic abuse, degradation and annihilation of a 'liberated' modern career woman.

The novel opens with O, the heroine, being taken by her young male lover to a chateau outside Paris, where she is stripped, bound, beaten and penetrated, both with penises and instruments, by men to whose whims (at her lover's behest) she submits herself without argument. Frightened, disgusted and frequently in pain, O nonetheless experiences profound emotional and sensual pleasure, and later, allowed to return to her life as a photographer – but instructed to dress in such a way that her breasts, vagina and anus are available to any man who understands the meaning of the iron ring that she wears – she glows with so great a dignity that her fellow workers observe it.

Next, O's lover hands her over to an older man, the English aristocrat Sir Stephen, who not only subjects her to greater pain but has her branded with his initials and has hammered through one of her labia a heavy, iron disk engraved with his name and a crest. And he, too, makes O available to friends and business associates, transforming her not only into an object but one of no special value. The novel ends in what might be O's death, or might be simply her extinction as a human.

Like much of this kind of 'extreme' pornography, *Story of O* is heavy with religious, especially Christian, connotations. Its fervent detailing of self-abnegation; of submission to an all-knowing, all-seeing master; of pleasure acquired through suffering; of the glorious triumph of martyrdom: all these have much in common with ecstatic literature. Which is interesting as a demonstration of the way in which sex, like religion, can be seen as a route to transcendence, but doesn't explain how such a novel can be sexually arousing to women who, in real life, struggle for autonomy and selfhood and against all forms of cruelty, humiliation and sexual abuse.

The explanation may be, in part, that all of us need a safe, fantasy retreat from the pressures of responsibility: especially in the realm of sexuality where decisions have recently become so complex. The structure and tone of this particular story, however, are also quite special. For a start, its stately, formal language holds its horrors in constant check, permitting the reader to relax as though into a game with understood limits. Besides, it is immediately clear (and is several times spelt out) that O is not simply colluding in but actually provoking the course of events. Her apparent abdication of will is, paradoxically, an act of will: allowing the reader who identifies with her to become, not a victim, but securely in control.

Second, unlike in most pornography, the pain-into-pleasure is convincingly described as though through a *woman's* body: as openness, crucially; but also as wetness; as arousal not simply of the genitals; as a slow, building rhythm of anticipation, retreat and great, rolling climaxes. Speech, too, is eroticized, the men devoting much of their powers to describing what they are about to do: obligingly giving voice to O's desires. And again unlike in most pornography, the underlying form of the book is not a loosely linked, picaresque adventure, whimsically stopping and starting, but a carefully constructed **romantic fiction** of the type perfected by Georgette **Heyer**. Albeit in unfamiliar guise, O is a 'feisty heroine' – we have flashbacks to her earlier life as a heartbreaker both of women and men – whose ultimate submission is to an older, richer, socially superior man, but only when he has at last conceded that he *loves* her. (At all times, the ambiguities of power and control are acknowledged.) In fact, the novel proceeds beyond Sir Stephen's confession of love for O into something darker and more sinister – the world, one could say, which lies beyond the marriage proposal at which romantic fiction traditionally stops – but then it is also true that, at this point, many women cease to find it erotic, reading on more with fascinated horror than arousal.

Called 'Pauline Réage' on the jacket, the author of *Story of O* could in fact be any of a number of people. At one time it was thought that it was Jean Paulhan, who wrote a preface when the novel originally appeared; more recently, the most serious guess has been that it is the critic Dominique Aury. Whoever it is – though a woman does seem to be the most plausible author – their pseudonym is also

attached to a rather perfunctory sequel, *Retour à Roissy/Story of O: Part II* (1969), which appears to be trying to further neither its author's literary reputation nor, with any great energy, the sexual pleasure of its readers. *HG*

Story of O (New York: Ballantine, 1981; London: Corgi, 1972); *Story of O: Part II* (New York: Grove Weidenfeld, 1980; London: Corgi, 1985)

See also **Ecstasy; Masochism; Sado-Masochism**

Strindberg, August (1849-1912)

'Can you understand my misogyny? Which is only the reverse image of a terrible desire for the other sex,' wrote the Swedish playwright August Strindberg to a friend in 1888.

Strindberg was almost forty when he wrote that. He had survived an unhappy childhood and early career disappointments and the first of his three unsatisfactory marriages was drawing to a close. He had also just completed *The Father*, *Miss Julie* and *Creditors*, plays of such power that, even if he had written nothing else, they alone would ensure his place in posterity. In fact, despite repeated mental crises, he was to continue writing for a further twenty-four years, completing over sixty plays (as well as novels, autobiography and pamphlets) covering historical drama, **fantasy** and symbolism. In the latter part of his life he produced *A Dream Play* and *The Ghost Sonata*, which were as ground-breaking in their use of expressionism as the earlier plays such as *Miss Julie* were in their embracement of naturalism.

The symbolism of these later plays – there are undoubtedly connections with Sigmund **Freud's** *The Interpretation of Dreams* – is full of images open to sexual interpretation, the image of male potency being particularly strong in *A Dream Play*. But it is the earlier, naturalistic plays where one can best see Strindberg's interest in the relation between sexuality and power, obsessive sexual attraction and an unending war between the sexes. 'The experience of many of his plays can be like watching a dramatization of one of Freud's case studies; their preoccupation with sexuality, irrationality and with the family as a site of struggle are more than open to Freudian interpretation,' writes Deborah Philips in *The Bloomsbury Theatre Guide* (London: Bloomsbury, 1988).

The Strindberg critic and translator Michael Meyer, in *File on Strindberg* (London: Methuen, 1986), puts it in a nutshell: 'Strindberg knew that people can fuck each other and hate each other; indeed, he believed that this was what sex and marriage were really about. This had been said by other writers in novels, but not in plays; in drama before Strindberg, fucking is done only by married people or wicked people. One has to use this verb when writing of Strindberg, because his characters do not make love; that is the tragedy of the couples in *The Father*, *Miss Julie* and *The Dance of Death*.'

Although it is impossible to deny Strindberg's **misogyny**, which is evident throughout his writings, his embittered attitude towards women resulted in an examination of issues of power and gender that could, on stage, be open to a feminist interpretation (many productions simply stress the sado-masochistic elements of the plays). *Miss Julie* is described by Strindberg, in the foreword to the play, as an example of 'the degeneracy of the half-woman, the man-hater', but in performance she can emerge as a great tragic heroine. Her defeat is sexual but, in choosing death, she exerts a moral superiority. Her failure lies in faltering in her move towards sexual independence; her strength in choosing her destiny, even if that means death. *LG*

See also **Munch**

Surrealism

In 1959 the poet André Breton – the grand old man of Surrealism – claimed that, however varied Surrealist works of art might appear, they had one thing in common: eroticism.

The Surrealist movement originated in Paris just after the First World War and was self-consciously outrageous. It set out to challenge esthetic and social conventions and to subvert the rationalism that had landed the world in such trouble. Breton and his friends invoked, a little vaguely, the ideas of Sigmund **Freud** about the **unconscious**, experimenting with 'automatic' writing, random juxtapositions of images, found objects, jokes and verbal or visual games, all designed to bypass rational thinking. Poets (Breton, Paul Eluard), painters and sculptors (René Magritte, Salvador Dali, Max Ernst), photographers (Man Ray) and filmmakers (Luis Buñuel) agreed in discarding a stale and superficial realism. They wanted to open up the secret world of dreams with its contradictions, symbolic transformations and punning substitutions; to explore ecstatic and hallucinatory states; to assert their kinship with madness, and with a childhood that was somehow more 'real' than adult life.

But it is, they argued, in our erotic yearnings that we are *most* real, *most* truly ourselves. Love – or sexual desire, the two are seen as identical – is insatiable, endlessly and perversely inventive, possessing the power to smash through a hundred years of bourgeois repression. It is revolutionary, revelatory, simultaneously destructive and regenerative. One quality sought by the Surrealists in art was 'convulsive beauty': a giddy (orgasmic) mix of excitement and panic that makes the ordinary world crack open or slip away. 'The fauna and flora of Surrealism are shameful and not to be confessed to,' Breton announced with a certain pride, and most Surrealists set out to scandalize the bourgeoisie. But they were also romantic idealists for whom love – equal and reciprocal – was a transforming power, offering glimpses of lost wholeness.

Breton, indeed, argued that 'masculinity' is bankrupt; the artist must turn towards the disregarded 'feminine', must 'exalt, or better still . . . appropriate . . . all which distinguishes woman from man'. The Surrealistic woman, seen as a bridge to that other world of the unconscious, is by turns small girl, mother-creator, sinister sorceress. A handful of images – they turn up in virtually every history of the movement – hint at her ambiguous

André Masson, *Metamorphosis of Gradiva*, 1939

role, her function as a screen onto which fantasies are projected. In the painter André Masson's 'Gradiva' a statue, contorted and broken, seems to be undergoing violent and orgasmic metamorphosis into flesh and blood. Magritte's ambiguous and disturbing 'Rape' superimposes a woman's naked body on her face, so that the breasts become eyes and the vulva a mouth. In Dali's 'Young Virgin Auto-Sodomized by Her Own Chastity' the naked body of a girl leaning through a window has been dismantled, her buttocks transformed into aggressively phallic shapes. Ernst's naked women, obscured by heavy feathered cloaks and bird masks, act out obscure and cruel pantomimes; impassively beautiful girls dream their way through Paul Delvaux's townscapes.

This simultaneous idealizing and violating of the female body is, of course, a commonplace in western art. Over the last twenty years, feminist art historians have pinpointed the conventionality lurking at the core of much Surrealist rebellion. But they have also rediscovered the many women who were drawn to the movement's anti-academic iconoclasm, and to its concern with an inner personal reality, with the fluid and shifting realm of fantasy where anything is possible. Women like Leonora **Carrington**, the Czechoslovakian painter who called herself Toyen, Dorothea Tanning, Eileen Agar, Leonor Fini, Remedios Varo and Meret Oppenheim (who are all treated perfunctorily in conventional histories) worked fruitfully and inventively, if sometimes uneasily, in association with

Surrealism. We are only just beginning to understand how much they achieved.   *MW*

Ed. José Pierre *Investigating Sex: Surrealist Discussions,
1928-1932* (London: Verso, 1992); Roger Cardinal and
Robert Stuart Short *Surrealism* (London: Studio Vista, 1970);
Whitney Chadwick *Women Artists and the Surrealist Move-
ment* (Boston: Little, Brown and Co., 1985); Mary Ann Caws
'Ladies Shot and Painted: Female Embodiment in Surrealist
Art' in ed. Susan Rubin Suleiman *The Female Body in Western
Culture* (Cambridge, Mass: Harvard University Press, 1986)

See also **Balthus; Bataille; Bourgeois; Ecstasy;
Kahlo; Kaplan; Klimt; Miller, Lee; Nude;
Repression**

Susann, Jacqueline (1921-1974)

Born in Philadelphia, the only child of a nationally
known portrait painter and his schoolteacher wife,
Jacqueline Susann was both a model and a minor
Broadway actress before achieving somewhat
greater success as a television personality. Having
co-written a play, *Lovely Me*, in 1946, she took seventeen years to publish again, making a small
splash with the non-fiction canine memoir *Every
Night, Josephine!* As a portrait of her bi-coastal
French poodle, up to his rhinestone collar in entertainment industry savvy, the book has undeniable
charm, but its admirers were not prepared for what
came next: the salacious ur-soap opera *Valley of the
Dolls* (1966). Even more disappointed, however,
were those *Dolls* fans who, unable to wait the three
years for Susann's next novel, *The Love Machine*,
ran to check *Josephine* out of the local library,
expecting another lurid stew of glamor groupies
and masochistic love affairs.

A tale of three attractive, ambitious and ultimately self-destructive young women, each with a
doomed show biz career, *Dolls* sold 350,000 copies
in its hard-cover edition, amazing for a first novel,
and went on to sell about 25 million paperback
copies worldwide. (The 'dolls' of the title is actually
a then-current Hollywood slang for pills.)

Critics soon delighted in regularly denouncing
Susann as the female avatar (Harold Robbins was

her male counterpart) of all that was hackneyed
and pandering, all that was vulgarly prurient in
bestselling pop literature. But Susann, her career
adroitly managed by her husband Irving Mansfield,
chose to combat her detractors and to encourage
allies, among them her loyal fans and those often-
overlooked workers at the lower levels of the publishing business, eager for any recognition from a
Big Name Author. Her strategy of incessant self-
promotion and personal-touch media marketing
has been much imitated in the years since Susann's
heyday, as has her now clichéd formula for *roman-
à-clef*ish novels about lust and love, viciousness and
vulnerability among the rich and famous.

It is worth noting, however, that Susann, like
Judith Krantz more recently, was a woman very
much at home in the gossip-ridden, artifice-
obsessed worlds of Manhatten and Los Angeles,
and familiarity does indeed breed contempt. Thus
Susann's creations, for all that they titillate ('Sex is
the most potent ingredient in Jacqueline Susann's
books. And she is quite a love machine in her own
right': *Daily Mirror*) also satirize. She takes as her
targets the single-minded, amoral opportunism and
the inevitable betrayals it engenders, along with the
emotionless seductions and the empty but mutually
profitable relationships found along the corridors
of power. Romance is rarely romantic in Susann's
novels, her characters are almost always dysfunc-
tional, and yet, even as one is vaguely repelled by
the goings-on, and even today when the stories'
milieus seem rather dated, it's hard to stop reading.
                                                  MiS

Valley of the Dolls (London: Corgi, 1968)

Barbara Seaman *Lovely Me: The Life of Jacqueline Susann*
(New York: William Morrow, 1987; London: Sidgwick &
Jackson, 1988)

See also **Masochism; Romantic Fiction**

T

Tantrism

All Hindu philosophies accept the duality of the masculine and the feminine principles; what distinguishes tantrism is its belief in the ascendancy of the feminine. Tantric sects worship female deities, especially Parvati, the consort of Lord Siva, in her form as Durga or Kali.

Tantrics practice special ceremonies which they believe to be of greater efficacy than those practiced by the ordinary, orthodox Hindu. Their rites involve the breaking of accepted taboos. Thus, initiates meet in such inauspicious places as cremation grounds, gathering around a magical diagram called *yantra*. The *yoni-yantra* is the symbolic representation of the divine mother and the cosmic womb. Not only do tantrics consider the *yoni* (the divine vulva or womb) to be sacred but, for them, there are no taboos attached to menstrual fluid, and their worship is performed before either the vulva of a living woman or its representation in paint, stone, wood or metal. Participants at these ceremonies also break vegetarian taboos and have **sexual intercourse** (often only symbolically) in order to accentuate the reversal of orthodox attitudes.

KV

See also **Hinduism**

Taylor, Valerie (1913-   )

Valerie Taylor has written popular lesbian paperback fiction since the late 1950s. She spent her childhood and college years in the rural expanse of Illinois, followed by a spell of schoolteaching and an unsuccessful marriage. When the marriage ended, in the early 1950s, she found employment as an editor and in advertising. Producing confessional stories for magazines provided another source of income to feed and clothe her three sons.

A contemporary of Ann **Bannon**, Taylor wrote about the provincial side of lesbian life as it was lived in the post-war, pre-**Gay Liberation** movement USA. Three of these novels follow the exploits of Erica Frohmann, a Jewish concentration-camp survivor. The first of the series, *Journey to Fulfillment* (1964), begins with Erica's last day in the camp, when she is beginning to explore her sexuality with another inmate. Erica is sexually and emotionally exploited by the daughter of the family that adopts her in the USA, but, when this is discovered, she is allowed to live with a young teacher. The narrative ends with a hint of the relationship to come between the two young women, rather than with the gloomy ending commonly deployed in lesbian novels of the time. At the end of the Erica trilogy, she is even settled with a married woman who has left her husband to live with her. Similarly, in *A World Without Men* (1963), in contrast to the predominant pathological interpretation of **lesbianism**, a Doctor Lieberman counsels a lesbian client not to worry about her sexuality.

Throughout these texts, sex with women is seen as a much more emotional and total experience than sex with men, although the descriptions of the act itself are clothed in the coy language of the time, with little made explicit and everything hinted.

Having been reprinted in the 1980s by the lesbian press Naiad, Taylor is experiencing something of a renaissance and, this time round, is far more explicit when describing sex between women. She has written a sequel to the Erica Frohmann series which picks the relationship up after twenty years and reflects on the enormous changes wrought by the gay and women's movements. She now covers issues of age, poverty, **AIDS**, along with other feminist concerns around the sexual politics of lesbian relationships.

CU

A World Without Men (Tallahasee: Naiad, 1982); *Journey to Fulfillment* (Tallahasee: Naiad, 1982); *Prism* (Tallahasee: Naiad, 1981); *Ripening* (Austin, Texas: Banned Books, 1988); *Rice and Beans* (Tallahasee: Naiad, 1989)

See also **Microcosm; Romantic Fiction; Rule; Wilhelm**

Theweleit, Klaus (1942-   )

The German Klaus Theweleit's work is concerned with applying psychoanalytic theory to the interpretation of history. His doctoral thesis, *Mannerphantasien/Male Fantasies*, was a controversial bestseller in West Germany where, in 1977, it was first issued. A provocative, eclectic collection of ideas, it analyzes fascist myths and fantasies in relation to sexuality. By returning fascism to its emotive and affective roots in family relationships, Theweleit manages to address both the difficulties of interpreting experiences located outside the 'norm' and the grip, on ordinary people, of myths of the abnormal.

Male Fantasies is ostensibly an account of German protofascism in the years immediately after the First World War, but it possesses wider implications for the creation of male sexual identities. Theweleit's theory, which has its ancestry in the work of Wilhelm **Reich**, is very much an interpretive psychology centered on the materiality of the human body: fascism and the culture of warfare represent a polarization of sexual politics where the feminine is viewed as a radical threat to the wholeness and hardness of the 'soldier male'. The fascist warrior is psychotic; his childhood does not take the normal path of development in the formation of an 'ego' and the establishment of bodily boundaries between self and other. As a result, the identities of these 'not-yet-fully-born' men are extremely fragile and achieved by proxy only through militarism and a disciplined régime.

Fear of ego dissolution leads to the fascist warrior's expulsion and denial of the feminine. He has a paranoia about the pleasures, softness, liquidity and flows of the female body, of woman as a 'terrain of desire'. Preoccupied with boundaries, hardness and discipline, his 'soldierly totality-body . . . made functional by drill' seeks continually to 'dam in, and to subdue any force that threatens to transform him back into the horribly disorganized jumble of flesh, hair, skin and bones, intestines, and feelings that calls itself human'. War is the only permissible outlet for the fascist warrior's expression of desire; sexualized, it 'holds the promise of massive velocities, explosions without number – the promise of consummate pleasure for the totality component' without having to engage with the reality of another human being. War guarantees the renewal of the mechanisms which structure the fascist persona by transforming the body into a site of destruction.

Ironically, Theweleit's indictment of fascism as the marginalization and derealization of women suffers from a similar problem: there is very little evidence in *Male Fantasies* of either the relation of women to fascism or an account of real, historical women under fascism.   *GCL*

Male Fantasies, Vol. 1 (Minneapolis: University of Minnesota Press, 1987; Cambridge: Polity Press, 1987); *Male Fantasies, Vol. 2* (Minneapolis: University of Minnesota Press, 1989; Cambridge: Polity Press, 1989)

See also **Shuihu Zhuan**; **Valenzuela**

Torture Garden, The

First published in 1898, Octave Mirbeau's *The Torture Garden* has long been recognized as one of the classics of decadent **pornography**. Mirbeau was a Parisian journalist noted for his rampant anticlericism and support of radical causes. He eventually became an anarchist. His novels, of which he published a number, were red in tooth, claw and politics and were largely philosophical treatises lightly disguised as fiction. *The Torture Garden*, his most notorious work, was swiftly condemned as obscene and has long enjoyed a sinister underground renown, a sort of literary half-life. It has been read in literal fashion as a prurient and arousing sado-masochistic fantasy, but in fact its excesses are a rhetorical device designed to illustrate philosophical debate. It is an uneven book which conveys a gripping if somewhat unbalanced force and vitality.

The construction of the book is similar to that of Sir Thomas More's *Utopia* and this serves to underline Mirbeau's satirical intentions. Both books have an introductory section preceding the main body of the text and, in both, the central section is divided into a critique of contemporary society followed by a description of an imaginary alternative. The narrator is a sophisticated and corrupt Parisian who, having become an embarrassment in political circles, is sent to the east in the guise of a scientist. Thus his basic fraudulence and bad faith are established. He meets Clara, an Englishwoman who can respond erotically only to torture and death. In an imaginary China, unfettered and barbaric, the narrator and reader are forced to confront their secret, primeval natures, normally restrained by the deathly grip of western civilization. The book is an allegory, a violent attack on the hypocrisy of the so-called civilized world, the frigidity and corruption of European society and on Catholicism which, Clara maintains, instills a fear of nature and a hatred of love.

But Mirbeau's intention is ironic as Clara hymns the 'natural' alternative, the 'vital scope . . . passionate poetry and stupendous pulse of all nature' which throbs to ecstasies of sex and blood. Together, the couple visit the local prison where the public are admitted once a week to feed rancid flesh to the pitiful convicts and witness appalling torture sessions. Clara criticizes European civilization which is content to torture people in secret rather than proudly and openly amid the rampant floral orgy of this mythical Chinese prison garden. Mirbeau spends much time describing the monstrous, bloated beauty of the flowers in the Torture Garden which, nourished by human compost, serve as a metaphor for unrestrained nature. Clara argues for the preservation of primitive cultures and this establishes the sub-Sadeian theme, which angers and confuses intellectuals today as much as it did then. However much they may wish for 'nature', they are unwilling to confront the barbarity and cruelty that logically attend the natural, whether it be in the form of **female genital mutilation** or monstrous, imaginary tortures.

In the first section of this book Mirbeau rips away the masks of civilized society, showing the rot and corruption underneath, and, in the Torture Garden section, reveals how the natural and primitive are not so much noble alternatives as bloody, gross and ignorant. In the face of such misanthropy and moral outrage, it would take a brave or exceptionally insensitive reader to respond sexually to the book.   *EY*

The Torture Garden (New York: Dedalus/Hippocrene Press, 1990)

See also **Obscenity; Sade; Sado-Masochism;** *Story of O*

Transexuality

Transexuality is a sexual variation in which individuals feel a strong identification with the other gender and urgently desire those physical therapies – surgery, hormones – which will make such identification more overt. They feel that their gender *identity* is a matter of essence, separate from such accidents as primary and secondary sexual characteristics, characteristics that they regard as repulsive or incongruous. Transvestites, drag queens and butch dykes are, by contrast, happy with their genders and seek to play with appearances.

The majority of those seeking gender reassignment are male; although a significant number of female-to-male transexuals also exists, in spite of the deficiencies of their surgical options. Both sexes are treated with hormones. Female-to-male transexuals will have mastectomies while male-to-female transexuals may have breast augmentation. Male-to-female transexuals will also have their testicles removed and a facsimile of female genitals constructed from the skin and flesh of the penis and scrotum; female-to-male transexuals will have a hysterectomy and a penis constructed from the skin and flesh of their thigh.

Before such surgery existed, many individuals lived in sub-cultures where the adoption of at least the appearance and social role of the opposite gender was possible; traditionally, these sub-cultures often involved sex work, and many pre- and post-operative male-to-female transexuals still work as prostitutes to pay for surgery or to provide existential validation of their identity. Some non-western cultures, notably various of the Plains tribes of Native Americans, provide a social niche for individuals who might, in western culture, identify as transexuals.

From Germaine **Greer** and Robin Morgan onwards, there has existed a vein of deep hostility to transexuality in the feminist movement, finding its most formulated expression in Janice Raymond's *The Transexual Empire* (1980). Raymond alleges that the entire existence not only of transexual surgery, but of the transexual community, is a fraud by surgeons and psychiatrists anxious to bolster **patriarchy** by using the desires of transexuals to legitimize it. She argues that the patriarchy is creating brain-washed feminine pseudo-females in order to render actual women redundant and that male-to-female transexuals who identify as feminists or lesbians are trojan horses of the patriarchy. Female-to-male transexuals she regards as having been tricked into acting as red herrings.

It is certainly the case that many doctors working with transexuals have attempted to police them into accepting stereotyped models of femininity, and that many transexuals have capitulated to this pressure, at least until after their surgery. The freedom of transexuals to criticize the medical profession is limited while access to treatment depends heavily on the medical model; the fact that surgery is available as a cure for alleged sickness rather than as a response to need and choice makes such criticism harder. Nonetheless, some male-to-female transexuals are feminists, and regard the dominance of the Raymond position as temporary. They point to the strategic role of Raymond's book, which claims an absolute immutability of gender identity, in the attempt by some feminists to claim the right to say who is, and who is not, a woman.

Transexuals of both adopted genders are not necessarily heterosexual; about a third, postoperatively, are bisexual or lesbian or gay. This has little correlation with pre-operative sexual identification. The hostility in the lesbian and gay communities is often based on the claim that people become transexual to avoid accepting gay identity. Given the constant discrimination that transexuals endure, hounding by the press and vulnerability to assault whenever their original gender is known, this seems beside the point. Many transexuals see themselves as not simply either the gender of their birth or of their adoption, but as a small community of identity separate from their gender of preference in training and, perhaps, skills, but with largely identical interests and needs. Others identify more strongly with their new gender, sometimes regarding their past with shame or horror, and regard their right to privacy as primary.

Attempts to provide an etiology of transexuality – like those that claim that **homosexuality** and **lesbianism** are the product of *in utero* hormone fluctuation – are seen as attempts to delegitimize the existence of transexuals and their human rights. Libertarian feminists are interested in transexuals as a demonstration of the arbitrariness of gender roles and sexual identities, and the capacity of will to overcome them.   *RK*

See also **Cross-Dressing; Prostitution, Male**

Ukiyo-E

An eighteenth-century school of Japanese art, Ukiyo-e, or Pictures of the Floating World, used a system of four-color, wood-block prints called 'shunga' to express the pleasure of the moment, including the pleasure of sex. Especially towards the end of the period the images were sometimes grotesquely fantastic, including depictions of monsters and **rape**, but many showed sex as mutually agreeable, sensual exploration without shame – as befits a country where prudery was imported only in the mid-nineteenth century from the west.

Nudity to the Japanese is not traditionally erotic, but unremarkable or even faintly disgusting ('It really does not have the slightest charm,' pronounced the eleventh-century novelist Lady Murasaki) so the figures in Ukiyo-e are usually draped, with only the genitals, of both the sexes,

Katsushika Hokusai, *A Couple Making Love*, (from *Picture Album of Couples*), *c*. 1810-15

presented in attention-grabbing, naturalistic detail and quite *un*natural proportion. Among the school's most famous practitioners were Utamaro and Harunobu.   *HG*

Charles Grosbois *Shunga, Images of Spring: Essay on Erotic Elements in Japanese Art* (Geneva, Paris and Munich: Nagel, 1966)

See also **Comics, Japanese; Erotica**

Unconscious, The

Sigmund **Freud** was by no means the first thinker to attach significance to unconscious processes, but he has undoubtedly done more than any other fig-ure in the history of ideas to revolutionize our con-ception of their significance. The Freudian uncon-scious can be thought of as an 'area' of the mind (although such topographical metaphors are prob-lematic); it can also be conceived of as a *mode* of thought, operating according to its own laws (pri-marily those of 'condensation' and 'displacement'), its contents atemporal and inaccessible to con-sciousness while exerting a continuous and dynamic influence on conscious thought and action.

That said, not all schools of **psychoanalysis** agree about the formation of the unconscious. Kleinians believe that the unconscious exists from birth (hence making possible unconscious **fantasy**), while the Lacanian reading of Freud emphasizes the unconscious in relation to **repression**: that is, the unconscious is constituted by the repression, at a slightly later phase of childhood, of unacceptable wishes. Freud himself reserved a place for 'phylo-genetic' contents – contents that have developed throughout the process of human evolution – that constitute the nucleus of the unconscious.

Subjectively, the unconscious makes itself felt in everyday life in the 'return of the repressed': in dreams, in slips of the tongue and other 'slips' of speech and, at the level of the subject's personal trajectory, in the 'repetition compulsion', the tendency for the subject to recreate or reproduce patterns of behavior or object choice which he or she is consciously opposed to but 'finds' himself or herself seeking out.

Feminist psychoanalytic reading of the 1970s, influenced by Juliet Mitchell's *Psychoanalysis and Feminism* (London: Allen Lane, 1974), saw the unconscious mind as the means or mechanism by which we acquire the necessary laws of human society. Such a reading inevitably poses an additional question: if the society is patriarchal, is the unconscious patriarchal in content? Freud's own concept of transcendent primal fantasies – the subject's phylogenetic inheritance referred to above – is a partial (and ambiguous) answer to this question at the level of Freud's text. But questions such as this have tended to come to a halt as more feminists have become involved in psychotherapy and psychoanalysis, as both patients and practitioners, and have found that the dilemmas of subjectivity are more absorbing than a generalized theorization of a 'patriarchal' unconscious. In addition, it has been difficult to know how to integrate a feminist perspective on questions of gender and historical change when the psychoanalytic literature itself tends to be ahistorical and individually focused, though with some important exceptions. The work on women of Marie Langer, the Austrian-born psychoanalyst who spent much of her working life in Latin America, is one. *AS*

Sigmund Freud 'The Unconscious' in *On Metapsychology: The Theory of Psychoanalysis* (Harmondsworth: Penguin, 1984) Marie Langer *From Vienna to Managua: Journey of a Psychoanalyst* (London: Free Association Books, 1989) J. Laplanche and J.-B. Pontalis *The Language of Psycho-Analysis* (London: Hogarth Press and the Institute of Psycho-Analysis, 1973)

See also **Kristeva; Lacan; Surrealism**

Valadon, Suzanne (1865-1938)

The French artist Suzanne Valadon is generally given credit as a painter of the **nude**, but, as a painter whose work directly addresses female sexuality, she has been effectively ignored. This relative neglect derives from the unease that she aroused both as a painter and a person: as a painter because of the way in which she represented women and their bodies; as a person because her manner of living challenged notions of female sexuality.

Valadon's artistic originality lies in the kinds of women she chose to represent – most of them far from the classical ideal of the nude – and the way she shows their relationship to their bodies and their sexuality. The best known example is 'Le Salon Bleu', a comment on and a challenge to **Manet**'s 'Olympia'. In it, typically, the model is shown as unambiguously in possession of her body. Her sexuality is hers; she is neither waiting for nor positioned in relation to a male lover or viewer. Some of Valadon's most powerful paintings are of young girls in the process of discovering their bodies'; in 'Nude at the Mirror' a girl is standing naked in a hallway looking at her genitals' reflection. Perhaps her most challenging painting, however, is the self-portrait done when she was sixty-six in which she is wearing nothing but make-up and a necklace. Through the juxtaposition of her firm, smooth breasts and her lined neck and face, she is disrupting a whole set of easy identifications: of the nude, of self-portraiture, of age, of sexuality.

Valadon the person is always portrayed in explicitly sexual terms: as a model who, at the age of eighteen, gave birth to an illegitimate son (who would grow up to be the alcoholic painter Maurice Utrillo); as a woman who took many lovers and, at the age of forty-four, married a man who was three years younger than her son. The three lived together in Montmartre and were notorious for their rows and excesses. Valadon in particular is seen as excessive,

Suzanne Valadon, *Nude with Mirror*, 1909

a castrating mother, masculine in her style of living and painting, her line described as 'virile' and her nudes as revealing her hatred of women.   *FE*

Musée National d'Art Moderne, Paris

See also **Balthus; Degas; Neel: Rego**

Valenzuela, Luisa (1938-   )

Luisa Valenzuela is an Argentine writer who has escaped from the shadow of Jorge Luis Borges to find her own style and a voice that takes account of her country's history and reality. Sex, in Valenzuela's novels and stories, is inextricably linked to power. Out of her country's political material – three successive military dictatorships waging a 'dirty war' against 'subversives' which, during the 1970s alone, claimed over 30,000 lives – she has woven a baroque literary construction that ultimately identifies male sexuality with sadism, power and torture.

Following Octavio Paz's famous dictum that Latin American literature defines 'woman' as 'the other', Valenzuela has called her latest novel *The Crime of the Other*. Although the plot concerns a man's murder of an unknown woman, it is not only his gratuitous violence that is examined – a violence as gratuitous as the attraction that preceded it – but the ways in which women become accomplices in their own destiny. Such investigations, even novelistically phrased, tread a fine line between anti-feminism ('there are as many compliant women as violent men') and a serious psychological study of how the interrelationship of the genders is determined by, and in turn determines, history.

Argentina's recent history is more explicitly encountered in *The Lizard's Tail*, whose apparently anodyne title in fact refers to a particular thong used by torturers to whip and blind the peasants who make it. In this novel, Valenzuela meets the male voice that questions: 'A woman writer? Don't be funny, women don't know how to write,' by documenting the monstrous fantasies of the President and emerging as witness and survivor of the final Armageddon. While, earlier, she has been tormented by the man who 'has more pressing passions than love', ultimately her salvation lies in trusting not man but herself.

Valenzuela's short stories often take a more humorous look at men's foibles and futilities. In 'The Censors' a censor succeeds in censoring not only the imaginary double entendres of everyone else's mail but, finally, his own love letter, destroying it and himself in the process. And, in 'The Minstrels', Jeanne the Strong One so far outbids her husband in their son's affections that she succeeds in persuading him that his true father is all nine of the eponymous minstrels.   *AmH*

The Lizard's Tail (New York: Farrar Straus, 1983: London: Serpent's Tail, 1987)

See also **Sade; Theweleit;** *Torture Garden*

Venereal Disease

A venereal disease is one that is mainly transmitted by **sexual intercourse**, or by such other intimate, physical acts as anal sex or **oral sex**. At different times and in different places, the most common have included gonorrhea, syphilis, herpes simplex and **AIDS** (although this last, to be precise, is not itself a disease, but a syndrome comprising a number of different possible diseases, tumors and cancers).

With the exception to date of **AIDS** the venereal diseases, now more frequently known as 'sexually transmitted diseases', are either containable or curable; most, however, were harder to deal with before the development of penicillin, streptomycin, actinospectacin and so on. Gonorrhea, the most common of all, and one familiar even to the Ancient Egyptians, was a major cause of pelvic pain and premature infertility in women until there were antibiotics capable of curing it. Syphilis, before there was treatment, could paralyze, blind, destroy the brain, or, in the form of congenital syphilis, either deform or kill the children born to infected women.

Very much frightened by such diseases, people logically tried to prevent them by using varieties of condom: from the small, linen sheath supposedly developed by an Italian, Gabriele Fallopius, in the middle of the sixteenth century, to the larger sheep-gut or fish-skin sheaths more generally used in the eighteenth century. But they also hurled blame about, wildly. Most commonly held responsible were foreigners (the particular sort depending upon the country doing the blaming), their own society (for having grown dissolute and thus earned divine displeasure) and, more prosaically, prostitutes. From China in the early sixteenth century to Britain in the middle of the nineteenth century, the prostitute was the principal culprit so far as medicine and the state were concerned: as though infection were not a two-way process involving men. But then – as is shown by the similar lack of logic surrounding **AIDS** – diseases connected with sex carry with them all the fear, guilt and power-abuse to which sexual activity itself so often gives rise.   *HG*

See also **Acton; Contagious Diseases Acts; Contraception; Prostitution**

Vidal, Gore (1925-   )

An American novelist and essayist, Gore Vidal has helped break down sexual stereotypes in US literature less by his work than by his example. Connected by cousinship to Jacqueline Kennedy, he is a patrician whose early novel *Williwaw* graphically represented military combat; at the same time he is entirely open and unashamed about being homosexual. One of the first to express sardonic reservations about the Kennedy era, his association with it has not harmed his career; Vidal has always found honorable ways of having his cake and eating it. His role as licensed establishment jester is at once the traditional role of gay male Trickster and something more sophisticated.

While Vidal's tone has often infuriated the progressive forces with which he has allied himself, he has consistently mocked sexual conformism as one of the scare tactics by which the US establishment defends its prerogatives. Specifically, he has cru-

saded against the **homophobia** which sections of the New Right have whipped up as a substitute for traditional anti-semitism. His tone of aristocratic scorn has given him access to journals and other media where a more radical voice could not have penetrated.

Some of Vidal's novels have dealt explicitly with sexual themes. *The City and the Pillar* (1948) and the pseudonymous detective story *Death in the Fifth Position* presented views of **homosexuality** and **bisexuality** unusually positive for their time, while *Myra Breckinridge* (1968) and its sequel *Myron* use the male-to-female transexual as the necessary outsider viewpoint in a generalized satire on US mores. Both those books also present Vidal's intensely double feelings towards unmanliness and have been criticized for their implicit hostility to transexuals and women in general.

Vidal exhibits a sometimes productive, sometimes limiting, ambivalence towards **camp**: liking its potential for verbally felicitous coinages and game-playing; distrusting its tendency to the merely irresponsible. If Vidal's politics and esthetic often smack of class privilege, they also have in them much of the patrician's sense of duty.   *RK*

The City and the Pillar (New York: Ballantine, 1986); *Death in the Fifth Position* (New York: Armchair Detective, 1991); *Myra Breckinridge* (New York: Random House, 1987; London: Grafton, 1989)

See also **Gay Liberation; Transexuality**

Virginity

At its most straightforward, virginity is the state, shared by most young females, of having the entrance to the vagina partially covered by a fold of mucous membrane called a hymen. As **Sade** put it in his novel *Justine*, virginity is essentially a matter of 'a little more or less skin'.

But that, of course, is not the whole story. Indeed, the full quote from Sade is as follows: 'How can a girl be so simple to believe that virtue depends upon a little more or less skin!' And the answer is:

men *tell* her it does, in almost every known civilization. Until her hymen is broken by **sexual intercourse** with her husband, she had better ensure – with her life, if needs be – that it remains intact. Today, in countries where women have some economic and social power, the injunction is frequently ignored; in Britain, for instance, it is estimated that only between six and twelve per cent of women who get married are virgins. But in countries where women are more dependent on men's protection, income and good will, they cannot be so cavalier. In Algeria, for instance, the wedding-night sheets are sometimes inspected for blood from the bride's broken hymen. While in Greece, in 1978, the parents of a sixteen-year-old girl who had been seduced by her language teacher were awarded 350,000 drachmae to add to the dowry they would now have to pay 'to compensate a man . . . for the loss of her virginity'.

On the practical level, men may want to know (however they behave themselves) that any woman whom they 'possess' has not been 'had' by another man, cannot be carrying another man's child and, as Nawal el **Saadawi** points out in *The Hidden Face of Eve*, cannot be in a position to judge them sexually. Besides this, some men appear to obtain a special erotic pleasure from sexual intercourse with a virgin: perhaps because they enjoy the component of pain that is sometimes involved for the woman; perhaps because of a gentler fantasy involving teaching and awakening; or perhaps because of a frisson to do with taboos. For of course, the more strongly that virginity is seen as something to be saved for a husband, the greater will be a thrill, for some, of taking it illicitly, even by force. And in Christian cultures, where virginity and the mother of God are inextricably linked, the condition has an additional kind of uneasy, half-acknowledged magic: recently shown in Britain by the alarm over virgins being allowed to conceive via artificial insemination. At all events, there is undoubtedly a market for virgin prostitutes, which is unlikely to be entirely a matter of caution about **venereal disease**.

The irony is that virginity, whether paid for in a brothel or obtained through marriage, is no sure guarantee of anything. On the one hand it is not unknown for brothel keepers to have young prostitutes sewn to *appear* like virgins; on the other hand a hymen may get broken through riding, gymnastics or some other non-sexual activity. That so many men place so much stress on an unreliable, physical sign could indicate that they understand women not as complex amalgams of thought, behavior and feeling like themselves, but as bodies which, like motor-cars, are all the more desirable when still wrapped up in their manufacturer's protective plastic.   *HG*

See also **Chastity; Christianity; Honor**

Von Gloeden, Baron Wilhelm (1856-1931)

After studying art in Weimar, in 1880 Wilhelm von Gloeden moved to Sicily, where he pursued an interest in photography that has earned him a place in the annals of **camp**. He specialized in staged scenes from pastoral antiquity with **nude** or scantily clothed Sicilian youths as stand-ins for gods, satyrs and other mythic figures. In common with the work of his acquaintances, fellow Prussian Wilhelm von Plüschow and the Italian Vincenzo Galdi, these overdone pseudo-Renaissance erotic poses had a wide circulation at the turn of the century on the European market for photographs of the male nude. The lines of class and north-south imperialism that cross these photographs evoke the colonial harem pictures of women that they in some ways resemble. In a brief essay on von Gloeden, Roland Barthes delighted in the naively adventurous 'kitsch' quality of his photographs: '. . . it is delectable, the contradiction between this whole literary apparatus of third-year Greek and the bodies of these young peasant gigolos . . .' Von Gloeden died in Taormina. The bulk of his work, both glass plates and prints, were destroyed by the fascists in the 1930s.   *LH*

Leo Kandl Collection, Vienna; Violett Collection, Paris

V

Baron Wilhelm von Gloeden, *Naples 1890-1900*

See also **Mapplethorpe; Paedophilia; Plato**

Voyeurism

'Voyeurism' is one of those slippery words that can be used technically (by psychoanalysts) or casually. Although it is a neutral term, referring to the sexual pleasure that derives from looking, it is all too frequently wielded with disapproval.

According to Sigmund **Freud**, voyeurism may be defined as a **perversion** when pleasure in looking is restricted to looking at the genitals, when the pleasure involves an overriding of disgust and when it supplants other forms of sexual excitement. On the other hand, Freud insisted that voyeurism is part of 'normal' development; all children are intensely curious about genitals, their own and

other people's, about bodily functions and about the 'primal scene' (**sexual intercourse** between the parents either witnessed or fantasized). Freud went on to point out that pleasure in looking at another person remains the primary source of sexual excitement, that our curiosity is constantly stimulated by civilized concealment and that, when voyeuristic pleasure is 'sublimated', in other words is 'shifted away from the genitals on to the shape of the body as a whole', it becomes a mainspring of our interest in art.

The concept is undoubtedly essential to an understanding of the centrality of the **nude**, particularly the female nude, in western art. Indeed, some common topics of this art – the biblical story of Susannah spied upon by the elders, for example – deal self-consciously with voyeuristic pleasure and outrage. And movie historians have always recognized the skill with which cinema plays on the audi-

262

ence's voyeuristic fantasies. The spectator, isolated in the dark, gazes at a dream world, private, impervious, that unfolds at a distance. (Again, many films, from Alfred **Hitchcock**'s *Rear Window* (1954) to Michael Powell's *Peeping Tom* (1960), from Krystsztof Kieslowski's *A Short Film About Love* (1988) to Patrice Leconte's *Monsieur Hire* (1989), take voyeurism as their theme.)

The last twenty years have seen a vigorous feminist debate over voyeurism and gender; in popular culture (studies of how **pornography** panders to male voyeurism), in art history (recognition of the links between the images purveyed by admen and pornographers and the idealized nudes of high art) and in cinema theory (analyses of the male as spectator, voyeuristic, sadistic, and the female as sex object). Laura Mulvey has put the feminist position most sharply: 'In a world ordered by sexual imbalance, pleasure in looking has been split between active/male and passive/female. The determining male gaze projects his fantasy on to the female figure . . . she holds the look; and plays to and signifies male desire.' The complexity of the issues under discussion is best understood by looking at the impassioned debates over certain key figures, such as Hitchcock and the painter Edgar **Degas**. Do the films of the former exploit or explore voyeuristic fantasies? Are the latter's extraordinary pictures of naked bathers from the 1860s merely 'keyhole nudes', aggressively misogynist, or genuine attempts to imagine the unseeable?

One strain in feminist theory has hardened into a self-parodying insistence that the whole of western art, including cinema, is a misogynist conspiracy that spies on, fetishizes, fragments and mutilates the female body. This denies the fact that the woman's body, partly because it is ultimately the mother's, will always arouse our most intense curiosity and a longing that is never very far away from terror or even disgust. But increasingly feminists recognize that, as Freud argued, the roots of voyeurism are often auto-erotic; that active and passive impulses – pleasure in looking, pleasure in being looked at – are neither rigidly separated nor, necessarily, divided according to gender; and that,

after all, gender itself is not something we can take for granted.   *MW*

John Berger *Ways of Seeing* (New York and London: Penguin, 1977) Ed. Thomas B. Hess and Linda Nochlin *Woman as Sex Object: Studies in Erotic Art 1730-1970* (London: Allen Lane, 1973) Wendy Lesser *His Other Half: Men Looking at Women Through Art* (Harvard: Harvard University Press, 1991) Laura Mulvey 'Visual Pleasure and Narrative Cinema' in *Screen* (Vol: 16, no. 3, 1975)

See also **Balthus; Bellocq; Brassai; Export; Graham; Infantile Sexuality; Mapplethorpe; Miller, Lee; Neel; Rape and Revenge Movies; Sensuality; Snuff Movies; Women's Images of Men**

Walker, Alice (1944-   )

Born in Eatonton, Georgia, the daughter of a sharecropper, Alice Walker is one of the few African-American authors to have gained a worldwide reputation in her lifetime. Poet, essayist, short-story writer and novelist, Walker thematizes issues that concern women of all races. These include **female genital mutilation, lesbianism, incest, rape** and have made her work very controversial for men, especially for black men.

Walker's book of essays *In Search of Our Mothers' Gardens* (1983) is subtitled 'womanist prose'. She called herself a 'womanist' as distinct from a 'feminist' because as a black woman, she realized that western feminism rarely addressed racial matters. Walker defines a 'womanist' as 'a black feminist or a feminist of color' and derives it from '"womanish" . . . usually referring to outrageous, audacious, courageous, or *willful* behavior'. Her second definition of a 'womanist' is: 'A woman who loves other women, sexually and/or nonsexually'.

In Walker's fourth volume of poetry, *Horses Make a Landscape Look More Beautiful* (1984), she considers sexism and rape. 'The Thing Itself' has a biting depiction of a man's belief that all 'real women/like rape'. It is in her short stories, however, that these themes are examined in depth. In her first volume, *In Love and Trouble* (1967), 'The Child

Who Favored Daughter' is a most disturbing depiction of incest. Although the act itself does not occur, the story ends horrifically in the father's mutilation of his daughter-lover.

With her second volume of stories, *You Can't Keep a Good Woman Down* (1971), Walker tackles **pornography** and its effect on the black middle class. In 'Porn' she shows vividly how pornographic stereotypes have distorted black women's experience, and in 'Advancing Luna and Ida B. Wells' she grapples with inter-racial rape. Another story, 'Coming Apart', has a preface in which Walker argues that 'the more ancient roots of modern pornography are to be found in the almost always pornographic treatment of black women, who, from the moment they entered slavery . . . were subjected to rape as the "logical" convergence of sex and violence': an argument that is fully developed in Toni Morrison's Pulitzer Prize-winning novel *Beloved* (New York; Knopf, 1987).

Walker won the Pulitzer Prize for her third novel, *The Color Purple* (1983). Like Morrison's *The Bluest Eye* (New York: Holt Rinehart & Winston, 1970) this novel contains an incestuous rape. Jean Wyatt believes that 'Alice Walker is concerned with incestuous rape not as an isolated problem, but as a part of a continuum of male sexual attitudes that dehumanize and objectify women'. Although *The Color Purple* addresses many of the problems facing the black community in the USA, its main theme is silencing. This is evident when, after being raped, its heroine is told: 'You better not tell anybody but God.' But Walker does tell and, in doing so, gives voice to the most silenced woman in US literature, a woman who is 'pore, black and ugly'. For Walker to choose a heroine who is the antithesis of the beautiful mulatta, and to have her triumph, was a major departure for black American fiction. Moreover, this is the first affirmative lesbian novel written by an African-American. It presents a lesbian relationship as nurturing and freeing, allowing creativity to flourish.

In her most recent, polemical novel *Possessing the Secret of Joy*, Walker turns her attention to female genital mutilation, presenting the practice as emotionally as well as physically damaging. But her suggestion that such mutilation, as practiced in Africa and elsewhere today, has a part in the spread of **AIDS** cannot be substantiated in a work of fiction.   *SRu*

In Love and Trouble (California: Harcourt Brace Jovanovich, 1974; London: Women's Press, 1984); *The Third Life of Grange Copeland* (New York: Pocket Books, 1989; London: Women's Press, 1985); *You Can't Keep a Good Woman Down* (California: Harcourt Brace Jovanovich, 1982; London: Women's Press, 1982); *In Search of Our Mothers' Gardens* (California: Harcourt Brace Jovanovich, 1984; London: Women's Press, 1984); *The Color Purple* (New York: Pocket Books, 1990; London: Women's Press, 1983); *Horses Make a Landscape Look More Beautiful* (California: Harcourt Brace Jovanovich, 1986; London: Women's Press, 1985); *Possessing the Secret of Joy* (California: Harcourt Brace Jovanovich, 1992; London: Jonathan Cape, 1992)

Barbara Christian *Black Feminist Criticism: Perspectives on Black Women Writers* (New York and Oxford: Pergamon Press, 1985)

See also Angelou; Hurston

Warhol, Andy (1928-1987)

Andy Warhol, painter and filmmaker, casts a silvery shadow over the decades between 1960 and 1990 and is arguably the greatest artist of the postwar period. Instantly recognizable with his silver-blond wig, dark glasses, ashen complexion, black leather jacket and skeletal amphetamine chic, his characteristic appearance was enhanced by the ingenuous, child-like nature of his responses. He was ultimately to become an American icon as famous as those he portrayed: Elvis Presley, Marilyn Monroe or Jackie Onassis.

Born Andrew Warhola, he came from a poor Ruthenian immigrant family in Pittsburgh and studied art at the Carnegie Institute of Technology. In New York he became a successful commercial artist before making the difficult transition to the fine-art world. By the early 1960s Abstract Expressionism was a spent force and a new generation of artists including Warhol, Jasper Johns, Robert Rauschenberg and Roy Lichtenstein were using images from popular culture, advertising and the mass media to create what became known as Pop Art. In 1962 Warhol exhibited his notorious silkscreens of Campbell's Soup cans. Shortly afterwards he established his famous studio, known as the Factory, and surrounded himself with an entourage of the beautiful and the damned: hustlers, transvestites, speed-freaks, street people and beautiful fag-hags like Edie Sedgwick and Viva. Warhol started to make experimental films using his brilliant, damaged acolytes as 'superstars'. Many of these early black-and-white films, such as *Sleep* (1963), *Kiss* (1963), *Blow-Job* (1964), *Couch* (1964) and *The Chelsea Girls* (1966) are partly exercises in **voyeurism**. Although Warhol himself was both very private and very homosexual, a certain stunted masochistic passivity in his psyche led him to focus compulsively on confrontational emotion and sexual scenes in these films.

Warhol films flesh with the fascinated intensity of one who is profoundly alienated from life. The films have great artistic significance: they are beautiful in the manner of abstract paintings and they raise important questions about the limits of boredom, the relation of film time to real time, the uncharted area between script and improvisation and the nature of 'performance' with regard to pose and affectation, reality and illusion. Eventually Warhol's filmmaking was taken over by one of his assistants, Paul Morissey, and the later films such as *Flesh* (1968), *Trash* (1969) and *Bad* (1976), although amusing, are almost entirely vacuous. Overall, however, Warhol's pathologically uncensorious approach to sexuality in his art contributed much to the changing sexual mores of the era. The films represent women as dominant and sexually demanding and give a vivid, accurate impression of the casual sexual encounters of the 1960s: the **bisexuality**, fluid sexual role-playing and general acceptance of sex as being completely divorced from notions of love. Warhol's nonchalant filmic approach to **homosexuality** paralleled the growing **Gay Liberation** movement.

The Factory garnered an unparalleled reputation as a sink of license and depravity and, as drug deaths and suicides took their toll, Warhol was increasingly seen as a sort of demonic Svengali. His association with a rock group, The Velvet Underground, whose lyrical paeans to narcotics and **sado-masochism** prefigured punk music, consolidated Warhol's image as a twisted manipulator of dark forces. Eventually, in 1968, one of his fringe followers, a deranged feminist called Valerie Solanas, shot him and he nearly died. Afterwards it was never the same. After flirting so long with death and doom, Warhol seemed permanently damaged by their reality. The Factory was cleaned up and moved to other premises. The speed freaks were replaced by aristocrats, businessmen and media personalities. Warhol started *Interview* magazine, moved like a pale ghost into high society and became a commissioned portrait painter to the rich and famous. His art became mechanical and slapdash – apart from his near-pornographic gay *Sex Parts* paintings of 1977-1978 and the *Piss Paintings* of the same period. His work was again revitalized in his final years by a collaboration with the young graffiti artist Jean-Michel Basquiat. Warhol died after a minor operation. *EY*

Ed. Pat Hackett *The Warhol Diaries* (New York: Warner Books, 1989) Victor Bockris *The Life and Death of Andy Warhol* (New York: Bantam, 1990; London: Muller, 1989)

See also **Masochism; Sexual Revolution**

Water Margin, The

See Shuihu Zhuan

Wa Thiong'o, Ngugi

A Kenyan whose highly complex novels reflect the evils inflicted by British colonialism, and its latter-day African inheritors, upon Kenyan society, Ngugi wa Thiong'o reached a crossroads in his writing career when, after publishing four novels in English, he rejected that language as a medium of imaginative expression, regarding it as his patriotic duty to write in the language of his country's peasants and workers, not of its bourgeoisie.

It is unsurprising that, in Ngugi's writing, sexuality is always 'political' in the wider sense. His female characters are generally strong-willed pragmatists who occupy symbolic positions; young women, often made pregnant by an older married man and rejected by their families, represent the disintegration of traditional values. Invariably they overcome their tribulations and come to represent the strength and rebirth possible in African society. Wanja in *Petals of Blood* (1977) is one such character. In a singularly cold-blooded act, she murders her newborn by flushing it into the sewer. Later, becoming a prostitute, she is exploited by all and sundry but soon becomes a brothel owner and learns to be the exploiter. When her brothel is burned down and she is hospitalized, Wanja makes a drawing which lifts her 'out of her own self' and grants her 'a kind of inner assurance of the possibilities of a new kind of power'. She thus represents both the new creative energy in Kenya and the vicissitudes to which it has been subjected.

Like many other Ngugi women, Wanja isn't a stereotypically feminine construct and, although she is obviously desirable, the novel never concentrates on her physical attributes. That she enjoys sex and fulfills her own yearnings is clear from her jokes with the other women about the sexual habits of their men and the 'rubber trousers' they sometimes cover their penises with. Men in Ngugi's novels do not fare well. When, as in *Weep Not Child* (1964), they are both powerful and selfless, they end up castrated. When they are good in bed, they are lousy outside it, and too immature to take responsibility for themselves or others. Even when morally courageous, they are also indecisive – like Remi in *The Black Hermit* (1968) who, with foresight, rails against tribalism and corruption but does not have the insight to save his wife from suicide – and their indecision often has tragic consequences. Remi may be the hero of his drama but it is really his mother who shows true character when she tells her daughter-in-law, 'I hate to see your

youth wearing away . . . I tell you take a man. If he does not marry you, he may at least give you a child.' *NOB*

Weep Not Child (London: Heinemann, 1987); *The Black Hermit* (London; Heinemann, 1968); *Petals of Blood* (London; Heinemann, 1986)

See also **Emecheta; Mizoguchi; Prostitution**

Wedekind, Benjamin Franklin (1864-1918)

With Lulu, the German-born playwright Benjamin Wedekind created a character who has become one of the most enduring sexual icons of the twentieth century. In *Die Erdgeist/The Earth Spirit* (1893) and *Die Büchse Der Pandora/Pandora's Box* (1894), Wedekind deployed her to celebrate a sensual pleasure that he believed was the prerogative of every man and woman. Yet his espousal of the Nietzschean idea that 'love is war' is predicated on the belief that there can be no *equality* between the sexes. Lulu's sexual freedom is paid for by sexual victimization: she dies horribly at the hands of Jack the Ripper.

And, if Lulu was the product of a nineteenth-century imagination attempting to escape a social morality that preached sexual intolerance and ignorance, in subsequent incarnations – Alban Berg's unfinished opera; Pabst's 1922 silent film starring Louise Brooks; many later stage adaptations – she has become all things to all men. Peter Skrine, in *Hauptmann, Wedekind and Schnitzler* (Basingstoke: Macmillan, 1989), has even argued that the Lulu plays 'gave tangible form to one of the twentieth century's most potent myths, the woman sex symbol in an amoral world; the myth was to take on reality eighty years later in the life and legend of Marilyn Monroe, who had much in common with Wedekind's heroine, though on a larger, more glamorous transatlantic scale.' Although Wedekind's Lulu plays broke a nineteenth-century taboo on imagining that women can and do enjoy sex as much as men, they also pandered to and perpetuated the pornographic male fantasy that the female sex needs to be tamed and subdued by men and that, as John Elsom writes in *Erotic Theatre* (London: Secker and Warburg, 1973), 'woman has not lived until she has been slaughtered'. *LG*

The Lulu Plays and Other Sex Tragedies (New York: Riverrun, 1979; London: John Calder, 1973)

See also **Strindberg**

Weeks, Jeffrey (1945-   )

Jeffrey Weeks is the major British historian and theorist of sexuality. Born in Rhondda, in Wales, and educated at local schools and at University College, London, he was among the early members of the **Gay Liberation** Front in 1970. Although he had published three substantial scholarly books and many articles, it proved difficult for him to find a permanent academic post and he had several short-term appointments before becoming Professor of Social Relations at Bristol Polytechnic in 1990.

Weeks's historical work has spanned the nineteenth and twentieth centuries, beginning with a pioneering study of the homosexual reform movements and moving on to a broader consideration of the social changes that affected sexuality in general. His history is informed by the belief that **homosexuality**, as we understand it, is not innate but a social construct that has not existed in the same way in all societies: an approach in whose development Weeks has played an important part, from its early sociological beginnings, when it focused on stigmatized roles such as the homosexual, towards a more overarching postmodernist concern with questioning identities and exploring the significance of sexuality in contemporary western identity construction.

In *Coming Out* (1977) Weeks argued that the full establishment of the male homosexual role and subculture occurred only in the second half of the nineteenth century (unlike Alan Bray in ***Homosexuality In Renaissance England***, who placed its emergence in the seventeenth century). In the medieval world, Weeks argued, homosexual behavior had been condemned as sinful; by the late nineteenth century, homosexuality was a *condition that some men had*, giving them a distinct identity and way of life. Part of Weeks's explanation for this was a loosely Marxist one: with industrialization and urbanization the family became a focus of bourgeois moral concern, men's and women's roles became more clearly defined and 'as sexuality was more closely harnessed ideologically to the reproduction of the population, so the social condemnation of male homosexuality increased'. By the time Weeks wrote *Sexuality and Its Discontents* (1985), he had broadened his concerns not only to discuss the identity politics of lesbian and gay male 'movements of affirmation', but also to address the extraordinary importance and enigmatic quality that modern societies attribute to sex. He examines the analytical and political implications of Sigmund **Freud**, Michel **Foucault** and other theorists, with a constant awareness of the specific tensions of the current crisis in sexuality.

Weeks's great contribution is to combine a strong sense of history – and rich historical scholarship – with a sophisticated theoretical awareness and to use both of these in the service of a radical sexual politics. Though scholarly, his work is never academic but speaks to, as well as about, the activists of the day. *MM*

Coming Out; Homosexual Politics in Britain from the 19th Century to the Present (London: Quartet, 1990); *Sex, Politics and Society: The Regulation of Sexuality Since 1800* (London: Longman, 1981); *Sexuality and Its Discontents: Meanings, Myths and Modern Sexualities* (London: Routledge and Kegan Paul, 1985); *Sexuality* (Chichester: Ellis Horwood, 1986; London: Tavistock, 1986); *Against Nature: Essays in History, Sexuality and Identity* (London: Rivers Oram, 1991)

See also **Ellis; Hocquenghem**

West, Mae (1892-1980)

The legendary Hollywood 'Sex Goddess' was forty when she made her first film, but Mae West was already notorious for her raunchy, irreverent and

W

non-judgmental approach to sex. The daughter of a Brooklyn heavyweight boxer, she played child parts in stock companies before embarking on a long career in vaudeville. In 1926 she wrote, produced, directed and starred in a Broadway show, *Sex*, in which the heroine was a Montreal prostitute who did not come to a bad end. The public flocked. The police raided. West was charged with **obscenity** and jailed for ten days. Unrepentant, she continued to flirt with danger. Other subjects she tackled in her plays included male **homosexuality** *(The Drag)* and female impersonation *(Pleasure Man)*.

Trailed by her reputation, West arrived in Hollywood and was at once in conflict with the censors. But *She Done Him Wrong* and *I'm No Angel* (both 1933), which contain some of her juiciest dialogue, escaped relatively unscathed. Although the Motion Picture Production Code, or **Hays Code**, ordaining what was and what was not permissible in Hollywood movies, had been adopted in 1930, it had been less than strictly imposed. With the formation of the influential National Legion of Catholic Decency in 1934, in direct response to West's 'immorality' and 'bad taste', the scissors began to be wielded in earnest and West's films became progressively limper until they were almost, one might say, totally emasculated.

West managed to look like a sex symbol and a parody of a sex symbol at the same time. On and off stage and screen, her appearance was old-fashioned, even for its day. Big, blowsy, bosomy and blonde, West favored a style in clothes, make-up and hair-dos which was – and still is – the envy of female impersonators. Indeed, there are those who seriously thought she was a female impersonator.

West's sexiness had nothing to do with fleshly revelations; it had everything to do with innuendo, insinuation and those immortal double entendres. It is in her witty one-liners, all of which she wrote herself, that the key to her uniqueness lies. 'It's not the men in my life that count, but the life in my men'; 'A man in the house is worth two in the street'; 'Is that a gun in your pocket or are you just pleased to see me?'; 'I used to be Snow White but I drifted'; and, when greeted by a score of virile young men at her office: 'I'm feeling a little tired today. One of those fellows'll have to go.' Lines like these show that in her attitude towards sex West was way before her time. They denote a woman in command, 'on top', who calls the shots; a woman who, instead of being a sex object, turned men into sex objects; a woman who could make fun of sex and find it fun. It was this sense of being in control of her own destiny, far more than her beckoning looks and undulating hips, that drove her fans wild and her detractors mad.   *MH*

She Done Him Wrong (1933); *I'm No Angel* (1933); *Belle of the Nineties* (1934); *Klondyke Annie* (1936); *Myra Breckinridge* (1969)

See also **Camp; Cross-Dressing**

Wharton, Edith (1862-1937)

Edith Wharton wrote interestingly about women at a time when women weren't supposed to be interesting. One of the clear themes that emerges from her books is the extent to which the respectable, upper-middle-class lady of her time had boringness thrust upon her, most literally in her sexual life. A lady must remain woefully ignorant, denied any explanation or description of sexuality, until she married. This ignorance is passed from mother to daughter like a curse, a congenital affliction which has devastating effects on the young woman's sexual awakening and subsequent adjustment. If, on the other hand, one was not a lady, one's life was not so much boring as poverty-stricken and isolated.

The two sorts of women, the 'innocent' lady and the knowledgeable 'fallen woman' clash quite openly in two of Wharton's most famous books, *The Age of Innocence* (1921), widely reckoned to be her best, and *The Reef* (1912). The 'reef' of the latter title is sexuality, dark, hidden and threatening, something upon which a life may unwittingly smash – at least, a female life. The danger and fatality of passion is also the theme of *Ethan Frome* (1911), her best known book. Ethan, the married hero, and young Mattie kindle real warmth between themselves, only to end as victims of their own desperation, horribly crippled by a sleigh ride down a moonlit hill meant to consummate their pathetically meager relationship in death.

The anguish of unfulfilled lives spent trapped in stifling marriages is Wharton's central theme. In this she seems to identify with the experience of her father, as she perceived it: an experience she was fated to repeat in her own life, until she divorced Teddy Wharton in 1913. According to her biographer R.W.B. Lewis, *Ethan Frome* is the most autobiographical of her books in its unrelenting depiction of the squalor and bitterness of a soured marriage.

Lewis's biography includes the famous 'Appendix C', which consists of a fragment of an unfinished, unpublished work called *Beatrice Palmato*. The fragment is a piece of 'pornography' (the biographer's description), certainly a piece of deeply erotic writing, in which the heroine, Beatrice Palmato, is not so much seduced as initiated into sexual pleasure by her father. She has already been inexpertly deflowered by her unfortunate husband, and we learn that the entire tale is meant to encompass her mother's madness and the incestuous relationship between her father and her sister which provokes her mother's suicide as well as her sister's madness. But we only hear about these details at secondhand; what is reprinted in full is the vivid scene in which Beatrice is made love to by her father. And the episode, though incestuous, is by no means an assault. Beatrice consents and participates fully, and both the experience and her sensations are described with a lack of inhibition that nothing else in Wharton's canon would lead us to expect. But then, in her life, she frequently defied expectation.   *ALT*

Ethan Frome (New York: Dover, 1991; London: Virago, 1990); *The Reef* (London: Virago, 1983); *The Age of Innocence* (London: Virago, 1988)

R.W.B. Lewis *Edith Wharton: A Biography* (New York: Harper & Row, 1975)

See also **Brontë, Charlotte; Incest**

Whitman, Walt (1819-1897)

Walt Whitman, who answered Ralph Waldo Emerson's call for a poet who would represent those things truly American, scandalized provincial readers with his explicitly sexual poems. What he seemed to be aiming for was an omni-self, one who could speak as a man or a woman, a slave or a master, an animal or a human, the grass itself or something sentient. One of the most famous sections of 'Song of Myself' is written from the viewpoint of a woman standing in the window of a house, secretly looking out and watching, with longing, twenty-eight young men bathing naked, imagining that she is the water and can touch their bodies. 'The beards of the young men glisten'd with wet, it ran from their long hair,/Little streams pass'd all over their bodies./An unseen hand also pass'd over their bodies,/It descended tremblingly from their temples and ribs.'

In 'I Sing the Body Electric' Whitman illustrates this humanist omni-self by speaking first of his attraction to women: 'This is the female form,/ . . . It attracts with fierce undeniable attraction,/ . . . the response likewise is ungovernable,/ . . . Limitless limpid jets of love hot and enormous, quivering jelly of love, whiteblow and delirious juice, . . .'/ Bridegroom night of love/ . . . lost in the sweet-flesh of day,' He then goes on to speak of the male body, then of the bodies of male and female slaves and their beauty, ending with: 'Do you not see that these are exactly the same to all in all nations and times all over the earth?' This emphasis on accepting sexuality, democratically, in everything, including religion and politics, certainly generated mixed responses to Whitman's poetry. 'To a Common Prostitute', with these lines, offended many: 'Be composed – be at ease with me – I am Walt Whitman, liberal and lusty as nature,/ Not till the sun excludes you, do I exclude you.' Another poem, 'Spontaneous Me', explicitly describes **masturbation**: '. . . young man that wakes, deep at night, his hot hand seeking to repress what would master him – the strange half-welcome pangs, vision, sweats,/The pulse pounding through palms and trembling encircling fingers – the young man all colored, red, ashamed, angry.

Whitman's poems glorify male comradeship in such a way that they can easily be read as homoerotic. However, it should not be forgotten that what Whitman's writings consistently portray is the freedom to love, for all beings, and with all beings, and that the Christian term 'brotherhood' was the focus of his poems. His 'barbaric yawp' was to take all beings out of slavery and 'Through me forbidden voices,/Voices of sexes and lusts, /. . . Voices indecent' would be 'clarified and transfigur'd'. *DW*

Walt Whitman: The Complete Poems (New York and London: Penguin, 1977)

See also **Carpenter; Christianity; Lawrence; Prostitution; Sensuality**

Wilde, Oscar (1854-1900)

Playwright, esthetician and poet; the son of an Irish patriotic writer and her doctor husband; Oscar Wilde used both university connections and late-Victorian publicity techniques to make himself famous, and only then justified that fame with his work.

Wilde's esthetic position was a development of Walter Pater's cult of perfect form combined with John Ruskin's emphasis on the need for art to be a spiritual nourishment for a wounded society. He reasoned himself into a theoretical support for Socialism based on absolute egoism: a just society is necessary so that the artist will not be continually distracted by the need to relieve human misery. Wilde played with paradox, but many of his paradoxes had a directly subversive edge to them.

His plays and children's stories play constantly with paradox, double lives and real identities. It is appreciation of the beauty of the Baptist's asceticism that leads Salome into an equally arid and self-concerned sensuality; it is leading a double life that makes it possible for Jack Worthing to discover his true identity as Ernest. Dorian Gray leads a variety of lives as seducer, murderer and sensualist and is corrupted by his seeming impunity; it is his attempt to regain unattainable innocence by destroying his portrait that kills him. There was, of course, good reason for Wilde's fascination with this theme: 'He that leads more lives than one/More deaths than one must die.'

In due course Wilde's own double life, as husband and frequenter of rent boys and selfish young aristocrats, was used to make of him a horrid example; new laws against male **homosexuality** were rigidly enforced and he was sentenced to prison. His health was wrecked; the vicious extra penalties imposed by society – the withdrawal of his work, the sequestration of his children – robbed him of any reason to work or live further. He became, for good and ill, a myth of the artist destroyed by the bourgeois world, and of the gay martyr, with a quip ever on the lips and a secret identity in his pocket, ground down by a cruel straight society. It is unfortunate that this has led to a comparative depreciation of his seriousness as a thinker and artist; it is a life and work all of a piece. *RK*

The Happy Prince (Oxford: Oxford University Press, 1980); *Lord Arthur Savile's Crime and Other Stories* (Harmondsworth: Penguin, 1973); *The Picture of Dorian Gray* (New York: Buccaneer Books, 1990; London: Dent, 1990); *Salomé* (London: Faber, 1989); *The Importance of Being Ernest* (Colorado: Fulcrum, 1991; London: Methuen, 1989)

See also **Beardsley**

Wilhelm, Gale (1908-)

Rescued from obscurity by the US lesbian publishing house Naiad, two of Gale Wilhelm's novels were reprinted in the 1980s. Both had originally been published in the 1930s by the respected publisher Random House; Wilhelm's work was mentioned in the first ever index of lesbian writing, *Sex Variant Women in Literature* (1956); and, as Barbara Grier points out in her introduction to the reprint of *We Too Are Drifting*, the literary merit of Wilhelm's books transcends the values of a USA that was in the throes of economic depression and had little, if any, tolerance for **homosexuality**.

Wilhelm was born, raised and educated in Oregon. She completed her education in Washington and followed this with ten years living in San Francisco. In 1935, when her first novel was published, she accepted work as an associate editor of a literary magazine, which necessitated a move to New York. She moved back to San Francisco and has lived in Berkeley since 1948. Both *We Too Are Drifting* (1935) and *Torchlight to Valhalla* (1938) are written in sparse but eloquent prose that gained much praise when the novels were first published. Both deal in characters who, unlike most in the later lesbian novels of Ann **Bannon**, move in circles that are far from being exclusively 'gay'. However, everyone is also far from poor, and all are in some way linked with the arts. The first of the two books has something of a classic bleak ending: having finished a fruitless affair with a married woman, artist Jan Morale has to watch her new love Victoria take a train ride out of her life and into the arms of a more acceptable, heterosexual trainee lawyer. *Torchlight to Valhalla*, on the other hand, ends with two women beginning a committed relationship. On the way, the main protagonist, a successful writer with the androgynous name of Morgan, has to shed the romantic and sexual interest of the pianist Royale. With great sensitivity, Wilhelm portrays the heterosexual act as one in which Morgan is unable to engage emotionally and from which she can obtain no physical pleasure. Even more subtle is the way she shows how little this affects the romantic feelings of Royale, who is devastated when he realizes the lesbian nature of Morgan's new friendship. Of great interest because of when they were written, these two texts offer a glimpse of a **lesbianism** that admitted social sanctions but demonstrated that one need not always abide by them. *CU*

We Too Are Drifting (Tallahassee: Naiad, 1985); *Torchlight to Valhalla* (Tallahassee: Naiad, 1985);

See also **Romantic Fiction; Taylor**

Wilson, Colin (1931-   )

Colin Wilson came to public attention very suddenly, in 1956, with his first book *The Outsider*. To the staid British press, Wilson seemed to be an authentic beatnik – with his polo-necked sweaters, square, black-rimmed glasses and shaggy hair – and he was accorded a great deal of publicity which served to obscure any real criticism of the book.

The Outsider attempted to define a certain sort of 'loner' personality which Wilson argued was symptomatic of twentieth-century alienation. This was a popular theme and Wilson had a rough and ready mix of philosophy and literature to hand. Thus he was considered to be an existentialist. The ecstatic reception afforded his book merely underscored the poor quality of intellectual debate in Britain; it was clear that few people understood contemporary European theorists.

Naturally there was a terrific backlash when the true nature of Wilson's intellectual credentials became clear. He was really interested in subjects without any academic legitimacy, principally criminology (especially when this involved murder) and the occult. He has now published over sixty books in the past thirty-five years, through which there run two main themes. Wilson believes in what Abraham Maslow called 'the dominant five per cent', a Nietzschean concept of natural leaders. Such charismatics can be murderers or mediums. Additionally, Wilson is interested in the search for higher states of consciousness and he sees these as being inextricably linked with sex. In this he is indebted to the works of Wilhelm **Reich** and he has published *The Quest for Wilhelm Reich*, *Origins of the Sexual Impulse* and *Sex and the Intelligent Teenager*. Wilson is particularly concerned with 'peak experiences', another idea derived from Maslow. This refers to occasional moments of hyperreal, super-charged experience, frequently glimpsed at the moment of **orgasm**. Wilson regards his use of others' ideas as evidence of his eclectic genius, whereas most critics see it as merely derivative. *EY*

See also **Crowley**

Winterson, Jeanette (1959-   )

A British lesbian author, Jeanette Winterson won the Whitbread Award for a first novel with *Oranges Are Not the Only Fruit* (1985), a semi-autobiographical account of her working-class childhood in the north of England. The book is a scathing and satirical indictment of the Pentecostal Evangelical church around which the narrator's life is made to revolve, with church becoming the site of conflict when her emerging lesbian sexuality is deemed a sin to be exorcised. Her fight against such repression is told with a mixture of sardonic recollection and incisive wit, while running through the narrative are skillfully crafted passages that employ the language of myth and legend to echo the battles being fought in the present. The text is divided into sections each of which is named after a book in the bible, which it echoes in style. So successful was this first novel that it was dramatized on British television in the winter of 1990. Scripted by the author, the television version left out the mystical interjections but made compelling and often hilarious drama from one young woman's journey to **lesbianism** and independence.

Successive novels have been well received by the critics and sales have enabled Winterson to become a full-time writer. Lesbianism is not the principal concern of these later works because, in relation to sex, Winterson has comments to make across the board. *The Passion* (1987), for instance, shows the passion in adherence to political leaders as well as in heterosexual and lesbian relationships. Set at the time of Napoleon, the narrative makes great play of the enormous shifts that were occurring in western thinking. Human nature, long assumed to be a simple given, was being placed under a new, 'rational' lens and inspected more closely. By subjecting sexual passion to this lens, Winterson is able to explore the relationship between sex and control: one main protagonist, Henri, turns down the offer of escape from prison because he knows that the woman he loves does not love him and he prefers to have some measure of control by staying in a concrete prison rather than living in freedom with the shackles of unrequited desire. Such complexities are communicated in a lucid and accessible style and this novel won Winterson the John Llewelyn Rhys literary prize of 1988.

In *Written on the Body* (1992) gender again takes a back seat as love is explored as a matter of inevitable loss. The sex in the narrative is between women but each relationship is presented as universally human, not specifically lesbian. Winterson nonetheless sees her own sexuality as not unconnected with her literary success. Interviewed in *Spare Rib* (February 1990), she stated: 'I've always said that if I was heterosexual I wouldn't be in this position because I'd have been undermined by a man.'   CU

Oranges Are Not the Only Fruit (New York: Atlantic Monthly, 1987; London: Pandora Press, 1985); *The Passion* (New York: Random House, 1990; Harmondsworth: Penguin, 1988); *Sexing the Cherry* (New York: Random House, 1991; London, Vintage, 1990); *Oranges Are Not the Only Fruit: The Script* (London: Pandora Press, 1990)

See also **Carter**

Wittig, Monique (1935-   )

Monique Wittig was born in the Haut-Rhin region of France and has lived and worked in Paris and the USA. Her first novel, *L'Opoponax* (1964), won her the prestigious Prix Médicis and was hailed by Marguerite Duras as 'the first modern book written about childhood'. It also heralds many of the concerns of Wittig's later writing, in particular a strong evocation of the power of female communities and of lesbian love.

Les Guérillères/The Guérillères (1969) is an account of a war of the sexes which is eventually won by the women. Its form is experimental: the narrative is fragmented, consisting of short lower-case passages, lists of women's names, poems and large black circles. The latter can be seen as symbolizing the vulva and, indeed, the text as a whole draws attention to the ways in which the female body has been represented and named. In that it is patriarchal, this process of representation is attacked and subverted: the symbols are set free, made to work with and for the warrior-women.

In all her later writings, Wittig aims to bring the lesbian subject into existence. *Le Corps lesbien/ The Lesbian Body* (1973) is a series of poems and fragments passionately exploring, dismantling and recreating the body in love. The poems are written in 'I-you' form but the 'I' is slashed ('j/e' in French), which hints both at the power of lesbian love which splits and recreates the lover's self, and at the problematic status of lesbian identity in a heteroppressive society. The violence of some of the poems is the subject of controversy among readers, but for Elaine Marks it is a vital and life-giving aspect of Wittig's task: '(D)estruction of one order of language and sensibility implies creation of a new order. The J/e of *Le Corps lesbien* is the most powerful lesbian in literature because as a lesbian-feminist she reexamines and redesigns the universe . . . She is, in fact, the only true anti-Christ, the willful assassin of Christian love.' This shift of perspective also underpins *Brouillon pour un dictionnaire des amantes/Lesbian People's Material for a Dictionary* (1976), written with Sande Zeig, an encyclopedic look at an exclusively lesbian world which weaves together myth and history, and *Virgile, non/Across the Acheron* (1985), a rewriting of Dante's *Inferno*.

VH

L'Opoponax (Paris: Editions de Minuit, 1964); *Les Guérillères/ The Guérillères* (Paris: Editions de Minuit, 1969; London: Peter Owen, 1971); *Le Corps lesbien/ The Lesbian Body* (Paris: Editions de Minuit, 1973; New York: Avon, 1975); *Brouillon pour un dictionnaire des amantes/ Lesbian People's Material for a Dictionary* (Paris: Grasset, 1976; London: Virago, 1979); *Virgile, non/Across the Acheron* (Paris: Editions de Minuit, 1985; London: Peter Owen, 1987)

See also **Brossard; Irigaray; Lesbianism; Lorde; Radicalesbianism; Stein**

Women Against Violence Against Women

Women Against Violence Against Women (WAVAW) was a nationwide anti-male-violence campaign which flourished in Britain in the early 1980s. It was set up at a Leeds women's conference on sexual violence in 1981, a year which coincided with the horrific multiple murders of women in the Yorkshire area by Peter Sutcliffe (the Yorkshire Ripper). There was felt to be a need for a campaigning group to supplement the practical 'rescue' work done by rape crisis centers and women's aid.

For a time WAVAW seemed to be the most visible and vocal feminist organization in the country. Although some groups were diverse in composition, there was a hard core of WAVAW activists who identified as revolutionary feminists and held sway over the organization as a whole. This led to WAVAW becoming the target of stinging criticisms from socialist feminists, in particular over issues relating to **pornography** and censorship. In fact, few WAVAW members endorsed censorship. They tended to favor civil disobedience and consciousness raising among women rather than a legislative response to pornography. WAVAW women picketed the trials of women who had killed in 'self-defense' as well as those of rapists and murderers of women; they picketed sex shops and newsagents stocking pornography and organized 'Reclaim the Night' marches. The 'guerilla wing' of WAVAW called itself 'Angry Women' and engaged in bold, direct action: it hurled paint-bombs at cinema screens showing violent, misogynist movies; went in groups to confront rapists who had been freed by the courts; fire-bombed sex shops; publicised descriptions of child-sex-abusers.

Some feminists felt that the WAVAW emphasis on the most brutal manifestations of male sexuality was disempowering to women; they believed that feminists should not lose sight of female pleasure as well as female victimization. Angry confrontations took place between 'pro-pleasure' and 'anti-male-violence' feminists throughout the 1980s especially in the context of US and British debates around pornography. Such polarizations were anathema to feminists who wanted simultaneously to fight male violence and affirm women's right to sexual pleasure.

WAVAW was spent as a strong political force within a few years of its inception. Some ex-members would claim that it foundered on the rocks of a narrow political agenda which was set by its 'informal' revolutionary feminist leadership. Others would attribute its demise to the growth of libertarian sexual attitudes among feminists.   JE

See also **Rape; Russell**

Women's Co-operative Guild

The Women's Co-operative Guild was formed in 1883 for women in the English consumers' co-operative movement. The majority of its members – 10,000 in 1897 and 30,000 by 1914 – were the wives of manual workers, a social group that had not previously been organized to promote its own interests. Accordingly, alongside its co-operative work, the Guild gradually developed a distinctive role advocating the rights of working-class women.

The Guild's concern with the condition of women as wives and mothers, as well as citizens and workers, led it to investigate married life, laying bare the seamier side of sexual relations hemmed in by poverty, overwork and a lack of **contraception**. The material collected by Guild members and presented to the Royal Commission on Divorce Law Reform in 1910 broke through the convention that marital relations should not be discussed in public and provides some of the earliest evidence we have about the sexual experience of working-class women. Predictably enough, pleasure is not one of its points of reference.

The existing divorce laws, enacted in 1857, illustrated the inequalities of class and gender underpinning Victorian society. Whereas a man could divorce his wife for a single act of **adultery**, a woman, assuming she was in a position to fight a

legal battle at all, had to prove cruelty or desertion as well as adultery. For most of the population the high cost of divorce made separation the only available course of action, ruling out the possibility of remarriage. The Guild's research demonstrated that, in a society which denied women legal protection and financial safeguards against oppressive husbands, the suffering experienced inside failed marriages was 'very much more on the side of women than on the side of men'. As the Guild's general secretary, Margaret **Llewelyn Davies** pointed out: 'No woman could inflict on a man the amount of degradation that a man may force on a woman.'

Guildswomen reported cases where 'a woman ill-used and kicked, has taken her husband back five times; of a diseased husband compelling co-habitation [**sexual intercourse**], resulting in deficient children; of excessive co-habitation regardless of the wife's health; of a man frightening his wife during pregnancy in order to bring on miscarriage.' In one particularly harrowing letter, a woman related how her first child had been born when her husband was out of work and the marriage already in ruins: 'The tenth day after the baby was born he came home drunk and compelled me to submit to him. Of course I had no strength and was at his mercy . . . Babies came rather fast. Then I got told I was like a rabbit for breeding and drugs was obtained, as he did not want children, although I was compelled to submit . . . I was so badly treated that when I knew my condition for the fourth time, I took something which nearly ended my existence. It poisoned me.'

As one Guildswoman asked: 'Is it not more degrading for these women to be living what is, after all, legalized prostitution, than for them to be divorced?' Yet the reforms recommended by the Guild – a cheapening of legal procedure, a removal of the sexual double standard and the inclusion of such grounds for divorce as mutual consent and serious incompatibility – took more than half a century to become statutory. Such proposals challenged the dominant view that a woman's duty was to fulfil her biological function as a childbearer.

Instead, the Guild underlined the need for legal changes and improvements in the economic position of women which would enable them to 'respect themselves more and really look upon their bodies as their own property and not so soon give in to the brutal desires of lazy, selfish men', objectives which remain fundamental to the struggle for sexual equality. *GS*

Ed. Margaret Llewelyn Davies, introductory letter by Virginia Woolf *Life as We Have Known It by Co-operative Working Women* (London: Virago, 1977)

See also **Marital Rape**

Women's Images Of Men

Women's Images of Men was an exhibition held at the Institute of Contemporary Arts in London in 1980 in which twenty-nine women artists revealed their perceptions of masculinity to outcries from male critics: 'An aura of sensationalism, of penises for penises' sake,' complained the *Guardian* newspaper. In fact, the penis was absent from most of the works, which dealt with male role-playing, the male body beautiful, the vulnerable male, male tyranny and male blindness. The artists depicted sexuality with humor, **sensuality** and violence.

Jo Brocklehurst, *Don, The Urban Cowboy II*, 1978

Mandy Havers, for example, used leather to present the muscles of the male torso as a gleaming, dark skin; 'Framed Figure' (1980) is a torso fixed to a frame, strong but also helpless, which addresses the links between lust and the victimized object.

Issues raised by the recurrent images of 'invalided men' in women's art are explored in a book, edited by Sarah Kent and Jacqueline **Morreau**, which grew out of the exhibition: *Women's Images of Men* (London: Pandora, 1990). The book also asks questions about picturing the male as erotic object. Can women present the male as gently sensual without denying his masculine power? Do male pin-up images merely reverse sexual power relations? Can women invent a language to depict a desirable male nude? What is a desirable male nude? *FB*

See also **Beale; Neel; Voyeurism**

Woolf, Virginia

See Orlando

Wright, Helena (1887-1982)

A British family-planning pioneer, and perhaps the country's first sex therapist, Helena Wright was born in Brixton and trained at the London School of Medicine for Women. Having held posts in various hospitals, at the end of the First World War she traveled to China with her surgeon husband, where the two of them worked as medical missionaries in Tsinan.

Wright's involvement with the birth-control movement began on her return to Britain in the late 1920s. First she established a training center where doctors, midwives, nurses and others could learn to give contraceptive advice; then, in 1930, she obtained from the church its qualified approval of birth control for married women, and obtained from the minister of health permission to provide birth-control advice in public welfare clinics. In the same year her first book was published. Called *The Sex Factor in Marriage*, it was in many ways a radical work. Not only did it defiantly assert that 'the attainment of complete sex-pleasure in a woman is the fine flowering of a healthy body' but, outrageously for the time, pointed out that 'the only purpose of the clitoris is to provide sensation; a full understanding of its capabilities and place in the sex-act is therefore of supreme importance'. In short, like many women involved in promoting knowledge of **contraception**, she was at least as much concerned with women's right to unfrightened sexual pleasure as with the more usual male preoccupation with limiting the population.

There were, however, problems with *The Sex Factor in Marriage*. Although it sold over one million copies and was reprinted eleven times between 1930 and 1942, readers consistently complained to Wright that, follow her instructions as they might, they still could not achieve an **orgasm**. Wright had insisted that all that was needed for women to reach a climax through **sexual intercourse** was that their **clitoris** should constantly be in contact with the man's body and that their hips should be allowed to move freely. In *More About the Sex Factor in Marriage* (1947), she confronted the idea that intercourse itself might not be perfectly designed for women's sexual pleasure. First she questioned the male belief that, during penetration, 'women will have an answering orgasm felt in the vagina induced by the movement of the penis', adding that 'so strongly held and widespread is this expectation that it can be said to amount to a penis-vagina fixation'. 'I began to criticize this universal demand . . . as soon as I began to shake myself free of the current ideal and expectations, and to doubt the efficacy of the penis-vagina combination for producing an orgasm for a woman, the path was cleared and progress began to be made.' Cleared the path might be but, needless to say, it was not one along which most of Wright's fellow professionals wanted to travel. It wasn't until there was too much supportive evidence even for them to ignore – via the later research of Alfred **Kinsey** and **Masters and John-**son, among others – and a women's movement to make sure that it got publicized, that Wright was finally vindicated; if, by and large, forgotten.   *HG*

See also **Besant; Koedt; Sanger; Stopes**

X, Laura

The feminist activist Laura X was at the forefront of the US women's liberation movement, editing and writing in its early newspapers and, in 1968, founding the Women's History Library in Berkeley, California. The library was not only used for research by writers such as Susan Griffin and Susan Brownmiller (the latter for *Against Our Will*) but, because there were no other women's centers or services in the country, became a women's refuge as well.

Laura was also responsible for the International Women's History Periodical Archive – nicknamed 'Herstory' – a collection of almost a million documents recording the voices of the women's liberation movement (theorists and activists) on subjects that range from women and health, women and mental health, women and law through to issues of color, **lesbianism, prostitution**, and even the epidemic of male impotence allegedly caused by the women's movement. Now published on microfilm, the archive is currently available in three hundred libraries in fourteen countries.

Because of its function as a refuge, the Women's History Library gave its volunteers an early awareness of the violence suffered by women: testimonies of battery and **rape** were documented there long before the subjects were taken up by the popular media. The library dispersed in 1974, but the work of collecting information on violence and on the abuse of women and girls was continued. Then, in 1978, there occurred the famous Rideout trial – the first in the USA where a husband was prosecuted for raping his wife while they were living together – and Laura saw a need to found the National Clearing House on Marital and Date Rape and to campaign, in California first, to make **marital rape** a crime.

Laura has been accused of turning the world upside down, because, after her successful 1979 campaign in California, there were forty-four states where marital rape was *not* a crime and, by the end of 1990, there were forty-four states where it *was*. Date rape, too, has moved from being a crime in forty-five states to being a crime in forty-nine, while rape by a cohabiter has moved from being a crime in thirty-seven states to forty-five.

Women's testimonies are once again heard as Laura invites them to share the platform with her on college campuses, legislative hearings and pulpits; she sees herself as a medium and a catalyst for empowering women to speak. Her most important contribution to feminist thinking about sex and rape, she believes, is her discovery that she (among others) had gone too far in thinking that rape was 'violence, not sex'. 'Yes, we wanted, in the mid-1970s, to get people away from thinking that "boys will be boys", "just trying to give a girl a good time", "totally controlled by their biological drives". It took the battered women speaking out to remind us of the sexual kick in violence, especially the woman on the program *Battered Wives, Shattered Lives* who said that her husband could not have an erection without beating her.'   *MS*

See also **Llewelyn Davies; Russell**

Yin and Yang

In China, sexual and gender relationships have, until quite recently, been popularly described as the complementary opposition of *yin* and *yang*: the cosmic principles that denote the weak and the strong, the female and the male, darkness and light. Early classical texts stressed that **sexual intercourse** was a manifestation of the cosmic forces of *yin* and *yang* and, as such, the foundation of universal life.

Sex, therefore, was ideally a harmonious meeting of different but complementary forces. Popular thought further suggested that the mutual interaction of *yin* and *yang* was a source of physical vitality and longevity. In immoderation, however, the harmonious balance between the two forces was lost. When not required for the purposes of reproduction, ejaculation was considered excessive and wasteful. Ideally, as Robert Van Gulik pointed out in his famous book *Sexual Life in Ancient China*, male retention of the *yang* essence by non-ejaculation was considered a means of attaining immortality. *Yang* essence could also be impaired by an excess of *yin* essence; many a story is told of the debilitating effects on men of over-indulgence in sexual activity with women.

While the female *yin* essence, in moderation, was thought to be beneficial to the male, it was also associated with polluting and dangerous powers. Menstrual blood, for instance, was considered a harmful *yin* essence and, to this day in China, sexual intercourse during menstruation is considered debilitating, if not positively dangerous. Similarly, during pregnancy and during the month of confinement after childbirth, male contact with female essences has been thought to be harmful to the male. Despite its apparent acceptance of the importance of female pleasure, the notion of harmony and balance in Chinese tradition was always assymmetrical. The female was invariably treated as the dependent and recipient of male action, while the bias was always towards preserving male strength and maximizing male pleasure.   *HE*

Robert Van Gulik *Sexual Life in Ancient China* (Leiden: Brill, 1974)

See also **Heterosexuality**

Yu Luojin

The Chinese writer Yu Luojin became, in 1980, a cause célèbre when she published a story describing her experiences of love, marriage and divorce. The revelations in 'A Winter's Fairy Tale' caused a sensation among university students and young urban dwellers, for they broke official and literary taboos by describing the social, moral and sexual pressures to which women in China commonly were, and still are, subject.

At the beginning of the Cultural Revolution in 1966, both Yu's parents (who had been labeled class enemies during 1957) lost their jobs. Her elder brother was arrested and eventually executed for his political activities, while Yu herself was condemned as a reactionary and eventually sent to 'reform through labor' in Hebei province. In response to her parents' pressure, Yu married a man for the advantages that his connections and wealth would bring to her parents, yet she never loved him and refused to sleep with him after their wedding night. After some years she met and fell in love with another man and gained a divorce in order that she might marry him. His parents, however, refused to allow their son to marry a woman who was both a reactionary and a divorcée. She thus found herself treated as an outcast, the object of scorn and moral condemnation. In 1977 she again married for convenience, in order to transfer her residence to Beijing, and there she fell in love again with a man who was more than twenty years her senior. She moved out of her husband's house and, despite his attempts to prevent it, was granted a second divorce.

For some people, Yu's case made her the symbol of the 'liberated woman' unintimidated by social opprobrium. For others, she symbolized the manipulative schemer, ready to use any opportunity to get what she wanted. And yet, despite the moral outrage voiced by her critics, her autobiography demonstrated some of the real difficulties encountered by young people, especially women, in China, when making choices concerning their affective and sexual lives. It showed that social and material considerations are still paramount in marriage, often with tragic consequences. It raised a series of questions about the meaning of love and sexual attraction, through exposing what passed for marital affection as little more than mutual use. It also indicated the need for the 'alienation of affection' clause, recently introduced in the Marriage Law of 1980, and the continuing difficulties of divorced women who, as the object of social scorn, suffer considerable discrimination in housing and employment.

Since Yu Luojin, a number of other women writers have begun to write about their experiences in love and marriage, of the horrors women have to endure in undergoing semi-coerced abortions, of the emptiness of loveless marriages and the difficulties endured by women who decide to remain unmarried. Between them, they have taken the first steps to opening up a debate about sexuality and love which has been absent from Chinese literature since 1949.   HE

Ed. Michael Duke *Modern Chinese Women Writers: Critical Appraisals* (London: M.E. Sharp, 1989)

See also **Chinese Marriage Laws; Das; Hui**

Zetterling, Mai (1925-   )

Internationally known as an actress, the Swede Mai Zetterling turned to directing in 1963. Having made several short documentaries, she completed her first feature film, *Älskande par/Loving Couples*, in 1966. It was based on a seven-volume novel written in the 1930s by the Swedish author Agnes von Krusenstjerna. Krusenstjerna, who has been called 'the Swedish Proust', deals in her novels with women's sexuality, especially the problems of growing into adulthood, and with madness as a response to repressed desire. Zetterling's sympathetic adaptation puts an emphasis on the theme of women being closely related to life's extremes.

Another great Zetterling theme, lust and loneliness, is treated in films such as *Doktor Glas/Doctor Glas* (1967) and *Nattlek/Night Games* (1966). The latter was adapted from Zetterling's own novel and deals with a young man haunted by childhood memories of a dissipated mother. Sexual excess, for Zetterling, seems to imply the loss of love; this has nothing to do with morals, however, but is rather the result of a logic which, in Zetterling's view, is inherent to love itself.

In *Flickorna/Girls* (1968) Zetterling deals ironically with the relations between the sexes, telling the story of a theater troup rehearsing Aristophanes's *Lysistrata*, about women on a love strike. As in *Loving Couples*, three women are at the center of the movie, complementing and contrasting with each other. Analyzing their parts in the play and fantasizing together, they gradually discover the play's connections to their own lives and relations with men. From this point on, the women's attempts at unmasking, provoking and confronting their partners expose the male inability for deeper sexual and emotional involvement.

In *Amorosa* (1986) Zetterling returns to Krusenstjerna in a film based on biographical material mingled with fictional episodes from her novels. In her autobiography *Osminkat/All Those Tomorrows* (Stockholm: Norstedts, 1984), Zetterling reveals the obvious connections between herself and Krusenstjerna. Both have focused in their work upon women's sexual relations, women faced with marriage, the links between women's sexuality and childbirth, women as prisoners in a male-defined world, the language that women do not master. Stylistically, Zetterling's cinematic work is characterized by the juxtaposition of contrasting elements: on the one hand, scenes of great sparsity; on the other, a markedly symbolic imagery combined with naturalistic details. Her straightforward and often provocative way of showing obsession, sexuality and desire has been much criticized; as have her deliberately feminist intentions. *ASW*

Älskande par/Loving Couples (1966); *Nattlek/Night Games* (1966); *Doktor Glas/Doctor Glas* (1967); *Flickorna/Girls* (1968); *Amorosa* (1986)

See also **Repression**

Zola, Émile (1840-1902)

Misunderstood through much of his life as a novelist who reveled in the sordid – in one view, in order to expose ugly social injustice; in another, in order to titillate middle-class readers with working-class brutishness – Émile Zola was more concerned with describing human existence as a natural evolution, a process of struggle, flux and progress in rhythm with plant and animal life. Although he was born in Paris and lived there for most of the time he was writing, his 'naturalism' was influenced by childhood periods in Provence, so that his fictional townscapes teem less with socially ordered comings and goings than with massive, organic energy.

And nature, for Zola, meant female. Thus the women in his books are not so much people as symbols of hope, fertility, barrenness, destruction. The prostitute Nana in his novel of that title (published in 1880 as part of the twenty-volume *Rougon-Macquart* series) is, to some extent, a social being, a woman who earns her living as she does because of poverty and early sexual exploitation; but more, and much more powerfully, she is the natural disaster awaiting a greedy and decadent Second Empire. Zola describes her career like this: 'The fly that had flown up from the ordure of the slums, bringing with it the ferments of social decay, had poisoned all these men by merely alighting on them. It was well done – it was just. She had avenged the beggars and the wastrels from whose cast she issued . . . her sex rose in a halo of glory and beamed over prostrate victims like a mounting sun . . .' Nana's death from smallpox, one of the most disgusting scenes in literature, is not the traditional punishment given by authors to strong-minded heroines but Zola's warning to his country.

Like most of those who, in art or life, conflate the 'female' with the 'natural', Zola was most at ease with the idea of women as mothers and nurturers, as distinct from as sexual beings with needs of their own. In many respects a courageous man, notably in protesting against the cynical, antisemitic 'Dreyfus Affair', his often sexually graphic novels are more revealing of nineteenth-century male fears than of female experience. *HG*

Thérèse Raquin (Cambridge, MA: Schoenhof, 1970; Harmondsworth: Penguin n.e. 1992); *Les Rougon-Macquart* (Cambridge, MA: Schoenhof, 1960-1968)

See also **Flaubert; Klimt; Manet; Prostitution**

The Contributors

YA   Yasmin Alibhai was born and brought up in Uganda, part of that dispossessed, far-flung Asian diaspora. She went to university there and was then forced to move to Britain as a refugee when Idi Amin expelled all Asians living in Uganda. An M.Phil. at Oxford in nineteenth-century literature followed and then the best thing of all, the birth of her lovely son Ari. She taught English to immigrants and foreign students for a few years and went on to become a journalist, writing mainly on racism, joining the staff of *New Society* (and then the *New Statesman and Society*) in 1987. She is now working for the BBC and also doing some more ambitious writing.

PA   Penny Ashbrook was born in Manchester in 1954. She is a freelance television producer and director who has contributed several items to Channel Four's lesbian and gay series *Out*. She was co-programmer of the London Lesbian and Gay Film Festival between 1989 and 1992, and for seven years was a programmer of London's Ritzy Cinema.

EB   Eleanor J. Bader is a teacher, editor and freelance writer from New York City. She has been a reproductive rights activist since the late 1970s and writes for progressive and feminist publications including *Belles Lettres, The Guardian, In These Times, Lilith, New Directions for Women* and *On the Issues*.

JB   Josephine Balmer is a freelance writer, translator and lecturer on classical civilization. She has published many translations and articles and her work includes *Sappho: Poems and Fragments* (London: Brilliance Books, 1984; Secaucus, NJ: Lyle Stuart, 1988).

AB   Adrianne Blue, an American who lives in London, is the author of four books on sport. She has written on sport and literary subjects for the *Sunday Times*, the *New Statesman*, *Vogue*, *Ms* magazine and *The Washington Post*.

FB   Frances Borzello is the author of *The Artist's Model* (London: Junction Books, 1982), *Women Artists: A Graphic Guide* (London: Camden Press, 1986), *Civilising Caliban: The Misuse of Art 1875-1980* (London: Routledge, 1987) and is the editor with A.L. Rees of *The New Art History* (London: Camden Press, 1986).

NOB   Nancee Oku Bright is a social anthropologist born in Liberia and educated at Wesleyan, Georgetown and Oxford Universities. She has worked for the United Nations and World Health Organization and has written for *The Guardian, The Independent, West Africa* and *New Statesman and Society*.

LBr   Lyndie Brimstone lives in London with her 'pretend family' and is currently preparing a full-length study of twentieth-century lesbian writing. She has contributed to a number of journals and critical anthologies including *Lesbian and Gay Writing* (London: Macmillan, 1990) edited by Mark Lilly, *What Lesbians Do In Books* (London: The Women's Press, 1991) edited by Elaine

Hobby and Chris White, and *Out of the Margins: Women's Studies in the Nineties* (London: Falmer Press, 1991) edited by Jane Aaron and Sylvia Walby.

LBu   Louisa Buck is a freelance journalist, broadcaster and art historian, specializing in twentieth-century art. After reading history of art at Cambridge University and the Courtauld Institute of Art she worked at the Tate Gallery, Bonham's auctioneers and *City Limits* magazine. She is currently a presenter for BBC Radio 4's *Kaleidoscope*, a regular contributor to *New Statesman and Society*, and a contributing editor of *GQ*. She has lectured on the visual arts at the Tate Gallery, the Royal Academy, Reading University and the Royal College of Art.

SB   Sandra Buckley teaches in the Department of East Asian Studies at McGill University, Montreal, Canada.

SuB   Susan Butler is a freelance writer and curator currently lecturing part-time on the MA Fine Art, Cardiff. She is a former editor of *Creative Camera* (1984-1986) and curated 'Shifting Focus' (1989, Arnolfini Gallery, Bristol and Serpentine Gallery, London), an international exhibition of recent photo-based work by women.

MC   Margaret M. Caffrey is an assistant professor in the Department of History, Memphis State University, Memphis, Tennessee, USA, with special interests in American history and Women's Studies. She is the author of *Ruth Benedict: Stranger in this Land*.

AC   Angela Carter died in February 1992. She was among the most important, intelligent, *enjoyable* novelists this century (for details, see entry about her in the body of this book). For the note about her here, she asked to be described as 'a middle-aged

writer who lives in London'. She is painfully missed.

SC   Scarlet Cheng has written frequently about film, books and the arts for various publications including *The Washington Post*, *The World & I* and *Asian Wall Street Journal*. She is currently the managing editor of *Asian Art News*, a leading magazine on the visual arts in Asia. Before locating to Hong Kong in 1992, she worked for Time-Life Books in Washington, D.C., for ten years.

LC   Leighton Cole is an American who has lived in Britain since 1968. She has a Diploma in Social Anthropology from University College, London. She is currently teaching anthropology and sociology at the City Lit and is a tutor/counselor at the Open University.

DC   Diana Collecott teaches American and British literature at the University of Durham, England. Her doctorate is from the University of Bristol and she has held research fellowships at Yale University for work in the manuscript collections there. She has contributed widely to journals and international symposia on modernism, feminist poetics and gay textuality, and is about to publish a full-length study of H.D.

RC   Ros Coward was a university lecturer in media studies and is now mainly looking after her family and working as a freelance writer. She is the author of *Female Desire* (London: Paladin, 1984) and *The Whole Truth: The Myth of Alternative Health* (London: Faber, 1989).

JD   Jane Dibblin earns her living as a writer, teacher, counselor and documentary filmmaker. She has published two books, *Day of Two Suns: US Nuclear Testing and the Pacific Islanders* (Virago) and *Wherever I Lay My Hat: Young Women and Homelessness*

(Shelter). She is currently working on a collection of short stories.

LD   Leslie Dick is an American writer who has lived in London since 1965. Her first novel, *Without Falling* (London: Serpent's Tail) was published in 1987, and her second *Kicking* (London: Secker & Warburg) in 1992. A collection of her stories, *The Skull of Charlotte Corday and Other Stories*, will appear in 1994.

jD   jay Dixon worked in publishing for ten years, including two at Mills & Boon, and for the last seven years has been researching the development of the romances published by Mills & Boon from their first year of operation, 1909, to 1989.

ED   Efua Dorkenoo is Ghanaian and an experienced health educator. She has been active in campaigns to improve women's health and to prevent female genital mutilation/circumcision. She has researched female circumcision in more than six African countries and works with grassroots African groups training and supporting self-help health-promotion activities. She has written extensively on African women's health and acts as an advisory consultant to many international and national groups.

CD   Carol Anne Douglas has been on the staff of the Washington DC-based feminist newspaper *off our backs* since 1973. She has written a book on feminist theory, *Love and Politics: Radical Feminist and Lesbian Theories* (San Francisco: ism press, 1990).

SD   Susan Dowell is a writer/journalist, Christian, mother (of four) and clergy wife. She is also co-Chair and publications editor of Christian CND and, since moving to Shropshire, a wine-maker. She is the author of *They Two Shall Be One: Monogamy in Reli-*

gion and History (London: Collins, 1990) and has edited and contributed to a number of other publications.

MD   Maureen Duffy was educated at King's College, London. A novelist, poet, playwright and activist for writers' rights, she has also written books on Aphra Behn, Virginia Woolf and Faery.

FE   Felicity Edholm has spent too long writing a biography of Suzanne Valadon. She also works for the Open University and tries to paint.

JE   Jane Egerton is currently working as a TV researcher and freelance writer. She has been active in lesbian and feminist politics for a decade, drifting from libertarian Marxism through revolutionary feminism to a place of eclectic confusion. She co-edited *Inventing Ourselves* (London: Routledge, 1989), a lesbian oral-history anthology.

HE   Harriet Evans lectures in modern Chinese history and Women's Studies at the University of Westminster. Her doctoral dissertation was on 'The Official Construction of Female Sexuality and Gender in the People's Republic of China, 1949-1959'. Her current research is on issues of gender and sexuality in post-Mao China. Among her publications are *La Historia Moderna de China desde 1800* (Mexico, 1989) and articles on women and gender in contemporary China.

ME   Mary Evans was educated at the London School of Economics and the University of Sussex. She teaches sociology and Women's Studies at the University of Kent at Canterbury and is the author of various books and editions, including *Jane Austen and the State* (London: Tavistock, 1987) and *Simone de Beauvoir: A Feminist Mandarin* (London: Tavistock, 1985).

LG   Lyn Gardner was the theatre editor of *City Limits* magazine.

EG   Elizabeth Grosz is Director of the Institute for Critical and Cultural Studies at Monash University in Australia. She is the author of *Sexual Subversions: Three French Feminists* (Sydney: Allen & Unwin, 1989), *Jacques Lacan: A Feminist Introduction* (London: Routledge, 1990) and *Volatile Bodies. Towards A Corporeal Feminism* (Bloomington: Indiana University Press, 1993).

DH   Diana Hamer is an Australian feminist living and working in London. She is doing postgraduate research in the Department of Cultural Studies at Birmingham University in between working as a television researcher. To date she has worked on *Out on Tuesday*, *The Media Show* and *Verdict*. She also teaches women's studies, lesbian and gay history and media studies in adult education.

KH   Kate Hamlyn was born in 1957. To date she has been a clerk, a secretary, a nanny, a teacher, a financial researcher, a merchant banker and a financial journalist. Nothing has ever lasted more than two years. Redundancy has now convinced her to do what *she* wants. If not now, when? She graduated in Latin and Greek from University College London.

VH   Valerie Hannagan teaches French at Queen Mary and Westfield College, University of London, and has been studying contemporary French women's writing since 1982. She writes poetry, literary criticism and essays on the experience of writing creatively as a woman. Her publications include 'Writing as a Daughter: Chantal Chawaf Revisited' in *Contemporary French Fiction by Women: Feminist Perspectives* (Manchester University Press, 1990), edited by Atack and Powrie.

MH   Madeleine Harmsworth is the film reviewer and the letters page editor of the *Sunday Mirror*. She has written for The *Guardian*, The *Telegraph*, the *New Statesman* and *The Times*.

AH   Alison Hennegan is a freelance writer.

LH   Liz Heron is a writer and translator. She edited *Truth, Dare or Promise: Girls Growing Up In the Fifties* (London: Virago, 1985) and is the author of *Changes of Heart: Reflections on Women's Independence* (London: Pandora, 1986). As a photography critic, she has written widely for many years contributing to British and US publications. Her most recent book is the anthology *Streets of Desire: Women's Fictions of the Twentieth Century* (London, Virago, 1993).

GH   Ginger Hjelmaa has degrees from Stanford University and the University of Newcastle upon Tyne. Her PhD was on *EM Forster's Fictional Sources: A Study of the Edwardian Novel*. She now teaches at Kilburn College in Brent.

AmH   Amanda Hopkinson is a freelance journalist and translator. She has written, broadcast and lectured widely on Latin American culture and edits the human rights magazine *Central America Report*. Her most recent books, to coincide with exhibitions she curated at the Photographers' Gallery, London, include *The Forbidden Rainbow* and *Desires and Disguises* (London: Serpent's Tail, 1992).

AkH   Akemi Horie is a theater director and heads the experimental theater group Workshop 5. She also lectures in Japanese drama at SOAS, University of London, and recently organized the International Theatre Symposium on Japanese Theatre and the West, held at the ICA, London. She is currently writing a book on Early Kabuki & Folk Religious Rites.

MyH   Myra Hunter is a clinical psychologist specializing in women's health at University College Hospital, London and a research fellow at Guy's Hospital Medical School. She has counseled menopausal women for many years and at King's College Hospital set up the South East England menopause project – the results of which have received international recognition and challenge traditional ideas about this phase of life. She lives in London with her husband and twin daughters.

SH   Shahrukh Husain is a practicing psychotherapist and lectures and writes on the Indian cinema, Asian women writers, mythology and folklore. Among her publications are *Urdu Literature* (Third World Pubns., 1986), *Demons, Gods and Holy Men from Indian Myth and Legend* (London: Eurobook, 1986), *Focus on India* (London: Hamish Hamilton, 1986), *Exploring Indian Food* (London: Mantra Publishing, 1988) and her forthcoming *Virago Book of Witches*, to be published by Virago in October 1993. Her screenplay adaptation of Anita Desai's *In Custody* is in production with Merchant Ivory Productions.

DJ   Darcie Conner Johnston has been an editor for *Belles Lettres: A Review of Books by Women* since 1986, and currently supports herself as a science writer for Time-Life Books and as a singer-songwriter. Originally from the Colorado Rockies, she now lives with her two children in the Washington DC area.

RK   Roz Kaveney is a journalist, author and publishers' reader living in London.

ALT   Aileen La Tourette is the author of *Nuns*

and *Mothers* and *Cry Wolf* (London: Virago, 1984 and 1986 respectively), of five radio plays broadcast on BBC Radio 4 and a collection of short stories with Sara Maitland, *Weddings and Funerals*. She has recently finished her third novel and is working on a book about the Blessed (un)virgin Mary. She is married to David Cohen and has two sons, Nicholas and Reuben.

SL   Sarah Lefanu has co-edited two anthologies of original fiction, *Despatches from the Frontiers of the Female Mind* (London: The Women's Press, 1985) and *Colours of a New Day: Writing for South Africa* (Lawrence and Wishart, 1990) and is the author of *In The Chinks of the World Machine: Feminism and Science Fiction* (London: The Women's Press, 1988).

GCL   Gail Ching-Liang Low is a postgraduate student at the University of East Anglia completing her thesis on colonialism and representation. She has taught nineteenth-century women's studies, popular culture, black literature and film part-time at both UEA and the University of Southampton.

SM   Sara Maitland is the author and editor of various books, both fiction and non-fiction, including *Vesta Tilley* (London: Virago, 1987), a cultural study of female cross-dressing, and, most recently, the novel *Home Truths* (London: Chatto & Windus, 1993). She is also a feminist theologian. She lives in east London.

MM   Mary McIntosh teaches sociology at the University of Essex. She has been involved in the National Deviancy Symposium, the Gay Liberation Front, the Women's Liberation Campaign for Financial and Legal Independence and *Feminist Review*. She published 'The Homosexual Role' in 1968 and has also written on social policy and on the family from a Marxist and feminist perspective.

TM   Toni McNaron is a professor of English and Women's Studies at the University of Minnesota where she has taught for 26 years. Her publications include *Voices in the Night: Women Speaking About Incest* (Cleis Press, 1982), *The Sister Bond: A Feminist View of a Timeless Connection* (London: Pergamon Press, 1985), articles on Virginia Woolf, lesbian literature and culture, and Feminist pedagogy. Her autobiography, *I Dwell in Possibility*, was published by the Feminist Press in 1991. Her interests include jogging, travel, gardening and household carpentry.

SMe   Sheryl L. Meyering teaches American literature at Southern Illinois University at Edwardsville. She has edited *Charlotte Perkins Gilman: The Woman and Her Work* (Ann Arbor, Michigan: UMI Research Press, 1989) and authored *Sylvia Plath: A Reference Guide, 1973-1988* (Boston: G.K. Hall, 1990). She is currently working on *A Reader's Guide to the Short Stories of Willa Cather*.

NM   Noriko Mizuta received her PhD in American Studies from Yale University in 1970. She is currently a professor of English and American literature and the director of the Center for Inter-Cultural Studies and Education at Josai University, Japan. Among her published works are *Heroine kara hero e: josei no jiga to hyogen/From Heroine to Hero: Female Ego and Expression* (Tokyo: Tabata Shoten, 1982), *Tsumi to yume: Edgar Allan Poe no sekai/Crime and Dream: A Study of Edgar Allan Poe* (Tokyo: Kenkyusha, 1982) and *Kagami no naka no sakuran: Sylvia Plath shisen to hyoron/A Disturbance in Mirrors: The Poetry of Sylvia Plath* (Tokyo: Seichisha, 1985). She

was co-editor and translator of *Stories by Contemporary Japanese Women Writers* (M.E. Sharp, 1982) and editor of *Josei to kazoku no henyo/Women and the Family* (Tokyo: Gakuyo Shobo, 1990).

CM   Carole Morin was born in Glasgow and went to school in New York. She studied at Harvard then worked briefly as Associate Editor of *Granta* Magazine, after which she converted to Catholicism. She wrote her first novel, *Lampshades*, while suffering from a tubercular toe. *Lampshades* has been described as 'exhilarating, clever and utterly new' (*Sunday Times*) and was recently published in paperback by Minerva. She now lives in Ladbroke Grove and organizes a Culture Club for lifers at Wormwood Scrubs prison, and is editing a book on Glamor.

JM   Jacqueline Morreau, a painter and printmaker, was born in Wisconsin, USA, in 1929. She is the mother of four children. She has lived in London since 1972 and in 1980 was one of the organizers of 'Women's Images of Men', an exhibition which is a landmark in the understanding and acceptance of women's feminist and figurative art. In 1985 she co-edited (with Sarah Kent) a book on the effects of the exhibition. She has participated in a number of important didactic group shows and has shown her own work widely. She is represented in many public and private collections.

JN   Julia Neuberger is a rabbi who was minister at the South London Liberal Synagogue for twelve years. She is now Visiting Fellow at the King's Fund Institute, London. She chairs the Patients' Association, is a trustee of the Runnymede Trust, the Citizenship Foundation, the North London Hospice Group, and a Council Member of St George's House, Windsor. She also teaches at Leo Baeck College and writes and broadcasts frequently.

TP   Tina Papoulias was born in Athens and has been living in Britain since 1985. After completing an MA in Psychoanalytic studies at the University of Kent, she moved to London, where she is currently working and pursuing research in the intersections between narratives of nationalism, memory and perversion.

DR   Daphne Read did her graduate work and taught women's studies at York University, Toronto, Canada. She is currently an assistant professor in English at the University of Alberta, Edmonton, Canada.

NR   Nasreen Rehman was born in Rawalpindi, Pakistan, and since 1970 has lived in England. A musicologist, she has worked as an arts development co-ordinator for the Asian Arts Group in Newham, and as a freelance consultant for arts and leisure planning. She writes for Pakistani, British and Indian publications. She has two daughters.

DiR   Diane Richardson is Senior Lecturer in the Department of Sociological Studies at the University of Sheffield. She has written extensively about the social construction of sexuality and is well known for her work on safer sex and how AIDS affects women. Her books include *The Theory and Practice of Homosexuality* (Pandora, 1981), *Women and the AIDS Crisis* (Pandora, 2nd edition, 1989), *Safer Sex: The Guide for Women Today* (Pandora, 1990), *Women, Motherhood and Childrearing* (Macmillan, 1993) and, with Victoria Robinson, *Introducing Women's Studies: Feminist Theory and Practice* (Pandora, 1993).

SR   Saba Risaluddin is a European (English father, Swiss mother) born in England and educated partly in England and partly in Switzerland. Drawing on her experience in creating and restoring gardens (some on behalf of the National Trust) she is the author of several books on plants and gardening. She is secretary of the executive committee of Action for Bosnia, a political advocacy group and a member of the committee of C21 (Minorities into the 21st century) and is an active member of a number of interfaith organizations and dialogue groups. She is the creator of The Calamus Foundation, a charity devoted to promoting harmony between adherents of the Abrahamic faiths.

MR   Michèle Roberts lives and works in London. She is half French. Her second solo collection of poems is *Psyche and the hurricane* (Methuen, 1991), and her most recent novel, *Daughters of the House* (Virago, 1992), was shortlisted for the 1992 Booker Prize. She has also published essays and short stories.

SRu   Sandi Russell grew up in Harlem and is currently living in Britain. As a professional jazz singer, she has performed throughout the USA and in Britain. An essay about her early singing career appeared in *Glancing Fires* (London: The Women's Press, 1987). Her interviews with African-American women writers and singers have appeared in *The Women's Review*. She is the author of *Render Me My Song: African Women Writers from Slavery to the Present* (London: Pandora Press, 1990) and a co-editor of *The Virago Book of Love Poetry* (1992). She is presently working on a book of short stories.

AR   Amanda Ryder was born and grew up in Australia and educated at Adelaide University, the Chinese University of Hong Kong and Leeds University. Her main research interests are traditional Chinese fiction and the conflicting influences of Western and traditional Chinese culture in modern China. She is presently working for the BBC World Service.

MS Mary Salome is a recent graduate from the University of California, where she read anthropology and women's studies.

PS Patricia Scanlan was born in 1958, in Cork, Ireland, and educated at University College Cork, reading History of Art, and Trinity College Dublin. She is presently completing a doctoral thesis on Surrealism in Britain at the University of London. She is also the editor of *SuperReal*, a journal on surrealism, and founder of an avant-garde arts journal, *Lovely Jobly*. She has four collections of poems published, the latest entitled *A Picture of Water* (1991).

AS Anne Scott is co-author, with the late Ruth First, of *Olive Schreiner: A Biography*. She has worked as an editor at Free Association Books, London, and in a state mental hospital in Boston, Massachusetts. Her writing on psychoanalysis has appeared in *Feminist Review* and *History Workshop* and she is working on a study of the work of women psychoanalysts.

GS Gill Scott completed a doctoral thesis on the Women's Co-operative Guild, at Sussex University, and is currently in the process of developing it into a book on the organisation of working-class women. She is employed as a senior lecturer in the Humanities Department at Brighton Polytechnic, teaching courses in Politics and Modern History.

DS Diana Scully is Coordinator of the Women's Studies Program and Associate Professor of Sociology at Virginia Commonwealth

University in Richmond, Virginia. She is the author of two books: *Men Who Control Women's Health: The Miseducation of Obstetrician-Gynecologists* (Boston: Houghton Mifflin, 1980) and *Understanding Sexual Violence: A Study of Convicted Rapists* (New York and London: Unwin Hyman/ Harper Collins Academic, 1990).

LyS Lynne Segal teaches psychology at Middlesex University. Her previous works include *Is the Future Female?: Troubled Thoughts on Contemporary Feminism* (Virago, 1987), *Slow Motion: Changing Masculinities, Changing Men* (Virago, 1990) and *Sex Exposed: Sexuality and the Pornography Debate*, edited with Mary McIntosh (Virago, 1992). She is currently writing a book on heterosexuality.

LS Linda Semple was for many years a bookseller at Silver Moon Women's Bookshop in London and has written many critical articles on women and crime fiction.

SS Susan Sheridan is the author of *Christina Stead* (London: Harvester Press, 1988), the editor of *Grafts: Feminist Cultural Criticism* (London: Verso, 1988) and reviews editor of *Australian Feminist Studies*. She has published widely on feminist theory, women's writing and Australian cultural history and is currently Senior Lecturer in Women's Studies at the Flinders University of South Australia.

US Ulrike Sieglohr lectures part-time in film studies for the extra-mural department at Birkbeck College, London. She has written an MA dissertation on German/Austrian feminist filmmakers and is currently researching Werner Schroeter and New German Cinema for a PhD at the University of East Anglia.

MiS   Michele Slung's works include *Crime on Her Mind* (New York: Pantheon, 1975; London: Michael Joseph, 1976), a historical anthology of fictional women detectives; *The Absent-Minded Professor's Memory Book* (New York: Ballantine Books, 1985); *The Only Child Book* (New York: Ballantine Books, 1989); *I Shudder at Your Touch: Tales of Sex and Horror* (New York: Dutton, 1991); and the best-selling Momilies books, *Momilies: As My Mother Used to Say* (New York: Ballantine Books, 1985) and *More Momilies* (1986), which have now been translated into French, German, Japanese and Italian. In addition, she was the editor of the Plume American Women Writers series, presenting long-out-of-print fiction in a uniform format, and has been an editor and columnist for *The Washington Post 'Book World'*. Her current project is a sequel to her 1992 collection of original contemporary women's erotica, *Slow Hand*.

ASW   Astrid Söderbergh Widding, born in 1963, received her BA in cinema studies in 1985. She works as a researcher, teacher and critic in Stockholm and is currently preparing a doctoral thesis in film theory.

DSp   Dale Spender is a feminist writer and researcher who divides her time between 'overseas' and Australia. An avid reader of nineteenth-century women's novels, she knows that, pre-Freud, there was a society which was not oriented towards sexual consumption.

DSt   Dorothy Stein is a developmental psychologist who has taught courses in psychology, demography and women's studies at the University of Hawaii. She is the author of *Ada: A Life and a Legacy* (MIT Press, 1986) and of papers on the history of science, literature and women in India.

HT   Helen Taylor is senior lecturer in American Literature at the University of Warwick. She has published and lectured widely on British and American women writers and popular culture. She is the author of *Gender, Race and Region in the Writings of Grace King, Ruth McEnery Stuart and Kate Chopin* (Louisiana State U.P., 1989) and *Scarlett's Women: Gone with the Wind and Its Female Fans* (Virago, 1989).

JT   Jenny Turner was books editor of *City Limits* magazine, London.

LU   Lee Upton's second book of poetry, *No Mercy*, was published in 1989 by Atlantic Monthly Press. She has published a critical study of the American poet Jean Garrigue, and her poetry, fiction and criticism have appeared in numerous journals.

CU   Carol Ann Uszkurat was born in Bristol in 1949. She is currently researching into the popular post-war paperback side of lesbian writing. She has had articles published in the gay, lesbian and feminist press and devised and taught gay and lesbian studies courses as a subversive in Adult Education. Since leaving a husband and coming out as lesbian in 1978 she has explored the range of lesbian sex, lesbian relationships, lesbian politics and feminist theory. She now considers herself to be variously situated but not exclusively aligned.

MV   Mariana Valverde is a writer and activist living in Toronto, Canada. She teaches Sociology at York University and is the author of *Sex, Power, and Pleasure* (Toronto: 1985; Philadelphia: 1987) and of *The Age of Light, Soap and Water: Moral Reform in English Canada 1880s-1920s* (forthcoming from McClelland and Stewart).

KV   Kiran Velagapudi was born in 1964 in

Madras, India. She has a degree in History and Social Anthropology from the School of Oriental and African Studies, University of London, and has run a development center for refugee women in Pakistan. She now shares her life between India and London, working as a reflexologist.

LWM Linda Wagner-Martin is Hanes Professor of English and Comparative Literature at the University of North Carolina, Chapel Hill. She has written extensively on American modernism (a recent book is *The Modern American Novel, 1914-1945*) and its writers: Hemingway, Faulkner, William Carlos Williams, T.S. Eliot, John Dos Passos, Ellen Glasgow, Edith Wharton and others. Her biography of Sylvia Plath appeared in 1987 and she is currently finishing a revisionist life of Gertrude Stein.

DW Diane Wakoski is an American poet from Southern California whose poetry career began in New York in the 1960s. Her books include *The Motorcycle Betrayal Poems*, *The Collected Greed*, *Emerald Ice* and, most recently, *Medea the Sorceress* from Black Sparrow Press. She is Writer in Residence at Michigan State University.

RW Ruth Wallsgrove is a 1970s-vintage radical feminist with a particular weakness for working on publications: among them *Spare Rib*, *Trouble and Strife*, *Women and Computing* and, her longest love, *off our backs*. She is currently an engineer in Milton Keynes. (It is possible to be both.)

MW Margaret Walters is a writer and broadcaster. She was film critic for the *Listener* for four years and has written a book on the male nude.

MWr Marina Warner is a novelist, historian and critic. Her most recent book was *Indigo*

(London: Chatto & Windus, 1992). She is now working on a study of fairytales, *From the Beast to the Blonde*.

KW Kathleene West is a poet who teaches at New Mexico State University in Las Cruces. Her latest books are *Water Witching* (Copper Canyon Press) and *The Farmer's Daughter* (Sandhills Press). Work on a new manuscript takes her frequently to Central America and the Yucatan.

MWd Margaret Whitford teaches French at Queen Mary and Westfield College, University of London. She is the author of *Luce Irigaray: Philosophy in the Feminine* (Routledge, 1991) and editor of *The Irigaray Reader* (Blackwell, 1991).

GW Gillian Wilce has worked as a secretary, a social worker and an editor, including five years as literary editor of the *New Statesman*, and is now training as a psychotherapist.

AW Angela Willans, a graduate of London University, has been the agony aunt on *Women's Own* since 1964 and a contributor to various journals, radio and TV. She is on the board of Brook Advisory Centres, a patron of the Eating Disorders Association and of the Gay Humanist Association, and a council member of One-Parent Families. The author of three non-fiction books and one novel, she is divorced, with two daughters and five grandchildren.

JW Jane Williams read theology in Cambridge and now lectures, teaches and writes about systematic and feminist theology. She is an Anglican and is on a number of Church commissions, including one on women bishops. She lives in Oxford and is married with one small daughter.

SW Sarah Wood is a filmmaker and film critic.

She is currently writing a book on the home in contemporary American culture.

LX Laura X is director of the National Clearing House on Marital and Date Rape, Women's History Research Center, Berkeley, California, and a speaker in North America, the Caribbean and Ireland for over two decades. She has been honored by the World Congress of Victimology, the American Library Association and the US Surgeon General, C. Everette Koop. Her name protests the legal slavery of women which enables marital and date rape.

EY Elizabeth Young was born in Lagos, Nigeria and grew up in West Africa, London and Scotland. She was educated at The Mount School, York, the Sorbonne and York University where she studied American Literature. She is now a full-time writer and literary journalist. Her first book (co-authored with Graham Caveney) was *Shopping in Space: Essays on 'Blank Generation' American Fiction* and she has also published a number of horror stories. She lives in London.

OY Olivia Young is currently a doctoral candidate in the Department of Political Science at the University of Missouri-St Louis. Her areas of concentration are public policy analysis and public law. A public health nurse/instructor and administrator, her career spans two and half decades in the business and public sectors. After being severely sexually harassed during a business meeting in 1980, she began what was to become a ten-year struggle in the American judiciary to effect adequate restitution and fair treatment for all victims of sexual harassment. She has since been an outspoken opponent of sexual harassment. She is also the mother of three sons.